# Welcome to Town & Country Homes

Thank you ┊
to 'The Irish ┊
almost 1,500 ┊
Ireland.

Using our guid┄┄┄┄┄┄┄ ┄. booking your
accommodatior ┄┄┄ ┄ith our homes before you
depart, contacting your Travel Agent, or our central
office through our website.   Plan your route and drive
to every corner of Ireland where you can stay in one of
our bed & breakfast homes.

This year, for your convenience, we have included precise instructions to locate
our homes which you will find on our website www.townandcountry.ie and
approximately 850 members now have their own websites.  Use our On Line
Reservation System and book direct with the Bed and Breakfast of your choice.

Experience the warm welcome and relaxed pace of life in our country.   Bed and
Breakfast offers total immersion into Irish life and culture.   Discuss politics,
education, make life long friends and trace your ancestors with the assistance of
our welcoming, hospitable hosts and their families.

Practical Tips to enhance your holiday:

- Prior to departure book your first and last nights accommodation
- Check in prior to 6.00pm and telephone if there are any alterations and confirm your booking
- Use our network of homes to book your next nights accommodation and assistance with route planning
- Follow the Shamrock - your guarantee of approved homes by the Irish Tourist Board
- Our customer care line is 071 9822271

We wish you a pleasant and memorable holiday and look forward to welcoming
you back to Ireland and Town and Country Homes.

*Carol O'Gorman*

**Carol O'Gorman, Chairperson**

# Tourist Regions of Ireland

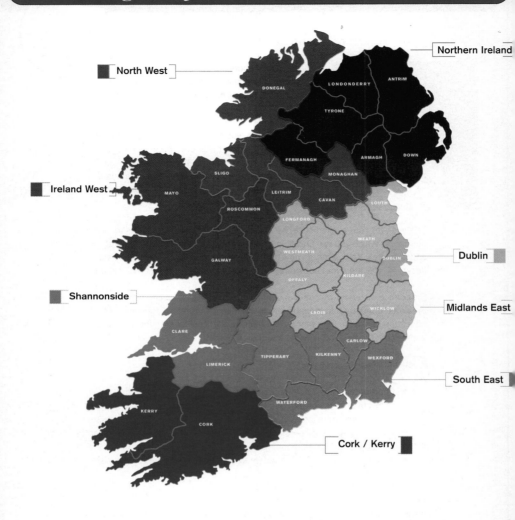

**North West**

**Northern Ireland**

**Ireland West**

**Dublin**

**Shannonside**

**Midlands East**

**South East**

**Cork / Kerry**

DONEGAL
LONDONDERRY
ANTRIM
TYRONE
FERMANAGH
ARMAGH
DOWN
SLIGO
MONAGHAN
MAYO
LEITRIM
CAVAN
ROSCOMMON
LOUTH
LONGFORD
MEATH
WESTMEATH
DUBLIN
GALWAY
OFFALY
KILDARE
LAOIS
WICKLOW
CLARE
CARLOW
LIMERICK
TIPPERARY
KILKENNY
WEXFORD
KERRY
WATERFORD
CORK

---

Northern Ireland Tourist Board

**Approved Accommodation Signs**
These signs will be displayed at most premises which are approved by Failte Ireland, the National Tourism Development Authority and Northern Ireland Tourist Board Standards.

**Plakette für Geprüfte Unterkunft**
Diese Plaketten werden an den meisten Häusern angezeigt, die von auf die Einhaltung der Normen der irischen Fremdenverkehrsbehörde überprüft und zugelassen wurden.

**Borden voor goedgekeurde accommodatie**
Deze borden vindt u bij de meeste huizen die zijn goedgekeurd door voor de normen van de Ierse Toeristenbond.

**Simbolo di sistemazione approvata**
Questi simboli saranno esposti nella maggior parte delle case approvate (associazione dei Bed & Breakfast approvati per qualità), rispondenti agli standard dell'Ente del Turismo Irlandese.

**Símbolo de alojamiento aprobado**
Estos símbolos se muestran en los establecimientos que han sido aprobados por bajos los estandars de la Oficina de Turismo Irlandesa.

**Skyltar för Godkänd logi**
Dessa skyltar finns vid de flesta gästhus som har godkänts (Föreningen för kvalitetsgodkända gästhus AB), enligt irländsk turisföreningens normer.

**Panneaux d'homologation des établissements**
Ces panneaux sont affichés dans la plupart des établissements homologués selon les normes de l'Office du tourisme irlandais.

# Contents

Regional Map ............................................ 2
Head Office and Officers of Association .............. 4
Using this Guide ....................................... 6
Tourism Ireland Offices ............................. 351
Hinweise für den Gebrauch dieses Führers ........... 352
Comment utiliser ce guide ........................... 353
Cómo utilizar esta guía ............................. 354
Uso di questa guida ................................. 355
Hoe u deze gids gebruikt ............................ 356
Hur man använder denna guidebok ..................... 357

## South East — 8

| Carlow | 10 |
| Kilkenny | 12 |
| Tipperary | 20 |
| Waterford | 32 |
| Wexford | 44 |

### Cork/Kerry — 52

| Cork | 54 |
| Kerry | 87 |

### Shannonside — 140

| Clare | 142 |
| Limerick | 169 |

### Ireland West — 180

| Galway | 182 |
| Mayo | 218 |
| Roscommon | 236 |

### Midlands East — 240

| Kildare | 242 |
| Laois | 245 |
| Longford | 247 |
| Louth | 248 |
| Meath | 252 |
| Offaly | 259 |
| Westmeath | 262 |
| Wicklow | 268 |

## North West — 278

| Cavan | 280 |
| Donegal | 282 |
| Leitrim | 298 |
| Monaghan | 300 |
| Sligo | 302 |

### Northern Ireland — 310

| Antrim | 312 |
| Armagh | 317 |
| Down | 319 |
| Fermanagh | 322 |
| Londonderry | 324 |
| Tyrone | 326 |

### Dublin — 328

| North City | 330 |
| North County | 335 |
| South City | 343 |
| South County | 347 |

**HEAD OFFICE**
Belleek Road, Ballyshannon, Co. Donegal.
Tel: 00353 71 9822222   Fax: 00353 71 9822207
*(Monday-Friday 9am-5pm)*
Email: admin@townandcountry.ie
Web: www.townandcountry.ie
WAP: www.bandbireland.com

# Head Office and Officers of Association

### Chairperson
Mrs Carol O'Gorman, Ashfort,
Galway/Knock Rd, Charlestown, Co Mayo.
Tel: 094 9255568, Fax: 094 9255885
Email: ashfortbb@eircom.net

### Vice-Chairman
Mr Jim Denby, Shelmalier House, Cartrontroy,
Athlone, Co. Westmeath.
Tel: 090 6472245, Fax: 090 6473190
Email: shelmalier@eircom.net

### Secretary
Mr Denis Fahey, Farrenwick Country House,
Poulmucka, Curranstown, Clonmel, Co. Tipperary.
Tel: 052 35130, Fax: 052 35377
Email: kayden@clubi.ie

### Treasurer
Mrs Lily Saunders, Rosedene, Limerick Road,
Portlaoise, Co. Laois.
Tel: 0502 22345, Fax: 0502 22345
Email: rosedenebb@eircom.net

**Please forward all correspondence & enquiries to:**

**Mrs Margaret Storey, Chief Executive,
Town & Country Homes Association Ltd.**

Belleek Road, Ballyshannon, Co. Donegal.

**Tel: 00353 71 9822222. Fax: 00353 71 9822207.**

Email: mstorey@townandcountry.ie  Web: www.townandcountry.ie
WAP: www.bandbireland.com

## TOWN & COUNTRY HOMES GIFT TOKENS

Why not share your experience of staying in a
Town & Country home
by purchasing our gift tokens.
They are available in €10, €20 or €50
and can be used in any home featured in this guide.

Contact us on email: accounts@townandcountry.ie
Telephone: 071 9822222   Fax: 071 9822207

# Ireland's Tourist Information Network

**W**ELCOME TO IRELAND and to the special services provided by our friendly staff in the Tourist Information Network.

In addition to tourist information and room reservations, our staff will provide a wide range of FREE services, all designed to aid you in your holiday planning and help you to enjoy to the full, all that Ireland has to offer.

Please ask for a copy of the list of all networked offices. It's available free anywhere you see the special 'i' symbol.

## OUR SERVICES AT A GLANCE

- Accommodation Booking Service
- Bureau de Change Facilities
- Computer-speeded Gulliver Info/Reservation Service
- Guide Books for Sale
- Itinerary and Route Planning
- Local and National Information

- Local Craft Displays
- Day Tours and Evening Entertainments
- Souvenirs & Map Sales
- Stamps and Postcards
- What's on in the Area and Nationally

*\* Some Tourist Information Offices may not provide all of the services or facilities listed here.*

## Follow the Shamrock

**L**OOK FOR THE SHAMROCK SIGN on accommodation. It is your guarantee that the premises has been inspected and approved as meeting the minimum national standard set by the National Tourism Authority. Only such premises may be pre-booked through Ireland's Tourist Information Network.

Ask for our free guide to the locations of all Tourist Information Offices throughout the country - your guide to better service and a happier holiday.

The guide is divided into eight geographical regions which are subdivided into counties (see page 2 for map of regions and counties). The regions are: **South East, Cork/Kerry, Shannonside, Ireland West, Midlands East, North West, Northern Ireland, Dublin.**

### Bed & Breakfast

The price for Bed & Breakfast is per person sharing. See explanation notes overleaf for full details on each entry in our guide.

### Booking Procedure

It is advisable to **book first and last night's accommodation** in advance at all times.

#### Room Availability in Dublin

Rooms in Dublin City and County can be difficult to find unless accommodation is pre-booked. If visiting the capital city, we strongly advise pre-booking all accommodation **well in advance.** Never count on finding rooms at short notice in Dublin. Always reserve in advance.

#### Onward Reservations:

During peak season, should problems arise finding accommodation when in Ireland, contact any Tourist Information Office, or seek advice and assistance from your host/hostess in Town & Country Homes. She/he will assist in booking subsequent night/nights for the cost of a telephone call. We recommend securing your following nights accommodation before leaving the B&B.

### Credit Card Bookings

Credit cards are accepted in homes with the [cc] symbol.

Telephone reservations may be guaranteed by quoting a valid credit card number. Check terms and conditions when booking.

### Travel Agents Vouchers

Please present your voucher on arrival. Vouchers are only valid in homes displaying (v).

**Standard Vouchers** cover B&B in room without private facilities. To **upgrade to ensuite** rooms, the maximum charge is **€2.00 per person.** The maximum charge for 3 or more sharing should **not exceed €5.00 per room.**

**Ensuite vouchers** cover a room with full private facilities. No extra charge is payable.

**Low/High Season Supplement:** For the months of July and August a supplement should be included on all vouchers. For more information please refer to head office.

### Dublin Supplement:

A room supplement for Dublin city and county of €7.50 per room applies for the months of **June, July August & September** on Travel Agency Vouchers. This charge is paid directly to the accommodation provider and is not included in the voucher.

### Cancellation policy

When a reservation has been confirmed, please check cancellation policy with establishment at the time of booking. The person making the reservation is responsible for the agreed cancellation fee.

Please telephone immediately in the event of a cancellation. Should it be necessary to cancel or amend a booking without sufficient prior notice, a financial penalty applies.

- 7-14 days notice – 50% of the 1st night
- 24 hours - 6 days notice – 75% of the 1st night
- Failure to show - 100% of the 1st night.

### Late Arrivals

Please note that late arrival – **i.e. after 6pm is by Special Agreement with home.** It would be much appreciated if time of arrival were given to your host/hostess.

### Advance Bookings

For advance bookings, a cheque or Credit Card number may be requested to guarantee arrival. Check Terms and Conditions.

### Check In/Out

Please advise of early arrival.
- Rooms available between 2pm and 6pm.
- Check out should be no later than 11am.
- Reservations should be taken up by 6pm.

### Reduction for Children

Applies where children share with a parent or three or more children share one room. Full rate applies when one or two children occupy separate rooms. Please check that the home is suitable for children when booking. Cots are available in some homes – there may be a nominal charge.

### Evening Meals

Book in advance preferably before 12 noon on the day. Light meals [X] available on request.

### Pets

With the exception of Guide Dogs, in the interest of hygiene pets are not allowed indoors.

### Disabled Persons/Wheelchair Users

Premises will only be listed with homes that have been approved by Comhairle or in the past by the National Rehabilitation Board.

**Family Name**
NAME OF TOWN OR
COUNTRY HOME
**Address**
Description of Town & Country Home

| Area | | |
|---|---|---|
| **TEL:** | | **FAX:** |
| **EMAIL:** | | |
| **WEB:** | | |
| **BUS NO:** | | |

| B&B | # | Ensuite | Min€/Max€ | Dinner | € |
|---|---|---|---|---|---|
| B&B | # | Standard | Min€/Max€ | Partial Board | Min€/Max€ |
| Single Rate | | | Min€/Max€ | Child reduction | % |

**Nearest Town** distance in km

**Facility Symbols:**

B+B PPS: Bed & Breakfast per person sharing
PARTIAL BRD: Bed & Breakfast, Evening meal for seven days.
# No of rooms.

**Open:**

Child Reduction % for Children sharing parents room or where three or more children share one room
ENSUITE: : Room with Bath/Shower & Toilet
SINGLE RATE: : Single Rate for Room

## Symbols

|  |  |
|---|---|
| CC | Credit Cards accepted |
| | Accessible to ambulant people |
| | Accessible to a wheelchair user able to walk a few paces and up at least 3 steps |
| | Accessible to an independant wheelchair user |
| | Accessible to a wheelchair user with assistance |
| S | Single Room |
| | Triple Room |
| P | Private off-street parking |
| | Irish spoken |
| | Facilities for Pets |
| | No smoking house |
| | No smoking bedrooms |
| | TV in bedrooms |
| | Direct dial telephone in bedrooms |
| | Tea/Coffee facilities in bedrooms |

|  |  |
|---|---|
| | Babysitter, normally to 12 midnight |
| | Cot available |
| | Light meals available |
| | Wine Licence |
| Inet | Internet Access |
| | Walking |
| | Cycling |
| | Golf within 5kms. |
| | Horse riding within 5kms. |
| | Facilities for Fishing |
| L | Lake fishing within 15km. |
| S | Sea Fishing within 15km. |
| R | River fishing within 15km. |
| V | Travel Agency Vouchers Accepted. |
| | Travel Agency Vouchers Not Accepted |

## Compliments and Comments

**Complaints should always be brought to the attention of the proprietor before departure.** Failing satisfaction and in the case of alleged overcharging, your receipt should be sent with your complaint to: **Customer Care, Town & Country Homes, Belleek Road, Ballyshannon, Co. Donegal.**

To maintain the high standards which the Association is renowned for, all comments on the general level of service and the standards you have experienced are welcome. All constructive criticisms will be taken seriously to ensure continued service improvement.

## Errors and Omissions

Every care has been taken to ensure accuracy in this publication in compliance with the Consumer Protection Laws of Ireland. The Town & Country Homes Association Ltd. cannot accept responsibility for errors, omissions or inaccurate particulars in material supplied by members for inclusion in this publication, or for any loss or disappointment caused by dependence on information contained herein. Where such are brought to our attention, future editions will be amended accordingly. There may be changes after going to press where properties are sold, and the home changes ownership.

 Page 352
 Page 353
 Page 354
 Page 355
 Page 356
 Page 357

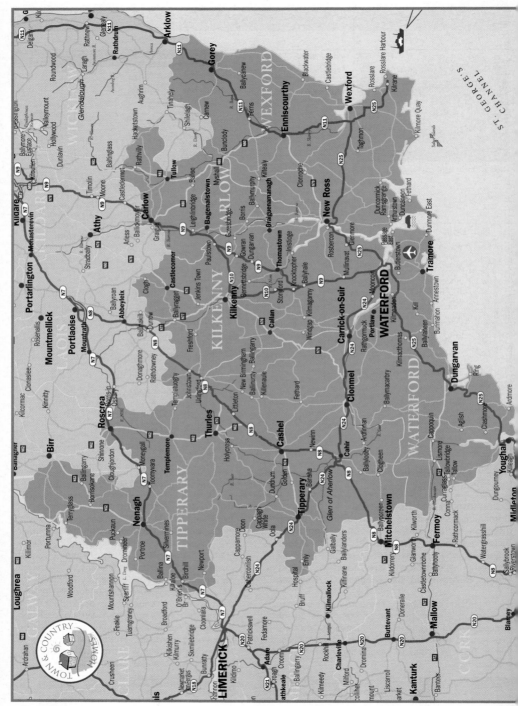

*South East*

# South East

The well-known term "Sunny South East" derives equally from the mildness of the climate and the warmth of the people in this lovely corner of Ireland.

There are five counties in the region - Carlow, Kilkenny, South Tipperary, Waterford and Wexford, and five major river systems - the Barrow, Blackwater, Nore, Slaney, and the Suir. Their undulating valleys criss-cross the region as they meander peacefully through the fertile landscape which is dotted with more heritage sites than virtually any other tourism region in Ireland.

**Cahir Castle**

The South East is a mix of seaside and activity - the coastal resorts from Courtown to Ardmore backed by a mix of opportunities to golf, fish, horse-ride, walk and cycle. For the more leisurely, there are gardens in abundance and riverside villages where time still stands still!

## Area Representatives

**CARLOW**
Mrs Mary Dwyer-Pender BARROW LODGE The Quay Carlow Town Co Carlow Tel: 059 9141173

**KILKENNY**
Mrs Helen Dunning DUNBOY 10 Parkview Drive off Freshford Road Kilkenny City
Co Kilkenny Tel: 056 7761460  Fax: 056 7761460
Mr Liam Holohan ALCANTRA Maidenhill Kells Road Kilkenny Co Kilkenny
Tel: 056 7761058  Fax: 056 7761058

**TIPPERARY**
Mr Pierce Duggan THE CASTLE Two Mile Borris Thurles Co Tipperary  Tel: 0504 44324  Fax: 0504 44352
Mr Denis Fahey FARRENWICK COUNTRY HOUSE Poulmucka Curranstown Clonmel Co
Tipperary  Tel: 052 35130  Fax: 052 35377

**WATERFORD**
Mrs Phyllis McGovern ASHLEIGH Holy Cross Cork Road Waterford Co Waterford
Tel: 051 375171  Fax: 051 375171
Mrs Margo Sleator ROSEBANK HOUSE Clonea Road (R675) Dungarvan Co Waterford Tel: 058 41561
Ms Maureen Wall SUNCREST Slieverue Ferrybank Via Waterford Co Waterford
Tel: 051 832732  Fax: 051 851861

**WEXFORD**
Mrs Ann Foley RIVERSDALE HOUSE Lr William Street New Ross Co Wexford
Tel: 051 422515
Mrs Ann Sunderland HILLSIDE HOUSE Tubberduff Gorey Co Wexford
Tel: 055 21726/22036  Fax: 055 22567

## ℹ️ Tourist Information Offices

**OPEN ALL YEAR**

REFER TO PAGE 5 FOR A LIST OF SERVICES AVAILABLE

Waterford
The Granary
The Quay
Tel: 051 875823

Waterford Tourist
Information Office
Waterford Crystal
Visitor Centre
Cork Road
Tel: 051 358397

Carlow
College St
Tel: 059 9131554

Clonmel
Sarsfield Street
Tel: 052 22960

Dungarvan
The Courthouse
Tel: 058 41741

Kilkenny
Shee Alms House
Rose Inn Street
Tel: 056 7751500

Wexford
Crescent Quay
Tel: 053 23111

Website: **www.southeastireland.com**

Carlow is Ireland's most charming inland county. It's central location offers the perfect base to explore the entire South East. Visitors can enjoy the hospitality and friendliness of it's people; a unique experience of outdoor activities; great golf; and a superb choice of restaurants and pubs. Enjoy real Ireland the Carlow way.

---

**Mairead Heffernan**
ORCHARD GROVE
N9 Wells, Bagenalstown,
Co Carlow

### Bagenalstown

TEL: **059 9722140**
EMAIL: **orchardgrove@eircom.net**
WEB: **www.orchardgrovebb.com**

Warm welcoming family home. Superb accomodation. Midway Carlow/Kilkenny. On N9. Breakfast Menu. Ideal base touring South East. Golf, Fishing, Walking. Childrens play area. AA ◆◆◆◆.

| | | | | | |
|---|---|---|---|---|---|
| B&B | 3 | Ensuite | €32-€35 | Dinner | €25-€25 |
| B&B | 1 | Standard | €32-€33 | Partial Board | €370 |
| Single Rate | | | €40-€45 | Child reduction | 50% |

Bagenalstown 2km

**Open:** 1st January-30th November

---

**Mrs Kathleen Tallon**
KNOCKRIGG HOUSE
Wells, Royal Oak N9,
Co Carlow

### Bagenalstown

TEL: **059 9722555**   FAX: **059 9722555**
EMAIL: **knockrigghse@eircom.net**
WEB: **www.knockrigghouse.com**

Luxurious family run B&B. TV/Hairdryer all rooms. Guest lounge. Midway Carlow/Kilkenny on N9. Near Bus/Rail route. Beside River Barrow. Dublin/Rosslare 1hr 15mins.

| | | | | | |
|---|---|---|---|---|---|
| B&B | 4 | Ensuite | €30-€35 | Dinner | €25-€25 |
| B&B | | Standard | - | Partial Board | €350 |
| Single Rate | | | €40-€45 | Child reduction | 50% |

Bagenalstown 2km

**Open:** 7th January-18th December

---

**Ms Valerie James**
TUDOR LODGE
Kilmeaney, Carlow, Co Carlow

### Carlow

TEL: **059 9142299**
EMAIL: **valeriejs@eircom.net**
WEB: **www.carlowtourism.com/tudorlodge.html**

Attractive house 4km from Carlow on N80. Warm welcome, spacious garden, home baking, scones on arrival. Breakfast menu. 1 hour from Dublin, Rosslare.

| | | | | | |
|---|---|---|---|---|---|
| B&B | 2 | Ensuite | €30-€35 | Dinner | - |
| B&B | 1 | Standard | €28-€32 | Partial Board | - |
| Single Rate | | | €38-€50 | Child reduction | 50% |

Carlow 4km

**Open:** 1st January-31st December

---

**Ann Moore**
QUARRY RIDGE B&B
Keelogue, Killeshin, Co Carlow

### Carlow

TEL: **059 9147875**   FAX: **059 9147875**
EMAIL: **quarry_ridge7@hotmail.com**

Set in picturesque area. 3 ensuite bedrooms. Private parking near historic monuments, Romanesque Doorway, St. Diarmuid's Well, Brownshill Dolmen. 6km Carlow, 3km river Barrow.

| | | | | | |
|---|---|---|---|---|---|
| B&B | 3 | Ensuite | €27.50-€31 | Dinner | €19 |
| B&B | 1 | Standard | €25.50-€28.50 | Partial Board | €392 |
| Single Rate | | | €38-€43.50 | Child reduction | 50% |

Carlow 6km

**Open:** 1st January-31st December

**Pat & Noeleen Dunne**
GREENLANE HOUSE
Dublin Road, Carlow Town,
Co Carlow

### Carlow Town

TEL: **059 91 42670**  FAX: **059 91 30903**
EMAIL: **greenlanehse@hotmail.com**

Highly recommended town house, spacious bedrooms, private parking. Situated N9. 1 hour from Dublin/Rosslare close to all amenities. Home from home. Award winning garden.

| B&B | 6 | Ensuite | €35-€40 | Dinner | - |
| B&B | - | Standard | | Partial Board | - |
| Single Rate | | | €40-€45 | Child reduction | - |

In Carlow

**Open:** 6th January-30th November

**Mrs Mary Dwyer-Pender**
BARROW LODGE
The Quay, Carlow Town,
Co Carlow

### Carlow Town

TEL: **059 9141173**
EMAIL: **georgepender@eircom.net**
WEB: **www.carlowtourism.com/barrowlodge.html**

Always a popular choice with visitors due to our central riverside location. A short stroll from Carlow's excellent Restaurants, Clubs and Pubs.

| B&B | 5 | Ensuite | €32-€35 | Dinner | - |
| B&B | - | Standard | - | Partial Board | - |
| Single Rate | | | €40-€45 | Child reduction | - |

In Carlow

**Open:** All Year

**Ms Maureen Walsh**
KILLAMASTER HOUSE
Killamaster, Carlow, Co Carlow

### Castledermot

TEL: **059 9163654**  FAX: **059 9163654**
EMAIL: **mairinwalsh@eircom.net**
WEB: **www.killamaster.com**

Luxury country home on R418 between Tullow & Castledermot. Guest sun lounge overlooking beautiful garden/mountains. Midway Dublin/Rosslare. Carlow 15mins. Kilkenny 45mins. Dublin 90mins.

| B&B | 3 | Ensuite | €28-€33 | Dinner | - |
| B&B | - | Standard | - | Partial Board | - |
| Single Rate | | | €40-€43.50 | Child reduction | 25% |

Tullow 7km

**Open:** 1st March-31st October

**Anne & Edward Byrne**
LABURNUM LODGE
Bunclody Road, Tullow,
Co Carlow

### Tullow

TEL: **059 9151718**
EMAIL: **lablodge@indigo.ie**
WEB: **laburnum-lodge.com**

Elegant Georgian house. Downstairs accommodation. Overlooking Mount Wolseley golf course. Altamount garden. Midway Dublin/Rosslare. Orthopaedic beds, Electric blankets, Hairdryers.

| B&B | 6 | Ensuite | €31-€34 | Dinner | - |
| B&B | - | Standard | - | Partial Board | - |
| Single Rate | | | €40-€43.50 | Child reduction | 25% |

Tullow 1km

**Open:** 3rd January-12th December

---

## TOWN & COUNTRY GIFT TOKENS

Why not share your experience of staying in a Town & Country home by buying our gift tokens. They are available in €10, €20 or €50 and can be used in any home featured in this guide.

Contact us on email: accounts@townandcountry.ie

Telephone: 071 9822222  Fax: 071 9822207

Kilkenny - Medieval Capital of Ireland, its splendid castle as its centre-piece is home to Ireland's best known craft centre. County Kilkenny offers visitors an ideal base for touring the South East, a couple of days here will reward the discerning visitor.

---

**In Bennettsbridge**

**Mrs Sheila Cole**
**NORELY THEYR**
**Barronsland, Bennettsbridge, Co Kilkenny**

### Bennettsbridge
TEL: **056 7727496**
EMAIL: **norelytheyr@eircom.net**

Friendly, luxurious, spacious house on R700. Quiet restful. Tea/coffee facilities. Breakfast selection. "A taste of the traditional".

| | | | | | |
|---|---|---|---|---|---|
| B&B | 3 | Ensuite | €27.50-€33 | Dinner | €19-€25 |
| B&B | 1 | Standard | €25.50-€30 | Partial Board | €294 |
| Single Rate | | | €38-€45 | Child reduction | 25% |

**Open:** All Year

---

**Kilkenny 8km**

**Mrs June Greer**
**AARD OAKLEIGH**
**Ballyreddin West, Bennettsbridge, Co Kilkenny**

### Bennettsbridge
TEL: **056 7727388**   FAX: **056 7727388**
EMAIL: **greer@iol.ie**
WEB: **www.aardoakleigh.com**

Two storey modern house with large garden. Close to Equestrian, Golf, Racing, Fishing Facilities. Local Craft & Pottery shops in picturesque village.

| | | | | | |
|---|---|---|---|---|---|
| B&B | 3 | Ensuite | €27.50-€31 | Dinner | €18-€19 |
| B&B | - | Standard | - | Partial Board | - |
| Single Rate | | | €40-€48 | Child reduction | 25% |

**Open:** 1st January-31st December

---

**Callan 6km**

**Mrs Mary Butler**
**HARTFORD HOUSE**
**Graigue, Kilmanagh, Co Kilkenny**

### Callan
TEL: **056 7769215**   FAX: **056 7769215**
EMAIL: **marypbutler@eircom.net**
WEB: **www.kilmanagh.com**

Comfortable home in tranquil location. Home baking. Traditional music. Close to woodland walk, Nature reserve and Ballykeeffe Amphitheatre on R695 Kilmanagh.

| | | | | | |
|---|---|---|---|---|---|
| B&B | 3 | Ensuite | €30-€36 | Dinner | €25-€25 |
| B&B | - | Standard | - | Partial Board | €320 |
| Single Rate | | | €42-€45 | Child reduction | 33.3% |

**Open:** 1st February-31st October

---

**Thomastown 5km**

**Jim & Elizabeth Byrne**
**KILBAWN COUNTRY HOUSE**
**Dungarvan, Co Kilkenny**

### Dungarvan
TEL: **056 7793883**
EMAIL: **eliz@kilbawnhouse.com**
WEB: **www.kilbawnhouse.com**

A luxury new B&B outside the village of Dungarvan on N9 10mls Kilkenny City, 5mls Mount Juliet, 2mls Gowran Park race track.

| | | | | | |
|---|---|---|---|---|---|
| B&B | 4 | Ensuite | €30-€35 | Dinner | - |
| B&B | - | Standard | - | Partial Board | - |
| Single Rate | | | €40-€45 | Child reduction | 50% |

**Open:** 1st January-23rd December

**In Freshford**

**Mrs Priscilla Flanagan**
POMADORA HOUSE
Clinstown Road, Freshford,
Co Kilkenny

### Freshford

Tᴇʟ: **056 8832256**
Eᴍᴀɪʟ: **info@pomadora.com**
Wᴇʙ: **www.pomadora.com**

Home on Hunter Stud on R693 to Cashel. Gardens, Fishing, Horseriding, Hunting in Winter. Stabling for Horses, Dog Kennels, meals.

| B&B | 3 | Ensuite | €30-€35 | Dinner | €20-€22.50 |
|---|---|---|---|---|---|
| B&B | - | Standard | - | Partial Board | - |
| Single Rate | | | €40-€45 | Child reduction | 25% |

**Open:** All Year

---

**Freshford 3km**

**Mrs Bridget Nolan**
CASTLE VIEW
Balleen, Freshford, Co Kilkenny

### Freshford

Tᴇʟ: **056 32181**
Eᴍᴀɪʟ: **bridgetnolan@eircom.net**
Wᴇʙ: **www.castleviewbb.com**

Bungalow, peaceful location, panoramic view of country side. Orthopaedic beds. 15 mins drive to Kilkenny City on route to Rock of Cashel.

| B&B | 3 | Ensuite | €27.50-€31 | Dinner | - |
|---|---|---|---|---|---|
| B&B | - | Standard | - | Partial Board | - |
| Single Rate | | | €40-€43.50 | Child reduction | 50% |

**Open:** All Year

---

**Graiguenamanagh 4km**

**Helen Doyle**
BRANDON VIEW
Ballyling Lower,
Graiguenamanagh,
Co Kilkenny

### Graiguenamanagh

Tᴇʟ: **059 9724625** Fᴀx: **059 9724625**
Eᴍᴀɪʟ: **hdoylebrandonview@eircom.net**
Wᴇʙ: **www.brandonviewbandb.com**

AA ◆◆◆◆. Luxurious country home on R729. Singing pubs and restaurants 10 min. Central to Waterford, Wexford, Kilkenny 25min. Tea/Coffee facility guest lounge T.V

| B&B | 3 | Ensuite | €30-€30 | Dinner | €20 |
|---|---|---|---|---|---|
| B&B | 1 | Standard | - | Partial Board | €300 |
| Single Rate | | | €42-€42 | Child reduction | 50% |

**Open:** 3rd January-12th December

---

**Kilkenny City 4km**

**Pat & Monica Banahan**
CHURCH VIEW
Cuffesgrange, Callan Road,
Kilkenny, Co Kilkenny

### Kilkenny

Tᴇʟ: **056 7729170** Fᴀx: **056 7729170**
Eᴍᴀɪʟ: **info@churchview.info**
Wᴇʙ: **www.churchview.info**

Warm comfortable luxurious home on the main Clonmel/Cork/Killarney route, N76. Only 4 minutes drive from the medieval city of Kilkenny. Peaceful location. A warm welcome assured.

| B&B | 4 | Ensuite | €30-€35 | Dinner | - |
|---|---|---|---|---|---|
| B&B | 2 | Standard | €28-€30 | Partial Board | - |
| Single Rate | | | €48-€55 | Child reduction | 25% |

**Open:** 1st January-23rd December

---

**In Kilkenny**

**Ms Miriam Banville**
BANVILLE'S B&B
49 Walkin Street, Kilkenny,
Co Kilkenny

### Kilkenny

Tᴇʟ: **056 7770182**
Eᴍᴀɪʟ: **mbanville@eircom.net**

Warm comfortable home near City Centre. Private parking. Rooms Ensuite, Multichannel TV, Hairdryers, Alarm Clocks.

| B&B | 4 | Ensuite | €32.50-€35 | Dinner | - |
|---|---|---|---|---|---|
| B&B | - | Standard | - | Partial Board | - |
| Single Rate | | | €45-€48 | Child reduction | 50% |

**Open:** 1st February-30th November

### Mrs Nuala Brennan
**MELROSE HOUSE**
Circular Road, Kilkenny,
Co Kilkenny

Kilkenny

TEL: **056 7765289**  FAX: **056 7765289**
EMAIL: **brennanpn@eircom.net**
WEB: **www.melrosehouse.com**

Modern family run B&B. N76 opposite Hotel Kilkenny. 8 mins walk to City Centre. Private parking. Guest garden, quiet location. Multi channel TV, Hairdryers, Radio in rooms.

| B&B | 4 | Ensuite | €32-€38 | Dinner | - |
| B&B | - | Standard | - | Partial Board | - |
| Single Rate | | | €42-€50 | Child reduction | 50% |

**In Kilkenny City**

**Open:** 4th January-20th December

---

### Ms Angela Byrne
**CELTIC HOUSE**
18 Michael Street,
Kilkenny City, Co Kilkenny

Kilkenny City

TEL: **056 7762249**  FAX: **056 7762249**
EMAIL: **john376@gofree.indigo.ie**
WEB: **www.celtic-house-bandb.com**

Excellent location, walk everywhere. In the heart of Kilkenny City. Built 1998. Private lock-up. Parking. 4 min walk Bus and Train Station. Excellent standards. TV, Tea/Coffee facilities.

| B&B | 4 | Ensuite | €32-€40 | Dinner | - |
| B&B | - | Standard | - | Partial Board | - |
| Single Rate | | | - | Child reduction | - |

**In Kilkenny City**

**Open:** All Year Except Christmas

---

### John & Sharon Cahill
**LAUNARD HOUSE**
Maiden Hill, Kells Road,
Kilkenny, Co Kilkenny

Kilkenny

TEL: **056 7751889**  FAX: **056 7771017**
EMAIL: **info@launardhouse.com**
WEB: **www.launardhouse.com**

Luxurious purpose built home. "Irish Experts" and Hidden Places Guides recommended. "A Touch of Class". Some superior rooms with king beds (supp).

| B&B | 5 | Ensuite | €28-€42.50 | Dinner | - |
| B&B | - | Standard | - | Partial Board | - |
| Single Rate | | | - | Child reduction | - |

**Kilkenny 1km**

**Open:** 1st March-30th November

---

### Mrs Marie Callan
**LICHFIELD HOUSE**
Bennettsbridge Rd, Kilkenny,
Co Kilkenny

Kilkenny

TEL: **056 7765232**  FAX: **056 7770614**
EMAIL: **lichfieldhouse@eircom.net**
WEB: **www.lichfieldhouse.com**

Georgian Country Home on 1 acre. Quiet location 5 min drive from Kilkenny City on R700. Recommended Le Routard~Edmonton Journal~West Australian.

| B&B | 3 | Ensuite | €30-€35 | Dinner | - |
| B&B | - | Standard | - | Partial Board | - |
| Single Rate | | | - | Child reduction | 33.3% |

**Kilkenny 2km**

**Open:** 1st February-30th November

---

### Mrs Joan Cody
**OAKLAWN B&B**
8 Oakwood, Kilfera,
Bennettsbridge Road, Kilkenny,
Co Kilkenny

Kilkenny

TEL: **056 7761208**

Modern detached bungalow on the R700 main New Ross/Rosslare Road. Quiet area. Tastefully decorated. Set in mature lawns.

| B&B | 3 | Ensuite | €30-€30 | Dinner | €18 |
| B&B | - | Standard | - | Partial Board | - |
| Single Rate | | | €40-€43.50 | Child reduction | 50% |

**Kilkenny 4km**

**Open:** 1st March-31st October

**Mrs Mary Cody**
OLINDA
**Castle Road, Kilkenny,
Co Kilkenny**

TEL: **056 7762964**

Comfortable house, quiet location. Large garden area for guests. Tea/Coffee facilities. Walking distance to Pubs and Restaurants. Private parking. Hairdryers, Alarm clocks.T.V. in bedrooms.

| B&B | 3 | Ensuite | €30-€40 | Dinner | - |
| B&B | 1 | Standard | €28-€35 | Partial Board | - |
| Single Rate | | | - | Child reduction | 25% |

In Kilkenny

**Open:** 1st March-1st November

---

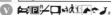

**Mrs Vicky Comerford**
PARK VILLA
**Castlecomer Road, Kilkenny,
Co Kilkenny**

TEL: **056 7761337**
EMAIL: **vicpat@eircom.net**
WEB: **www.kilkennybedandbreakfast.com**

Failte!! Modern family run home. Opposite Newpark Hotel. Prize gardens. Kettle always boiling. Warm welcome guaranteed. Rooms ensuite TV/Hairdryers. Convenient to Bus, Rail, Pubs, Golf etc.

| B&B | 5 | Ensuite | €30-€35 | Dinner | - |
| B&B | - | Standard | - | Partial Board | - |
| Single Rate | | | €40-€50 | Child reduction | 25% |

In Kilkenny

**Open:** 1st January-22nd December

---

**Ms Breda Dore**
AVILA B&B
**Freshford Road, Kilkenny City,
Co Kilkenny**

TEL: **056 7751072**   FAX: **056 7751072**
EMAIL: **doreb@indigo.ie**
WEB: **www.avilakilkenny.com**

Family run B&B within 15 minutes walk of City Centre. Located in quiet area. Warm welcome and best Irish breakfast guaranteed. Beside St. Lukes and Auteven Hospital R693.

| B&B | 4 | Ensuite | €28-€35 | Dinner | - |
| B&B | - | Standard | - | Partial Board | - |
| Single Rate | | | - | Child reduction | 33.3% |

Kilkenny City

**Open:** 6th January-18th December

---

**Mrs Margaret Drennan**
HILLGROVE
**Warrington,
Bennettsbridge Road, Kilkenny,
Co Kilkenny**

TEL: **056 7751453/7722890**
EMAIL: **hillgrove@esatclear.ie**
WEB: **http://homepage.eircom.net/~hillgrove**

National Breakfast Award-Winning Country Home, furnished with antiques, on R700. Orthopaedic beds, Electric blankets. Recommended Frommer, Dillard/Causin, Denver Post.

| B&B | 5 | Ensuite | €30-€35 | Dinner | - |
| B&B | - | Standard | - | Partial Board | - |
| Single Rate | | | €40-€43.50 | Child reduction | 50% |

Kilkenny 2km

**Open:** 1st February-12th December

---

**Mrs Helen Dunning**
DUNBOY
**10 Parkview Drive,
off Freshford Road,
Kilkenny City, Co Kilkenny**

TEL: **056 7761460**   FAX: **056 7761460**
EMAIL: **dunboy@eircom.net**
WEB: **www.dunboy.com**

Le Routard recommended. Quiet location. Close to City Centre. Take Freshford Road (R693) turn left at roundabout before St. Lukes Hospital, then right into cul-de-sac.

| B&B | 4 | Ensuite | €30-€35 | Dinner | - |
| B&B | - | Standard | - | Partial Board | - |
| Single Rate | | | - | Child reduction | - |

In Kilkenny City

**Open:** 1st March-31st October

**Mrs Bernadette Egan**
**KNOCKAVON HOUSE**
**Dublin/Carlow Road, Kilkenny,**
**Co Kilkenny**

**Kilkenny City**
TEL: **056 7764294**

Town house 3 mins walk to bus and train station. Parking. Beside Langtons and Rivercourt Hotels. 7 mins walk to castle and heritage sites and lovely gardens at rear of house.

| B&B | 5 | Ensuite | €30-€36 | Dinner | - |
| B&B | - | Standard | - | Partial Board | - |
| Single Rate | | | €45-€45 | Child reduction | 50% |

In Kilkenny City

**Open:** 1st January-30th December

**Mrs Oonagh Egan Twomey**
**CARRAIG RUA**
**Dublin Rd, Kilkenny City,**
**Co Kilkenny**

**Kilkenny City**
TEL: **056 7722929**   FAX: **056 7722929**

Elegant two storey city house on N10. 4 mins walk to bus and rail station. Close to City Centre, Kilkenny Castle, Langtons, Hotels and Restaurants.

| B&B | 5 | Ensuite | €27.50-€35 | Dinner | - |
| B&B | 1 | Standard | €26-€30 | Partial Board | - |
| Single Rate | | | €40-€45 | Child reduction | 25% |

In Kilkenny City

**Open:** 1st January-18th December

**Liam & Brigid Holohan**
**ALCANTRA**
**Maidenhill, Kells Road,**
**Kilkenny, Co Kilkenny**

**Kilkenny**
TEL: **056 7761058**   FAX: **056 7761058**
EMAIL: **alcantra@eircom.net**
WEB: **homepage.eircom.net/~alcantra**

Spacious comfortable home with guest lounge and conservatory, located on R697. Exactly 1km from City Centre. Numerous recommendations. AA ◆◆◆◆.

| B&B | 4 | Ensuite | €30-€36 | Dinner | - |
| B&B | - | Standard | - | Partial Board | - |
| Single Rate | | | - | Child reduction | - |

Kilkenny 1km

**Open:** 1st January-15th December

**Mrs Mary Lawlor**
**RODINI**
**Waterford Road,**
**(R910 off N10), Kilkenny,**
**Co Kilkenny**

**Kilkenny City**
TEL: **056 21822/70836**
EMAIL: **rodini@eircom.net**

Comfortable home. Convenient Hotels, City Centre, Castle and other amenities. Family room. Electric blankets, Hairdryers available. Ideal base to tour the beautiful historic South East.

| B&B | 5 | Ensuite | €30-€35 | Dinner | - |
| B&B | - | Standard | - | Partial Board | - |
| Single Rate | | | €40-€45 | Child reduction | 50% |

Kilkenny 1km

**Open:** All Year

**Ms Katherine Molloy**
**MENA HOUSE**
**Castlecomer Road (N77),**
**Kilkenny, Co Kilkenny**

**Kilkenny**
TEL: **056 7765362**
EMAIL: **menahouse@eircom.net**
WEB: **www.menahousekilkennybandb.com**

Antique furnished luxurious home. Prize gardens. TV all rooms. Tea making facilities. Breakfast choice, homemade preserves. Adjacent New Park Hotel, Golf, Swimming, Horse-riding.

| B&B | 7 | Ensuite | €30-€35 | Dinner | - |
| B&B | 2 | Standard | €28-€32 | Partial Board | - |
| Single Rate | | | €38-€45 | Child reduction | 50% |

In Kilkenny City

**Open:** 1st January-21st December

**Mrs Maud Morrissey**
BEECH LODGE B&B
Bennettsbridge Road, Kilkenny,
Co Kilkenny

### Kilkenny
TEL: **056 7764083** FAX: **056 7764083**

Warm friendly home, quiet location on main New Ross/Rosslare road. Picturesque garden. Spacious rooms. Orthopaedic beds, Electric blankets. Conservatory for guests.

| B&B | 4 | Ensuite | €30–€34 | Dinner | - |
| B&B | - | Standard | | Partial Board | - |
| Single Rate | | | €40–€45 | Child reduction | **25%** |

Kilkenny City 2km

**Open:** 1st January–1st December

---

**Ms Carmel Nolan**
THE RISE
Dunmore, Kilkenny,
Co Kilkenny

### Kilkenny
TEL: **056 7764534** FAX: **056 7764534**
EMAIL: **carmeljn@gofree.indigo.ie**

A warm welcome awaits our guests at our newly renovated 19th Century family farm home. Tea/Coffee on arrival. Stroll through our fields at your leisure.

| B&B | 4 | Ensuite | €27.50–€31 | Dinner | - |
| B&B | - | Standard | - | Partial Board | - |
| Single Rate | | | €40–€43.50 | Child reduction | **33.3%** |

Kilkenny 2km

**Open:** 1st February–31st October

---

**Mrs Nora O'Connor**
SUNDOWN
Freshford Rd, Kilkenny,
Co Kilkenny

### Kilkenny City
TEL: **056 7721816**
EMAIL: **sundownbandb@eircom.net**

Welcoming friendly home situated on Freshford road R693. Walking distance City Centre. Large car park. TV, Radio, Hairdryers all rooms. New Greyhound Stadium and Hospital nearby.

| B&B | 4 | Ensuite | €30–€35 | Dinner | - |
| B&B | 1 | Standard | €30–€34 | Partial Board | - |
| Single Rate | | | €44–€44 | Child reduction | **33.3%** |

Kilkenny City 1km

**Open:** 1st March–1st November

---

**Josephine O'Reilly**
CARRIGLEA
Archers Avenue, Castle Road,
Kilkenny, Co Kilkenny

### Kilkenny City
TEL: **056 7761629**
EMAIL: **archers@iol.ie**
WEB: **www.iol.ie/~archers**

Spacious elegant home. 5 min walk to City Centre, Pubs, Restaurants etc. Situated in quiet residential cul-de-sac. 3 min walk past Castle on right. Private parking.

| B&B | 3 | Ensuite | €30–€33 | Dinner | - |
| B&B | - | Standard | - | Partial Board | - |
| Single Rate | | | - | Child reduction | **33.3%** |

In Kilkenny

**Open:** 1st March–31st October

---

**Mrs V Rothwell**
DUNROMIN
Dublin Rd, Kilkenny,
Co Kilkenny

### Kilkenny City
TEL: **056 7761387** FAX: **056 7770736**
EMAIL: **valtom@oceanfree.net**
WEB: **www.dunrominkilkenny.com**

A warm welcome to our 19th Century family home (on Dublin road N10). Walking distance Medieval City Centre. Golf, Horse Riding nearby. Kettle always boiling.

| B&B | 5 | Ensuite | €30–€36 | Dinner | - |
| B&B | - | Standard | - | Partial Board | - |
| Single Rate | | | - | Child reduction | - |

In Kilkenny City

**Open:** 1st April–30th November

17

**Kathleen Ryan**
THE MEADOWS
6 Greenfields Road,
Bishops Meadows,
Kilkenny City, Co Kilkenny

### Kilkenny

Tel: **056 7721649**  Fax: **056 7721649**
Email: **kryan@indigo.ie**
Web: **www.the-meadows.net**

Quiet area off R693. Home baking. Menu. Walking distance City. Orthopaedic beds, Electric blankets, Hairdryer, Ironing facilities in room. Itinerary planned.

| B&B | 3 | Ensuite | €30-€35 | Dinner | - |
|-----|---|---------|---------|--------|---|
| B&B | - | Standard | - | Partial Board | - |
| Single Rate | | | €40-€45 | Child reduction | 25% |

Kilkenny City 1km  (V)  cc S ⚲ P ⊗ ᴿ ⟋ ☐ 🍽 ☂ 🐾 🐾 ᵣ  **Open:** All Year

---

**Mrs Helen Sheehan**
CNOC MHUIRE
Castle Road, Kilkenny,
Co Kilkenny

### Kilkenny

Tel: **056 7762161**  Fax: **056 7762161**
Email: **cnocmhuire@eircom.net**
Web: **www.cnocmhuire.com**

Warm comfortable home off Rosslare Road (R700). Quiet location. Orthopaedic beds, electric blankets. Hairdryers. Parking. 10 minute walk to centre and Castle.

| B&B | 4 | Ensuite | €30-€36 | Dinner | - |
|-----|---|---------|---------|--------|---|
| B&B | - | Standard | - | Partial Board | - |
| Single Rate | | | €40-€45 | Child reduction | 25% |

Kilkenny City 1km  (V)  cc P ⊗ ᴿ ⟋ ☐ 🍽 ☂ 🐾 🐾 ᵣ  **Open:** 12th January-15th December

---

**Jim & Joan Spratt**
CHAPLINS
Castlecomer Road, Kilkenny,
Co Kilkenny

### Kilkenny

Tel: **056 7752236**
Email: **chaplins@eircom.net**
Web: **www.chaplinsbandb.com**

Spacious Town house N77. All rooms equipped with Multi-Channel TV. Hairdryers, Tea/Coffee. RAC selected AA ◆◆◆.

| B&B | 6 | Ensuite | €28-€45 | Dinner | - |
|-----|---|---------|---------|--------|---|
| B&B | - | Standard | - | Partial Board | - |
| Single Rate | | | | Child reduction | 25% |

In Kilkenny City  (V)  cc ⚲ P ✿ ⊗ ᴿ ⟋ ☐ 🍽 ☂ 🐾 ᵣ  **Open:** 1st January-20th December

---

**Mrs Marie Trait**
ARD ALAINN
Keatingstown, Kilkenny,
Co Kilkenny

### Kilkenny

Tel: **056 7767680**

Nice country home on outskirts of Kilkenny. Central heating, lovely view of country side. Peaceful and quiet location.

| B&B | 4 | Ensuite | €27.50-€31 | Dinner | - |
|-----|---|---------|------------|--------|---|
| B&B | - | Standard | - | Partial Board | - |
| Single Rate | | | €40-€43.50 | Child reduction | 25% |

Kilkenny 3km  (V)  S ⚲ P ⊗ ᴿ ⟋ ♿ ✈ 🏃 🎠 🍽 ☂ 🐾 ᵣ  **Open:** 6th January-15th December

---

**Mary & Eamonn Wogan**
TIR NA NOG
Greenshill,
(off Castlecomer Rd), Kilkenny,
Co Kilkenny

### Kilkenny City

Tel: **056 7765250/7762345**  Fax: **056 7763491**
Email: **emw@iol.ie**
Web: **www.tirnanog-kilkenny.com**

Luxurious ensuite rooms, incl. TV/Radio, Trouserpress/Iron, Hairdryer, Breakfast menu. Convenient to Bus/Rail Station and City Centre.

| B&B | 5 | Ensuite | €30-€35 | Dinner | - |
|-----|---|---------|---------|--------|---|
| B&B | - | Standard | - | Partial Board | - |
| Single Rate | | | €40-€45 | Child reduction | - |

In Kilkenny City  (V)  cc ⚲ P ⊗ ᴿ ⟋ ☐ 🍽 🐾 ᵣ  **Open:** All Year

**Mrs Julie Doyle**
**CARRICKMOURNE HOUSE**
**New Ross Road, Thomastown,**
**Co Kilkenny**

### Thomastown

TEL: **056 7724124**   FAX: **056 7724124**
EMAIL: **carrickmournehouse@eircom.net**
WEB: **www.southeastireland.com/carrickmourne**

Elevated site, surrounded by scenic views peaceful country setting. Convenient Jerpoint Abbey, Mount Juliet Golf, Fishing, Restaurants. 2km off New Ross Rd.

| B&B | 5 | Ensuite | €30-€38 | Dinner | - |
|---|---|---|---|---|---|
| B&B | - | Standard | - | Partial Board | - |
| Single Rate | | | - | Child reduction | 25% |

Thomastown 3km

**Open:** 15th January-15th December

19

The loveliest and most scenic inland county in Ireland. Known as the Golden Vale county, lends itself to a longer stopover with its rolling plains and mountains. The River Suir transverses its entire length. Visit - Abbeys, Castles, and historic moats. Pony Trekking, Golf, Fishing, Greyhound and Horse racing. Hill Walking, Birdwatching. Many walking tours available.

**Marie Ryan & Mark Langton**
**LACKEN LODGE**
Cooleen, Birdhill, Co Tipperary

### Birdhill

Tel: **061 379083**
Email: **ryan.mp@iolfree.ie**
Web: **www.lackenlodge.com**

Attractive newlybuilt home just off N7 in Birdhill (R504) midway between Limerick and Nenagh 5 mins from Killaloe/Ballina on Lough Derg, train bus service in village.

| B&B | 3 | Ensuite | €30-€32 | Dinner | €20-€20 |
|-----|---|---------|---------|--------|---------|
| B&B | 1 | Standard | €28-€30 | Partial Board | - |
| Single Rate | | | €40-€43.50 | Child reduction | 25% |

Birdhill 2km

**Open:** 1st January-31st December

---

**Carmen & Wolfgang Rodder**
**DANCER COTTAGE**
Curraghmore, Borrisokane, Co Tipperary

### Borrisokane

Tel: **067 27414** Fax: **067 27414**
Email: **dcr@eircom.net**
Web: **dancercottage.cjb.net**

Comfortable house, quiet rural location. Large garden for guests. Fresh seasonal home cooking/baking, children welcome, Bicycles. Golf, Lough Derg nearby.

| B&B | 4 | Ensuite | €31-€34 | Dinner | €24 |
|-----|---|---------|---------|--------|-----|
| B&B | - | Standard | - | Partial Board | - |
| Single Rate | | | €40-€43.50 | Child reduction | 33.3% |

Borrisokane 1.9km

**Open:** 5th January-5th December

---

**Butler Family**
**CARRIGEEN CASTLE**
Cahir, Co Tipperary

### Cahir

Tel: **052 41370**
Email: **carrigeencastle@yahoo.co.uk**
Web: **www.tipp.ie/butlerca.htm**

Manor of Cahir. Historic (prison) home. Warm, comfortable, spacious, overlooking Town. Walled garden. Walking distance Bus/Train. Ideal touring base.

| B&B | 3 | Ensuite | €33-€33 | Dinner | - |
|-----|---|---------|---------|--------|---|
| B&B | 4 | Standard | €28-€28.50 | Partial Board | - |
| Single Rate | | | €45-€60 | Child reduction | - |

Cahir 1km

**Open:** 2nd January-15th December

---

**Ms Kay Byrne**
**ARBUTUS**
Tipperary Road, Cahir, Co Tipperary

### Cahir

Tel: **052 41617**
Email: **byrnearbutus-bb-@yahoo.co.uk**

Comfortable family home. Spacious en-suite rooms, TV, Hairdryers. Tea/Coffee all rooms. View Galtee mountains. On N24 off N8 roundabout. Walking distance town centre. Private parking.

| B&B | 2 | Ensuite | €28-€31 | Dinner | - |
|-----|---|---------|---------|--------|---|
| B&B | 1 | Standard | €27-€28.50 | Partial Board | - |
| Single Rate | | | €38-€45 | Child reduction | 25% |

Cahir 1km

**Open:** 1st May-30th October

**Mrs Jo Doyle**
KILLAUN
Clonmel Road, Cahir,
Co Tipperary

**Cahir**

TEL: **052 41780**
EMAIL: **killaunbandb@eircom.net**
WEB: **www.killaun.com**

Bungalow, bedrooms overlooking spacious gardens, 5 mins walk from town, Bus and Train Station. Golf, Fishing and Horseriding closeby. On N24

| B&B | 3 | Ensuite | €27.50-€31 | Dinner | - |
|-----|---|---------|-----------|--------|---|
| B&B | - | Standard | - | Partial Board | - |
| Single Rate | | | €40-€43.50 | Child reduction | 25% |

n Cahir

**Open:** All Year Except Christmas

**Gerard & Marian Duffy**
THE HOMESTEAD
Mitchelstown Road, Cahir,
Co Tipperary

**Cahir**

TEL: **052 42043**
EMAIL: **homesteadcahir@msn.com**

Spacious modern bungalow near Town Centre, TV in bedrooms ; Large off street private car park; Families welcome; Ideal Touring Base; Tea/Coffee on arrival

| B&B | 4 | Ensuite | €27.50-€31 | Dinner | - |
|-----|---|---------|-----------|--------|---|
| B&B | - | Standard | - | Partial Board | - |
| Single Rate | | | €40-€43.50 | Child reduction | 25% |

n Cahir

**Open:** 2nd January-30th November

**Mrs Mary English**
BROOKFIELD HOUSE
Old Cashel Road, Cahir,
Co Tipperary

**Cahir**

TEL: **052 41936**

Comfortable homely residence. All rooms have TV., Hairdryers, Tea/Coffee making facilities. Private parking. Conservatory and Guest Lounge.

| B&B | 2 | Ensuite | €27.50-€31 | Dinner | - |
|-----|---|---------|-----------|--------|---|
| B&B | 1 | Standard | €25.50-€28.50 | Partial Board | - |
| Single Rate | | | €38-€43.50 | Child reduction | 25% |

Cahir 1km

**Open:** 1st May-30th September

**Margaret Neville**
HOLLYMOUNT HOUSE
Upper Cahir Abbey, Cahir,
Co Tipperary

**Cahir**

TEL: **052 42888**
EMAIL: **hollymounthouse@msn.com**
WEB: **www.dirl.com/tipperary/cahir/hollymount.htm**

Get away from it all! Wind your way to the top of the mountain road, for peace and tranquillity. Only 5 minutes drive from town. Spectacular view. Quiet.

| B&B | 2 | Ensuite | €27.50-€31 | Dinner | - |
|-----|---|---------|-----------|--------|---|
| B&B | 2 | Standard | €25.50-€28.50 | Partial Board | - |
| Single Rate | | | €38-€43.50 | Child reduction | 25% |

Cahir 2km

**Open:** 1st January-31st December

**Mrs Hannah-Mai O'Connor**
SILVER ACRE
Clonmel Road, Cahir,
Co Tipperary

**Cahir**

TEL: **052 41737**
EMAIL: **hoconnor315@eircom.net**

Modern bungalow, Tourism award winner, in quiet cul-de-sac. Private parking. Bus, Train, Fishing, Golf nearby. Tea and Coffee in sitting room.

| B&B | 3 | Ensuite | €27.50-€31 | Dinner | - |
|-----|---|---------|-----------|--------|---|
| B&B | - | Standard | - | Partial Board | - |
| Single Rate | | | €40-€43.50 | Child reduction | 25% |

n Cahir

**Open:** 1st February-30th November

*In Cahir*

### Liam and Patricia Roche
**TINSLEY HOUSE**
The Square, Cahir,
Co Tipperary

TEL: **052 41947**  FAX: **052 41947**
EMAIL: **tinsleyhouse@eircom.net**

19th Century Town House. Former antique shop with bedrooms upstairs. Separate sitting room for guests with Tea/Coffee making facilities. Period decor and Roof Garden accessible to guests.

| B&B | 3 | Ensuite | €31 | Dinner | - |
|------|---|---------|-----|--------|---|
| B&B | - | Standard | - | Partial Board | - |
| Single Rate | | | - | Child reduction | 25% |

**Open:** 1st February-30th November

---

*Cahir 1.5km*

### The Hyland Family
**COUNTRY HOUSE B&B AND EQUESTRIAN CENTRE**
Ardfinnan Road R670, Cahir,
Co Tipperary

TEL: **052 41426**  FAX: **052 41426**
EMAIL: **familyhyland@eircom.net**
WEB: **www.dirl.com/tipperary/cahir/cahir-equestrian.htm**

Beautiful country home with equestrian centre set among spacious gardens. Ideally located for fishing, golfing and touring local beauty spots. Brochure on request.

| B&B | 3 | Ensuite | €30-€31 | Dinner | - |
|------|---|---------|---------|--------|---|
| B&B | 1 | Standard | €28-€28.50 | Partial Board | - |
| Single Rate | | | €38-€43.50 | Child reduction | 33.3% |

**Open:** 1st January-31st December

---

*Carrick-on-Suir 11km*

### The Coady Family
**THE GRAND INN**
Nine-Mile-House, Carrick-On-Suir, Co Tipperary

TEL: **051 647035**  FAX: **051 647035**
EMAIL: **thegrandinn9@eircom.net**

Former 17th century Bianconi Inn Family Home. In scenic Valley of Slievenamon. Spacious gardens. Antique furnishings. On Clonmel/Kilkenny Road N76.

| B&B | 3 | Ensuite | €35-€35 | Dinner | - |
|------|---|---------|---------|--------|---|
| B&B | 2 | Standard | €30-€30 | Partial Board | - |
| Single Rate | | | €40-€45 | Child reduction | 25% |

**Open:** All Year

---

*Carrick-on-Suir 1km*

### John & Dolores Lonergan
**HILLCREST**
Greenhill Close, Carrick-on-Suir, Co Tipperary

TEL: **051 640847**
EMAIL: **hillcrestdj@hotmail.com**

Family run B&B opposite Sean Kelly Sports Centre on N24. Ideal for touring the south east. Carrick is the home of cycling.

| B&B | 4 | Ensuite | €30-€32 | Dinner | - |
|------|---|---------|---------|--------|---|
| B&B | - | Standard | - | Partial Board | - |
| Single Rate | | | €40-€43.50 | Child reduction | 50% |

**Open:** 1st January-23rd December

---

*Cashel 5km*

### Joan Brett Moloney
**TIR NA NOG**
Dualla, Cashel, Co Tipperary

TEL: **062 61350**  FAX: **062 62411**
EMAIL: **tnanog@indigo.ie**
WEB: **www.tirnanogbandb.com**

Award winning - friendly country home. Landscaped gardens. Peaceful surroundings. Home Baking, , Orthopaedic Beds. R691 Cashel/Kilkenny Road. Dinner/Breakfast Menu.

| B&B | 5 | Ensuite | €27.50-€37.50 | Dinner | €19-€28 |
|------|---|---------|---------------|--------|---------|
| B&B | 1 | Standard | €25.50-€34 | Partial Board | - |
| Single Rate | | | €38-€46 | Child reduction | 25% |

**Open:** All Year Except Christmas

**Eileen Creed**
**ARD RI HOUSE**
Dualla Road, Cashel,
Co Tipperary

### Cashel
Tel: **062 63143**   Fax: **062 63037**
Email: **donalcreed@eircom.net**
Web: **www.ardrihouse.com**

Warm friendly luxurious country home. Peaceful surroundings. Orthopaedic beds. Ground floor bedrooms. Gourmet breakfast menu. Home baking. Dulla/Kilkenny Road R691.

| B&B | 4 | Ensuite | €30-€35 | Dinner | - |
| B&B | - | Standard | | Partial Board | - |
| Single Rate | | | €40-€50 | Child reduction | 25% |

Cashel 1km

**Open:** 1st February-30th November

---

**Maria Dunne**
**WATTIE'S B&B**
Dominic Street, Cashel,
Co Tipperary

### Cashel
Tel: **062 61923**

Situated bwtween Dominic's Abbey and Rock of Cashel, warm welcome, breakfast menu, jacussi ensuite option, tea/coffee facilities, tv, hairdryer, clock/radio in spacious rooms.

| B&B | 3 | Ensuite | €32-€36 | Dinner | - |
| B&B | - | Standard | - | Partial Board | - |
| Single Rate | | | €45-€50 | Child reduction | 25% |

Cashel

**Open:** 1st January-22nd December

---

**Mrs Mary Hally**
**CARRON HOUSE**
Carron, Cashel, Co Tipperary

### Cashel
Tel: **052 62142**   Fax: **052 62168**
Email: **hallyfamily@eircom.net**
Web: **www.carronhouse.com**

Beautifully decorated award winning country home and farm in peaceful surroundings. (No children). Minutes from Cashel take N8 (St. Bound) for 2 miles signposted left of cross roads.

| B&B | 4 | Ensuite | €33 | Dinner | - |
| B&B | - | Standard | - | Partial Board | - |
| Single Rate | | | €50 | Child reduction | - |

Cashel 5km

**Open:** 1st April-1st October

---

**Anna & Patrick Hayes**
**ROCKVILLE HOUSE**
Cashel, Co Tipperary

### Cashel
Tel: **062 61760**

Located between 12th Century Abbey and the famous Royal Historic Castle. Recommended family home, relaxing garden. Local amenities. Secure car park.

| B&B | 6 | Ensuite | €27.50-€31 | Dinner | - |
| B&B | - | Standard | | Partial Board | - |
| Single Rate | | | €40-€43.50 | Child reduction | 25% |

In Cashel Town

**Open:** All Year

---

**Helen Hayes**
**COLLEGE VIEW**
Carrigeen, Cashel,
Co Tipperary

### Cashel
Tel: **052 62317**   Fax: **052 42996**
Email: **collegeview@eircom.net**
Web: **www.holidayireland.8k.ie**

B/B Country house. Country home with large gardens & Pet farm. Located on N8 between Cashel & Caher Co. Tipperary.

| B&B | 4 | Ensuite | €30-€35 | Dinner | - |
| B&B | - | Standard | | Partial Board | - |
| Single Rate | | | €40-€45 | Child reduction | 25% |

Cashel 3km

**Open:** 1st March-1st December

**Cashel 7km**

### Mrs Mary Hickey
GORT-NA-CLOC
Ardmayle, Cashel, Co Tipperary

Tel: **0504 42362**  Fax: **0504 42002**
Email: **gortnaclocbandb@hotmail.com**
Web: **www.tipperarybandb.com**

Comfortable home in peaceful countryside, North West of Cashel on Gooldscross Road. Fishing, Golf, Walks. Private parking. Orthopaedic beds. Internet access.

| B&B | 4 | Ensuite | €27.50-€31 | Dinner | - |
| B&B | 1 | Standard | €25.80-€28.50 | Partial Board | - |
| Single Rate | | | €38-€43.50 | Child reduction | 50% |

**Open:** 1st March-31st November

**In Cashel**

### Rem & Joan Joy
ROCKSIDE HOUSE B&B
Rock Villas, Cashel,
Co Tipperary

Tel: **062 63813**  Fax: **062 63813**
Email: **joyrocksidehouse@eircom.net**

Located at foot of Rock of Cashel (50 meters) and Bru Boru Centre. Warm welcome, orthopaedic beds, tv, hairdryer, tea/coffee all rooms, private parking.

| B&B | 4 | Ensuite | €30-€40 | Dinner | - |
| B&B | - | Standard | | Partial Board | - |
| Single Rate | | | - | Child reduction | 25% |

**Open:** 15th February-15th November

### Mrs Mary A Kennedy
THORNBROOK HOUSE
Dualla/Kilkenny Rd (R691),
Cashel, Co Tipperary

Tel: **062 62388**  Fax: **062 61480**
Email: **thornbrookhouse@eircom.net**
Web: **www.thornbrookhouse.com**

Elegant country home. Antique furnishing, Landscaped gardens. Orthopaedic beds, Hairdryers, Tea/coffee, TV in all bedrooms. AA ♦♦♦♦ Internationally acclaimed.

| B&B | 3 | Ensuite | €30-€35 | Dinner | - |
| B&B | 2 | Standard | €27-€30 | Partial Board | - |
| Single Rate | | | €40-€55 | Child reduction | 25% |

**Cashel 1km**

**Open:** 1st April-16th October

### Ellen, Ryan & Carmel Lawrence
ABBEY HOUSE
1 Dominic Street, Cashel,
Co Tipperary

Tel: **062 61104**  Fax: **062 61104**
Email: **teachnamainstreach@eircom.net**
Web: **www.southeastireland.com/michelle**

Town House, opposite Dominic's Abbey. 150 metres Rock of Cashel. Television/Tea/Coffee all bedrooms. Parking. Town Centre 50 metres.

| B&B | 4 | Ensuite | €35 | Dinner | - |
| B&B | 1 | Standard | €32 | Partial Board | - |
| Single Rate | | | €41-€45 | Child reduction | 25% |

**In Cashel**

**Open:** 1st February-30th November

### Mr & Mrs Kevin & Beatrice Leahy
LADYSWELL HOUSE
Ladyswell Street, Cashel,
Co Tipperary

Tel: **062 62985**
Email: **ladyswellhouse@eircom.net**
Web: **www.tipp.ie/ladyswell.htm**

19th century elegance and modern amenities under shadow of rock. Chauffeur tours available. 5 star base for tours of S.E. region. Come visit and enjoy our home.

| B&B | 4 | Ensuite | €27.50-€40 | Dinner | - |
| B&B | - | Standard | | Partial Board | - |
| Single Rate | | | €40-€60 | Child reduction | 33.3% |

**In Cashel**

**Open:** 1st January-24th December

### Mrs Dorothy Mason
**GEORGESLAND**
**Dualla/Kilkenny Road, Cashel, Co Tipperary**

**Cashel**

TEL: **062 62788**  FAX: **062 62788**
EMAIL: **georges_land@hotmail.com**
WEB: **www.georgesland.net**

Modern Country Home, situated R691 Dualla/Kilkenny road. Set in peaceful landscaped gardens, surrounded by scenic countryside. Secure parking.  Orthopedic beds

| B&B | 4 | Ensuite | €28-€31 | Dinner | - |
| B&B | - | Standard | - | Partial Board | - |
| Single Rate | | | €40-€43.50 | Child reduction | **33.3%** |

Cashel 1km

**Open:** 1st February-30th November

---

### Mrs Sarah Murphy
**INDAVILLE**
**Cashel, Co Tipperary**

**Cashel**

TEL: **062 62075**
EMAIL: **indaville@eircom.net**
WEB: **www.indaville.com**

Charming period home. Superb view of Rock of Cashel. Built in 1729 on 4 acres of Beechwood. Centrally located on N8, south of Main Street. Large comfortable rooms.

| B&B | 3 | Ensuite | €30-€35 | Dinner | - |
| B&B | - | Standard | - | Partial Board | - |
| Single Rate | | | €45-€50 | Child reduction | **50%** |

Cashel

**Open:** 1st March-31st October

---

### Mrs Breda O'Grady
**ROCKVIEW HOUSE**
**Bohermore, Cashel, Co Tipperary**

**Cashel**

TEL: **062 62187**

Modern bungalow situated in the Town of Cashel. Panoramic view of the Rock of Cashel. Tea & Coffee in Bedrooms. Breakfast Menu. Friendly hospitality.

| B&B | 3 | Ensuite | €30-€32 | Dinner | - |
| B&B | - | Standard | - | Partial Board | - |
| Single Rate | | | - | Child reduction | **25%** |

Cashel

**Open:** 17th March-31st October

---

### Michael & Laura Ryan
**ASHMORE HOUSE**
**John Street, Cashel, Co Tipperary**

**Cashel**

TEL: **062 61286**  FAX: **062 62789**
EMAIL: **ashmorehouse@eircom.net**
WEB: **www.ashmorehouse.com**

Georgian Family Home, heart of Cashel, Warm Welcome, Spacious Gardens, Private Parking, Residents Lounge, Touring Base, all amenities nearby. AA ◆◆◆.

| B&B | 5 | Ensuite | €30-€40 | Dinner | €30-€38 |
| B&B | - | Standard | - | Partial Board | - |
| Single Rate | | | €40-€60 | Child reduction | **25%** |

Cashel

**Open:** All Year

---

### Thomas & Margaret Ryan
**WESTON'S LOT**
**Grove Lawn, Dundrum, Co Tipperary**

**Cashel**

TEL: **062 71915**  FAX: **062 71915**
EMAIL: **info@westonslot.com**
WEB: **www.westonslot.com**

Luxurious spacious home on the edge of Dundrum House Hotel and Golf Course. An ideal base for touring the southeast. AA ◆◆◆◆.

| B&B | 4 | Ensuite | €32-€37.50 | Dinner | €20-€20 |
| B&B | - | Standard | - | Partial Board | €315 |
| Single Rate | | | €40-€50 | Child reduction | **25%** |

Cashel 8km

**Open:** All Year

### Cashel

**Mary & Matt Stapleton**
PALM GROVE HOUSE
**Dualla/Kilkenny Road, Cashel, Co Tipperary**

TEL: **062 61739**   FAX: **062 61739**
EMAIL: **sstapleton@eircom.net**

Highly recommended family home. Scenic view in quiet location. Take R688 from Cashel, turn left after Church on R691 and "Palm Grove" 1km on right.

| B&B | 3 | Ensuite | €30-€32 | Dinner | - |
| B&B | 2 | Standard | €27.50-€30 | Partial Board | - |
| Single Rate | | | €38-€43.50 | Child reduction | 25% |

Cashel 1km

**Open:** 1st May-31st October

---

### Clonmel

**Denis & Kay Fahey**
FARRENWICK COUNTRY HOUSE
**Poulmucka, Curranstown, Clonmel, Co Tipperary**

TEL: **052 35130**   FAX: **052 35377**
EMAIL: **kayden@clubi.ie**
WEB: **www.farrenwick.com**

Bed and breakfast accommodation on R687, 3km NW off N24 and 6.5km SE off N8. Family Rooms. Credit Cards. Tour Guide Service.

| B&B | 3 | Ensuite | €26.50-€35 | Dinner | - |
| B&B | - | Standard | €25.50-€33 | Partial Board | - |
| Single Rate | | | €38-€45 | Child reduction | 33.3% |

Clonmel 9km

**Open:** 1st February-30th November

---

### Clonmel

**Ms Agnes McDonnell**
CLUAIN FHIA
**25 Ballingarrane, Clonmel, Co Tipperary**

TEL: **052 21431**
EMAIL: **mcdonnell25@eircom.net**

Family home, quiet cul de sac. Main Limerick, Cork, Waterford, Rosslare Rd N24. Private parking.

| B&B | 2 | Ensuite | €28-€32 | Dinner | - |
| B&B | 2 | Standard | €26-€28.50 | Partial Board | - |
| Single Rate | | | €38-€43.50 | Child reduction | 50% |

Clonmel 1km

**Open:** All Year

---

### Clonmel

**Mr Michael J Moran**
LISSARDA
**Old Spa Road, Clonmel, Co Tipperary**

TEL: **052 22593/22294**

Spacious purpose built residence within walking distance of Town Centre. Landscaped gardens. Power showers, TV, Tea/Coffee, Hairdryers. Breakfast menu.

| B&B | 4 | Ensuite | €30-€35 | Dinner | - |
| B&B | - | Standard | - | Partial Board | - |
| Single Rate | | | €40-€45 | Child reduction | 33.3% |

In Clonmel

**Open:** 1st January-20th December

---

### Clonmel

**Mrs Rita Morrissey**
HILLCOURT
**Marlfield, Clonmel, Co Tipperary**

TEL: **052 21029/29711**
EMAIL: **ejmorrissey@hotmail.com**
WEB: **www.hillcourt.com**

Bungalow in peaceful surroundings 300 metres off main Cork/Limerick Rd (N24). Golf, Fishing within 2 miles. TV.

| B&B | 5 | Ensuite | €27.50-€31 | Dinner | - |
| B&B | - | Standard | - | Partial Board | - |
| Single Rate | | | €40-€43.50 | Child reduction | - |

Clonmel 1.5km

**Open:** All Year

**Anna O'Donnell**
WOODROOFFE HOUSE
**Cahir Road, Clonmel,**
**Co Tipperary**

Tel: **052 35243**
Email: **woodrooffe@eircom.net**
Web: **woodrooffe@eircom.net**

Country house in secluded setting situated 1km off N24 between Clonmel and Cahir. Ideal stopover on Rosslare/Galway route. Breakfast menu available. Tea/Coffee on arrival.

| B&B | 3 | Ensuite | €30-€32 | Dinner | - |
| B&B | - | Standard | €29-€29 | Partial Board | - |
| Single Rate | | | €38-€43.50 | Child reduction | - |

Cahir 6km

**Open:** 20th April-20th September

---

**Ms Breda O'Shea**
ASHBOURNE
**Mountain Road, Clonmel,**
**Co Tipperary**

Tel: **052 22307**  Fax: **052 22307**
Email: **ashbourn@iol.ie**

Period spacious home overlooking River, a few minutes walk from Town Centre, Shops, Pubs and Clubs. TV, hairdryers and tea/coffee facilities, all rooms. Private parking. Via Mountain Road.

| B&B | 3 | Ensuite | €30-€33 | Dinner | - |
| B&B | - | Standard | - | Partial Board | - |
| Single Rate | | | €40-€43.50 | Child reduction | 50% |

Clonmel

**Open:** 2nd January-18th December

---

**Mrs Margaret Whelan**
AMBERVILLE
**Glenconnor Rd,**
**(off Western Rd), Clonmel,**
**Co Tipperary**

Tel: **052 21470**
Email: **amberville@eircom.net**
Web: **www.southeastireland.com/amberville**

Spacious bungalow off Western road near Hospitals. Ideal base for touring, Hillwalking, Golf, Fishing. Guests TV lounge with Tea/Coffee facilities. Visa Cards.

| B&B | 3 | Ensuite | €27.50-€31 | Dinner | - |
| B&B | 2 | Standard | €25.50-€28.50 | Partial Board | - |
| Single Rate | | | €38-€43.50 | Child reduction | 33.3% |

Clonmel

**Open:** 1st January-1st November

---

**The Stanley Family**
BALLINACOURTY HOUSE
**Glen of Aherlow, Co Tipperary**

Tel: **062 56000/56230**
Email: **info@ballinacourtyhse.com**
Web: **ballinacourtyhse.com**

Situated in a beautiful valley. Our 18th Century modernised home was once a stable courtyard. Restaurant with resident Chef. Tennis, Forest walks start at gate.

| B&B | 5 | Ensuite | €28-€31 | Dinner | €30 |
| B&B | - | Standard | - | Partial Board | €400 |
| Single Rate | | | €40-€43.50 | Child reduction | 50% |

Tipperary 13km

**Open:** 19th January-10th December

---

**Brian & Mary Devine**
WILLIAMSFERRY HOUSE
**Fintan Lalor Street, Nenagh,**
**Co Tipperary**

Tel: **067 31118**
Email: **williamsferry@eircom.net**
Web: **www.williamsferry.com**

AA ◆◆◆. Elegant townhouse 1830. Private parking. Guest lounge. TV, Hairdryer, Tea/Coffee facilities in rooms. Central to Town. Very comfortable. Warm welcome.

| B&B | 6 | Ensuite | €29-€31 | Dinner | - |
| B&B | - | Standard | - | Partial Board | - |
| Single Rate | | | €40-€43.50 | Child reduction | 33.3% |

Nenagh

**Open:** 1st January-22nd December

**Mary & William Hayes**
**MARYVILLE**
Ballycommon, Near Dromineer,
Nenagh, Co Tipperary

### Nenagh
Tel: **067 32531**
Email: **maryvilleguest@eircom.net**
Web: **www.maryvillebandb.com**

Comfortable spacious home with breakfast conservatory, tranquil location in Ballycommon Village. On R495 to Dromineer Bay on Lough Derg. 150mts to renowned Bar/Restaurant.

| B&B | 3 | Ensuite | €27.50-€31 | Dinner | €19 |
|---|---|---|---|---|---|
| B&B | - | Standard | | Partial Board | €294 |
| Single Rate | | | €40-€43.50 | Child reduction | **33.3%** |

Nenagh 4km

**Open:** All Year

---

**Mrs Joan Kennedy**
**THE COUNTRY HOUSE**
Thurles Road, Kilkeary,
Nenagh, Co Tipperary

### Nenagh
Tel: **067 31193**

Luxurious residence recommended Frommer Guide. Large parking. Rooms Tea/coffee facilities. Breakfast menu. Orthopaedic beds. Fishing, Golf, Horse riding nearby.

| B&B | 3 | Ensuite | €30-€32.50 | Dinner | - |
|---|---|---|---|---|---|
| B&B | 2 | Standard | €28-€30 | Partial Board | - |
| Single Rate | | | €38-€43.50 | Child reduction | **33.3%** |

Nenagh 6km

**Open:** 1st January-31st December

---

**Mary & Joseph Kirwan**
**SEÓIDÍN**
Nenagh, Co Tipperary

### Nenagh
Tel: **067 22136**  Fax: **067 22278**
Email: **maryhenrykirwan@eircom.net**

Brown brick bungalow in outskirts of Terryglass village with beautiful landscape gardens. Close to lake amenities, water sports, fishing (very private).

| B&B | 1 | Ensuite | €30-€35 | Dinner | €20-€30 |
|---|---|---|---|---|---|
| B&B | 2 | Standard | €28-€30 | Partial Board | |
| Single Rate | | | - | Child reduction | **33.3%** |

Portumna 10km

**Open:** 15th January-20th December

---

**Mrs Mary Lynch**
**SHANNONVALE HOUSE**
Dromineer, Nenagh,
Co Tipperary

### Nenagh
Tel: **067 24102**  Fax: **067 24102**
Email: **shannonvalehouse@eircom.net**

Modern two storey house, close to Lough Derg. Quiet location in an idyllic setting. All the comforts of home.

| B&B | 3 | Ensuite | €30-€31 | Dinner | €25-€25 |
|---|---|---|---|---|---|
| B&B | - | Standard | | Partial Board | |
| Single Rate | | | €40-€43.50 | Child reduction | **50%** |

Dromineer 3km

**Open:** 17th March-30th September

---

**Tom & Patricia McKeogh**
**WILLOWBROOK**
Belleen (Portroe Rd), Nenagh,
Co Tipperary

### Nenagh
Tel: **067 31558**  Fax: **067 41222**
Email: **willowbrook@oceanfree.net**
Web: **www.willowbrook.ie**

Spacious, Modern home. Ideal base for touring / business. Internet use available, gardens for guest use, restaurants nearby. 1.5km Nenagh, N52 / R494 (Portroe Road junction)

| B&B | 6 | Ensuite | €29-€31 | Dinner | - |
|---|---|---|---|---|---|
| B&B | - | Standard | | Partial Board | - |
| Single Rate | | | €40-€43.50 | Child reduction | **33.3%** |

Nenagh 2km

**Open:** All Year

**Mary McGeeney**
COOLANGATTA
Brocka, Ballinderry, Nenagh,
Co Tipperary

### Nenagh Lough Derg

Tel: **067 22164**
Email: **coolangatta@eircom.net**

Spectacular views of Lough Derg and surrounding Countryside. Breakfast menu, Tea/Coffee, Lounge with TV/Video. Use of landscaped garden. Folk dancing classes.

| B&B | 3 | Ensuite | €27.50-€31 | Dinner | - |
|---|---|---|---|---|---|
| B&B | - | Standard | €25.50-€28.50 | Partial Board | - |
| Single Rate | | | €40-€43.50 | Child reduction | 50% |

enagh 20km

**Open:** All Year

**Margaret & PJ Mounsey**
ASHLEY PARK HOUSE
Ashley Park, Nenagh,
Co Tipperary

### Nenagh Lough Derg

Tel: **067 38223**   Fax: **067 38013**
Email: **margaret@ashleypark.com**
Web: **www.ashleypark.com**

17th Century house stands on the shores of Lough Orna. Centrally located, ideal for those who love tranquillity. Golfing, private Lake with boat for fishing. Woodlands for private walks.

| B&B | 5 | Ensuite | €45-€55 | Dinner | €32-€38 |
|---|---|---|---|---|---|
| B&B | - | Standard | - | Partial Board | - |
| Single Rate | | | - | Child reduction | 50% |

enagh

**Open:** All Year Except Christmas

**Marie Warren**
SLÍ DÁLA B&B
Dublin Road, Roscrea,
Co Tipperary

### Roscrea

Tel: **0505 23270**   Fax: **0505 23270**
Email: **slidala@eircom.net**
Web: **www.slidala.com**

Friendly home situated on the N7 at the entrance to Roscrea Heritage town.

| B&B | 5 | Ensuite | €30-€35 | Dinner | - |
|---|---|---|---|---|---|
| B&B | - | Standard | - | Partial Board | - |
| Single Rate | | | €40-€43.50 | Child reduction | 33.3% |

oscrea 1km

**Open:** 1st January-24th December

**Sheila & Oliver Darcy**
LAKE LAND LODGE
Terryglass, Nenagh,
Co Tipperary

### Terryglass

Tel: **067 22069**   Fax: **067 22069**
Email: **lakelandlodge@eircom.net**

Luxurious accommodation in beautiful scenic area. "A home away from home" Close to all Lake amenities eg. Fishing, Water Sports, Traditional Music, Golf etc.

| B&B | 2 | Ensuite | €32-€32 | Dinner | - |
|---|---|---|---|---|---|
| B&B | 1 | Standard | €32-€32 | Partial Board | - |
| Single Rate | | | €40-€45 | Child reduction | 33.3% |

Terryglass

**Open:** 1st January-23rd December

**Pierce & Joan Duggan**
THE CASTLE
Two Mile Borris, Thurles,
Co Tipperary

### Thurles

Tel: **0504 44324**   Fax: **0504 44352**
Email: **b&b@thecastletmb.com**
Web: **www.thecastletmb.com**

ITC. House Adjacent to Castle. Superior Accommodation, deluxe ensuite bedrooms. The Castle is on the N75 near the village of Two Mile Borris. AA ◆◆◆◆◆.

| B&B | 4 | Ensuite | €35-€40 | Dinner | €40 |
|---|---|---|---|---|---|
| B&B | - | Standard | - | Partial Board | - |
| Single Rate | | | €45-€50 | Child reduction | 25% |

hurles 4km

**Open:** All Year

**Mary Flanagan Hunt**
ABBEYVALE HOUSE B&B
Cashel Road, Holy Cross,
Thurles, Co Tipperary

### Thurles

TEL: **0504 43032**
EMAIL: **abbeyval@gofree.indigo.ie**
WEB: **abbeyvalehouse.com**

Enjoy Irish hospitality at its best in a spacious, luxurious home, between Cashel and Thurles, in tranquil surroundings. Fishing, Golf nearby. Ideal touring base. Bord Failte Merit Award. AA ◆◆◆◆.

| B&B | 4 | Ensuite | €30-€32.50 | Dinner | €19-€25 |
|-----|---|---------|------------|--------|---------|
| B&B | - | Standard | - | Partial Board | - |
| Single Rate | | | €40-€43.50 | Child reduction | 50% |

Thurles 6km

**Open:** 1st February-30th November

---

**Anna Stakelum**
BOHERNA LODGE
Clohane, Tipperary Road (R661),
Holycross, Thurles,
Co Tipperary

### Thurles

TEL: **0504 43121**
EMAIL: **boherna@oceanfree.net**
WEB: **www.dirlcom/tipperary/boherna-lodge.htm**

Elegant country house, peaceful surrounding. Warm professional welcome. Ideal base for touring Holycross Abbey, Rock of Cashel. Golf, Fishing, Riding nearby.

| B&B | 3 | Ensuite | €27.50-€31 | Dinner | €19 |
|-----|---|---------|------------|--------|-----|
| B&B | 1 | Standard | €25.50-€28.50 | Partial Board | - |
| Single Rate | | | €38-€43.50 | Child reduction | 25% |

Thurles 6km

**Open:** All Year Except Christmas

---

**Mrs Noreen Collins**
PURT HOUSE
Bohercrowe, Emly Road,
Tipperary Town, Co Tipperary

### Tipperary

TEL: **062 51938**
EMAIL: **purthouse@eircom.net**

Warm welcome R515 to Killarney, Tea/Coffee, TV, Hairdryers in bedrooms, hot scones, Credit cards, laundry facilities, Irish Night arranged

| B&B | 5 | Ensuite | €31 | Dinner | €25-€25 |
|-----|---|---------|-----|--------|---------|
| B&B | 1 | Standard | €31 | Partial Board | - |
| Single Rate | | | €41-€43.50 | Child reduction | 33.3% |

Tipperary 1.5km

**Open:** 1st April-31st October

---

**Mrs Kay Crowe**
RIVERSIDE HOUSE
Galbally Road, Tipperary Town,
Co Tipperary

### Tipperary

TEL: **062 51219/51245**   FAX: **062 51219**
EMAIL: **riversidehouse@hotmail.com**
WEB: **http://welcome.to/riversidehouse**

Superbly situated home, main Cork route (R662). 5 mins walk Town Centre. All facilities in bedrooms. Guests Lounge, Sports Complex, Swimming Pool, Tennis, Golf & Cinema nearby, available to guests.

| B&B | 3 | Ensuite | €30-€32 | Dinner | - |
|-----|---|---------|---------|--------|---|
| B&B | 1 | Standard | €28-€30 | Partial Board | - |
| Single Rate | | | €40-€45 | Child reduction | 33.3% |

In Tipperary

**Open:** 1st March-31st October

---

**Douglas & Angela Edinborough**
BALLYKISTEEN LODGE
Monard, Co Tipperary

### Tipperary

TEL: **062 33403**   FAX: **062 33711**
EMAIL: **ballykisteenlodge@oceanfree.net**
WEB: **www.ballykisteenlodgebandb.net**

Luxurious residence. Adjacent to Ballykisteen Golf & Leisure Centre, Tipperary Racecourse. 10 minutes to Tipperary. Breakfast menu. TV, Tea/Coffee facilities. TV lounge.

| B&B | 4 | Ensuite | €35-€35 | Dinner | - |
|-----|---|---------|---------|--------|---|
| B&B | - | Standard | - | Partial Board | - |
| Single Rate | | | €45-€45 | Child reduction | 25% |

Tipperary Town 3km

**Open:** 30th April-31st October

**Mrs Margaret Merrigan**
TEACH GOBNATHAN
Glen of Aherlow,
Golf Links Road, Brookville,
Tipperary, Co Tipperary

**Tipperary**

Tel: **062 51645**
Email: **teachgobnathan@iolfree.ie**

Suburban home in scenic location beside Golf Club. Close to all amenities. Turn down at traffic lights, centre of Tipperary town, right at roundabout, two bends past Golf Club. Failte.

| B&B | 3 | Ensuite | €27.50-€31 | Dinner | - |
| B&B | 1 | Standard | €25.50-€28.50 | Partial Board | - |
| Single Rate | | | €38-€43.50 | Child reduction | 25% |

Tipperary 1.5km

**Open:** 1st March-31st October

---

**Mrs Mary Quinn**
CLONMORE HOUSE
Cork/Galbally Rd,
Tipperary Town, Co Tipperary

**Tipperary**

Tel: **062 51637**
Email: **clonmorehouse@eircom.net**

Bungalow 5 mins walk town, scenic surroundings, overlooking Galtee Mountains, Frommer, Birnbaun, Best B&B Guides recommended. Ground floor bedrooms, Electric blankets.

| B&B | 4 | Ensuite | €30-€31 | Dinner | - |
| B&B | - | Standard | - | Partial Board | - |
| Single Rate | | | €40-€43.50 | Child reduction | - |

n Tipperary

**Open:** 1st March-31st October

---

**Mrs Mairín Chuirc**
AISLING
Glen of Aherlow Road,
Tipperary, Co Tipperary

**Tipperary**

Tel: **062 33307** Fax: **062 82955**
Email: **ladygreg@oceanfree.net**

Welcome to Aisling. Now you are home. Tea/Coffee on arrival. Central to Glen of Aherlow, Lakes, Rock of Cashel, Cahir Castle, Local Ancestor Tracing Centre, Golf, Fishing.

| B&B | 4 | Ensuite | €30-€31 | Dinner | - |
| B&B | - | Standard | €25.50-€28.50 | Partial Board | - |
| Single Rate | | | €38-€43.50 | Child reduction | 50% |

Tipperary 1.5km

**Open:** All Year Except Christmas

---

**Mrs Teresa Russell**
BANSHA CASTLE
Bansha, Co Tipperary

**Tipperary**

Tel: **062 54187** Fax: **062 54294**
Email: **trese@banshacastle.com**
Web: **www.banshacastle.com**

Historic country house. Private gardens, Mature trees. Snooker room. Superb cooking. Walking/cycling. Pre booking recommended. 10 mins south Tipperary N24.

| B&B | 5 | Ensuite | €45 | Dinner | €25-€25 |
| B&B | 1 | Standard | €42 | Partial Board | €490 |
| Single Rate | | | €52-€55 | Child reduction | 25% |

Tipperary 8km

**Open:** 10th January-20th December

---

## TELEPHONE

- Operator assisted calls within Ireland — Dial 10
- International telephone operator — Dial 11818
- Directory Enquiries — Dial 11811

**FOR TROUBLE-FREE TELEPHONE CALLS FROM PUBLIC PAY PHONES IT IS ADVISABLE TO PURCHASE A TELEPHONE CALLCARD AVAILABLE IN POST OFFICES AND WHEREVER YOU SEE A CALLCARD SIGN.**

**TO DIAL IRELAND FROM ABROAD:** Country Access Code + 353 + Area Code (omit first zero) + Local Number

Waterford, The Crystal County boasts of splendid scenery, mountain passes, miles of spectacular coastline with safe and sandy beaches. The city of Waterford is a bustling maritime city, with 1,000 years of History, Museums and Heritage centres to see and explore.

---

**Ms Theresa Troy**
CUSH
**Duffcarrick, Ardmore,
Co Waterford**

### Ardmore

TEL: **024 94474**
EMAIL: **mttroy@eircom.net**

Situated adjacent picturesque Ardmore, off N25, with views of Bay, historic Ancient sites and surrounding countryside. Warm personal welcome assured.

| | | | | | |
|---|---|---|---|---|---|
| B&B | 2 | Ensuite | €29-€31 | Dinner | - |
| B&B | 1 | Standard | €28-€30 | Partial Board | - |
| Single Rate | | | - | Child reduction | - |

**Ardmore 2km**

**Open:** 1st April-30th September

---

**Richard & Nora Harte**
CNOC-NA-RI
**Nire Valley, Ballymacarby,
Via Clonmel, Co Waterford**

### Ballymacarbry Nire Valley

TEL: **052 36239**   FAX: **052 36243**
EMAIL: **richardharte@eircom.net**
WEB: **homepage.eircom.net/~cnocnaricountryhome/**

Luxurious friendly home. Spacious ensuite rooms with every comfort for guests. Elevated site surrounded by scenic views. Causin & Dillard Rec. Extensive breakfast menu. Walking, golf, fishing, touring.

| | | | | | |
|---|---|---|---|---|---|
| B&B | 4 | Ensuite | €35-€40 | Dinner | - |
| B&B | - | Standard | - | Partial Board | - |
| Single Rate | | | €45-€45 | Child reduction | 25% |

**Clonmel 14km**

**Open:** 1st February-1st November

---

**Una Mason**
BELLE VISTA
**Melleray Road R669,
Cappoquin, Co Waterford**

### Cappoquin

TEL: **058 54296**
EMAIL: **masonuna@hotmail.com**

Scenic peaceful surroundings on edge of town. Melleray Road. Good golf fishing and walking. Blackwater Valley and mountain drives. Dungarvan and sea 15 mins Failte.

| | | | | | |
|---|---|---|---|---|---|
| B&B | 2 | Ensuite | €35-€35 | Dinner | - |
| B&B | 1 | Standard | €30-€30 | Partial Board | - |
| Single Rate | | | €43-€45 | Child reduction | 25% |

**In Cappoquin**

**Open:** 1st April-30th September

---

**Mrs Catherine Mary Scanlan**
COOLHILLA
**Ballyhane, Cappoquin,
Co Waterford**

### Cappoquin

TEL: **058 54054**   FAX: **058 54054**
EMAIL: **coolhilla@eircom.net**

'Ambassador of Tourism' winner. Home Cooking, Tea/Coffee facilities, All rooms en-suite with TV. Ideal location for Walking, Fishing, Golfing. Excellent food and Irish music. Main N72. Credit cards accepted.

| | | | | | |
|---|---|---|---|---|---|
| B&B | 3 | Ensuite | €35-€35 | Dinner | €28 |
| B&B | - | Standard | - | Partial Board | - |
| Single Rate | | | €45-€45 | Child reduction | 25% |

**Cappoquin 5km**

**Open:** 10th January-30th November

**Sheila Lane**
BALLINAMORE HOUSE
**Ballyduff, Dungarvan,**
**Co Waterford**

TEL: **058 42146**

Just off R672, 2.5km west Dungarvan. Superior ground floor accommodation homely atmosphere in idyllic setting. Near Town, Fishing, Golf, Horseriding and Walking. Patio, garden for guests.

| B&B | 3 | Ensuite | €27.50-€31 | Dinner | - |
|---|---|---|---|---|---|
| B&B | - | Standard | | Partial Board | - |
| Single Rate | | | €40-€43.50 | Child reduction | **33.3%** |

Dungarvan 2.5km

**Open:** 1st January-21st December

---

**Sheila Norris**
BAYSIDE
**Gold Coast Road, Dungarvan,**
**Co Waterford**

TEL: **058 44318**  FAX: **058 44318**
EMAIL: **pnorris@gofree.indigo.ie**
WEB: **www.bayside.s5.com**

Seafront dormer bungalow in a rural setting, overlooking Dungarvan Bay. Private car park.

| B&B | 4 | Ensuite | €33-€35 | Dinner | - |
|---|---|---|---|---|---|
| B&B | - | Standard | - | Partial Board | - |
| Single Rate | | | €43-€45 | Child reduction | - |

Dungarvan 5km

**Open:** 1st March-31st October

---

**Helen O'Connell**
HILLCREST
**Waterford Road, Tarr's Bridge,**
**Dungarvan, Co Waterford**

TEL: **058 42262**
EMAIL: **hillcrestdungarvan@eircom.net**

Bungalow on Waterford/Cork road(N25). Adjacent 18 hole Golf Course. Rosslare 1.5 hours. Electric blankets. Safe Parking. Ideal touring centre. Early breakfasts served.

| B&B | 2 | Ensuite | €27.50-€31 | Dinner | - |
|---|---|---|---|---|---|
| B&B | 1 | Standard | €25.50-€28.50 | Partial Board | - |
| Single Rate | | | €38-€43.50 | Child reduction | **50%** |

Dungarvan 3km

**Open:** 1st May-30th October

---

**Mrs R Prendergast**
THE OLD RECTORY
**Waterford Rd, Dungarvan,**
**Co Waterford**

TEL: **058 41394**  FAX: **058 41394**
EMAIL: **theoldrectory@cablesurf.com**
WEB: **homepage.eircom.net/~1108**

Waterford side of town on N25, Offstreet Parking. Walking distance of Town Centre. TV, Tea/Coffee facilities in bedrooms. 3x18 Hole Golf Courses nearby.

| B&B | 4 | Ensuite | €32-€36 | Dinner | - |
|---|---|---|---|---|---|
| B&B | - | Standard | | Partial Board | - |
| Single Rate | | | €40-€44 | Child reduction | **50%** |

n Dungarvan

**Open:** 1st February-31st December

---

**Mrs Alice Shanley**
TOURNORE HOUSE
**Abbeyside, Dungarvan,**
**Co Waterford**

TEL: **058 44370**
EMAIL: **tournore.house@oceanfree.net**
WEB: **www.tournorehouse.com**

Magnificent 18th Century country house located just off N25 and close to Town Centre/Golf/Beaches etc. Private parking. Tennis Court. Warm welcome assured.

| B&B | 3 | Ensuite | €32-€38 | Dinner | - |
|---|---|---|---|---|---|
| B&B | 1 | Standard | €30-€32 | Partial Board | - |
| Single Rate | | | €45 | Child reduction | - |

Dungarvan 1km

**Open:** 1st January-20th December

**Mrs Margo Sleator**
**ROSEBANK HOUSE**
Clonea Road (R675),
Dungarvan, Co Waterford

## Dungarvan

TEL: **058 41561**
EMAIL: **msleator@eircom.net**
WEB: **www.rosebankhouse.com**

Take R675 from Dungarvan, following signposting for Clonea Strand, own signposting en-route, Tea/Coffee in lounge. Highly recommended. Gourmet Breakfast menu.

| B&B | 3 | Ensuite | €34 | Dinner | - |
| B&B | 1 | Standard | €30 | Partial Board | - |
| Single Rate | | | €42-€45 | Child reduction | - |

Dungarvan 3km

**Open:** 1st March-22nd December

---

**Winnie & Tony Brooke**
**SPRINGFIELD**
Dunmore East, Co Waterford

## Dunmore East

TEL: **051 383448**
EMAIL: **springfieldbb@esatclear.ie**
WEB: **www.springfield-dunmore.com**

Ideally located in village in quiet, beautiful area 200mts from beach, pubs & restaurants. Luxurious home, recommended Lonely Planet/Routard. "Seaside Charmer" LA Times 2003. Secure parking.

| B&B | 6 | Ensuite | €29-€33 | Dinner | - |
| B&B | - | Standard | - | Partial Board | - |
| Single Rate | | | €40-€50 | Child reduction | 25% |

In Dunmore East

**Open:** 1st March-31st October

---

**Phyllis & Ed Lannon**
**CHURCH VILLA**
Dunmore East, Co Waterford

## Dunmore East

TEL: **051 383390**   FAX: **051 383187**
EMAIL: **churchvilla@eircom.net**
WEB: **homepage.eircom.net/~churchvilla**

A warm welcome awaits you at this beautiful, well established Victorian Town House. Multi guide recommended. Close to all Restaurants, Pubs, Beach. 5 Golf courses nearby. Email access.

| B&B | 6 | Ensuite | €29-€33 | Dinner | - |
| B&B | - | Standard | - | Partial Board | - |
| Single Rate | | | €40-€45 | Child reduction | - |

In Dunmore East

**Open:** All Year Except Christmas

---

**Mrs Kathleen Martin**
**CREADEN VIEW**
Harbour Road, Dunmore East,
Co Waterford

## Dunmore East

TEL: **051 383339**   FAX: **051 385792**
EMAIL: **creadenvw@eircom.net**

Highly Recommended charming friendly home centre of Village. Walking distance Restaurants, Bars, Beaches, Golf club 2km. Recommended Frommer/Lonely Planet. Breakfast menu.

| B&B | 6 | Ensuite | €29-€33 | Dinner | - |
| B&B | - | Standard | - | Partial Board | - |
| Single Rate | | | €40-€45 | Child reduction | 25% |

In Dunmore East

**Open:** 1st March-31st October

---

**Mrs Carmel McAllister**
**MC ALLISTERS**
4 Wellington Terrace,
Dunmore East, Co Waterford

## Dunmore East

TEL: **051 383035**
EMAIL: **mcallisterbb@hotmail.com**
WEB: **www.indunmoreeast.com**

Period luxurious townhouse combining old world charm & all modern comforts. Overlooking Beach & Harbour. Peaceful location yet central.

| B&B | 3 | Ensuite | €28-€33 | Dinner | - |
| B&B | - | Standard | - | Partial Board | - |
| Single Rate | | | - | Child reduction | 25% |

In Dunmore East

**Open:** 1st April-16th October

### Dunmore East

**The Sutton Family**
GLOR NA MARA
Kilmacleague, Dunmore East,
Co Waterford

TEL: **051 383361** FAX: **051 383361**
EMAIL: **peggysutton@eircom.net**

Country home, peaceful scenic surroundings. Golf, Fishing, Scenic Walks. Good food locally. All rooms ensuite with TV, Tea/Coffee facilities. Dunmore East 5km.

| B&B | 3 | Ensuite | €28-€31 | Dinner | - |
| B&B | - | Standard | | Partial Board | - |
| Single Rate | | | €40-€43.50 | Child reduction | 50% |

Dunmore East 5km

**Open:** All Year Except Christmas

### Lismore

**Daphne & Shaun Power**
PINE TREE HOUSE
Ballyanchor, Lismore,
Co Waterford

TEL: **058 53282**
EMAIL: **pinetreehouse@oceanfree.net**
WEB: **www.pinetreehouselismore.com**

Comfortable family home on outskirts of heritage town of Lismore. Walking distance to Lismore Castle & gardens. Very peaceful pleasant surroundings. Large private gardens. N72.

| B&B | 3 | Ensuite | €28.50-€33 | Dinner | - |
| B&B | - | Standard | - | Partial Board | - |
| Single Rate | | | €40-€50 | Child reduction | 25% |

Lismore

**Open:** 2nd January-24th December

### Lismore

**John Power**
BEECHCROFT
Deerpark Road, Lismore,
Co Waterford

TEL: **058 54273** FAX: **058 54273**
EMAIL: **beechcroftbandb@eircom.net**
WEB: **www.beechcroftbandb.ie**

A warm welcome awaits you in our home. TV, Hairdryers, Electric blankets in all bedrooms. Tea/Coffee facilities. Large mature award winning gardens. Leave N72 at Lismore. Located opposite infants school.

| B&B | 2 | Ensuite | €27.50-€31 | Dinner | - |
| B&B | 1 | Standard | €25.50-€28.50 | Partial Board | - |
| Single Rate | | | €38-€43.50 | Child reduction | 25% |

Lismore

**Open:** 1st January-23rd December

### Tramore

**John Buckley**
ASHBOURNE LODGE
1 Glen Road, Tramore,
Co Waterford

TEL: **051 330570** FAX: **051 330570**

House beside race course, walking distance Tramore with all its amenities, all bedrooms with tv tea/coffee and en suite facilities private parking.

| B&B | 4 | Ensuite | €30-€35 | Dinner | - |
| B&B | - | Standard | | Partial Board | - |
| Single Rate | | | €45-€50 | Child reduction | 33.3% |

Tramore

**Open:** All Year

### Tramore

**Frank & Majella Heraughty**
GLENART HOUSE
Tivoli Rd, Tramore,
Co Waterford

TEL: **051 381236** FAX: **051 391236**
EMAIL: **tourismse@eircom.net**

Elegant restored 1920's detached residence. Convenient Racecourse, Splashworld, Beach & Golf. Friendly atmosphere. Breakfast menu. Tea/coffee facilities. Ideal touring base.

| B&B | 4 | Ensuite | €35-€45 | Dinner | - |
| B&B | - | Standard | | Partial Board | - |
| Single Rate | | | €45-€50 | Child reduction | 50% |

Tramore

**Open:** 1st March-1st December

**Anne Lawlor**
**FERN HILL**
Newtown, Tramore,
Co Waterford

### Tramore

TEL: **051 390829**  FAX: **051 390829**
EMAIL: **fernhill@tramore.net**
WEB: **www.fernhillhouse.com**

Warm and luxurious house opposite Tramore Golf Club and 1 km from Beach. Beautiful views of Tramore Bay. All facilities within the area.

| B&B | 5 | Ensuite | €30-€36 | Dinner | - |
| B&B | - | Standard | - | Partial Board | - |
| Single Rate | | | €40-€50 | Child reduction | 33.3% |

**In Tramore**

**Open:** 1st April-31st October

---

**Mrs Anne McCarthy**
**SEAMIST**
Newtown, Tramore,
Co Waterford

### Tramore

TEL: **051 381533**  FAX: **051 381533**
EMAIL: **annflor@iol.ie**
WEB: **www.tramore.net/seamist/**

Luxurious spacious home. Renowned generous breakfast. On site parking at rear. On coastal historical walk. 250 metres from Tramore Golf club, signposted on R675.

| B&B | 3 | Ensuite | €28-€34 | Dinner | - |
| B&B | - | Standard | - | Partial Board | - |
| Single Rate | | | €40-€50 | Child reduction | 25% |

**In Tramore**

**Open:** 1st February-30th November

---

**Mrs Olive McCarthy**
**OBAN**
1 Eastlands, Pond Road,
Tramore, Co Waterford

### Tramore

TEL: **051 381537**
EMAIL: **obanhouse@eircom.net**

"Breakfast over the Bay" in central comfortable home. Walking distance to Racecourse, Beach, Pubs, Restaurants etc. Extensive Breakfast menu. Ideal touring base.

| B&B | 3 | Ensuite | €28-€32 | Dinner | - |
| B&B | 1 | Standard | €26-€30 | Partial Board | - |
| Single Rate | | | €38-€43.50 | Child reduction | 33.3% |

**In Tramore**

**Open:** 8th January-11th December

---

**Thomas & Elizabeth Moran**
**SEA COURT**
Tivoli Road, Tramore,
Co Waterford

### Tramore

TEL: **051 386244/393367**  FAX: **051 393367**
EMAIL: **seacourthouse@eircom.net**

Friendly home. All rooms with multi-channel TV, Tea/Coffee facilities. Guest lounge. Secure parking. Breakfast menu. Premises not suitable for children under twelve.

| B&B | 6 | Ensuite | €30-€35 | Dinner | - |
| B&B | - | Standard | - | Partial Board | - |
| Single Rate | | | €45-€50 | Child reduction | 25% |

**In Tramore**

**Open:** 1st May-30th September

---

**Mrs Marie Murphy**
**GLENORNEY BY THE SEA**
Newtown, Tramore,
Co Waterford

### Tramore

TEL: **051 381056**  FAX: **051 381103**
EMAIL: **glenoney@iol.ie**
WEB: **www.glenorney.com**

Award winning luxurious home panoramic sea views. RAC, AA ◆◆◆◆'s (Red Diamonds highest rating). Recommended by all top class guides. Family suites. Extensive menu.

| B&B | 6 | Ensuite | €30-€40 | Dinner | - |
| B&B | - | Standard | - | Partial Board | - |
| Single Rate | | | €50-€80 | Child reduction | 20% |

**In Tramore**

**Open:** All Year Except Christmas

### Niall & Penny Nordell
**NORLANDS**
**Glen Road, Tramore,**
**Co Waterford**

TEL: **051 391132**
EMAIL: **nordell@eircom.net**
WEB: **www.norlands.ie**

Established luxurious family home with recently added guest sun lounge beside Racecourse - 10 min drive to Waterford Crystal. Tranquil surroundings. Ideal base for touring south east. Mins from sandy beaches & mountains.

| B&B | 3 | Ensuite | €32-€34 | Dinner | - |
| B&B | - | Standard | - | Partial Board | - |
| Single Rate | | | €42-€44 | Child reduction | **33.3%** |

Tramore

**Open:** 6th January-20th December

---

### Mrs Áine O'Brien
**SILVER BIRCH**
**Crobally, Tramore,**
**Co Waterford**

TEL: **051 391849**   FAX: **051 391849**

Family run, homely atmosphere, quiet location, private parking. Walking distance to town. Relax in mature rambling garden, breakfast menu, tea coffee all rooms.

| B&B | 3 | Ensuite | €35-€45 | Dinner | - |
| B&B | - | Standard | - | Partial Board | - |
| Single Rate | | | €40-€45 | Child reduction | **50%** |

Tramore

**Open:** All Year Except Christmas

---

### Ann & John O'Meara
**KNOCKVILLE**
**Moonvoy, Tramore,**
**Co Waterford**

TEL: **051 381084**
EMAIL: **knockville@iolfree.ie**

Country home in rural area on R682, 7km from N25. Owner chef. Breakfast/Dinner menu. Bring your own wine. Tea/Coffee facilities. Private parking. Credit cards.

| B&B | 3 | Ensuite | €27.50-€31 | Dinner | €19 |
| B&B | 2 | Standard | €25.50-€28.50 | Partial Board | - |
| Single Rate | | | €38-€43.50 | Child reduction | **50%** |

amore 2km

**Open:** 1st March-1st November

---

### Pat & Hilary O'Sullivan
**CLIFF HOUSE**
**Cliff Road, Tramore,**
**Co Waterford**

TEL: **051 381497/391296**   FAX: **051 381497**
EMAIL: **hilary@cliffhouse.ie**
WEB: **www.cliffhouse.ie**

Panoramic view Tramore Bay. Luxury AA ◆◆◆◆ Le Routard, Dillard/Causin, Fran Sullivan Guides, Family suites, extensive menu, private parking. Superior room with balconies extra.

| B&B | 6 | Ensuite | €33-€37.50 | Dinner | - |
| B&B | - | Standard | - | Partial Board | - |
| Single Rate | | | €40-€50 | Child reduction | **25%** |

Tramore

**Open:** 10th March-15th December

---

### Mrs Evelyne Power
**WESTCLIFFE**
**5 Newtown, Tramore,**
**Co Waterford**

TEL: **051 381365**
EMAIL: **evepower@yahoo.com**
WEB: **www.west-cliffe.com**

Welcoming, comfortable, home overlooking Tramore Bay opposite Tramore Golf Club, spacious en-suite rooms with seaview, extensive breakfast menu.

| B&B | 3 | Ensuite | €30-€37 | Dinner | - |
| B&B | - | Standard | - | Partial Board | - |
| Single Rate | | | €40-€50 | Child reduction | **25%** |

Tramore

**Open:** 1st February-30th November

In Tramore

**Neil & Maria Skedd**
CLONEEN
Love Lane, Tramore,
Co Waterford

**Tramore**
TEL: **051 381264**   FAX: **051 381264**
EMAIL: **cloneen@iol.ie**
WEB: **www.cloneen.net**

Family run bungalow set in landscaped gardens. Sun Lounge and Patio for guests. Quiet location with private parking. Beach, Golf and Splashworld nearby.

| B&B | 5 | Ensuite | €32-€35 | Dinner | €19-€19 |
|---|---|---|---|---|---|
| B&B | - | Standard | - | Partial Board | - |
| Single Rate | | | €50-€50 | Child reduction | 50% |

**Open:** All Year

---

In Tramore

**Frank & Margaret Walsh**
SUMMERHILL LODGE
Summerhill, Tramore,
Co Waterford

**Tramore**
TEL: **051 381938**   FAX: **051 391333**
EMAIL: **summerhilllodge@eircom.net**
WEB: **www.summerhilllodge.com**

Quality welcoming home with private parking and gardens. 10 mins walk Beach. Approach via Main Street and Summerhill 200 yards past Credit Union and Catholic Church.

| B&B | 6 | Ensuite | €30-€35 | Dinner | - |
|---|---|---|---|---|---|
| B&B | - | Standard | - | Partial Board | - |
| Single Rate | | | €40-€50 | Child reduction | - |

**Open:** 2nd January-23rd December

---

**Áine & Joe Whelan**
TURRET HOUSE
2 Church Road, Town Centre,
Tramore, Co Waterford

**Tramore**
TEL: **051 386342**
EMAIL: **turrethouse@hotmail.com**

"Tramore at it's Best". Quiet home in the heart of Tramore with superb views. All facilities. Family suite. Private parking.

| B&B | 4 | Ensuite | €32-€35 | Dinner | - |
|---|---|---|---|---|---|
| B&B | - | Standard | - | Partial Board | - |
| Single Rate | | | €40-€45 | Child reduction | 50% |

In Tramore

**Open:** 1st May-31st October

---

Waterford 5km

**Susan Bailey - Daunt**
SAMUELS HERITAGE
Ballymaclode, Halfway House,
Dunmore Rd, Waterford,
Co Waterford

**Waterford**
TEL: **051 875094**   FAX: **051 304013**
EMAIL: **samuelsheritage@eircom.net**
WEB: **www.samuelsheritage.com**

Family home, panoramic views, quiet and peaceful country surroundings, close proximity to Beaches, Golf, Angling, Walking, Horseriding and wide choice of Restaurants.

| B&B | 3 | Ensuite | €30-€33 | Dinner | - |
|---|---|---|---|---|---|
| B&B | - | Standard | - | Partial Board | - |
| Single Rate | | | €40-€45 | Child reduction | 50% |

**Open:** 1st January-31st December

---

Waterford 7km

**Mrs Eithne Brennan**
HILLVIEW LODGE
Kilmeaden, Co Waterford

**Waterford**
TEL: **051 384230**
EMAIL: **hillviewlodgebandb@eircom.net**
WEB: **homepage.eircom.net/~hillviewlodge**

Two storey house with large mature garden on N25. Horse Riding and Golf, Driving Range nearby. Convenient to Waterford Crystal.

| B&B | 4 | Ensuite | €30-€33 | Dinner | - |
|---|---|---|---|---|---|
| B&B | 1 | Standard | €30-€30 | Partial Board | - |
| Single Rate | | | €40-€45 | Child reduction | 25% |

**Open:** 1st March-31st October

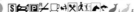

### Annette Comiskey
**OLD PAROCHIAL HOUSE**
Priests Lane, Robinstown,
Glenmore (via Waterford),
Co Waterford

**Waterford**

TEL: **051 880550**  FAX: **051 880550**
EMAIL: **anastasiacomiskey@hotmail.com**
WEB: **www.southeastireland.com/oldparochialhouse**

Built in 1870 this former Parochial House is set in beautiful gardens with fountain, gazebo & orchards. Modern facilities with old world charm. 50m off N25.

| B&B | 2 | Ensuite | €28-€31 | Dinner | - |
| B&B | 1 | Standard | €25.50-€28.50 | Partial Board | - |
| Single Rate | | | €38-€43.50 | Child reduction | - |

ew Ross/Waterford 12km

**Open:** 10th January-22nd December

### Miriam Corcoran
**CLADDAGH**
Lr Newrath, Ferrybank,
Waterford, Co Waterford

**Waterford**

TEL: **051 854797**
EMAIL: **mashacorcoran@yahoo.com**
WEB: **www.southeastireland.com/claddagh**

Modern spacious home, quiet location, off N9/N24, beside Waterford. 18 hole Golf Course. Ground floor accommodation. Private Car Park, Tea/Coffee bedrooms. TV, Hairdryers. On city bus route.

| B&B | 5 | Ensuite | €32 | Dinner | - |
| B&B | - | Standard | - | Partial Board | - |
| Single Rate | | | €40-€45 | Child reduction | 50% |

aterford 2.5km

**Open:** 1st April-31st October

### Patrick & Noreen Dullaghan
**LOUGHDAN**
Newrath, Dublin Rd, Waterford,
Co Waterford

**Waterford**

TEL: **051 876021**
EMAIL: **info@loughdan.net**
WEB: **www.loughdan.net**

Modern house Dublin/Limerick Rd. N9/N24. Convenient Golf, Bus/Train Station. Tea/Coffee facilities, TV, Hairdryers in bedrooms. Breakfast menu.

| B&B | 5 | Ensuite | €30-€32 | Dinner | - |
| B&B | 1 | Standard | €27-€30 | Partial Board | - |
| Single Rate | | | €40-€45 | Child reduction | 25% |

aterford 1km

**Open:** 1st February-30th November

### Mrs Catherine Evans
**ROSEWOOD**
Slieverue, Via Waterford,
Co Waterford

**Waterford**

TEL: **051 832233**  FAX: **051 358389**
EMAIL: **cevans@rosewood-waterford.com**
WEB: **www.rosewood-waterford.com**

Family run purpose built B&B, beautiful gardens. Located in the small country village of Slieverue on the N25, 3km from Waterford City. Convenient to Waterford Crystal and Golf.

| B&B | 4 | Ensuite | €32-€34 | Dinner | - |
| B&B | - | Standard | - | Partial Board | - |
| Single Rate | | | €40-€44 | Child reduction | - |

aterford City 3km

**Open:** 1st February-15th December

### Mrs Ann Fitzgerald
**DAWN B&B**
Kildarmody, Kilmeaden,
Co Waterford

**Waterford**

TEL: **051 384465**
EMAIL: **dawnb.and.b@esatclear.ie**
WEB: **www.southeastireland.com/dawnbed&breakfast**

Modern single storey bunglow in very quiet rural area. With mature garden and private lake. Restaurant/ Bar walking distance. Waterford Crystal 10km. Private parking. Garden for guests.

| B&B | 3 | Ensuite | €28-€32 | Dinner | - |
| B&B | - | Standard | - | Partial Board | - |
| Single Rate | | | €40-€43.50 | Child reduction | 25% |

lmeaden 3km

**Open:** All Year Except Christmas

**Margaret C Fitzmaurice**
BLENHEIM HOUSE
Blenheim Heights, Waterford,
Co Waterford

Waterford

TEL: **051 874115**
EMAIL: **blenheim@eircom.net**
WEB: **homepage.tinet.ie/~blenheim/**

Georgian residence C1763. Furnished throughout with Antiques & object d'art. Surrounded by lawns and private Deer Park. Convenient to Waterford Castle and Faithlegg Golf clubs.

| B&B | 6 | Ensuite | €32 | Dinner | - |
| B&B | - | Standard | - | Partial Board | - |
| Single Rate | | | €40 | Child reduction | - |

Waterford 3.5km

**Open:** 1st January-22nd December

---

**Phil Harrington**
BROOKDALE HOUSE
Carrigrue, Ballinaneeshagh,
Waterford, Co Waterford

Waterford

TEL: **051 375618**

Quiet location,Joint Award of Excellence. Spacious Car Park - 400 metres of Cork/Waterford Road (N25). Power showers in Rooms - 1km Waterford Crystal Factory.

| B&B | 3 | Ensuite | €30-€33 | Dinner | - |
| B&B | - | Standard | - | Partial Board | - |
| Single Rate | | | €40-€45 | Child reduction | 25% |

Waterford 3km

**Open:** 1st March-31st October

---

**Mrs Margaret Hayes**
ARRIVISTE
Holycross, Cork Road,
Butlerstown, Co Waterford

Waterford

TEL: **051 354080**  FAX: **051 354080**
EMAIL: **arriviste@iolfree.ie**

Country house, central heated. Private car park. Lounge, TV rooms, Tea/Coffee facilities. Large relaxing Conservatory. Landscaped gardens. Situated on N25. 2km from Waterford Crystal.

| B&B | 6 | Ensuite | €30-€32 | Dinner | €19 |
| B&B | - | Standard | - | Partial Board | - |
| Single Rate | | | €40-€43.50 | Child reduction | 25% |

Waterford 4.5km

**Open:** 15th January-15th December

---

**Bernadette Kiely**
ASHFIELD B&B
Belmount Road, Ferrybank,
Waterford, Co Waterford

Waterford

TEL: **051 832266**
EMAIL: **ashfieldwfd@eircom.net**

Comfortable family home on N25. Rosslare 55 mins. Close to Golf, Shops, Crystal Factory and Beaches. Ideal for touring Southeast. TV Lounge with Tea/Coffee Facilities.

| B&B | 3 | Ensuite | €30-€33 | Dinner | - |
| B&B | 1 | Standard | - | Partial Board | - |
| Single Rate | | | €38-€41 | Child reduction | 25% |

Waterford 2km

**Open:** 1st March-31st October

---

**Mrs Eileen Landy**
BELMONT HOUSE
Belmont Road, Rosslare Road,
Ferrybank, Waterford,
Co Waterford

Waterford

TEL: **051 832174**  FAX: **051 832174**
EMAIL: **belmonthouse@eircom.net**

Easy to find on Waterford/Rosslare Rd N25. Spacious Modern house. No smoking. Private parking. AA & RAC listed. Tea/Coffee. Convenient to Crystal Factory, Golf, Train & Bus City 2km.

| B&B | 4 | Ensuite | €30-€33 | Dinner | - |
| B&B | 2 | Standard | €27-€30 | Partial Board | - |
| Single Rate | | | €45-€60 | Child reduction | - |

Waterford City 2km

**Open:** 1st May-31st October

**Phyllis McGovern**
ASHLEIGH
Holy Cross, Cork Road,
Waterford, Co Waterford

### Waterford

TEL: **051 375171**   FAX: **051 375171**
EMAIL: **ashleighhouse@eircom.net**
WEB: **www.ashleigh-house.com**

Award of Excellence winner. Spacious home, gardens, carpark. On N25 close to Waterford Crystal, Pub & Restaurant. TV, Tea/Coffee in rooms. Breakfast menu. **Stg: Ensuite £18.50-£20.35 Single Rate £25-£27.75.**

| B&B | 6 | Ensuite | €30-€33 | Dinner | - |
| B&B | - | Standard | | Partial Board | - |
| Single Rate | | | €40-€45 | Child reduction | - |

Waterford 4km   V   CC S ⊠ P ⊗ ⁿ✕ ⊡ ⊑ 🗡 ➤ J Jₗ Jₛ Jᵣ     **Open:** 1st February-10th December

**Mrs Marian O'Keeffe**
ST ANTHONY'S
Ballinaneesagh, Cork Road,
Waterford, Co Waterford

### Waterford

TEL: **051 375887**   FAX: **051 353063**
EMAIL: **reservation@stanthonyswaterford.com**
WEB: **www.stanthonyswaterford.com**

Landscaped garden. On N25 near Waterford Crystal. Breakfast menu. Hairdryers, Electric blankets. Frommer recommended. CIE award of excellence 1998,1999, & 2000.

| B&B | 6 | Ensuite | €30-€33 | Dinner | - |
| B&B | - | Standard | - | Partial Board | - |
| Single Rate | | | €40-€43.50 | Child reduction | 33.3% |

Waterford 2km   V   CC 🗝 P ⊗ ⁿ✕ ⊡ ⊑ 🗡 ➤     **Open:** 8th January-20th December

**Terence & Anne O'Neill**
ST. JOSEPH'S
Ballinaneeshagh, Cork Road,
Waterford, Co Waterford

### Waterford

TEL: **051 376893**

Spacious friendly home. Waterford/Cork N25 2 mins. Crystal Factory. Cable TV, Tea/Coffee facilities in bedrooms. City Bus service. Breakfast menu.

| B&B | 3 | Ensuite | €31 | Dinner | - |
| B&B | - | Standard | | Partial Board | - |
| Single Rate | | | €43.50 | Child reduction | - |

Waterford 1.5km   V   S P ⊗ ⁿ✕ ⊡ ⊑ 🗡 ➤ J Jₗ Jₛ Jᵣ     **Open:** 15th January-1st December

**Mrs Phyllis O'Reilly**
ANNVILL HOUSE
1 The Orchard, Kingsmeadow,
Waterford, Co Waterford

### Waterford

TEL: **051 373617**   FAX: **051 373617**

From City turn right at N25 roundabout, at lights turn left. 2 mins from Crystal factory. Winner of CIE Int'l Awards of Excellence. Frommer Recommended. Tea/Coffee, Hairdryers. City Bus.

| B&B | 4 | Ensuite | €30-€33 | Dinner | - |
| B&B | 1 | Standard | €27-€29 | Partial Board | - |
| Single Rate | | | €39-€45 | Child reduction | - |

Waterford City 1km   V   🗝 P ⊗ ⁿ✕ 🗡 ➤ Jₛ     **Open:** 1st January-21st December

**Paul & Breda Power**
DUNROVEN B&B
Ballinaneesagh, Cork Rd N25,
Waterford City, Co Waterford

### Waterford

TEL: **051 374743**   FAX: **051 377050**
EMAIL: **dunroven@iol.ie**
WEB: **www.dunroven-ireland.com**

Modern home. Cork/Waterford road N25. 2 minutes Crystal Factory, W.I.T. College. Cable TV, Tea/Coffee, Hairdryers. Breakfast menu. City bus IMP. No Smoking house. **Stg: Ensuite £18-£20.35 Single Rate £25-£27.75.**

| B&B | 6 | Ensuite | €30-€33 | Dinner | - |
| B&B | - | Standard | | Partial Board | - |
| Single Rate | | | €40-€45 | Child reduction | - |

Waterford City 1.5km   V   CC S 🗝 P ⊗ ⁿ✕ ⊡ ⊑ 🗡 ➤ J Jₗ Jₛ Jᵣ     **Open:** 1st January-21st December

**Mrs Rena Power**
GLENCREE
The Sweep, Kilmeaden,
Co Waterford

**Waterford**

TEL: 051 384240

Country home off Cork/Waterford Road (N25). Crystal Factory, Horse Riding, Pubs, Restaurants locally. Ideal for Coastal, Mountain or Heritage tours.

| B&B | 3 | Ensuite | €30-€33 | Dinner | - |
| B&B | 2 | Standard | €30-€30 | Partial Board | - |
| Single Rate | | | €40-€45 | Child reduction | 25% |

Waterford 9km

**Open:** 1st March-31st October

---

**Mrs Marie Prendergast**
TORY VIEW
Mullinavat, Co Waterford

**Waterford**

TEL: **051 885513**  FAX: **051 885513**
EMAIL: **toryviewbandb@eircom.net**
WEB: **www.southeastireland.com/toryview**

Modern house on N9 Dublin/Kilkenny Road. Tea/Coffee Facilities, TV, Hairdryers in Bedrooms. Convenient Golf & Waterford Crystal.

| B&B | 4 | Ensuite | €28-€32 | Dinner | - |
| B&B | 1 | Standard | €26-€28.50 | Partial Board | - |
| Single Rate | | | €38-€43.50 | Child reduction | 25% |

Waterford 8km

**Open:** 1st February-30th November

---

**Helen Quinn**
WHITE WEBBS
Ballinaneeshagh, Waterford,
Co Waterford

**Waterford**

TEL: 051 370696

Joint Award of excellence 1998, 1999 & 2000. Quiet location, landscaped gardens, car park. 1km Waterford Crystal. 400m off Cork/Waterford Road (N25).

| B&B | 3 | Ensuite | €30-€33 | Dinner | - |
| B&B | - | Standard | - | Partial Board | - |
| Single Rate | | | €40-€45 | Child reduction | 25% |

Waterford 3km

**Open:** 1st March-31st October

---

**Maureen Wall**
SUNCREST
Slieverue,
Ferrybank Via Waterford,
Co Waterford

**Waterford**

TEL: **051 832732**  FAX: **051 851861**
EMAIL: **maurwal@eircom.net**
WEB: **www.southeastireland.com/suncrest**

Split level bungalow in quiet rural location 600 metres off N25 Waterford/Rosslare road. In Slieverue village, Waterford City 3kms, Rosslare 50 mins. Ideal base for touring South East.

| B&B | 6 | Ensuite | €31-€34 | Dinner | - |
| B&B | - | Standard | - | Partial Board | - |
| Single Rate | | | €40-€45 | Child reduction | - |

Waterford 3km

**Open:** 1st February-30th November

---

**Mrs Patricia Wall**
SAN-MARTINO
Ballinaneeshagh, Cork Rd,
Waterford, Co Waterford

**Waterford**

TEL: 051 374949

Modern bungalow on main Waterford/Cork road. 3 mins from Waterford Crystal Factory. Tea/Coffee facilities. Winner of Award of Excellence for 1998 and 1999, 2000 and 2001. **Stg: Ensuite £21 Single Rate £28.50.**

| B&B | 5 | Ensuite | €33 | Dinner | - |
| B&B | - | Standard | - | Partial Board | - |
| Single Rate | | | €45 | Child reduction | 25% |

Waterford City 2km

**Open:** 1st April-30th September

**Aedamar Walsh**
AISLING HOUSE
Polerone, Mooncoin,
Via Waterford, Co Waterford

## Waterford

TEL: **051 895456**  FAX: **051 895456**
EMAIL: **aislingbb@eircom.net**
WEB: **www.aislingbb.com**

Spacious friendly home on N24 Waterford/Limerick Rd. Large Bedrooms, generous breakfast menu, tea/coffee facilities, scenic surroundings, Mount Juliet 30mins.

| B&B | 5 | Ensuite | €33-€33 | Dinner | - |
| B&B | 1 | Standard | €30-€30 | Partial Board | - |
| Single Rate | | | €40-€45 | Child reduction | 50% |

Waterford 9km

Open: All Year

---

## RESERVATIONS

- Confirm phone bookings in writing without delay with agreed deposit.
- To avoid misunderstandings later, check rate on booking and clarify any additional changes which may apply to your booking.
- Give details of any special requirements.
- State clearly day, date of arrival and departure date.

---

## APPROVED ACCOMMODATION SIGNS

Northern Ireland Tourist Board

### Approved Accommodation Signs
These signs will be displayed at most premises which are approved by Failte Ireland, the National Tourism Development Authority and Northern Ireland Tourist Board Standards.

### Panneaux d'homologation des établissements
Ces panneaux sont affichés dans la plupart des établissements homologués selon les normes de l'Office du tourisme irlandais.

### Plakette fúr Geprúfte Unterkunft
Diese Plaketten werden an den meisten Häusern angezeigt, die von auf die Einhaltung der Normen der irischen Fremdenverkehrsbehörde überprüft und zugelassen wurden.

### Borden voor goedgekeurde accommodatie
Deze borden vindt u bij de meeste huizen die zijn goedgekeurd door voor de normen van de Ierse Toeristenbond.

### Simbolo di sistemazione approvata
Questi simboli saranno esposti nella maggior parte delle case approvate (associazione dei Bed & Breakfast approvati per qualità), rispondenti agli standard dell'Ente del Turismo Irlandese.

### Símbolo de alojamiento aprobado
Estos símbolos se muestran en los establecimientos que han sido aprobados por bajos los estandars de la Oficina de Turismo Irlandesa.

### Skyltar för Godkänd logi
Dessa skyltar finns vid de flesta gästhus som har godkänts (Föreningen för kvalitetsgodkända gästhus AB), enligt irländska turisföreningens normer.

A region rich in history, landscaped with ancient Castles, Abbeys and Museums. Savor the dramatic scenery of Hook peninsula or leisurely enjoy the sunny South East's golden beaches. Gateway to Britain and Europe - Wexford is famous for its Opera Festival.

### Mrs Ann Crosbie
**GLENDINE COUNTRY HOUSE**
**Arthurstown, Co Wexford**

**Arthurstown**
TEL: **051 389258/389500**   FAX: **051 389677**
EMAIL: **glendinehouse@eircom.net**
WEB: **www.glendinehouse.com**

We invite you to our charming 1830 Georgian home. We offer superb accommodation, bedrooms enjoy sweeping views of the Estuary. From N25, take R733/R783. AA ◆◆◆◆.

| | | | | | |
|---|---|---|---|---|---|
| B&B | 4 | Ensuite | €45-€55 | Dinner | - |
| B&B | - | Standard | - | Partial Board | - |
| Single Rate | | | €65-€80 | Child reduction | 25% |

Waterford 7km

**Open:** 1st February-30th November

### Mary Gilsenan
**MOSS COTTAGE**
**Bunclody, Enniscorthy,**
**Co Wexford**

**Bunclody**
TEL: **054 77828**
EMAIL: **bgilsenan@eircom.net**
WEB: **www.mosscottageireland.com**

Victorian style house in mature gardens. Visitor's lounge with tv. Easy walk to town. Beside Blackstairs Mountains and Slaney River. One hour Rosslare.

| | | | | | |
|---|---|---|---|---|---|
| B&B | 2 | Ensuite | €30-€35 | Dinner | - |
| B&B | 1 | Standard | €30-€32 | Partial Board | - |
| Single Rate | | | €38-€44 | Child reduction | 50% |

In Bunclody

**Open:** 1st April-30th October

### Ms Phil Kinsella
**MEADOW SIDE B&B**
**Ryland Street, Bunclody,**
**Co Wexford**

**Bunclody**
TEL: **054 76226/77459**   FAX: **054 75997**

Elegant stone Georgian Town House ideally situated. Tea/Coffee on arrival, TV Lounge, spacious rooms ensuite. Private Car Park.

| | | | | | |
|---|---|---|---|---|---|
| B&B | 3 | Ensuite | €35-€40 | Dinner | - |
| B&B | 1 | Standard | €30-€35 | Partial Board | - |
| Single Rate | | | €40-€50 | Child reduction | - |

In Bunclody

**Open:** All Year Except Christmas

### Ann & Joe Delany
**ST JUDES**
**Munfin, Tomnalossitt,**
**Enniscorthy, Co Wexford**

**Enniscorthy**
TEL: **054 33011**   FAX: **054 37831**
EMAIL: **anndelany@eircom.net**

Home located 2km off the N30 on Bree Rd. Scenic countryside. Nearest B&B to Enniscorty Golf club. Early Breakfast. Rosslare Ferryport 38km. Bedrooms ground floor.

| | | | | | |
|---|---|---|---|---|---|
| B&B | 4 | Ensuite | €27.50-€31 | Dinner | - |
| B&B | - | Standard | - | Partial Board | - |
| Single Rate | | | €40-€43.50 | Child reduction | 25% |

Enniscorthy 4km

**Open:** 1st January-30th November

rns 2km

## Enniscorthy

**Ms Anne Marie Hobbs**
KILBORA
Camolin, Enniscorthy,
Co Wexford

TEL: 054 67089
EMAIL: stay@kilborabandb.com
WEB: www.kilborabandb.com

Spacious modern home, rooms ensuite with tv and hairdryer, tea/coffee. Beautiful views, pub/restaurant 2km. Located on N11 between Gorey and Enniscorthy.

| | | | | | |
|---|---|---|---|---|---|
| B&B | 4 | Ensuite | €30-€35.50 | Dinner | - |
| B&B | - | Standard | - | Partial Board | - |
| Single Rate | | | €40-€43.50 | Child reduction | 50% |

**Open:** 1st January-31st December

orey 8km

## Gorey

**Mrs Noreen Byrne**
PERRYMOUNT COUNTRY HOME
Inch, Gorey, Co Wexford

TEL: 0402 37418 FAX: 0402 21931
EMAIL: perrymount@eircom.com
WEB: www.perrymountcountryhome.com

Situated 50 metres of N11 at Inch & North of Gorey. T.V., tea/coffee in room. Breakfast menu. Pub, restaurant 50 metres. Signposted at 'Toss Byrnes Pub'.

| | | | | | |
|---|---|---|---|---|---|
| B&B | 4 | Ensuite | €30-€35 | Dinner | €25-€25 |
| B&B | - | Standard | - | Partial Board | €350 |
| Single Rate | | | €40-€45 | Child reduction | 50% |

**Open:** 1st January-20th December

orey 2km

## Gorey

**Mrs Martina Redmond**
CARRAIG VIEW
Ballycale, Gorey, Co Wexford

TEL: 055 21323 FAX: 055 21323
EMAIL: carraigview@eircom.net
WEB: www.southeastireland.com

Located 2km from Gorey. Standing on 1.5 acres of magnificent gardens. The dining room is located to take in the view while enjoying breakfast. Cleanliness/comfort is a No. 1 priority.

| | | | | | |
|---|---|---|---|---|---|
| B&B | 2 | Ensuite | €30-€33.50 | Dinner | - |
| B&B | 1 | Standard | €28-€30 | Partial Board | - |
| Single Rate | | | €38-€45 | Child reduction | 33.3% |

**Open:** 1st January-20th December

orey 5km

## Gorey

**Mrs Ann Sunderland**
HILLSIDE HOUSE
Tubberduff, Gorey, Co Wexford

TEL: 055 21726/22036 FAX: 055 22567
EMAIL: hillsidehouse@eircom.net
WEB: www.hillsidehouse.net

Spacious modern hse, ideal for touring South East. 3 km off N11, North of Gorey. All rooms Tea/Coffee, TV, Hairdryers, Electric blankets. Guest lounge with open fire. AA ◆◆◆◆.

| | | | | | |
|---|---|---|---|---|---|
| B&B | 6 | Ensuite | €30-€35 | Dinner | €30-€30 |
| B&B | - | Standard | - | Partial Board | €350 |
| Single Rate | | | €45-€50 | Child reduction | - |

**Open:** 1st January-20th December

lmore Quay 5km

## Kilmore Quay

**Mary Cousins**
GROVESIDE
Ballyharty, Kilmore, Co Wexford

TEL: 053 35305 FAX: 053 35305
EMAIL: grovesidefarmb-b@iolfree.ie
WEB: www.iolfree.ie/grovesidefarmb_b

Arable farm on quiet country road. TV,hairdryer, guest T.V. lounge. Home Baking, early ferry break-fast, restaurants locally, sandy beaches, golf Rosslare/Wexford 20 mins.

| | | | | | |
|---|---|---|---|---|---|
| B&B | 3 | Ensuite | €28-€30 | Dinner | - |
| B&B | - | Standard | - | Partial Board | - |
| Single Rate | | | €36-€38 | Child reduction | 25% |

**Open:** 20th April-30th September

**In Kilrane**

**Mr & Mrs Tony & Vivienne Close**
**VICTORIA HOUSE**
**Kilrane, Co Wexford**

TEL: **053 61965**   FAX: **053 61191**
EMAIL: **victoriahouse@eircze.net**
WEB: **www.victoriahse.vze.com**

Spacious country house 4 mins from pubs and restaurants and 4 mins drive to ferry. TV and Tea/Coffee in each room. Two golf courses 10 mins and Wexford town just 15mins.

| | | | | | |
|---|---|---|---|---|---|
| B&B | 3 | Ensuite | €28-€31 | Dinner | - |
| B&B | - | Standard | | Partial Board | - |
| Single Rate | | | €40-€43.50 | Child reduction | **50%** |

**Open:** 1st February-30th November

---

**New Ross 14km**

**Mr Colin Campbell**
**WOODLANDS HOUSE**
**Carrigbyrne, Co Wexford**

TEL: **051 428287**   FAX: **051 428287**
EMAIL: **woodwex@eircom.net**
WEB: **www.woodwex.com**

Beautifully situated between Wexford and Waterford (N25). 30 Minutes to Rosslare. Tastefully refurbished. Guest lounge. Country walks. Early Breakfast. AA ◆◆◆.

| | | | | | |
|---|---|---|---|---|---|
| B&B | 4 | Ensuite | €30-€35 | Dinner | €25-€25 |
| B&B | - | Standard | - | Partial Board | |
| Single Rate | | | €42.50-€45 | Child reduction | |

**Open:** 18th March-31st October

---

**New Ross 1km**

**Ms Catherine Casey**
**CARBERY**
**Mountgarrett, New Ross, Co Wexford**

TEL: **051 422742**
EMAIL: **caseycolin@eircom.net**
WEB: **www.southeastireland.com/carbery**

Tudor style, walk to town. Golf , boating, fishing near. Private gardens, views river and mountains. Dunbrodyship, Inistioge, pub close, private parking, patio, tv lounge.

| | | | | | |
|---|---|---|---|---|---|
| B&B | 2 | Ensuite | €32-€34 | Dinner | - |
| B&B | 1 | Standard | €30-€32 | Partial Board | - |
| Single Rate | | | €40-€44 | Child reduction | **50%** |

**Open:** 1st May-30th September

---

**New Ross 2km**

**Mrs Noreen Fallon S.R.N. S.C.M.**
**KILLARNEY HOUSE**
**The Maudlins, New Ross, Co Wexford**

TEL: **051 421062**
EMAIL: **noreenfallon@eircom.net**

Frommer recommended. Rooms ground floor. Breakfast menu. Peaceful. Electric blankets. Reduction more than 1 nt. Complimentary Tea/Coffee, Breakfast anytime. Rosslare Ferry 45 mins.

| | | | | | |
|---|---|---|---|---|---|
| B&B | 2 | Ensuite | €30-€33 | Dinner | - |
| B&B | 1 | Standard | €28-€30 | Partial Board | - |
| Single Rate | | | €38-€43.50 | Child reduction | |

**Open:** 1st April-15th October

---

**In New Ross**

**Mrs Ann Foley**
**RIVERSDALE HOUSE**
**Lr William Street, New Ross, Co Wexford**

TEL: **051 422515**
EMAIL: **riversdalehouse@eircom.net**
WEB: **www.riversdalehouse.com**

Spacious ensuite bedrooms (two triple) with TV, Tea/Coffee, Electric blankets, Hairdryers. Parking. Sun Lounge. Gardens. Non smoking home. 5 mins walk to Town Centre.

| | | | | | |
|---|---|---|---|---|---|
| B&B | 4 | Ensuite | €35-€35 | Dinner | - |
| B&B | - | Standard | - | Partial Board | - |
| Single Rate | | | €50-€50 | Child reduction | - |

**Open:** 1st March-1st December

### New Ross

**Mrs Philomena Gallagher**
ROSVILLE HOUSE
Knockmullen, New Ross,
Co Wexford

TEL: **051 421798**
EMAIL: **rosvillehouse@oceanfree.net**
WEB: **www.rosville.com**

Modern home in peaceful surroundings. Guaranteed hospitality/comfort. Overlooking river Barrow. Rosslare Ferries 40mins. Early breakfast. Private Parking.

| B&B | 4 | Ensuite | €30-€33 | Dinner | - |
| B&B | 1 | Standard | €28-€30 | Partial Board | - |
| Single Rate | | | €38-€43.50 | Child reduction | 25% |

ew Ross 1km

**Open:** 1st March-1st November

---

### New Ross

**Susan & John Halpin**
OAKWOOD HOUSE
Ring Road (N30), Mountgarrett,
New Ross, Co Wexford

TEL: **051 425494**   FAX: **051 425494**
EMAIL: **susan@oakwoodhouse.net**
WEB: **www.oakwoodhouse.net**

Luxury purpose built non-smoking home, with a view. Spacious bedrooms with TV, tea/coffee facilities. AA ◆◆◆◆ selected. Peaceful setting with landscape gardens. Private parking.

| B&B | 4 | Ensuite | €35-€35 | Dinner | - |
| B&B | - | Standard | - | Partial Board | - |
| Single Rate | | | €50-€50 | Child reduction | - |

ew Ross 1km

**Open:** 1st April-31st October

---

### New Ross

**Annette Kinsella**
GREENPARK
Creakan Lower, New Ross,
Co Wexford

TEL: **051 421028**   FAX: **051 421028**

Greenpark is an Olde Worlde country house. Just off the R733, 4km from New Ross. 45 mins drive from Rosslare. Peaceful rural setting. No weddings. No parties. **Stg: Ensuite £23 Standard £19 Single Rate £25-£28.**

| B&B | 2 | Ensuite | €35-€35 | Dinner | - |
| B&B | 1 | Standard | €30-€30 | Partial Board | - |
| Single Rate | | | €40-€50 | Child reduction | 25% |

ew Ross 4km

**Open:** 1st February-30th November

---

### Rosslare Harbour

**Sue & Neil Carty**
MARIANELLA
Kilrane, Rosslare Harbour,
Co Wexford

TEL: **053 33139**
EMAIL: **marianella@ireland.com**

Comfortable bungalow on N25. 1km Ferry Port. All rooms on ground floor with TV & Tea/Coffee facilities. Guest lounge. Early breakfast. Restaurants nearby.

| B&B | 4 | Ensuite | €27.50-€31 | Dinner | - |
| B&B | 2 | Standard | €25.50-€28.50 | Partial Board | - |
| Single Rate | | | €38-€43.50 | Child reduction | - |

osslare Harbour 1km

**Open:** All Year Except Christmas

---

### Rosslare Harbour

**Kay Crean**
OLD ORCHARD LODGE
Kilrane, Rosslare Harbour,
Co Wexford

TEL: **053 33468**
EMAIL: **oldorchardlodge@eircom.net**
WEB: **homepage.eircom.net/~oldorchardlodge/**

1km Ferry. Early breakfast available. Private Parking. All rooms ensuite, Tea/Coffee & TV. Beside good Restaurants & Pubs. On quiet country road opposite Pubs in Kilrane village.

| B&B | 5 | Ensuite | €28-€31.50 | Dinner | - |
| B&B | - | Standard | - | Partial Board | - |
| Single Rate | | | €40-€50 | Child reduction | 50% |

osslare Harbour 1km

**Open:** 1st January-22nd December

47

## Rosslare Harbour

**Mrs Margaret Day**
ASHLEY LODGE B&B
Ballycowan, Tagoat,
Rosslare Harbour, Co Wexford

TEL: **053 31991**
EMAIL: **margaret@ashley-lodge.com**
WEB: **www.ashley-lodge.com**

The house is 400 metres off the N25 to Rosslare Harbour. Turn on to R736 at Tagoat Village, Ashley Lodge is on the Right, 400 metres off N25.

| B&B | 4 | Ensuite | €28-€31 | Dinner | - |
| B&B | - | Standard | | Partial Board | - |
| Single Rate | | | €40-€43.50 | Child reduction | 25% |

Rosslare Harbour 5km

**Open:** All Year Except Christmas

---

## Rosslare Harbour

**Anne Gleeson**
WAYSIDE HOUSE
Ballygeary, Kilrane,
Rosslare Harbour, Co Wexford

TEL: **053 33475**  FAX: **053 33475**

Country house on quiet road off N25. 1km Rosslare Port. Rooms with shower/toilet, TV, Tea/Coffee. Private Parking . Early breakfast.

| B&B | 3 | Ensuite | €27.50-€31 | Dinner | - |
| B&B | - | Standard | - | Partial Board | - |
| Single Rate | | | €40-€43.50 | Child reduction | - |

Rosslare Harbour 1.5km

**Open:** 31st March-31st October

---

## Rosslare Harbour

**Dermot & Philomena Kelly**
BALLYKELSH HOUSE
Tagoat, Rosslare Harbour,
Co Wexford

TEL: **053 31675**  FAX: **053 31675**
EMAIL: **ballykelsh@eircom.net**
WEB: **www.ballykelsh.com**

Georgian style house on peaceful quiet country lane only 1.5km off N25, 10 mins to ferry. All rooms en-suite with tv and tea/coffee making facilities.

| B&B | 3 | Ensuite | €27.50-€31 | Dinner | - |
| B&B | - | Standard | - | Partial Board | - |
| Single Rate | | | €40-€43.50 | Child reduction | 33.3% |

Rosslare Harbour 5km

**Open:** 1st January-31st December

---

## Rosslare Harbour

**Mrs Kathleen Lawlor**
CARRAGH LODGE
Station Road,
Rosslare Harbour, Co Wexford

TEL: **053 33492**

Modern bungalow on quiet side road off N25. 3 minutes drive from Ferryport. TV, Tea & Coffee facilities.

| B&B | 3 | Ensuite | €27.50-€31 | Dinner | - |
| B&B | 1 | Standard | €25.50-€28.50 | Partial Board | - |
| Single Rate | | | €38-€43.50 | Child reduction | 50% |

Rosslare Harbour Village 1km

**Open:** 1st March-30th November

---

## Rosslare Harbour

**Mrs Carmel Lonergan**
CLOVER LAWN
Kilrane, Rosslare Harbour,
Co Wexford

TEL: **053 33413**
EMAIL: **cloverlawn@eircom.net**
WEB: **homepage.eircom.net/~cloverlawn**

Highly recommended comfortable home. 1km from Ferry Port. In Kilrane Village turn left between pubs 3rd house on right. Early Breakfast. Golf, Beaches, Restaurants, Bus and Rail nearby.

| B&B | 3 | Ensuite | €28-€32 | Dinner | - |
| B&B | 1 | Standard | €28-€30 | Partial Board | - |
| Single Rate | | | €38-€50 | Child reduction | 33.3% |

Rosslare Harbour 2km

**Open:** 1st March-30th November

**Christina Mason**
ARCHWAYS B&B
**Rosslare Road (N25), Tagoat, Co Wexford**

Tel: **053 58111**
Email: **thearchways@eircom.net**

Warm comfortable home on N25, 5 mins drive to ferry. Early Breakfast. TV, Tea/Coffee in bedrooms. Private Parking. Sitting room and garden for guests.

| B&B | 4 | Ensuite | €27.50-€31 | Dinner | - |
|-----|---|---------|------------|--------|---|
| B&B | - | Standard | - | Partial Board | - |
| Single Rate | | | - | Child reduction | **50%** |

Rosslare Harbour 5km

**Open:** All Year

---

**Mary McDonald**
OLDCOURT HOUSE
**Rosslare Harbour, Co Wexford**

Tel: **053 33895**
Email: **oldcrt@gofree.indigo.ie**
Web: **http://gofree.indigo.ie/~oldcrt**

Modern house in the village of Rosslare Harbour close to ferry port, train and bus station near beaches, golf and fishing.

| B&B | 4 | Ensuite | €30-€31 | Dinner | - |
|-----|---|---------|---------|--------|---|
| B&B | - | Standard | - | Partial Board | - |
| Single Rate | | | €40-€43.50 | Child reduction | - |

Wexford 12km

**Open:** 1st March-18th December

---

**Catherine McHugh**
BALLYCOWAN LODGE
**Tagoat, Co Wexford**

Tel: **053 31596**   Fax: **053 31596**
Email: **ballycowanlodge1@eircom.net**

Secluded peaceful location only 150m off N25. 5 mins to Ferry. Early Breakfast. All rooms TV & Tea/Coffee making facilities.

| B&B | 4 | Ensuite | €27.50-€31 | Dinner | - |
|-----|---|---------|------------|--------|---|
| B&B | - | Standard | - | Partial Board | - |
| Single Rate | | | €40-€43.50 | Child reduction | **50%** |

Rosslare Harbour 5km

**Open:** 6th January-18th December

---

**Mr & Mrs D O'Donoghue**
LAUREL LODGE
**Rosslare Harbour, Co Wexford**

Tel: **053 33291**

Comfortable home on quiet road off Rosslare Harbour Village. 1km from Ferry. Within walking distance of 3 Hotels.

| B&B | 4 | Ensuite | €27.50-€31 | Dinner | - |
|-----|---|---------|------------|--------|---|
| B&B | - | Standard | - | Partial Board | - |
| Single Rate | | | €40-€43.50 | Child reduction | - |

In Rosslare Harbour

**Open:** 1st March-31st October

---

**Ms Una Stack**
DUNGARA B&B
**Kilrane, Rosslare Harbour, Co Wexford**

Tel: **053 33391**   Fax: **053 33391**
Email: **unastack@eircom.net**

Comfortable home with friendly athmosphere on N25. 1km to Ferry. TV, Electric Blankets, Tea/Coffee in rooms. Early Breakfast. Shops and Restaurants nearby.

| B&B | 6 | Ensuite | €27.50-€31 | Dinner | - |
|-----|---|---------|------------|--------|---|
| B&B | - | Standard | - | Partial Board | - |
| Single Rate | | | €40-€43.50 | Child reduction | **50%** |

In Rosslare

**Open:** 1st January-23rd December

**Ms Siobhan Whitehead**
KILRANE HOUSE
Kilrane, Rosslare Harbour,
Co Wexford

### Rosslare Harbour

TEL: **053 33135**  FAX: **053 33739**
EMAIL: **siobhanwhitehead@eircom.net**
WEB: **southeastireland.com/kilranehouse**

Period house. Many original features, superb ornate. Guest lounge. Opposite Pub, Restaurants. 3 mins drive from Ferry. Recommended by many guides.

| B&B | 6 | Ensuite | €28-€31 | Dinner | - |
|-----|---|---------|---------|--------|---|
| B&B | - | Standard | - | Partial Board | - |
| Single Rate | | | €43.50 | Child reduction | - |

Rosslare Harbour 2km

**Open:** 2nd January-23rd December

---

**Ms Grainne Cullen**
GRANVILLE HOUSE
Clonard Road, Wexford,
Co Wexford

### Wexford

TEL: **053 22648**
EMAIL: **emmetcullen@eircom.net**
WEB: **www.accommodationireland.net**

Luxury accomodation in warm friendly family home surrounded by award winning gardens. Interior designed to the highest standards. Close to N11 and N25

| B&B | 6 | Ensuite | €35-€40 | Dinner | - |
|-----|---|---------|---------|--------|---|
| B&B | - | Standard | - | Partial Board | - |
| Single Rate | | | €45-€45 | Child reduction | - |

Wexford 1.5km

**Open:** 15th January-15th December

---

**Mrs Angela Doocey**
TOWNPARKS HOUSE
Coolcotts, Wexford,
Co Wexford

### Wexford

TEL: **053 45191**
EMAIL: **angeladoocey@eircom.net**

Purpose-built Georgian house off R769. 10mins walk Town Centre. 20mins Rosslare Ferries. Tea/Coffee facilities, Set Clock Radios, Hairdryers. Early Breakfast.

| B&B | 4 | Ensuite | €30-€32.50 | Dinner | - |
|-----|---|---------|------------|--------|---|
| B&B | 1 | Standard | €30-€32.50 | Partial Board | - |
| Single Rate | | | €40-€43.50 | Child reduction | 33.3% |

In Wexford

**Open:** 1st February-23rd December

---

**Mr & Mrs Dave & Dianne Doyle**
COLIEMORE HOUSE
Ballycrane, Castlebridge,
Co Wexford

### Wexford

TEL: **053 59091**  FAX: **053 59091**
EMAIL: **coliemorehouse@hotmail.com**
WEB: **coliemorehouse.com**

Large modern home. Guest lounge. Rooms ensuite with power showers, TV, Tea/Coffee. On R742 Wexford 5 mins, Curracloe beach 5 mins. Your home from home.

| B&B | 3 | Ensuite | €30-€35 | Dinner | - |
|-----|---|---------|---------|--------|---|
| B&B | - | Standard | - | Partial Board | - |
| Single Rate | | | €40-€45 | Child reduction | 50% |

Wexford 3km

**Open:** 3rd January-20th December

---

**Mrs Maureen Keogh**
ELMLEIGH
Coolcots, Wexford Town,
Co Wexford

### Wexford

TEL: **053 44174**
EMAIL: **maureenkeogh2003@yahoo.com**

Modern home in peaceful residential area. Secure parking. Guests garden. Family rooms. 1 minute from N11/N25. 10 mins walk to Town Centre. 20 mins to Ferry, Rosslare.

| B&B | 3 | Ensuite | €27.50-€31 | Dinner | - |
|-----|---|---------|------------|--------|---|
| B&B | 1 | Standard | €25.50-€28.50 | Partial Board | - |
| Single Rate | | | €38-€43.50 | Child reduction | 50% |

Wexford Town

**Open:** 1st January-20th December

**Ms Mary D Moore**
ROCKVILLE
Rocklands, Rosslare Road,
Wexford Town, Co Wexford

**Wexford**
Tel: **053 22147**   Fax: **053 22147**
Email: **marydm@indigo.ie**
Web: **www.bedandbreakfastwexford.com**

Comfortable home with large garden in peaceful location. Southern fringe Wexford town (R730). Guest sitting room, private parking, walking distance Town Centre. Rosslare ferry 15 mins drive.

| B&B | 3 | Ensuite | €27.50-€31 | Dinner | - |
| B&B | 1 | Standard | €25.50-€28.50 | Partial Board | - |
| Single Rate | | | €40-€43.50 | Child reduction | 50% |

In Wexford

**Open:** 1st January-20th December

---

**Nicholas & Kathleen Murphy**
GLENHILL
Ballygoman, Barntown,
Co Wexford

**Wexford**
Tel: **053 20015**

Modern home peaceful surroundings. Guaranteed hospitality. On N25 15 mins Rosslare Ferries. Early breakfast. Private car park. Ferrycarrig 2km. Wexford 4km.

| B&B | 5 | Ensuite | €30-€33 | Dinner | - |
| B&B | - | Standard | - | Partial Board | - |
| Single Rate | | | - | Child reduction | 25% |

Wexford 4km

**Open:** 1st January-20th December

---

**Mrs Ellen O'Connor**
BROMPTON
Newtown Road, Wexford,
Co Wexford

**Wexford**
Tel: **053 40863**   Fax: **053 40863**

Luxury home, rooms ensuite tea/coffee. Private parking. Sitting room & garden. 10 mins walk Town Centre, 15mins car ferry, close to race course & heritage centre.

| B&B | 3 | Ensuite | €28-€32 | Dinner | - |
| B&B | 1 | Standard | €25.50-€28.50 | Partial Board | - |
| Single Rate | | | €38-€43.50 | Child reduction | 50% |

In Wexford

**Open:** All Year

---

**Ms Margaret Redmond**
FERRYCARRIG LODGE
Park, Ferrycarrig Road,
Wexford, Co Wexford

**Wexford**
Tel: **053 42605**   Fax: **053 42606**
Email: **ferrycarrig@wexford-accommodation.com**
Web: **www.wexford-accommodation.com**

Charming, relaxing residence, nestled on riverbank. Individually designed rooms, 10 min walk Heritage Park, Hotel, Quality Restaurants, Ferries 15 mins.

| B&B | 4 | Ensuite | €37.50-€40 | Dinner | - |
| B&B | - | Standard | - | Partial Board | - |
| Single Rate | | | €50-€60 | Child reduction | 50% |

Wexford 2km

**Open:** 1st February-31st December

---

**Eamonn & Margaret Sreenan**
MAPLE LODGE
Castlebridge, Wexford,
Co Wexford

**Wexford**
Tel: **053 59195**   Fax: **053 59195**
Email: **sreenan@eircom.net**
Web: **www.maplelodgewexford.com**

Quality approved AA ◆◆◆◆. Refreshments in guest lounge overlooking landscaped gardens. On R741 20 mins. Rosslare Port, 10 mins Beaches. Breakfast menu, home baking.

| B&B | 4 | Ensuite | €35-€37.50 | Dinner | - |
| B&B | - | Standard | - | Partial Board | - |
| Single Rate | | | €45-€55 | Child reduction | - |

Wexford 4km

**Open:** 12th March-12th November

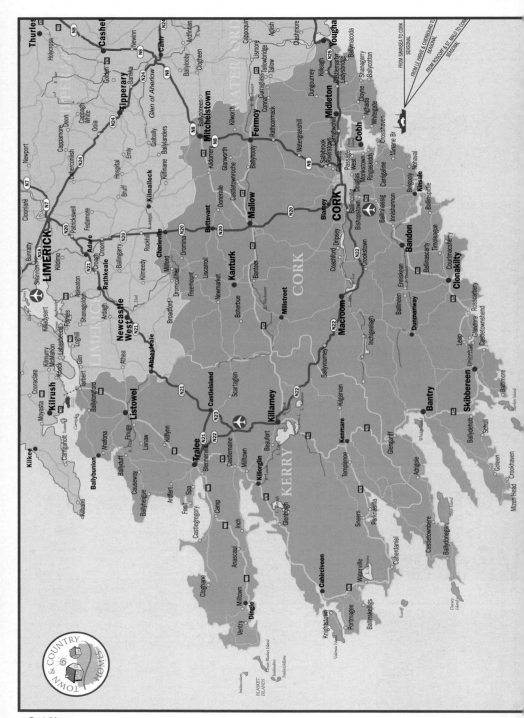

*Cork/Kerry*

Located in the south-west corner of Ireland, the Cork and South Kerry region offers its visitors a great diversity of scenery, culture and leisure activities. The region claims some of the most varied and spectacular scenery in the country. Here you will find the full range of holiday options to ensure a memorable, refreshing and very different holiday.

The South Western coastline, sculptured by the ice-age and influenced by the warm waters of the Gulf Stream, is steeped in ancient history and folklore from the East and West Cork coasts, The Beara and Dingle Peninsulas, and from the Ring of Kerry to the Lakes of Killarney and the Bandon, Lee and Blackwater Valleys.

**Ross Castle, Killarney**

Some of Ireland's best international festivals are hosted in the region and attractions for all the family, guarantees a fun filled holiday.

## Area Representatives

**CORK**

Ms Patricia Blanchfield BLANCHFIELD HOUSE Rigsdale (Cork/Bandon N71) Halfway Ballinahassig Co Cork Tel: 021 4885167   Fax: 021 4885805
Mrs Georgina Coughlan GLEBE HOUSE Tay Road Cobh Co Cork
Tel: 021 4811373   Fax: 021 4811373
Ms Peggie Downing BRU NA PAIRCE 7 Slip Park Bantry Co Cork
Tel: 027 51603

**KERRY**

Mrs Margaret Brown THE OLD CABLE HOUSE B&B Milestone Site Award
Old Cable Station Waterville Ring of Kerry
Tel: 066 9474233   Fax: 066 9474869
Mrs Coleen Burke BEENOSKEE Tralee Road Killarney Co Kerry
Tel: 064 32435   Fax 064 32435
Mr Maurice O'Shea BALLYMORE HOUSE Ballymore Ventry Dingle Co Kerry
Tel: 066 9159050

## Tourist Information Offices
**OPEN ALL YEAR**

REFER TO PAGE 5 FOR A LIST OF SERVICES AVAILABLE

Cork
Aras Failte
Grand Parade
Tel: 021 4255100

Blarney
Tel: 021 4381624

Dingle
Strand Street
Tel: 066 9151188

Killarney
Beech Road
Tel: 064 31633

Kinsale
Pier Road
Tel: 021 4772234

Skibbereen
Town Hall
Tel: 028 21766

Website: **www.corkkerry.ie**

Cork, the southern capital, Ireland's largest county. West Cork warmed by the Gulf stream with spectacular scenic beauty. Experience the tranquillity of East Cork with its sandy beaches. Get lost in nature in North Cork through rolling hills and valleys.

---

Ballincollig 11.5km

**John & Elizabeth Plaice**
MUSKERRY HOUSE
**Farnanes, Co Cork**

### Ballincollig

TEL: **021 7336469**   FAX: **021 7336469**
EMAIL: **muskerryhouse@hotmail.com**

Cork/Killarney road N22. Entry from N22/R619 intersection. Ballincollig 11.5km. Spacious rooms, full bathrooms. Central - Airport, Ferry, Blarney, West Cork and Kerry. Restaurant 5 min walk.

| B&B | 6 | Ensuite | €28-€31 | Dinner | - |
|---|---|---|---|---|---|
| B&B | - | Standard | - | Partial Board | - |
| Single Rate | | | €40-€43.50 | Child reduction | 25% |

**Open:** 6th January-20th December

---

Halfway Village 3km

**Ms Patricia Blanchfield**
BLANCHFIELD HOUSE
**Rigsdale (Cork/Bandon N71), Halfway, Ballinahassig, Co Cork**

### Ballinhassig Kinsale

TEL: **021 4885167**   FAX: **021 4885805**
EMAIL: **blanchfield@eircom.net**

Period country home on N71, near City Airport, Ferry Port, Kinsale. Good tour base West Cork/Kerry.  Private Salmon, Trout Fishing. Breakfast/Dinner menus.

| B&B | 2 | Ensuite | €28-€34 | Dinner | €19-€25 |
|---|---|---|---|---|---|
| B&B | 4 | Standard | €26-€32 | Partial Board | €400 |
| Single Rate | | | €38-€45 | Child reduction | 25% |

**Open:** 15th March-31st October

---

Ballycotton 3km

**Mrs Anna Casey**
SUNVILLE HOUSE
**Sunville, Ballycotton, Co Cork**

### Ballycotton

TEL: **021 4646271**
EMAIL: **Sunvillehouse@eircom.net**
WEB: **www.sunville.net**

Sea and shore angling. Salmon rivers. Bird sanctuary. 5 min from beach. Tranquil setting near Ballycotton. Lovely cliff walks. Sun lounge. Home baking. A warm welcome.

| B&B | 6 | Ensuite | €28-€35 | Dinner | €19-€22 |
|---|---|---|---|---|---|
| B&B | - | Standard | - | Partial Board | €294 |
| Single Rate | | | €40-€45.50 | Child reduction | 50% |

**Open:** All Year

---

Fermoy 8km

**Billy & Majella Mulqueen**
THE OLD TRAIN HOUSE B&B
**Station Road, Ballyhooly, Co Cork**

### Ballyhooly

TEL: **025 39337**   FAX: **025 39962**
EMAIL: **oldtrainhouse@eircom.net**
WEB: **www.oldtrainhouse.com**

Old stone railway building with large rooms, mature gardens, classic cars and great breakfasts. On N72 between Fermoy and Mallow. All rooms ensuite with tv.

| B&B | 3 | Ensuite | €30-€35 | Dinner | - |
|---|---|---|---|---|---|
| B&B | - | Standard | - | Partial Board | - |
| Single Rate | | | €40-€45 | Child reduction | 50% |

**Open:** 3rd January-20th December

### Mrs Peggy Twomey
**WESTON HOUSE**
The Mills, Ballyvourney,
Macroom, Co Cork

**Ballyvourney**

TEL: **026 45097/45936**   FAX: **026 45936**
EMAIL: **weston_house@hotmail.com**

Cead Mile Fáilte to a charming family run 18th century Georgian house on N22. Prize winning gardens. Local amenities, Golf, Fishing, Walking, Horse Riding, Pubs and Restaurants next door.

| B&B | 5 | Ensuite | €31 | Dinner | €25 |
|-----|---|---------|-----|--------|-----|
| B&B | - | Standard | | Partial Board | |
| Single Rate | | | €43.50 | Child reduction | 25% |

Killarney 14km

**Open:** All Year Except Christmas

---

### Mrs Margaret Harrington
**CHANNEL VIEW**
Baltimore, Co Cork

**Baltimore**

TEL: **028 20440**
EMAIL: **channelview@eircom.net**
WEB: **www.channelviewbb.com**

Spacious Dormer Bungalow, private car park, spectacular views overlooking the Bay. Sailing, Fishing, Island Trips, Diving, Scenic Walks, Golf, Tea/Coffee facilities.

| B&B | 5 | Ensuite | €28-€35 | Dinner | - |
|-----|---|---------|---------|--------|---|
| B&B | - | Standard | - | Partial Board | - |
| Single Rate | | | €40-€60 | Child reduction | 33.3% |

Baltimore 1km

**Open:** 1st March-31st October

---

### Marguerite O'Driscoll
**RATHMORE HOUSE**
Baltimore, Co Cork

**Baltimore**

TEL: **028 20362**   FAX: **028 20362**
EMAIL: **rathmorehouse@eircom.net**
WEB: **www.baltimore-ireland.com**

Rathmore house, overlooking harbour and islands, is the perfect place to relax and unwind. An area of understated beauty. A warm welcome awaits you.

| B&B | 6 | Ensuite | €30-€32.50 | Dinner | €20 |
|-----|---|---------|------------|--------|-----|
| B&B | - | Standard | | Partial Board | €325 |
| Single Rate | | | €40-€45 | Child reduction | 50% |

Baltimore 2km

**Open:** All Year

---

### Mrs Anne Buckley
**ST ANNE'S**
Clonakilty Road, Bandon,
Co Cork

**Bandon**

TEL: **023 44239**   FAX: **023 44239**
EMAIL: **stannesbandon@eircom.net**

Georgian house. Walled gardens. Near Town Centre. Convenient to Golf, Beaches, Fishing and Walking. Teamaking facilities. Airport 16 miles.

| B&B | 5 | Ensuite | €31-€33 | Dinner | - |
|-----|---|---------|---------|--------|---|
| B&B | - | Standard | | Partial Board | - |
| Single Rate | | | €43.50 | Child reduction | - |

Bandon 1km

**Open:** All Year Except Christmas

---

### Mrs Carmel Nash
**RIVERVIEW**
7 Riverview Estate, Bandon,
Co Cork

**Bandon**

TEL: **023 41080**   FAX: **023 41607**
EMAIL: **cfnash@eircom.net**

Friendly relaxed home edge of town. Scenic views. 30 mins to Airport, Ferry. Convenient Golf, Beaches and Kinsale. Ideal touring West Cork, Kerry.

| B&B | 4 | Ensuite | €30-€33 | Dinner | - |
|-----|---|---------|---------|--------|---|
| B&B | - | Standard | - | Partial Board | - |
| Single Rate | | | €40-€43.50 | Child reduction | - |

In Bandon

**Open:** All Year

Bandon 1km

**Mrs Theresa O'Connor**
ASHGROVE HOUSE
Castle Road, Bandon, Co Cork

Tel: **023 41033**   Fax: **023 41033**

Patio back and front, 5 minutes from Town Centre. House on Golf Club road. Beach 6km from House. Kinsale 20km.

| B&B | 4 | Ensuite | €27.50-€31 | Dinner | - |
|-----|---|---------|------------|--------|---|
| B&B | - | Standard | | Partial Board | - |
| Single Rate | | | €40-€43.50 | Child reduction | 25% |

**Open:** 1st January-20th December

---

In Bandon

**Kathleen O'Donovan**
AR NEAMH
Knockbrogan, Bandon, Co Cork

Tel: **023 41129**
Email: **arneamh@yahoo.com**

New dormer style house built on private site with landscaped garden.

| B&B | 4 | Ensuite | €35-€40 | Dinner | - |
|-----|---|---------|---------|--------|---|
| B&B | - | Standard | - | Partial Board | - |
| Single Rate | | | €40-€50 | Child reduction | - |

**Open:** 5th January-14th December

---

**Ms Peggie Downing**
BRU NA PAIRCE
7 Slip Park, Bantry, Co Cork

Tel: **027 51603**
Email: **pdowning1@eircom.net**

Modern home quiet locality, overlooking Caha mountains. 5 minutes walk from Town. Centre of West Cork and South Kerry.

| B&B | 2 | Ensuite | €30-€31 | Dinner | - |
|-----|---|---------|---------|--------|---|
| B&B | 1 | Standard | €30-€30 | Partial Board | - |
| Single Rate | | | €40-€43.50 | Child reduction | - |

**Open:** 1st January-31st December

---

Bantry 1km

**Maggie Doyle**
ATLANTIC SHORE
Newtown, Bantry, Co Cork

Tel: **027 51310**   Fax: **027 52175**
Email: **divebantry@eircom.net**

A spacious purpose built bungalow with a panoramic view of Bantry Bay. 50 metres past 30mph speed sign off Bantry/Glengarriff road N71.

| B&B | 5 | Ensuite | €29-€31 | Dinner | - |
|-----|---|---------|---------|--------|---|
| B&B | 1 | Standard | - | Partial Board | - |
| Single Rate | | | €40-€45 | Child reduction | - |

**Open:** 1st March-30th November

---

Bantry 1km

**Mrs Phyllis Foley**
ARD NA GREINE
Newtown, Bantry, Co Cork

Tel: **027 51169**
Email: **info@ardnagreine.net**
Web: **www.ardnagreine.net**

Country home, peaceful scenic setting overlooking nature gardens & countryside. One mile Bantry. Off N71 off Glengarriff/Killarney Rd. House signs on main N71 Rd.

| B&B | 4 | Ensuite | €30-€32 | Dinner | - |
|-----|---|---------|---------|--------|---|
| B&B | - | Standard | - | Partial Board | - |
| Single Rate | | | €40-€45 | Child reduction | - |

**Open:** 1st April-30th November

**Mrs Brenda Harrington**
LEYTON
23 Slip Lawn, Bantry, Co Cork

**Bantry**

TEL: 027 50665
EMAIL: **leyton@iolfree.ie**
WEB: **www.leytonbb.com**

Friendly relaxing home, quiet area. Breakfast menu. Car park. Bicycle garage. Off N71.
Signposted at junction Glengarriff Rd end of Bantry Town. 5 mins to Town Centre.

| B&B | 3 | Ensuite | €27.50-€31 | Dinner | - |
| B&B | 1 | Standard | €25.50-€28.50 | Partial Board | - |
| Single Rate | | | €38-€41 | Child reduction | 25% |

In Bantry

**Open:** 1st April-31st October

---

**Mrs Sheila Harrington**
ELMWOOD HOUSE
6 Slip Lawn, Bantry, Co Cork

**Bantry**

TEL: **027 50087**
EMAIL: **sheilaharrington@oceanfree.net**

Warm friendly home off main road. Tea/Cakes on arrival, Town 5 minutes. Turf fire, Bicycle garage.
Archivist. Off N71. Signposted end of Town near Peace Park.

| B&B | 2 | Ensuite | €27.50-€31 | Dinner | - |
| B&B | 2 | Standard | €25.50-€28.50 | Partial Board | - |
| Single Rate | | | - | Child reduction | 50% |

In Bantry

**Open:** 1st January-31st December

---

**Mrs Tosca Kramer**
THE MILL
Newtown, Bantry, Co Cork

**Bantry**

TEL: **027 50278**  FAX: **027 50278**
EMAIL: **bbthemill@eircom.net**
WEB: **www.the-mill.net**
BUS NO: **8**

Well established accommodation, (N71) Bantry (1km), AA ◆◆◆'s. Own art on display. All rooms
with TV. Laundry service.

| B&B | 6 | Ensuite | €30-€32 | Dinner | - |
| B&B | - | Standard | - | Partial Board | - |
| Single Rate | | | €40-€60 | Child reduction | 25% |

Bantry 1km

**Open:** 1st April-31st October

---

**Mrs Cait Murray**
ROCKLANDS
Gurteenroe, Bantry, Co Cork

**Bantry**

TEL: **027 50212**
EMAIL: **rocklandsbantry@eircom.net**

Modern Bungalow on Bantry/Glengarriff Rd. N71. Magnificent views Bantry Bay, Lake, Sea,
Mountains. Rooms with Tea/Coffee, TV & hairdryers. Private parking. Close to all tourist amenities.

| B&B | 3 | Ensuite | €30-€32 | Dinner | - |
| B&B | - | Standard | - | Partial Board | - |
| Single Rate | | | €45 | Child reduction | 50% |

Bantry 4km

**Open:** 1st March-10th October

---

**Mrs Margaret O'Sullivan**
PARK VIEW
Newtown, Bantry, Co Cork

**Bantry**

TEL: **027 51174**  FAX: **027 51174**
EMAIL: **margaret_o_sullivan3@hotmail.com**

Modern home, ideal touring centre. On main Bantry Glengarriff (N71). Beaches, Golf, Fishing,
Horse Riding convenient. Scenic drives. Choice of breakfast.

| B&B | 3 | Ensuite | €28-€31 | Dinner | - |
| B&B | 1 | Standard | €26-€28.50 | Partial Board | - |
| Single Rate | | | €38-€45 | Child reduction | 25% |

Bantry 1km

**Open:** 1st February-30th November

**Bantry 2km**

### Vincent & Margaret O'Sullivan
**SONAMAR**
**Dromleigh South, Bantry, Co Cork**

**Bantry**

TEL: **027 50502**
EMAIL: **sonamar@iol.ie**

Distinctive bungalow with extensive gardens, overlooking town, unsurpassed view of Bantry Bay, Scenic walks, quiet location. Signposted from the square.

| | | | | |
|---|---|---|---|---|
| B&B | 3 | Ensuite | €28-€32 | Dinner — |
| B&B | 1 | Standard | €26-€30 | Partial Board — |
| Single Rate | | | €40-€43.50 | Child reduction 25% |

**Open:** 1st April-1st October

---

**In Bantry**

### Ursula Schiesser
**SHANGRI-LA**
**Glengarriff Road, Newtown/Bantry, Co Cork**

**Bantry**

TEL: **027 50244**  FAX: **027 50244**
EMAIL: **schiesserbb@eircom.net**

Bungalow with spectacular views of Bantry Bay. Spacious garden. Tea/Coffee making facilities. Credit Cards welcome, Golf nearby. German/French spoken.

| | | | | |
|---|---|---|---|---|
| B&B | 6 | Ensuite | €28-€31 | Dinner €19 |
| B&B | - | Standard | - | Partial Board — |
| Single Rate | | | €40-€44 | Child reduction 25% |

**Open:** 1st March-1st November

---

**Bantry 1km**

### Mrs Joan Sweeney
**HIGHFIELD**
**Newtown, Bantry, Co Cork**

**Bantry**

TEL: **027 50791**
EMAIL: **highfieldbantry@eircom.net**

Situated on main Bantry/Glengarriff Road. Overlooking Bantry Bay. Electric blankets, hairdryers available. Garage for bicycles. Close to all amenities.

| | | | | |
|---|---|---|---|---|
| B&B | 4 | Ensuite | €28-€31 | Dinner — |
| B&B | - | Standard | - | Partial Board — |
| Single Rate | | | €43.50 | Child reduction 50% |

**Open:** 20th April-15th October

---

### Helen Allcorn
**ALLCORN'S COUNTRY HOME**
**Shournagh Road, Blarney, Co Cork**

**Blarney**

TEL: **021 4385577**  FAX: **021 4382828**
EMAIL: **info@allcorns.com**
WEB: **www.allcorns.com**

Really spacious country home/gardens beside Shournagh river. Surrounded by mature woods and meadows. Just off R617 Blarney/Killarney Road.

| | | | | |
|---|---|---|---|---|
| B&B | 3 | Ensuite | €30-€35 | Dinner — |
| B&B | 1 | Standard | €30-€30 | Partial Board — |
| Single Rate | | | €38-€45 | Child reduction 25% |

**Blarney 2km**

**Open:** 1st March-31st October

---

**Blarney 1km**

### Mrs Veronica Annis-Sisk
**YVORY HOUSE**
**Killowen, Blarney, Co Cork**

**Blarney**

TEL: **021 4381128**
EMAIL: **yvoryhouse@eircom.net**

Modern luxury bungalow in scenic farming location. Horseriding, Golf, Music locally, TV in bedrooms, Tea/Coffee facilities. 1km off Blarney/Killarney Rd. (R617)

| | | | | |
|---|---|---|---|---|
| B&B | 2 | Ensuite | €30-€32 | Dinner — |
| B&B | 1 | Standard | €28-€28.50 | Partial Board — |
| Single Rate | | | €40-€50 | Child reduction 25% |

**Open:** 1st February-30th November

**In Blarney**

### Pat & Regina Coughlan
**THE WHITE HOUSE**
Shean Lower, Blarney, Co Cork

**Blarney**

TEL: **021 4385338**
EMAIL: **info@thewhitehouseblarney.com**
WEB: **www.thewhitehouseblarney.com**

Well heated luxurious home, overlooking Castle. All rooms with Satellite TV, Tea/coffee facilities, hairdryers. AA ◆◆◆◆ selected. Breakfast menu.

| B&B | 6 | Ensuite | €30-€35 | Dinner | - |
|-----|---|---------|---------|--------|---|
| B&B | - | Standard | - | Partial Board | - |
| Single Rate | | | €40-€50 | Child reduction | 25% |

**Open:** 1st January-23rd December

---

**Blarney 1.5km**

### Anne & Christopher Cremin
**ASHCROFT**
Stoneview, Blarney, Co Cork

**Blarney**

TEL: **021 4385224**   FAX: **021 4385224**
EMAIL: **info@ashcroftblarney.com**
WEB: **www.ashcroftblarney.com**

Ashcroft offers magnificent views of Blarney Castle and Golf course. Rooms with TV, Tea/Coffee, Hairdryers and Power Showers. Breakfast menu. Follow signs for Blarney Golf course.

| B&B | 4 | Ensuite | €28-€32 | Dinner | - |
|-----|---|---------|---------|--------|---|
| B&B | - | Standard | - | Partial Board | - |
| Single Rate | | | €40-€45 | Child reduction | 25% |

**Open:** 5th January-20th December

---

**Blarney 1km**

### Fran & Tony Cronin
**HILLVIEW HOUSE**
Killard, Blarney, Co Cork

**Blarney**

TEL: **021 4385161**
EMAIL: **hillview_blarney@yahoo.co.uk**
WEB: **www.blarneyaccommodation.com**

Beautiful view. Ground floor rooms. Car park. Sun Lounge. Pressurised showers, Cable TV, Hairdryers. Extensive Breakfast Menu. Walking distance to Blarney.

| B&B | 4 | Ensuite | €30-€32 | Dinner | - |
|-----|---|---------|---------|--------|---|
| B&B | - | Standard | - | Partial Board | - |
| Single Rate | | | | Child reduction | 25% |

**Open:** 10th January-30th November

---

**Blarney**

### Eileen Desmond
**BUENA VISTA**
Station Road, Blarney, Co Cork

**Blarney**

TEL: **021 4383537**
EMAIL: **info@blarneybb.com**
WEB: **www.blarneybb.com**

Modern comfortable house, with private car park, landscaped gardens, all rooms with TV, Tea/Coffee facilities, Hairdryers, 1km to Blarney Village.

| B&B | 3 | Ensuite | €30-€32 | Dinner | - |
|-----|---|---------|---------|--------|---|
| B&B | - | Standard | - | Partial Board | - |
| Single Rate | | | €42-€45 | Child reduction | - |

**Open:** 15th January-15th December

---

**Blarney 9km**

### Neil & Noreen Finnegan
**THAR AN UISCE**
Magoola, Dripsey, Co Cork

**Blarney**

TEL: **021 7334788**
EMAIL: **tharanuisce@eircom.net**
WEB: **http://homepage.eircom.net/~tharanuisce**

Lakeside setting on Blarney/Killarney route R618. All rooms ensuite with TV, Tea/Coffee, Hairdryers. Fishing, Waterskiing, Riverside walk all alongside.

| B&B | 3 | Ensuite | €28-€31 | Dinner | - |
|-----|---|---------|---------|--------|---|
| B&B | - | Standard | - | Partial Board | - |
| Single Rate | | | €40-€43.50 | Child reduction | 50% |

**Open:** 17th March-31st October

**Blarney**

**Anne Fogarty**
**GLENMAROON HOUSE**
Paud's Cross, Blarney, Co Cork

TEL: **021 4385821**
EMAIL: **glenmaroonhouse@hotmail.com**

Luxurious country home in private tranquil location. Modern, spacious, colour coordinated bedrooms. 1km from Blarney. First left off Blarney-Killarney road (R617).

| B&B | 4 | Ensuite | €30-€34 | Dinner | - |
| B&B | - | Standard | - | Partial Board | - |
| Single Rate | | | €45-€50 | Child reduction | 25% |

Blarney 1km

**Open:** 8th January-17th December

---

**Blarney**

**Eucharia Hannon**
**WESTWOOD COUNTRY HOUSE**
Dromin, Blarney, Co Cork

TEL: **021 4385404**
EMAIL: **westwood.country.house@oceanfree.net**
WEB: **www.westwoodcountryhouse.com**

Luxurious home. Elegantly furnished. TV's, Hairdryers. Tea, scones on arrival. Convenient to Blarney Castle, Shops, Pubs, Restaurants. Superb base for touring Killarney, Kinsale, Cobh.

| B&B | 3 | Ensuite | €32.50-€35 | Dinner | - |
| B&B | - | Standard | - | Partial Board | - |
| Single Rate | | | €45-€50 | Child reduction | - |

Blarney 4km

**Open:** 1st January-20th December

---

**Blarney**

**Bridget & Pat Harrington**
**CURRAC BUI**
30 Castle Close Drive, Blarney, Co Cork

TEL: **021 4385424**
EMAIL: **curracbui@tinet.ie**
WEB: **www.curracbui.com**

Personally run modern home. 5 min walk Blarney Castle/Local amenities/Cork Bus route. Bedrooms with TV, Hairdryers, Tea/Coffee. Home baking, Breakfast choice.

| B&B | 3 | Ensuite | €30-€32 | Dinner | - |
| B&B | 1 | Standard | €26-€29 | Partial Board | - |
| Single Rate | | | €38-€44 | Child reduction | 33.3% |

In Blarney

**Open:** 1st February-30th November

---

**Blarney**

**Mrs Eileen Hempel**
**EDELWEISS HOUSE**
Leemount, Carrigrohane, Co Cork

TEL: **021 4871888**   FAX: **021 4871888**

Swiss style home overlooking river Lee. TV in rooms, Hairdryers. Credit cards accepted. 4.5 miles Blarney, Cork City 2 miles on N22. Killarney road signposted. House is on the R618.

| B&B | 3 | Ensuite | €32-€32 | Dinner | - |
| B&B | 1 | Standard | €29-€29 | Partial Board | - |
| Single Rate | | | €40-€44 | Child reduction | 25% |

Cork City 6km

**Open:** 16th March-18th December

---

**Blarney**

**Mrs Anne Hennessy**
**BLARNEY VALE HOUSE**
Cork Road (R617), Blarney, Co Cork

TEL: **021 4381511**
EMAIL: **info@blarneyvale.com**
WEB: **www.blarneyvale.com**

Luxurious home on private grounds overlooking village. AA ◆◆◆◆ selected, friendly atmosphere. Bedrooms with TV, Hairdryers, Tea/Coffee facilities. Breakfast menu. Cork City 8 mins.

| B&B | 4 | Ensuite | €30-€35 | Dinner | - |
| B&B | - | Standard | - | Partial Board | - |
| Single Rate | | | €45-€55 | Child reduction | 25% |

In Blarney

**Open:** 1st March-30th November

**In Blarney**

### Mrs Margaret Kearney
SUNVILLE
**1 Castle Close Lawn, Blarney, Co Cork**

**Blarney**

Tᴇʟ: **021 4381325**

Modern comfortable home 5 mins walk to Castle, Restaurants, Shops, Entertainment. Adjacent to bus route and beautiful country walk. Tea/Coffee facilities.

| B&B | 2 | Ensuite | €29-€32 | Dinner | - |
|-----|---|---------|---------|--------|---|
| B&B | 1 | Standard | - | Partial Board | - |
| Single Rate | | | €38-€45 | Child reduction | 25% |

**Open:** 1st March-1st December

---

**Blarney 1km**

### Susan & Brian Kenna
LANESVILLE B&B
**Killard, Blarney, Co Cork**

**Blarney**

Tᴇʟ: **021 4381813**
Eᴍᴀɪʟ: **info@lanesvillebandb.com**
Wᴇʙ: **www.lanesvillebandb.com**

Luxurious family run home. Walking distance to Blarney Castle. Rooms with TV, tea/coffee, hairdryers & pressurised showers. Breakfast menu. Private car park.

| B&B | 4 | Ensuite | €28-€32 | Dinner | - |
|-----|---|---------|---------|--------|---|
| B&B | - | Standard | - | Partial Board | - |
| Single Rate | | | €40-€43.50 | Child reduction | 25% |

**Open:** 2nd January-10th December

---

**Blarney 5km**

### Mrs Cecilia Kiely
CLARAGH
**Waterloo Road, Blarney, Co Cork**

**Blarney**

Tᴇʟ: **021 4886308**  Fᴀx: **021 4886308**
Eᴍᴀɪʟ: **claraghbandb@eircom.net**
Wᴇʙ: **www.claragh.com**

Complimentary Home Baking on arrival. Bedrooms have TV, Tea/Coffee, Electric Blankets, Hairdryers. Breakfast menu includes French Toast. Private Parking.

| B&B | 4 | Ensuite | €30-€32 | Dinner | - |
|-----|---|---------|---------|--------|---|
| B&B | - | Standard | - | Partial Board | - |
| Single Rate | | | €40-€45 | Child reduction | - |

**Open:** 1st April-31st October

---

**Blarney 2km**

### Michael & Anne Lynch
THE GABLES
**Stoneview, Blarney, Co Cork**

**Blarney**

Tᴇʟ: **021 4385330**
Eᴍᴀɪʟ: **anne@gablesblarney.com**
Wᴇʙ: **www.gablesblarney.com**

Former Victorian Rectory on two acres, overlooking Blarney Castle. Golf course - Bar & Restaurant alongside. Home baking. Private parking. Itineraries arranged.

| B&B | 3 | Ensuite | €28-€31 | Dinner | - |
|-----|---|---------|---------|--------|---|
| B&B | - | Standard | - | Partial Board | - |
| Single Rate | | | €40-€45 | Child reduction | - |

**Open:** 1st March-30th November

---

**Blarney 1km**

### Mrs Caroline Morgan
KILLARNEY HOUSE
**Station Road, Blarney, Co Cork**

**Blarney**

Tᴇʟ: **021 4381841**  Fᴀx: **021 4381841**
Eᴍᴀɪʟ: **info@killarneyhouseblarney.com**
Wᴇʙ: **www.killarneyhouseblarney.com**

Purpose built luxury home on 1 acre of landscaped gardens, overlooking village. AA ◆◆◆◆. Breakfast menu, bedrooms with power showers, TV, hairdryers, tea/coffee. Private car park.

| B&B | 6 | Ensuite | €28-€36 | Dinner | - |
|-----|---|---------|---------|--------|---|
| B&B | - | Standard | - | Partial Board | - |
| Single Rate | | | €40-€50 | Child reduction | 25% |

**Open:** 1st January-31st December

Blarney 1km

**Mrs Janet Murphy-Hallissey**
**PINE FOREST HOUSE**
Elmcourt, Blarney, Co Cork

### Blarney

TEL: **021 4385979**   FAX: **021 4382917**
EMAIL: **info@pineforestbb.com**
WEB: **www.pineforestbb.com**

Spacious bungalow situated in peaceful wooded area with large landscaped garden. 1km on Blarney/Killarney Road (617). Tea and Coffee on arrival.  Private parking.

| B&B | 4 | Ensuite | €30-€32.50 | Dinner | - |
| B&B | - | Standard | - | Partial Board | - |
| Single Rate | | | €40-€45 | Child reduction | 25% |

**Open:** All Year Except Christmas

---

Blarney 4km

**Mrs Marian Nugent**
**COOLIM**
Cooflugh, Tower, Blarney, Co Cork

### Blarney

TEL: **021 4382848**
EMAIL: **nugent.coolim@oceanfree.net**
WEB: **www.coolimbb.com**

Spacious, friendly home in a picturesque country setting. Private Parking. Refreshments on arrival. Home baking. Close to Blarney Castle, Golf, Pubs, Shop and Restaurants.

| B&B | 3 | Ensuite | €32-€34 | Dinner | - |
| B&B | - | Standard | - | Partial Board | - |
| Single Rate | | | €45 | Child reduction | 33.3% |

**Open:** 4th January-20th December

---

Blarney 6km

**Mrs Ita O'Donovan**
**KNOCKAWN WOOD**
Curraleigh, Inniscarra, Co Cork

### Blarney

TEL: **021 4870284**   FAX: **021 4870284**
EMAIL: **odknkwd@iol.ie**
WEB: **homepages.iol.ie/~odknkwd/**

Picturesque, restful. Tea & scones on arrival. Electric blankets. Hairdryers. Cork, Ferry, Airport 30 mins. N25 west/N22/R618. From Blarney-Killarney R617/R618. Fishing.

| B&B | 4 | Ensuite | €28-€32 | Dinner | €20 |
| B&B | - | Standard | - | Partial Board | - |
| Single Rate | | | €40-€45 | Child reduction | 50% |

**Open:** All Year

---

Blarney 4km

**Mrs Gertie O'Shea**
**TRAVELLERS JOY**
Tower, Blarney, Co Cork

### Blarney

TEL: **021 4385541**
EMAIL: **travellersjoy@iolfree.ie**

Blarney/Killarney R617. Recommended in many guides. Private parking. Prizewinning gardens. Tea/Coffee & T.V. in bedrooms. Quality breakfasts. Close to all amenities.

| B&B | 3 | Ensuite | €29-€33 | Dinner | - |
| B&B | - | Standard | - | Partial Board | - |
| Single Rate | | | €41-€45 | Child reduction | 50% |

**Open:** 10th January-20th December

---

Blarney 1km

**Mrs Rose O'Sullivan**
**AVONDALE LODGE**
Killowen, Blarney, Co Cork

### Blarney

TEL: **021 4381736**
EMAIL: **info@avondalelodge.com**
WEB: **www.avondalelodge.com**

Warm friendly home with superb views. Walking distance to village/castle. Golf, horseriding, music locally. Tea/coffee, hairdryers and TV in rooms. Breakfast menu. Private garden/parking.

| B&B | 4 | Ensuite | €30-€32 | Dinner | - |
| B&B | - | Standard | - | Partial Board | - |
| Single Rate | | | - | Child reduction | - |

**Open:** 1st February-30th November

**Blarney**

### Chef Billie & Catherine Phelan
**PHELAN'S WOODVIEW HOUSE**
Tweedmount, Blarney, Co Cork

Tel: **021 4385197**  Fax: **021 4385197**
Email: **info@phelanswoodviewhouse.com**
Web: **www.phelanswoodviewhouse.com**

Enjoy Gourmet Cooking at Phelans, Seafood a speciality. TV in bedrooms. Tea/coffee facilities, Credit Cards. Frommer & Eye Witness Guides recommended.

| B&B | 7 | Ensuite | €30-€35 | Dinner | €28-€45 |
| B&B | 1 | Standard | €26-€30 | Partial Board | - |
| Single Rate | | | €39-€45 | Child reduction | **50%** |

Blarney 3km

**Open:** 1st April-31st October

---

**Blarney**

### Mrs Olwen Venn
**MARANATHA COUNTRY HOUSE**
Tower, Blarney, Co Cork

Tel: **021 4385102**  Fax: **021 4382978**
Email: **douglasvenn@eircom.net**
Web: **www.maranathacountryhouse.com**

Stroll through the beautiful private gardens and woodlands surrounding this lovely Victorian mansion. Spacious romantic bedrooms. Beautiful historic antiques throughout.

| B&B | 4 | Ensuite | €30-€60 | Dinner | - |
| B&B | 1 | Standard | €30 | Partial Board | - |
| Single Rate | | | €40-€80 | Child reduction | **50%** |

Blarney 2km

**Open:** 1st February-10th December

---

**Carrigaline Cork Ferryport Airport**

### Mrs Ann O'Leary
**THE WILLOWS**
Ballea Road, Carrigaline, Co Cork

Tel: **021 4372669**  Fax: **021 4372669**
Email: **info@willowsbb.com**
Web: **www.willowsbb.com**

Split level house with gardens front and rear. Fishing, Golfing, Horse Riding, and Beaches 3km. Cork Airport 6km. Ringaskiddy Ferry 5km.

| B&B | 4 | Ensuite | €32-€35 | Dinner | - |
| B&B | - | Standard | - | Partial Board | - |
| Single Rate | | | €40-€45 | Child reduction | **33.3%** |

Carrigaline 1km

**Open:** 7th January-20th December

---

**Carrigtwohill**

### Miss Margot Seymour
**DUN-VREEDA HOUSE**
Carrigtwohill, Co Cork

Tel: **021 4883169**

Off N25 Cork, Waterford/Rosslare road at Carrigtwohill. Near Fota Wildlife, Cobh, and Jameson Heritage Centre. Golf, Fishing, Riding nearby. Bus route. Church in area. Snacks, light meals.

| B&B | 2 | Ensuite | €27.50-€31 | Dinner | - |
| B&B | 2 | Standard | €25.50-€28.50 | Partial Board | - |
| Single Rate | | | | Child reduction | **50%** |

In Carrigtwohill

**Open:** 1st January-31st December

---

**Castletownbere**

### Mrs Mary Donegan
**REALT-NA-MARA**
Castletownbere, Co Cork

Tel: **027 70101**  Fax: **027 71101**
Email: **realtnamaractb@eircom.net**
Web: **www.realtnamara.org**

Friendly home big garden, overlooks sea on Glengarriff Castletownbere road. Near Beara Way walking route. Near Town, Golf, Fishing. Tea/Coffee facilities on request.

| B&B | 4 | Ensuite | €30-€33 | Dinner | - |
| B&B | 1 | Standard | €28-€31 | Partial Board | - |
| Single Rate | | | €38-€43.50 | Child reduction | **33.3%** |

Castletownbere 1km

**Open:** All Year

Castletownbere 1km

**Mrs Noralene McGurn**
SEA BREEZE
Derrymihan, Castletownbere,
Beara Penïnsula, Co Cork

### Castletownbere

Tel: **027 70508**  Fax: **027 70508**
Email: **seabreez@eircom.net**
Web: **www.seabreez.com**

Warm friendly home. Situated on seafront overlooking Bere Island. Near Beara Way walking route. Ideal base for touring. Beara a peaceful spot.

| B&B | 6 | Ensuite | €30-€33 | Dinner | - |
| B&B | - | Standard | | Partial Board | - |
| Single Rate | | | €40-€43.50 | Child reduction | 25% |

**Open:** All Year Except Christmas

---

Ardgroom Village 5km

**Mary & John Gerard O'Sullivan**
SEA VILLA
Castletownberehaven Cst Rd,
Ardgroom Inward,
Beara Peninsula, Co Cork

### Castletownberehaven Ardgroom

Tel: **027 74369**  Fax: **027 74369**
Email: **seavilla1@eircom.net**
Web: **www.seavilla1.com**

New luxury home, tranquil scenic location on Beara Peninsula Rd, Beara way, sea, mountains & unspoilt landscape. Breakfast menu. T.V., hairdryer in all rooms. Sea trips locally.

| B&B | 3 | Ensuite | €31-€31 | Dinner | - |
| B&B | - | Standard | - | Partial Board | - |
| Single Rate | | | €40-€43.50 | Child reduction | - |

**Open:** 1st April-31st October

---

Clonakilty 1km

**Sean & Eileen Clancy**
SEA BREEZE
Carhue, Clonakilty, Co Cork

### Clonakilty

Tel: **023 34427**
Email: **seabreezeclon@eircom.net**
Web: **http://homepage.eircom.net/~seabreezeclonakilty**

Tranquility and total relaxation in this idyllic home, just off N71, less than 1km from town. Close to all amenities. Power showers, hairdryers. A warm welcome assured.

| B&B | 4 | Ensuite | €28-€35 | Dinner | - |
| B&B | - | Standard | | Partial Board | - |
| Single Rate | | | €40-€45 | Child reduction | 50% |

**Open:** All Year

---

In Clonakilty

**Tony & Noreen Driscoll**
BAY VIEW HOUSE
Old Timoleague Road,
Clonakilty, Co Cork

### Clonakilty

Tel: **023 33539**
Email: **bayviewhouse@eircom.net**
Web: **www.bayviewclonakilty.com**

Luxury home. Numerous awards & recommendations. Extensive menu. Delightful gardens. Quiet, scenic, seashore location off N71 at roundabout Cork approach. Town 3 mins walk.

| B&B | 5 | Ensuite | €28-€35 | Dinner | - |
| B&B | 1 | Standard | | Partial Board | - |
| Single Rate | | | €38-€53 | Child reduction | 33.3% |

**Open:** 1st March-31st October

---

In Clonakilty

**Mrs Marie Hanly**
GLENDINE
Tawnies Upper, Clonakilty,
Co Cork

### Clonakilty

Tel: **023 34824**
Email: **glendine@eircom.net**
Web: **www.glendine.com**

Charming family home, magnificent views. Generously sized, beautifully decorated rooms. Extensive breakfast menu. Warm hospitality comes with delicious home baking. Where good food is never rushed.

| B&B | 3 | Ensuite | €30-€35 | Dinner | - |
| B&B | - | Standard | | Partial Board | - |
| Single Rate | | | - | Child reduction | - |

**Open:** 1st February-31st October

**In Clonakilty**

### Mrs Clare Hayes
**WYTCHWOOD**
**Emmet Square, Clonakilty,**
**Co Cork**

TEL: **023 33525**   FAX: **023 35673**
EMAIL: **wytchost@iol.ie**

Georgian house with walled garden in a peaceful and tranquil setting. Breakfast choice. Le Guide du Routard and Lonely Planet recommended.

| B&B | 6 | Ensuite | €30-€35 | Dinner | - |
|-----|---|---------|---------|--------|---|
| B&B | - | Standard | - | Partial Board | - |
| Single Rate | | | €40-€60 | Child reduction | - |

**Open:** 1st March-30th September

---

**Clonakilty 4km**

### Mrs Ann Lehane
**BALARD HOUSE**
**Ballymacowen, Clonakilty,**
**Co Cork**

TEL: **023 33865**   FAX: **023 33865**

Modern home in peaceful location on Kinsale/Clonakilty road R600. Restaurants, Beaches, Sailing, Golf & Horseriding within easy reach.

| B&B | 3 | Ensuite | €28-€32 | Dinner | - |
|-----|---|---------|---------|--------|---|
| B&B | - | Standard | - | Partial Board | - |
| Single Rate | | | €45-€45 | Child reduction | 50% |

**Open:** 1st May-30th September

---

**In Clonakilty**

### Noreen & David McMahon
**NORDAV**
**off Western Road,**
**(Fernhill Rd) Clonakilty,**
**Co Cork**

TEL: **023 33655**   FAX: **023 33655**
EMAIL: **nordav@eircom.net**
WEB: **www.nordav-bed-and-breakfast.com**

Very private, 300 mts West Church & Town Centre. Award winning gardens. 1 Family suite (includes 2 bedrooms & lounge). 1 suite with verandah,€40 p.p.s. Studio apartment.

| B&B | 4 | Ensuite | €27.50-€35 | Dinner | - |
|-----|---|---------|------------|--------|---|
| B&B | - | Standard | - | Partial Board | - |
| Single Rate | | | €40-€60 | Child reduction | 25% |

**Open:** 1st April-30th September

---

**Clonakilty 2km**

### Mrs Breda Moore
**SHALOM**
**Ballyduvane, Clonakilty,**
**Co Cork**

TEL: **023 33473**

Modern bungalow in rural setting on main Clonakilty - Skibbereen road (N71). 2km Clonakilty Town, 6km beautiful sandy Inchydoney Beach.

| B&B | 2 | Ensuite | €28-€32 | Dinner | - |
|-----|---|---------|---------|--------|---|
| B&B | 1 | Standard | €26-€29 | Partial Board | - |
| Single Rate | | | - | Child reduction | 50% |

**Open:** 1st March-31st October

---

### Mrs Chris O'Brien
**MELROSE**
**The Miles, Clonakilty, Co Cork**

TEL: **023 33956/33961**   FAX: **023 33961**
EMAIL: **melroseclon@eircom.net**
WEB: **www.melrosewestcork.com**

Warm welcoming home 200mtrs off N71. Large gardens. Power showers. Tranquil location, ideal for touring Cork and Kerry. Restaurants, beaches, all amenities nearby.

| B&B | 4 | Ensuite | €30-€35 | Dinner | - |
|-----|---|---------|---------|--------|---|
| B&B | 1 | Standard | €30-€35 | Partial Board | - |
| Single Rate | | | €45-€50 | Child reduction | 50% |

**In Clonakilty**

**Open:** 1st January-30th November

In Clonakilty

**Ms Maeve O'Grady Williams**
MACLIAM LODGE
Western Road, Clonakilty,
Co Cork

### Clonakilty

TEL: **023 35195**
EMAIL: **macliamlodge@eircom.net**
WEB: **www.westcorkbandb.com**

National Award of Excellence winner. All rooms T.V. tea/coffee, power showers, hairdryers. Quiet location on N71. 5 min walk to town centre. Warm welcome assured.

| B&B | 6 | Ensuite | €30-€35 | Dinner | - |
| B&B | - | Standard | - | Partial Board | - |
| Single Rate | | | €40-€55 | Child reduction | 50% |

**Open:** All Year

Clonakilty 3km

**Mrs Nora O'Regan**
ASSUMPTION HOUSE
Ballinascarthy, Clonakilty,
Co Cork

### Clonakilty

TEL: **023 39268**
EMAIL: **assumptionhse@eircom.net**
WEB: **http://homepage.eircom.net/-assumptionhse**

Situated on N71, in Ballinascarthy. Warm welcoming home. Freshly prepared wholesome food. Home baking a speciality. Ideal location to beaches & day tours.

| B&B | 2 | Ensuite | €30-€35 | Dinner | - |
| B&B | 1 | Standard | €30-€35 | Partial Board | - |
| Single Rate | | | €40-€50 | Child reduction | 50% |

**Open:** 1st March-31st October

Cobh 2km

**Mrs Georgina Coughlan**
GLEBE HOUSE
Tay Road, Cobh, Co Cork

### Cobh

TEL: **021 4811373**   FAX: **021 4811373**
EMAIL: **info@glebehousecobh.com**
WEB: **www.glebehousecobh.com**

Warm spacious friendly home. Convenient Fota, Golf, Ferryport, Airport. Over bridge at Fota, turn left 2 miles to Crossroads, turn left. Breakfast menu. French spoken.

| B&B | 4 | Ensuite | €29-€34 | Dinner | - |
| B&B | - | Standard | - | Partial Board | - |
| Single Rate | | | €43-€45 | Child reduction | 25% |

**Open:** 1st April-30th November

Cobh 2km

**Mrs Bernadette de Maddox**
TEARMANN
Ballynoe, Cobh, Co Cork

### Cobh

TEL: **021 4813182**   FAX: **021 4814011**
EMAIL: **tearmanncobh@eircom.net**
WEB: **www.tearmanncobh.com**

19th Century Traditional House. Lovely garden. Car park. Close Heritage Centres, FOTA, Golf etc. Airport and Port 25 mins. Follow R624, pass by cross river ferry, 1st left up road on left.

| B&B | 2 | Ensuite | €28-€31 | Dinner | €20-€20 |
| B&B | 1 | Standard | €28-€30 | Partial Board | - |
| Single Rate | | | €40-€43.50 | Child reduction | - |

**Open:** 1st April-31st October

In Cobh

**Mrs Phyllis Fortune**
ARDEEN B&B
3 Harbour Hill, Cobh, Co Cork

### Cobh

TEL: **021 4811803**
EMAIL: **ardeenbandb@hotmail.com**

Period house, central location. Adjacent to St. Colmans Cathedral. Offers magnificent sea views. The Town Heritage Centre and Railway Station within a walk.

| B&B | 4 | Ensuite | €28-€32 | Dinner | - |
| B&B | - | Standard | - | Partial Board | - |
| Single Rate | | | €40-€44 | Child reduction | 50% |

**Open:** 1st January-22nd December

**In Cobh**

### Mrs Noreen Hickey
**MOUNT VIEW**
Beechmount, Cobh, Co Cork

**Cobh**

Tel: **021 4814260**   Fax: **021 4814260**
Email: **mountview8@eircom.net**
Web: **http://homepage.eircom.net/~mountainview8**

Town house spectacular view of Cathedral and harbour. Close to International and local ferries and Queenstown Story. Private car park. Signposted at Cathedral. Ground floor room.

| B&B | 4 | Ensuite | €27.50-€32 | Dinner | - |
| B&B | - | Standard | | Partial Board | - |
| Single Rate | | | €40-€49 | Child reduction | - |

**Open:** 1st January-10th December

---

**Cobh 1.4km**

### Pat & Martha Hurley
**HIGHLAND**
Carrignafoy Road, Ballywilliam, Cobh, Co Cork

**Cobh**

Tel: **021 4813873**   Fax: **021 4813873**
Email: **highlandcobh@eircom.net**
Web: **http://homepage.eircom.net/~highlandcobh**

Modern home with panoramic views, close to Local and International Ferries, Fota Golf, Wildlife Park, Queenstown Story. Ground floor rooms on request.

| B&B | 5 | Ensuite | €27.50-€33 | Dinner | - |
| B&B | - | Standard | - | Partial Board | - |
| Single Rate | | | €40-€49 | Child reduction | 25% |

**Open:** 1st March-31st October

---

**In Cobh**

### Ms Bernadette O'Shea
**ARD NA LAOI**
15 Westbourne Place, Cobh, Co Cork

**Cobh**

Tel: **021 4812742**

House is adjacent to promenade, it's the nearest B&B to Heritage Centre and railway station 2-3 mins walk. Spacious guest lounge, side yard for cycles.

| B&B | 5 | Ensuite | €30-€34 | Dinner | - |
| B&B | - | Standard | - | Partial Board | - |
| Single Rate | | | €40-€45 | Child reduction | 33.3% |

**Open:** 1st March-30th November

---

**Cobh**

### Cathal & Paula Rasmussen
**ROSEMOUNT**
Bishops Road, Cobh, Co Cork

**Cobh**

Tel: **021 4813547**   Fax: **021 4813873**
Email: **rosemountcobhl@eircom.net**
Web: **http://homepage.tinet.ie/~dodonovan/rosemount.html**

Luxurious home situated overlooking Cork harbour & St Colmans cathedral. Within walking distance of town centre, railway station & heritage centre. Large car park & mature gardens.

| B&B | 2 | Ensuite | €29-€33 | Dinner | - |
| B&B | 1 | Standard | €29-€33 | Partial Board | - |
| Single Rate | | | €39-€45 | Child reduction | 25% |

**Open:** 10th January-30th November

---

**Tallow 2km**

### Kevin Ryan
**THE GRANGE**
Curraglass, Conna, Near Tallow, Co Cork

**Conna**

Tel: **058 56247**   Fax: **058 56124**
Email: **kevin.ryan@thegrangehousetallow.com**
Web: **thegrangehousetallow.com**

Large three storey Georgian house dating back to 1840. Set on 8 acres of mature gardens and woodlands. Ideally based. Fishing on the Blackwater 5 mile. Nine excellent Golf courses within 12 miles.

| B&B | 3 | Ensuite | €35-€35 | Dinner | - |
| B&B | - | Standard | - | Partial Board | - |
| Single Rate | | | €40-€43.50 | Child reduction | 33.3% |

**Open:** 8th January-8th December

**Cork City 1km**

### Mrs Breeda Higgins
**7 Ferncliff**
**Bellevue Park, St Lukes,**
**Cork City, Co Cork**

**Cork City**

TEL: **021 4508963**  FAX: **021 4508963 (man)**
BUS NO: **7 & 8**

Victorian home, quiet cul-de-sac. Bus/Train Stations/City Centre 1km. Take left at T after Ambassador Hotel, then straight ahead, and on right.

| B&B | 2 | Ensuite | €27.50-€31 | Dinner | - |
| B&B | 2 | Standard | €25.50-€28.50 | Partial Board | - |
| Single Rate | | | €38-€43.50 | Child reduction | **33.3%** |

**Open:** 10th March-10th November

---

**Cork City 5km**

### Mrs Mary Bayer
**WHITE LODGE**
**Airport Cross, Kinsale Road,**
**Cork, Co Cork**

**Cork City Airport Kinsale Road**

TEL: **021 4961267**  FAX: **021 4967909**
EMAIL: **bayerfamily@eircom.net**

Take Airport road to roundabout at Airport gates, take Cork exit off roundabout, 100m on, turn left down side road. We are first B&B on left. City 6km.

| B&B | 3 | Ensuite | €28-€32 | Dinner | €22-€25 |
| B&B | 1 | Standard | €26-€29 | Partial Board | €300 |
| Single Rate | | | €39-€44 | Child reduction | **25%** |

**Open:** 11th January-20th December

---

**Cork City 6km**

### Mrs Breeda Savage
**GREEN ISLE**
**Ballygarvan Village,**
**Off Airport/Kinsale Road,**
**Co Cork**

**Cork City Airport Kinsale Road**

TEL: **021 4888171**

Country Home in scenic valley off Cork/Kinsale road. Airport 2km. Near Kinsale. Ferryport 8km. Tea/Coffee, Hairdryer in rooms. Visa.

| B&B | 2 | Ensuite | €29-€32 | Dinner | - |
| B&B | 1 | Standard | €28-€30 | Partial Board | - |
| Single Rate | | | €41-€44 | Child reduction | **25%** |

**Open:** 12th January-12th December

---

**Cork City 2km**

### Mrs Kay O'Donovan
**DUNDERG**
**38 Westgate Road,**
**Bishopstown, Cork City,**
**Co Cork**

**Cork City Bishopstown**

TEL: **021 4543078**  FAX: **021 4543078**
EMAIL: **dunderg@eircom.net**
WEB: **www.dunderg.com**
BUS NO: **5 & 8**

Quiet location 400m off N71 Bishopstown Bar. Convenient to N25 Greyhound Stadium, Leisure centre, University Hospital, UCC, FAS, West Cork, Killarney, Ferry, Airport. CIT.

| B&B | 4 | Ensuite | €32-€35 | Dinner | - |
| B&B | - | Standard | - | Partial Board | - |
| Single Rate | | | - | Child reduction | - |

**Open:** 1st January-15th December

---

**Cork City 2Km**

### Finbarr & Rebecca Sheehan
**BROOKSIDE HOUSE**
**8 Stratton Pines, Bishopstown,**
**Cork City, Co Cork**

**Cork City Bishopstown**

TEL: **021 4543564**  FAX: **021 4543564**
EMAIL: **rebecca@brooksidecork.com**
WEB: **www.brooksidecork.com**
BUS NO: **8**

Modern family run B&B. quiet location. 100m off N71 Bishopstown Bar. Convenient to Ferry, Airport, Greyhound Stadium, FAS, University Hospital, City Centre. Ideal base for touring the south.

| B&B | 3 | Ensuite | €30-€35 | Dinner | - |
| B&B | - | Standard | - | Partial Board | - |
| Single Rate | | | - | Child reduction | **25%** |

**Open:** 11th January-17th December

**Mrs Pauline Hickey**
BERKLEY LODGE B&B
Model Farm Road, Cork,
Co Cork

### Cork City Dennehy's Cross-Wilton

Tel: **021 4341755**  Fax: **021 4347522**
Email: **info@berkleylodge.com**
Web: **www.berkleylodge.com**
Bus No: **5 & 8**

Comfortable home in western suburbs near University Hospital/Wilton between South Ring N25 West and N22 Killarney Road. Ext N71 at Dennehys Cross to Model Farm Road. R608. City 2km.

| B&B | 4 | Ensuite | €32.50-€35 | Dinner | - |
| B&B | - | Standard | | Partial Board | - |
| Single Rate | | | - | Child reduction | 50% |

Cork City 2km

**Open:** 1st January-17th December

**Mrs Catherine Edwards**
RIVER VIEW
Douglas East, Cork, Co Cork

### Cork City Douglas

Tel: **021 4893762**  Fax: **021 4893762**
Email: **edwardsc@eircom.net**
Bus No: **7**

Victorian 1890 home in Douglas Village, near Barrys Pub. Convenient Restaurants Shopping Centres, Churches, Airport, Ferry. Cable TV all bedrooms. Access via tunnel to Douglas Village.

| B&B | 3 | Ensuite | €30-€37.50 | Dinner | - |
| B&B | - | Standard | | Partial Board | - |
| Single Rate | | | €39-€47.50 | Child reduction | - |

Cork 3km

**Open:** 15th January-15th December

**Mrs Elizabeth O'Shea & Family**
FATIMA HOUSE
Grange Road, Douglas,
Cork City, Co Cork

### Cork City Douglas

Tel: **021 4362536**  Fax: **021 4362536**
Email: **fatimabandb@eircom.net**
Bus No: **6 & 7**

South ring = N25. Kinsale road roundabout. Airport exit = N27 immediate left Little Chef/Brog Maker Pub. 2km. Parking. City buses. Taxi. Menu. Room rates. Visa.

| B&B | 4 | Ensuite | €27.50-€37.50 | Dinner | - |
| B&B | - | Standard | | Partial Board | - |
| Single Rate | | | €40-€48 | Child reduction | - |

Cork City 4km

**Open:** 1st January-21st December

**Mrs Ann Ryan**
HILLCREST HOUSE
South Douglas Road, Cork,
Co Cork

### Cork City Douglas

Tel: **021 4891178**
Bus No: **6**

Detached family home. Bedrooms overlooking large garden. Walking distance City Centre, Golf, Swimming, Shops nearby. Airport, Ferry, TV all bedrooms.

| B&B | 2 | Ensuite | €33-€36 | Dinner | - |
| B&B | 1 | Standard | €30-€32.50 | Partial Board | - |
| Single Rate | | | €45-€50 | Child reduction | - |

Cork 3km

**Open:** 1st January-23rd December

**Lorraine & John Dineen**
KENT HOUSE
47 Lower Glanmire Road, Cork,
Co Cork

### Cork City Lower Glanmire Road

Tel: **021 4504260**
Email: **kenthouse@eircom.net**

Family run, end of terrace, Victorian town house. Adjacent railway station. City Centre/Bus Station within 5 min walk. Breakfast menu. Secure parking within 50mts. Safe on street parking.

| B&B | 4 | Ensuite | €29-€42 | Dinner | - |
| B&B | 1 | Standard | €26-€36 | Partial Board | - |
| Single Rate | | | €40-€50 | Child reduction | 25% |

In Cork City

**Open:** 1st January-22nd December

In Cork City

**Mr Kevin Flynn**
AARAN HOUSE B&B
**49 Lower Glanmire Road,
Cork City, Co Cork**

### Cork City Lower Glanmire Road

TEL: **021 4551501**   FAX: **021 4551501**
EMAIL: **aarankev@hotmail.com**

Town House, adjacent to Train Station. Easy walking distance to Bus Station and City Centre 5 mins. Early Breakfast

| B&B | 6 | Ensuite | €30-€31 | Dinner | - |
|-----|---|---------|---------|--------|---|
| B&B | - | Standard | - | Partial Board | - |
| Single Rate | | | €40-€45 | Child reduction | 33.3% |

**Open:** 2nd January-30th December

---

In Cork

**Ellen Murray**
OAKLAND B&B
**51 Lower Glanmire Road, Cork,
Co Cork**

### Cork City Lower Glanmire Road

TEL: **021 4500578**
BUS NO: **11**

Our house was built in the 18th Century. It is a terraced house within 5 mins walk of the Bus Station, City Centre and adjacent to the Railway Station.

| B&B | 5 | Ensuite | €31-€33 | Dinner | - |
|-----|---|---------|---------|--------|---|
| B&B | - | Standard | - | Partial Board | - |
| Single Rate | | | €40-€45 | Child reduction | 25% |

**Open:** 1st January-23rd December

---

In Cork

**Jerry Spillane**
NUMBER FORTY EIGHT
**48 Lr. Glanmire Rd, Cork,
Co Cork**

### Cork City Lower Glanmire Road

TEL: **021 4505790**   FAX: **021 4505790**
EMAIL: **jerryspillane48@hotmail.com**

Victorian town house on Cork/Dublin road (N8). Adjacent to Railway Station. Walking distance to City Centre/Bus Station. Home baking.

| B&B | 6 | Ensuite | €40-€45 | Dinner | - |
|-----|---|---------|---------|--------|---|
| B&B | - | Standard | - | Partial Board | - |
| Single Rate | | | €45-€50 | Child reduction | 50% |

**Open:** 1st January-31st December

---

Cork City 2km

**Mrs Rita O'Herlihy**
55 Wilton Gardens
**off Wilton Road, Cork City,
Co Cork**

### Cork City Wilton University

TEL: **021 4541705**
BUS NO: **8 & 5**

Situated quiet park, off Wilton Road, convenient to West Cork, Killarney roads, Airport, University, Hospital, College. Frommer recommended.

| B&B | 2 | Ensuite | €30-€31 | Dinner | - |
|-----|---|---------|---------|--------|---|
| B&B | 1 | Standard | €27-€28.50 | Partial Board | - |
| Single Rate | | | €38-€43.50 | Child reduction | - |

**Open:** 1st February-1st November

---

In Crookhaven

**Maureen & James Newman**
GALLEY COVE HOUSE
**Crookhaven, West Cork,
Co Cork**

### Crookhaven Mizen Head

TEL: **028 35137**   FAX: **028 35137**
EMAIL: **info@galleycovehouse.com**
WEB: **www.galleycovehouse.com**

Ireland's most south-westerly award winning approved B&B in peaceful scenic location. Overlooking Atlantic Ocean and Fastnet lighthouse. Near Mizen head and Barleycove.

| B&B | 4 | Ensuite | €35-€40 | Dinner | - |
|-----|---|---------|---------|--------|---|
| B&B | - | Standard | - | Partial Board | - |
| Single Rate | | | €45-€55 | Child reduction | 33.3% |

**Open:** 15th March-31st December

**Drimoleague 2km**

### Mrs Marian Collins
**ROSELAWN HOUSE**
Derrygrea, Drimoleague,
Co Cork

## Drimoleague Skibbereen

TEL: **028 31369**
EMAIL: **roselawnhouse@eircom.net**

Elegant country house on Cork/Bantry R586 route. Local amenities. Skibbereen 12km. Bantry 20km. Homely atmosphere. Painting tuition available locally.

| B&B | 2 | Ensuite | €27.50-€31 | Dinner | €19-€19 |
| B&B | 1 | Standard | €25.50-€28.50 | Partial Board | €294 |
| Single Rate | | | €38-€43.50 | Child reduction | 50% |

**Open:** 1st March-31st October

---

**Fermoy 1km**

### Mrs Patricia O'Leary
**PALM RISE**
Barrys Boreen,
Duntahane Road, Fermoy,
Co Cork

## Fermoy

TEL: **025 31386**
EMAIL: **palmrisebb@yahoo.com**

Friendly modern home in peaceful scenic surroundings. Close to fishing, horse riding, Leisure Centre and scenic walks. 1km from N8-main Dublin/Cork road.

| B&B | 3 | Ensuite | €28-€31 | Dinner | - |
| B&B | 1 | Standard | €28-€31 | Partial Board | - |
| Single Rate | | | €40-€43.50 | Child reduction | - |

**Open:** 1st January-20th December

---

**In Glengarriff**

### Niamh Barry-Murphy
**COIS COILLE**
Glengarriff, Co Cork

## Glengarriff

TEL: **027 63202**
EMAIL: **coiscoille@eircom.net**
WEB: **www.coiscoille.com**

Warm hospitality in comfortable home overlooking Glengarriff harbour. Award winning garden in quiet woodland setting. Extensive breakfast menu, home baking.

| B&B | 6 | Ensuite | €32-€34 | Dinner | - |
| B&B | - | Standard | | Partial Board | - |
| Single Rate | | | €45-€50 | Child reduction | 25% |

**Open:** 15th May-30th September

---

**Glengarriff 3km**

### Mrs Kathleen Connolly
**CARRAIG DUBH HOUSE**
Droumgarriff, Glengarriff,
Co Cork

## Glengarriff

TEL: **027 63146**
EMAIL: **carraigdubhhouse@hotmail.com**

Lovely family home in quiet peaceful location. 150m off main road overlooking Harbour and Golf club. Nice walking area. Tea/Coffee and Hairdryer in bedrooms. Lovely breakfast menu.

| B&B | 4 | Ensuite | €27.50-€31 | Dinner | - |
| B&B | 1 | Standard | €25.50-€28.50 | Partial Board | - |
| Single Rate | | | €38-€43.80 | Child reduction | 25% |

**Open:** 1st January-15th December

---

**In Glengarriff**

### Imelda Lyne
**ISLAND VIEW HOUSE**
Glengarriff, Co Cork

## Glengarriff

TEL: **027 63081** FAX: **027 63600**
EMAIL: **info@islandviewhouse.net**
WEB: **www.islandviewhouse.net**

Comfortable family home in peaceful scenic area. 10 minutes walk to town - 150 metres off main road. Ideal touring centre. Breakfast menu. Hairdryers all rooms.

| B&B | 6 | Ensuite | €28-€34 | Dinner | - |
| B&B | - | Standard | - | Partial Board | - |
| Single Rate | | | €40-€45 | Child reduction | 50% |

**Open:** 23rd March-24th October

In Glengarriff

**Mrs Maureen MacCarthy**
MAUREENS
Glengarriff Village Home,
Glengarriff, Co Cork

### Glengarriff
TEL: **027 63201**   FAX: **027 63526**
EMAIL: **info@maureensglengarriff.com**
WEB: **www.maureensglengarriff.com**

Stone fronted house adjacent/picturesque village. Beside ancient Oak Forest, Sea, Mountains, Lakes and Rivers. Opposite entrance to Garinish island.

| B&B | 4 | Ensuite | €27.50-€45 | Dinner | - |
|---|---|---|---|---|---|
| B&B | 2 | Standard | €26.50-€30 | Partial Board | - |
| Single Rate | | | €38-€43.50 | Child reduction | **33.3%** |

**Open:** 1st January-31st December

In Goleen

**Ms Sue Hill**
THE HERON'S COVE
The Harbour, Goleen,
West Cork, Co Cork

### Goleen
TEL: **028 35225**   FAX: **028 35422**
EMAIL: **suehill@eircom.net**
WEB: **www.heronscove.com**

Comfortable rooms, good food, wine. Near Barleycove, Mizen Head. Hairdryers, Electric blankets. A la carte Restaurant. Fresh fish/local produce. AA ◆◆◆◆. On harbour. Mini hifi.

| B&B | 5 | Ensuite | €35-€35 | Dinner | - |
|---|---|---|---|---|---|
| B&B | - | Standard | - | Partial Board | - |
| Single Rate | | | | Child reduction | - |

**Open:** 2nd January-23rd December

Innishannon 3km

**Mrs Kathleen Cummins**
ELLAMORE
Ballymountain, Innishannon,
Co Cork

### Innishannon near Kinsale
TEL: **021 4775807**
EMAIL: **ellamore@oceanfree.net**
WEB: **www.ellamore.com**

Country residence, convenient to Airport, Ferryport. Follow signpost for Ballymountain House off N71 at Innishannon Bridge. Next house on left.

| B&B | 3 | Ensuite | €30-€35 | Dinner | - |
|---|---|---|---|---|---|
| B&B | - | Standard | - | Partial Board | - |
| Single Rate | | | €40-€45 | Child reduction | **50%** |

**Open:** 1st January-20th December

Kinsale 1km

**John & Eleanor Bateman**
ROCKLANDS HOUSE
Compass Hill, Kinsale, Co Cork

### Kinsale
TEL: **021 4772609**   FAX: **021 4702149**
EMAIL: **rocklandshouse@eircom.net**
WEB: **www.kinsaletown.com**

Set on scenic walking trail, 3 minutes drive from Town Centre. Balcony rooms overlooking the inner harbour; Guest Lounge. Recommended by Lonely Planet Guide Book & La Guide du Routard.

| B&B | 6 | Ensuite | €32.50-€45 | Dinner | - |
|---|---|---|---|---|---|
| B&B | - | Standard | - | Partial Board | - |
| Single Rate | | | €50-€80 | Child reduction | - |

**Open:** 1st March-31st October

Kinsale 1km

**Mrs Joan Collins**
WATERLANDS
Cork Road, Kinsale, Co Cork

### Kinsale
TEL: **021 4772318**   FAX: **021 4774873**
EMAIL: **info@collinsbb.com**
WEB: **www.collinsbb.com**

Luxury accommodation, extensive menu, breakfast conservatory overlooking beautiful gardens, guest patio, AA ◆◆◆◆ Diamond Award. Highly recommended, Ideal touring base. Airport 15 mins & Ferryport 30 mins.

| B&B | 4 | Ensuite | €30-€35 | Dinner | - |
|---|---|---|---|---|---|
| B&B | - | Standard | - | Partial Board | - |
| Single Rate | | | €50-€50 | Child reduction | **25%** |

**Open:** 1st March-1st December

### Phyllis & PJ Crowe
**WATERSIDE HOUSE**
**Dromderrig, Kinsale, Co Cork**

Tel: **021 4774196**   Fax: **021 4774196**
Email: **Info@waterside.ie**
Web: **www.waterside.ie**

Picturesque setting in spacious seaside garden. View of inner Harbour. Kinsale is a pleasant 1km waterside walk. Golf courses, Beaches nearby. R600 from Kinsale, right by Big Bridge.

| B&B | 4 | Ensuite | €35-€45 | Dinner | - |
| B&B | - | Standard | - | Partial Board | - |
| Single Rate | | | - | Child reduction | - |

insale 1km

**Open:** 1st February-1st December

---

### Mrs Kathleen Cummins
**BAY VIEW**
**Clasheen, Kinsale, Co Cork**

Tel: **021 4774054**
Email: **info@bayviewkinsale.com**
Web: **www.bayviewkinsale.com**

Comfortable modern spacious home. Panoramic views overlooking Bay and countryside from dining room. Breakfast menu. "Le guide du Routard" recommended.

| B&B | 3 | Ensuite | €30-€33 | Dinner | - |
| B&B | - | Standard | - | Partial Board | - |
| Single Rate | | | - | Child reduction | - |

insale 1km

**Open:** 1st April-30th September

---

### Peggy & Eamonn Foley
**FERNVILLE**
**Lower Cove, Kinsale, Co Cork**

Tel: **021 4774874**   Fax: **021 4774874**
Email: **fernville@oceanfree.net**
Web: **www.dirl.com/cork/fernville.htm**

Luxury B&B with Sea views on Kinsales outer Harbour. 1 min to Beach/Fishing. 10 mins drive to Kinsale, signs from Charles Fort. Airport/Ferry 30 mins.

| B&B | 3 | Ensuite | €32.50-€35 | Dinner | - |
| B&B | - | Standard | - | Partial Board | - |
| Single Rate | | | €50-€55 | Child reduction | 25% |

insale 4km

**Open:** 17th March-31st October

---

### Ms Gillian Good
**GLEBE COUNTRY HOUSE**
**Ballinadee, Nr Kinsale, Bandon, Co Cork**

Tel: **021 4778294**   Fax: **021 4778456**
Email: **glebehse@indigo.ie**
Web: **http://indigo.ie/~glebehse/**

Charming family run Georgian Rectory close to Beaches, Bandon & Kinsale. Take N71 to Innishannon Bridge, follow signs for Ballinadee. AA ◆◆◆◆.

| B&B | 4 | Ensuite | €40-€50 | Dinner | €35 |
| B&B | - | Standard | - | Partial Board | - |
| Single Rate | | | €55-€65 | Child reduction | 50% |

insale 10km

**Open:** 3rd January-20th December

---

### Mrs Teresa Gray
**ROCKVILLE**
**The Rock, Kinsale, Co Cork**

Tel: **021 4772791**

Modern well appointed split level home overlooking Kinsale Town and Harbour and within five minutes walk of Town Centre.

| B&B | 3 | Ensuite | €30-€34 | Dinner | - |
| B&B | - | Standard | - | Partial Board | - |
| Single Rate | | | €45-€50 | Child reduction | 25% |

Kinsale

**Open:** 31st March-30th November

**Mrs Margaret Griffin**
HILLSIDE HOUSE
Camp Hill, Kinsale, Co Cork

### Kinsale

TEL: **021 4772315**   FAX: **021 4772315**
EMAIL: **info@griffinhillside.com**
WEB: **www.griffinhillside.com**

Beautiful spacious home. Award winning gardens. On 1601 battle site, overlooks Town. Frommer recommended. Car park. Guests conservatory. 10-15 mins walk Town. Menu.

| B&B | 6 | Ensuite | €30-€35 | Dinner | - |
| B&B | - | Standard | - | Partial Board | - |
| Single Rate | | | - | Child reduction | 25% |

Kinsale 1km

**Open:** 2nd January-15th December

---

**Orla Griffin**
GRIFFIN'S RIVERSIDE HOUSE
Kippagh, Kinsale, Co Cork

### Kinsale

TEL: **021 4774917**
EMAIL: **info@griffinsriversidehouse.com**
WEB: **www.griffinsriversidehouse.com**

Panoramic ocean view. Luxury accommodation. TVs, Hairdryers, Tea/coffee, private gardens. Car park. All amenities. Walking distance, Golf/Fishing arranged. Power showers.

| B&B | 5 | Ensuite | €33-€35 | Dinner | - |
| B&B | - | Standard | - | Partial Board | - |
| Single Rate | | | €40-€45 | Child reduction | 25% |

Kinsale 1km

**Open:** 1st February-1st December

---

**Brian & Valerie Hosford**
WOODLANDS HOUSE
Cappagh, Kinsale, Co Cork

### Kinsale

TEL: **021 4772633**   FAX: **021 4772649**
EMAIL: **info@woodlandskinsale.com**
WEB: **www.woodlandskinsale.com**

Modern luxurious accommodation. Beautiful views of Kinsale Town and Harbour. 7 mins walk to Town Centre. En suite. Private parking. TV, DD Telephone, breakfast menu. King-size beds.

| B&B | 4 | Ensuite | €32-€45 | Dinner | - |
| B&B | - | Standard | - | Partial Board | - |
| Single Rate | | | €50-€70 | Child reduction | 25% |

In Kinsale

**Open:** 1st March-15th November

---

**Mrs Joan Hurley**
FOYLE
Acres, Kinsale, Co Cork

### Kinsale

TEL: **021 4772363**
EMAIL: **info@foylebb.com**
WEB: **www.foylebb.com**

Modern bungalow in rural setting with conservatory/patio for guests use. On R600 Coast road. Old Head Golf course, Beaches nearby. Airport/Ferryport 20km.

| B&B | 4 | Ensuite | €30-€35 | Dinner | - |
| B&B | - | Standard | - | Partial Board | - |
| Single Rate | | | €50-€55 | Child reduction | 25% |

Kinsale 3km

**Open:** 1st March-7th November

---

**Mrs Mary Hurley**
SCEILIG HOUSE
Ard Brack, Scilly, Kinsale, Co Cork

### Kinsale

TEL: **021 4772832**   FAX: **021 4772832**
EMAIL: **hurleyfamily@eircom.net**

Town house set in layered gardens overlooking Kinsale Harbour. Seaview from bedrooms with private patio/balcony. Frommer and "La Guide" recommended. Follow Scilly sign on entry to Town.

| B&B | 3 | Ensuite | €30-€45 | Dinner | - |
| B&B | - | Standard | - | Partial Board | - |
| Single Rate | | | €60-€80 | Child reduction | 33.3% |

In Kinsale

**Open:** 1st January-31st December

### Kinsale

**Mrs Teresa Hurley**
**CEPHAS HOUSE**
Compass Hill, Kinsale, Co Cork

TEL: **021 4772689**  FAX: **021 4772985**
EMAIL: **thurley@eircom.net**

Town house, beautiful private garden. Magnificent seaviews from bedrooms with balcony. Scenic walk to town. Guide du Routard recommended.

| B&B | 3 | Ensuite | €30-€45 | Dinner | - |
| B&B | - | Standard | - | Partial Board | - |
| Single Rate | | | €60-€80 | Child reduction | 25% |

Kinsale

**Open:** 1st March-31st October

---

### Kinsale

**Mr & Mrs Fearghal &**
**Katherine Kelly**
**LEIGHMONEYMORE**
Dunderrow, Kinsale, Co Cork

TEL: **021 4775312**  FAX: **021 4775692**
EMAIL: **rooms@leighmoneymore.ie**
WEB: **www.leighmoneymore.ie**

Secluded and tranquil family run B&B in several acres of garden by the river Bandon. Great base to explore West Cork from. Kinsale 5 mins airport 20 mins.

| B&B | 3 | Ensuite | €35-€40 | Dinner | - |
| B&B | - | Standard | - | Partial Board | - |
| Single Rate | | | €55-€55 | Child reduction | 50% |

insale 5km

**Open:** 15th January-15th December

---

### Kinsale

**Margaret Kelly**
**ASHGROVE**
Bandon Road, Kinsale, Co Cork

TEL: **021 4774127**  FAX: **021 4774127**
EMAIL: **ashgroveguesthouse@eircom.net**
WEB: **http://homepage.eircom.net/~ashgrovebb**

Extremely comfortable home set in landscape gardens. Great Irish Breakfast. 5 minutes walk from Historic Kinsale Town, Museums, Churches, Pubs & Gourmet Restaurants. Tranquil, home from home.

| B&B | 4 | Ensuite | €35-€45 | Dinner | - |
| B&B | 1 | Standard | €30-€35 | Partial Board | - |
| Single Rate | | | €40-€55 | Child reduction | 50% |

Kinsale

**Open:** 1st February-15th November

---

### Kinsale

**Mrs Nora Kelly**
**VALLEY-VIEW**
Hospital Road, Coolvalanane,
Kinsale, Co Cork

TEL: **021 4772842**
EMAIL: **valleyview@iol.ie**

Spacious bungalow in scenic farming area. Overlooking open countryside, close to Beaches, Golf and Fishing. Airport, Ferry, half hour drive.

| B&B | 2 | Ensuite | €28-€30 | Dinner | - |
| B&B | 2 | Standard | €26-€28 | Partial Board | - |
| Single Rate | | | €45-€45 | Child reduction | 50% |

insale 2km

**Open:** 1st January-31st December

---

### Kinsale

**Mrs Myrtle Levis**
**WALYUNGA**
Sandycove, Kinsale, Co Cork

TEL: **021 4774126**  FAX: **021 4774126**
EMAIL: **info@walyunga.com**
WEB: **www.walyunga.com**

Bright spacious modern bungalow. Unique design, landscaped gardens, outstanding ocean & valley views, Sandy Beaches, Scenic Coastal walks. Recommended by many guides.

| B&B | 4 | Ensuite | €30-€38 | Dinner | - |
| B&B | 1 | Standard | - | Partial Board | - |
| Single Rate | | | €27-€32.50 | Child reduction | 25% |

insale 3.5km

**Open:** 17th March-31st October

**Anthony & Fiona McCarthy**
SEA BREEZE
**Featherbed Lane, Kinsale,
Co Cork**

### Kinsale
TEL: **021 4774854**
EMAIL: **seabreezebb@eircom.net**
WEB: **www.seabreezebb.com**

Modern Dormer Bungalow, view of Harbour from some bedrooms. 3 mins walk Town Centre. Carpark. Internationally famous for Gourmet restaurants. Tea/coffee/biscuits on arrival.

| B&B | 4 | Ensuite | €34-€40 | Dinner | - |
| B&B | - | Standard | - | Partial Board | - |
| Single Rate | | | €46-€62 | Child reduction | 25% |

In Kinsale

**Open:** 1st May-31st October

---

**Mr & Mrs Michael McCarthy**
HILL TOP B&B
**Sleaveen Heights, Kinsale,
Co Cork**

### Kinsale
TEL: **021 4772612**

Modern spacious bungalow, conservatory overlooking Kinsale Harbour and James's Fort. Close Museum, Beaches, Golf, Yachting, Marina, Fishing. 3 mins walk Town.

| B&B | 6 | Ensuite | €34-€40 | Dinner | - |
| B&B | - | Standard | - | Partial Board | - |
| Single Rate | | | €45-€60 | Child reduction | 25% |

In Kinsale

**Open:** 1st January-31st October

---

**Mrs Catherine Murphy**
MURCHU
**Barrells Cross, Kinsale,
Co Cork**

### Kinsale
TEL: **021 4778906**
EMAIL: **omurchu2004@yahoo.co.uk**

A warm welcome awaits you in our comfortable home. Peaceful country setting R600 West Cork. Beaches, Old Head Golf Links, 4km ferryport. 20km Airport.

| B&B | 3 | Ensuite | €28-€32 | Dinner | - |
| B&B | - | Standard | - | Partial Board | - |
| Single Rate | | | €35-€45 | Child reduction | - |

Kinsale 5km

**Open:** 1st April-31st October

---

**Martina Murphy**
FOUR WINDS
**Watersland, Kinsale, Co Cork**

### Kinsale
TEL: **021 4774822**
EMAIL: **info@fourwindsbb.com**
WEB: **www.fourwindsbb.com**

New accomodation set in peaceful area on 1 acre of beautiful garden. Kinsale 1km/Airport 20 mins/Ferry 30 mins.

| B&B | 3 | Ensuite | €30-€32 | Dinner | - |
| B&B | 1 | Standard | €28-€30 | Partial Board | - |
| Single Rate | | | €40-€45 | Child reduction | 25% |

Kinsale 1km

**Open:** 1st February-30th November

---

**Mrs Theresa Murphy**
TESBEN HOUSE
**Old Head/Golf Links Road,
Barrells Cross, Kinsale,
Co Cork**

### Kinsale
TEL: **021 4778354**
EMAIL: **info@tesben.com**
WEB: **www.tesben.com**

Tranquil surroundings unrivalled. Picturesque view R600 West Cork/Kerry. "Old Head" Golf Links 4km. "Le Guide du Routard" recommended. Ferryport 20km.

| B&B | 2 | Ensuite | €29-€33 | Dinner | - |
| B&B | 2 | Standard | €28-€30 | Partial Board | - |
| Single Rate | | | €50-€55 | Child reduction | 25% |

Kinsale 5km

**Open:** 1st March-5th December

**Mrs Eileen O'Connell**
**DOONEEN HOUSE**
Ardcarrig, Bandon Road,
Kinsale, Co Cork

**Kinsale**

TEL: **021 4772024**
EMAIL: **info@dooneenhouse.com**
WEB: **www.dooneenhouse.com**

Modern house in peaceful setting with views of inner and outer Harbour, TV lounge, private parking, garage for cycles, secluded gardens. Town area.

| B&B | 4 | Ensuite | €30-€35 | Dinner | - |
|-----|---|---------|---------|--------|---|
| B&B | - | Standard | | Partial Board | - |
| Single Rate | | | €40-€50 | Child reduction | - |

Kinsale

**Open:** All Year Except Christmas

**Carol O'Connor**
**GOLDEN GATE HOUSE**
Barrack Street, Kinsale,
Co Cork

**Kinsale**

TEL: **021 4773934**

Purpose built B&B, dormer bungalow style. 3 mins walk to town centre, rooms ensuite with TV's, Tea/Coffee, Breakfast Menu, Private Garden, Car Park.

| B&B | 3 | Ensuite | €27.50-€31 | Dinner | - |
|-----|---|---------|-----------|--------|---|
| B&B | - | Standard | - | Partial Board | - |
| Single Rate | | | €40-€45 | Child reduction | 50% |

Kinsale

**Open:** 1st January-31st December

**Mrs Phil O'Donovan**
**ROSSBRIN**
Harbour Heights, Cappagh,
Kinsale, Co Cork

**Kinsale**

TEL: **021 4772112**

Luxury bungalow, quiet residential park. Panoramic views, gardens. Breakfast menu. Rooms TV, Tea/Coffee. From St Multose Church on Bandon road, drive 630m, turn left as signposted.

| B&B | 3 | Ensuite | €30-€34 | Dinner | - |
|-----|---|---------|---------|--------|---|
| B&B | - | Standard | - | Partial Board | - |
| Single Rate | | | - | Child reduction | - |

Kinsale

**Open:** 1st March-1st November

**Mrs Mary O'Neill**
**SEA GULL HOUSE**
Cork Street, Kinsale, Co Cork

**Kinsale**

TEL: **021 4772240**
EMAIL: **marytap@iol.ie**
WEB: **seagullhouse.com**

Next door to "Desmond Castle", wine museum built 1500. Near Beach, Fishing & Golf. Kinsale Gourmet Town. Groups welcome. Family run home.

| B&B | 5 | Ensuite | €30-€35 | Dinner | - |
|-----|---|---------|---------|--------|---|
| B&B | 1 | Standard | | Partial Board | - |
| Single Rate | | | €40-€45 | Child reduction | - |

Kinsale

**Open:** 1st March-31st October

**Mrs Claire O'Sullivan**
**RIVERMOUNT HOUSE**
Barrells Cross, Kinsale,
Co Cork

**Kinsale**

TEL: **021 4778033**   FAX: **021 4778225**
EMAIL: **rivermnt@iol.ie**
WEB: **www.rivermount.com**

Award winning luxurious home overlooking the river, AA  RAC  ◆◆◆◆'s (red diamonds are highest rating). Extensive Breakfast menu. Recommended by many guides. Just off R600.

| B&B | 6 | Ensuite | €30-€40 | Dinner | - |
|-----|---|---------|---------|--------|---|
| B&B | - | Standard | - | Partial Board | - |
| Single Rate | | | €50-€80 | Child reduction | 25% |

nsale 4km

**Open:** 1st February-1st December

**In Kinsale**

**Mrs Phil Price**
DANABEL
**Feather Bed Lane, Sleaveen,
Kinsale, Co Cork**

### Kinsale

Tel: **021 4774087**
Email: **info@danabel.com**
Web: **www.danabel.com**

Modern house, quiet area. Town 3 mins walk. Orthopaedic beds. Hairdryers, Teamaking. Airport/Ferry 20 mins. Harbour view some bedrooms. Frommer recommended/Star Rating.

| B&B | 5 | Ensuite | €30-€45 | Dinner | - |
| B&B | - | Standard | | Partial Board | - |
| Single Rate | | | €55-€75 | Child reduction | 25% |

**Open:** 1st January-20th December

---

**In Kinsale**

**Margo Searls**
LANDFALL HOUSE
**Cappagh, Kinsale, Co Cork**

### Kinsale

Tel: **021 4772575**  Fax: **021 4772575**
Email: **info@landfallhouse.com**
Web: **www.landfallhouse.com**

Luxury spacious home and gardens. Panoramic views over River, Harbour and Town. Recommended by many guides. Private parking, breakfast menu, power showers, hairdryers.

| B&B | 4 | Ensuite | €30-€35 | Dinner | - |
| B&B | - | Standard | - | Partial Board | - |
| Single Rate | | | €50-€65 | Child reduction | 25% |

**Open:** 25th March-31st October

---

**In Town**

**June & Jack Sheehan**
VILLA MARIA
**Cork Road, Kinsale, Co Cork**

### Kinsale

Tel: **021 4772627**
Email: **villamaria@oceanfree.net**

Comfortable Villa, Scenic views, Conservatory, Garden. Cork-Kinsale Bus route. Quiet, 3 mins walk Town. On R600 near Music, Pubs, Restaurants, Golf, Beaches, Airport, Ferryport.

| B&B | 6 | Ensuite | €27-€34 | Dinner | - |
| B&B | - | Standard | - | Partial Board | - |
| Single Rate | | | - | Child reduction | 50% |

**Open:** 1st April-31st October

---

**In Macroom**

**Mrs Geraldine Manning**
RICHALDINE HOUSE
**Gurteenroe, Macroom,
Co Cork**

### Macroom

Tel: **026 41966**  Fax: **026 41966**

Two storey town house with garden. Family run. 0.5km from Town Centre. On N22 Killarney direction opposite Statoil petrol station.

| B&B | 3 | Ensuite | €28-€31 | Dinner | - |
| B&B | - | Standard | | Partial Board | - |
| Single Rate | | | €40-€43.50 | Child reduction | 50% |

**Open:** 4th January-22nd December

---

**Macroom 1km**

**Eileen McCarthy**
FIRMOUNT
**Killarney Road, Macroom,
Co Cork**

### Macroom

Tel: **026 41186**

Two storey town house on N22. Ideal touring base, overlooking Golf Course, access to river, opposite Auld Triangle Restaurant.

| B&B | 3 | Ensuite | €31-€33 | Dinner | - |
| B&B | 1 | Standard | €30-€31 | Partial Board | - |
| Single Rate | | | €40-€45 | Child reduction | 50% |

**Open:** 1st May-1st December

**Macroom**

**Sean & Margaret Moynihan**
AN CUASAN
Coolavokig, Macroom, Co Cork

Tel: **026 40018**
Email: **cuasan@eircom.net**
Web: **www.welcome.to/cuasan**

Tranquil setting on N22, Blarney/Killarney. Dilliard/Causin recommended. Landscaped gardens, Walking, Golf, Traditional music family. Downstairs rooms. Bicycle shed.

| B&B | 5 | Ensuite | €27.50-€31 | Dinner | - |
| B&B | 1 | Standard | €25.50-€28.50 | Partial Board | - |
| Single Rate | | | €38-€43.50 | Child reduction | 50% |

Macroom 9km

**Open:** 1st April-31st October

---

**Macroom**

**Kathleen & Brendan Mulcahy**
FOUNTAIN HOUSE
Cork Road, Macroom, Co Cork

Tel: **026 43813**   Fax: **026 43813**

Lakeside N22 landscaped gardens. Ground floor rooms. Private parking. Warm hospitality. Breakfast menu, Home baking. Touring base Blarney, Killarney, Bantry.

| B&B | 6 | Ensuite | €29-€31 | Dinner | - |
| B&B | - | Standard | - | Partial Board | - |
| Single Rate | | | €40-€43.50 | Child reduction | 50% |

Macroom 5km

**Open:** 1st March-30th November

---

**Mallow**

**Mrs B Courtney**
RATHMORE HOUSE
Fermoy Road, Mallow, Co Cork

Tel: **022 21688**

Peaceful setting beside Fermoy/Waterford Mitchelstown/Dublin road. Rosslare Ferryport route. Spacious grounds, parking. Home baking. Tea/coffee in rooms.

| B&B | 3 | Ensuite | €27.50-€31 | Dinner | - |
| B&B | 1 | Standard | €25.50-€28.50 | Partial Board | - |
| Single Rate | | | €38-€43.50 | Child reduction | - |

Mallow 2km

**Open:** 1st June-1st November

---

**Mallow**

**Anne Doolan**
RIVERVALE LODGE
Bearforest, Mallow, Co Cork

Tel: **022 22218**   Fax: **022 22955**
Email: **rivervale_lodge@yahoo.co.uk**

In tranquil setting with panoramic views overlooking River Blackwater, Castle and Deerpark. Access to riverside walks. 4 minutes walk to Town Centre.

| B&B | 3 | Ensuite | €30-€31 | Dinner | - |
| B&B | - | Standard | - | Partial Board | - |
| Single Rate | | | €40-€43.50 | Child reduction | 50% |

Mallow

**Open:** 2nd January-20th December

---

**Mallow**

**Mrs Mary Kiely**
HILL TOP VIEW
Navigation Road, Mallow,
Co Cork

Tel: **022 21491**   Fax: **022 21491**
Email: **mkhilltopview@eircom.net**

Country residence adjacent Racecourse/Fishing, Golf, Horseriding nearby. Touring centre. TV, Tea/Coffee facilities, Hairdryers, Breakfast menu, Conservatory, Secluded gardens.

| B&B | 4 | Ensuite | €30-€32 | Dinner | - |
| B&B | - | Standard | - | Partial Board | - |
| Single Rate | | | €40-€43.50 | Child reduction | 25% |

Mallow

**Open:** 1st April-31st October

79

**Mrs Eva Lane**
PARK SOUTH
**Doneraile, Mallow, Co Cork**

TEL: **022 25296**
EMAIL: **parksouth@eircom.net**
WEB: **www.park-south.com**

Situated 1km off N73. Dublin, Killarney, Cork, Ringaskiddy, Rosslare, Ferry. Fishing, Golf, Racecourse, Parks, Gardens (Ann's Grove). Bicycle shed. Qualified Cert cook. Hot scones on arrival.

| B&B | 3 | Ensuite | €27.50-€31 | Dinner | €20-€20 |
| B&B | 1 | Standard | €25.50-€28.50 | Partial Board | |
| Single Rate | | | €38-€43.50 | Child reduction | 25% |

**Mallow 15km**   (V)   **Open:** All Year

**Mrs Winifred O'Donovan**
OAKLANDS
**Springwood,
Off Killarney Road, N72,
Mallow, Co Cork**

TEL: **022 21127**   FAX: **022 21127**
EMAIL: **oaklands@eircom.net**

AA ◆◆◆◆, Le Guide du Routard recommended. Quiet location, Breakfast conservatory. Short walk to town, train, races. N20/N72 Roundabout (150 yds) signposted at railway bridge.

| B&B | 4 | Ensuite | €30-€35 | Dinner | - |
| B&B | - | Standard | - | Partial Board | - |
| Single Rate | | | €45 | Child reduction | 25% |

**In Mallow**   (V)   **Open:** 1st April-1st November

**O'Leary Family**
DROMAGH CASTLE
**Mallow, Co Cork**

TEL: **029 78013**
EMAIL: **dromaghcastle@eircom.net**

House on grounds of Dromagh Castle 16th century Principal Castle of chieftains of Duhallow the O'Keefe. Mid-way between Mallow & Killarney on N72. Kanturk 5km. Millstreet 5km.

| B&B | 3 | Ensuite | €27.50-€31 | Dinner | - |
| B&B | - | Standard | - | Partial Board | - |
| Single Rate | | | €40-€43.50 | Child reduction | 25% |

**Mallow 20km**   (V)   **Open:** 1st January-23rd December

**Mrs Eileen O'Shea**
ASHFIELD
**Woodpark, Lombardstown,
Mallow, Co Cork**

TEL: **022 47979**
EMAIL: **info@ashfieldbb.com**
WEB: **www.ashfieldbb.com**

New luxury home 2 acres of gardens. 5 mins town. Tea/coffee on arrival. Hairdryers, electric blankets, orthopaedic beds, breakfast menu, private car park.

| B&B | 3 | Ensuite | €30-€32 | Dinner | - |
| B&B | - | Standard | - | Partial Board | - |
| Single Rate | | | €40-€43.50 | Child reduction | 25% |

**Mallow 7km**   (V)   **Open:** 1st January-1st December

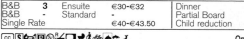

**Sean & Margaret O'Shea**
ANNABELLA LODGE
**Mallow, Co Cork**

TEL: **022 43991**
EMAIL: **moshea@esatclear.ie**
WEB: **http://www.annabella-lodge.com**

Purpose built luxury accommodation. Conservatory dining room, Hairdryers, Electric Blankets. Ideally situated 5 mins walk Town Centre, Railway Station. Adjacent Race Course, Golf. On N72.

| B&B | 6 | Ensuite | €32-€35 | Dinner | - |
| B&B | - | Standard | - | Partial Board | - |
| Single Rate | | | €40-€45 | Child reduction | 33.3% |

**In Mallow**   (V)   **Open:** 1st January-31st December

### Ms Catherine Palmer
TOWER LODGE B&B
New Two Pot House, mallow,
Co Cork

TEL: **022 22953**   FAX: **022 22953**
EMAIL: **tower_lodge@hotmail.com**

Situated in small vilage tea and coffee on arrival. All upstairs all ensuite spacious.

| B&B | 4 | Ensuite | €30-€31 | Dinner | - |
| B&B | - | Standard | - | Partial Board | - |
| Single Rate | | | €40-€43.50 | Child reduction | **25%** |

allow 5km

**Open:** 1st January-31st December

### Mrs M Walsh
RIVERSIDE HOUSE
Navigation Road, Mallow,
Co Cork

TEL: **022 42761**

Country house set in scenic area overlooking river Blackwater on N72. Ideal base for touring.
Convenient Town Centre, Racecourse, Railway Station.

| B&B | 6 | Ensuite | €28-€31 | Dinner | - |
| B&B | - | Standard | - | Partial Board | - |
| Single Rate | | | €40-€43.50 | Child reduction | **25%** |

Mallow

**Open:** All Year

### Mrs Eileen Dowling
AMANDA
Cahermone, Midleton, Co Cork

TEL: **021 4631135**   FAX: **021 4631135**
EMAIL: **amandabnb@hotmail.com**

Situated on the (N25). Waterford side of Midleton Town, near Jameson and Cobh Heritage Centre,
Ballymaloe House, Fishing and Golf nearby.

| B&B | 4 | Ensuite | €27.50-€31 | Dinner | - |
| B&B | - | Standard | - | Partial Board | - |
| Single Rate | | | €40-€43.50 | Child reduction | **50%** |

idleton 1km

**Open:** 1st February-1st November

### Mrs Margaret Harty
SWAN LAKE
Loughaderra, Castlemartyr,
Co Cork

TEL: **021 4667261**
EMAIL: **swanlakebnb@eircom.net**

Overlooking Loughaderra Lake, 400m off N25, between Midleton and Castlemartyr.  Convenient
Midleton & Cobh, Heritage Centre, Ballymaloe Hse, Fota Wildlife.

| B&B | 2 | Ensuite | €27.50-€31 | Dinner | - |
| B&B | 1 | Standard | €25.50-€28.50 | Partial Board | - |
| Single Rate | | | €38-€43.50 | Child reduction | **50%** |

idleton 4km

**Open:** 17th March-31st October

### Mrs Mary Quinlan
SUNDOWN HOUSE
Kilmountain, Castlemartyr,
Midleton, Co Cork

TEL: **021 4667375**
EMAIL: **sundownhouse@eircom.net**

0.5km off Midleton to Waterford N 25, near Jameson Heritage Centre.  Ballymaloe House,
Blarney Castle, Deep Sea Angling/Lake Fishing, Golf nearby.

| B&B | 4 | Ensuite | €27.50-€31 | Dinner | - |
| B&B | 2 | Standard | €25.50-€28.50 | Partial Board | - |
| Single Rate | | | €38-€43.50 | Child reduction | **50%** |

idleton 5km

**Open:** 1st April-1st November

## Mitchelstown

**Mrs Betty Luddy**
RIVERSDALE
**Limerick Road R513,**
**Mitchelstown, Co Cork**

TEL: **025 24717** FAX: **025 24717**
EMAIL: **bettyluddy@eircom.net**

Situated just off N8 (Dublin/Cork Rd.) Golf Course at rear. Fishing rivers. Parks/Gardens. Convenient to Mitchelstown Caves.

| B&B | 2 | Ensuite | €27.50-€31 | Dinner | - |
| B&B | 1 | Standard | €25.50-€28.50 | Partial Board | - |
| Single Rate | | | €38-€43.50 | Child reduction | 33.3% |

Mitchelstown 1km

**Open:** 1st February-30th November

## Mitchelstown

**Mrs Mary O'Connell**
PALM LODGE
**Limerick Road R513,**
**Mitchelstown, Co Cork**

TEL: **025 24687** FAX: **025 24687**
EMAIL: **palmlodgebb@hotmail.com**
WEB: **www.dirl.com/cork/palm-lodge.htm**

Peaceful scenic home/gardens. Just off N8. At centre of South via Dublin/Kerry/Rosslare. Mountains view, 18 hole golf course, hairdryers.

| B&B | 2 | Ensuite | €27.50-€31 | Dinner | €20 |
| B&B | 1 | Standard | €25.50-€28.50 | Partial Board | - |
| Single Rate | | | €38-€43.50 | Child reduction | 33.3% |

Mitchelstown 1km

**Open:** 1st February-20th December

## Schull

**Nancy Brosnan**
STANLEY HOUSE
**Schull, West Cork, Co Cork**

TEL: **028 28425** FAX: **028 27887**
EMAIL: **stanleyhouse@eircom.net**
WEB: **www.stanley-house.net**

A home away from home modernised house providing every comfort with spectacular views of sea and mountains set in beautiful garden 1km from Schull.

| B&B | 4 | Ensuite | €32 | Dinner | - |
| B&B | - | Standard | - | Partial Board | - |
| Single Rate | | | €42-€43.50 | Child reduction | - |

Schull 1km

**Open:** 1st March-31st October

## Skibbereen Town

**Mrs Cathy Gill**
SUNNYSIDE
**42 Mardyke Street,**
**Skibbereen, Co Cork**

TEL: **028 21365** FAX: **028 21365**
EMAIL: **sunnysideskibb@eircom.net**

Highly recommended, excellent breakfasts hospitality and comfort. Very peaceful, in Town. Orthopaedic beds. Electric blankets. Bicycle storage. Signposted on R595.

| B&B | 3 | Ensuite | €28-€32.50 | Dinner | - |
| B&B | 1 | Standard | €26-€30 | Partial Board | - |
| Single Rate | | | €38-€48 | Child reduction | - |

In Skibbereen

**Open:** All Year

## Skibbereen

**Mrs Marguerite McCarthy**
MARGUERITES
**Baltimore Road, Coronea,**
**Skibbereen, Co Cork**

TEL: **028 21166**
EMAIL: **marguerites@eircom.net**

Luxury accommodation in landscaped private grounds. Very peaceful, highly recommended. Ideal base for touring West Cork. Signposted on R595.

| B&B | 3 | Ensuite | €28-€33 | Dinner | - |
| B&B | - | Standard | - | Partial Board | - |
| Single Rate | | | €40-€50 | Child reduction | - |

Skibbereen 1km

**Open:** All Year

**Kathleen & Pat O'Donovan**
P.K. LODGE
Smorane, Skibbereen, Co Cork

**Skibbereen**

TEL: **028 21749**
EMAIL: **info@pklodgecork.com**
WEB: **www.pklodgecork.com**

Welcome to our highly commended spacious luxurious home set in beautiful peaceful surroundings. On eastern side of town 200 mts off N71. Complimentary Tea/Coffee, Home Baking. Erdvig recommended.

| B&B | 4 | Ensuite | €28-€32 | Dinner | - |
| B&B | - | Standard | | Partial Board | - |
| Single Rate | | | €40-€50 | Child reduction | 33.3% |

Skibbereen 1km

**Open:** 1st January-31st December

---

**Breda O'Driscoll**
SANDYCOVE HOUSE
Castletownend, Skibbereen, Co Cork

**Skibbereen**

TEL: **028 36223**
EMAIL: **sandycovehouse@eircom.net**

Seaside location with superb view of Cliffs and Ocean. Beautiful sandy Beach adjacent (100m). Ideal for Rock Fishing, Swimming, Windsurfing, Cliffwalking.

| B&B | 4 | Ensuite | €30-€31 | Dinner | - |
| B&B | - | Standard | - | Partial Board | - |
| Single Rate | | | €45-€50 | Child reduction | - |

Skibbereen 7km

**Open:** 1st March-31st October

---

**Mrs Eileen O'Driscoll**
PALM GROVE
Coolnagurrane, Hospital Road, Skibbereen, Co Cork

**Skibbereen**

TEL: **028 21703**   FAX: **028 21703**
EMAIL: **info@palmgrovebb.com**
WEB: **www.palmgrovebb.com**

Spacious bungalow overlooking open countryside, 1km off N71 on R593/R594 Bantry/Drimoleague Road, close to Hospital. Frommer recommended.

| B&B | 2 | Ensuite | €30-€32 | Dinner | - |
| B&B | 2 | Standard | €26-€29 | Partial Board | - |
| Single Rate | | | €38-€48 | Child reduction | 25% |

Skibbereen 1km

**Open:** 1st March-31st October

---

**Mrs Sheila Poillot**
WHITETHORN LODGE
Schull Road, Skibbereen, Co Cork

**Skibbereen**

TEL: **028 22372**   FAX: **028 22372**
EMAIL: **whitethornlodge@eircom.net**
WEB: **www.cork-guide.ie/skibbereen/whitethornlodge/welcome.html**

Luxury home & large garden on N71 town suburbs. Near West Cork Hotel. Extensive breakfast menu, complimentary tea/coffee. Golf arranged. Warm welcome.

| B&B | 5 | Ensuite | €30-€35 | Dinner | - |
| B&B | - | Standard | | Partial Board | - |
| Single Rate | | | €42-€50 | Child reduction | - |

Skibbereen

**Open:** 1st March-31st October

---

**Mrs Mary Holland**
ATLANTIC SUNSET
Kilsillagh, Butlerstown, Bandon, Co Cork

**Timoleague**

TEL: **023 40115**

First class accommodation overlooking Atlantic. Dunworley sandy beaches 1km. Golf, Tennis, Fishing locally. Coastal walks. Leisure Centre 6km.

| B&B | 2 | Ensuite | €30-€31 | Dinner | - |
| B&B | 2 | Standard | €28-€28.50 | Partial Board | - |
| Single Rate | | | €42-€43.50 | Child reduction | - |

Butlerstown 1km

**Open:** 30th January-20th December

**Pat & Jo O'Donovan**
**HARBOUR HEIGHTS**
**Timoleague, Bandon, Co Cork**

## Timoleague

TEL: **023 46232**  FAX: **023 46232**
EMAIL: **harbourheights@fsmail.net**
WEB: **www.harbourheightsb&b.webworld.ie**

Modern bungalow set in tranquil surroundings overlooking Timoleague Abbey & Courtmacsherry Bay. Guest Lounge, Conservatory. Private Car Park. On R600 between Kinsale & Clonakilty.

| B&B | 3 | Ensuite | €30-€32 | Dinner | - |
| B&B | 1 | Standard | €28-€28.50 | Partial Board | - |
| Single Rate | | | €38-€43.50 | Child reduction | 25% |

Clonakilty 8km

**Open:** 7th March-7th November

---

**Ann O'Connell**
**ARDAGH HOUSE**
**Union Hall, West Cork, Co Cork**

## Union Hall Glandore

TEL: **028 33571**  FAX: **028 33970**
EMAIL: **arhouse@indigo.ie**
WEB: **www.ardaghhouse.com**

100 year old townhouse beautifully restored, wonderful sea views, in fishing village, very homely atmosphere. Lonely Planet Guide recommended.

| B&B | 4 | Ensuite | €30-€31 | Dinner | - |
| B&B | - | Standard | - | Partial Board | - |
| Single Rate | | | €40-€43.50 | Child reduction | 50% |

Union Hall

**Open:** All Year

---

**Noreen Cashman**
**CLONVILLA B&B**
**Clonpriest, Youghal, Co Cork**

## Youghal

TEL: **024 98288**
EMAIL: **clonvilla@hotmail.com**

4km off N25 Ballymacoda Road. Close to Beaches, Golf, Villages. (Guide du Routard recommended). Tv, Tea/Coffee facilities in rooms. Car Park, Warm Welcome.

| B&B | 2 | Ensuite | €27.50-€31 | Dinner | €20 |
| B&B | 1 | Standard | €25.50-€28.50 | Partial Board | - |
| Single Rate | | | €38-€43.50 | Child reduction | 50% |

Youghal 6km

**Open:** 1st January-15th December

---

**Mrs Therese Cliffe**
**THE GABLES**
**Kinsalebeg, Youghal, Co Cork**

## Youghal

TEL: **024 92739**
EMAIL: **theresecliffe@hotmail.com**

Two storey building on 1.25 acres site off the N25 with Tennis Court. Close to sandy Beaches, Fishing, Golf, Fota, Jameson Heritage Centre. Ardmore, Youghal, Lismore.

| B&B | 1 | Ensuite | €27.50-€31 | Dinner | - |
| B&B | 2 | Standard | €25.50-€28.50 | Partial Board | - |
| Single Rate | | | €38-€41 | Child reduction | 50% |

Youghal 8km

**Open:** 1st March-31st October

---

**Mrs Nuala Connor**
**LAGILE LODGE**
**Killeagh, Youghal, Co Cork**

## Youghal

TEL: **024 95323**  FAX: **024 95323**
EMAIL: **lagilelodge@eircom.net**
WEB: **www.lagilelodge.com**

Enjoy farm animals, wildlife on 10 acres, gardens, paddocks, 200m off N25. Nearby pub food, walks. Spacious bedrooms. Breakfast menu, home baking. We enjoy meeting guests.

| B&B | 3 | Ensuite | €30-€34 | Dinner | - |
| B&B | - | Standard | - | Partial Board | - |
| Single Rate | | | - | Child reduction | 25% |

Youghal 8km

**Open:** 1st May-30th September

**Maura Coughlan**
CARN NA RADHARC
Ardsallagh, Youghal, Co Cork

**Youghal**

TEL: **024 92703**
EMAIL: **carnnaradharc@eircom.net**

2km off N25, Youghal Bridge. Magnificent views river, mountains, quiet cul-de-sac. Locally Beaches, Heritage Centres, Fota. Comfortable bedrooms, TV lounge.

| | | | | | | |
|---|---|---|---|---|---|---|
| B&B | 2 | Ensuite | €27.50-€31 | Dinner | | - |
| B&B | 1 | Standard | €25.50-€28.50 | Partial Board | | - |
| Single Rate | | | €38-€41 | Child reduction | | 50% |

oughal 6km

**Open:** 1st February-31st November

**Mrs Phyllis Foley**
ROSEVILLE
New Catherine St., Youghal, Co Cork

**Youghal**

TEL: **024 92571**
EMAIL: **rosevillebandb@eircom.net**
WEB: **www.rosevillebb.com**

Attractive detached residence situated within the "Olde Town" off N25 on R634 Rosslare/Cork route. Within easy access to all amenities. Extensive breakfast menu. A warm welcome awaits you.

| | | | | | | |
|---|---|---|---|---|---|---|
| B&B | 5 | Ensuite | €29.50-€33 | Dinner | | - |
| B&B | - | Standard | - | Partial Board | | - |
| Single Rate | | | €40-€45 | Child reduction | | 33.3% |

Youghal

**Open:** 20th January-20th December

**Paddy, Mary & Esther Forde**
DEVON VIEW
Pearse Square, Youghal, Co Cork

**Youghal**

TEL: **024 92298** FAX: **024 92557**
EMAIL: **devonview@eircom.net**
WEB: **http://www.devonview.com**

Charming well preserved Georgian house with antique furniture and modern house. Centrally located to all amenities. Car park.

| | | | | | | |
|---|---|---|---|---|---|---|
| B&B | 6 | Ensuite | €27.50-€31 | Dinner | | - |
| B&B | - | Standard | - | Partial Board | | - |
| Single Rate | | | €40-€43.50 | Child reduction | | 25% |

Youghal

**Open:** 1st January-31st December

**Mrs Eileen Gaine**
AVONMORE HOUSE
South Abbey, Youghal, Co Cork

**Youghal**

TEL: **024 92617** FAX: **024 92617**
EMAIL: **avonmoreyoughal@eircom.net**

Elegant 18th Century Georgian House at the entrance to Youghal Harbour within 3 min walk of Youghal's famous clock tower.

| | | | | | | |
|---|---|---|---|---|---|---|
| B&B | 6 | Ensuite | €27.50-€35 | Dinner | | - |
| B&B | - | Standard | - | Partial Board | | - |
| Single Rate | | | €40-€45 | Child reduction | | 25% |

Youghal

**Open:** 10th January-20th December

**Mrs Angela Leahy**
LEAHYS B&B
29 Friar Street, Youghal, Co Cork

**Youghal**

TEL: **024 92292**
EMAIL: **leahyangela@hotmail.com**
WEB: **http://www.leahysyoughalbandb.com**

R634 Cork/Rosslare. Comfortable townhouse, central to restaurants, pubs, shops, laundrette, cinema, heritage centre, etc. Beach 5 mins. Private parking. Visa. Family room.

| | | | | | | |
|---|---|---|---|---|---|---|
| B&B | 4 | Ensuite | €28-€33 | Dinner | | - |
| B&B | - | Standard | - | Partial Board | | - |
| Single Rate | | | €40-€43.50 | Child reduction | | 50% |

Youghal

**Open:** All Year

**Barbara Murray**
SUMMERFIELD LODGE
Summerfield, Youghal,
Co Cork

### Youghal

Tel: **024 92838**
Email: **summerfieldlodge@eircom.net**

Comfortable family home on acre of elevated garden overlooking the sea. 5 mins walk from beach. Farrells pub 2mins, after Perks Family Entertainment. Take 2nd right at cross.

| B&B | 3 | Ensuite | €27.50-€31 | Dinner | - |
| B&B | - | Standard | - | Partial Board | - |
| Single Rate | | | €40-€43.50 | Child reduction | 25% |

Youghal 2km

**Open:** 1st May-1st October

---

**Mrs Mary Scanlon**
GREENLAWN
Summerfield, Youghal,
Co Cork

### Youghal

Tel: **024 93177**
Email: **tjscanlon@eircom.net**

Modern 2 storey home, 2km from Town Centre on the N25. Blue Flag Beach within 5 mins walk. Friendly welcome. Take exit R634 coming from Cork.

| B&B | 4 | Ensuite | €28-€32 | Dinner | - |
| B&B | - | Standard | - | Partial Board | - |
| Single Rate | | | €40-€44 | Child reduction | 25% |

Youghal 2km

**Open:** 1st February-31st October

---

**Ms Monica Yeomans**
BAYVIEW HOUSE
Front Strand, Youghal, Co Cork

### Youghal

Tel: **024 92824**   Fax: **024 92824**
Email: **bayview6@eircom.net**

Beautiful Victorian house, 50 metres from Blue Flag Beach. 1km from Youghal Town. "Guide du Routard" recommended. TV lounge. Warm welcome.

| B&B | 4 | Ensuite | €27.50-€32 | Dinner | - |
| B&B | - | Standard | - | Partial Board | - |
| Single Rate | | | €40-€43.50 | Child reduction | 50% |

Youghal 1km

**Open:** 1st February-30th November

Discover the magic of Kerry, with its enthralling mountain and coastal scenery and wide diversity of culture and leisure activities. Enjoy the superb hospitality and friendliness of its people in a county that is rich in heritage and history.

---

**Mrs Kathleen O'Connor**
FOUR WINDS
Annascaul, Co Kerry

### Annascaul (Dingle Peninsula)
TEL: **066 9157168**   FAX: **066 9157174**

Recommended Dillard Causin Guide. Outstanding views, Walks, Mountain Climbing, Beaches, Fishing, Lake/River. Golfing.

| B&B | 3 | Ensuite | €28-€31 | Dinner | - |
| B&B | 1 | Standard | €27-€28.50 | Partial Board | - |
| Single Rate | | | €38-€43.50 | Child reduction | **25%** |

Annascaul

**Open:** 1st March-30th October

---

**Katherine Higgins**
ARDKEEL HOUSE
Ardfert, Co Kerry

### Ardfert
TEL: **066 7134288**   FAX: **066 7134288**
EMAIL: **ardkeelhouse@oceanfree.net**
WEB: **www.ardfert.com/ardkeelhouse**

Warm welcoming hospitality. Luxurious home, quiet location off Ardfert/Fenit Road. Walking distance Bars, Restaurants, Tralee Golf Course 4km, Banna Beach 3km.

| B&B | 3 | Ensuite | €30-€33 | Dinner | €20 |
| B&B | | Standard | - | Partial Board | - |
| Single Rate | | | €40-€48 | Child reduction | **33.3%** |

Ardfert

**Open:** All Year

---

**Mrs Bridie Sweeney**
FAILTE
Tralee Road, Ardfert, Co Kerry

### Ardfert
TEL: **066 7134278**
EMAIL: **bridiesweeney@iolfree.ie**
WEB: **www.stayinkerry.com/trbb.htm**

Luxurious Bungalow on Tralee/Banna/Ballyheigue road (R551) in historical Ardfert village near Tralee Golf course. Banna beach 3km. Restaurant 2 min walk.

| B&B | 4 | Ensuite | €27.50-€31 | Dinner | - |
| B&B | - | Standard | - | Partial Board | - |
| Single Rate | | | €40-€43.50 | Child reduction | **50%** |

Ardfert

**Open:** 1st March-31st October

---

**Mrs Bridie O'Connor**
BEACH COVE
St Finian's, Ballinskelligs, Co Kerry

### Ballinskelligs
TEL: **066 9479301**
EMAIL: **beachcove@eircom.net**
WEB: **www.stayatbeachcove.com**

Superb beachfront location on Skellig Ring, majestic views of Skellig Michael and Atlantic Ocean. Highly recommended. Beach on doorstep. Trips to Skellig arranged. Extensive breakfast menu.

| B&B | 2 | Ensuite | €30-€32 | Dinner | - |
| B&B | 1 | Standard | €28-€30 | Partial Board | - |
| Single Rate | | | €38-€43.50 | Child reduction | - |

allinskelligs 6km

**Open:** 15th March-31st October

### Maurice & Patricia Boyle
THE OLD COURSE
Golf Links Road, Ballybunion,
Co Kerry

**Ballybunion**

Tel: **068 27171**   Fax: **068 27171**
Email: **oldcourse@eircom.net**
Web: **www.oldcoursebb.com**

A warm welcome awaits you in our luxurious, spacious home at Ballybunion's famous Old Course. Green fee reduction. Private car park. Early Breakfasts.

| B&B | 3 | Ensuite | €35-€50 | Dinner | - |
|---|---|---|---|---|---|
| B&B | - | Standard | | Partial Board | - |
| Single Rate | | | €45-€80 | Child reduction | - |

In Ballybunion

**Open:** 1st April-23rd October

### Michael & Ann Kissane
SEASHORE
Doon East, Ballybunion,
Co Kerry

**Ballybunion**

Tel: **068 27986**
Email: **seashorebandb@eircom.net**
Web: **homepage.eircom.net/~seashorebandb**

Modern spacious home with sea views. Car park, early Breakfast, Power Showers. Near Beach and Golf. Tarbert Car Ferry 20 mins drive. Green fee reduction.

| B&B | 4 | Ensuite | €30-€40 | Dinner | - |
|---|---|---|---|---|---|
| B&B | - | Standard | - | Partial Board | - |
| Single Rate | | | €40-€50 | Child reduction | 25% |

In Ballybunion

**Open:** 1st March-1st November

### Mrs Anne McCaughey
DOON HOUSE
Doon Road, Ballybunion,
Co Kerry

**Ballybunion**

Tel: **068 27411/27073**   Fax: **068 27411**
Email: **doonhouse@eircom.net**

Overlooking Ballybunion and Atlantic Ocean. Beautiful panoramic Sea/Mountain view. (Golfers home away from home). Green fee reductions. Early Breakfasts.

| B&B | 3 | Ensuite | €30-€50 | Dinner | - |
|---|---|---|---|---|---|
| B&B | - | Standard | - | Partial Board | - |
| Single Rate | | | €40-€50 | Child reduction | - |

In Ballybunion

**Open:** All Year

### Sean & Nora Stack
SEANOR HOUSE
Listowel Rd, Ballybunion,
Co Kerry

**Ballybunion**

Tel: **068 27055**   Fax: **068 27055**
Email: **bed@eircom.net**
Web: **www.seanorhouse.com**

Luxurious welcoming family home 5 mins from Golf & Beach. Early breakfast. Green fee reduction. Tea/Coffee on arrival. Ballybunion/Listowel Rd.(553)

| B&B | 3 | Ensuite | €30-€40 | Dinner | - |
|---|---|---|---|---|---|
| B&B | - | Standard | - | Partial Board | - |
| Single Rate | | | €40-€50 | Child reduction | 50% |

Ballybunion 1km

**Open:** 10th January-20th December

### Eileen Walsh
THE COUNTRY HAVEN
Ballybunion, Co Kerry

**Ballybunion**

Tel: **068 27103**
Email: **countryhaven@eircom.net**

Rooms with seaview, miles of private walks, own tennis court, near golf course. Early breakfasts catered for. On R551 road towards Tarbert Car Ferry.

| B&B | 5 | Ensuite | €30-€35 | Dinner | - |
|---|---|---|---|---|---|
| B&B | - | Standard | | Partial Board | - |
| Single Rate | | | €40-€45 | Child reduction | 50% |

Ballybunion 2km

**Open:** 1st April-30th October

**Ballyduff**

**Mrs Nuala Sowden**
SHANNON VIEW
**Ferry Road, Ballyduff, Tralee, Co Kerry**

TEL: **066 7131324**

Chef owned, evening meals, excellent food. 5 mins to Ballybunion, golf and sandy beaches. Ballyheigue 20 mins. Enroute to Cliffs of Moher, Dingle, Ring of Kerry.

| B&B | 2 | Ensuite | €27.50-€31 | Dinner | €25-€27 |
|-----|---|---------|------------|--------|---------|
| B&B | 2 | Standard | €25.50-€30 | Partial Board | €294 |
| Single Rate | | | €38-€45 | Child reduction | 25% |

Ballyduff

**Open:** All Year

**Ballylongford**

**Patricia & Garrett Dee**
CASTLE VIEW HOUSE
**Carrig Island, Ballylongford, Co Kerry**

TEL: **068 43304**  FAX: **068 43304**
EMAIL: **castleviewhouse@eircom.net**
WEB: **www.castleviewhouse.com**

Relax in peaceful setting on scenic Island (entry by bridge). Facing Carrigafoyle Castle. Tarbert - Killimer Ferry. Ballybunion Golf course nearby. Scenic walks. Good food, Warm welcome.

| B&B | 6 | Ensuite | €27.50-€31 | Dinner | €19-€19 |
|-----|---|---------|------------|--------|---------|
| B&B | - | Standard | - | Partial Board | - |
| Single Rate | | | €40-€43.50 | Child reduction | 50% |

allylongford 2.5km

**Open:** 2nd January-20th December

**Ballylongford**

**Mrs Noreen Heaphy**
GLEBE HOUSE
**Rushy Park, Ballylongford, Co Kerry**

TEL: **068 43555**  FAX: **068 43555**
EMAIL: **glebeh@iol.ie**
WEB: **www.glebehouse.ie**

Period residence, beautifully restored, blending modern convenience with olde world ambiance. Tarbert - Killimer Car Ferry, Ballybunion Golf Course & Beaches nearby.

| B&B | 4 | Ensuite | €28-€32 | Dinner | €20 |
|-----|---|---------|---------|--------|-----|
| B&B | - | Standard | - | Partial Board | - |
| Single Rate | | | €40-€43.50 | Child reduction | 50% |

Ballylongford

**Open:** All Year Except Christmas

**Caherdaniel Ring of Kerry**

**Mrs Cathy Fitzmaurice**
THE OLDE FORGE
**Caherdaniel, Ring of Kerry, Co Kerry**

TEL: **066 9475140**  FAX: **066 9475170**
EMAIL: **theoldeforge@eircom.net**
WEB: **www.theoldeforge.com**

Family run, overlooking Kenmare Bay. Access to Sea. Breakfast menu. Dillard Causin Guide. Horseriding, Hill walking, Sea sport, Golf, Fishing, Diving. Kerry Way. Skellig Trips.

| B&B | 6 | Ensuite | €27.50-€31 | Dinner | - |
|-----|---|---------|------------|--------|---|
| B&B | - | Standard | - | Partial Board | - |
| Single Rate | | | €40-€43.50 | Child reduction | 33.3% |

aherdaniel 1km

**Open:** All Year

**Caherdaniel Ring of Kerry**

**Donal & Monica Hunt**
DERRYNANE BAY HOUSE
**Caherdaniel, Co Kerry**

TEL: **066 9475404**  FAX: **066 9475436**
EMAIL: **derrynanebayhouse@eircom.net**
WEB: **www.ringofkerry.net**

Superb accommodation, overlooking Derrynane Bay. Breakfast menu. Golf, Horse-riding, Fishing, Diving, Beaches nearby. Adjacent Kerry Way. AA ◆◆◆◆.

| B&B | 5 | Ensuite | €28-€33 | Dinner | - |
|-----|---|---------|---------|--------|---|
| B&B | - | Standard | - | Partial Board | - |
| Single Rate | | | €43.50-€43.50 | Child reduction | 25% |

aherdaniel 1km

**Open:** 16th March-1st November

### Mrs Irene Curran
**HARBOUR HILL**
Knockeens, Cahirciveen,
Co Kerry

**Cahirciveen**

TEL: **066 9472844**  FAX: **066 9472844**
EMAIL: **harbourhill@eircom.net**
WEB: **www.dirl.com/kerry/harbour-hill.htm**

Luxurious home. Panoramic sea views. Close to all amenities. Skeilig trips. Suitable for allergy sufferers. Single and Family rooms. Special low season rates.

| B&B | 4 | Ensuite | €27.50-€31 | Dinner | - |
| B&B | - | Standard | | Partial Board | - |
| Single Rate | | | €40-€43.50 | Child reduction | 33.3% |

Cahirciveen 3km

**Open:** 1st May-30th September

---

### Mrs Eilis Dennehy
**SEA BREEZE**
Renard Road, Cahersiveen,
Co Kerry

**Cahirciveen**

TEL: **066 9472609**  FAX: **066 9473275**
EMAIL: **seabreezebandb@eircom.net**
WEB: **homepage.eircom.net/~seabreezebandb**

Friendly atmosphere, spectacular views, Sea, Islands, Castle, Forts. Skellig trips. Recommended Routard, Michelin, Restaurants walking distance. Breakfast menu. Orthapaedic beds.

| B&B | 4 | Ensuite | €28-€31 | Dinner | - |
| B&B | 2 | Standard | €26-€31 | Partial Board | - |
| Single Rate | | | €38-€44 | Child reduction | 25% |

Cahirciveen 1km

**Open:** 1st March-31st October

---

### Mary Guirey
**FERRYVIEW**
Renard, Cahirciveen, Co Kerry

**Cahirciveen**

TEL: **066 9472052**
EMAIL: **info@ferryview-cahersiveen.com**
WEB: **www.ferryview-cahersiveen.com**

Luxury country home. Peaceful setting, spacious rooms. Panoramic sea, Mountain view. Skellig trips. Jacuzzi and Steamroom facility. Tea/Coffee on arrival.

| B&B | 4 | Ensuite | €31 | Dinner | - |
| B&B | - | Standard | - | Partial Board | - |
| Single Rate | | | €43.50 | Child reduction | 33.3% |

Cahirciveen 2.5km

**Open:** All Year

---

### Breda & Alan Landers
**SAN ANTOINE**
Valentia Rd, Cahirciveen,
Co Kerry

**Cahirciveen**

TEL: **066 9472521**  FAX: **066 9472521**
EMAIL: **sanantoine@eircom.net**
WEB: **www.sanantoine.com**

Set in peaceful landscaped gardens overlooking the Bay. Sea Sports, Golf, Angling, Horse-riding, sandy beaches, scenic walks locally. Breakfast menu.

| B&B | 6 | Ensuite | €27.50-€31 | Dinner | - |
| B&B | - | Standard | | Partial Board | - |
| Single Rate | | | €40-€45 | Child reduction | 33.3% |

In Cahirciveen

**Open:** 1st April-20th October

---

### Ian & Ann Nugent
**CUL DRAIOCHTA**
Points Cross, Cahirciveen,
Co Kerry

**Cahirciveen**

TEL: **066 9473141**  FAX: **066 9473141**
EMAIL: **inugent@esatclear.ie**
WEB: **www.culdraiochta.com**

Charming family home with panoramic scenery. Excellent location on N70. Highly recommended. Tea/Coffee on arrival. Extensive breakfast menu.

| B&B | 4 | Ensuite | €27.50-€31 | Dinner | €20 |
| B&B | - | Standard | - | Partial Board | - |
| Single Rate | | | €40-€43.50 | Child reduction | 50% |

Cahirciveen 1km

**Open:** 1st January-31st December

**Mrs Claire O'Donoghue**
OCEAN VIEW
Renard Road, Cahirciveen,
Co Kerry

### Cahirciveen

TEL: **066 9472261**  FAX: **066 9472261**
EMAIL: **oview@eircom.net**
WEB: **www.oceanview.mainpage.net**

Luxury home overlooking Cahirciveen Bay on Waterville side on famous Skellig ring. Spectacular Sea & mountain view. Rec. by numerous guides. Orthapaedic beds, extensive menu.

| B&B | 6 | Ensuite | €27.50-€31 | Dinner | - |
| B&B | - | Standard | - | Partial Board | - |
| Single Rate | | | €40-€43.50 | Child reduction | 25% |

ahirciveen 1km

**Open:** 3rd January-19th December

**Mrs Christina O'Neill**
IVERAGH HEIGHTS
Carhan Rd, Cahirciveen,
Co Kerry

### Cahirciveen

TEL: **066 9472545**  FAX: **066 9472545**
EMAIL: **iveraghheights@eircom.net**
WEB: **www.iveraghheights.com**

Luxury spacious rooms overlooking Atlantic Ocean. Trip to Skellig Michael arranged. Ideal for exploring Iveragh Peninsula, Archaeological sites. Recommended Routard, Michelin Guide.

| B&B | 6 | Ensuite | €27.50-€31 | Dinner | €19 |
| B&B | - | Standard | - | Partial Board | - |
| Single Rate | | | - | Child reduction | 50% |

Cahirciveen

**Open:** All Year

**Eileen O'Shea**
O'SHEAS B&B
Church St, Cahirciveen,
Co Kerry

### Cahirciveen

TEL: **066 9472402**
EMAIL: **osheasbnb@eircom.net**
WEB: **osheasbnb.com**

Friendly family run home. Relax in quiet peaceful location with breathtaking view of Mountain and Sea. Group and Low season reduction. Blue flag Beaches.

| B&B | 4 | Ensuite | €30-€31 | Dinner | - |
| B&B | - | Standard | - | Partial Board | - |
| Single Rate | | | €40-€43.50 | Child reduction | 25% |

Cahirciveen

**Open:** All Year

**Mrs Mary Ferriter**
BEENOSKEE
Cappateige, Conor Pass Road,
Castlegregory, Co Kerry

### Castlegregory Dingle Peninsula

TEL: **066 7139263**  FAX: **066 7139263**
EMAIL: **beenoskee@eircom.net**
WEB: **www.beenoskee.com**

Tastefully decorated rooms overlooking ocean. Spectacular views - Mountains, Islands, Lake. Warm hospitality, Breakfast menu. Homebaking. "Routard" recommended. 1KM West Stradbally.

| B&B | 5 | Ensuite | €30-€35 | Dinner | €25 |
| B&B | - | Standard | - | Partial Board | €385 |
| Single Rate | | | €42.50-€45 | Child reduction | 50% |

tradbally 1km

**Open:** 12th January-31st December

**Mrs Mary Ellen Flynn**
BEDROCK
Stradbally, Conor Pass Road,
Castlegregory, Co Kerry

### Castlegregory Dingle Peninsula

TEL: **066 7139401**
EMAIL: **bedrockbandb@eircom.net**
WEB: **homepage.eircom.net/~bedrockbandb**

Family run, overlooking Brandon Bay, Maharees Islands, Golf course, Restaurant, Beaches, Fishing, Water Sports, Horse Riding, Mountain Climbing. Breakfast menu.

| B&B | 4 | Ensuite | €30-€35 | Dinner | - |
| B&B | - | Standard | - | Partial Board | - |
| Single Rate | | | €42.50-€45 | Child reduction | - |

astlegregory 2.5km

**Open:** All Year Except Christmas

---

**Mrs Catherine Griffin**
GRIFFIN'S PALM BEACH
COUNTRY HOUSE
Goulane, Conor Pass Road,
Castlegregory, Co Kerry

### Castlegregory Dingle Peninsula

TEL: **066 7139147**  FAX: **066 7139073**
EMAIL: **griffinspalmbeach@eircom.net**

Luxury home on Dingle Peninsula far from madding crowd. Half a mile to safe sandy beaches and mountains. AA ◆◆◆, Formmer recommended. Ideal for ornithologists/artists. Golf, surfing, hand-gliding on beach.

| B&B | 4 | Ensuite | €35-€40 | Dinner | - |
| B&B | 2 | Standard | €32-€32 | Partial Board | - |
| Single Rate | | | €40-€45 | Child reduction | 25% |

Dingle 14km

**Open:** 1st March-1st November

---

**Ms Mary Kelliher**
KELLIHERS
The Station, Castlegregory,
Co Kerry

### Castlegregory

TEL: **066 7139295**
EMAIL: **kellihers@hotmail.com**

Perfect location in peaceful setting on Dingle Way. Close to beach and all amenities. Ideal touring base for Dingle Peninsula. Private parking.

| B&B | 4 | Ensuite | €29-€31 | Dinner | - |
| B&B | - | Standard | - | Partial Board | - |
| Single Rate | | | €43.50-€43.50 | Child reduction | - |

Castlegregory

**Open:** 1st January-31st December

---

**Mrs Mary Lynch**
STRAND VIEW HOUSE
Kilcummin, Conor Pass Road,
Castlegregory, Co Kerry

### Castlegregory Dingle Peninsula

TEL: **066 7138131**  FAX: **066 7138386**
EMAIL: **strandview@eircom.net**
WEB: **www.strandview.com**

Spacious luxury home on sea front overlooking Brandon Bay. AA ◆◆◆◆ Quality Award. Highly recommended in Guides. 3km West of Stradbally.

| B&B | 4 | Ensuite | €30-€35 | Dinner | - |
| B&B | - | Standard | | Partial Board | - |
| Single Rate | | | €55-€55 | Child reduction | 50% |

Stradbally 3km

**Open:** 6th January-15th December

---

**Mrs Catherine Lyons**
ORCHARD HOUSE
Castlegregory, Co Kerry

### Castlegregory

TEL: **066 7139164**
EMAIL: **orchardh@gofree.indigo.ie**
WEB: **www.kerryview.com**

Family home in idyllic village - on Dingle Way walk route. Convenient to all cultural, sporting and leisure amenities. Beach 5 minutes walk. Home baking.

| B&B | 3 | Ensuite | €28-€31 | Dinner | - |
| B&B | 1 | Standard | €30 | Partial Board | - |
| Single Rate | | | €40-€43.50 | Child reduction | 50% |

In Castlegregory

**Open:** 1st March-31st October

---

**Mrs Annette O'Mahony**
THE SHORES COUNTRY HOUSE
Cappatigue, Conor Pass Rd,
Castlegregory, Co Kerry

### Castlegregory Dingle Peninsula

TEL: **066 7139196/7139195**  FAX: **066 7139196**
EMAIL: **theshores@eircom.net**
WEB: **www.theshorescountryhouse.com**

Highest Award winning AA ◆◆◆◆◆, luxurious spacious "Laura Ashley" style rooms all panoramic Sea-view. Breakfast/Dinner menu. Highly recommended. 1 mile west Stradbally.

| B&B | 6 | Ensuite | €30-€40 | Dinner | €28-€30 |
| B&B | - | Standard | - | Partial Board | €460 |
| Single Rate | | | €40-€80 | Child reduction | 33.3% |

Dingle 14km

**Open:** 15th February-20th November

**Castlegregory**

**Mrs Sheila Rohan**
CASTLE HOUSE
Castlegregory, Co Kerry

## Castlegregory Dingle Peninsula

Tᴇʟ: **066 7139183**
Eᴍᴀɪʟ: **castlebnb@unison.ie**
Wᴇʙ: **www.castlehouse-bnb.com**

Stylish house on Dingle-way. Peaceful surroundings with sea view. Comfort assured. Home Baking. Former Calor Housewife of the year.

| B&B | 6 | Ensuite | €30-€35 | Dinner | - |
|---|---|---|---|---|---|
| B&B | - | Standard | - | Partial Board | - |
| Single Rate | | | €42.50-€45 | Child reduction | 50% |

**Open:** All Year

**ngle 14km**

**Mrs Paula Walsh**
SEA-MOUNT HOUSE
Cappatigue, Conor Pass Road,
Castlegregory, Co Kerry

## Castlegregory Dingle Peninsula

Tᴇʟ: **066 7139229**  Fᴀx: **066 7139229**
Eᴍᴀɪʟ: **seamount@unison.ie**
Wᴇʙ: **www.seamounthouse.com**

Relax in our award winning AA ◆◆◆◆ stylishly decorated home on seafront. Rooms are spacious and luxurious. Near restaurants. 1km west Stradbally.

| B&B | 3 | Ensuite | €30-€35 | Dinner | - |
|---|---|---|---|---|---|
| B&B | - | Standard | - | Partial Board | - |
| Single Rate | | | €42-€45 | Child reduction | 50% |

**Open:** 1st March-30th November

**astleisland 3km**

**Lilian Dillon**
THE GABLES
Dooneen, Limerick Rd (N21),
Castleisland, Co Kerry

## Castleisland

Tᴇʟ: **066 7141060**  Fᴀx: **066 7141060**
Eᴍᴀɪʟ: **gablesdillon@eircom.net**
Wᴇʙ: **homepage.eircom.net/~gablesbnb**

Luxurious home overlooking 18 hole golf course (1 min drive) and beautiful landscape. Ideal touring/golfing base. Breakfast menu. Two triple rooms.

| B&B | 3 | Ensuite | €28-€30 | Dinner | - |
|---|---|---|---|---|---|
| B&B | 1 | Standard | €26-€28 | Partial Board | - |
| Single Rate | | | €38-€43.50 | Child reduction | 50% |

**Open:** 1st January-15th December

**astleisland 3km**

**Mrs Eileen O'Connor**
GLENBROOK HOUSE
Airport Road, Currow Village,
Castleisland, Killarney,
Co Kerry

## Castleisland

Tᴇʟ: **066 9764488**  Fᴀx: **066 9764488**
Eᴍᴀɪʟ: **glenbrookhse@eircom.net**

Highly recommended home. Ideal for touring Kerry. Home cooking a speciality. Signposted off N23. Airport 1 km. Visa/Access/Mastercard accepted.

| B&B | 3 | Ensuite | €28-€31 | Dinner | - |
|---|---|---|---|---|---|
| B&B | 1 | Standard | €26-€29 | Partial Board | - |
| Single Rate | | | €39-€44 | Child reduction | 50% |

**Open:** 31st January-31st November

**Castleisland**

**Breda O'Sullivan**
TAILORS LODGE
Killegane, Castleisland,
Co Kerry

## Castleisland

Tᴇʟ: **066 7142170**
Eᴍᴀɪʟ: **tailorlodge@eircom.net**

Luxurious purpose built house on the R577 Castleisland/Scartaglen road. Power showers, hairdryers, guest lounge, breakfast menu. Airport 8km. Ideal touring base for Kerry.

| B&B | 5 | Ensuite | €30-€32 | Dinner | - |
|---|---|---|---|---|---|
| B&B | - | Standard | - | Partial Board | - |
| Single Rate | | | €40-€43.50 | Child reduction | - |

**Open:** 1st January-20th December

**Mrs Betty Riordan**
RONNOCO LODGE
Limerick Rd, Castleisland,
Co Kerry

### Castleisland
TEL: **066 7141325**  FAX: **066 7141325**
EMAIL: **betty_riordan@hotmail.com**

Experience comfort in family run home, adjacent to golf course. All ground floor bedrooms. TV, Tea/Coffee, radio clock alarms, hairdryers, electric blankets. Family room. Pub transport.

| | | | | | | |
|---|---|---|---|---|---|---|
| B&B | 2 | Ensuite | €27.50-€31 | Dinner | | - |
| B&B | 1 | Standard | €25.50-€28.50 | Partial Board | | - |
| Single Rate | | | €38-€43.50 | Child reduction | | 50% |

Castleisland 2km    **Open:** 1st April-31st October

**Mrs Joan Burke**
MOUNTAIN VIEW
Ballinamona, Castlemaine,
Co Kerry

### Castlemaine
TEL: **066 9767249**
EMAIL: **mountainview02@eircom.ie**

Modern two storey new house with panoramic view. Central for touring Ring of Kerry and Dingle Peninsula. Access/Visa/Euro.

| | | | | | | |
|---|---|---|---|---|---|---|
| B&B | 2 | Ensuite | €27.50-€31 | Dinner | | €20 |
| B&B | 1 | Standard | €25.50-€28.50 | Partial Board | | - |
| Single Rate | | | €38-€43.50 | Child reduction | | 25% |

Castlemaine 1km  **Open:** 1st April-30th October

**Mrs Elizabeth O'Sullivan**
CAHER HOUSE
Caherfilane, Keel, Castlemaine,
Co Kerry

### Castlemaine
TEL: **066 9766126**
EMAIL: **caherf1@eircom.net**

Comfortable residence overlooking Dingle Bay. Central for Dingle, Ring of Kerry, Killarney, Kerry Airport, 15kms, between Castlemaine & Inch, Scenic Walks.

| | | | | | | |
|---|---|---|---|---|---|---|
| B&B | 5 | Ensuite | €28-€31 | Dinner | | €20 |
| B&B | 1 | Standard | €26-€28.50 | Partial Board | | - |
| Single Rate | | | €38-€43.50 | Child reduction | | 50% |

Castlemaine 4km    **Open:** 1st April-31st October

**Robert Ashe**
ASHES B&B
Spa Road, Dingle, Co Kerry

### Dingle
TEL: **066 9151197**
EMAIL: **ashesdingle@eircom.net**
WEB: **www.ashesdingle.com**

Charming townhouse, 1 minute walk from Main St. private car park and garden, non smoking, power showers, walking distance from all pubs and local amenities.

| | | | | | | |
|---|---|---|---|---|---|---|
| B&B | 6 | Ensuite | €30-€45 | Dinner | | - |
| B&B | - | Standard | | Partial Board | | - |
| Single Rate | | | €40-€90 | Child reduction | | 25% |

In Dingle  **Open:** All Year Except Christmas

**Brid Bowler Sheehy**
BALLINVOUNIG HOUSE
Ballinvounig, Dingle, Co Kerry

### Dingle
TEL: **066 9152104**
EMAIL: **ballinvounighouse@eircom.net**
WEB: **homepage.eircom.net/~dbsheehy**

Welcoming family home, tranquil location, panoramic views. Off main Tralee/Dingle Rd (N86). 5 mins town centre. Spacious comfortable bedrooms, homebaking, varied quality breakfast.

| | | | | | | |
|---|---|---|---|---|---|---|
| B&B | 4 | Ensuite | €28-€35 | Dinner | | - |
| B&B | - | Standard | - | Partial Board | | - |
| Single Rate | | | €50-€55 | Child reduction | | - |

Dingle 1.5km    **Open:** 1st March-31st October

**Mrs Kitty Brosnan**
ABHAINN MHOR
Cloghane, Co Kerry

### Dingle

TEL: **066 7138211**
EMAIL: **brosnankitty@hotmail.com**
WEB: **www.kerryweb.ie**

Beside village. On Dingle way, foot of Brandon Mountain. Near Dingle, Beaches, Hill walking, Fishing, Archaeology. Coeliacs welcome.

| B&B | 3 | Ensuite | €31 | Dinner | - |
| B&B | 1 | Standard | €28.50 | Partial Board | - |
| Single Rate | | | €41 | Child reduction | **33.3%** |

ngle 10km

**Open:** 1st April-1st October

---

**Ms Camilla Browne**
BROWNE'S B&B
Ladyscross, Milltown, Dingle,
Co Kerry

### Dingle

TEL: **066 9151259**
EMAIL: **jbrownes@iol.ie**
WEB: **www.iol.ie/~jbrownes**

Comfortable home with bay harbour and mountain views on Ventry Slea Head Drive. Tea on arrival, varied breakfast menu and orthopaedic beds.

| B&B | 4 | Ensuite | €28-€35 | Dinner | - |
| B&B | - | Standard | - | Partial Board | - |
| Single Rate | | | €42-€45 | Child reduction | **25%** |

ngle 1km

**Open:** 16th March-31st October

---

**Ms Eileen Carroll**
FIÚISE
Miltown, Dingle, Co Kerry

### Dingle

TEL: **066 9152850**
EMAIL: **fiuise@eircom.net**
WEB: **www.fiuise.com**

Quiet home with panoramic views spacious rooms with tv, hairdryer, powershowers, tea/coffee, breakfast menu, home baking, private parking. 10 minutes walk to Dingle.

| B&B | 4 | Ensuite | €30-€35 | Dinner | - |
| B&B | - | Standard | - | Partial Board | - |
| Single Rate | | | - | Child reduction | - |

ngle 1km

**Open:** 15th February-15th November

---

**Mrs Mary Carroll**
CEANN TRA HEIGHTS
Ventry (Ceann Trá), Dingle,
Co Kerry

### Dingle

TEL: **066 9159866**
EMAIL: **ventry@iol.ie**
WEB: **www.dingle-vacation.com**

Quiet country home in peaceful scenic area overlooking Ventry Harbour/Dingle Bay. Seaview from rooms. In Ventry village. 5 minutes walk to blue flag Beach. Breakfast menu. Tea making facilities.

| B&B | 4 | Ensuite | €28-€32.50 | Dinner | - |
| B&B | - | Standard | - | Partial Board | - |
| Single Rate | | | €40-€45 | Child reduction | **33.3%** |

ngle 4km

**Open:** 12th March-15th November

---

**Michael & Barbara Carroll**
MILESTONE HOUSE
Dingle, Co Kerry

### Dingle

TEL: **066 9151831**   FAX: **066 9151831**
EMAIL: **milestonedingle@eircom.net**

Quiet detached family home overlooking Dingle bay, Mount Brandon. All rooms with phone, t.v., clock radio, hairdryer, tea/coffee available. Breakfast menu. Private car park.

| B&B | 4 | Ensuite | €28-€35 | Dinner | - |
| B&B | 1 | Standard | €28-€35 | Partial Board | - |
| Single Rate | | | €40-€45 | Child reduction | **25%** |

ingle 1km

**Open:** 16th March-31st October

### Eileen Collins
**KIRRARY**
**Avondale, Dingle, Co Kerry**

TEL: **066 9151606**
EMAIL: **collinskirrary@eircom.net**

Personal touch. In centre of Town, private gardens. Ideal Walkers/Cyclists. Sciuird Archaelogy Tours,, Rent - A - Bike. Recommended by Rick Steeves, famous American Tour Guide.

| | | | | | |
|---|---|---|---|---|---|
| B&B | 2 | Ensuite | €33-€38 | Dinner | - |
| B&B | 1 | Standard | €32-€36 | Partial Board | - |
| Single Rate | | | €40-€55 | Child reduction | - |

**In Dingle**

**Open:** 1st January-20th December

---

### Geraldine and Kevin Devane
**DEVANE'S**
**Goat Street, Dingle, Co Kerry**

TEL: **066 9151193**
EMAIL: **devanesdingle@eircom.net**
WEB: **homepage.eircom.net/~devanesdingle/index.html**

Townhouse, family run, overlooking Dingle Bay. Within walking distance to all amenities. Ideal touring base. TV, clock-radios, hairdryers, Tea/Coffee in bedrooms. Quiet location.

| | | | | | |
|---|---|---|---|---|---|
| B&B | 5 | Ensuite | €30-€35 | Dinner | - |
| B&B | 1 | Standard | €30-€33 | Partial Board | - |
| Single Rate | | | - | Child reduction | 33.3% |

**In Dingle**

**Open:** 12th March-1st November

---

### Marie Dolores NicGearailt
**NIC GERAILTS B&B**
**Bothar Bui, Ballydavid, Dingle,**
**Co Kerry**

TEL: **066 9155142**   FAX: **066 9155142**
EMAIL: **mnicgear@indigo.ie**
WEB: **www.nicgearailt.com**

Warm friendly home, Gaelic area. Breakfast menu, Home baking. Walkers & hill climbers paradise. Pubs, Restaurants, Beach, Gallarus Oratory, Dingle Way nearby.

| | | | | | |
|---|---|---|---|---|---|
| B&B | 4 | Ensuite | €28-€31 | Dinner | - |
| B&B | - | Standard | - | Partial Board | - |
| Single Rate | | | €40-€43.50 | Child reduction | 33.3% |

**Dingle 11km**

**Open:** 1st April-1st October

---

### Mrs Bridie Fitzgerald
**DINGLE HEIGHTS**
**Ballinboula, High Road, Dingle,**
**Co Kerry**

TEL: **066 9151543**   FAX: **066 9152445**
EMAIL: **dingleheights@hotmail.com**
WEB: **www.dingleheights.com**

Warm friendly home overlooking Dingle Bay and Harbour. Private parking, Walking distance to Town and all amenities. Quiet location.

| | | | | | |
|---|---|---|---|---|---|
| B&B | 5 | Ensuite | €29-€34 | Dinner | - |
| B&B | - | Standard | - | Partial Board | - |
| Single Rate | | | - | Child reduction | - |

**In Dingle**

**Open:** 1st March-20th November

---

### Beatrice Flannery
**THE PLOUGH**
**Ventry, Dingle, Co Kerry**

TEL: **066 9159727**
EMAIL: **theplough@iol.ie**
WEB: **www.ireland-discover.com/plough.htm**

Warm friendly home, Ventry Village. Walking distance all amenities. Enjoy Panoramic Sea/Mountain views from deck area. Breakfast menu. Restaurant in village. Guest Lounge, Orthopaedic beds.

| | | | | | |
|---|---|---|---|---|---|
| B&B | 4 | Ensuite | €28-€32 | Dinner | - |
| B&B | - | Standard | - | Partial Board | - |
| Single Rate | | | €40-€45 | Child reduction | - |

**Dingle 4km**

**Open:** 1st January-1st December

**Dingle**

### Robbie & Mary Griffin
**TOWER VIEW**
The High Road, Dingle,
Co Kerry

Tel: **066 9152990**   Fax: **066 9152989**
Email: **towerviewdingle@eircom.net**
Web: **www.towerviewdingle.com**

New home, overlooking Dingle harbour, quiet location. Parking. Mins walk Town, close to all local amenities. Guest lounge, multi-channel TV, Tea/Coffee. Breakfast menu. 5ft beds power showers.

| B&B | 5 | Ensuite | €32-€37.50 | Dinner | - |
|---|---|---|---|---|---|
| B&B | - | Standard | | Partial Board | - |
| Single Rate | | | €45-€55 | Child reduction | 33.3% |

Dingle

**Open:** 1st March-1st November

---

**Dingle**

### Noeline Hand
**DUNROMAN**
Lispole, Co Kerry

Tel: **066 9151049**   Fax: **066 9151779**
Email: **info@dunroman.com**
Web: **www.dunroman.com**

New purpose built guesthouse. Located on N86, 5 mins drive to Dingle, Private Parking, Sat TV, Powershowers, Tea/Coffee home baking on arrival, Quiet Location, Breakfast Menu.

| B&B | 3 | Ensuite | €28-€32 | Dinner | - |
|---|---|---|---|---|---|
| B&B | - | Standard | | Partial Board | - |
| Single Rate | | | €40-€45 | Child reduction | 50% |

ingle 5km

**Open:** 17th March-31st October

---

**Dingle**

### Mrs Alice Hannafin
**AN SPEICE**
Ballyferriter West, Dingle,
Co Kerry

Tel: **066 9156254**
Email: **speice@eircom.net**
Web: **www.dinglewest.com**

A warm welcome awaits you at our family run B&B. Tea/Coffee on arrival. Home baking and Breakfast menu. On Slea Head drive. Sea/Mountain views. Close to Village, Golf, Sea & Walks.

| B&B | 3 | Ensuite | €28-€32 | Dinner | - |
|---|---|---|---|---|---|
| B&B | - | Standard | - | Partial Board | - |
| Single Rate | | | €40-€44 | Child reduction | 50% |

Ballyferriter

**Open:** 1st February-31st October

---

**Dingle**

### Kerry & Michael Hennessy
**CONOR PASS HOUSE**
Ballybeg, Conor Pass, Dingle,
Co Kerry

Tel: **066 9152184**
Email: **conorpasshouse@eircom.net**
Web: **www.conorpasshouse.com**

New home, quiet. Close to town & all amenities. Private Parking, guest lounge, Cable T.V. Orthopadic beds, powershowers, Tea/Coffee on arrival. Panoramic views. Breakfast menu.

| B&B | 4 | Ensuite | €32-€37.50 | Dinner | - |
|---|---|---|---|---|---|
| B&B | - | Standard | - | Partial Board | - |
| Single Rate | | | | Child reduction | - |

ingle 1km

**Open:** 1st February-23rd December

---

**Dingle**

### Tom & Veronica Houlihan
O'Neill
**OLD MILL HOUSE**
3 Avondale Street, Dingle,
Co Kerry

Tel: **066 9152349**   Fax: **066 9151120**
Email: **verhoul@iol.ie**
Web: **www.oldmillhousedingle.com**

Local family run. 1 min walk to pubs, Fungi and bus stop. Spacious comfortable ensuite rooms with TV. Ideal base walkers/cyclists. Angling, Golf, Archeology tours from house.

| B&B | 3 | Ensuite | €29.90-€40.50 | Dinner | - |
|---|---|---|---|---|---|
| B&B | - | Standard | | Partial Board | - |
| Single Rate | | | €40-€43.50 | Child reduction | 33.3% |

Dingle

**Open:** All Year

**Denise Kane**
**DUNLAVIN HOUSE**
**Milltown, Dingle, Co Kerry**

### Dingle

TEL: **066 9152375**
EMAIL: **dunlavin@gofree.indigo.ie**
WEB: **www.dunlavin/house.com**

Panoramic Harbour Views. 10 minutes walk to town. Private Car Parking. Tea/Coffee facilities. Extensive breakfast.

| | | | | | | |
|---|---|---|---|---|---|---|
| B&B | 4 | Ensuite | €30-€35 | Dinner | | - |
| B&B | - | Standard | - | Partial Board | | - |
| Single Rate | | | €50-€55 | Child reduction | | - |

In Dingle .05km

**Open:** All Year

---

**Ms Marguerite Kavanagh**
**KAVANAGH'S B&B**
**Garfinny, Dingle, Co Kerry**

### Dingle

TEL: **066 9151326**
EMAIL: **mkavan@iol.ie**
WEB: **www.iol.ie/~mkavan/**

Country family run home located on N86, 5 minutes drive to Dingle. Spacious bedrooms, Hairdryers, TV, Tea/Coffee, Electric Blankets in rooms. Family bedroom available.

| | | | | | | |
|---|---|---|---|---|---|---|
| B&B | 3 | Ensuite | €27.50-€32 | Dinner | | - |
| B&B | 1 | Standard | €25.50-€30 | Partial Board | | - |
| Single Rate | | | €38-€45 | Child reduction | | 50% |

Dingle 3km

**Open:** 1st April-30th September

---

**James & Hannah Kelliher**
**BALLYEGAN HOUSE**
**Upper John Street, Dingle, Co Kerry**

### Dingle

TEL: **066 9151702**

Luxury home, magnificent views overlooking Dingle Harbour. Car parking. Minutes walk to Town. Guest lounge. AA recommended. Pass Doyles Restaurant. We are at top of Johns Street on left.

| | | | | | | |
|---|---|---|---|---|---|---|
| B&B | 6 | Ensuite | €34-€35 | Dinner | | - |
| B&B | - | Standard | - | Partial Board | | - |
| Single Rate | | | - | Child reduction | | - |

In Dingle

**Open:** 2nd February-1st December

---

**Angela Long**
**TIGH AN DUNA**
**Fahan, Slea Head, Ventry, Dingle, Co Kerry**

### Dingle

TEL: **066 9159822**
EMAIL: **ventrysleahead@hotmail.com**

Peaceful home at Dunbeg Fort, near spectacular Slea Head. Atlantic Ocean. Views from bedrooms/diningroom. Near Beehives, Blasket Ferry, Restaraunts, Beaches. On Dingle Way walk route.

| | | | | | | |
|---|---|---|---|---|---|---|
| B&B | 2 | Ensuite | €30-€32 | Dinner | | - |
| B&B | 1 | Standard | €29-€30 | Partial Board | | - |
| Single Rate | | | €40-€45 | Child reduction | | 50% |

Dingle 12km

**Open:** 1st May-30th September

---

**Mrs Angela McCarthy**
**CILL BHREAC HOUSE**
**Milltown, Dingle, Co Kerry**

### Dingle

TEL: **066 9151358**
EMAIL: **info@cillbhreachouse.com**
WEB: **www.cillbhreachouse.com**

Panoramic harbour views. Recommended by 400 Best B&Bs, International Travel Magazine, Ireland Expert, Guide de Routard. Breakfast menu. Electric blankets. Satellite TV. Orthopaedic beds.

| | | | | | | |
|---|---|---|---|---|---|---|
| B&B | 6 | Ensuite | €28-€35 | Dinner | | - |
| B&B | - | Standard | - | Partial Board | | - |
| Single Rate | | | - | Child reduction | | 33.3% |

Dingle 1km

**Open:** 15th February-30th November

**Mrs Ann Murphy**
ARD-NA-MARA COUNTRY HOUSE
**Ballymore, Ventry, Dingle, Co Kerry**

TEL: **066 9159072**
EMAIL: **annmurphybnb@hotmail.com**

Elevated peaceful country home beside the sea overlooking Ventry Harbour. Rooms en-suite, Breakfast menu. Complimentary Tea/Coffee.

| B&B | 4 | Ensuite | €29-€32 | Dinner | - |
| B&B | - | Standard | - | Partial Board | - |
| Single Rate | | | €41-€44 | Child reduction | 50% |

Dingle 3km

**Open:** 1st March-14th November

---

**Mrs Mary Murphy**
THE LIGHTHOUSE
**The High Road, Ballinaboula, Dingle, Co Kerry**

TEL: **066 9151829**
EMAIL: **info@lighthousedingle.com**
WEB: **www.lighthousedingle.com**

Spacious home, magnificent harbour views. Dillard/Causin recommended. Mins walk town.TV lounge, clock radios, hairdryers, breakfast menu. From Main St on to Ashmount Ter we're 3rd B&B on right.

| B&B | 6 | Ensuite | €30-€37 | Dinner | - |
| B&B | - | Standard | - | Partial Board | - |
| Single Rate | | | €40-€50 | Child reduction | 50% |

n Dingle

**Open:** 1st February-11th November

---

**Anne & Pat Neligan**
DUININ HOUSE
**Conor Pass Road, Dingle, Co Kerry**

TEL: **066 9151335**  FAX: **066 9151335**
EMAIL: **pandaneligan@eircom.net**
WEB: **homepage.tinet.ie/~pandaneligan/**

Award winning B&B. Superb location with magnificent views. Recommended by Frommer, Berlitz and 300 Best B&B's. Extensive Breakfast menu. Luxurious Guest conservatory - lounge.

| B&B | 5 | Ensuite | €28-€35 | Dinner | - |
| B&B | - | Standard | - | Partial Board | - |
| Single Rate | | | - | Child reduction | - |

Dingle 1km

**Open:** 1st February-30th November

---

**Mrs Margaret Noonan**
CLUAIN MHUIRE HOUSE
**Spa Road, Dingle, Co Kerry**

TEL: **066 9151291**

4 Bedrooms with satellite TV. Tea/Coffee facilities, electric blankets, hairdryer. Private large car park. Credit Cards. House well signposted.

| B&B | 4 | Ensuite | €30-€35 | Dinner | - |
| B&B | - | Standard | - | Partial Board | - |
| Single Rate | | | - | Child reduction | - |

n Dingle

**Open:** 1st January-31st December

---

**Diarmuid & Denise O'Beaglaoi**
AN RIASC
**Fheothanach, Ballydavid, Dingle, Co Kerry**

TEL: **066 9155446**  FAX: **066 9155446**
EMAIL: **denisebegley@eircom.net**
WEB: **www.anriasc.com**

Idyllic location surrounded by mountain and sea close to beaches, golf, angling, walks, historical sites. Breakfast delights using organic produce homebaking.

| B&B | 3 | Ensuite | €30-€35 | Dinner | - |
| B&B | - | Standard | - | Partial Board | - |
| Single Rate | | | €45-€50 | Child reduction | 50% |

Dingle 12km

**Open:** 1st February-30th November

**Mrs Helen O'Neill**
DOONSHEAN VIEW
High Road, Garfinny, Dingle,
Co Kerry

TEL: **066 9151032**
EMAIL: **doonsheanview@eircom.net**
WEB: **homepage.eircom.net/~doonsheanview**

Tranquil area, sea & mountain views. Off N86 Tralee/Killarney Rd. Ideal for touring Dingle peninsula. Warm welcome. TV lounge, breakfast menu, home baking.

| B&B | 4 | Ensuite | €30-€35 | Dinner | - |
|---|---|---|---|---|---|
| B&B | - | Standard | | Partial Board | - |
| Single Rate | | | €40-€45 | Child reduction | 25% |

Dingle 2km

**Open:** 16th March-31st October

---

**Mrs Mary O'Neill**
John Street
Dingle, Co Kerry

TEL: **066 9151639**

Purpose built home. Quiet location. 2 minutes walk to Town Centre. Tea/Coffee making facilities, TV, Clock radio, Hairdryer. Guest TV Lounge, choice of Breakfast.

| B&B | 6 | Ensuite | €30-€35 | Dinner | - |
|---|---|---|---|---|---|
| B&B | - | Standard | - | Partial Board | - |
| Single Rate | | | €45-€50 | Child reduction | 25% |

In Dingle

**Open:** 17th March-30th September

---

**Mrs Jacqueline O'Shea**
TORANN NA DTONN
Ventry, Dingle, Co Kerry

TEL: **066 9159952**
EMAIL: **torann@iol.ie**
WEB: **www.dingle-peninsula.com**

Country Home beside Ventry village, on Slea Head drive. Magnificent Sea view overlooking Bay. 5 mins walk sandy beach. Fishing, Watersports, Scenic walks, Golf, Horse-riding. Breakfast menu.

| B&B | 5 | Ensuite | €30-€32.50 | Dinner | - |
|---|---|---|---|---|---|
| B&B | - | Standard | | Partial Board | - |
| Single Rate | | | €40-€45 | Child reduction | 25% |

Dingle 4km

**Open:** 1st March-13th November

---

**Maurice & Therese O'Shea**
BALLYMORE HOUSE
Ballymore, Ventry, Dingle,
Co Kerry

TEL: **066 9159050**
EMAIL: **info@ballymorehouse.com**
WEB: **www.ballymorehouse.com**

Spacious Country Home with Sea view, tranquil location. Guest TV & reading room. Open coal fire. Extensive Breakfast & Dinner menu. Home cooking our speciality. Numerous recommendations.

| B&B | 5 | Ensuite | €32-€32 | Dinner | €25-€30 |
|---|---|---|---|---|---|
| B&B | 1 | Standard | €30-€30 | Partial Board | €380 |
| Single Rate | | | €45-€50 | Child reduction | |

Dingle 3km

**Open:** 1st January-31st December

---

**Eric & Eleanor Prestage**
MOUNT EAGLE LODGE
Ventry, Dingle, Co Kerry

TEL: **066 9159754**
EMAIL: **lodging@iol.ie**
WEB: **www.dinglelodging.com**

AA ◆◆◆◆. Magnificent views from spacious rooms overlooking Ventry Bay. Electric blankets, acclaimed buffet and breakfast menu mins walk to beach village, restaurant. Drying room: see website.

| B&B | 4 | Ensuite | €30-€45 | Dinner | - |
|---|---|---|---|---|---|
| B&B | - | Standard | - | Partial Board | - |
| Single Rate | | | €40-€55 | Child reduction | 50% |

Dingle 5km

**Open:** 1st March-30th November

### Mrs Mary Russell
**RUSSELL'S B&B**
**The Mall, Dingle, Co Kerry**

**Dingle**

TEL: **066 9151747**   FAX: **066 9152331**
EMAIL: **maryr@iol.ie**
WEB: **homepage.eircom.net/~maryrussell**

Detached house in Town Centre. Private parking, 2 minute walk to bus stop, Restaurants etc. Recommended by Guide du Routard, Reise, Fodors close up.

| B&B | 6 | Ensuite | €29-€36 | Dinner | - |
| B&B | - | Standard | - | Partial Board | - |
| Single Rate | | | €40-€52 | Child reduction | 33.3% |

**Dingle**

**Open:** 1st January-10th December

---

### Mrs Mary Sheehy
**SHEEHY'S**
**Milltown, Dingle, Co Kerry**

**Dingle**

TEL: **066 9151453**
EMAIL: **marycsheehy@eircom.net**
WEB: **homepage.eircom.net/~sheehyshome**

Peaceful home on the Cuas - Feoghanach road. Dingle 1km. Close to all amenities. Private parking. Choices of Breakfast. Irish speaking.

| B&B | 4 | Ensuite | €29-€33 | Dinner | - |
| B&B | - | Standard | - | Partial Board | - |
| Single Rate | | | - | Child reduction | 50% |

ingle 1km

**Open:** 1st March-1st November

---

### Mrs Mary B Ui Chiobhain
**ARD NA CARRAIGE**
**Carraig, Ballydavid, Dingle,**
**Co Kerry**

**Dingle**

TEL: **066 9155295**
EMAIL: **ardnacarr@eircom.net**
WEB: **http://www.dingle-region.com/carraige.htm**

Scenic Gaelic area. Close to Beach, Pubs, Restaurants, Dingle Way Walk, Gallarus Oratory, Kilmaolceadar. Tea/Coffee facilities. Breakfast menu.

| B&B | 4 | Ensuite | €28-€31 | Dinner | - |
| B&B | - | Standard | - | Partial Board | - |
| Single Rate | | | €40-€45 | Child reduction | - |

ingle 10km

**Open:** 1st May-30th September

---

### Mrs Josephine Walsh
**WALSHS TOWNHOUSE B&B**
**Main Street, Dingle, Co Kerry**

**Dingle**

TEL: **066 9151147**
EMAIL: **walshbb@iol.ie**
WEB: **www.iol.ie/~walshtownhouse/**

Luxury Town house in Town centre. Close to Shops, Restaurants & Bus. Ideal location for touring Dingle Peninsula. Breakfast menu. Low season reductions.

| B&B | 6 | Ensuite | €29-€37.50 | Dinner | - |
| B&B | - | Standard | - | Partial Board | - |
| Single Rate | | | €40-€50 | Child reduction | - |

Dingle

**Open:** All Year Except Christmas

---

### Doreen Caulfield
**FOREST VIEW**
**Glenbeigh, Co Kerry**

**Glenbeigh**

TEL: **066 9768140**
EMAIL: **forestviewglenbeigh@eircom.net**
WEB: **www.forestviewhouse.com**

Elegant home in panoramic tranquil setting. Excellent touring location on Ring of Kerry. Adjacent to beach, horseriding, Dooks Golf Club and Kerry Way.

| B&B | 3 | Ensuite | €30-€34 | Dinner | - |
| B&B | 1 | Standard | - | Partial Board | - |
| Single Rate | | | €42-€45 | Child reduction | 25% |

lenbeigh 1.2km

**Open:** 27th March-31st October

---

**Della Doyle**
GLENCURRAH HOUSE
Curraheen, Glenbeigh,
Co Kerry

### Glenbeigh

Tel: **066 9768133** Fax: **066 9768691**
Email: **info@glencurrahhouse.com**
Web: **www.glencurrahhouse.com**

Delightful country house with picturesque gardens overlooking Dingle Bay on the Ring of Kerry route N70. 1km from Glenbeigh village, Dooks Golf Links nearby.

| B&B | 5 | Ensuite | €32-€35 | Dinner | - |
|-----|---|---------|---------|--------|---|
| B&B | - | Standard | | Partial Board | - |
| Single Rate | | | €42-€45 | Child reduction | - |

Glenbeigh 1km

**Open:** 1st March-31st October

---

**Mrs Bridget McSweeney**
HILLCREST HOUSE
Ballycleave, Glenbeigh,
Co Kerry

### Glenbeigh Ring of Kerry

Tel: **066 9769165** Fax: **066 9769165**
Email: **2mcsweeney@eircom.net**
Web: **www.stayathillcrest.com**

On Glenbeigh Killorglin Road in peaceful scenic area. Close to Lake, Beaches, Dooks Golf, Fishing. Red Fox Restaurant/Bar, Irish music. Bog Museum walking distance. 200m off Main Road.

| B&B | 3 | Ensuite | €27.50-€31 | Dinner | - |
|-----|---|---------|------------|--------|---|
| B&B | 1 | Standard | €25.50-€28.50 | Partial Board | - |
| Single Rate | | | €38-€43.50 | Child reduction | **50%** |

Glenbeigh 4km

**Open:** 1st April-31st October

---

**Mrs Anne O'Riordan**
MOUNTAIN VIEW
Mountain Stage, Glenbeigh,
Co Kerry

### Glenbeigh

Tel: **066 9768541** Fax: **066 9768541**
Email: **mountainstage@eircom.net**

Quiet peaceful location with breathtaking views. 200 mtrs off Ring of Kerry. Adjacent to Beaches, Fishing - "Kerry Way". Low season reductions.

| B&B | 4 | Ensuite | €27.50-€31 | Dinner | €19 |
|-----|---|---------|------------|--------|-----|
| B&B | - | Standard | | Partial Board | €295 |
| Single Rate | | | €40-€43.50 | Child reduction | **50%** |

Glenbeigh 4.2km

**Open:** 1st April-31st October

---

**Mrs Eileen Kennedy**
WATERSIDE
Inch, Annascaul, Co Kerry

### Inch Dingle Peninsula

Tel: **066 9158129**
Email: **watersideinch@hotmail.com**

Modern, spacious, friendly, quality accommodation. Convenient to Beach, Pub, Restaurant. Guest Lounge. Superb, central, scenic seaside setting. Ideal touring base. Private shoreline.

| B&B | 4 | Ensuite | €27.50-€31 | Dinner | - |
|-----|---|---------|------------|--------|---|
| B&B | - | Standard | - | Partial Board | - |
| Single Rate | | | - | Child reduction | **25%** |

In Inch

**Open:** 1st April-15th October

---

**Mrs Hannah Boland**
MUXNAW LODGE
Castletownbere Rd, Kenmare,
Co Kerry

### Kenmare

Tel: **064 41252**
Email: **muxnawlodge@eircom.net**

Enchanting house built in 1801. Furnished throughout with antiques. Overlooking Kenmare Bay. All weather Tennis Court. Breakfast menu. Many recommendations.

| B&B | 5 | Ensuite | €35-€40 | Dinner | €30 |
|-----|---|---------|---------|--------|-----|
| B&B | - | Standard | - | Partial Board | - |
| Single Rate | | | - | Child reduction | - |

Kenmare 1km

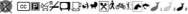

**Open:** All Year Except Christmas

### Mary Brennan
**ASHFIELD**
**Killowen Road, Kenmare,**
**Co Kerry**

TEL: **064 42234**
EMAIL: **wosbery@yahoo.com**
WEB: **www.neidin.net/ashfield**

Purpose built B&B, all rooms with view over Kenmare river & mountains. Ajacent to golf course. 10 mins walk to town. Good base for touring Kerry. Spacious ensuites. Route R569.

| B&B | 4 | Ensuite | €30-€35 | Dinner | - |
|-----|---|---------|---------|--------|---|
| B&B | - | Standard | - | Partial Board | - |
| Single Rate | | | €40-€45 | Child reduction | **50%** |

enmare 0.50km   **Open:** 1st March-30th November

---

### Dan Carraher O'Sullivan
**ANNAGRY HOUSE**
**Sneem Road (N70), Kenmare,**
**Co Kerry**

TEL: **064 41283**
EMAIL: **info@annagryhouse.com**
WEB: **www.annagryhouse.com**

Ideal location on Ring of Kerry road (N70). Kenmare centre 6 mins walk. Peaceful. Spacious ensuite rooms. Bathtubs/Showers. Extensive breakfast menu. Fresh ground coffee. Home baking.

| B&B | 6 | Ensuite | €30-€32.50 | Dinner | - |
|-----|---|---------|------------|--------|---|
| B&B | - | Standard | - | Partial Board | - |
| Single Rate | | | - | Child reduction | **33.3%** |

Kenmare   **Open:** 1st April-30th November

---

### Brendan & Geraldine Ceallaigh
**ABBEY COURT**
**Killowen, Kilgarvan Road,**
**Kenmare, Co Kerry**

TEL: **064 42735**  FAX: **064 42735**
EMAIL: **info@abbeycourtkenmare.com**
WEB: **www.abbeycourtkenmare.com**

Luxury house on acres of landscaped gardens and metres from the seashore. Adjacent to golf course. Excellent breakfast. Ideal touring base for Ring of Kerry/Beara.

| B&B | 3 | Ensuite | €30-€35 | Dinner | - |
|-----|---|---------|---------|--------|---|
| B&B | - | Standard | - | Partial Board | - |
| Single Rate | | | €40-€50 | Child reduction | **33.3%** |

Kenmare   **Open:** All Year Except Christmas

---

### Mrs Anne Clifford
**CHERRY HILL**
**Killowen, Kenmare, Co Kerry**

TEL: **064 41715**
EMAIL: **cherryhill@eircom.net**

Located on Cork/Kilgarvan road off N22 on R569. Beautiful view of Kenmare river. Near Town, Golf course. Ideal base for touring Ring of Kerry, Beara.

| B&B | 2 | Ensuite | €28-€32 | Dinner | - |
|-----|---|---------|---------|--------|---|
| B&B | 1 | Standard | €26-€29 | Partial Board | - |
| Single Rate | | | | Child reduction | **25%** |

enmare 1km   **Open:** 1st May-30th September

---

### Noreen Cronin
**WATERSEDGE**
**Muxnaw, Kenmare, Co Kerry**

TEL: **064 41707**
EMAIL: **vnk@gofree.indigo.ie**

New purpose built B&B. Set in oak woods overlooking Kenmare Bay. Scenic, peaceful location, but only 10 min walk to town centre. Full facilities, spacious rooms.

| B&B | 4 | Ensuite | €28-€31 | Dinner | - |
|-----|---|---------|---------|--------|---|
| B&B | - | Standard | - | Partial Board | - |
| Single Rate | | | €43-€45 | Child reduction | **50%** |

enmare 1km   **Open:** 1st January-31st November

**Mrs Edel Dahm**
ARD NA MARA
**Pier Road, Kenmare, Co Kerry**

### Kenmare
TEL: **064 41399**  FAX: **064 41399**

Family home with garden overlooking Kenmare Bay at the front & MacGillycuddy Reeks at the back on the N71 road to Bantry. 5 mins walk into Town. German spoken.

| | | | | | |
|---|---|---|---|---|---|
| B&B | 4 | Ensuite | €30-€32 | Dinner | - |
| B&B | - | Standard | - | Partial Board | - |
| Single Rate | | | €40-€40 | Child reduction | **50%** |

**In Kenmare**

**Open:** All Year Except Christmas

---

**Mrs B Dinneen**
LEEBROOK HOUSE
**Killarney Road, Kenmare, Co Kerry**

### Kenmare
TEL: **064 41521**
EMAIL: **leebrookhouse@eircom.net**

Experience genuine hospitality in elegant family home. Located on N71 convenient to Kenmare Town. Ideal touring base Ring of Kerry/Beara.

| | | | | | |
|---|---|---|---|---|---|
| B&B | 4 | Ensuite | €30-€32.50 | Dinner | - |
| B&B | - | Standard | - | Partial Board | - |
| Single Rate | | | - | Child reduction | **25%** |

**Kenmare 1km**

**Open:** 14th March-20th November

---

**Mrs Kathleen Downing O'Shea**
MELROSE
**Gortamullen, Kenmare, Co Kerry**

### Kenmare
TEL: **064 41020**
EMAIL: **kathleenmelrose@eircom.net**
WEB: **www.melrosekenmare.com**

Bungalow situated off N71 Killarney road. 5 mins walk to Town Centre. Located in a scenic country area overlooking the Town. Central to all amenities.

| | | | | | |
|---|---|---|---|---|---|
| B&B | 3 | Ensuite | €28-€33 | Dinner | - |
| B&B | 1 | Standard | €28-€31 | Partial Board | - |
| Single Rate | | | - | Child reduction | - |

**In Kenmare**

**Open:** 1st April-30th October

---

**Mrs Marian Dwyer**
ROCKCREST HOUSE
**Gortamullen, Kenmare, Co Kerry**

### Kenmare
TEL: **064 41248**
EMAIL: **dodwy@eircom.net**
WEB: **www.rockcresthouse.com**

Elegant home, spacious rooms, quiet rd. Off N71 Killarney Rd. Scenic location overlooking Druid Circle & Kenmare Town/Mts./Valley, 5 min. walk to Town Centre.

| | | | | | |
|---|---|---|---|---|---|
| B&B | 6 | Ensuite | €30-€32.50 | Dinner | - |
| B&B | - | Standard | - | Partial Board | - |
| Single Rate | | | - | Child reduction | **33.3%** |

**In Kenmare**

**Open:** 1st January-31st December

---

**Ian & Sue Eccles**
FERN HEIGHT
**Lohart, Castletownbere Road, Kenmare, Co Kerry**

### Kenmare
TEL: **064 84248**  FAX: **064 84248**
EMAIL: **Fernheight@eircom.net**
WEB: **www.neidin.com/fernheight**

Situated on R571. Some 15 mins drive towards Castletown Bearhaven. Rural location with views of the Bay, Mountains & Castle. Good food comes as standard.

| | | | | | |
|---|---|---|---|---|---|
| B&B | 3 | Ensuite | €30-€35 | Dinner | €26-€26 |
| B&B | 1 | Standard | €28-€30 | Partial Board | €340 |
| Single Rate | | | €40-€45 | Child reduction | **25%** |

**Kenmare 11km**

**Open:** 1st May-31st October

### Mrs Mary Fitzgerald
**WHISPERING PINES**
**Glengarriff Road, Kenmare, Co Kerry**

**Kenmare**

TEL: **064 41194**  FAX: **064 40813**
EMAIL: **wpines@eircom.net**

Modernised period home. Spacious gardens, 3 minutes walk to Town, Golf course and Kenmare Bay. Recommended Dillard Causin/Sullivan Guide. Breakfast menu.

| | | | | | |
|---|---|---|---|---|---|
| B&B | 4 | Ensuite | €30-€40 | Dinner | - |
| B&B | - | Standard | - | Partial Board | - |
| Single Rate | | | - | Child reduction | - |

n Kenmare

**Open:** 1st March-1st November

### Antoinette Galvin
**VALHALLA**
**Blackwater Bridge, Kenmare, Co Kerry**

**Kenmare**

TEL: **064 82941**  FAX: **064 82941**
EMAIL: **galvina@gofree.indigo.ie**
WEB: **www.neidin.net/valhalla**

Luxury country house. Panoramic views of Kenmare Bay/Caha Mountains. On Ring Of Kerry route, 10 mins drive from Kenmare town. Breakfast choice.

| | | | | | |
|---|---|---|---|---|---|
| B&B | 4 | Ensuite | €28-€32.50 | Dinner | - |
| B&B | - | Standard | - | Partial Board | - |
| Single Rate | | | €40-€45 | Child reduction | 25% |

Kenmare 10km

**Open:** 1st March-31st October

### Margaret & Michael Gavin
**BEARA WAY B&B**
**Killaha East, Kenmare, Co Kerry**

**Kenmare**

TEL: **064 42482**  FAX: **064 42482**
EMAIL: **bearaway@eircom.net**
WEB: **www.neidin.net/bearaway**

New B&B, large individually designed bedrooms, cosy guest lounge, breakfast menu, scenic peaceful location close to town, sea, mountains and forest.

| | | | | | |
|---|---|---|---|---|---|
| B&B | 3 | Ensuite | €30-€35 | Dinner | - |
| B&B | - | Standard | - | Partial Board | - |
| Single Rate | | | €40-€50 | Child reduction | 50% |

Kenmare 2km

**Open:** 1st March-31st October

### Mrs Gretta Gleeson-O'Byrne
**WILLOW LODGE**
**Convent Garden, Kenmare, Co Kerry**

**Kenmare**

TEL: **064 42301**
EMAIL: **willowlodgekenmare@yahoo.com**

Quietly located, 2 minutes from Town Centre. Ideal base to tour Ring of Kerry & Beara Peninsula. Full facilities and jacuzzi bath. Good Restaurants, Golf, Walking, Horse Riding & Fishing.

| | | | | | |
|---|---|---|---|---|---|
| B&B | 5 | Ensuite | €35-€42 | Dinner | - |
| B&B | - | Standard | - | Partial Board | - |
| Single Rate | | | €50-€80 | Child reduction | - |

n Kenmare

**Open:** All Year

### Mrs Bernadette Goldrick
**DRUID COTTAGE**
**Sneem Road, Kenmare, Co Kerry**

**Kenmare**

TEL: **064 41803**

19th Century Classic stone residence, luxuriously renovated without losing olde world charm. Complimentary tea/coffee. Hill walking enthusiast.

| | | | | | |
|---|---|---|---|---|---|
| B&B | 2 | Ensuite | €28-€31 | Dinner | - |
| B&B | 1 | Standard | €27.50-€28.50 | Partial Board | - |
| Single Rate | | | €38-€43.50 | Child reduction | - |

Kenmare 1km

**Open:** 1st February-30th November

**Kenmare 4km**

**Mr & Mrs Tony & Joyce Hughes**
**SHAMINIR**
**Dawros, Kenmare, Co Kerry**

### Kenmare

TEL: **064 42678**
EMAIL: **joyce@shaminir.com**
WEB: **www.shaminir.com**

Ideal base for exploring Beara Peninsular and Ring of Kerry. House 50 metres from Kenmare Bay. Walking, fishing, golf, bar/food all close by.

| B&B | 4 | Ensuite | €30-€40 | Dinner | - |
| B&B | - | Standard | | Partial Board | - |
| Single Rate | | | €40-€45 | Child reduction | **50%** |

**Open:** 1st January-31st December

---

**Kenmare 6km**

**Mrs Maureen McCarthy**
**HARBOUR VIEW**
**Castletownbere Haven Road, Dauros, Kenmare, Co Kerry**

### Kenmare

TEL: **064 41755**   FAX: **064 42611**
EMAIL: **maureenmccarthy@eircom.net**
WEB: **www.kenmare.net/harbourviewhouse**

Award winning luxurious seashore home, panoramic views Kenmare Bay R571. AA4 ◆◆◆◆ award. Conservatory Breakfast room. Seafood. Satellite TV/Video, Trouserpress, Iron, Tea/Coffee. Jacuzzi bath.

| B&B | 4 | Ensuite | €35-€40 | Dinner | - |
| B&B | 2 | Standard | €35-€40 | Partial Board | - |
| Single Rate | | | €50-€70 | Child reduction | **20%** |

**Open:** 1st April-31st October

---

**In Kenmare**

**Ms Helen McGonigle**
**OLDCHURCH HOUSE**
**Killowen, Kenmare, Co Kerry**

### Kenmare

TEL: **064 42054**
EMAIL: **oldchurchkenmare@hotmail.com**
WEB: **www.kenmare.com/oldchurch**

Luxury house situated on Kenmare-Cork road R569. Ideal place to relax surrounded by mountains, golf course and old church ruin. Excellent Breakfast.

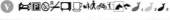

| B&B | 3 | Ensuite | €27.50-€35 | Dinner | - |
| B&B | - | Standard | - | Partial Board | - |
| Single Rate | | | - | Child reduction | **25%** |

**Open:** 1st February-5th October

---

**Kenmare 8km**

**Mrs Lisa O'Brien**
**THE FORD**
**Glengarriff Road, Bonane, Kenmare, Co Kerry**

### Kenmare

TEL: **064 42431**
EMAIL: **sobrien1@eircom.net**
WEB: **www.neidin.net/ford**

Nestled in Caha mountains off N71. Bank of Sheen river. Unique family home. Hospitality assured. Base for Ring of Kerry, Beara Peninsula. Walkers haven.

| B&B | 3 | Ensuite | €30-€32 | Dinner | - |
| B&B | - | Standard | | Partial Board | - |
| Single Rate | | | €48-€48 | Child reduction | **25%** |

**Open:** 17th March-17th October

---

**In Kenmare**

**Julia O'Connor**
**AN BRUACHAN**
**Killarney Road, Kenmare, Co Kerry**

### Kenmare

TEL: **064 41682**   FAX: **064 41682**
EMAIL: **bruachan@iol.ie**
WEB: **www.kenmare.com**

Friendly home in 1 acre of mature gardens on N71. Own riverfront very quiet 3 minutes drive to town centre. Hill walking experience breakfast choice.

| B&B | 4 | Ensuite | €30-€32.50 | Dinner | - |
| B&B | - | Standard | - | Partial Board | - |
| Single Rate | | | €40-€43.50 | Child reduction | - |

**Open:** 1st June-31st October

**Anne O'Doherty**
BRANDYLOCHS
**Lodge Wood, Kenmare,
Co Kerry**

### Kenmare

TEL: **064 42147**
EMAIL: **brandylochs@eircom.net**
WEB: **www.kenmare.com/brandylochs**

Spacious quality country house overlooking 18 hole Golf club with scenic mountain backdrop - 2 minutes walk to award winning quality Restaurants in town of Kenmare.

| B&B | 4 | Ensuite | €30-€40 | Dinner | - |
| B&B | - | Standard | - | Partial Board | - |
| Single Rate | | | - | Child reduction | - |

Kenmare

**Open:** 1st March-15th November

---

**Mrs Lynne O'Donnell**
O'DONNELLS OF ASHGROVE
**Ashgrove, Kenmare, Co Kerry**

### Kenmare

TEL: **064 41228**   FAX: **064 41228**
EMAIL: **odonnellsofashgrove@hotmail.com**

Beautiful home in peaceful setting. Many antiques. Mature garden. Guests welcomed as friends. German spoken. Angling enthusiast. Recommended Dillard/Causin.

| B&B | 3 | Ensuite | €30-€34 | Dinner | - |
| B&B | 1 | Standard | €28-€32 | Partial Board | - |
| Single Rate | | | €40-€46 | Child reduction | - |

enmare 5km

**Open:** 1st April-31st October

---

**Eilish & Pat O'Shea**
THE CAHA'S
**Hospital Road, Kenmare,
Co Kerry**

### Kenmare

TEL: **064 41271**   FAX: **064 41271**
EMAIL: **osheacahas@eircom.net**
WEB: **www.kenmare.com/caha**

Spacious family home in peaceful location with landscaped garden. Extensive Breakfast menu. Just 7 minutes walk from Town past Catholic Church.

| B&B | 4 | Ensuite | €28-€34 | Dinner | - |
| B&B | - | Standard | - | Partial Board | - |
| Single Rate | | | - | Child reduction | 25% |

Kenmare

**Open:** 1st April-1st November

---

**Therese O'Shea**
O'SHEAS CEOL NA HABHANN
**Killarney Road, Kenmare,
Co Kerry**

### Kenmare

TEL: **064 41498**
EMAIL: **osheasfarmhouse@eircom.net**
WEB: **www.osheasceolnahabhann.com**

Friendly home, excellent spacious accommodation. Breakfast menu, quiet scenic location on the N71 Killarney Road. TV, Tea/Coffee.  Large triple / family rooms.

| B&B | 4 | Ensuite | €30-€32.50 | Dinner | - |
| B&B | 1 | Standard | €29-€31 | Partial Board | - |
| Single Rate | | | €40-€48 | Child reduction | 33.3% |

enmare 1km

**Open:** 1st February-10th November

---

**Bernie O'Sullivan**
CARRIGMORE HOUSE
**Hospital Road, Kenmare,
Co Kerry**

### Kenmare

TEL: **064 41563**

Comfortable home, spacious rooms. Scenic balcony views. Semi orthopaedic beds, Hairdryers. 5 minutes walk Town Centre. Location haven of rest. Non smoking.

| B&B | 3 | Ensuite | €28-€32.50 | Dinner | - |
| B&B | - | Standard | - | Partial Board | - |
| Single Rate | | | - | Child reduction | 25% |

Kenmare

**Open:** 1st February-31st October

---

**Fiona & John O'Sullivan**
MYLESTONE HOUSE
Killowen Road, Kenmare,
Co Kerry

### Kenmare

TEL: **064 41753**
EMAIL: **mylestonehouse@eircom.net**
WEB: **www.kenmare.com/mylestone**

Excellent spacious accommodation, friendly hospitality. Extensive Breakfast menu. Opposite Golf Course. Ideal Touring base, Ring of Kerry/ Beara Peninsula.

| B&B | 5 | Ensuite | €32-€35 | Dinner | - |
| B&B | - | Standard | | Partial Board | - |
| Single Rate | | | €42-€48 | Child reduction | 25% |

In Kenmare

**Open:** 1st March-10th November

---

**Mrs Marian O'Sullivan**
OAKFIELD
Castletownberehaven Rd R571,
Dauros, Kenmare, Co Kerry

### Kenmare

TEL: **064 41262**   FAX: **064 42888**
EMAIL: **oakfield@eircom.net**
WEB: **www.oakfield-kenmare.com**

Luxury country home, spacious warm bedrooms. Situated 5 mins drive on R571, with spectacular views of the bay and mountains. Breakfast choice. Home from home.

| B&B | 4 | Ensuite | €32-€35 | Dinner | - |
| B&B | 1 | Standard | €32-€35 | Partial Board | €340 |
| Single Rate | | | €50-€50 | Child reduction | 25% |

Kenmare 5km

**Open:** 1st April-15th October

---

**Mrs Sheila O'Sullivan**
MOUNTAIN VIEW
Healy Pass Road, Lauragh,
Near Kenmare, Co Kerry

### Kenmare Lauragh

TEL: **064 83143**
EMAIL: **mountainview@eircom.net**
WEB: **www.oldstonecottage.com**

Take R571 towards Beara for 25 mins at Lauragh Cross take left and follow signs. 3 day special P.B. €135 seafood speciality. Bring own wine.

| B&B | 2 | Ensuite | €28-€31 | Dinner | €20-€22 |
| B&B | 1 | Standard | €28-€28.50 | Partial Board | €310 |
| Single Rate | | | €38-€43.50 | Child reduction | 50% |

Lauragh 1km

**Open:** 1st March-31st October

---

**Mrs Eileen M Ryan**
RIVER MEADOWS
Sneem Road, Kenmare,
Co Kerry

### Kenmare

TEL: **064 41306**   FAX: **064 41306**
EMAIL: **rivermeadows@eircom.net**
WEB: **www.rivermeadowsbnb.com**

Enjoy breakfast in our garden room against a magnificent mountain backdrop. Uniquely rustic area close to Town. Private road leading to seashore. Off N70 Ring of Kerry road.

| B&B | 4 | Ensuite | €28-€31 | Dinner | - |
| B&B | - | Standard | - | Partial Board | - |
| Single Rate | | | €40-€43.50 | Child reduction | - |

Kenmare 2km

**Open:** 1st March-30th November

---

**Mrs Maureen Sayers**
GREENVILLE
Lansdown Lodge, Kenmare,
Co Kerry

### Kenmare

TEL: **064 41769**

Superb residence overlooking Golf course. Full central heating. Town Centre 1 mins walk. Private parking. Extensive breakfast menu. TV in rooms.

| B&B | 4 | Ensuite | €30-€40 | Dinner | - |
| B&B | - | Standard | - | Partial Board | - |
| Single Rate | | | | Child reduction | 33.3% |

In Kenmare

**Open:** 1st March-31st October

**Mrs Geraldine Topham**
GRENANE HEIGHTS
Greenane, Ring of Kerry Road,
Kenmare, Co Kerry

### Kenmare

Tel: **064 41760**  Fax: **064 41760**
Email: **topham@iol.ie**
Web: **www.grenaneheights.com**

Open-planned, spacious home, pine interior. Spectacular views of Kenmare Bay & Caha Mountains. Ideal base for Ring of Kerry/Beara. Tea/Coffee, Fax/E-mail.

| B&B | 4 | Ensuite | €28.50-€31 | Dinner | - |
| B&B | 1 | Standard | €27.50-€31 | Partial Board | - |
| Single Rate | | | - | Child reduction | 33.3% |

Kenmare 5km

**Open:** 1st May-30th September

---

**Robert Phillips & Vanessa Hedger**
2 MILE LODGE
Killarney Road, Kenmare,
Co Kerry

### Kenmare

Tel: **064 42430**  Fax: **064 42913**
Email: **bobphillips@eircom.net**
Web: **www.2milelodge.com**

Enjoy warm friendly hospitality in our beautiful spacious architect designed home. Picturesque country setting. Superb base for touring Kerry.

| B&B | 4 | Ensuite | €30-€35 | Dinner | €19-€30 |
| B&B | - | Standard | - | Partial Board | - |
| Single Rate | | | €40-€50 | Child reduction | 25% |

Kenmare 3km

**Open:** All Year

---

**Alison & Andy Whelton**
SEANUA
Gortagass, Crossroads,
Kenmare, Co Kerry

### Kenmare

Tel: **064 42505**  Fax: **064 32366**
Email: **info@seanua.com**
Web: **www.seanua.com**

Old style country cottage located 3km from Kenmare, just off Kilgarven/Cork Rd (R569). Activities centre nearby. Ideal base touring, Golf, Walking, Fishing.

| B&B | 3 | Ensuite | €29-€32.50 | Dinner | - |
| B&B | - | Standard | - | Partial Board | - |
| Single Rate | | | €40-€50 | Child reduction | 33.3% |

Kenmare 3km

**Open:** 1st May-31st October

---

**Mr & Mrs Peter & Mignonne Williams**
DRIFTWOOD
Killowen, Kenmare, Co Kerry

### Kenmare

Tel: **064 89147**
Email: **driftwood-kenmare@iolfree.ie**
Web: **www.driftwoodkenmare.com**

Luxury house with natural furnishings giving a feel of open space bright and airy adjacent to golf course and 8 mins walk to town, menu available.

| B&B | 4 | Ensuite | €27.50-€40 | Dinner | - |
| B&B | - | Standard | - | Partial Board | - |
| Single Rate | | | €40-€43.50 | Child reduction | 33.3% |

In Kenmare

**Open:** 1st March-31st October

---

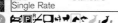

**Mrs Mary MacDonnell**
BIRCHWOOD
Churchground, Kilgarvan,
Co Kerry

### Kilgarvan

Tel: **064 85473**  Fax: **064 85570**
Email: **birchwood1@eircom.net**
Web: **www.birchwood-kilgarvan.com**

Home set in 1.5 acre garden in peaceful natural surroundings off R569. AA ◆◆◆◆ Approved. Ideal for touring Ring of Kerry/Beara. Golf, Fishing arranged.

| B&B | 5 | Ensuite | €27.50-€31 | Dinner | €22-€22 |
| B&B | - | Standard | - | Partial Board | - |
| Single Rate | | | €40-€43.50 | Child reduction | 50% |

Kilgarvan 1km

**Open:** 1st January-31st December

**Kilgarvan**

Valerie O'Connor
**ARDTULLY HOUSE**
Kilgarvan, Co Kerry

Tel: **064 85518**   Fax: **064 85518**
Email: **ardtullyhouse1@eircom.net**
Web: **www.kilgarvan.com**

Luxurious family run country home peaceful location on the R569 with beautiful mountains views. Walking distance from Roughty River, home baking. Ideal for touring Ring of Kerry/Beara.

| B&B | 3 | Ensuite | €27.50-€31 | Dinner | €25-€25 |
|---|---|---|---|---|---|
| B&B | - | Standard | | Partial Board | |
| Single Rate | | | €40-€43.50 | Child reduction | 33.3% |

Kilgarvan 2km   **Open:** 8th January-21st December

---

**Killarney Tralee Road**

Mrs Delia Ruth Adams
**BRIDGE HOUSE**
Coolgarrive, Tralee Road,
Killarney, Co Kerry

Tel: **064 31425**

200 metres off Killarney-Limerick road. All credit cards accepted and vouchers. Riding Stables and Golf Course nearby. Golfers welcome.

| B&B | 3 | Ensuite | €30-€31 | Dinner | - |
|---|---|---|---|---|---|
| B&B | - | Standard | - | Partial Board | - |
| Single Rate | | | €40-€43.50 | Child reduction | - |

Killarney 2km   **Open:** 14th May-14th September

---

**Killarney**

Mary Ahern-Nolan
**WINDWAY HOUSE**
New Road, Killarney, Co Kerry

Tel: **064 32835**   Fax: **064 37887**
Email: **windwayhouse@eircom.net**
Web: **www.windwayhouse.com**

This modern home is nestled along a quiet tree-lined avenue in the heart of Killarney 3 minute walk to town centre. Recommended by all best guide books.

| B&B | 6 | Ensuite | €30-€37.50 | Dinner | - |
|---|---|---|---|---|---|
| B&B | - | Standard | | Partial Board | - |
| Single Rate | | | €45-€55 | Child reduction | - |

In Killarney   **Open:** All Year Except Christmas

---

**Killarney Gap of Dunloe**

Mrs Margaret Blake
**CHARLWOOD TOMIES**
Gap of Dunloe, Beaufort,
Killarney, Co Kerry

Tel: **064 44117**

Just off Gap of Dunloe Road Lake District- Fishing, Golf, Horse Riding, Scenic woodland and Hill walks. Tours Dingle, Ring of Kerry. Restaurant, Music 2km.

| B&B | 2 | Ensuite | €27.50-€31 | Dinner | - |
|---|---|---|---|---|---|
| B&B | 1 | Standard | €25.50-€28.50 | Partial Board | - |
| Single Rate | | | €38-€43.50 | Child reduction | 25% |

Killarney 8km   **Open:** 17th March-31st October

---

**Killarney Town**

Kathy Brosnan
**APPLECROFT HOUSE**
Woodlawn Road, Killarney,
Co Kerry

Tel: **064 32782**
Email: **applecroft@eircom.net**
Web: **http://homepage.eircom.net/~applecroft/**

Luxury accommodation off N71, peaceful country setting. 12 min walk Killarney Town. Winner of Killarney Looking Good Competition. AA -◆◆◆◆

| B&B | 5 | Ensuite | €30-€35 | Dinner | - |
|---|---|---|---|---|---|
| B&B | - | Standard | - | Partial Board | - |
| Single Rate | | | €40-€50 | Child reduction | 50% |

Killarney 1km   **Open:** 1st February-1st December

**In Killarney**

**Padraig & Margaret Brosnan**
CLOGHROE
14 Scrahan Court, Killarney,
Co Kerry

Tel: **064 34818**
Email: **cloghroe@gofree.indigo.ie**
Web: **www.geocities.com/cloghroebandb**

Enjoy warm friendly hospitality in our beautiful home. Quiet location 2 mins walk Town/Bus/Rail.
Near Ross Castle/National Park/Lakes/Golf. Tours arranged.

| B&B | 3 | Ensuite | €28-€33 | Dinner | - |
|------|---|----------|---------|--------|---|
| B&B | - | Standard | - | Partial Board | - |
| Single Rate | | | €40-€44 | Child reduction | **33.3%** |

**Open:** 1st March-31st October

---

**Killarney 5km**

**Mrs Colleen Burke**
BEENOSKEE
Tralee Rd, Killarney, Co Kerry

Tel: **064 32435**  Fax: **064 32435**
Email: **burkemc@eircom.net**
Web: **www.geocities.com/beenoskeebandb**

Country home on Limerick Rd/N22. Twice National Award of Excellence winner. All rooms
TV/Video, Hairdryer, Tea/Coffee. Credit Cards accepted. Landscaped garden. Home Baking.

| B&B | 4 | Ensuite | €28-€31 | Dinner | €19-€19 |
|------|---|----------|---------|--------|---------|
| B&B | - | Standard | - | Partial Board | - |
| Single Rate | | | €40-€43.50 | Child reduction | **50%** |

**Open:** 1st April-31st October

---

**Killarney 2km**

**Mrs Veronica Caesar**
CAESAR'S
Lissyvigeen, Cork Road,
Killarney, Co Kerry

Tel: **064 31821**  Fax: **064 31821**

Picturesque residence on N22. Superb location. Chosen and recommended by Irish Times Special
Travel Correspondent on South West Ireland.

| B&B | 4 | Ensuite | €30-€34 | Dinner | - |
|------|---|----------|---------|--------|---|
| B&B | - | Standard | - | Partial Board | - |
| Single Rate | | | €40-€43 | Child reduction | **25%** |

**Open:** 1st June-30th September

---

**In Killarney**

**Mrs Eileen Carroll**
THE MOUNTAIN DEW
3 Ross Road, Killarney,
Co Kerry

Tel: **064 33892**  Fax: **064 31332**
Email: **mountain.dew@oceanfree.net**

Modern house in quiet area, 2 mins walk Town, Rail/Bus. Private Car Park. Tours arranged.
Breakfast menu. In Killarney. Low season reductions

| B&B | 6 | Ensuite | €27.50-€33 | Dinner | - |
|------|---|----------|---------|--------|---|
| B&B | - | Standard | - | Partial Board | - |
| Single Rate | | | €40-€50 | Child reduction | **50%** |

**Open:** All Year

---

**Killarney 3km**

**Mrs Marie Carroll**
CEDAR HOUSE
Loreto Road,
(off Muckross Rd), Killarney,
Co Kerry

Tel: **064 32342**  Fax: **064 35156**
Email: **info@cedar-bnb.com**
Web: **www.cedar-bnb.com**

House adjacent to Lakes, Gleneagle Complex, National Event centre, Ross Golf Club. Spacious
bedrooms with Hairdryers and Televisions. Tea facilities in rooms. Tours arranged.

| B&B | 3 | Ensuite | €35-€35 | Dinner | - |
|------|---|----------|---------|--------|---|
| B&B | - | Standard | - | Partial Board | - |
| Single Rate | | | - | Child reduction | - |

**Open:** 31st March-31st October

**Mrs Eileen Casey**
CASEYS HOMEDALE
Dunrine, Tralee Road, Killarney,
Co Kerry

### Killarney

TEL: **064 33855**
EMAIL: **homedale@eircom.net**
WEB: **homepage.eircom.net/~homedale**

Friendly welcome assured, Family run. Ground floor ensuite bedrooms. Panoramic views. Complimentary Tea/Coffee. On N22. Ideal touring base. All tours arranged.

| B&B | 3 | Ensuite | €28.50-€32.50 | Dinner | - |
| B&B | - | Standard | - | Partial Board | - |
| Single Rate | | | €43.50 | Child reduction | 50% |

Killarney 5km        **Open:** 1st April-31st October

---

**Margaret Casey**
MAGGIE O'S
14 Muckross View, Dromhale,
Killarney, Co Kerry

### Killarney

TEL: **064 37229** FAX: **064 37229**
EMAIL: **maggieos14@eircom.net**

Relax in the cosy, friendly atmosphere of Maggieo's, with breathtaking views of Killarney's Lakes/Mts/National Park. Quiet area, only 5 mins walk town centre. 24hr taxi service.

| B&B | 3 | Ensuite | €30-€35 | Dinner | - |
| B&B | - | Standard | - | Partial Board | - |
| Single Rate | | | | Child reduction | - |

In Killarney        **Open:** All Year

---

**Mrs Mary Casey**
DIRREEN HOUSE
Tralee/Limerick Road N22,
Killarney, Co Kerry

### Killarney Tralee Road

TEL: **064 31676** FAX: **064 31676**
EMAIL: **dirreenhouse@eircom.net**
WEB: **homepage.eircom.net/~dirreenhouse**

Comfortable ground floor bedrooms. TV, Tea making facilities. Breakfast menu, Golf/Tours arranged. Coach pick up/drop off from premises. Expanding views of Countryside and Mountains.

| B&B | 4 | Ensuite | €27.50-€31 | Dinner | €19-€25 |
| B&B | - | Standard | - | Partial Board | - |
| Single Rate | | | €40-€43.50 | Child reduction | - |

Killarney 5km        **Open:** 15th March-1st November

---

**Liam & Anne Chute**
CHUTEHALL
Lower Park Road, Killarney,
Co Kerry

### Killarney Town

TEL: **064 37177** FAX: **064 37178**
EMAIL: **chutehall@eircom.net**
WEB: **www.killarneyaccommodation.net**

New quality accommodation, quiet location. 3 min walk Town Centre, Rail, Bus. Spacious rooms, bath/pressurised shower. Private Car Park. All Tours arranged. Lakes nearby.

| B&B | 5 | Ensuite | €33-€40 | Dinner | - |
| B&B | - | Standard | - | Partial Board | - |
| Single Rate | | | - | Child reduction | - |

In Killarney    **Open:** 1st May-31st October

---

**Mrs Peggy Coffey**
HOLLY GROVE
Glencar Road, Gap of Dunloe,
Beaufort, Killarney, Co Kerry

### Killarney Gap of Dunloe

TEL: **064 44326** FAX: **064 44326**
EMAIL: **dunloe@eircom.net**
WEB: **www.stayathollygrove.com**

Killorglin N72 road. Spacious bedrooms, 1 with 3 beds. Tea/Coffee facilities, Electric blankets. Pony riding, Golf , Fishing, Climbing, Music nearby. Ideal for touring Kerry Ring/Dingle.

| B&B | 3 | Ensuite | €27.50-€31 | Dinner | €25-€25 |
| B&B | 1 | Standard | €25.50-€28.50 | Partial Board | - |
| Single Rate | | | €38-€43.50 | Child reduction | 50% |

Killarney 9km    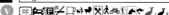    **Open:** 1st March-31st October

**Mary & Avril Connell**
ST ANTHONY'S LODGE
Cork Road, Killarney, Co Kerry

### Killarney

Tel: **064 31534**
Email: **info@best-bb-killarney.com**
Web: **www.best-bb-killarney.com**

Uniquely decorated comfortable home on edge of town. Frommer recommended since 1966.
Ensuite rooms TV, Tea/Coffee, Hairdryers, Private Parking, Breakfast Menu.

| B&B | 4 | Ensuite | €30-€36.50 | Dinner | - |
| B&B | - | Standard | - | Partial Board | - |
| Single Rate | | | €40-€45 | Child reduction | 50% |

In Killarney        **Open:** All Year

---

**Mrs Eileen Cremin**
MOUNTAIN VIEW
Gap of Dunloe, Beaufort,
Co Kerry

### Killarney Gap of Dunloe

Tel: **064 44212**

Scenic area. 4km west of Killarney on N72. Turn left for Gap of Dunloe. Continue for 4km more.
Golf, Lakes, Hill walking, Horse riding, Restaurant, Music locally.

| B&B | 2 | Ensuite | €27.50-€31 | Dinner | - |
| B&B | 1 | Standard | €25.50-€28.50 | Partial Board | - |
| Single Rate | | | €38-€43.50 | Child reduction | 50% |

Killarney 8km    **Open:** 1st May-30th September

---

**Mrs Betty Cronin**
DUNROSS HOUSE
Tralee Road, Killarney, Co Kerry

### Killarney Tralee Road

Tel: **064 36322**
Email: **dunrosshouse@eircom.net**

Luxurious home (N22) Kerry Airport 8km - all rooms TV/Tea making, Breakfast menu. Excellent
location for National Park, Ring of Kerry / Dingle. Tours arranged.

| B&B | 4 | Ensuite | €27.50-€31 | Dinner | €25-€25 |
| B&B | - | Standard | - | Partial Board | - |
| Single Rate | | | - | Child reduction | 50% |

Killarney 5km    **Open:** 30th March-31st October

---

**Mrs Lily Cronin**
CRAB TREE COTTAGE AND
GARDENS
Mangerton Road, Muckross,
Killarney, Co Kerry

### Killarney Muckross Road

Tel: **064 33169**
Email: **crabtree@eircom.net**
Web: **www.crabtreebnb.com**

Picturesque cottage in the heart of Killarney, National Park, Lakes. Award winning landscaped
gardens. Prime location for hillwalking, mountain climbing. On route of "Kerry Way"

| B&B | 3 | Ensuite | €28-€32 | Dinner | - |
| B&B | 1 | Standard | €26-€30 | Partial Board | - |
| Single Rate | | | €38-€42 | Child reduction | - |

Killarney 4km    **Open:** 20th March-30th September

---

**Mrs Noreen Cudden**
THE AMBER LANTERN
Fossa, Killarney, Co Kerry

### Killarney Fossa

Tel: **064 31921**
Email: **cudden@eircom.net**

Well appointed home with balconies, opposite Golf Club, Lakes. Ring of Kerry/Dingle road.
Horse riding, Hill walking. Tours arranged.

| B&B | 5 | Ensuite | €30-€32.50 | Dinner | - |
| B&B | 1 | Standard | €30-€30 | Partial Board | - |
| Single Rate | | | €40-€45 | Child reduction | 25% |

Killarney 2km    **Open:** 1st April-30th September

Killarney 5km

### Mrs Agnes Curran
ARBOUR VILLA
Golf Course Road, Fossa,
Killarney, Co Kerry

TEL: **064 44334**
EMAIL: **agnescurran@eircom.net**

Ring Kerry/Golf Course road, near Lakes, Gap of Dunloe, Fishing, Horse Riding, Golf 2 km. Ideal Walkers/Climbers. Tours arranged.

| B&B | 4 | Ensuite | €28-€38 | Dinner | €30 |
| B&B | - | Standard | | Partial Board | |
| Single Rate | | | €40-€45 | Child reduction | 50% |

**Open:** 1st May-30th September

---

Killarney 3km

### Mrs K Davies
HAVENS REST
Tralee Road N22, Killarney,
Co Kerry

TEL: **064 32733**  FAX: **064 32237**
EMAIL: **havensrest@oceanfree.net**
WEB: **gofree.indigo.ie/~haverest**

Lake Zurich Travel (USA) recommended - Luxury accommodation with antique furniture. Highly recommended. Real Irish welcome. On N22, 3 mins from Town Centre.

| B&B | 3 | Ensuite | €30-€35 | Dinner | - |
| B&B | - | Standard | - | Partial Board | - |
| Single Rate | | | €40-€50 | Child reduction | 33.3% |

**Open:** 31st March-31st October

---

Killarney 1km

### Mrs Catherine Dero-Spillane
BEAUTY'S HOME
Cleeney, Tralee Road, Killarney,
Co Kerry

TEL: **064 31836/31251**  FAX: **064 34077**
EMAIL: **deroscoachtours@eircom.net**
WEB: **www.beautyshome.com**

Luxurious Bungalow. TV, Video, Movie Channel, Tea/Coffee Facilities. Orthopaedic Beds. Free collection Rail/Bus Station.. 1km from Killarney National Park.  Off season special rates.

| B&B | 2 | Ensuite | €27.50-€40 | Dinner | - |
| B&B | 2 | Standard | €25.50-€35 | Partial Board | - |
| Single Rate | | | €38-€55 | Child reduction | 33.3% |

**Open:** 5th January-31st December

---

Killarney 3km

### Mrs Deborah Devane
GLENMILL HOUSE
Nunstown, Aghadoe, Killarney,
Co Kerry

TEL: **064 34391**
EMAIL: **glenmillhouse@eircom.net**
WEB: **www.kerry-insight.com/glenmill/**

Luxurious home with panoramic views Lakes, Golf Course, McGillicuddy Reeks, National Park. Orthopaedic beds. Airport 15km. Adjacent to Aghadoe Heights Hotel. Tours arranged.

| B&B | 4 | Ensuite | €28-€31 | Dinner | - |
| B&B | - | Standard | | Partial Board | - |
| Single Rate | | | €40-€44 | Child reduction | 33.3% |

**Open:** 1st March-30th September

---

### Mrs Mary Devane
REEKS VIEW
Spa, Killarney, Co Kerry

TEL: **064 33910**  FAX: **064 33910**
EMAIL: **devane@eircom.net**
WEB: **www.reeksview.com**

Luxurious bungalow off Killarney/Cork road. Signposted at Parkroad roundabout. N22 Cork/Killarney road, take industrial estate exit off roundabout.

| B&B | 5 | Ensuite | €27.50-€32 | Dinner | --€20 |
| B&B | - | Standard | - | Partial Board | €325 |
| Single Rate | | | €40-€43.50 | Child reduction | 50% |

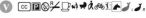

Killarney 2km

**Open:** 1st March-1st November

**Killarney 2km**

**Mrs Noreen Dineen**
MANOR HOUSE
18 Whitebridge Manor,
Ballycasheen, Killarney,
Co Kerry

### Killarney Cork Road

TEL: **064 32716**   FAX: **064 32716**

Modern Georgian Style house in peaceful area. Fishing, Golfing, Swimming. National Park and Lakes, Cabaret and Local Tours arranged.

| B&B | 4 | Ensuite | €27.50-€32 | Dinner | - |
| B&B | - | Standard | - | Partial Board | - |
| Single Rate | | | €40-€43.50 | Child reduction | - |

**Open:** 1st May-30th September

**In Killarney**

**Mrs Aileen Doherty**
BEECHWOOD HOUSE
Cahernane Meadows,
Muckross Road, Killarney,
Co Kerry

### Killarney Muckross Road

TEL: **064 34606**
EMAIL: **jdoh1@gofree.indigo.ie**

Luxurious home, 5 mins Town. Near Muckross House, National Park, Lakes, Mountains, Leisure Centre, Gleneagle/Dromhall Hotels. N71 Muckross Rd from Town, right at Holiday Inn then 2nd right.

| B&B | 3 | Ensuite | €30-€35 | Dinner | - |
| B&B | - | Standard | - | Partial Board | - |
| Single Rate | | | €50-€50 | Child reduction | 25% |

**Open:** 1st April-30th September

**Killorglin 8km**

**Mrs Tess Doona**
HOLLYBOUGH HOUSE
Cappagh, Kilgobnet, Beaufort,
Co Kerry

### Killarney Beaufort

TEL: **064 44255**
EMAIL: **hollyboughhouse@eircom.net**
WEB: **homepage.eircom.net/~hollyboughhouse**

Quiet scenic location central for Ring of Kerry, near Ireland's highest and most majestic mountains, The McGillycuddy Reeks. Visa accepted.

| B&B | 3 | Ensuite | €27.50-€31 | Dinner | - |
| B&B | 2 | Standard | €25.50-€28.50 | Partial Board | - |
| Single Rate | | | €38-€43.50 | Child reduction | 25% |

**Open:** 25th March-31st October

**In Killarney**

**Mrs Greta Doyle**
ALGRET HOUSE
80 Countess Grove,
Off Countess Rd, Killarney,
Co Kerry

### Killarney Countess Road

TEL: **064 32337**   FAX: **064 30936**
EMAIL: **gretad@gofree.indigo.ie**
WEB: **www.algret.com**

Friendly home, quiet area. Town 5 min walk. All rooms have multi-channel TV, Tea/Coffee facilities and Hairdryers. Breakfast menu. N71 Muckross road, 1st left, 2nd right.

| B&B | 6 | Ensuite | €28-€36 | Dinner | - |
| B&B | - | Standard | - | Partial Board | - |
| Single Rate | | | €40-€50 | Child reduction | 25% |

**Open:** 1st February-31st October

**In Killarney**

**Mary Theresa & Derry Doyle**
ELYOD HOUSE
Ross Road, Killarney, Co Kerry

### Killarney Town

TEL: **064 36544**   FAX: **064 36544**
EMAIL: **elyod@eircom.net**
WEB: **www.elyodhouse.ie**

Luxurious friendly home situated verge of National Park, Golf, Fishing, Horse-riding nearby. Tours arranged. Breakfast menu. Tea/Coffee facilities available.

| B&B | 6 | Ensuite | €30-€35 | Dinner | - |
| B&B | - | Standard | - | Partial Board | - |
| Single Rate | | | €50-€55 | Child reduction | - |

**Open:** 1st February-15th December

**Killarney 5km**

### Mrs Julia Egan
ASHBROOK
Tralee Road, Killarney, Co Kerry

**Killarney Tralee Road**

Tel: **064 22507**
Email: **juliaegan@eircom.net**

Luxury accomodation with spacious ensuite bedrooms. Home baking and orthopaedic beds. Excellent location on N22. 5 mins drive to Killarney, 10 mins drive to Kerry Airport.

| | | | | | |
|---|---|---|---|---|---|
| B&B | 4 | Ensuite | €27.50-€31 | Dinner | €19-€19 |
| B&B | - | Standard | - | Partial Board | |
| Single Rate | | | €40-€43.50 | Child reduction | 50% |

**Open:** 1st January-31st December

---

**Killarney 4km**

### Mrs Sheila Falvey
FALSHEA HOUSE
Tralee Road, Killarney, Co Kerry

**Killarney Tralee Road**

Tel: **064 34871**
Email: **stay@falsheahouse.com**
Web: **www.falsheahouse.com**

Purpose built luxury home in scenic peaceful surroundings. All rooms with TV, Tea/Coffee making facilities, Hairdryers. National Award of Excellence Winner. Tours arranged.

| | | | | | |
|---|---|---|---|---|---|
| B&B | 4 | Ensuite | €32-€34 | Dinner | - |
| B&B | - | Standard | - | Partial Board | |
| Single Rate | | | €42-€45 | Child reduction | 50% |

**Open:** 8th January-23rd December

---

**Killarney 8km**

### Mrs Theresa Ferris
WAYSIDE
Gap of Dunloe, Killarney, Co Kerry

**Killarney Gap of Dunloe**

Tel: **064 44284**   Fax: **064 44284**
Email: **www.waysideguesthouse@hotmail.com**
Web: **http://www.dirl.com/kerry/wayside.htm**

Peaceful lake/mountain district. Restaurants, Irish music & dancing 1km. Horse riding, Fishing & Golf Courses 1km. Dingle & Ring of Kerry 2km. Breakfast Menu. Off R562.

| | | | | | |
|---|---|---|---|---|---|
| B&B | 2 | Ensuite | €30-€31 | Dinner | - |
| B&B | 2 | Standard | €27.50-€30 | Partial Board | - |
| Single Rate | | | €40-€43.50 | Child reduction | 50% |

**Open:** All Year Except Christmas

---

### Carmel Fitzgerald
ACARA
10 St Anne's Road, Killarney, Co Kerry

**Killarney**

Tel: **064 35415**
Email: **carmelfitzgerald@eircom.net**

Excellent quiet location 2 mins walk to town centre, bus/train station. 10 min walk to national event centre/national park. Tours/golf tees arranged.

| | | | | | |
|---|---|---|---|---|---|
| B&B | 3 | Ensuite | €25-€40 | Dinner | - |
| B&B | 1 | Standard | €25-€40 | Partial Board | - |
| Single Rate | | | €40-€50 | Child reduction | 25% |

**In Killarney**

**Open:** All Year

---

**Killarney 6km**

### Mrs Anne Fleming
GLENDALE HOUSE
Dromadeesirt, Tralee Road, Killarney, Co Kerry

**Killarney Tralee Road**

Tel: **064 32152/34952**   Fax: **064 32152**
Email: **gdalehse@eircom.net**
Web: **www.glendalehse.com**

Luxurious house on Tralee road (N22). Killarney 6km. Kerry Airport 5 mins drive. All rooms with TV, Tea/Coffee making facilities, Hairdryers. Ground floor bedrooms. Tours arranged.

| | | | | | |
|---|---|---|---|---|---|
| B&B | 6 | Ensuite | €27.50-€31 | Dinner | - |
| B&B | - | Standard | - | Partial Board | - |
| Single Rate | | | €40-€43.50 | Child reduction | 33.3% |

**Open:** 1st March-1st November

**Mrs Maureen Fleming**
SHRAHEEN HOUSE
Ballycasheen (off N22),
Killarney, Co Kerry

### Killarney Cork Road

TEL: **064 31286/37959**   FAX: **064 37959**
EMAIL: **info@shraheenhouse.com**
WEB: **www.shraheenhouse.com**

Highly recommended home set in 2.5 acres. Home baking. Satellite T.V.. Tea/Coffee, hairdryers. Breakfast menu. AA ◆◆◆◆. Tours arranged. Off N22 at Whitebridge sign.

| B&B | 6 | Ensuite | €30-€35 | Dinner | - |
|-----|---|---------|---------|--------|---|
| B&B | - | Standard | - | Partial Board | - |
| Single Rate | | | €40-€55 | Child reduction | 33.3% |

Killarney 2km    **Open:** 1st February-30th November

**Mrs Moira Gorman**
GORMAN'S
Tralee Road, Killarney, Co Kerry

### Killarney Tralee Road

TEL: **064 33149**   FAX: **064 33149**
EMAIL: **mgormans@eircom.net**
WEB: **homepage.eircom.net/~gormanscountryhome**

No smoking house, smoking room available. Former B.F. garden prize winners. Low season reductions. Afternoon tea free on arrival. Visa & Vouchers welcome.

| B&B | 4 | Ensuite | €31-€32 | Dinner | €19-€19.99 |
|-----|---|---------|---------|--------|------------|
| B&B | - | Standard | - | Partial Board | €294 |
| Single Rate | | | €40-€45 | Child reduction | 33.3% |

Killarney 5km    **Open:** 1st January-23rd December

**Louise Griffin**
CHELMSFORD HOUSE
Muckross View,
Countess Grove, Killarney,
Co Kerry

### Killarney

TEL: **064 36402**   FAX: **064 33806**
EMAIL: **info@chelmsfordhouse.com**
WEB: **www.chelmsfordhouse.com**

Highly recommended luxurious spacious home, 5 mins walk to town. Magnificent view of Lakes & Mountains. Delicious breakfasts home made pancakes etc. Guest Lounge, open log fire. All tours arranged.

| B&B | 4 | Ensuite | €32-€36 | Dinner | - |
|-----|---|---------|---------|--------|---|
| B&B | - | Standard | - | Partial Board | - |
| Single Rate | | | | Child reduction | - |

n Killarney    **Open:** 1st February-1st December

**Mary & Pat Hayes**
PINE CREST
Woodlawn Road, Killarney,
Co Kerry

### Killarney Muckross Road

TEL: **064 31721**

Luxurious bungalow in scenic area, convenient to Lakes, National Park, Golf Courses, Airport, Ring of Kerry, Dingle. 1km from Gleneagle National Events Centre.

| B&B | 6 | Ensuite | €27.50-€35 | Dinner | - |
|-----|---|---------|------------|--------|---|
| B&B | - | Standard | - | Partial Board | - |
| Single Rate | | | €38-€41 | Child reduction | 50% |

Killarney 1km    **Open:** 1st January-31st December

**Catherine Howe**
DUN-A-RI HOUSE
Ross Road, Killarney, Co Kerry

### Killarney Ross Road

TEL: **064 36629**
EMAIL: **dunari@eircom.net**

Located in scenic peaceful area. Opposite Ross Castle Holiday Homes adjacent to Ross Golf Club, National Park. Breakfast Menu, Hairdryers.

| B&B | 4 | Ensuite | €28-€33 | Dinner | - |
|-----|---|---------|---------|--------|---|
| B&B | - | Standard | - | Partial Board | - |
| Single Rate | | | €44-€48 | Child reduction | - |

n Killarney    **Open:** All Year Except Christmas

Killarney 2km

**Mr Tom Kearney**
CILLCEARN HOUSE
Ballycasheen Road, Killarney,
Co Kerry

## Killarney Cork Road

Tel: **064 35670**  Fax: **064 34127**
Email: **info@cillcearn.com**
Web: **www.cillcearn.com**

Award winning luxurious home off N22, set in picturesque surroundings. Forest and river walks. Warm homely atmosphere, cable T.V lounge. Golf locally. Tours arranged.

| B&B | 5 | Ensuite | €30-€35 | Dinner | - |
| B&B | - | Standard | - | Partial Board | - |
| Single Rate | | | - | Child reduction | 33.3% |

**Open:** 1st January-31st December

---

Killarney 1km

**Mrs Nora Kelliher**
HAZELWOOD
Park Rd Upper, Ballyspillane,
Killarney, Co Kerry

## Killarney Cork Road

Tel: **064 34363**  Fax: **064 34335**
Email: **hazelwood_kelliher@yahoo.com**

Comfortable bungalow, 300m from Park Road roundabout on N22, walking distance from Town. Ideal touring base. Refreshments available. Tours arranged.

| B&B | 6 | Ensuite | €28-€32.50 | Dinner | €20 |
| B&B | - | Standard | - | Partial Board | - |
| Single Rate | | | €40-€43.50 | Child reduction | 25% |

**Open:** 15th March-1st November

---

In Killarney

**Sean & Carol Landers**
MARIAN HOUSE
Woodlawn, Muckross Road,
Killarney, Co Kerry

## Killarney Muckross Road

Tel: **064 31275**  Fax: **064 31275**
Email: **marianguests@eircom.net**

Friendly home close to town centre, Gleneagle Hotel, National Park, Lakes. Ideal base for touring south west, Golfing. Quiet area. Private Parking.

| B&B | 6 | Ensuite | €27.50-€35 | Dinner | - |
| B&B | - | Standard | - | Partial Board | - |
| Single Rate | | | €40-€45 | Child reduction | 25% |

**Open:** 15th January-15th December

---

Killarney 3km

**William & Anne Leahy**
AVONDALE HOUSE
Tralee Road, Killarney, Co Kerry

## Killarney Tralee Road

Tel: **064 35579**  Fax: **064 35197**
Email: **avondalehouse@eircom.net**
Web: **www.avondale-house.com**

Modern family run home. Large bedrooms, Scenic views, TV, Tea facilities, Hairdryers, Electric blankets. Breakfast menu. Kerry Airport 10 mins drive.

| B&B | 5 | Ensuite | €30-€34 | Dinner | - |
| B&B | - | Standard | - | Partial Board | - |
| Single Rate | | | €42-€46 | Child reduction | 50% |

**Open:** 1st February-30th November

---

In Killarney

**Siobhan Leen**
LEENS
22 Marian Terrace, Killarney,
Co Kerry

## Killarney Town

Tel: **064 32819**
Email: **siobhanleen@eircom.net**
Web: **www.stayatleens.com**

Modern house in residential area. At Lewis Rd go straight at roundabout, take 1st left, sign for house on right.

| B&B | 4 | Ensuite | €28-€35 | Dinner | - |
| B&B | - | Standard | - | Partial Board | - |
| Single Rate | | | €40-€45 | Child reduction | 25% |

**Open:** All Year

In Killarney

**Ms Pauline Lyne**
PARKFIELD HOUSE
**Park Road, Killarney, Co Kerry**

### Killarney Town

TEL: **064 37022**   FAX: **064 37022**
EMAIL: **paulinelyne@eircom.net**
WEB: **www.parkfieldhouse.com**

Luxurious townhouse backing on to farmland within 5 mins walking distance to Town Centre and Bus/Rail station. Spacious parking. Tours arranged.

| B&B | 6 | Ensuite | €28-€38 | Dinner | - |
|---|---|---|---|---|---|
| B&B | - | Standard | | Partial Board | - |
| Single Rate | | | €45-€55 | Child reduction | 25% |

**Open:** 1st January-31st December

---

In Killarney

**Mrs Chriss Mannix**
FLESK LODGE
**Muckross Road, Killarney, Co Kerry**

### Killarney Muckross Road

TEL: **064 32135**   FAX: **064 32135**
EMAIL: **fleskldg@gofree.indigo.ie**
WEB: **www.flesklodge.com**

Luxury bungalow walking distance from Town. Close to all amenities. Beside Gleneagle Hotel Complex. Landscaped garden.

| B&B | 6 | Ensuite | €30-€35 | Dinner | €20 |
|---|---|---|---|---|---|
| B&B | - | Standard | | Partial Board | - |
| Single Rate | | | €42-€45 | Child reduction | - |

**Open:** All Year Except Christmas

---

In Killarney

**Joan McCarthy**
THE HARP
**Muckross Road, Killarney, Co Kerry**

### Killarney

TEL: **064 31272**
EMAIL: **ourhomeinkillarney@eircom.net**
WEB: **www.kerrypages.com/theharp**

On N71 walking distance from Town. All room ensuite TV, hairdryers. Tea/Coffee facilities in Lounge. Breakfast Menu. Private Parking. Please email for web page.

| B&B | 4 | Ensuite | €28-€32 | Dinner | - |
|---|---|---|---|---|---|
| B&B | - | Standard | - | Partial Board | - |
| Single Rate | | | - | Child reduction | 50% |

**Open:** 1st January-30th December

---

**Mrs Kathleen McCarthy**
SANCTA MARIA
**53 Park Drive, Off Park Road, Killarney, Co Kerry**

### Killarney Town

TEL: **064 32447**   FAX: **064 32447**
EMAIL: **sanctamariabb@eircom.net**

Comfortable house in residential area. Walking distance of Town, close to all amenities. Private parking. Tours arranged. Complimentary tea on arrival.

| B&B | 3 | Ensuite | €30-€35 | Dinner | - |
|---|---|---|---|---|---|
| B&B | 1 | Standard | €28-€33 | Partial Board | - |
| Single Rate | | | €38-€45 | Child reduction | 25% |

**Open:** 1st January-31st December

---

In Killarney

**Mrs Peggy McCarthy**
DROMHALL HEIGHTS
**Off Countess Road, Killarney, Co Kerry**

### Killarney Countess Road

TEL: **064 32662**   FAX: **064 32662**
EMAIL: **peggymccarthy@eircom.net**
WEB: **http://homepage.eircom.net/~peggymccarthy/**

Family home, quiet private location. View mountains, Lakes. Only minutes walk to Town from Countess road through Countess Grove, to top of Hill, then left road.

| B&B | 2 | Ensuite | €28-€31 | Dinner | - |
|---|---|---|---|---|---|
| B&B | 1 | Standard | €26-€28.50 | Partial Board | - |
| Single Rate | | | €38-€43.50 | Child reduction | - |

**Open:** 1st March-30th November

**Killarney 7km**

**Mrs Betty McSweeney**
HILTON HEIGHTS
Glebe, off Tralee Road,
Killarney, Co Kerry

### Killarney Tralee Road

TEL: **064 33364**
EMAIL: **bettymcsweeney@eircom.net**
WEB: **www.hiltonheightsbnb.com**

All rooms with TV, Hairdryers, Tea/making. From Killarney take Tralee Road for 7km. Sign for Hilton Heights on left, turn right at sign. Farranfore airport 10 minutes.

| B&B | 4 | Ensuite | €27.50-€31 | Dinner | - |
|-----|---|---------|------------|--------|---|
| B&B | | Standard | | Partial Board | - |
| Single Rate | | | €40-€43.50 | Child reduction | 25% |

**Open:** 1st April-31st October

---

**In Killarney Town**

**Miss Christine McSweeney**
EMMERVILLE HOUSE
Muckross Drive,
Off Muckross Rd, Killarney,
Co Kerry

### Killarney Muckross Road

TEL: **064 33342**

Quiet private residential road, mins to town centre. Award winning comfortable home, guest lounge. Reduction low season. Close to scenic areas, nightly entertainment. Close to Bus, Rail.

| B&B | 4 | Ensuite | €30-€33 | Dinner | - |
|-----|---|---------|---------|--------|---|
| B&B | - | Standard | - | Partial Board | - |
| Single Rate | | | €40-€43.50 | Child reduction | 25% |

**Open:** All Year

---

**Killarney 5km**

**Frances Moriarty**
MORIARTY'S
Dunrine, Tralee Road, Killarney,
Co Kerry

### Killarney Tralee Road

TEL: **064 36133**   FAX: **064 36133**
EMAIL: **francesmoriarty@eircom.net**
WEB: **www.geocities.com/moriartysbandb**

Friendly home. N22 (Limerick/Tralee Rd). Convenient to Lakes, Ring of Kerry, National Park, Golf, Fishing, Riding Stables, Airport. Tours arranged.

| B&B | 4 | Ensuite | €29-€32 | Dinner | - |
|-----|---|---------|---------|--------|---|
| B&B | - | Standard | - | Partial Board | - |
| Single Rate | | | €42-€44 | Child reduction | 50% |

**Open:** 1st March-31st October

---

**Killarney 4km**

**Margaret Moriarty**
BENISKA HOUSE
Lackabane, Fossa, Killarney,
Co Kerry

### Killarney

TEL: **064 32200**   FAX: **064 32200**
EMAIL: **beniska@utvinternet.com**
WEB: **www.beniskahouse.com**

New luxurious home on Ring of Kerry/Dingle (R563) roads. Take N72 West 2.5 miles. Adjacent Killarney 3 Golf Courses and 5* Hotel Europe. Next to Pub and Restaurant.

| B&B | 4 | Ensuite | €27.50-€40 | Dinner | - |
|-----|---|---------|------------|--------|---|
| B&B | - | Standard | - | Partial Board | - |
| Single Rate | | | | Child reduction | - |

**Open:** 15th April-15th October

---

**Killarney 8km**

**Tim & Nora Moriarty**
THE PURPLE HEATHER
Glencar Rd, Gap of Dunloe,
Beaufort, Killarney, Co Kerry

### Killarney Gap of Dunloe

TEL: **064 44266**   FAX: **064 44266**
EMAIL: **purpleheather@eircom.net**
WEB: **http://homepage.eircom.net/~purpleheather**

Breakfast Conservatory panoramic view. Breakfast menu. Rooms with TV, Electric Blanket, Hairdryer, Tea/Coffee, Pool Room, Irish Music, Restaurant, Golf 1km.

| B&B | 5 | Ensuite | €28-€31 | Dinner | - |
|-----|---|---------|---------|--------|---|
| B&B | | Standard | | Partial Board | - |
| Single Rate | | | €40-€48 | Child reduction | 50% |

**Open:** 1st March-31st October

**Mrs Maura Moynihan**
KELARE LODGE
Muckross Drive,
Off Muckross Rd, Killarney,
Co Kerry

### Killarney Muckross Road

Tᴇʟ: **064 32895**

Luxury award winning home. 3 Minutes walk from Town Centre. National Park, Bus, Rail station. Quiet location off Muckross road. Tours arranged.

| B&B | 6 | Ensuite | €30-€33 | Dinner | - |
|------|---|----------|---------|--------|---|
| B&B | | Standard | - | Partial Board | - |
| Single Rate | | | - | Child reduction | - |

Killarney

**Open:** 31st March-31st October

---

**Michael & Oonagh Moynihan**
KYLEMORE
Ballydowney, Killarney,
Co Kerry

### Killarney

Tᴇʟ: **064 31771**  Fᴀx: **064 31771**
Eᴍᴀɪʟ: **kylemorehousekillarney@eircom.net**

Friendly home on route N72 (Ring of Kerry and Dingle road). Adjacent to Killarney, Golf and Fishing club, Riding stables and National Park.

| B&B | 6 | Ensuite | €27.50-€31 | Dinner | - |
|------|---|----------|------------|--------|---|
| B&B | - | Standard | - | Partial Board | - |
| Single Rate | | | €40-€43.50 | Child reduction | 50% |

llarney 1km

**Open:** 4th January-30th November

---

**Mrs Eileen Murphy**
GREEN ACRES
Fossa, Killarney, Co Kerry

### Killarney Fossa

Tᴇʟ: **064 31454**  Fᴀx: **064 31454**

Modern family home 2km from Killarney on the main Ring of Kerry road. In the midst of three famous Golf courses, Horse riding, Fishing 1km. Walks. AA listed.

| B&B | 4 | Ensuite | €30-€33 | Dinner | - |
|------|---|----------|---------|--------|---|
| B&B | 2 | Standard | €28.50-€30 | Partial Board | - |
| Single Rate | | | €40-€45 | Child reduction | 25% |

llarney 2km

**Open:** 1st April-30th September

---

**Mrs Evelyn Murphy**
REDWOOD
Tralee/Limerick Road N22,
Killarney, Co Kerry

### Killarney Tralee Road

Tᴇʟ: **064 34754**  Fᴀx: **064 34178**
Eᴍᴀɪʟ: **redwd@indigo.ie**
Wᴇʙ: **www.redwoodireland.com**

AA ◆◆◆◆ highly recommended spacious home on 15 acres. Breakfast menu, home baking some queensize beds. Magnificent mountain view. Tours arranged. Kerry airport 12 minutes.

| B&B | 6 | Ensuite | €30-€40 | Dinner | - |
|------|---|----------|---------|--------|---|
| B&B | - | Standard | - | Partial Board | - |
| Single Rate | | | €40-€65 | Child reduction | 50% |

llarney 3km

**Open:** 1st January-31st December

---

**Mrs Sheila Murphy**
SERENIC VIEW
Coolcorcoran, Killarney,
Co Kerry

### Killarney

Tᴇʟ: **064 33434**  Fᴀx: **064 33578**
Eᴍᴀɪʟ: **info@serenicview.com**
Wᴇʙ: **www.serenicview.com**

Luxury balcony rooms and ground floor accommodation. 5 min drive from Killarney, on Ring of Kerry. Signposted on Killarney/Limerick road. Quiet scenic area. Breakfast menu. Tours arranged.

| B&B | 4 | Ensuite | €32-€35 | Dinner | - |
|------|---|----------|---------|--------|---|
| B&B | - | Standard | - | Partial Board | - |
| Single Rate | | | €45-€47 | Child reduction | 25% |

llarney 2km

**Open:** 1st March-31st August

**David & Vivienne Nash**
NASHVILLE
Tralee Road, Killarney, Co Kerry

### Killarney Tralee Road

TEL: **064 32924**  FAX: **064 32924**
EMAIL: **nashville@eircom.net**
WEB: **www.nashvillekillarney.com**

Modern family home on Tralee N22 road. Colour TV's, Hairdryers, Tea/Coffee facilities. Payphone for guests. Ideal centre for touring Kerry - all tours arranged.

| | | | | Dinner | - |
|---|---|---|---|---|---|
| B&B | 6 | Ensuite | €28-€35 | Partial Board | - |
| B&B | - | Standard | | Child reduction | 33.3% |
| Single Rate | | | €40-€45 | | |

Killarney 3km

**Open:** 1st January-20th December

**Mrs Triona Neilan**
ROSSARNEY HOUSE
St Margaret's Road, Killarney, Co Kerry

### Killarney Town

TEL: **064 34630**
EMAIL: **rossarneyhouse@eircom.net**

Quiet private residential road. Walk to town. Award winning cosy family home. Guest T.V. lounge with tea/coffee. Golf, riding stables, Itinerary planned. Reduction low season. Peat fire in winter.

| | | | | Dinner | - |
|---|---|---|---|---|---|
| B&B | 4 | Ensuite | €27.50-€33 | Partial Board | - |
| B&B | - | Standard | | Child reduction | - |
| Single Rate | | | - | | |

In Killarney

**Open:** 1st January-20th December

**Mrs Rosemary O'Connell**
OAKLAWN HOUSE
Muckross Drive, Off Muckross Road, Killarney, Co Kerry

### Killarney Muckross Road

TEL: **064 32616**
EMAIL: **oaklawnhouse@eircom.net**
WEB: **www.oaklawn-house.com**

Award winning house. Winner of prestigious Killarney looking good and best Town & Country Home '95-'98. Golden Circle Award '99, 2000, 2001, 2002 & 2003. Two minutes to Town Centre.

| | | | | Dinner | - |
|---|---|---|---|---|---|
| B&B | 6 | Ensuite | €28-€35 | Partial Board | - |
| B&B | - | Standard | | Child reduction | 33.3% |
| Single Rate | | | €40-€55 | | |

In Killarney

**Open:** All Year

**Mrs Mary O'Connor Donoghue**
THE LOST BALL
Gortroe, Killarney, Co Kerry

### Killarney Fossa

TEL: **064 37449**
EMAIL: **thelostball@eircom.net**
WEB: **www.thelostball.com**

2km west of Killarney town off N72 (Ring of Kerry). Golf club, riding stables, hotel leisure centre, national park close by. All rooms ensuite with TV, Tea/Coffee.

| | | | | Dinner | - |
|---|---|---|---|---|---|
| B&B | 5 | Ensuite | €32-€35 | Partial Board | - |
| B&B | - | Standard | | Child reduction | - |
| Single Rate | | | €40-€43.50 | | |

Killarney 2km

**Open:** 1st May-30th September

**Annette O'Donoghue**
DUNN COURT HOUSE
Pike Hill, Lissivigeen, Killarney, Cork Road, Co Kerry

### Killarney

TEL: **064 34622**
EMAIL: **dunncourt@eircom.net**

House Quiet location with excellent view of mountains, family run. Spacious bedrooms with T.V. 3 mins drive to town centre adjacent to National Park, Lakes, golf, tours arranged.

| | | | | Dinner | - |
|---|---|---|---|---|---|
| B&B | 5 | Ensuite | €27.50-€35 | Partial Board | - |
| B&B | - | Standard | | Child reduction | - |
| Single Rate | | | €40-€45 | | |

Killarney 3km

**Open:** All Year

**Mrs Bridie O'Donoghue**
MUCKROSS DRIVE HOUSE
Muckross Drive,
Off Muckross Road, Killarney,
Co Kerry

### Killarney Muckross Road

TEL: **064 34290**   FAX: **064 39818**
EMAIL: **muckrossdrive@eircom.net**
WEB: **www.muckross.8m.com**

Award-winning purpose built B&B. 3 minute walk Town Centre. Bus/Rail. Situated in a quiet cul-de-sac. Overlooking mountains & National Park. All tours arranged.

| B&B | 5 | Ensuite | €28-€33 | Dinner | - |
| B&B | - | Standard | - | Partial Board | - |
| Single Rate | | | €40-€44 | Child reduction | **50%** |

Killarney

**Open:** 1st January-30th November

---

**Patrick & Julia O'Donoghue**
WOODLANDS
Ballydowney, Killarney,
Co Kerry

### Killarney

TEL: **064 31467**   FAX: **064 31467**
EMAIL: **stayatwoodlands@eircom.net**
WEB: **stayatwoodlands.com**

Friendly home walking distance Town. Ring of Kerry road N72. Riding stables, Golf, Fishing, Lakes/National Park nearby. Ideal walkers/climbers/cycling.

| B&B | 5 | Ensuite | €28-€35 | Dinner | - |
| B&B | 1 | Standard | €26-€29 | Partial Board | - |
| Single Rate | | | €38-€45 | Child reduction | **25%** |

Killarney 1km

**Open:** 1st February-20th December

---

**Mrs Phil O'Donohoe**
MAYWOOD
Mill Road, Killarney, Co Kerry

### Killarney Muckross Road

TEL: **064 31263**

Spacious, bungalow in scenic area near National Park. Golf, Fishing, Mountains, Lakes nearby. Tours arranged.

| B&B | 3 | Ensuite | €27.50-€31 | Dinner | - |
| B&B | 2 | Standard | €25.50-€28.50 | Partial Board | - |
| Single Rate | | | €38-€43.50 | Child reduction | **50%** |

Killarney 1.5km

**Open:** 1st March-31st October

---

**Mrs Eileen O'Grady**
FORREST HILLS
Muckross Road, Killarney,
Co Kerry

### Killarney Muckross Road

TEL: **064 31844**

Modern, well-heated home in scenic area, a few hundred yards from Town Centre. Spacious Parking. Home cooking.

| B&B | 4 | Ensuite | €30-€35 | Dinner | - |
| B&B | 2 | Standard | €28.50-€30 | Partial Board | - |
| Single Rate | | | €40-€50 | Child reduction | **50%** |

Killarney 1km

**Open:** 1st March-1st November

---

**Denis & Rosaleen O'Leary**
ROSS CASTLE LODGE
Ross Road, Killarney, Co Kerry

### Killarney Ross Road

TEL: **064 36942**   FAX: **064 36942**
EMAIL: **rosscastlelodge@eircom.net**
WEB: **killarneyb-and-b.com**

Luxurious house, edge of town amidst magical woodland and lakeshore walks. Golf, Lake cruising, Fishing 10 mins walk. Spacious bedrooms. RAC ◆◆◆◆ Award Winner.

| B&B | 4 | Ensuite | €30-€40 | Dinner | - |
| B&B | - | Standard | - | Partial Board | - |
| Single Rate | | | €40-€50 | Child reduction | - |

Killarney

**Open:** 15th March-15th November

**Killarney 2km**

**Miss Noreen O'Mahoney**
**MYSTICAL ROSE**
Woodlawn Road, Killarney,
Co Kerry

### Killarney Town
Tel: **064 31453**  Fax: **064 35846**
Web: **www.mysticalrosekillarney.com**

Award winning guest home. Frommer Guide recommended. Beautiful country home convenient to Mountain, Lake District. All tours arranged.

| B&B | 6 | Ensuite | €30-€35 | Dinner | - |
|-----|---|---------|---------|--------|---|
| B&B | - | Standard | | Partial Board | - |
| Single Rate | | | €40-€50 | Child reduction | - |

**Open:** All Year

---

**Killarney 1km**

**Sean & Sheila O'Mahony**
**O'MAHONY'S**
Park Road, Killarney, Co Kerry

### Killarney Town
Tel: **064 32861**
Email: **omahonysbandb@eircom.net**

Warm comfortable family run home opposite Ryan Hotel. TV, Hairdryers, Breakfast menu, Private parking. Walking distance Town centre. Tours arranged. Tea/Coffee facilities.

| B&B | 6 | Ensuite | €28-€31 | Dinner | - |
|-----|---|---------|---------|--------|---|
| B&B | - | Standard | - | Partial Board | - |
| Single Rate | | | €40-€43.50 | Child reduction | - |

**Open:** 1st January-30th November

---

**Killarney 2km**

**Mrs Norrie O'Neill**
**ALDERHAVEN COUNTRY HOME**
Ballycasheen Cork Road,
Killarney, Co Kerry

### Killarney Ballycasheen
Tel: **064 31982**  Fax: **064 31982**
Email: **alderhaven@eircom.net**
Web: **www.alderhaven.com**

Secluded Tudor style house off N22 at Whitebridge. 5 acres woodlands, Private avenue. Tranquil setting. Breakfast conservatory, Menu, Hairdryers. Tours arranged.

| B&B | 6 | Ensuite | €33-€34 | Dinner | - |
|-----|---|---------|---------|--------|---|
| B&B | - | Standard | | Partial Board | - |
| Single Rate | | | €45-€45 | Child reduction | 25% |

**Open:** 1st March-1st December

---

**In Killarney**

**Mrs Patricia O'Neill**
**LORENZO HOUSE**
Lewis Road, Killarney Town,
Killarney, Co Kerry

### Killarney Town
Tel: **064 31869**
Email: **lorenzokillarney@eircom.net**

Modern town house, 3 minutes walk to Town centre, Bus and Railway, National Park, Golf, Riding stables nearby. Tours arranged.

| B&B | 4 | Ensuite | €30-€33 | Dinner | - |
|-----|---|---------|---------|--------|---|
| B&B | - | Standard | - | Partial Board | - |
| Single Rate | | | - | Child reduction | - |

**Open:** 1st April-31st October

---

**Killarney 1km**

**Joan & Patrick O'Riordan**
**ST RITAS VILLA**
Mill Road, Killarney, Co Kerry

### Killarney Muckross Road
Tel: **064 31517**  Fax: **064 37631**
Email: **joan@kerrypages.com**
Web: **www.kerrypages.com/stritasvilla**

House adjacent to Lakes, Muckross House, Gleneagle Hotel. Tea/Coffee served, Orthopaedic beds, Hairdryers available. Tours arranged. Private parking.

| B&B | 4 | Ensuite | €31-€32 | Dinner | - |
|-----|---|---------|---------|--------|---|
| B&B | 1 | Standard | €29-€30 | Partial Board | - |
| Single Rate | | | €40-€45 | Child reduction | 25% |

**Open:** 10th April-31st October

**Mrs Anne O'Rourke**
SILVER SPRINGS
Tralee Road, Killarney, Co Kerry

TEL: **064 31016**   FAX: **064 31016**
EMAIL: **silverspringsbnb@eircom.net**
WEB: **homepage.eircom.net/~silversprings/s.html**

Country home. 4km Killarney on Tralee-Limerick road N22. Bedrooms ensuite, with TV, Coffee and Tea making facilities. Tours, Golf, Horse riding and Cycling near.

| B&B | 3 | Ensuite | €28-€32 | Dinner | - |
| B&B | 1 | Standard | €25.50-€29 | Partial Board | - |
| Single Rate | | | €40-€43.50 | Child reduction | - |

llarney 4km

**Open:** 1st March-1st December

**Mrs Kay O'Shea**
SPRINGFIELD LODGE
Rookery Rd, Ballycasheen,
Killarney, Co Kerry

TEL: **064 32944**
EMAIL: **springfieldlodge@eircom.net**
WEB: **www.springfieldlodgebb.com**

Modern, comfortable, welcoming home. Tranquil setting, adjacent to woodlands. Central location, private parking off N22. All tours arranged.

| B&B | 4 | Ensuite | €30-€35 | Dinner | - |
| B&B | - | Standard | - | Partial Board | - |
| Single Rate | | | - | Child reduction | 25% |

llarney 1km

**Open:** 1st February-31st November

**Mrs Eileen O'Sullivan**
KINGDOM VIEW
Glencar Road, Kilgobnet,
Beaufort, Killarney, Co Kerry

TEL: **064 44343**
EMAIL: **jos@iol.ie**
WEB: **www.iol.ie/~kingdomview**

On Killarney/Glencar Road, Slopes of McGillycuddy Mountains. Spectacular Countryside. Seafood speciality. Turf Fire. Cot available. Traditional musicians in family.

| B&B | 5 | Ensuite | €27.50-€31 | Dinner | €25 |
| B&B | 1 | Standard | €25.50-€28.50 | Partial Board | - |
| Single Rate | | | €38-€43.50 | Child reduction | 50% |

llorglin 8km

**Open:** 1st February-30th November

**Mr Eugene A O'Sullivan**
NORAVILLE HOUSE
St Margarets Road, Killarney,
Co Kerry

TEL: **064 36053**
EMAIL: **noraville@eircom.net**
WEB: **homepage.eircom.net/~noraville/**

Highly recommended modern townhouse. Select residential location. Tea/Coffee facilities and Hairdryers in all rooms. Tours arranged. Reduction low season. Personal attention.

| B&B | 5 | Ensuite | €30-€35 | Dinner | - |
| B&B | - | Standard | | Partial Board | - |
| Single Rate | | | €45-€50 | Child reduction | 25% |

Killarney

**Open:** All Year

**Mrs Rosaleen O'Sullivan**
KILLARNEY VILLA
Cork/Mallow Road (N72),
Killarney, Co Kerry

TEL: **064 31878**   FAX: **064 31878**
EMAIL: **killarneyvilla@eircom.net**
WEB: **www.killarneyvilla.com**

AA ◆◆◆◆ Award. RAC Sparkling Diamond Award. Scenic. Providing modern comforts. We pride ourselves in our roof top conservatory that overlooks magnificent gardens.

| B&B | 6 | Ensuite | €27.50-€35 | Dinner | - |
| B&B | - | Standard | - | Partial Board | - |
| Single Rate | | | €40-€44 | Child reduction | 25% |

llarney 3km

**Open:** 1st May-30th September

**Joan & Jerry Ryan**
THE GROTTO
Fossa, Killarney, Co Kerry

### Killarney

Tel: **064 33283**
Email: **the_grotto@hotmail.com**

On Ring of Kerry/Dingle, opposite Lake and Killarney Golf & Fishing Club. Tea facilities. Riding stables nearby. Near Castlerosse Hotel. Tours arranged.

| | | | | |
|---|---|---|---|---|
| B&B | 6 | Ensuite | €30-€32.50 | Dinner | - |
| B&B | - | Standard | | Partial Board | - |
| Single Rate | | | €40-€45 | Child reduction | 33.3% |

Killarney 2km

**Open:** 1st March-31st October

---

**Mrs Mary Tuohy**
FRIARY VIEW
Dennehy's, Bohereen,
Killarney, Co Kerry

### Killarney Town

Tel: **064 32996**  Fax: **064 32996**

Peaceful home in secluded area off main road. Walking distance to Town, Bus, Rail. Tours arranged. Breakfast Menu. Small road beside Friary Church.

| | | | | |
|---|---|---|---|---|
| B&B | 4 | Ensuite | €27.50-€31 | Dinner | - |
| B&B | - | Standard | - | Partial Board | - |
| Single Rate | | - | | Child reduction | - |

In Killarney

**Open:** 1st May-30th September

---

**Mrs Eileen Twomey**
GOLDEN OAKES
Dromhale,
(Off Countess Grove),
Killarney, Co Kerry

### Killarney

Tel: **064 32737**
Email: **jandetwomey@eircom.net**

Excellent accomodation on private grounds. Superb view of Lakes and Mountains. 5 min from Town Centre. Tea/Coffee provided on request.

| | | | | |
|---|---|---|---|---|
| B&B | 3 | Ensuite | €28-€35 | Dinner | - |
| B&B | - | Standard | - | Partial Board | - |
| Single Rate | | | €40-€45 | Child reduction | 25% |

In Killarney

**Open:** 1st April-30th September

---

**Mrs Agnes Walsh**
WUTHERING HEIGHTS
Knockeenduff, Killarney,
Co Kerry

### Killarney

Tel: **064 32756**
Email: **wutheringheights_@hotmail.com**
Web: **www.kerrypages.com/detail.php?id=179**

Bungalow in peaceful location signposted on Killarney/Limerick road (N22). Tea/Coffee making facilities, Orthopaedic beds, Electric blankets, Hairdryer. Low season reduction.

| | | | | |
|---|---|---|---|---|
| B&B | 4 | Ensuite | €28-€32.50 | Dinner | - |
| B&B | - | Standard | | Partial Board | - |
| Single Rate | | | €40-€45 | Child reduction | 50% |

Killarney 2km

**Open:** 1st February-15th December

---

**Kevin & Breege Woods**
BROOKFIELD HOUSE
Aghadoe, Killarney, Co Kerry

### Killarney Aghadoe

Tel: **064 32077**
Email: **brookfieldhouse@eircom.net**
Web: **http://homepage.eircom.net/~brookfieldhouse**

Country Residence: signposted 1km Killarney/Tralee/Limerick road N22. Convenient for touring Ring of Kerry, Best Guides Recommended.

| | | | | |
|---|---|---|---|---|
| B&B | 6 | Ensuite | €30-€32 | Dinner | - |
| B&B | - | Standard | | Partial Board | - |
| Single Rate | | | €40-€42.50 | Child reduction | 25% |

Killarney 2km

**Open:** 1st March-31st October

**Killarney**

### Patricia Wright
SUNFLOWER COTTAGE
Cleeney, Tralee Road, Killarney,
Co Kerry

TEL: **064 32101**
EMAIL: **lesw@indigo.ie**

First class accommodation close to Town. Ideal for touring Ring of Kerry, Dingle and Lakes. A warm welcome to be expected. Situated on N22.

| B&B | 4 | Ensuite | €30-€37 | Dinner | - |
|---|---|---|---|---|---|
| B&B | - | Standard | - | Partial Board | - |
| Single Rate | | | €45-€53 | Child reduction | **33.3%** |

**Open:** 1st March-31st October

---

**illorglin 3km**

### Mrs Irma Clifford
FERN ROCK
Tinnahalla N70, Milltown,
Co Kerry

TEL: **066 9761848**   FAX: **066 9761848**
EMAIL: **fernrock@eircom.net**
WEB: **www.stayatfernrock.com**

Excellent accommodation (on N70 Tralee Rd) superb view. Tours arranged. Golf .5 km. Also 10 Golf courses within 1hour drive. Central for Ring of Kerry/Dingle/Killarney. Beaches close by.

| B&B | 4 | Ensuite | €27.50-€31 | Dinner | - |
|---|---|---|---|---|---|
| B&B | - | Standard | - | Partial Board | - |
| Single Rate | | | €40-€43.50 | Child reduction | - |

**Open:** 2nd January-15th December

---

**illorglin**

### Mrs Marie Clifford
HILLCREST
Killarney Road, Killorglin,
Co Kerry

TEL: **066 9761552**
EMAIL: **hillcrest_clifford@hotmail.com**
WEB: **www.hillcrest-bb.com**

Georgian styled residence on N72, spectacular views Irelands Highest Mountain and countryside. Orthopaedic Beds, Hairdryers. Frommer Recommended.

| B&B | 5 | Ensuite | €27.50-€31 | Dinner | - |
|---|---|---|---|---|---|
| B&B | - | Standard | - | Partial Board | - |
| Single Rate | | | €40-€43.50 | Child reduction | **50%** |

**Open:** 1st April-30th September

---

**Killorglin**

### Mrs Bridie Evans
ORGLAN HOUSE
Killarney Road N72, Killorglin,
Co Kerry

TEL: **066 9761540**
EMAIL: **orglanhouse@eircom.net**
WEB: **www.orglanhouse.com**

Peaceful hilltop residence with magnificent mountain views, overlooking River and Town. 5 mins walk from Town. Golf, Fishing, Beaches, Hillwalking all within 20 mins of Town centre.

| B&B | 3 | Ensuite | €27.50-€31 | Dinner | - |
|---|---|---|---|---|---|
| B&B | 1 | Standard | €25.50-€28.50 | Partial Board | - |
| Single Rate | | | €38-€43.50 | Child reduction | **25%** |

**Open:** 1st April-1st October

---

**Killorglin**

### Noreen Evans
LAUNE BRIDGE HOUSE
Killarney Rd N72, Killorglin,
Co Kerry

TEL: **066 9761161**
EMAIL: **launebridgehouse@hotmail.com**
WEB: **www.launebridgehouse.com**

At the Bridge Killorglin scenic location overlooking River. Purpose built on Ring of Kerry. Walking distance high class restaurants. Golf, fishing & hillwalking. Ideal touring base.

| B&B | 6 | Ensuite | €32 | Dinner | - |
|---|---|---|---|---|---|
| B&B | - | Standard | - | Partial Board | - |
| Single Rate | | | €40-€45 | Child reduction | **25%** |

**Open:** 1st March-1st December

**Killorglin 2km**

**Mrs Christine Griffin**
ARDRAHAN HOUSE
Ownagarry, Killorglin, Co Kerry

TEL: **066 9762219**
EMAIL: **cdgriffin@eircom.net**

Family run peaceful homely accommodation, quiet location. 2km from Town. Central for Mountain and Hill walking, Cycling, Fishing, Ring of Kerry, Dingle, Killarney, Seaside, Caragh Lake.

| B&B | 2 | Ensuite | €27.50-€31 | Dinner | - |
|-----|---|---------|------------|--------|---|
| B&B | 1 | Standard | €25.50-€28.50 | Partial Board | - |
| Single Rate | | | €38-€43.50 | Child reduction | 50% |

**Open:** 1st January-20th December

---

**Killorglin**

**Mrs Catherine Lyons**
TORINE HOUSE
Sunhill Road, Killorglin,
Ring of Kerry, Co Kerry

TEL: **066 9761352** FAX: **066 9761352**
EMAIL: **torinehouse@eircom.net**
WEB: **www.torinehouse.com**

Comfortable accommodation. Base for Ring of Kerry, Dingle, Killarney. Golf & Fishing nearby. Tea/Coffee, TV in rooms. Orthopaedic beds. Guide du Routard recommended.

| B&B | 5 | Ensuite | €27.50-€31 | Dinner | €25-€25 |
|-----|---|---------|------------|--------|---------|
| B&B | 1 | Standard | €25.50-€28.50 | Partial Board | - |
| Single Rate | | | €38-€43.50 | Child reduction | 50% |

**Open:** 1st March-30th November

---

**In Killorglin**

**Mrs Geraldine Mangan**
RIVERSIDE HOUSE
Killorglin, Ring of Kerry,
Co Kerry

TEL: **066 9761184** FAX: **066 9761184**
EMAIL: **riversidehousebnb@eircom.net**
WEB: **www.riversidehousebnb.com**

Comfortable family home, superb view from rooms overlooking River. Golfing, Walking. Ideal touring base. Killarney, Ring/Kerry, Dingle. Information route N70.

| B&B | 5 | Ensuite | €27.50-€31 | Dinner | - |
|-----|---|---------|------------|--------|---|
| B&B | 1 | Standard | €25.50-€28.50 | Partial Board | - |
| Single Rate | | | €38-€43.50 | Child reduction | 33.3% |

**Open:** 15th March-15th November

---

**In Killorglin**

**Christina & Jerome O'Regan**
O'REGANS COUNTRY HOME
& GARDENS
Bansha, Killorglin, Co Kerry

TEL: **066 9761200** FAX: **066 9761200**
EMAIL: **jeromeoregan@eircom.net**
WEB: **www.oreganscountryhomeandgardens.com**

Luxurious modern home on award winning gardens. Golf, Fishing nearby. Ideal touring base. Home baking. AA ♦♦♦ Award. Tea/Coffee facilities. TV, Hairdryer in rooms.

| B&B | 3 | Ensuite | €27.50-€31 | Dinner | €28-€30 |
|-----|---|---------|------------|--------|---------|
| B&B | 1 | Standard | €25.50-€28.50 | Partial Board | - |
| Single Rate | | | €38-€43.50 | Child reduction | 33.3% |

**Open:** 1st March-30th November

---

**Killorglin 1km**

**Ms Carina O'Shea**
DUIBHLEAS
Dunmaniheen, Killorglin,
Co Kerry

TEL: **066 9761002**
EMAIL: **duibhleas@eircom.net**

Luxurious dormer bungalow set in scenic private grounds on Ring of Kerry. Close to horseriding, golf, beaches, fishing, gourmet restaurants. Warm welcome.

| B&B | 3 | Ensuite | €28-€31 | Dinner | - |
|-----|---|---------|---------|--------|---|
| B&B | 1 | Standard | €26-€29 | Partial Board | - |
| Single Rate | | | €38-€45 | Child reduction | 33.3% |

**Open:** 1st March-31st October

**Jacinta Sheehan**
THE FAIRWAYS
**Tinnahalla, Killorglin, Co Kerry**

### Killorglin Ring of Kerry

Tᴇʟ: **066 9762391**
Eᴍᴀɪʟ: **fairways@gofree.indigo.ie**
Wᴇʙ: **www.fairways-killorglin.com**

Luxurious friendly B&B near Golf course. Ideal base for Ring of Kerry/Dingle/Tralee/Killarney. Tea/Coffee available. Warm welcome.

| B&B | 4 | Ensuite | €27.50-€31 | Dinner | - |
| B&B | | Standard | - | Partial Board | - |
| Single Rate | | | €45-€45 | Child reduction | 33.3% |

illorglin 2km

**Open:** 1st February-30th November

---

**Mrs Joan Carmody**
PALMGROVE HOUSE
**Tarbert Rd, Listowel, Co Kerry**

### Listowel

Tᴇʟ: **068 21857**
Eᴍᴀɪʟ: **joan@palmgrove-listowel.com**
Wᴇʙ: **palmgrove-listowel.com**

Comfortable home on Tarbert N69 Car Ferry road. Tarbert Ferry 10 min. Spacious bedrooms, laundry service, Tea/Coffee. Fishing and Golfing nearby. Permits available. Private Car park.

| B&B | 3 | Ensuite | €28-€31 | Dinner | - |
| B&B | 1 | Standard | €26-€28.50 | Partial Board | - |
| Single Rate | | | €38-€43.50 | Child reduction | 50% |

istowel 2.5km

**Open:** 1st March-30th November

---

**Mrs Mary Costello**
ARAS MHUIRE
**Ballybunion Road, Listowel, Co Kerry**

### Listowel

Tᴇʟ: **068 21515/23612**　Fᴀx: **068 23612**
Eᴍᴀɪʟ: **marycos@eircom.net**
Wᴇʙ: **homepage.eircom.net/~doniec**

Near Town Centre Lartique monorail on R553. Ideal for Ballybunion Beach and Golf and Tarbert Car Ferry. Reduction for more than 1 night. Irish Independent recommended.

| B&B | 4 | Ensuite | €28-€35 | Dinner | - |
| B&B | - | Standard | - | Partial Board | - |
| Single Rate | | | €40-€45 | Child reduction | 33.3% |

n Listowel

**Open:** 10th January-28th December

---

**Anne & Ian Everard**
CLAREVILLA
**Skehenerin, Tarbert Road, Listowel, Co Kerry**

### Listowel

Tᴇʟ: **068 23723**　Fᴀx: **068 23723**
Eᴍᴀɪʟ: **everardian@eircom.net**

Dormer Bungalow. Landscaped Gardens. 2kms from Listowel on main N69, Tarbert Ferry Rd. Ferry 15 mins. Golf, Salmon, Trout fishing. Good Bass fishing from shore in winter.

| B&B | 4 | Ensuite | €28-€35 | Dinner | - |
| B&B | - | Standard | - | Partial Board | - |
| Single Rate | | | €40-€43.50 | Child reduction | 50% |

istowel 2km

**Open:** All Year

---

**Mrs Teresa Keane**
WHISPERING PINES
**Bedford, Listowel, Co Kerry**

### Listowel

Tᴇʟ: **068 21503**
Eᴍᴀɪʟ: **t_keane@unison.ie**

Comfort assured in luxurious home in peaceful location on Ballylongford Road. Ballybunion and Listowel Golf Courses, Tarbert Ferry, Beaches 10 mins.

| B&B | 3 | Ensuite | €27.50-€31 | Dinner | - |
| B&B | 1 | Standard | €25.50-€28.50 | Partial Board | - |
| Single Rate | | | €38-€43.50 | Child reduction | 25% |

istowel 1.5km

**Open:** 1st January-31st December

129

In Listowel

### Mrs Breda Mahony
**ASHFORD LODGE**
Tarbert Road, Listowel,
Co Kerry

TEL: **068 21280**  FAX: **068 24406**
EMAIL: **ashfordlodge@eircom.net**

Nearest approved B&B to Town Centre on Car Ferry Road (N69). Leaving Listowel, turn right at end of bypass road. Recommended by Rough Guide to Ireland.

| B&B | 3 | Ensuite | €28-€31 | Dinner | - |
| B&B | 1 | Standard | €28-€30 | Partial Board | - |
| Single Rate | | | €38-€45 | Child reduction | 50% |

**Open:** All Year

---

Listowel 1km

### Mrs Nancy O'Neill
**ASHGROVE HOUSE**
Ballybunion Road, Listowel,
Co Kerry

TEL: **068 21268**  FAX: **068 21268**
EMAIL: **nancy.oneill@ireland.com**
WEB: **www.ashgrovebandb.com**

Luxury home near Town R553. Frommer/Sullivan Guide recommended. TV-Tea-Coffee all rooms. Golf - Car Ferry 15 mins. See www.dirl.com

| B&B | 3 | Ensuite | €28-€31 | Dinner | - |
| B&B | 1 | Standard | €28-€29 | Partial Board | - |
| Single Rate | | | €40-€45 | Child reduction | 33.3% |

**Open:** 15th March-31st October

---

### Mrs Monica Quille
**NORTH COUNTY HOUSE**
67 Church St, Listowel,
Co Kerry

TEL: **068 21238**  FAX: **068 22831**
EMAIL: **bryanmonica1@eircom.net**

Centre of Town. Luxurious family run home. Convenient to Ballybunion Golf Courses (fee reduction). Tarbert Car Ferry. Ideal touring base.

| B&B | 8 | Ensuite | €29-€37 | Dinner | - |
| B&B | - | Standard | | Partial Board | - |
| Single Rate | | | €41-€49 | Child reduction | 50% |

In Listowel

**Open:** All Year

---

Milltown 1km

### Ms Agnes Shortt
**SHORTCLIFF HOUSE**
Lyre, Milltown, Killarney,
Co Kerry

TEL: **066 9767106**  FAX: **066 9767106**
EMAIL: **shortcliffhouse@eircom.net**
WEB: **homepage.eircom.net/~shortcliffhouse**

Peaceful country location 1km off N70. Ring of Kerry route. Mature gardens, Riding stables on site, Golf 5 mins. Ideal for Golf, Walking, Touring & Horse riding.

| B&B | 3 | Ensuite | €27.50-€31 | Dinner | - |
| B&B | - | Standard | | Partial Board | - |
| Single Rate | | | €40-€44 | Child reduction | 25% |

**Open:** 1st April-30th September

---

Portmagee 5km

### Mrs Kathleen Lynch
**HARBOUR GROVE**
Aghadda, Portmagee, Co Kerry

TEL: **066 9477116**  FAX: **066 9477116**
EMAIL: **harbourgrove@eircom.net**
WEB: **www.harbourgrove.com**

Friendly home, 6km Ring of Kerry N70. Panoramic views. Harbour setting. Mature trees. Spacious bathrooms. Skellig tours, boat, fishing, riding, walking arranged. Restaurant, pub, music near.

| B&B | 3 | Ensuite | €28-€31 | Dinner | - |
| B&B | - | Standard | | Partial Board | - |
| Single Rate | | | €40-€45 | Child reduction | 50% |

**Open:** 1st May-30th September

Portmagee

**Christina Murphy**
THE WATERFRONT
**Portmagee, Co Kerry**

TEL: **066 9477208**
EMAIL: **thewaterfront@eircom.net**

At entrance Portmagee village on scenic Skellig Ring near bridge linking Valentia Island to mainland. Adjacent to Skellig Heritage Centre

| B&B | 5 | Ensuite | €27.50-€31 | Dinner | - |
|---|---|---|---|---|---|
| B&B | - | Standard | | Partial Board | - |
| Single Rate | | | €40-€43.50 | Child reduction | 50% |

**Open:** 1st April-31st October

---

Sneem

**Ann Cronin**
SNEEM RIVER LODGE
**Sneem, Co Kerry**

Sneem Ring of Kerry

TEL: **064 45578**  FAX: **064 45277**
EMAIL: **sneemriverlodge@eircom.net**

Newly built guesthouse with magnificent mountain views, overlooking Sneem river. Every comfort provided for our guests. Close to all amenities. Private parking.

| B&B | 4 | Ensuite | €28-€31 | Dinner | - |
|---|---|---|---|---|---|
| B&B | - | Standard | - | Partial Board | - |
| Single Rate | | | €40-€43.50 | Child reduction | 50% |

**Open:** 1st February-6th December

---

neem

**Mrs Gretta Drummond**
ROCKVILLE HOUSE
**Sneem, Co Kerry**

Sneem Ring of Kerry

TEL: **064 45135**
EMAIL: **rockville@oceanfree.net**

Luxurious dormer bungalow set in private grounds. Kerry Way walking route, Golf, Fishing nearby. Bicycle shed. Breakfast menu.

| B&B | 4 | Ensuite | €27.50-€31 | Dinner | - |
|---|---|---|---|---|---|
| B&B | - | Standard | - | Partial Board | - |
| Single Rate | | | €40-€43.50 | Child reduction | 25% |

**Open:** 1st March-15th November

---

Sneem

**Mrs Margaret Harrington**
BANK HOUSE
**North Square, Sneem,**
**Killarney, Co Kerry**

Sneem Ring of Kerry

TEL: **064 45226**

Georgian house with antiques and charm situated in the heart of Ireland's most picturesque Village. Frommer and French Guide recommended. Breakfast menu.

| B&B | 3 | Ensuite | €27.50-€31 | Dinner | - |
|---|---|---|---|---|---|
| B&B | 2 | Standard | €25.50-€28.50 | Partial Board | - |
| Single Rate | | | €38-€43.50 | Child reduction | - |

**Open:** 1st March-1st November

---

Sneem

**Mrs Alice O'Sullivan**
OLD CONVENT HOUSE
**Pier Road, Sneem, Co Kerry**

Sneem Ring of Kerry

TEL: **064 45181**  FAX: **064 45181**
EMAIL: **conventhouse@oceanfree.net**
WEB: **www.oldconventhouse.com**

Unique, comfortable, old world stone house (1866), on Sneem estuary. Private grounds with access to fishing river. Numerous  recommendations. Walkers welcome.

| B&B | 6 | Ensuite | €27.50-€31 | Dinner | - |
|---|---|---|---|---|---|
| B&B | - | Standard | - | Partial Board | - |
| Single Rate | | | €40-€43.50 | Child reduction | 25% |

**Open:** 1st March-30th November

**In Tralee**

**Mrs Patricia Canning**
BRICRIU
20 Old Golf Links Road,
Oakpark, Tralee, Co Kerry

### Tralee

Tel: **066 7126347**   Fax: **066 7126347**
Web: **canningpj@yahoo.co.uk**

Quiet area off N69 pass Railway. Take 1st right, left, right again (10 mins walk). Adjacent Sports Complex. Convenient Golf, Beaches.

| B&B | 3 | Ensuite | €28-€35 | Dinner | - |
| B&B | - | Standard | | Partial Board | - |
| Single Rate | | | €40.50-€45 | Child reduction | 10% |

**Open:** 1st June-31st October

---

**Tralee 2km**

**Mrs Eileen Curley**
MOUNTAIN VIEW HOUSE
Ballinorig West, Tralee,
Co Kerry

### Tralee

Tel: **066 7122226**

Ideal golf/touring base. Approaching Tralee on N21. Pass McDonalds on Left, straight through small roundabout, second exit on right at Maxol gas station.

| B&B | 3 | Ensuite | €31 | Dinner | - |
| B&B | 1 | Standard | €28.50 | Partial Board | - |
| Single Rate | | | €41-€43.50 | Child reduction | 25% |

**Open:** 1st April-31st October

---

**Tralee 1.5km**

**Mrs Gertie Deady**
GURRANE
50 Derrylea, Tralee, Co Kerry

### Tralee

Tel: **066 7124734**
Email: **deadysgurrane@eircom.net**

Modern two storey house on N69 Listowel Tarbert Car Ferry road. Convenient to Rail, Bus, Town, Golf, Greyhound Track, Hotel, Restaurant, Sports complex.

| B&B | 2 | Ensuite | €27.50-€31 | Dinner | - |
| B&B | 2 | Standard | €25.50-€28.50 | Partial Board | - |
| Single Rate | | | €38-€43.50 | Child reduction | 25% |

**Open:** 8th January-20th December

---

**Tralee 1km**

**Mrs Hannah Devane**
EASTCOTE
34 Oakpark Demesne, Tralee,
Co Kerry

### Tralee

Tel: **066 7125942**

Select accommodation in peaceful location. All facilities in rooms. Ideal touring base. 200 metres off N69 route, Tarbert Car ferry road. Warm welcome.

| B&B | 2 | Ensuite | €27.50-€31 | Dinner | - |
| B&B | 1 | Standard | €25.50-€28.50 | Partial Board | - |
| Single Rate | | | €38-€43.50 | Child reduction | - |

**Open:** 7th January-20th December

---

**Tralee 2km**

**Mrs Patricia Dooley**
TEACH AN PHIOBAIRE
Laharn, Listowel Rd, Tralee,
Co Kerry

### Tralee

Tel: **066 7122424**   Fax: **066 7122424**
Email: **info@tanp.ie**
Web: **www.tanp.ie**

The Piper's House, on the N69 Ferry route. Tea/coffee on arrival. Music, golf, fishing, touring, nearby. Trad Irish Music Uilleann Pipes Workshop on site.

| B&B | 4 | Ensuite | €27.50-€31 | Dinner | - |
| B&B | - | Standard | - | Partial Board | - |
| Single Rate | | | €40-€45 | Child reduction | 50% |

**Open:** All Year Except Christmas

**Mrs Maura Dowling**
LEESIDE
Oakpark, Tralee, Co Kerry

### Tralee

TEL: **066 7126475**
EMAIL: **www.dowlingsleeside-bnb.com**
WEB: **info@dowlingsleeside-bnb.com**

N69 Ferry route. Near Bus/Rail. Antique Irish Furniture. Recommended Lets Go/Routard/Rough Guides. Orthopaedic beds. TV's. Power showers. Home baking. Tea/Coffee facilities.

| B&B | 3 | Ensuite | €27.50-€31 | Dinner | - |
| B&B | - | Standard | | Partial Board | - |
| Single Rate | | | €40-€43.50 | Child reduction | - |

n Tralee

**Open:** 1st March-1st November

---

**Mrs Ann Gleeson**
ROSEDALE LODGE
Oakpark Road, Tralee,
Co Kerry

### Tralee

TEL: **066 7125320**

All spacious en-suite ground floor bedrooms on "N69 Car Ferry Road". Adjacent to Hotel and Restaurant. Recommended "Bed and Breakfast Ireland".

| B&B | 3 | Ensuite | €28-€35 | Dinner | - |
| B&B | - | Standard | - | Partial Board | - |
| Single Rate | | | €40-€45 | Child reduction | - |

n Tralee

**Open:** 1st March-30th November

---

**Mary Ann Hanafin**
GLENOGUE HOUSE
Ballymakegogue, The Spa,
Tralee, Co Kerry

### Tralee Fenit Road

TEL: **066 7136476**   FAX: **066 7136476**
EMAIL: **mahanafin@eircom.net**
WEB: **glenoguehouse.com**

Quiet, family run guesthouse in the heart of the countryside, with superb views of Slieve Mish Mountains. Ideal for touring Dingle,the ring of Kerry or if you just fancy a game of golf.

| B&B | 4 | Ensuite | €28-€32 | Dinner | - |
| B&B | - | Standard | | Partial Board | - |
| Single Rate | | | €40-€43.50 | Child reduction | 50% |

Tralee 6km

**Open:** 1st April-31st October

---

**Mrs Mary Hannafin**
SHANGRI-LA
The Spa, Tralee, Co Kerry

### Tralee Fenit Road

TEL: **066 7136214**
EMAIL: **shangrila_spa@hotmail.com**

Secluded country residence overlooking Tralee Bay. Walk to Beach, Pub & Restaurant. Golf Courses nearby. Ideal Golfing/Touring base. Walking route locally. On R558. (Coastal drive).

| B&B | 4 | Ensuite | €28-€32 | Dinner | - |
| B&B | - | Standard | | Partial Board | - |
| Single Rate | | | €40-€43.50 | Child reduction | 50% |

Tralee 4km

**Open:** 1st January-1st December

---

**Mrs Eileen Hooker**
SHERIDAN LODGE
Listellick, Tralee, Co Kerry

### Tralee

TEL: **066 7123272**   FAX: **066 7123272**
EMAIL: **eileenhooker@eircom.net**
WEB: **www.traleebnb.ht.st**

A warm welcome awaits you. Scenic location. Ideal Golfing/Touring base. Private Car Parking. Tea/Coffee. TV room with Log/Turf fire.

| B&B | 4 | Ensuite | €28-€31 | Dinner | - |
| B&B | 1 | Standard | €28-€30 | Partial Board | - |
| Single Rate | | | €39-€43.50 | Child reduction | 50% |

Tralee 3km

**Open:** 8th January-18th December

# Kerry

**Mrs Sheila Horgan**
ALVERNA
26 Liosdara, Oakpark, Tralee,
Co Kerry

**Tralee**

Tel: **066 7126970**
Email: **alvernatralee@hotmail.com**

Off N69. First turn right after Swimming pool and Sports Centre. Fourth house on left. Convenient to many Golf clubs. 10 mins walk Town Centre, 5 mins walk Railway/Bus depot.

| B&B | 2 | Ensuite | €30-€33 | Dinner | - |
| B&B | 2 | Standard | €28-€30 | Partial Board | - |
| Single Rate | | | €38-€42 | Child reduction | 50% |

Tralee 1km

**Open:** 1st March-1st December

---

**Mrs Sheila Kerins**
BALLINGOWAN HOUSE
Mile Height, Killarney Road,
Tralee, Co Kerry

**Tralee Killarney Road**

Tel: **066 7127150**  Fax: **066 7120325**
Email: **ballingowan@eircom.net**
Web: **www.kerryview.com/ballingowanhouse**

All spacious rooms with TV, Tea/Coffee, Hairdryer. Private parking. Approaching Tralee on N21/N22 on left before McDonalds on Kerry Airport Road.

| B&B | 4 | Ensuite | €28-€32 | Dinner | - |
| B&B | - | Standard | - | Partial Board | - |
| Single Rate | | | €40-€50 | Child reduction | 50% |

Tralee 1km

**Open:** 16th April-30th September

---

**Mrs Eileen Lynch**
ST ENDAS
Oakpark, Tralee, Co Kerry

**Tralee**

Tel: **066 7126494**  Fax: **066 7126494**
Email: **eileenmlynch@eircom.net**

Town house convenient Sports Complex, Aqua Dome, Golf, Beaches, Greyhound Racing. 5 mins Bus and Train Depot. Private parking. Ideal touring base. N69.

| B&B | 4 | Ensuite | €27.50-€31 | Dinner | - |
| B&B | - | Standard | - | Partial Board | - |
| Single Rate | | | €40-€43.50 | Child reduction | 50% |

In Tralee

**Open:** 1st January-21st December

---

**Helen Lyons**
KNOCKBRACK
Oakpark Road, Tralee,
Co Kerry

**Tralee**

Tel: **066 7127375**
Email: **knockbrackguests@eircom.net**
Web: **www.dirl.com/kerry/knockbrack.htm**

Newly built home. TV in bedrooms, tea-making facilities, power showers, private parking. Separate TV lounge for guests. Adjacent to hotel/restaurant. On N69 (car ferry route).

| B&B | 3 | Ensuite | €30-€36 | Dinner | - |
| B&B | - | Standard | - | Partial Board | - |
| Single Rate | | | €50 | Child reduction | 25% |

In Tralee

**Open:** 16th March-30th November

---

**Mrs Juliette O'Callaghan**
GREEN GABLES
1 Clonmore Villas,
Ballymullen road, Tralee,
Co Kerry

**Tralee**

Tel: **066 7123354**  Fax: **066 7123354**
Email: **info@greengablestralee.com**
Web: **www.greengablestralee.com**

Listed Victorian period town house. Town Centre location adjacent County Library, Town park, on N70. 5 min walk Bus/Train station.

| B&B | 3 | Ensuite | €27.50-€35 | Dinner | - |
| B&B | 1 | Standard | €25.50-€28.50 | Partial Board | - |
| Single Rate | | | €38-€45 | Child reduction | - |

In Tralee

**Open:** 23rd February-30th November

### Mrs Joan O'Connor
**SKEHANAGH LODGE**
**Skehanagh Cross,**
**Castlemaine Road, Tralee,**
**Co Kerry**

**Tralee**

Tel: **066 7124782**   Fax: **066 7124782**
Email: **Skehanaghlodge@eircom.net**

Bright spacious comfortable bungalow on Killorglin/Ring of Kerry road N70. Tea/Coffee facilities with TV in bedrooms. Guide de Routard recommended. Two large family rooms. Touring base.

| B&B | 3 | Ensuite | €29-€31 | Dinner | - |
| B&B | 1 | Standard | €26-€28.50 | Partial Board | - |
| Single Rate | | | €38-€43.50 | Child reduction | 50% |

alee 1km

**Open:** 1st April-31st October

---

### Rose O'Keeffe
**ASHVILLE HOUSE**
**Ballyard, Tralee, Co Kerry**

**Tralee Ballyard**

Tel: **066 7123717**   Fax: **066 7123898**
Email: **ashville@eircom.net**

Architect designed, country setting off Dingle Road (N86). Tralee 2 minutes drive, TV, Hairdryers, Power Showers, Breakfast Menu, Drying Room.

| B&B | 6 | Ensuite | €30-€32 | Dinner | - |
| B&B | - | Standard | - | Partial Board | - |
| Single Rate | | | €43-€45 | Child reduction | 50% |

alee 1km

**Open:** 1st March-31st December

---

### Mrs Mary O'Neill
**BEECH GROVE**
**Oakpark, Tralee, Co Kerry**

**Tralee**

Tel: **066 7126788**   Fax: **066 7180971**
Email: **oneillbeechgrove@eircom.net**
Web: **www.beechgrove.irishhouse.net**

On Car Ferry Rd N69. Near Railway/Bus Station, Sports Complex, Town Centre. Secure car park. Siamsa tickets. Tours arranged.

| B&B | 3 | Ensuite | €27.50-€31 | Dinner | - |
| B&B | 1 | Standard | €25.50-€28.50 | Partial Board | - |
| Single Rate | | | €38-€43.50 | Child reduction | 50% |

alee 1km

**Open:** 24th January-20th December

---

### Mrs Helen O'Shea
**CLUAIN MOR HOUSE**
**Boherbee, Tralee, Co Kerry**

**Tralee**

Tel: **066 7125545**
Email: **cluainmorguesthousetralee@eircom.net**

On 1 acre garden. 5 mins Rail Station, Aqua Dome. Golf, Angling, Beaches 5 miles. Kerry Airport 20 mins. 5 mins walk to Tralee Town. Private Car parking.

| B&B | 5 | Ensuite | €28-€31 | Dinner | - |
| B&B | - | Standard | - | Partial Board | - |
| Single Rate | | | €40-€43.50 | Child reduction | 25% |

Tralee

**Open:** 1st January-20th December

---

### Mrs Catherine O'Sullivan
**MARINA LODGE**
**Cloherbrien, (Fenit Road Area),**
**Tralee, Co Kerry**

**Tralee**

Tel: **066 7123565**
Email: **marinalodge@eircom.net**

Warm welcome awaits you. Family run B&B. Scenic location. Complimentary Tea/Coffee. Golf, Seafood Restaurants nearby. Private parking. Tours arranged.

| B&B | 3 | Ensuite | €27.50-€35 | Dinner | - |
| B&B | - | Standard | - | Partial Board | - |
| Single Rate | | | - | Child reduction | - |

ralee 2 km

**Open:** 30th March-30th September

135

**Mrs Joan Smith**
BRIANVILLE
Clogherbrien, Fenit Road Area,
Tralee, Co Kerry

### Tralee Fenit Road

Tᴇʟ: **066 7126645**
Eᴍᴀɪʟ: **michsmit@gofree.indigo.ie**
Wᴇʙ: **www.brianville-tralee.com**

Luxurious bungalow. AA ◆◆◆◆. Frommer guide recommended, Best B&B in Ireland. Tea/Coffee, Hairdryers, TV in rooms, all on ground floor. 18 hole Golf Links. Seafood Restaurants nearby.

| B&B | 3 | Ensuite | €30-€35 | Dinner | - |
| B&B | - | Standard | - | Partial Board | - |
| Single Rate | | | - | Child reduction | 50% |

Tralee 1.5km

**Open:** All Year

---

**Paddy & Deirdre Stack**
WOODBROOK HOUSE
Laharn, Listowel Road(N69),
Tralee, Co Kerry

### Tralee

Tᴇʟ: **066 7180078**
Eᴍᴀɪʟ: **woodbrookhouse@esatclear.ie**
Wᴇʙ: **www.esatclear.ie/~woodbrookhouse**

Luxurious hillside residence with breathtaking views of Slieve Mish mountains. Ideal base for Touring, Golfing, Hillwalking with excellent restaurants nearby. Groundfloor rooms. Car ferry road.

| B&B | 4 | Ensuite | €30-€35 | Dinner | - |
| B&B | - | Standard | - | Partial Board | - |
| Single Rate | | | €40-€50 | Child reduction | 33.3% |

Tralee 3km

**Open:** 3rd January-18th December

---

**Tim & Mary Walshe**
THE WILLOWS
5 Clonmore Terrace,
Moyderwell, Tralee, Co Kerry

### Tralee

Tᴇʟ: **066 7123779**  Fᴀx: **066 7123779**
Eᴍᴀɪʟ: **2thewillows@eircom.net**
Wᴇʙ: **www.thewillowsbnb.com**

Friendly Victorian townhouse - Olde world charm - On N70. 5 mins walk Town/Bus/Train. Breakfast menu. TV, Tea/Coffee, Hairdryers in rooms. Ideal touring base.

| B&B | 3 | Ensuite | €30-€32 | Dinner | - |
| B&B | 1 | Standard | €27.50-€28.50 | Partial Board | - |
| Single Rate | | | €40-€43.50 | Child reduction | 33.3% |

In Tralee

**Open:** 1st February-19th December

---

**Ms Maureen Young**
MAUREEN'S B&B
Leeside, Oak Park, Tralee,
Co Kerry

### Tralee

Tᴇʟ: **066 7127740**
Eᴍᴀɪʟ: **youngmaureens@yahoo.co.uk**

N69 ferry route. Tea coffee on arrival. Home baking. Breakfast menu. Beside Hotel Restaurant Bar. Orthopaedic beds. Sky TV. Private parking. Ideal tourning base.

| B&B | 4 | Ensuite | €27.50-€31 | Dinner | - |
| B&B | - | Standard | - | Partial Board | - |
| Single Rate | | | €40-€43.50 | Child reduction | 33.3% |

In Tralee

**Open:** 1st January-31st December

---

**Mrs Mary Foran**
SPRING ACRE
Knightstown, Valentia Island,
Co Kerry

### Valentia Island

Tᴇʟ: **066 9476141**  Fᴀx: **066 9476377**
Eᴍᴀɪʟ: **rforan@indigo.ie**

Superb accommodation located on the seafront, panoramic scenery, peaceful setting beside restaurants, pubs, scenic walks, skellig and angling boats closeby.

| B&B | 4 | Ensuite | €30-€32 | Dinner | - |
| B&B | - | Standard | - | Partial Board | - |
| Single Rate | | | €40-€44 | Child reduction | 50% |

In Town

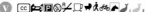

**Open:** 1st March-1st November

### Mary Lane
**SHEALANE COUNTRY HOUSE**
Corha-Mor, Valentia Island, Co Kerry

TEL: **066 9476354**
EMAIL: **marylane@eircom.net**
WEB: **www.shealane.com**

Peaceful setting on Road bridge entrance adjacent to Skelig Experience Centre. Skelig trips, Fishing, Walking arranged. Restaurants, Traditional music nearby.

| B&B | 3 | Ensuite | €30-€32 | Dinner | - |
| B&B | - | Standard | | Partial Board | - |
| Single Rate | | | €40-€45 | Child reduction | - |

Portmagee 1km    Ⓥ    **Open:** 1st May-30th September

---

### Mrs Julie O'Sullivan
**GLENREEN HEIGHTS**
Knightstown Road, Valentia Island, Co Kerry

TEL: **066 9476241**   FAX: **066 9476241**
EMAIL: **glenreen@eircom.net**
WEB: **www.glenreenheights.com**

Panoramic view, sea/mountains. Breakfast menu, orthopaedic beds, 3 power showers, tea/coffee facilities, group reductions. Boat trips to Skellig arranged.

| B&B | 3 | Ensuite | €27.50-€31 | Dinner | €18-€18 |
| B&B | 1 | Standard | €25.50-€28.50 | Partial Board | - |
| Single Rate | | | €38-€43.50 | Child reduction | 50% |

Knightstown 2km    Ⓥ    **Open:** 1st April-1st November

---

### Mrs Breda Barry
**GOLF LINKS VIEW**
Murreigh, Waterville, Co Kerry

TEL: **066 9474623**   FAX: **066 9474623**
EMAIL: **jbar@eircom.net**
WEB: **www.golflinksview.com**

AA ◆◆◆ recommended, luxury home downstairs bedrooms. Power showers, Hairdryers, TV, open peat fire. Golf Course, Fishing, Horse Riding, Beach, trips to Skelligs.

| B&B | 6 | Ensuite | €27.50-€31 | Dinner | €19-€22 |
| B&B | - | Standard | | Partial Board | - |
| Single Rate | | | €40-€43.50 | Child reduction | 25% |

Waterville 1km    Ⓥ    **Open:** 1st March-30th November

---

### Mrs Margaret Brown
**THE OLD CABLE HOUSE**
Milestone Heritage Site, Old Cable Station, Waterville Village, Co Kerry

TEL: **066 9474233**   FAX: **066 9474869**
EMAIL: **interestingstay@iol.ie**
WEB: **www.oldcablehouse.com**

Interesting stay. Origins First Transatlantic Telegraph Cable from Ireland to USA - Victorian Internet, 1866. Waterville Golf Links, Free Salmon - Trout fishing Lough Currane.

| B&B | 4 | Ensuite | €27.50-€35 | Dinner | €19 |
| B&B | 2 | Standard | €25.50-€30 | Partial Board | €300 |
| Single Rate | | | €38-€50 | Child reduction | 25% |

n Waterville    Ⓥ    **Open:** 1st January-31st December

---

### Mrs Abbie Clifford
**CLIFFORDS B&B**
Waterville, Co Kerry

TEL: **066 9474283**   FAX: **066 9474283**
EMAIL: **cliffordbandb@eircom.net**

Family run B+B in Waterville, Ring of Kerry, overlooking the Atlantic Ocean, close to all amenities, Golf, Fishing, Walking, Cycling etc. Skeelig trips arranged. Drying facilities available.

| B&B | 4 | Ensuite | €27.50-€31 | Dinner | - |
| B&B | 1 | Standard | €25.50-€28.50 | Partial Board | - |
| Single Rate | | | €40-€43.50 | Child reduction | 33.3% |

n Waterville    Ⓥ    **Open:** 15th March-31st October

**In Waterville**

**Mrs Angela Grady**
O'GRADYS TOWNHOUSE
Spunkane, Waterville, Co Kerry

TEL: **066 9474350**  FAX: **066 9474730**
EMAIL: **paogrady@eircom.net**
WEB: **www.stayatogradys.com**

Ideally located B&B. Close to all amenities, Golf, Fishing, trips to Skellig Rock arranged. Spacious ensuite rooms, Visitors lounge, Breakfast Menu.

| B&B | 6 | Ensuite | €27.50-€31 | Dinner | €19 |
|-----|---|---------|-----------|--------|-----|
| B&B | - | Standard | - | Partial Board | - |
| Single Rate | | | €40-€43.50 | Child reduction | 33.3% |

**Open:** 1st March-31st October

**In Waterville**

**Mrs Cirean Morris**
KLONDYKE HOUSE
New Line Road, Waterville,
Co Kerry

TEL: **066 9474119**  FAX: **066 9474666**
EMAIL: **klondykehouse@eircom.net**
WEB: **http://homepage.eircom.net/~klondykehouse**
BUS NO: **279, 280**

Luxurious accommodation with sun-lounge on N70, fantastic ocean views, town 3 mins walk, recommended by all leading giudebooks. Golf, Fishing on Lough Currane, Skellig trips arranged.

| B&B | 6 | Ensuite | €27.50-€31 | Dinner | €19-€19 |
|-----|---|---------|-----------|--------|---------|
| B&B | - | Standard | - | Partial Board | €280 |
| Single Rate | | | €40-€43.50 | Child reduction | 25% |

**Open:** All Year Except Christmas

# Heritage ISLAND
## IRELAND'S VISITOR ATTRACTIONS

The centres range from historic houses, castles, heritage towns, monuments, museums, galleries, national parks, interpretative centres, gardens and theme parks.

Visitors can avail of big savings by displaying this *Heritage Island Explorer* at the following attractions, which will entitle them to reduced admission, many two for one's and special offers...

**ANTRIM**
- Giant's Causeway
- Ulster Museum
- whowhatwherewhenwhy W5

**ARMAGH**
- Armagh Planetarium
- Saint Patrick's Trian

**CAVAN**
- Cavan County Museum

**CLARE**
- Aillwee Cave
- Bunratty Castle & Folk Park
- Clare Museum
- Craggaunowen

**CLARE (CONT)**
- Killaloe/Ballina Heritage Town*
- Kilrush Heritage Town*

**CORK**
- Bantry House & Gardens
- Blarney Castle
- Cobh Heritage Town*
- Fota House

**CORK (CONT)**
- Kinsale Heritage Town*
- Mizen Head Visitor Centre
- Old Midleton Distillery
- Skibbereen Heritage Centre
- Youghal Heritage Town*

**DONEGAL**
- Donegal County Museum

**DOWN**
- Castle Ward
- Mount Stewart House and Gardens
- Saint Patrick Centre
- Somme Heritage Centre
- Ulster Folk & Transport Museum

**DUBLIN**
- Bank of Ireland Arts Centre
- Chimney Viewing Tower
- Dalkey Heritage Town*
- Dublin City Gallery The Hugh Lane

**DUBLIN (CONT)**
- Dublinia
- Dublin's City Hall, The Story of the Capital
- GAA Museum
- Guinness Storehouse
- Old Jameson Distillery
- Saint Patrick's Cathedral

**DUBLIN (CONT)**
- Trinity College Library and Dublin Experience

**FERMANAGH**
- Belleek Pottery Visitor Centre
- Castle Coole

**FERMANAGH (CONT)**
- Enniskillen Castle & Museums
- Marble Arch Caves

**GALWAY**
- Galway Atlantaquaria
- Galway Irish Crystal Heritage Centre

**GALWAY (CONT)**
- Horseworld at Dartfield - Ireland's Horse Museum & Equestrian Park
- Kylemore Abbey and Garden
- Rathbaun Farm

**KERRY**
- Crag Cave
- Kerry County Museum
- Listowel Heritage Town*
- Siamsa Tíre

**KILDARE**
- Irish National Stud, Japanese Gardens & St. Fiachra's Garden

**LIMERICK**
- Adare Heritage Centre
- Hunt Museum, Limerick

**LIMERICK (CONT)**
- King John's Castle

**MAYO**
- Westport Heritage Town*
- Westport House

**MEATH**
- Kells Heritage Town*

**MEATH (CONT)**
- Trim Heritage Town*

**OFFALY**
- Birr Heritage Town*
- Birr Castle Demesne & Ireland's Historic Science Centre

**OFFALY (CONT)**
- Tullamore Dew Heritage Centre

**ROSCOMMON**
- Cruachan Aí
- King House
- Lough Key Forest Park

**ROSCOMMON (CONT)**
- Strokestown Park

**TIPPERARY**
- Brú Ború
- Cashel Heritage Town*
- Killaloe/Ballina Heritage Town*

**TIPPERARY (CONT)**
- Roscrea Heritage Town*
- Tipperary Heritage Town*

**TYRONE**
- Ulster American Folk Park

**WATERFORD**
- Lismore Heritage Town*

**WATERFORD (CONT)**
- Waterford Crystal Visitor Centre
- Waterford Museum of Treasures

**WESTMEATH**
- Athlone Castle

**WESTMEATH (CONT)**
- Belvedere House

**WEXFORD**
- Dunbrody Emigrant Ship
- Hook Lighthouse
- Irish National Heritage Park

**WICKLOW**
- Avondale House
- National Sealife Centre
- Powerscourt House and Gardens
- Russborough

scount available at Visitor Centre in Heritage Town
ritage Island members confirmed as at September 2004. Heritage Island cannot accept responsibility for any errors or omissions.

or further details on each of the attractions and Heritage Towns listed above, why not visit

**www.heritageisland.com**

# Heritage ISLAND
## IRELAND'S VISITOR ATTRACTIONS
# EXPLORER
Display this Explorer at any Heritage Island Centre to qualify for reduced admission

eritage Island, Ground Floor, Marina House, 11-13 Clarence Street, Dun Laoghaire, Co. Dublin. Email:info@heritageisland.com

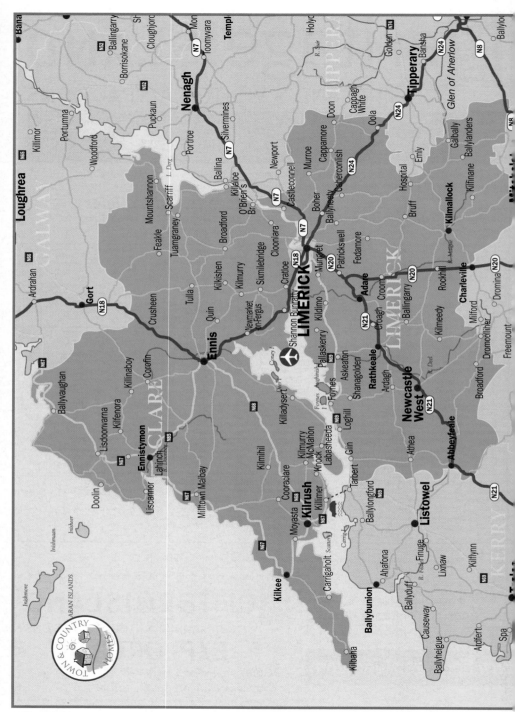

*Shannonside*

# Ireland's Shannonside

Δe Shannon Region comprise counties Clare, Limerick, North Tipperary, North Kerry and South ffaly. It is a particularly beautiful part of Ireland and is dominated by water. The Shannon river, e longest river in Ireland or the UK flows through its centre and gives the Region its name. 1annon's Lough Derg - Ireland's pleasure lake - touches on three counties, Clare, Tipperary and alway. The Region also boasts hundreds of smaller lakes and many rivers.

Δe Shannon Region has a dramatic Atlantic coastline, with beautiful beaches and a purity of air at refreshes the Region and invigorates the visitor.

Δough the Shannon Region is compact, only 100 miles (166 Kms), from end to end, there is

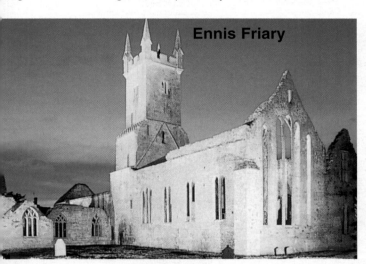

**Ennis Friary**

tremendous diversity in its scenery from the Slieve Bloom mountains to lakelands, golden beaches, the awesome Cliffs of Moher and the Burren District.

The Region offers great visitor attractions and night-time entertainment options and is also perfect for the activity enthusiast interested in Golfing, Angling, Horse Riding, Walking, Cycling or water based activities.

## rea Representatives

**ARE**
rs Patricia Byrnes RATHMORE HOUSE Ballina Killaloe Co Clare
l: 061 379296
rs Mary Corcoran GRANGE Wood Road Cratloe Co Clare
l: 061 357389   Fax: 061 357389
rs Phil Fleming KNOCKNAGOW Leimaneighmore Newmarket-on-Fergus
Clare  Tel: 061 368685   Fax: 061 368685

**MERICK**
s Agnes Callinan MOYRHEE Phares Road off N18 Meelick Co Limerick
l: 061 326300
rs Eileen Murphy THE ORCHARD Limerick Road Newcastle West
Limerick  Tel: 069 61029   Fax: 069 61029

 ## Tourist Information Offices
**OPEN ALL YEAR**
REFER TO PAGE 5 FOR A LIST OF SERVICES AVAILABLE

Ennis
Arthurs Row
(off O'Connell
Square)
Tel: 065 6828366

Shannon Airport
Arrivals Hall
Tel: 061 471664

Limerick City
Arthur's Quay
Tel: 061 317522

Tralee
Ashe Memorial Hall
Tel: 066 7121288

Website: **www.shannon-dev.ie**

Clare is renowned for traditional music, its rugged beauty with Shannon Airport at its gateway.
Attractions: Bunratty Folk Park, Ennis, The famous Burren, Cliffs of Moher, Lisdoonvarna Spa Wells & Doolin. Championship Golf at Lahinch. Great fishing, excellent beaches, walks & trails.

---

**PJ & Margaret Fitzpatrick**
SEACOAST LODGE
**Craggagh, Fanore,**
**Ballyvaughan, Co Clare**

### Ballyvaughan
TEL: **065 7076250**
EMAIL: **seacoasbb@eircom.net**
WEB: **www.seacoastbb.com**

Family run home near blue flag beach on R477, beautiful views, Burren trails, beside shop, traditional pub and restaurant.

| B&B | 4 | Ensuite | €27.50-€32.50 | Dinner | - |
|---|---|---|---|---|---|
| B&B | - | Standard | - | Partial Board | - |
| Single Rate | | | €40-€43.50 | Child reduction | 25% |

Ballyvaughan 5km

**Open:** 15th March-1st November

---

**Annette Flanagan**
LOUGHRASK LODGE
**Ballyvaughan, Co Clare**

### Ballyvaughan
TEL: **00353 657077151**
EMAIL: **aflanagan77@eircom.net**
WEB: **www.loughrasklodge.com**

Beautifully positioned friendly home over looking Galway Bay and the Burren mountains guest sitting room with tv, tea & coffee available at all times.

| B&B | 4 | Ensuite | €30-€35 | Dinner | - |
|---|---|---|---|---|---|
| B&B | - | Standard | - | Partial Board | - |
| Single Rate | | | €40-€55 | Child reduction | 50% |

Ballyvaughan 1km

**Open:** 1st February-31st October

---

**Mr Gerard Flanagan**
THE CORE HOUSE
**Ballyvaughan, Co Clare**

### Ballyvaughan
TEL: **065 7077310**
EMAIL: **corehouse@eircom.net**
WEB: **www.thecorehouse.net**

Overlooking panoramic views of Galway Bay and The Burren Mountains. Guest sitting room with a TV. Tea & Coffee available at all times. Breakfast menu.

| B&B | 4 | Ensuite | €28-€33 | Dinner | - |
|---|---|---|---|---|---|
| B&B | - | Standard | - | Partial Board | - |
| Single Rate | | | €45-€59 | Child reduction | 33.3% |

Ballyvaughan 1km

**Open:** 1st February-31st October

---

**Hilde Schultheiss**
COOLSHINE B&B
**Green Road, Ballyvaughan,**
**Co Clare**

### Ballyvaughan
TEL: **065 7077163**
EMAIL: **coolshine@eircom.net**
WEB: **homepage.eircom.net/~coolshine**

Beautiful, quiet, friendly home. 0.1km off Galway road. Maps & Books for your use. German spoken. Organic homemade bread & jams. Family & 3 bedded Room.

| B&B | 3 | Ensuite | €28-€31 | Dinner | - |
|---|---|---|---|---|---|
| B&B | - | Standard | - | Partial Board | - |
| Single Rate | | | €40-€45 | Child reduction | 33.3% |

Ballyvaughan

**Open:** 27th March-31st October

**Mairead Bateman**
PARK HOUSE
Low Road, Bunratty, Co Clare

TEL: **061 369902**  FAX: **061 369903**
EMAIL: **parkhouse@eircom.net**
WEB: **homepage.eircom.net/~parkhouse**

Luxurious peaceful home. Full menu. Home baking. Bunratty Castle 1km. Airport 10 minutes drive. Orthopaedic beds, TV, Tea/Coffee, Curling tongs, Hairdryer. AA ◆◆◆◆

| B&B | 6 | Ensuite | €35-€35 | Dinner | - |
|---|---|---|---|---|---|
| B&B | - | Standard | | Partial Board | - |
| Single Rate | | | €50-€50 | Child reduction | 25% |

Bunratty 1km

**Open:** 10th January-20th December

---

**Kathleen Browne**
HEADLEY COURT
Deerpark, Bunratty,
Six Mile Bridge Post Office,
Co Clare

TEL: **061 369768**
EMAIL: **headleycourt@eircom.net**
WEB: **www.headleycourt.net**

Luxurious countryside residence, spacious heated rooms with large showers. Every convenience. Sullivan, Erdvig McQuillan recommended. End low road go right.

| B&B | 5 | Ensuite | €33.50-€33.50 | Dinner | - |
|---|---|---|---|---|---|
| B&B | - | Standard | - | Partial Board | - |
| Single Rate | | | - | Child reduction | 33.3% |

Bunratty 3km

**Open:** 15th February-15th November

---

**Mrs Mary Browne**
BUNRATTY LODGE
Sixmilebridge P.O., Bunratty,
Co Clare

TEL: **061 369402**
EMAIL: **reservations@bunrattylodge.com**
WEB: **www.bunrattylodge.com**

Luxurious, well heated rooms on ground floor with every convenience. Award winning breakfast. Recommended by all leading guides. Airport 10 minutes.

| B&B | 5 | Ensuite | €35 | Dinner | - |
|---|---|---|---|---|---|
| B&B | - | Standard | - | Partial Board | - |
| Single Rate | | | | Child reduction | - |

Bunratty 3km

**Open:** 1st March-15th November

---

**Mrs Jackie Burns**
BUNRATTY VILLA
Bunratty East, Co Clare

TEL: **061 369241**  FAX: **061 369947**
EMAIL: **bunrattyvilla@eircom.net**
WEB: **www.bunrattyvilla.com**

Luxurious B&B, All rooms ensuite with tea/coffee facilities, TV & Hairdryers.Bunratty Castle 5 minutes. Recommended by Hidden Ireland.

| B&B | 6 | Ensuite | €35-€35 | Dinner | - |
|---|---|---|---|---|---|
| B&B | - | Standard | - | Partial Board | - |
| Single Rate | | | €50-€50 | Child reduction | - |

Shannon 6km

**Open:** 20th March-30th November

---

**Mrs Mary Corcoran**
GRANGE
Wood Road, Cratloe, Co Clare

TEL: **061 357389**  FAX: **061 357389**
EMAIL: **alfie@iol.ie**
WEB: **www.grangebedandbreakfast.com**

Off N18 at Radisson Hotel. Spacious house, rooms ground floor. Shannon Airport 15 mins, Bunratty 5 mins.  Frommer, Lonely Planet recommended. Electric blankets. Early arrivals welcome.

| B&B | 3 | Ensuite | €27.50-€31 | Dinner | €19 |
|---|---|---|---|---|---|
| B&B | 2 | Standard | €25.50-€28.50 | Partial Board | - |
| Single Rate | | | €38-€43.50 | Child reduction | 50% |

Limerick 6km

**Open:** 1st January-31st December

**Mrs Trish Cronin**
BRIAR LODGE
Hill Road, Bunratty, Co Clare

TEL: **061 363388**  FAX: **061 363161**
EMAIL: **briarlodge@eircom.net**
WEB: **www.briarlodge.com**

Turn left between Gallaghers seafood restaurant & Fitzpatricks hotel, 1 mile on right. Hairdryers, Curling Irons all rooms. Guest lounge. Breakfast menu. AM arrivals welcome.

| B&B | 6 | Ensuite | €30-€32 | Dinner | - |
| B&B | - | Standard | | Partial Board | - |
| Single Rate | | | €40-€45 | Child reduction | 25% |

**Bunratty 1.5km**

**Open:** 1st March-31st October

---

**Mrs Patricia Darcy**
BUNRATTY HEIGHTS
Low Road, Bunratty, Co Clare

TEL: **061 369324**  FAX: **061 369324**
EMAIL: **bunrattyheights@eircom.net**
WEB: **www.bb-house.com/bunrattyheights.htm**

Morning guests welcome. Situated on Low Road 1 mile from Bunratty Castle/Durty Nellies. Airport 10 minutes. TV's, Hairdryers, Tea/Coffee facilities all rooms.

| B&B | 4 | Ensuite | €31-€31 | Dinner | - |
| B&B | - | Standard | | Partial Board | - |
| Single Rate | | | €40-€44 | Child reduction | 50% |

**In Bunratty 6km**

**Open:** 6th January-14th December

---

**T.M. Dennehy**
TUDOR LODGE
Hill Road, Bunratty, Co Clare

TEL: **061 362248**  FAX: **061 362248**
EMAIL: **tudorlodge@esatclear.ie**

Tudor style residence, Sylvan setting. All rooms have private facilities, TVs, Hairdryers. Bunratty Castle 5 mins walk. Shannon Airport 10 mins drive.

| B&B | 5 | Ensuite | €35-€35 | Dinner | - |
| B&B | - | Standard | - | Partial Board | - |
| Single Rate | | | €50-€50 | Child reduction | 25% |

**In Bunratty**

**Open:** 1st February-30th November

---

**Mrs Anne Fuller**
LEAVALE
Bunratty, Moyhill, Cratloe, Co Clare

TEL: **061 357439**
EMAIL: **leavale@eircom.net**
WEB: **www.leavale.com**

South of Bunratty on N18. Airport 10 mins. Inside Ireland recommended. Ground floor rooms. Orthopaedic beds, Clock Radio, Tea/Coffee in rooms. Guest garden.

| B&B | 2 | Ensuite | €28-€33 | Dinner | - |
| B&B | 1 | Standard | €27-€31 | Partial Board | - |
| Single Rate | | | €40-€45 | Child reduction | 25% |

**Bunratty 1km**

**Open:** 15th March-31st October

---

**Mrs Teresa Grady**
BUNRATTY ARMS
Bunratty, Six Mile Bridge, Co Clare

TEL: **061 369530**  FAX: **061 369256**
EMAIL: **catherineteresa@eircom.net**
WEB: **www.bunratty.net/bunrattyarms**

R471 off N18 1 mile, or take Road between Castle & Durty Nelly's, at end turn right.

| B&B | 4 | Ensuite | €32-€35 | Dinner | - |
| B&B | - | Standard | | Partial Board | - |
| Single Rate | | | €47-€52 | Child reduction | 50% |

**Bunratty 3km**

**Open:** 1st February-30th November

**Bunratty**

**Denis Hegarty**
DUNEDIN LODGE
Low Road, Bunratty, Co Clare

TEL: **061 369966**  FAX: **061 369953**
EMAIL: **dunedinhouse2000@eircom.net**
WEB: **www.dunedin-lodge.com**

Luxurious hillside home, rooms ensuite, tv/hairdryers, orthopaedic beds, tea/coffee on request, Shannon Airport 10 mins, Bunratty Castle 1km private car park.

| B&B | 5 | Ensuite | €32-€35 | Dinner | - |
| B&B | - | Standard | | Partial Board | - |
| Single Rate | | | €45-€45 | Child reduction | - |

Bunratty 1km

**Open:** 14th January-16th December

---

**Bunratty**

**Mrs Maureen McCabe**
McCabe's B+B
Clonmoney North (R471 Rd),
Bunratty, Co Clare

TEL: **061 364330**  FAX: **061 364330**
EMAIL: **mccabe@bunratty.net**
WEB: **www.bunratty.net/hillside**

Morning guests welcome. Dillard/Causin recommended. Airport 10 mins, Bunratty 2 km, off N18 at Sixmilebridge R471. Guests collected from Airport & Bus Stop.

| B&B | 4 | Ensuite | €30-€31 | Dinner | - |
| B&B | 2 | Standard | €28-€28.50 | Partial Board | - |
| Single Rate | | | €40-€43.50 | Child reduction | 25% |

Shannon 2km

**Open:** 1st January-31st December

---

**Bunratty**

**Mrs Imelda McCarthy**
INNISFREE
Low Road, Bunratty, Co Clare

TEL: **061 369773**  FAX: **061 369926**
EMAIL: **innisfree@unison.ie**
WEB: **bedandbreakfastireland.net**

Airport 10 mins. Road between Castle/Durty Nelly's. Tea/Coffee facilities, Hairdryers.  Frommer Readers recommended.  Breakfast menu, morning guests welcome.

| B&B | 4 | Ensuite | €30-€32 | Dinner | - |
| B&B | - | Standard | | Partial Board | - |
| Single Rate | | | €45-€50 | Child reduction | 50% |

n Bunratty

**Open:** 1st February-8th December

---

**Bunratty**

**Freddie & Deirdre McInerney**
AVAREST B&B
Hurlers Cross, Bunratty,
Co Clare

TEL: **061 360278**  FAX: **061 360414**
EMAIL: **avarest@eircom.net**
WEB: **www.avarest.ie**

New luxurious purpose-built home. Spacious rooms. TV, Telephones, Orthopaedic beds. Off N18 at Hurlers Cross. Bunratty/Airport 2 miles. Ideal touring base.

| B&B | 4 | Ensuite | €30-€35 | Dinner | - |
| B&B | - | Standard | | Partial Board | - |
| Single Rate | | | €40-€48 | Child reduction | 25% |

Shannon 3km

**Open:** 3rd January-20th December

---

**Bunratty**

**Paula McInerney**
RIVERSIDE B&B
Clonmoney West, Bunratty,
Co Clare

TEL: **061 364148**  FAX: **061 364148**
EMAIL: **riversideguests@eircom.net**
WEB: **www.riversidebnb.net**

Custom built luxurious B&B. Spacious bedrooms with TV. Breakfast menu. Early Breakfast available. Situated on N18. Airport 10 mins, Bunratty 5 mins.

| B&B | 4 | Ensuite | €32.50-€32.50 | Dinner | - |
| B&B | - | Standard | | Partial Board | - |
| Single Rate | | | €45-€50 | Child reduction | 25% |

n Bunratty

**Open:** 7th January-20th December

**Mrs Mary McKenna**
GALLOW'S VIEW
Bunratty East, Co Clare

### Bunratty

TEL: **061 369125**  FAX: **061 369125**
EMAIL: **gallowsview@eircom.net**
WEB: **www.bunratty.net/gallowsview**

Warm and friendly home. Frommer Recommended. Airport 10 mins. Breakfast Menu. TV, Hairdryers, Tea/Coffee. Road between Castle/Durty Nellies, through carpark, 7th house on right.

| B&B | 5 | Ensuite | €32-€35 | Dinner | - |
| B&B | - | Standard | | Partial Board | - |
| Single Rate | | | €45-€45 | Child reduction | **25%** |

Shannon 6km

**Open:** 15th February-30th November

**Jan & Jim Moloney**
HUNTING LODGE B&B
Wood Road, Cratloe, Co Clare

### Bunratty

TEL: **061 357216**  FAX: **061 357216**
EMAIL: **moloneyjj@eircom.net**

Spacious house, scenic views, quiet location, Bunratty 5 minutes, Limerick 10 minutes, Airport 15 minutes. 1 mile off N18 at Radisson SAS.

| B&B | 2 | Ensuite | €27.50-€31 | Dinner | - |
| B&B | 2 | Standard | €25.50-€28.50 | Partial Board | - |
| Single Rate | | | €38-€43.50 | Child reduction | **50%** |

Limerick 6km

**Open:** 2nd January-20th December

**Mrs Penny O'Connor**
DUNAREE
Low Road, Bunratty, Co Clare

### Bunratty

TEL: **061 369131**
EMAIL: **dunaree@eircom.net**
WEB: **www.dunaree.com**

Hillside residence with panoramic view, walking distance to Bunratty Castle. Luxurious bedrooms, all en-suite. Shannon Airport 10 minutes.

| B&B | 5 | Ensuite | €35 | Dinner | - |
| B&B | - | Standard | - | Partial Board | - |
| Single Rate | | | €50 | Child reduction | - |

Bunratty Village 1km

**Open:** 1st April-20th October

**Mrs Rosemary Ormston**
HIGHBURY HOUSE
Ballymorris, Cratloe, Co Clare

### Bunratty

TEL: **061 357212**
EMAIL: **cormston@iol.ie**

Tudor style Country Home on N18. 2 miles from Bunratty Castle travelling south towards Limerick or 6 miles from Limerick City travelling north. Hairdryers, Electric Blankets.

| B&B | 4 | Ensuite | €30-€35 | Dinner | - |
| B&B | - | Standard | - | Partial Board | - |
| Single Rate | | | €40-€45 | Child reduction | **50%** |

Bunratty 3km

**Open:** 1st January-15th December

**Mrs Kathleen O'Shea**
MANDERLEY
Deer Park, Bunratty,
Sixmilebridge, Co Clare

### Bunratty

TEL: **061 369572**
EMAIL: **manderley@oceanfree.net**
WEB: **http://gofree.indigo.ie/~manderly**

Two storey country home with mature gardens. Take road between Durty Nellys and Castle, turn right at end of road, third house on left handside.

| B&B | 4 | Ensuite | --€32.50 | Dinner | - |
| B&B | - | Standard | | Partial Board | - |
| Single Rate | | | --€45 | Child reduction | **25%** |

Shannon 8km

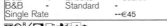

**Open:** 14th January-30th November

**Mary Slattery**
ROCKLANDS B&B
Hill road, Bunratty, Co Clare

### Bunratty

Tel: **061 363169**   Fax: **061 363169**
Email: **rocklandsbunratty@eircom.net**

Excellent accomm in homely and friendly atmosphere. All conveniences, all ground floor accommodation. Bunratty Castle 2 mins, turn left at Fitzpatricks Hotel 1 mile on left.

| B&B | 3 | Ensuite | €27.50-€31 | Dinner | - |
| B&B | - | Standard | - | Partial Board | - |
| Single Rate | | | €40-€43.50 | Child reduction | 33.3% |

n Bunratty

**Open:** 20th February-1st November

---

**Dariena Sutton**
BUNRATTY MEADOWS
Clonmoney West, Bunratty,
Co Clare

### Bunratty

Tel: **061 364725**   Fax: **061 718872**
Email: **relax@bunrattymeadows.com**
Web: **www.bunrattymeadows.com**

Beautifully positioned luxurious new custom built home overlooking the Shannon Estuary and Islands. Orthopaedic beds, Tv. Airport 2km, Castle and Folk Park 1km.

| B&B | 4 | Ensuite | €33-€36 | Dinner | - |
| B&B | - | Standard | - | Partial Board | - |
| Single Rate | | | €45-€50 | Child reduction | 25% |

Bunratty 1km

**Open:** 1st January-12th December

---

**Sheila Tiernan**
ASHGROVE HOUSE
Lowroad, Bunratty, Co Clare

### Bunratty

Tel: **061 369332**
Email: **sheila@ashgrovehouse.com**
Web: **www.ashgrovehouse.com**

Take low road between Bunratty Castle and Durty Nellies. 10 min drive to Airport. Free carpark. Private entrances. 3 min drive to Bunratty. Warm rooms. Good beds. All facilities.

| B&B | 4 | Ensuite | €27.50-€33 | Dinner | - |
| B&B | - | Standard | - | Partial Board | - |
| Single Rate | | | €40-€50 | Child reduction | 50% |

n Bunratty

**Open:** 1st January-20th December

---

**Mrs Mary Cleary**
LAKEFIELD LODGE
Ennis Road, Corofin, Co Clare

### Corofin

Tel: **065 6837675**   Fax: **065 6837299**
Email: **mcleary.ennis@eircom.net**

Recommended by "Le Guide du Routard". On periphery of Burren National Park. Cliffs of Moher, Shannon Airport 40 mins. Fishing locally. Tea/Coffee facilities.

| B&B | 4 | Ensuite | €28-€31 | Dinner | - |
| B&B | - | Standard | - | Partial Board | - |
| Single Rate | | | €40-€45 | Child reduction | 33.3% |

n Corofin

**Open:** 1st March-31st October

---

**Mrs Anne Connole**
CONNOLES
Killeen, Corofin, Co Clare

### Corofin

Tel: **065 6837773**
Email: **connolesbandb@eircom.net**
Web: **www.connolesbandb.com**

A luxury family run home by Ballycullian Lake. The gateway to the Burren. 10 mins from Ennis. Leisurely activities closeby. Breakfast menu.

| B&B | 4 | Ensuite | €29-€31 | Dinner | - |
| B&B | - | Standard | - | Partial Board | - |
| Single Rate | | | €40-€45 | Child reduction | 33.3% |

Corofin 2km

**Open:** 1st March-30th November

**Corofin**

**Mr Brendan Kearney**
SHAMROCK & HEATHER
Station Road, Corofin, Co Clare
TEL: **065 6837061**  FAX: **065 6837061**
EMAIL: **bmkearney@eircom.net**

Shannon Airport 40 minutes. Lake District, Cliffs of Moher, Burren National Park, Traditional Music, Clare Heritage Centre, Museum. Hairdryer, Tea/Coffee.

| B&B | 2 | Ensuite | €27.50-€31 | Dinner | - |
| B&B | 1 | Standard | €25.50-€28.50 | Partial Board | - |
| Single Rate | | | €38-€43.50 | Child reduction | **33.3%** |

**Corofin**

**Open:** 1st March-31st October

---

**Corofin**

**Mary Shannon**
COROFIN COUNTRY HOUSE
Station Road, Corofin, Co Clare
TEL: **065 6837791**  FAX: **065 6837791**

Luxury accommodation within walking distance of Corofin village with its pubs music and restaurants. Recommended by Lets Go Ireland.

| B&B | 4 | Ensuite | €27.50-€31 | Dinner | - |
| B&B | - | Standard | - | Partial Board | - |
| Single Rate | | | €40-€44 | Child reduction | **25%** |

**In Corofin**

**Open:** 1st March-30th November

---

**Doolin**

**Mrs Kathleen Cullinan**
HARBOUR VIEW
Doolin, Co Clare
TEL: **065 7074154**  FAX: **065 7074935**
EMAIL: **clarebb@eircom.net**
WEB: **www.harbourviewdoolin.com**

Spacious ground floor bedrooms. Breathtaking views - Cliffs of Moher, Burren, Aran Islands. Airport 1 hour. Hairdryers, Electric blankets. Rick Steeves.

| B&B | 4 | Ensuite | €32-€32 | Dinner | - |
| B&B | - | Standard | €30-€30 | Partial Board | - |
| Single Rate | | | €50-€50 | Child reduction | **25%** |

**Doolin 2km**

**Open:** 20th February-5th November

---

**Doolin**

**Susan Daly**
DALY'S HOUSE
Doolin, Co Clare
TEL: **065 7074242**  FAX: **065 7074668**
EMAIL: **susan@daly-doolin.com**
WEB: **www.dalys-doolin.com**

Situated 150 yards from Doolin Village-home of Traditional Music. Panoramic views of the Sea, Cliffs of Moher, Burren. Family run.

| B&B | 5 | Ensuite | €30-€32 | Dinner | - |
| B&B | - | Standard | - | Partial Board | - |
| Single Rate | | | - | Child reduction | **25%** |

**In Doolin**

**Open:** All Year

---

**Doolin**

**Ms Olive Dowling**
TOOMULLIN HOUSE
Doolin Village, Co Clare
TEL: **065 7074723**
EMAIL: **toomullin@eircom.net**
WEB: **www.toomullin.com**

Lovely country cottage in Doolin Village. 1 mins walk to traditional music Pubs and Restaurants. Tea/Coffee. Breakfast menu. Cliffs, Burren, Aran Ferry nearby.

| B&B | 3 | Ensuite | €30-€32 | Dinner | - |
| B&B | - | Standard | - | Partial Board | - |
| Single Rate | | | €45-€50 | Child reduction | **25%** |

**In Doolin**

**Open:** 1st January-28th December

### Brid & Val Egan
**ATLANTIC SUNSET HOUSE**
**Cliffs of Moher Road, Doolin, Co Clare**

**Doolin**

TEL: **065 7074080** FAX: **065 7074922**
EMAIL: **sunsethouse@esatclear.ie**
WEB: **www.atlanticsunsetdoolin.com**

Warm hospitable home conveniently located on R478. Near Cliffs of Moher, Aran Ferry, Burren, Music, Pubs. Breakfast Menu. Airport 1hour. Highly recommended by Travel Guides.

| B&B | 6 | Ensuite | €30-€33 | Dinner | - |
| B&B | - | Standard | | Partial Board | - |
| Single Rate | | | €45-€50 | Child reduction | 25% |

Doolin 2km

**Open:** 1st January-20th December

---

### Olwyn & Desmond Egan
**ASHBROOK LODGE**
**Boherbue, Doolin, Co Clare**

**Doolin/Cliffs of Moher**

TEL: **065 7074100**
EMAIL: **ashbrooklodge@eircom.net**
WEB: **www.ashbrooklodge-doolin.com**

Luxurious family home. Spacious rooms all with panoramic sea views, island, Galway Bay. Village 10 mins walk. Near Cliffs of Moher, Aran ferry, golf, pubs.

| B&B | 3 | Ensuite | €32-€37 | Dinner | - |
| B&B | - | Standard | - | Partial Board | - |
| Single Rate | | | | Child reduction | 25% |

Doolin Village 2km

**Open:** 1st April-30th September

---

### Mrs Maeve Fitzgerald
**CHURCHFIELD**
**Doolin, Co Clare**

**Doolin**

TEL: **065 7074209** FAX: **065 7074622**
EMAIL: **churchfield@eircom.net**
WEB: **www.doolinaccomodations.com**

House in Doolin Village. View - Cliffs Moher, Sea/Countryside. Traditional music. Burren. Frommer recommended. Breakfast menu. Tea/Coffee. At bus stop.

| B&B | 6 | Ensuite | €30-€33 | Dinner | €20-€22 |
| B&B | - | Standard | - | Partial Board | - |
| Single Rate | | | €45-€55 | Child reduction | 33.3% |

Doolin Village

**Open:** All Year Except Christmas

---

### Darra Hughes
**SEA VIEW HOUSE**
**Fisher Street, Doolin, Co Clare**

**Doolin**

TEL: **065 7074826** FAX: **065 7074849**
EMAIL: **info@ireland-doolin.com**
WEB: **www.ireland-doolin.com**

Luxury accommodation in the Village of Doolin overlooking the Atlantic Ocean. Extensive breakfast menu. Minutes walk music pubs, restaurants, Aran Ferry.

| B&B | 4 | Ensuite | €30-€40 | Dinner | - |
| B&B | - | Standard | - | Partial Board | - |
| Single Rate | | | - | Child reduction | 25% |

n Doolin

**Open:** 4th January-20th December

---

### Marian & Martin McDonagh
**GLASHA MEADOWS**
**Glasha, Doolin, Co Clare**

**Doolin**

TEL: **065 7074443** FAX: **065 7074443**
EMAIL: **glameadows@eircom.net**
WEB: **www.glashameadows.com**

Family bungalow 1.5km from Doolin Village. Quiet location R479. Cliffs of Moher, Aran Ferries, Airport 1 hour. Breakfast menu. All guests bedrooms on ground floor.

| B&B | 6 | Ensuite | €27.50-€31 | Dinner | - |
| B&B | - | Standard | - | Partial Board | - |
| Single Rate | | | - | Child reduction | 25% |

Doolin 1.5km

**Open:** All Year Except Christmas

**Mrs Josephine Moloney**
**HORSESHOE HOUSE**
Fisher Street, Doolin, Co Clare

**Doolin/Cliffs of Moher**

TEL: **065 7074006**
EMAIL: **horseshoe@iol.ie**
WEB: **www.horseshoehouse.com**

Scenic area overlooking village beside sea. Walking distance to music, pubs, restaurants, Cliffs of Moher, boats to Aran Islands. Shannon Airport 1 hr. Tennis court. R478.

| B&B | 4 | Ensuite | €30-€36 | Dinner | - |
|-----|---|---------|---------|--------|---|
| B&B | - | Standard | - | Partial Board | - |
| Single Rate | | | - | Child reduction | - |

In Doolin    Open: 4th March-31st October

---

**Mary Jo O'Connell**
**SEASCAPE B&B**
Roadford, Doolin, Co Clare

**Doolin**

TEL: **065 7074451** FAX: **065 7074451**
EMAIL: **seascape@eircom.net**
WEB: **www.doolin-bandb.com**

Located on a quiet cul-de-sac in the heart of Doolin village. Close to Pubs, Burren, Cliffs of Moher, Aran Islands Ferries.

| B&B | 4 | Ensuite | €29-€33 | Dinner | - |
|-----|---|---------|---------|--------|---|
| B&B | - | Standard | - | Partial Board | - |
| Single Rate | | | €45-€55 | Child reduction | 25% |

In Doolin    Open: 15th January-15th December

---

**Adrian & Bev O'Connor**
**CRAGGY ISLAND B&B**
Ardeamush, Doolin, Co Clare

**Doolin**

TEL: **065 7074595**
EMAIL: **cragisle@gofree.indigo.ie**
WEB: **homepage.eircom.net/~craggyisland/**

Peaceful, scenic location off R477 Lisdoonvarna/Ballyvaughan Coast road. Near Cliffs of Moher, Burren, Traditional music pubs. Traditional/Vegetarian breakfasts.

| B&B | 5 | Ensuite | €27.50-€31 | Dinner | - |
|-----|---|---------|------------|--------|---|
| B&B | - | Standard | - | Partial Board | - |
| Single Rate | | | €40-€43.50 | Child reduction | - |

Doolin 4km    Open: 7th January-30th November

---

**Martin & Joan Reilly**
**DUBHLINN HOUSE**
Doolin, Co Clare

**Doolin**

TEL: **065 7074770**
EMAIL: **martreilly@eircom.net**
WEB: **www.dubhlinnhouse.com**

Bright spacious family home. Less than 10 min walk from all 3 of Doolin's traditional music pubs. 6 breakfasts. Near Cliffs, Burren, Aran Island ferry.

| B&B | 3 | Ensuite | €30-€32 | Dinner | - |
|-----|---|---------|---------|--------|---|
| B&B | - | Standard | - | Partial Board | - |
| Single Rate | | | €45-€46 | Child reduction | 33.3% |

In Doolin    Open: All Year Except Christmas

---

**Ms Lorraine Spencer**
**NELLIE DEE'S**
Killilagh, Doolin Village,
Co Clare

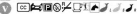
**Doolin/Cliffs of Moher**

TEL: **065 7074020**
EMAIL: **lorspencer@eircom.net**
WEB: **www.nelliedees-doolin.com**

Located in the heart of Doolin Village. Minutes walk to music, pubs, restaurants, Burren, Cliffs, Aran Ferry nearby. Breakfast menu. Ground floor bedrooms.

| B&B | 4 | Ensuite | €30-€32 | Dinner | - |
|-----|---|---------|---------|--------|---|
| B&B | - | Standard | - | Partial Board | - |
| Single Rate | | | - | Child reduction | 33.3% |

In Doolin    Open: 1st February-30th November

In Ennis

**Mrs Martina Brennan**
CLONEEN
Clonroad, Ennis, Co Clare

Ennis

TEL: **065 6829681**

Hiking, biking, driving ideal stop. Town Centre, Station 5 minutes walk. Airport, Burren, Cliffs, Castles 30 mins drive. Spacious gardens. Bicycle shed.

| B&B | 1 | Ensuite | €27.50-€31 | Dinner | - |
| B&B | 2 | Standard | €25.50-€28.50 | Partial Board | - |
| Single Rate | | | €38-€43.50 | Child reduction | 25% |

**Open:** 1st April-31st October

---

In Town

**Denis & Kathleen Cahill**
RAILWAY VIEW HOUSE
Tulla Road, Ennis, Co Clare

Ennis

TEL: **065 6821646**

Very secluded premises, 8 mins walk from Town Centre. Large private car park. No traffic noise. Shannon Airport 20 mins. Convenient to Cliffs of Moher, Burren & Castles.

| B&B | 3 | Ensuite | €27.50-€31 | Dinner | - |
| B&B | - | Standard | - | Partial Board | - |
| Single Rate | | | €40-€43.50 | Child reduction | 50% |

**Open:** 1st February-30th November

---

Ennis 1.5km

**Mrs Mary Connole**
SHANLEE
Lahinch Road, Ennis, Co Clare

Ennis

TEL: **065 6840270**
EMAIL: **mac.ennis@eircom.net**
WEB: **www.dirl.com/clare/shanlee.htm**

Comfortable home with ground floor rooms on N85 to the Burren, Cliffs of Moher, Bunratty Castle, Golf, Fishing. Traditional music. Morning guests welcome.

| B&B | 2 | Ensuite | €29.50-€32 | Dinner | - |
| B&B | 2 | Standard | €27.50-€30 | Partial Board | - |
| Single Rate | | | €38-€43.50 | Child reduction | 50% |

**Open:** 3rd January-23rd December

---

**Nathalie Crowe**
GORT NA MBLATH
Ballaghboy, Doora, Quin Road,
Ennis, Co Clare

Ennis

TEL: **065 6822204**  FAX: **065 6822204**
EMAIL: **crowe.ennis@eircom.net**

Peaceful comfortable family run home. Warm welcome. Ideal starting point for exploring the Burren. Detailed help in planning itinerary. Shannon Airport 15mins. French spoken.

| B&B | 2 | Ensuite | €32-€32 | Dinner | - |
| B&B | 2 | Standard | €29-€29 | Partial Board | - |
| Single Rate | | | €42-€44 | Child reduction | 50% |

Ennis 3km

**Open:** 1st January-31st December

---

Ennis 2km

**Teresa & Tom Crowe**
SHALOM
Ballybeg, Killadysert Road,
Ennis, Co Clare

Ennis

TEL: **065 6829494**

Comfortable, warm, hospitable home. All rooms ground floor. Spacious bathrooms. Quiet location on R473 route, 2km to Ennis Town Centre. Spacious private parking. Shannon Airport 18km.

| B&B | 3 | Ensuite | €30-€32 | Dinner | - |
| B&B | - | Standard | - | Partial Board | - |
| Single Rate | | | €40-€43.50 | Child reduction | - |

**Open:** 1st May-30th September

### Mrs Antoinette Diamond
**CARRAIG MHUIRE B&B**
Bearnafunshin, Barefield,
Ennis, Co Clare

**Ennis**

TEL: **065 6827106**  FAX: **065 6827375**
EMAIL: **info@carraigmhuire.com**
WEB: **http://www.carraigmhuire.com**

Country home, family friendly. Ennis/Galway road N18. Convenient to Cliffs of Moher/Burren & beaches. TV, hairdryers, tea/coffee all rooms.

| B&B | 4 | Ensuite | €35-€37.50 | Dinner | - |
| B&B | - | Standard | | Partial Board | - |
| Single Rate | | | €40-€45 | Child reduction | 25% |

Ennis 8km

**Open:** 1st March-31st October

---

### Seamus Fitzgerald
**SYCAMORE HOUSE**
Tulla Road, Lifford, Ennis,
Co Clare

**Ennis**

TEL: **065 6821343**
EMAIL: **info@sycamorehousebb.com**
WEB: **sycamorehousebb.com**

Friendly family home. Ennis town centre 6 mins walk. Private car park. TV/Radio in bedrooms. Airport, cliffs, and Banquets 30 mins.

| B&B | 3 | Ensuite | €30-€35 | Dinner | - |
| B&B | - | Standard | - | Partial Board | - |
| Single Rate | | | €40-€45 | Child reduction | 33.3% |

In Ennis

**Open:** All Year

---

### Evelyn Freeman
**GREYSTONE HOUSE**
Ballymaley, Barefield, Ennis,
Co Clare

**Ennis**

TEL: **065 6843070**  FAX: **065 6821868**
EMAIL: **pfeng@eircom.net**
WEB: **www.accommodationennisireland.com**

Large country house in quiet scenic area set back from Galway road 5 mins from Ennis town centre. Spacious rooms, tv, tea coffee facilities in rooms.

| B&B | 3 | Ensuite | €30-€35 | Dinner | - |
| B&B | - | Standard | | Partial Board | - |
| Single Rate | | | €40-€50 | Child reduction | 25% |

Ennis 2km

**Open:** 1st March-31st October

---

### Sean & Teresa Grogan
**ST PATRICK'S**
Corebeg, Doora, Ennis,
Co Clare

**Ennis**

TEL: **065 6840122**  FAX: **065 6840124**
EMAIL: **grogandoora@eircom.net**

Quiet scenic area. Beside Doora Church and Equestrian Centre. Ideal location for Banquets, Cragganowen, Burren, Cliffs of Moher. Traditional Music. Morning guests welcome.

| B&B | 3 | Ensuite | €27.50-€31 | Dinner | €20 |
| B&B | 1 | Standard | €25.50-€28.50 | Partial Board | €300 |
| Single Rate | | | €38-€43.50 | Child reduction | 25% |

Ennis 4km

**Open:** 7th February-30th November

---

### Mrs Maura Healy
**BROOKVILLE HOUSE**
Tobartaoscan,
Off Limerick Road, Ennis,
Co Clare

**Ennis**

TEL: **065 6829802**

Tranquil location, garden. Bus station, Town 10 mins walk, adjacent West Co. Hotel, Golf Courses. Airport, Cliffs, Castles 30 mins.

| B&B | 3 | Ensuite | €30-€32 | Dinner | - |
| B&B | - | Standard | - | Partial Board | - |
| Single Rate | | | - | Child reduction | - |

In Ennis

**Open:** 1st March-30th November

**Mrs Maureen Langan**
ST ANNES
Limerick Road, Ennis, Co Clare

### Ennis

TEL: **065 6828501**
EMAIL: **jlangan.ennis@eircom.net**

On N18, Airport 20 mins. Adjacent to West County Hotel. Convenient to Cliffs of Moher, Burren, Golf. Tea/facilities, TV, Hairdryers in bedrooms.

| B&B | 3 | Ensuite | €30-€35 | Dinner | - |
| B&B | - | Standard | - | Partial Board | - |
| Single Rate | | | - | Child reduction | - |

Ennis 1km

**Open:** 1st February-12th December

---

**Mrs Marie McDermott**
BROOKE LODGE
Ballyduff, Barefield, Ennis,
Co Clare

### Ennis

TEL: **065 6844830**
EMAIL: **brookelodge@eircom.net**
WEB: **www.brookelodge.com**

Luxurious country home within 5 minutes of Ennis and 20 minutes drive from Shannon Airport. An ideal base to visit Clare's tourist attractions.

| B&B | 3 | Ensuite | €30-€35 | Dinner | - |
| B&B | - | Standard | - | Partial Board | - |
| Single Rate | | | €40-€45 | Child reduction | 25% |

Ennis 2km

**Open:** 1st January-30th November

---

**Mrs Carmel McMahon**
ASHVILLE
Galway Rd, Ennis, Co Clare

### Ennis

TEL: **065 6822305**

New purpose built house on N18 Galway Road near Auburn Lodge Hotel. Ideal for touring Burren area, Cliffs of Moher & Ailwee Cave. Shannon Airport 15km.

| B&B | 3 | Ensuite | €30-€35 | Dinner | - |
| B&B | - | Standard | - | Partial Board | - |
| Single Rate | | | - | Child reduction | 25% |

Ennis 1km

**Open:** 6th January-23rd December

---

**The Meere Family**
FOUR WINDS
Limerick Road, Ennis, Co Clare

### Ennis

TEL: **065 6829831**
EMAIL: **fourwinds.ennis@eircom.net**

Large home on main Airport road (N18). Private Car park at rear. Golf, Pitch/Putt nearby. 5 mins walk Town centre.

| B&B | 5 | Ensuite | €27.50-€35 | Dinner | - |
| B&B | - | Standard | - | Partial Board | - |
| Single Rate | | | €40-€45 | Child reduction | 33.3% |

In Ennis

**Open:** 15th March-15th October

---

**Brian & Pauline Mulhern**
GLEN COVE B&B
Clarecastle, Ennis, Co Clare

### Ennis

TEL: **065 6824561**
EMAIL: **glencove@hotmail.com**

Comfortable, friendly, family run home. Convenient to Shannon Airport 20 mins, Burren, Cliffs of Moher, Castles, Trad Music, Golf.

| B&B | 3 | Ensuite | €27.50-€31 | Dinner | - |
| B&B | - | Standard | - | Partial Board | - |
| Single Rate | | | €40-€43.50 | Child reduction | 25% |

Ennis 2km

**Open:** All Year

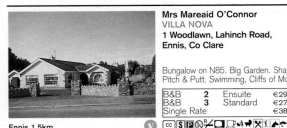

## Ennis

**Mrs Mareaid O'Connor**
VILLA NOVA
**1 Woodlawn, Lahinch Road,
Ennis, Co Clare**

TEL: 065 6828570

Bungalow on N85. Big Garden. Shannon 25 mins. Restaurant, Pub with music 2 mins walk. Golf, Pitch & Putt, Swimming, Cliffs of Moher, Bunratty Castle, Aillwee Caves nearby.

| B&B | 2 | Ensuite | €29.50-€32 | Dinner | €23-€25 |
|------|---|----------|------------|--------|---------|
| B&B | 3 | Standard | €27.50-€30 | Partial Board | |
| Single Rate | | | €38-€43.50 | Child reduction | 50% |

Ennis 1.5km    **Open:** 3rd January-23rd December

---

## Ennis

**Mrs Teresa O'Donohue**
SANBORN HOUSE
**Edenvale, Kilrush Road, Ennis,
Co Clare**

TEL: **065 6824959**
EMAIL: **sanbornbandb@eircom.net**
WEB: **www.bb-house.com/sanborn.htm**

Spacious neo-Georgian house in peaceful scenic setting on Kilrush/Car ferry road(N68). Convenient Airport, Cliffs of Moher, Burren, Castles. Early guests welcome.

| B&B | 4 | Ensuite | €30-€32 | Dinner | - |
|------|---|----------|---------|--------|---|
| B&B | - | Standard | - | Partial Board | - |
| Single Rate | | | €40-€43.50 | Child reduction | 33.3% |

Ennis 2km    **Open:** 2nd January-20th December

---

## Ennis

**Catriona & Thomas O'Keeffe**
RYEHILL B&B
**Tulla Road, Ennis, Co Clare**

TEL: **065 6824313**   FAX: **065 6824313**
EMAIL: **RyehillBandB@eircom.net**

Easy to find R352. Town Centre 3-4 mins by car. Ideal touring base. Golf, Fishing, Horse riding nearby. Limerick 40 mins. Shannon 25 mins. Pub and Restaurant 5 mins walk.

| B&B | 6 | Ensuite | €30-€35 | Dinner | - |
|------|---|----------|---------|--------|---|
| B&B | - | Standard | - | Partial Board | - |
| Single Rate | | | €40-€45 | Child reduction | 50% |

Ennis 2km    **Open:** All Year

---

## Ennis

**Mary O'Sullivan**
OGHAM HOUSE
**3 Abbey Court, Clare Road,
Ennis, Co Clare**

TEL: **065 6824878**
EMAIL: **oghamhouseennis@eircom.net**

On N18 opposite West County Hotel. Enjoy our warm hospitality in comfortable home. Bus/Train 10 mins walk. Shannon 20 mins drive. Ideal touring base.

| B&B | 2 | Ensuite | €32.50-€35 | Dinner | - |
|------|---|----------|------------|--------|---|
| B&B | 1 | Standard | €30-€32.50 | Partial Board | - |
| Single Rate | | | €40-€50 | Child reduction | - |

Ennis 1km    **Open:** 1st January-21st December

---

## Ennis

**Mrs Brigid Pyne**
KILMOON HOUSE
**Kildysart Road,
Off Limerick Rd, Ennis,
Co Clare**

TEL: **065 6828529**

Spacious home in peaceful environment, 20 mins from Shannon Airport. Convenient to Bunratty Castle, Knappogue, Burren and Cliffs of Moher.

| B&B | 2 | Ensuite | €30-€32 | Dinner | - |
|------|---|----------|---------|--------|---|
| B&B | 1 | Standard | €28-€30 | Partial Board | - |
| Single Rate | | | €38-€44 | Child reduction | 25% |

Ennis 1km    **Open:** 1st April-30th October

**Joan & George Quinn**
LAKESIDE COUNTRY LODGE
Barntick, Clarecastle, Ennis,
Co Clare

TEL: **065 6838488**   FAX: **065 6838488**
EMAIL: **lakesidecountry@eircom.net**
WEB: **www.lakeside.ie**

Home overlooking Killone Lake and Abbey, on coast road (R473) to Car Ferry. Convenient Airport.
Conservatory overlooking lake. "Le Guide Du Routard" Recommended.

| B&B | 4 | Ensuite | €30-€32 | Dinner | - |
| B&B | - | Standard | €40-€43.50 | Partial Board | - |
| Single Rate | | | - | Child reduction | 50% |

Ennis 3km

**Open:** 1st February-11th December

---

**T J & Pauline Roberts**
CARBERY HOUSE
Kilrush Road/Car Ferry Rd,
Ennis, Co Clare

TEL: **065 6824046**   FAX: **065 6824046**

Route 68, morning visitors welcome. Orthopaedic beds, Electric blankets, Hospitality trays,
Hairdryers. Continental breakfast reduced rate. Convenient Airport.

| B&B | 4 | Ensuite | €28-€31 | Dinner | - |
| B&B | - | Standard | - | Partial Board | - |
| Single Rate | | | - | Child reduction | - |

In Ennis

**Open:** 1st April-1st October

---

**Ms Nuala Ryan**
ADOBE
21 Fernhill, Galway Road,
Ennis, Co Clare

TEL: **065 6823919**
EMAIL: **johnryan.ennis@eircom.net**
WEB: **www.ennisbedandbreakfast.com**

Modern Detached house in quiet cul-de-sac. Breakfast menu. 5 mins walk to Town Centre, 100
metres off N18.

| B&B | 2 | Ensuite | €30-€32.50 | Dinner | - |
| B&B | 2 | Standard | €28-€30 | Partial Board | - |
| Single Rate | | | €45-€55 | Child reduction | 25% |

Ennis

**Open:** 1st January-20th December

---

**Mrs Ina Troy**
HAZELDENE
Barefield, Ennis, Co Clare

TEL: **065 6827212**   FAX: **065 6890988**
EMAIL: **hazeldenebarefield@eircom.net**

Ennis/Galway road. Morning guests welcome. Airport 30mins distance. TV in bedrooms.
Convenient Cliffs of Moher. Banquets, Golf, Fishing.

| B&B | 5 | Ensuite | €30-€35 | Dinner | - |
| B&B | - | Standard | - | Partial Board | - |
| Single Rate | | | €40-€45 | Child reduction | 25% |

Ennis 8km

**Open:** 1st February-30th November

---

**Mrs Kathleen Cahill**
STATION HOUSE
Ennis Road, Ennistymon,
Co Clare

TEL: **065 7071149**   FAX: **065 7071709**
EMAIL: **cahilka@indigo.ie**
WEB: **www.bb-stationhouse.com**

Route N85. Spacious home. Hospitality tray, Hairdryer, Telephone, TV in bedrooms. Breakfast
menu. Horse riding, Fishing, Golf, Cliffs of Moher, Burren nearby. Guide du Routard recommended.

| B&B | 6 | Ensuite | €27.50-€31 | Dinner | - |
| B&B | - | Standard | - | Partial Board | - |
| Single Rate | | | €40-€43.50 | Child reduction | - |

In Ennistymon

**Open:** 1st January-20th December

### Mrs Geraldine McGuane
SUNSET B&B
Kilcornan, Ennistymon,
Co Clare

**Ennistymon**

Tel: **065 7071527**
Email: **sunsetbb2002@yahoo.co.uk**
Web: **www.sunsetbb.com**

Situated on hill top with panoramic views of sea and countryside on R85 with peat fires and home baking. Cliffs of Moher, the Burren, Golf, Fishing.

| B&B | 2 | Ensuite | €27.50-€31 | Dinner | - |
| B&B | 1 | Standard | €25.50-€28.50 | Partial Board | - |
| Single Rate | | | €38-€43.50 | Child reduction | 25% |

Ennistymon 1km

**Open:** 1st May-1st October

---

### Mrs Patsy Flanagan
HARBOUR LODGE
6 Marine Parade, Kilkee,
Co Clare

**Kilkee**

Tel: **065 9056090**

Town Home across road from Beach in scenic area, adjacent all amenities.  Recommended by "The Irish Bed & Breakfast Book".

| B&B | 3 | Ensuite | €27.50-€31 | Dinner | - |
| B&B | 1 | Standard | €25.50-€28.50 | Partial Board | - |
| Single Rate | | | - | Child reduction | - |

In Kilkee

**Open:** 1st April-31st October

---

### Mary Hickie
BAYVIEW
O'Connell Street, Kilkee,
Co Clare

**Kilkee**

Tel: **065 9056058**
Email: **bayview3@eircom.net**
Web: **www.hickiesbayview.com**

Enjoy warm friendly hospitality in our tastefully decorated home. Magnificent view of Kilkee Bay, Cliffs. Central all amenities, Breakfast menu.

| B&B | 8 | Ensuite | €28-€31 | Dinner | - |
| B&B | - | Standard | - | Partial Board | - |
| Single Rate | | | €40-€43.50 | Child reduction | 50% |

In Kilkee

**Open:** 1st January-20th December

---

### Mrs Ann Nolan
NOLANS B&B
Kilrush Road, Kilkee, Co Clare

**Kilkee**

Tel: **065 9060100**
Email: **nolansbandb@eircom.net**
Web: **www.accommodation-clare.com**

Spacious family run accommodation in comfortable dormer house. Breakfast menu. Private parking. Ideal touring base. Tea and Coffee available on arrival.

| B&B | 6 | Ensuite | €27.50-€31 | Dinner | - |
| B&B | - | Standard | - | Partial Board | - |
| Single Rate | | | €40-€43.50 | Child reduction | 25% |

In Kilkee

**Open:** 2nd January-20th December

---

### Eileen Brennan
CARRAMORE LODGE
Roolagh, Ballina, Killaloe,
Co Clare

**Killaloe**

Tel: **061 376704**
Email: **carramorelodge@oceanfree.net**
Web: **www.carramorelodge.net**

Spacious family home on 1.5 acres of beautiful gardens, panoramic views beside River Shannon on Lough Derg. 5 mins walk Village, Pubs, Restaurants, Churches.

| B&B | 4 | Ensuite | €27.50-€31 | Dinner | - |
| B&B | - | Standard | - | Partial Board | - |
| Single Rate | | | €40-€43.50 | Child reduction | 33.3% |

In Killaloe

**Open:** 1st March-30th October

**Mrs Patricia Byrnes**
RATHMORE HOUSE
Ballina, Killaloe, Co Clare

**Killaloe**

TEL: **061 379296**
EMAIL: **rathmorebb@oceanfree.net**
WEB: **www.rathmorehouse.com**

On R494. Comfortable, relaxing & peaceful, near Killaloe overlooking Lough Derg on River Shannon. Pubs, restaurants, heritage town, close to Shannon airport.

| B&B | 5 | Ensuite | €27.50-€32.50 | Dinner | - |
| B&B | 1 | Standard | €27.50-€32.50 | Partial Board | - |
| Single Rate | | | €40-€45 | Child reduction | 33.3% |

Killaloe 2km

**Open:** 1st March-31st October

---

**Celine King**
SHANNARRA
Killaloe, Co Clare

**Killaloe**

TEL: **061 376548**
EMAIL: **celineking@hotmail.com**
WEB: **www.kingsbandb.com**

Comfortable family run accommodation 7km north of Killaloe on Scarriff road. Scenic views. Convenient to music Pubs, Restaurants, Water Sport & Hillwalking.

| B&B | 4 | Ensuite | €27.50-€31 | Dinner | - |
| B&B | - | Standard | - | Partial Board | - |
| Single Rate | | | €40-€43.50 | Child reduction | 25% |

Killaloe 7km

**Open:** 1st February-30th November

---

**Anne O'Connor**
WHITETHORN LODGE
1 Shannon View, Ballina, Killaloe, Co Clare

**Killaloe**

TEL: **061 375257**
EMAIL: **whitethornlodgebb@eircom.net**

Modern, friendly home in tranquil setting - walking distance to village pubs, shops, hotels, restaurants. Shannon Airport 20 mls. Limerick/University 14 mls.

| B&B | 3 | Ensuite | €27.50-€30 | Dinner | - |
| B&B | - | Standard | - | Partial Board | - |
| Single Rate | | | €40-€43.50 | Child reduction | 33.3% |

Killaloe

**Open:** 1st March-30th November

---

**Imy Kerrigan**
COIS-NA-SIONNA
Ferry Junction, Killimer, Kilrush, Co Clare

**Killimer**

TEL: **065 9053073** FAX: **065 9053073**
EMAIL: **coisnasionna@eircom.net**
WEB: **www.bb-house.com/cois-na-sionna.htm**

Spectacularly located, overlooking the beautiful Shannon Estuary and just 50 mins Shannon Airport. On the N67. Ideal touring base to tour the West of Ireland. AA ◆◆◆ approved.

| B&B | 4 | Ensuite | €30-€33 | Dinner | - |
| B&B | - | Standard | - | Partial Board | - |
| Single Rate | | | €40-€45 | Child reduction | 50% |

Killimer

**Open:** All Year

---

**Michael & Mary Clarke**
BRUACH NA COILLE
Killimer Road - N67, Kilrush, Co Clare

**Kilrush**

TEL: **065 9052250** FAX: **065 9052250**
EMAIL: **clarkekilrush@hotmail.com**
WEB: **www.clarkekilrush.com**

On N67 opposite Vandeleur walled gardens. Rooms with views. Family run. Frommer reader recommended and AA Award Winner 2003. Tea/Coffee on arrival. Comprehensive Breakfast menu.

| B&B | 2 | Ensuite | €28-€36 | Dinner | - |
| B&B | 2 | Standard | €26-€32 | Partial Board | - |
| Single Rate | | | €38-€55 | Child reduction | - |

Kilrush 1km

**Open:** 1st January-31st December

Kilrush 1km

### Brendan & Rita Griffin
**ASHGROVE**
**Ballynote West, Killimer Road, Kilrush, Co Clare**

Tel: **065 9051329**

Bungalow on N67, 1km from Kilrush, 8km from Killimer Car Ferry. Clean, comfortable, welcoming, close to wood and beach. Tea and coffee on arrival.

| B&B | 2 | Ensuite | €34 | Dinner | - |
|-----|---|---------|-----|--------|---|
| B&B | 2 | Standard | €32 | Partial Board | - |
| Single Rate | | | €45 | Child reduction | - |

**Open:** 1st May-30th September

---

Kilrush 1km

### Austin & Ethna Hynes
**HILLCREST VIEW**
**Doonbeg Road (off N67), Kilrush, Co Clare**

Tel: **065 9051986** Fax: **065 9051900**
Email: **ethnahynes@eircom.net**
Web: **www.hillcrestview.com**

Luxurious B&B. Spacious rooms. AA ◆◆◆◆ Award. Off N67. 5 mins walk Kilrush, Killimer Ferry 8km, Airport 1 hr drive. Conservatory. Quiet area. Breakfast menu.

| B&B | 6 | Ensuite | €28-€35 | Dinner | - |
|-----|---|---------|---------|--------|---|
| B&B | - | Standard | - | Partial Board | - |
| Single Rate | | | €40-€50 | Child reduction | 50% |

**Open:** All Year

---

### Ms Rosemary Donohue
**COIS FARRAIGE**
**Milton Malbay Road, Cregg, Lahinch, Co Clare**

Tel: **065 7081580** Fax: **065 7081580**
Email: **rosie@coisfarrraige.net**
Web: **www.coisfarraige.net**

Family run magnificent ocean views. Large family room(sleeps 5). Rooms with Electric Blankets and Hairdryers. Routard, Dillard Causin recommended.

Lahinch 1km

| B&B | 6 | Ensuite | €27.50-€31 | Dinner | - |
|-----|---|---------|------------|--------|---|
| B&B | - | Standard | - | Partial Board | - |
| Single Rate | | | €40-€43.50 | Child reduction | 50% |

**Open:** 1st March-30th November

---

### Mr & Mrs Pat & Margaret Donovan
**CASTLEVIEW LODGE**
**Ennistymon, Lahinch, Co Clare**

Tel: **065 7081648** Fax: **065 7086832**
Email: **lahinchok@eircom.net**
Web: **www.visitlahinch.com**

Spacious family run B&B on N67 main Ennis Shannon Road overlooking golf courses. Walking distance from award winning Restaurants, Pubs, Beach, Leisure Centre.

In Lahinch

| B&B | 5 | Ensuite | €27.50-€31 | Dinner | - |
|-----|---|---------|------------|--------|---|
| B&B | - | Standard | - | Partial Board | - |
| Single Rate | | | €40-€43.50 | Child reduction | 50% |

**Open:** 2nd January-31st December

---

### Mrs Brid Fawl
**MULCARR HOUSE**
**Ennistymon Road, Lahinch, Co Clare**

Tel: **065 7081123** Fax: **065 7081123**
Email: **mulcarrhouse@esatclear.ie**
Web: **www.esatclear.ie/~mulcarrhouse**

Smoke free home, walking distance to Beach, Golf Course. Convenient Cliffs of Moher, Doolin, Burren. Tea making facilities. Hair Dryers. On N67.

In Lahinch

| B&B | 4 | Ensuite | €27.50-€31 | Dinner | - |
|-----|---|---------|------------|--------|---|
| B&B | - | Standard | - | Partial Board | - |
| Single Rate | | | - | Child reduction | 33.3% |

**Open:** 16th March-31st October

### Lahinch

**Mrs Anita Gallery**
TUDOR LODGE
Ennistymon Road, Lahinch,
Co Clare

TEL: **065 7081270**

Comfortable home, personally run. Adjacent to Golf Courses. Early breakfasts if required. Special rate single room.

| B&B | 4 | Ensuite | €27.50-€31 | Dinner | - |
| B&B | - | Standard | - | Partial Board | - |
| Single Rate | | | €40-€43.50 | Child reduction | 33.3% |

Lahinch

**Open:** 1st April-12th November

---

### Lahinch

**Annie O'Brien**
LE BORD DE MER
Milltown Malbay Rd., Lahinch,
Co Clare

TEL: **065 7081454**   FAX: **065 7081454**
EMAIL: **annieobrien@eircom.net**
WEB: **http://homepage.eircom.net/~annieobrien**

Breathtaking Ocean View, Lahinch Championship Golf, French speaking, beside Beach. Ideal base Cliffs of Moher, Burren, Aran Islands, Routard recommended.

| B&B | 4 | Ensuite | €27.50-€31 | Dinner | - |
| B&B | - | Standard | - | Partial Board | - |
| Single Rate | | | €40-€43.50 | Child reduction | 25% |

hinch 1km

**Open:** 1st March-31st October

---

### Lahinch

**Mrs Margaret Skerritt**
MOHER VIEW
Ennistymon Road, Lahinch,
Co Clare

TEL: **065 7081206**   FAX: **065 7081206**
EMAIL: **moherview@esatclear.ie**
WEB: **moherview-lahinch.com**

Elevated dormer bungalow overlooking golf course. Convenient to Cliffs of Moher, Doolin, Burren, Tea/Coffee making facilities. Route N85.

| B&B | 4 | Ensuite | €27.50-€31 | Dinner | - |
| B&B | - | Standard | - | Partial Board | - |
| Single Rate | | | €40-€43.50 | Child reduction | 25% |

hinch 1km

**Open:** 1st May-30th September

---

### Lahinch

**Nanno & Cathy Vuyk**
AUBURN HOUSE
School Rd, Lahinch, Co Clare

TEL: **065 7082890**
EMAIL: **auburnhse@eircom.net**
WEB: **auburnhouse.ie**

Family run dormer house on N67 with ocean view. French, german, dutch spoken. Ideal for Clifs of Moher, Burren, Aran Islands, golf and surf.

| B&B | 6 | Ensuite | €27.50-€35 | Dinner | - |
| B&B | - | Standard | - | Partial Board | - |
| Single Rate | | | €40-€45 | Child reduction | 50% |

Lahinch

**Open:** 1st February-31st October

---

### Lahinch

**Mrs Marian White**
SEA BREEZE
Carrowgar,
Miltown Malbay Road, Lahinch,
Co Clare

TEL: **065 7081073**
EMAIL: **mariantwhite@eircom.net**

Family run bungalow on N67 in rural setting. 2km Lahinch. Convenient Beach, Cliffs of Moher, Burren, trips to Aran Islands, Golf Courses, Pony Trekking, Swimming Pools, Sauna, Jacuzzi.

| B&B | 3 | Ensuite | €28-€31 | Dinner | - |
| B&B | - | Standard | - | Partial Board | - |
| Single Rate | | | €40-€43.50 | Child reduction | 25% |

hinch 2km

**Open:** 1st May-30th September

**Ms Marie Dowling**
CLIFF VIEW LODGE
Lislarkin, Liscannor, Co Clare

### Liscannor

TEL: **065 7081783**
EMAIL: **cliffviewlodge@eircom.net**
WEB: **www.cliffview-liscannor.com**

Modern family run home, set in rural country surround. Adjacent to Cliffs of Moher, Burren. Doolin-Aran Islands Ferry. Direct contact: 086 8346450.

| B&B | 3 | Ensuite | €27.50-€31 | Dinner | - |
| B&B | - | Standard | €25.50-€28.50 | Partial Board | - |
| Single Rate | | | €38-€43.50 | Child reduction | 25% |

Liscannor 2km

**Open:** 1st January-31st December

---

**James & Sheila Lees**
SEA HAVEN
Liscannor, Co Clare

### Liscannor

TEL: **065 7081385**   FAX: **065 7081474**
EMAIL: **seahaven@eircom.net**

Sea-Haven with sea views. On main Lahinch - Cliffs of Moher road. Orthopaedic beds. 5 minutes walk to Liscannor Village.

| B&B | 6 | Ensuite | €28-€32 | Dinner | - |
| B&B | - | Standard | - | Partial Board | - |
| Single Rate | | | €40-€45 | Child reduction | 25% |

In Liscannor

**Open:** 1st January-30th November

---

**Kevin & Ann Thynne**
SEAMOUNT
Liscannor, Co Clare

### Liscannor

TEL: **065 7081367**

Family run home on road to Cliffs of Moher. In quiet secluded garden. 5 minutes walk from Liscannor Village. Close to Golf, Fishing, Pubs & Restaurants.

| B&B | 3 | Ensuite | €27.50-€31 | Dinner | - |
| B&B | - | Standard | - | Partial Board | - |
| Single Rate | | | €40-€43.50 | Child reduction | 50% |

In Liscannor

**Open:** 17th March-31st October

---

**Mrs Eileen Barrett**
MARCHMONT
Lisdoonvarna, Co Clare

### Lisdoonvarna

TEL: **065 7074050**

Town House, Car Park. TV Lounge. Hairdryers in rooms. Bicycle lock-up. Rick Steves recommended.

| B&B | 5 | Ensuite | €28-€32 | Dinner | - |
| B&B | - | Standard | - | Partial Board | - |
| Single Rate | | | €40-€42 | Child reduction | - |

In Lisdoonvarna

**Open:** 1st March-30th November

---

**Mrs Bernie Cosgrove**
ST JUDES
Coast Road, Lisdoonvarna,
Co Clare

### Lisdoonvarna

TEL: **065 7074108**

Elevated site overlooking countryside on N67 - tea/scones on arrival, real home baking, breakfast menu, electric blankets (1) three bedded room - 10 mins walk to village. Failte.

| B&B | 4 | Ensuite | €28-€31 | Dinner | - |
| B&B | - | Standard | - | Partial Board | - |
| Single Rate | | | €40-€43.50 | Child reduction | 50% |

Lisdoonvarna 1km

**Open:** 1st May-30th September

**Mrs Monica Droney**
CROSSWINDS
Lisdoonvarna, Co Clare

TEL: **065 7074469**
EMAIL: **crwinds@mail.com**
WEB: **http://crwinds.cjb.net**

Situated on Cliffs of Moher Rd, (R478). 10 mins drive Doolin, Island Ferries, Burren & Lisdoonvarna. Walking distance to nightly entertainment.

| | | | | | | |
|---|---|---|---|---|---|---|
| B&B | 2 | Ensuite | €27.50-€32 | Dinner | | - |
| B&B | 1 | Standard | €25.50-€28.50 | Partial Board | | - |
| Single Rate | | | €38-€43.50 | Child reduction | | 33.3% |

sdoonvarna 2km    **Open:** 10th April-10th October

---

**Mrs Mary Finn**
ST ENDA'S
Church Street, Lisdoonvarna,
Co Clare

TEL: **065 7074066**

Five minutes walk to Town Centre. Two storey house with sun lounge. Leading to main Galway Road. Welcoming tea/coffee and home baking. Bicycle lock up. Ideal base Burren, Cliffs of Moher.

| | | | | | | |
|---|---|---|---|---|---|---|
| B&B | 3 | Ensuite | €27.50-€31 | Dinner | | - |
| B&B | - | Standard | - | Partial Board | | - |
| Single Rate | | | €40-€43.50 | Child reduction | | 50% |

Lisdoonvarna    **Open:** 14th March-1st November

---

**Patricia Fitzpatrick**
BLACKBRIDGE HOUSE
St Brendans Road,
Lisdoonvarna, Co Clare

TEL: **065 7075934**
EMAIL: **fitzpatricktr@iolfree.ie**
WEB: **www.blackbridgehouse.com**

Dormer bungalow house. Built with the guest in mind. Friendly welcoming home, all rooms decorated to a high standard. Set on a hill where beautiful scenery awaits you. Cliffs of Moher 10 mins.

| | | | | | | |
|---|---|---|---|---|---|---|
| B&B | 4 | Ensuite | €28-€36 | Dinner | | - |
| B&B | - | Standard | - | Partial Board | | - |
| Single Rate | | | €40-€43.50 | Child reduction | | 33.3% |

Lisdoonvarna    **Open:** 1st March-14th October

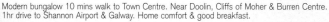

---

**Vera Fitzpatrick**
FERMONA HOUSE
Bog Road, Lisdoonvarna,
Co Clare

TEL: **065 7074243**
EMAIL: **fermona@eircom.net**
WEB: **www.fermonahouse.com**

Modern bungalow 10 mins walk to Town Centre. Near Doolin, Cliffs of Moher & Burren Centre. 1hr drive to Shannon Airport & Galway. Home comfort & good breakfast.

| | | | | | | |
|---|---|---|---|---|---|---|
| B&B | 5 | Ensuite | €28-€35 | Dinner | | - |
| B&B | - | Standard | - | Partial Board | | - |
| Single Rate | | | €40-€45 | Child reduction | | 33.3% |

Lisdoonvarna    **Open:** 17th March-1st October

---

**Mrs Ann Green**
HILLTOP
Doolin Road, Lisdoonvarna,
Co Clare

TEL: **065 7074134**
WEB: **www.bb-house.com/hilltop.htm**

Elevated site on N67, quiet location. 7 minutes walk to Village. One large family room. Convenient to Cliffs of Moher, Doolin and the Burren. Traditional music locally. Boat trips to Aran.

| | | | | | | |
|---|---|---|---|---|---|---|
| B&B | 3 | Ensuite | €27.50-€31 | Dinner | | - |
| B&B | - | Standard | - | Partial Board | | - |
| Single Rate | | | €40-€43.50 | Child reduction | | 33.3% |

sdoonvarna 1km    **Open:** 15th May-1st November

**Mrs Cathleen O'Connor**
RONCALLI
**Doolin Road, Lisdoonvarna,
Co Clare**

### Lisdoonvarna

Tel: **065 7074115**
Email: **cathleen@doolincoastalcottages.com**
Web: **www.bb-house.com/roncalli.html**

7 mins walk village N67. 5 houses from Emo Filling Station. Quiet location. "Lets Go" recommended. Close to Burren, Cliffs of Moher, Aran Ferry, Traditional Music. TV, Hairdryer.

| B&B | 3 | Ensuite | €27.50-€31 | Dinner | - |
| B&B | - | Standard | - | Partial Board | - |
| Single Rate | | | €40-€43.50 | Child reduction | 33.3% |

Lisdoonvarna 1km    **Open:** 1st April-1st November

---

**Mrs Joan O'Flaherty**
GOWLAUN
**St Brendan's Road,
Lisdoonvarna, Co Clare**

### Lisdoonvarna

Tel: **065 7074369**
Email: **gowlaun@eircom.net**
Web: **www.lisdoonvarnagowlaunb-b.com**

Situated on a quiet location off N67. 5 mins walk from Town Centre and bus stop. One hour drive from Shannon Airport. Burren and Cliffs of Moher closeby.

| B&B | 3 | Ensuite | €30-€32 | Dinner | - |
| B&B | - | Standard | - | Partial Board | - |
| Single Rate | | | €40-€43.50 | Child reduction | 33.3% |

In Lisdoonvarna    **Open:** 15th March-31st October

---

**Anne & Denis O'Loughlin**
BURREN BREEZE
**The Wood Cross,
Lisdoonvarna, Co Clare**

### Lisdoonvarna

Tel: **065 7074263**   Fax: **065 7074820**
Email: **burrenbb@iol.ie**
Web: **www.burrenbreeze.com**

Rooms with Bathtub & Shower, TV, Tea/coffee, Hairdryers. 2/3/4 night Specials. NO ENSUITE SUPPLEMENT. Internet access. Junction N67/R477 - Doolin/Coast Road.

| B&B | 5 | Ensuite | €27.50-€31 | Dinner | €15-€19 |
| B&B | 1 | Standard | €25.50-€28.50 | Partial Board | - |
| Single Rate | | | €38-€55 | Child reduction | 50% |

Lisdoonvarna 1km    **Open:** 15th January-15th December

---

**The Petty Family**
SUNVILLE
**Off Doolin Road, Lisdoonvarna,
Co Clare**

### Lisdoonvarna

Tel: **065 7074065**   Fax: **065 7074065**
Email: **tpetty@gofree.indigo.ie**
Web: **http://indigo.ie/~pettyt/**

Situated off N67, quiet area with private parking. Near Cliffs of Moher, Burren, Golf at Lahinch, Trips to Aran Island. Frommer recommended. Electric blankets, Hairdryers. Off season rates.

| B&B | 4 | Ensuite | €28-€31 | Dinner | - |
| B&B | - | Standard | - | Partial Board | - |
| Single Rate | | | €40-€44 | Child reduction | 33.3% |

In Lisdoonvarna    **Open:** All Year

---

**Mrs Helen Stack**
ORE-A-TAVA HOUSE
**Lisdoonvarna, Co Clare**

### Lisdoonvarna

Tel: **065 7074086**   Fax: **065 7074547**
Email: **oreatava@eircom.net**
Web: **www.oreatavahouse.com**

House in quiet area on landscaped gardens with patio for visitors use. Cliffs of Moher, Burren, Aran Islands nearby. Shannon-Galway 1 hour. Breakfast menu available. Credit cards accepted.

| B&B | 6 | Ensuite | €28-€35 | Dinner | - |
| B&B | - | Standard | - | Partial Board | - |
| Single Rate | | | €40-€45 | Child reduction | 33.3% |

Lisdoonvarna 1km    **Open:** 20th March-10th October

**Mrs Irene Vaughan**
WOODHAVEN
**Doolin Coast Road,
Lisdoonvarna, Co Clare**

TEL: **065 7074017**

Junction off N67/R477 scenic, peaceful surroundings. Near Doolin ferry. Traditional music. Cliffs of Moher. Electric Blankets, Homebaking, Private car park, Bicycle shed, Hairdryers.

| B&B | 4 | Ensuite | €28-€31 | Dinner | - |
| B&B | - | Standard | - | Partial Board | - |
| Single Rate | | | €41-€44.50 | Child reduction | 25% |

sdoonvarna 1km  **Open:** All Year Except Christmas

**Mary Burke**
ANCHOR LODGE
**Spanish Point Road,
Miltown Malbay, Co Clare**

TEL: **065 7084298**

Family run home on N67, 0.25km from Miltown Malbay, rooms ensuite, tea/coffee, convenient to Beach, Golf Course.

| B&B | 3 | Ensuite | €27.50-€31 | Dinner | - |
| B&B | - | Standard | - | Partial Board | - |
| Single Rate | | | €40-€43.50 | Child reduction | - |

Miltown Malbay  **Open:** 1st May-30th September

**Mary Hughes**
AN GLEANN
**Ennis Road, Miltown Malbay,
Co Clare**

TEL: **065 7084281**
EMAIL: **angleann@oceanfree.net**
WEB: **www.angleann.com**

Friendly family run home, rooms ensuite, TV, Tea/Coffee. Located 1km Ennis road. Recommended "New York Times". Close to all amenities. All credit cards welcome.

| B&B | 5 | Ensuite | €27.50-€32.50 | Dinner | - |
| B&B | - | Standard | - | Partial Board | - |
| Single Rate | | | €40-€43.50 | Child reduction | 33.3% |

iltown Malbay 1km  **Open:** 7th January-20th December

**Mrs Maura Keane**
SEA CREST
**Rineen, Miltown Malbay,
Co Clare**

TEL: **065 7084429**
EMAIL: **seacrestguesthouse@eircom.net**

On N67 overlooking Cliffs of Moher, Golf Courses and Beaches nearby. Rooms ensuite. TV Lounge for guests, use of kitchen for Tea/Coffee facilities.

| B&B | 5 | Ensuite | €27.50-€31 | Dinner | - |
| B&B | - | Standard | - | Partial Board | - |
| Single Rate | | | €40-€43.50 | Child reduction | 50% |

iltown Malbay 4.5km  **Open:** 1st January-31st December

**Howe Family**
OAK HOUSE
**Mountshannon, Co Clare**

TEL: **061 927185**  FAX: **061 927185**
EMAIL: **howemaureen@eircom.net**

Country home, panoramic view, overlooking Lough Derg. Private Beach, Boats, excellent facilities for Fishermen. Ideal base for touring. 200m village.

| B&B | 4 | Ensuite | €28.50-€32 | Dinner | - |
| B&B | - | Standard | - | Partial Board | - |
| Single Rate | | | €40-€43.50 | Child reduction | 25% |

Mountshannon  **Open:** 1st April-1st November

**Mountshannon**

### Mountshannon

**Vera O'Rourke**
**SUNRISE B&B**
**Mountshannon, Co Clare**

TEL: **061 927343**
EMAIL: **sunrise4bnb@eircom.net**
WEB: **sunrisebandb.com**

Panoramic views overlooking Lough Derg. Two minutes walk from village, restaurants, pubs. Ideal base for touring the west. Convenient to Shannon Airport.

| B&B | 2 | Ensuite | €30-€32 | Dinner | - |
| B&B | 1 | Standard | €28-€30 | Partial Board | - |
| Single Rate | | | €41-€43 | Child reduction | 33.3% |

**Open:** 1st April-1st November

---

**In Newmarket on Fergus**

### Newmarket-on-Fergus

**Colette Gilbert**
**FERGUS LODGE**
**Ennis Road, Newmarket-on-Fergus, Co Clare**

TEL: **061 368351**   FAX: **061 368351**
EMAIL: **ferguslodge@eircom.net**

Morning guests welcome, tours arranged. On R458 beside Texaco Station, Shannon Airport, Bunratty & Knappogue Castles 10 mins Dromoland Castle & Clare Inn Hotel 2 mins. Walking distance restaurants & bars.

| B&B | 5 | Ensuite | €35-€35 | Dinner | - |
| B&B | - | Standard | - | Partial Board | - |
| Single Rate | | | €45-€45 | Child reduction | 25% |

**Open:** 1st January-31st December

---

**Newmarket-on-Fergus 2km**

### Newmarket-on-Fergus

**David & Caroline Molloy**
**VALHALLA B&B**
**Urlanbeg, Newmarket-on-Fergus, Co Clare, Co Clare**

TEL: **061 368293**
EMAIL: **valhalla@esatclear.ie**

Quiet country home, ideal access to Shannon Airport, 5 mins drive on R472 from Shannon, 5 mins from Bunratty, 10 mins from Knappogue Castle. Morning guests welcome.

| B&B | 3 | Ensuite | €27.50-€31 | Dinner | - |
| B&B | - | Standard | - | Partial Board | - |
| Single Rate | | | €45-€50 | Child reduction | 25% |

**Open:** 1st January-20th December

---

**Shannon 4km**

### Newmarket-on-Fergus

**Pauline O'Brien**
**KELLS**
**Urlanmore, Newmarket-On-Fergus, Co Clare**

TEL: **061 476876**   FAX: **061 476884**
EMAIL: **roundtower8@excite.com**
WEB: **www.kellscountryhouse.com**

Castle type country house on 5 acres. Views over Shannon Estuary. Private Parking. Gardens for visitors use. Morning guests welcome. Airport, Bunratty and Golf Courses 10 mins.

| B&B | 3 | Ensuite | €40-€45 | Dinner | - |
| B&B | - | Standard | - | Partial Board | - |
| Single Rate | | | €50-€55 | Child reduction | - |

**Open:** 15th January-15th December

---

**Newmarket-on-Fergus 2km**

### Newmarket-on-Fergus

**Mrs Sheila Ryan**
**THE DORMER**
**Lisduff, Newmarket-On-Fergus, Co Clare**

TEL: **061 368354**   FAX: **061 368354**
EMAIL: **gerandsheilaryan@eircom.net**
WEB: **www.thedormer.com**

Peaceful rural setting, Airport side of Newmarket-on-Fergus off N18. Shannon Airport 10mins, Bunratty 10 mins. Dromoland Castle 5 mins. Fine Restaurants locally.

| B&B | 3 | Ensuite | €27.50-€31 | Dinner | - |
| B&B | - | Standard | - | Partial Board | - |
| Single Rate | | | €40-€43.50 | Child reduction | 50% |

**Open:** 1st March-31st October

### Mrs Antoinette Fitzgerald
SCAPAFLOW
O'Brien's Bridge, Co Clare

TEL: **061 377144**
EMAIL: **scapaflow@eircom.net**
WEB: **www.scapaflowobriensbridge.com**

Scapaflow is overlooking the River Shannon. 5 minutes walk from all facilities. Bar, restaurants, Post Office, tennis, fishing.

| B&B | 3 | Ensuite | €30-€32 | Dinner | - |
| B&B | - | Standard | - | Partial Board | - |
| Single Rate | | | €40-€43.50 | Child reduction | 25% |

Illaloe 8km

**Open:** 5th January-12th December

### Anne & Dave Hyland
SHANNON COTTAGE
O'Brien's Bridge, Co Clare

TEL: **061 377118**
EMAIL: **bandb@shannoncottage.com**
WEB: **www.shannoncottage.com**

Traditional 200 year old refurbished Cottage, on the banks of the River Shannon at O'Brien's Bridge Village. Restaurants, Fishing, Walking, Golf nearby. Near Limerick city.

| B&B | 6 | Ensuite | €30-€50 | Dinner | - |
| B&B | - | Standard | - | Partial Board | - |
| Single Rate | | | €50-€90 | Child reduction | 25% |

Illaloe 8km

**Open:** 15th January-15th December

### Mrs Joan Murphy
ROOSKA HOUSE
Quin, Co Clare

TEL: **065 6825661**
EMAIL: **rooskaguest@eircom.net**

Modern house in village. Convenient Quin Abbey, Knappogue & Craggaunowen. Shannon Airport 30 mins, Ennis 15 mins, Limerick 30 mins.

| B&B | 2 | Ensuite | €28-€31 | Dinner | - |
| B&B | 2 | Standard | €26-€29 | Partial Board | - |
| Single Rate | | | €38-€43.50 | Child reduction | 25% |

Quin

**Open:** 1st April-31st October

### Mr John Boland
FORT LACH
Drumline, Newmarket-on-Fergus, Co Clare

TEL: **061 364003**   FAX: **061 364059**
EMAIL: **johnboland@eircom.net**
WEB: **http://homepage.eircom.net/~johnboland**

Modern house, rural setting, 600 yds off N18. Shannon Airport, Bunratty, Golf, Horse Riding, Fishing all 10 mins. Ideal touring centre.

| B&B | 6 | Ensuite | €31 | Dinner | - |
| B&B | - | Standard | - | Partial Board | - |
| Single Rate | | | €45 | Child reduction | 25% |

hannon 7km

**Open:** 1st February-30th November

### Mr & Mrs Jerry & Martina Breen
SHANNON LODGE
2 Rosan Oir, Ballycasey, Shannon, Co Clare

TEL: **061 362655**
EMAIL: **gerrybreen5@hotmail.com**

Luxurious newly built B&B 5 minutes to airport and Bunratty. Located in Shannon Town, turn off at Old Lodge pub Comfort Inn Hotel, 100 metres from bus stop.

| B&B | 3 | Ensuite | €31-€31 | Dinner | - |
| B&B | - | Standard | - | Partial Board | - |
| Single Rate | | | €45-€45 | Child reduction | - |

hannon

**Open:** 1st March-15th November

165

---

### Catherine Collier
**AIRPORT MANOR**
**Ballycasey, Shannon Town, Co Clare**

TEL: **061 363010**
EMAIL: **seancollierirl@yahoo.com**

Luxury purpose built B&B. 5 mins drive to Airport & Bunratty. On old Airport Rd R471. Near Oakwood Arms Hotel. 5 mins walk to town centre & bus stop.

| B&B | 4 | Ensuite | €28-€32.50 | Dinner | - |
| B&B | - | Standard | - | Partial Board | - |
| Single Rate | | | €45-€50 | Child reduction | 50% |

**In Shannon**

**Open:** 15th January-30th November

---

### Mrs Geraldine Enright
**TRADAREE**
**Drumline, Newmarket-on-Fergus, Co Clare**

TEL: **061 364386**
EMAIL: **genright@gofree.indigo.ie**

Old style dormer house 100m off N18 to Ennis. Bunratty Castle, Shannon Airport 5 mins. Morning guests welcome. Visitors Garden.

| B&B | 2 | Ensuite | €27.50-€31 | Dinner | - |
| B&B | 1 | Standard | €25.50-€28.50 | Partial Board | - |
| Single Rate | | | €38-€41 | Child reduction | 25% |

**Shannon 4km**

**Open:** 15th March-15th October

---

### Mrs Phil Fleming
**KNOCKNAGOW**
**Leimaneighmore, Newmarket-on-Fergus, Co Clare**

TEL: **061 368685**   FAX: **061 368685**
EMAIL: **knocknagowbandb@eircom.net**
WEB: **homepage.eircom.net/~knocknagow**

Purpose built B&B. 8km from Shannon Airport on R472 Shannon/Newmarket-on-Fergus road. Convenient to Bunratty & Knappogue Castles. Morning guests welcome.

| B&B | 4 | Ensuite | €27.50-€31 | Dinner | - |
| B&B | - | Standard | - | Partial Board | - |
| Single Rate | | | €40-€43.50 | Child reduction | 25% |

**Shannon 5km**

**Open:** 5th January-20th December

---

### Mrs Sheila Hanrahan
**THE CROOKED CHIMNEY**
**Hurlers Cross, Co Clare**

TEL: **061 364696**   FAX: **061 364696**
EMAIL: **thecrookedchimney@eircom.net**
WEB: **www.thecrookedchimney.com**

Off main road N18 (Exit Hurlers Cross). 3 miles Shannon, 2 miles Bunratty. Private gardens for guest viewing. Tea/Coffee facilities.

| B&B | 5 | Ensuite | €28-€32 | Dinner | - |
| B&B | - | Standard | - | Partial Board | - |
| Single Rate | | | €40-€43.50 | Child reduction | 25% |

**Shannon 3km**

**Open:** 8th January-16th December

---

### Mrs Brede Lohan
**35 Tullyglass Crescent**
**Shannon, Co Clare**

TEL: **061 364268**   FAX: **061 364358**

Home overlooking River Shannon. Cul-de-sac. Airport Terminal 1.5 miles. Leisure Centre, Swimming Pool, Sauna 200 yds. Take Tullyglass Rd off Roundabout N19.

| B&B | 6 | Ensuite | €29-€31 | Dinner | €29-€29 |
| B&B | - | Standard | - | Partial Board | - |
| Single Rate | | | €42.50-€43.50 | Child reduction | 25% |

**In Shannon**

**Open:** 1st January-22nd December

**Mrs Kay Moloney**
MOLONEY'S B&B
**21 Coill Mhara, Shannon,
Co Clare**

TEL: **061 364185**

Home situated 5 mins from Airport Terminal. Shannon Town Centre 400 yds. Third road on left after Texaco filling station.

| B&B | 2 | Ensuite | €30-€30 | Dinner | - |
|-----|---|---------|---------|--------|---|
| B&B | 2 | Standard | €27-€27 | Partial Board | - |
| Single Rate | | | - | Child reduction | 50% |

Shannon    **Open:** 10th January-20th December

---

**Mrs Betty Nally**
IVORY LODGE
**Drumline, Newmarket-on-Fergus, Co Clare**

TEL: **061 364039**
EMAIL: **nallyivorylodge@eircom.net**

Situated in Drumline 400 yds off main N18 interchange for Shannon Airport (N19). Bunratty, Airport, Golf, Horse Riding all 10 mins. Ideal touring base.

| B&B | 4 | Ensuite | €31 | Dinner | - |
|-----|---|---------|-----|--------|---|
| B&B | - | Standard | - | Partial Board | - |
| Single Rate | | | - | Child reduction | 25% |

Shannon 2km    **Open:** 15th January-15th December

---

**Mrs Wiestawa O'Brien**
TARA GREEN
**Ballycally/Aerospace Rd, Newmarket-on-Fergus, Co Clare**

TEL: **061 363789**
EMAIL: **tarag@iol.ie**
WEB: **www.iol.ie/~tarag**

4 miles Shannon Airport. Welcome to Irish/Polish home. Organic garden. Home cooking. Golfing. Phone or use website for direction.

| B&B | 4 | Ensuite | €27.50-€31 | Dinner | €19-€30 |
|-----|---|---------|------------|--------|---------|
| B&B | - | Standard | - | Partial Board | €300 |
| Single Rate | | | €40-€48 | Child reduction | - |

Shannon 3km    **Open:** 15th January-10th December

---

**Mary O'Loughlin**
AVALON
**11 Ballycaseymore Hill, Shannon Town, Co Clare**

TEL: **061 362032**   FAX: **061 362032**
EMAIL: **avalonbnb@eircom.net**
WEB: **www.avalonbnb.net**

Spacious modern home in quiet cul-de-sac overlooking Shannon. 5 min drive to Airport. Near Bunratty. Turn off R471 at Comfort Inn Hotel/Old Lodge Pub.

| B&B | 2 | Ensuite | €27.50-€31 | Dinner | - |
|-----|---|---------|------------|--------|---|
| B&B | 1 | Standard | €25.50-€28.50 | Partial Board | - |
| Single Rate | | | €42-€52 | Child reduction | 50% |

Shannon    **Open:** 10th January-15th December

---

**Marian O'Meara**
ESTUARY VIEW
**20 Coill Mhara, Shannon,
Co Clare**

TEL: **061 364602**

Family home situated 5 mins from Airport. Shannon town centre 400 yards, local bus stop nearby. Third road on left after Texaco filling station.

| B&B | 2 | Ensuite | €30-€31 | Dinner | - |
|-----|---|---------|---------|--------|---|
| B&B | 2 | Standard | €27.50-€28.50 | Partial Board | - |
| Single Rate | | | - | Child reduction | 50% |

Shannon    **Open:** 2nd January-20th December

**Mrs Mary Tobin**
SHANNONSIDE
Clonlohan,
Shannon/ Newmarket Road R472,
Newmarket-on-Fergus, Co Clare

### Shannon

TEL: **061 364191**   FAX: **061 362069**
EMAIL: **tobins.shannonside@oceanfree.net**

Morning guests welcome, Highly recommended home offering warm hospitality for over 30 years on R472, 5 mins from Airport. Own putting green.

| B&B | 6 | Ensuite | €27.50-€31 | Dinner | - |
|---|---|---|---|---|---|
| B&B | - | Standard | - | Partial Board | - |
| Single Rate | | | €40-€43.50 | Child reduction | 50% |

Shannon 1km

**Open:** 7th January-15th December

---

**Mrs Mary Hoey**
GORTEEN COUNTRY HOUSE
Dangan, Tulla, Co Clare

### Tulla-Quin

TEL: **065 6835140**
EMAIL: **mary_hoey@hotmail.com**
WEB: **homepage.eircom.net/~gorteenfarmhouse**

Tree lined tarmac avenue leads to refurbished warm home, power showers, orthopaedic sanitized beds, guest's garden, full menu some organic. Airport 20 mins.

| B&B | 3 | Ensuite | €30-€35 | Dinner | - |
|---|---|---|---|---|---|
| B&B | - | Standard | - | Partial Board | - |
| Single Rate | | | €40-€46 | Child reduction | 50% |

Tulla 5km

**Open:** 1st February-1st November

---

## RESERVATIONS

- Confirm phone bookings in writing without delay with agreed deposit.
- To avoid misunderstandings later, check rate on booking and clarify any additional changes which may apply to your booking.
- Give details of any special requirements.
- State clearly day, date of arrival and departure date.

---

## FREQUENTLY ASKED QUESTIONS

**Q. Are the prices based on per person sharing or a room rate?**
A. The price for bed & breakfast is per person sharing.

**Q. What does an "ensuite" room mean?**
A. An ensuite room means the room has a private bath/shower and toilet

**Q. What are the check-in times?**
A. The check-in times are normally between 2pm and 6pm, unless agreed with your host/hostess

**Q. Where do I get directions to the B&B I have booked?**
A. Our website www.townandcountry.ie hosts directions to our homes. Alternatively, over 80% of our homes are accessible by email/fax and will be happy to forward directions on request.

A pleasant county of lush green pastures, bordered by the Shannon. Adare, where you will find quaint cottages nestling in the prettiest village in Ireland.

Experience the welcome in historic Limerick. Visit King John's Castle, St. Mary's Cathedral, Hunt Museum and Georgian Pery Square. Partake of the many attractions including golf, horse-riding, fishing, festivals and evening entertainment.

**Noreen & Tom Browne**
PARK LODGE
**Killarney Rd, Abbeyfeale,
Co Limerick**

## Abbeyfeale

TEL: **068 31312**
EMAIL: **info@parklodge.ie**
WEB: **www.parklodge.ie**

Spacious modern home, family run. Situated on N21. Ideal base for touring South West, convenient to Ballybunion, Tralee, Killarney, Dingle and Crag Cave.

| B&B | 4 | Ensuite | €30-€32.50 | Dinner | - |
| B&B | - | Standard | - | Partial Board | - |
| Single Rate | | | €40-€45 | Child reduction | 25% |

Abbeyfeale

**Open:** All Year

**Mrs Bridie Collins**
CASTLEVIEW HOUSE
**Clonshire, Adare, Co Limerick**

## Adare

TEL: **061 396394**
EMAIL: **castleview@eircom.net**
WEB: **www.bedandbreakfastireland.net**

Warm welcoming country home off N21. Peaceful location, with breathtaking gardens. Highly recommended. Extensive menu including pancakes. Golf & Horseriding locally.

| B&B | 3 | Ensuite | €30-€31 | Dinner | - |
| B&B | 1 | Standard | €30-€30 | Partial Board | - |
| Single Rate | | | €40-€45 | Child reduction | 33.3% |

dare 2km

**Open:** 1st March-30th November

**Bridie & Pat Donegan**
BERKELEY LODGE
**Station Road, Adare,
Co Limerick**

## Adare

TEL: **061 396857**   FAX: **061 396857**
EMAIL: **berlodge@iol.ie**
WEB: **www.adare.org**

Superb warm spacious home away from home. AA ◆◆◆◆, RAC ◆◆◆◆ Awards. Breakfast menu. Near Hotels Churches Golf Tour base. Turn at roundabout. Shannon 30 mins. Early arrivals welcome.

| B&B | 5 | Ensuite | €35-€35 | Dinner | - |
| B&B | 1 | Standard | €35-€35 | Partial Board | - |
| Single Rate | | | €58-€58 | Child reduction | 25% |

Adare

**Open:** All Year

**Mrs Maura Galvin**
EAGLE HOUSE
**Smithfield, Croagh, Adare,
Co Limerick**

## Adare

TEL: **069 64701**   FAX: **069 64701**

Luxury quality georgian house, ground floor bedrooms, breakfast menu, country setting, golf, horse riding, fishing, Shannon Airport 35 mins. Early arrivals welcome, sunlounge for guests.

| B&B | 3 | Ensuite | €27.50-€31 | Dinner | - |
| B&B | - | Standard | - | Partial Board | - |
| Single Rate | | | €40-€43.50 | Child reduction | 25% |

dare 3km

**Open:** 3rd January-20th December

**Adare Village 1km** Ⓥ

**Mrs Pauline Hedderman**
**ELM HOUSE**
**Mondellihy, Adare, Co Limerick**

### Adare
TEL: **061 396306**

Gracious restored 1892 Georgian Home with character. "Lonely Planet" recommended. Hidden in garden of mature trees. Shannon Airport 30 mins. Tea Coffee on arrival.

| | | | | Dinner | - |
|---|---|---|---|---|---|
| B&B | 1 | Ensuite | €33-€33 | Dinner | - |
| B&B | 3 | Standard | €33-€33 | Partial Board | - |
| Single Rate | | | €45-€45 | Child reduction | 33.3% |

**Open:** 7th January-15th December

---

**Adare 1km** Ⓥ

**Nora Hennessy**
**DUHALLOW HOUSE**
**Ballingarry Road (R519), Adare,**
**Co Limerick**

### Adare
TEL: **061 395030**
EMAIL: **duhallow@adare-ireland.com**
WEB: **www.adare-ireland.com**

Charming Rustic Family home at edge of Village. Warm friendly atmosphere. Satellite TV's, Hairdryers in rooms. First on right after N21/R519 junction.

| | | | | Dinner | - |
|---|---|---|---|---|---|
| B&B | 3 | Ensuite | €28-€32 | Dinner | - |
| B&B | - | Standard | - | Partial Board | - |
| Single Rate | | | €40-€45 | Child reduction | 25% |

**Open:** 1st April-30th November

---

**Adare Village 1km** Ⓥ

**Florence & Donal Hogan**
**COATESLAND HOUSE B&B**
**Tralee/Killarney Road,**
**Adare N21, Co Limerick**

### Adare
TEL: **061 396372**   FAX: **061 396833**
EMAIL: **coatesfd@indigo.ie**
WEB: **http://indigo.ie/~coatesfd/**

Modern warm home, RAC & AA ◆◆◆◆ awards. Friendly atmosphere. Nice gardens. Good restaurants. Online facilities. Also : RAC (Warm welcome & Sparkling Diamond Awards).

| | | | | Dinner | - |
|---|---|---|---|---|---|
| B&B | 6 | Ensuite | €35-€38 | Dinner | - |
| B&B | - | Standard | - | Partial Board | - |
| Single Rate | | | €45-€50 | Child reduction | 25% |

**Open:** 1st January-10th December

---

**In Adare** Ⓥ

**Elizabeth Jordan**
**ABBEY VILLA**
**Station Road, Adare,**
**Co Limerick**

### Adare
TEL: **061 396113**   FAX: **061 396969**
EMAIL: **abbeyvilla@eircom.net**
WEB: **abbeyvilla.net**

Spacious warm friendly home, Frommer recommended, Tea/Coffee in guest lounge, near Hotel, Restaurants, Golf, Horseriding and Shannon Airport. Turn at roundabout.

| | | | | Dinner | - |
|---|---|---|---|---|---|
| B&B | 5 | Ensuite | €30-€33 | Dinner | - |
| B&B | - | Standard | - | Partial Board | - |
| Single Rate | | | €45-€50 | Child reduction | - |

**Open:** 1st January-20th December

---

**Adare 2km** Ⓥ

**Mrs Maura Linnane**
**CARRIGANE HOUSE**
**Reinroe, Adare, Co Limerick**

### Adare
TEL: **061 396778**
EMAIL: **carrigane.house@oceanfree.net**
WEB: **http://carrigane.adarevillage.com**

Award winning AA ◆◆◆◆ Luxurious home just off main road. Morning guests welcome, near Woodlands Hotel. King size bed available. Extensive breakfast menu.

| | | | | Dinner | - |
|---|---|---|---|---|---|
| B&B | 6 | Ensuite | €32.50-€32.50 | Dinner | - |
| B&B | - | Standard | - | Partial Board | - |
| Single Rate | | | - | Child reduction | 50% |

**Open:** 15th January-10th December

Adare 2km

**Mrs Margaret Liston**
GLENELG
Mondelihy, Adare, Co Limerick

**Adare**

TEL: **061 396077**   FAX: **061 396077**

Luxurious superwarm home. Quiet location. Highly recommended "Karen Brown" 30 mins Shannon Airport, tea/coffee facilities, hairdryers, warm welcome.

| B&B | 2 | Ensuite | €33–€33 | Dinner | - |
|-----|---|---------|---------|--------|---|
| B&B | 1 | Standard | €33–€33 | Partial Board | - |
| Single Rate | | | €45–€45 | Child reduction | 25% |

**Open:** 1st January–20th December

---

Adare 4km

**Ms Christina O'Connell**
RIVERWOOD HOUSE
Castleroberts, Adare,
Co Limerick

**Adare**

TEL: **061 395810**   FAX: **061 395810**
EMAIL: **info@riverwoodhouse.com**
WEB: **www.riverwoodhouse.com**

Luxurious family home surrounded by 30 acres of woodland. Country walks and a mile of private fishing. Championship golf course 5 mins. Shannon 30 mins.

| B&B | 3 | Ensuite | €30–€32 | Dinner | - |
|-----|---|---------|---------|--------|---|
| B&B | - | Standard | | Partial Board | - |
| Single Rate | | | €45–€45 | Child reduction | 50% |

**Open:** 1st February–31st December

---

n Adare

**Richard Carter & Olive Fitzpatrick**
ADARE LODGE
Station Road, Adare,
Co Limerick

**Adare**

TEL: **061 396629**   FAX: **061 395060**
EMAIL: **info@adarelodge.com**
WEB: **www.adarelodge.com**

House located in centre of town within walking distance of shops, pubs, restaurants, golf, fishing and horseriding.

| B&B | 5 | Ensuite | €35–€40 | Dinner | - |
|-----|---|---------|---------|--------|---|
| B&B | - | Standard | - | Partial Board | - |
| Single Rate | | | €50–€60 | Child reduction | - |

**Open:** All Year Except Christmas

---

Adare 5km

**Michael & Jennie Power**
HILLCREST COUNTRY HOME
Clonshire, Croagh, Adare,
Co Limerick

**Adare**

TEL: **061 396534**   FAX: **061 396534**
EMAIL: **hillcrest_irl@hotmail.com**
WEB: **www.dirl.com/limerick/hillcrest.htm**

Hospitable, relaxed home. Amidst beautiful, tranquil pastures where nature abounds. Traditional farming. Forest and nature trails. Medieval ruins. Frommer recommended.

| B&B | 3 | Ensuite | €31–€33 | Dinner | - |
|-----|---|---------|---------|--------|---|
| B&B | - | Standard | | Partial Board | - |
| Single Rate | | | €45–€50 | Child reduction | - |

**Open:** 1st March–30th November

---

Adare

**Mrs Bridie Riordan**
CHURCHVIEW HOUSE
Adare, Co Limerick

**Adare**

TEL: **061 396371**   FAX: **061 396191**

Warm, friendly home in Ireland's prettiest village. Tea facilities in lounge, sun lounge for guests. Adjacent Dunraven Arms Hotel, Church, Golf, Shannon, Airport 45 mins.

| B&B | 4 | Ensuite | €29.50–€32 | Dinner | - |
|-----|---|---------|------------|--------|---|
| B&B | 2 | Standard | €28–€28.50 | Partial Board | - |
| Single Rate | | | €38–€43.50 | Child reduction | 25% |

**Open:** 1st January–18th December

**Mrs Phil Clancy**
**DROMINACLARA HOUSE**
Pallaskenry, Co Limerick

### Askeaton Pallaskenry

TEL: **061 393148**
EMAIL: **clancydrominaclara@hotmail.com**

2km from Kilcornan House off N69, scenic route. Country setting, peaceful surroundings. 3km Curragh Chase Forest Park, Celtic Park, Animal Farm. Golf and Fishing locally. 40 mins Airport.

| B&B | 4 | Ensuite | €27.50-€31 | Dinner | €20-€22 |
| B&B | - | Standard | - | Partial Board | - |
| Single Rate | | | €40-€43.50 | Child reduction | **25%** |

Askeaton 6km

**Open:** 3rd January-20th December

---

**Mrs Marie Keran**
**KILLEEN HOUSE**
Cow Park, Kilcornan,
Palaskenry, Co Limerick

### Askeaton

TEL: **061 393023**
EMAIL: **keran@eircom.net**

Spacious friendly home, lovely gardens on N69 scenic route. Beside Curragh Caravan Forest Park, Celtic Park. Shannon Airport 40 mins. Limerick City 15 min, Askeaton 5 min.

| B&B | 5 | Ensuite | €27.50-€31 | Dinner | - |
| B&B | 1 | Standard | - | Partial Board | - |
| Single Rate | | | €38-€43.50 | Child reduction | **25%** |

Askeaton 5km

**Open:** 1st January-31st December

---

**Mrs Mary Conway Ryan**
**FOUR SEASONS**
Boherlode, Ballyneety,
Co Limerick

### Ballyneety

TEL: **061 351365**  FAX: **061 351365**
EMAIL: **fourseasonsselfcatering@eircom.net**
WEB: **www.fourseasonsselfcatering.com**

Relaxing home, landscaped gardens, sandwiched between Limerick (Ballyclough) R511 and Limerick County Golf Clubs. R512, off N20, N21, N24, N7, N18. TV, hairdryers, tea coffee rooms.

| B&B | 3 | Ensuite | €27.50-€31 | Dinner | - |
| B&B | - | Standard | - | Partial Board | - |
| Single Rate | | | €40-€43.50 | Child reduction | **50%** |

Ballyneety 2km

**Open:** 1st January-21st December

---

**Mrs Margaret Ryan**
**GLENGROVE**
Glen, Ballyneety, Co Limerick

### Ballyneety

TEL: **061 351399**  FAX: **061 351399**
EMAIL: **glengrove@iolfree.ie**

Warm welcoming elegant home. Extensive breakfasts. Walk to Golf, Restaurant, Pubs. On R512 parallel with( N7, N24, N20, N21). Turn at Kilmallock roundabout on Childers road. Ideal Shannon etc.

| B&B | 3 | Ensuite | €27.50-€31 | Dinner | - |
| B&B | 1 | Standard | €25.50-€28.50 | Partial Board | - |
| Single Rate | | | €38-€43.50 | Child reduction | **50%** |

Limerick 7km

**Open:** 10th January-18th December

---

**Ms Breda McGrath Sadlier**
**THE OLD BANK**
Bruff, Co Limerick

### Bruff

TEL: **061 389969**
EMAIL: **info@theoldbank.ie**

House in town centre with parking, four poster beds, jacuzzi baths. Close to Lough Gur Lake, 8 golf courses and beautiful restaurants in house Holestic Therapist.

| B&B | 5 | Ensuite | €35-€45 | Dinner | - |
| B&B | - | Standard | - | Partial Board | - |
| Single Rate | | | €45-€55 | Child reduction | **50%** |

Limerick City 15 miles

**Open:** All Year Except Christmas

**Siobhan Moloney**
BARKER HOUSE
Glin, Co Limerick

### Glin

TEL: **068 34027**
EMAIL: **wmoloney@iol.ie**
WEB: **www.barkerhouse.net**

Elegant Town House on 3 acres, near Glin Castle. Offers luxury ensuite accomodation. Ideal touring base. Shannon Airport 1 hr drive. Tarbert Car Ferry 6km.

| B&B | 3 | Ensuite | €27.50-€31 | Dinner | - |
| B&B | - | Standard | | Partial Board | - |
| Single Rate | | | €40-€43.50 | Child reduction | **50%** |

Glin

**Open:** 1st January-22nd December

---

**Estelle O'Driscoll**
O'DRISCOLL'S B&B
Main Street, Glin, Co Limerick

### Glin

TEL: **068 34101**
EMAIL: **odriscollsbandb@eircom.net**
WEB: **www.odriscolls-accommodation.com**

Town house, welcoming and friendly. Glin is a picturesque Village on the N69. Near to Tarbert Car Ferry. Ballybunion Golf course 20 min.

| B&B | 3 | Ensuite | €32 | Dinner | - |
| B&B | 1 | Standard | €30 | Partial Board | - |
| Single Rate | | | €40-€45 | Child reduction | - |

Glin

**Open:** 10th January-16th December

---

**Mrs Catherine Sweeney**
SCENIC VIEW HOUSE
Ballyculhane, Glin, Co Limerick

### Glin

TEL: **068 34242**
EMAIL: **scenicviewhouse@eircom.net**

Bungalow, 7 mins Tarbert Car Ferry. Panoramic view of Shannon Estuary. Enroute from Shannon to Ring of Kerry on N69.

| B&B | 3 | Ensuite | €30-€32 | Dinner | - |
| B&B | 1 | Standard | €28-€30 | Partial Board | - |
| Single Rate | | | €40-€45 | Child reduction | **25%** |

Tarbert 4km

**Open:** All Year

---

**Mrs Anne O'Sullivan**
DEEBERT HOUSE
Kilmallock, Co Limerick

### Kilmallock

TEL: **063 98106** FAX: **063 82002**
EMAIL: **deeberthouse@eircom.net**
WEB: **www.deeberthouse.com**

Splendid Georgian residence, award winning gardens. Ideal touring centre. Adjacent to historic sites, golf, hill walking, horse riding. Loughgur Heritage Centre. On R515.

| B&B | 4 | Ensuite | €27.50-€31 | Dinner | €19-€25 |
| B&B | 1 | Standard | €25.50-€28.50 | Partial Board | €294 |
| Single Rate | | | €38-€43.50 | Child reduction | **25%** |

Kilmallock

**Open:** 1st February-30th November

---

**Terry Quish**
AUBURN HOUSE
Bruree Road, Kilmallock,
Co Limerick

### Kilmallock

TEL: **063 98761**

Elegant residence, scenic views, mature garden, adj to historic sites, hill walking, golf, horse riding, lough Gur heritage centre, the Ballyhouras, on R518.

| B&B | 2 | Ensuite | €27.50-€31 | Dinner | - |
| B&B | 1 | Standard | €25.50-€28.50 | Partial Board | - |
| Single Rate | | | €40-€43.50 | Child reduction | **25%** |

Kilmallock

**Open:** 1st March-30th November

**Agnes Callinan**
MOYRHEE
Phares Road Off N18, Meelick,
Co Limerick

TEL: **061 326300**
EMAIL: **agnesbnb@eircom.net**

Bungalow 1km off N18. Coming from Shannon Airport to Limerick City, turning after Radisson Hotel. Overlooking Clare Hills. Early arrivals welcome. Chiropractic clinic on premises.

| B&B | 3 | Ensuite | €28.50-€32 | Dinner | €20 |
|-----|---|---------|------------|--------|-----|
| B&B | - | Standard | - | Partial Board | - |
| Single Rate | | | €40-€43.50 | Child reduction | - |

Limerick 5km

**Open:** 1st January-1st December

---

**Mrs Bergie Carroll**
COONAGH LODGE
Coonagh, Off Ennis Rd,
Limerick, Co Limerick

TEL: **061 327050**
EMAIL: **coonagh@iol.ie**
WEB: **www.ireland-discover.com/coonaghlodge.htm**

Family run home. 10 minutes drive Shannon Airport, 5 minutes to Bunratty and Limerick City. Off Ennis Road roundabout at Travel Lodge Hotel.

| B&B | 6 | Ensuite | €28-€31 | Dinner | - |
|-----|---|---------|---------|--------|---|
| B&B | - | Standard | - | Partial Board | - |
| Single Rate | | | €40-€43.50 | Child reduction | 50% |

Limerick City 3km

**Open:** 7th January-15th December

---

**Patrick & Helen Daly**
GLEN EAGLES
12 Vereker Gardens,
Ennis Road, Limerick,
Co Limerick

TEL: **061 455521**   FAX: **061 455521**

Quiet cul-de-sac nearest B&B to City Centre. Train, bus, tourist office, off N18 beside Limerick Strand Hotel. TV, Hairdryers, Tea/Coffee facilities in rooms.

| B&B | 4 | Ensuite | €27.50-€31 | Dinner | - |
|-----|---|---------|------------|--------|---|
| B&B | - | Standard | - | Partial Board | - |
| Single Rate | | | €40-€43.50 | Child reduction | 25% |

In Limerick

**Open:** 1st February-15th December

---

**Elizabeth Gordon**
AVONDALE B&B
Old Cratloe Road, Limerick,
Co Limerick

TEL: **061 451697**

Warm, comfortable, country family home, peaceful surroundings. Ensuite bedrooms. Choice restaurants. Leisure activities. Tea/Coffee. Bunratty 3 miles, Airport 9 miles.

| B&B | 2 | Ensuite | €27.50-€31 | Dinner | - |
|-----|---|---------|------------|--------|---|
| B&B | 1 | Standard | €25.50-€28.50 | Partial Board | - |
| Single Rate | | | €40-€43.50 | Child reduction | 50% |

Limerick 3km

**Open:** 4th January-23rd December

---

**Lelia & Bernard Hanly**
SANDVILLA
Monaleen Road, Castletroy,
Co Limerick

TEL: **061 336484**   FAX: **061 336484**
EMAIL: **sandvilla@indigo.ie**

Warm welcoming haven off N7 & N24. Landscaped gardens. Award winning breakfast menu. Orthopaedic beds, TV in rooms. Near Castletroy, Kilmurry Hotels, University, Golf. Airport 30 mins.

| B&B | 2 | Ensuite | €27.50-€31 | Dinner | - |
|-----|---|---------|------------|--------|---|
| B&B | 2 | Standard | €26-€29 | Partial Board | - |
| Single Rate | | | €38-€43.50 | Child reduction | 25% |

Limerick 5km

**Open:** 6th January-16th December

**Martin & Patricia C Keane**
SANTOLINA
**Coonagh, Ennis Road,
Limerick, Co Limerick**

### Limerick City Ennis Road

TEL: **061 451590/328321**
EMAIL: **patriciaCkeane@eircom.net**
WEB: **http://homepage.eircom.net/~santolina**

Spacious country home. Ground floor accommodation. Coonagh is off N18 roundabout between Travelodge and Elm Garage. Convenient for City, Bunratty, Shannon.

| B&B | 6 | Ensuite | €28-€31 | Dinner | - |
| B&B | - | Standard | - | Partial Board | - |
| Single Rate | | | €40-€43.50 | Child reduction | 50% |

merick 3km

**Open:** 1st March-31st October

---

**Mrs Joan McSweeney**
TREBOR
**Ennis Road, Limerick City,
Co Limerick**

### Limerick City Ennis Road

TEL: **061 454632**  FAX: **061 454632**
EMAIL: **treborhouse@eircom.net**
WEB: **http://homepage.eircom.net/~treborhouse/index.html**

Old fashioned Town House, short walk City Centre on Bunratty Castle/Shannon Airport road. Tea/Coffee.

| B&B | 5 | Ensuite | €28-€31 | Dinner | - |
| B&B | - | Standard | - | Partial Board | - |
| Single Rate | | | €40-€43.50 | Child reduction | 25% |

Limerick

**Open:** 1st April-1st November

---

**Mrs Evelyn Moore**
AVONDOYLE COUNTRY-HOME
**Dooradoyle Road, Limerick,
Co Limerick**

### Limerick City

TEL: **061 301590**  FAX: **061 301590**
EMAIL: **avondoyl@iol.ie**
WEB: **http://welcome.to/avondoyle**

Dooradoyle exit off N20 highway. Follow golf club signs for 1km. Warm welcome. Extensive breakfast menu. TV, Tea/Coffee in rooms

| B&B | 2 | Ensuite | €30-€32 | Dinner | - |
| B&B | 2 | Standard | €28-€30 | Partial Board | - |
| Single Rate | | | €40-€44 | Child reduction | 50% |

merick City 3km

**Open:** All Year Except Christmas

---

**Noreen O'Farrell**
DOONEEN LODGE
**Caher Road, Mungret,
Near Limerick, Co Limerick**

### Limerick

TEL: **061 301332**
EMAIL: **dooneenlodge@eircom.net**
WEB: **www.dooneenlodge.net**

0.5 km off R526 between Limerick and Patrickswell, sign-posted. Tea/Coffee, TV all rooms. Convenient Adare, Bunratty, Shannon Airport, Limerick 5 km.

| B&B | 2 | Ensuite | €29-€32 | Dinner | - |
| B&B | 1 | Standard | €27.50-€30 | Partial Board | - |
| Single Rate | | | €38-€44 | Child reduction | 33.3% |

merick 5km

**Open:** 1st April-30th October

---

**Mrs Helen Quinn**
ASHGROVE HOUSE
**42 Rossroe Avenue,
Caherdavin, Ennis Road,
Limerick, Co Limerick**

### Limerick City Ennis Road

TEL: **061 453338**
EMAIL: **ashgrovehouse42@hotmail.com**
WEB: **www.limerickbandb.com**

5 mins City, L.I.T. College. Near, Bunratty. Approaching City from Shannon Airport turn left off Ennis Rd traffic lights at Ivans Cross to N7W. 3 mins walk Thomond Rugby Grounds & Gaelic Grounds.

| B&B | 4 | Ensuite | €31-€62 | Dinner | €20-€20 |
| B&B | - | Standard | - | Partial Board | - |
| Single Rate | | | €39-€43.50 | Child reduction | 25% |

merick City 2km

**Open:** 1st February-15th December

**Mr Ken Ryan**
**ARMADA LODGE**
**1 Elm Drive, Caherdavin,**
**Ennis Road, Limerick,**
**Co Limerick**

### Limerick City Ennis Road

TEL: **061 326993**
BUS NO: **302, 305**

Modern town house, convenient to Shannon Airport, City Centre, Bunratty and King Johns Castle. Opposite Greenhills Hotel. Private car parking.

| B&B | 4 | Ensuite | €31 | Dinner | - |
|---|---|---|---|---|---|
| B&B | - | Standard | - | Partial Board | - |
| Single Rate | | | €43.50 | Child reduction | - |

Limerick 2km    **Open:** 1st February-15th December

---

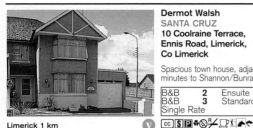

**Dermot Walsh**
**SANTA CRUZ**
**10 Coolraine Terrace,**
**Ennis Road, Limerick,**
**Co Limerick**

### Limerick City Ennis Road

TEL: **061 454500**
EMAIL: **dermotwa@yahoo.com**
WEB: **www.santacruzb-and-b.com**

Spacious town house, adjacent to Woodfield Hotel, Shannon bus stop. City Centre bus stop. 15 minutes to Shannon/Bunratty. 5 minutes Town. Tea/Coffee facilities. TV in bedrooms.

| B&B | 2 | Ensuite | €30-€33 | Dinner | - |
|---|---|---|---|---|---|
| B&B | 3 | Standard | €27-€30 | Partial Board | - |
| Single Rate | | | €39-€49 | Child reduction | 25% |

Limerick 1 km    **Open:** All Year

---

**Noreen Walshe**
**SHANVILLE B&B**
**Loughanleagh, Mungret,**
**Co Limerick**

### Limerick City

TEL: **061 353887**
EMAIL: **shanvillehouse@eircom.net**

Friendly home, peaceful surroundings/gardens. Secure parking. Fishing, ghillie boat hire arranged. Horse Riding, Limerick 5 mins, Airport 20 mins, on route N69.

| B&B | 3 | Ensuite | €30-€31 | Dinner | - |
|---|---|---|---|---|---|
| B&B | - | Standard | - | Partial Board | - |
| Single Rate | | | €40-€43.50 | Child reduction | 50% |

Limerick City 5km    **Open:** 1st January-20th December

---

**Mrs Mary Walsh-Seaver**
**RINNAKNOCK**
**Glenstal, Murroe, Co Limerick**

### Murroe

TEL: **061 386189**   FAX: **061 386263**
EMAIL: **walshseaver@eircom.net**
WEB: **homepage.eircom.net/~rinnaknock/**

Spacious residence beside Glenstal Abbey. Off N7 and N24. On Slieve Felim Cycling and Walking Trails.

| B&B | 5 | Ensuite | €30-€35 | Dinner | - |
|---|---|---|---|---|---|
| B&B | - | Standard | - | Partial Board | - |
| Single Rate | | | €45-€50 | Child reduction | 25% |

Murroe 2km    **Open:** 1st April-31st October

---

**Nuala Duffy**
**SHANAGARRY B&B**
**Killarney Rd, Newcastle West,**
**Co Limerick**

### Newcastle West

TEL: **069 61747**
EMAIL: **killarneyroad@eircom.net**
WEB: **homepage.eircom.net/~shanagarry/**

Welcoming home on outskirts of old market town (N21). Tea/Coffee on arrival. 13th century castle open after extensive renovation. Home of Ballygowan Spring Water.

| B&B | 2 | Ensuite | €28-€32 | Dinner | - |
|---|---|---|---|---|---|
| B&B | 1 | Standard | €25.50-€29 | Partial Board | - |
| Single Rate | | | €38-€43.50 | Child reduction | 50% |

Newcastle West 1km    **Open:** 1st April-31st October

**Mrs Joan King**
RANCH HOUSE
Cork Road, Newcastle West,
Co Limerick

TEL: **069 62313**
EMAIL: **bookings@ranch-house.ie**
WEB: **www.ranch-house.ie**

Luxurious home on large landscape gardens, quiet peaceful setting halfway between Shannon/Killarney/Tralee, adjacent to 18 hole Golf Course.

| B&B | 5 | Ensuite | €31 | Dinner | - |
|---|---|---|---|---|---|
| B&B | - | Standard | | Partial Board | - |
| Single Rate | | | €43.50 | Child reduction | 25% |

ewcastle West 1km

**Open:** 1st January-1st December

---

**Mrs Eileen Murphy**
THE ORCHARD
Limerick Road,
Newcastle West, Co Limerick

TEL: **069 61029**  FAX: **069 61029**
EMAIL: **eileentheorchard1@eircom.net**
WEB: **www.mrsapples.com**

Century old home with spacious rooms. Own farm produce. Breakfast menu. Homemade Breads/Jams. Near speed limit sign, on N21. Tea/Coffee on arrival.

| B&B | 5 | Ensuite | €27.50-€31 | Dinner | €25 |
|---|---|---|---|---|---|
| B&B | - | Standard | - | Partial Board | |
| Single Rate | | | €40-€43.50 | Child reduction | 50% |

ewcastle West 1km

**Open:** 1st January-31st December

---

**Mrs Carmel O'Brien**
BALLINGOWAN HOUSE
Limerick Road,
Newcastle West, Co Limerick

TEL: **069 62341**  FAX: **069 62457**
EMAIL: **ballingowanhouse@tinet.ie**

Luxurious pink Georgian house with distinctive features. Dillard Causin recommended. Landscaped gardens. N21 half way stop between Shannon/Killarney. 18 hole Golf course nearby.

| B&B | 5 | Ensuite | €27.50-€31 | Dinner | - |
|---|---|---|---|---|---|
| B&B | - | Standard | - | Partial Board | - |
| Single Rate | | | €40-€43.50 | Child reduction | 25% |

ewcastle West 2km

**Open:** 1st January-21st December

---

**Eilish Buckley**
LAUREL LODGE
Adare Road, Newboro,
Patrickswell, Co Limerick

TEL: **061 355059**  FAX: **061 355059**
EMAIL: **buckleyhome@yahoo.com**
WEB: **laurellodge.tourguide.net**

Secluded luxurious country home, highly recommended. Take R526 off N21 between Limerick and Adare to Patrickswell, at Church, Laurel Lodge is signposted.

| B&B | 4 | Ensuite | €31 | Dinner | - |
|---|---|---|---|---|---|
| B&B | - | Standard | | Partial Board | - |
| Single Rate | | | €43.50 | Child reduction | 33.3% |

atrickswell 3km

**Open:** 1st May-31st October

---

**The Geary Family**
CARNLEA HOUSE
Caher Road, Cloughkeating,
Patrickswell, Co Limerick

TEL: **061 302902**  FAX: **061 302902**
EMAIL: **carnleahouse@hotmail.com**
WEB: **www.carnleahouse.com**

Spacious bungalow midway between Limerick City and Patrickswell on R526 (off N20/21). Ideal stopover, Cork/Kerry/Bunratty/Shannon. Friendly atmosphere. Highly recommended.

| B&B | 3 | Ensuite | €28-€31 | Dinner | - |
|---|---|---|---|---|---|
| B&B | 1 | Standard | €26-€29 | Partial Board | - |
| Single Rate | | | €38-€43.50 | Child reduction | 50% |

atrickswell 3km

**Open:** 1st March-31st October

### Mrs Margaret Kearney
**BEECH GROVE**
**Barnakyle, Patrickswell,**
**Co Limerick**

**Patrickswell**

TEL: **061 355493**
EMAIL: **beechgrovehouse@yahoo.com**

On R526 off N20/21 at Patrickswell exit. Walking distance Village, Airport 20 mins. Near horse racing, golf, greyhound track. Ideal stopover Cork/Kerry.

| B&B | 2 | Ensuite | €30-€32 | Dinner | - |
| B&B | 1 | Standard | €28-€30 | Partial Board | - |
| Single Rate | | | €44-€44 | Child reduction | 33.3% |

Patrickswell

**Open:** 1st May-31st September

### Noreen O'Leary
**CEDAR LODGE**
**Patrickswell, Co Limerick**

**Patrickswell**

TEL: **061 355137**

Situated between Limerick and Patrickswell off N20/21 on the R526. Experience quality and comfort in our friendly family-run home.

| B&B | 4 | Ensuite | €30-€32 | Dinner | - |
| B&B | - | Standard | - | Partial Board | - |
| Single Rate | | | €40-€45 | Child reduction | - |

Patrickswell 2km

**Open:** 5th April-31st October

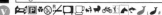

### Mrs Lily Woulfe
**LURRIGA LODGE**
**Patrickswell, Co Limerick**

**Patrickswell**

TEL: **061 355411** FAX: **061 355411**
EMAIL: **woulfe@esatclear.ie**
WEB: **www.lurrigalodge.com**

Award Winning Home, landscaped gardens. Breakfast menu. R526 off N20/N21 between Limerick/Adare to Patrickswell. Shannon Airport 25 mins, Adare 5 mins.

| B&B | 4 | Ensuite | €30-€32 | Dinner | - |
| B&B | - | Standard | - | Partial Board | - |
| Single Rate | | | €45.50 | Child reduction | 25% |

Patrickswell Village 1km

**Open:** 1st May-15th October

# Town & Country Gift Tokens

## TOWN & COUNTRY HOMES GIFT TOKENS

Why not share your experience of staying in a Town & Country home
by purchasing our gift tokens.
They are available in €10, €20 or €50 and can be used
in any home featured in this guide.

Contact us on email: accounts@townandcountry.ie
Telephone: 071 9822222   Fax: 071 9822207

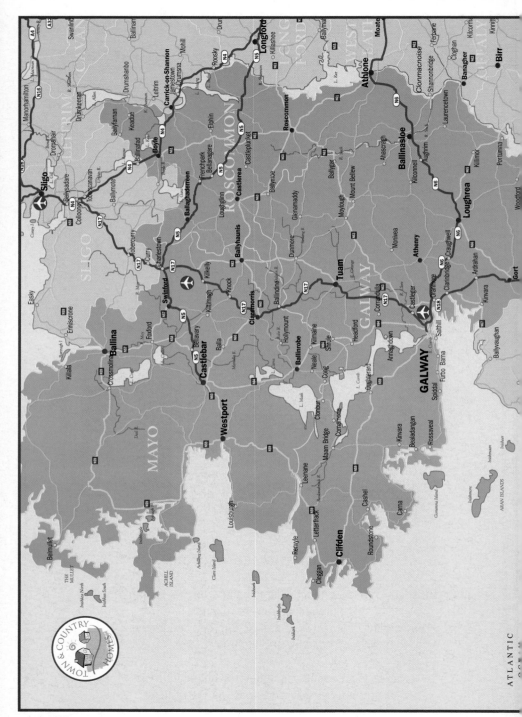

*Ireland West*

There is a special quality about these three beautiful Counties in the West of Ireland that is unique in Europe. The welcome is heartwarming, the quality of life, people and land-scape is all there for our visitor to share.

The spectacularly beautiful countryside, the coast that has been etched by the Atlantic, rambling hills and mountains and the lovely lakes and bays that mirror that special light from the clear skies over the countryside. Each County has its own special attractions and rich in all that is best in Irish folklore, music and song. There is something here for everyone, you will not be disappointed.

**Connemara National Park**

## Area Representatives

**GALWAY**

Bernadette Donoghue KILTEVNA 24 Grattan Park Coast Road Galway Co Galway
Tel: 091 588477   Fax: 091 581173
Mrs Bernie McTigue ABBEY VIEW Bushy Park Galway Co Galway
Tel: 091 524488   Fax: 091 524488
Mrs Mary Noone ASHBROOK HOUSE Dublin Road Oranmore Co Galway
Tel: 091 794196   Fax: 091 794196

**MAYO**

Mrs Maureen Daly WOODVIEW LODGE Breaffy (Breaghwy) Castlebar Co Mayo
Tel: 094 9023985   Fax: 094 9023985
Mr Robert Kilkelly ST ANTHONY'S Distillery Rd Westport Co Mayo
Tel: 098 28887   Fax: 098 25172
Mrs Carol O'Gorman ASHFORT Galway/Knock Road Charlestown Co Mayo
Tel: 094 9254706   Fax: 094 9255885

**ROSCOMMON**

Ms Mary Cooney CESH CORRAN Abbey Tce Sligo Rd Boyle Co Roscommon
Tel: 071 9662265   Fax: 071 9662265

## Tourist Information Offices
**OPEN ALL YEAR**

REFER TO PAGE 5 FOR A LIST OF SERVICES AVAILABLE

Galway City
Forster Street
Off Eyre Square
Tel: 091 537700

Westport
James St
Tel: 098 25711

Aran Islands
Inishmore
Tel: 099 61263

Oughterard
Main Street
Tel: 091 552808

Website: **www.irelandwest.ie**

Galway - A vibrant University City renowned for its Festivals, Music and Theatre. Archeological sites, Golf courses, Rivers, Lakes and the Aran Islands combine to make this county a magical place. Connemara dominated by the Twelve Pins is a delight to explore.

---

**Galway City 9km**

**Mrs Veronica Marley**
SILVER BIRCH
Clonboo, Annaghdown,
Co Galway

### Annaghdown
TEL: **091 791036**
EMAIL: **jmarley@eircom.net**

Family run home, on route Cong/Connemara/Westport on N84 road. Private parking, walking distance to pub, food served. Galway City 9km, Lough Corrib 4km.

| B&B | 4 | Ensuite | €27.50-€31 | Dinner | - |
|-----|---|---------|------------|--------|---|
| B&B | - | Standard | | Partial Board | - |
| Single Rate | | | €40-€43.50 | Child reduction | 25% |

**Open:** 1st April-31st October

---

**Kilronan 4.5km**

**Mrs Bridie Conneely**
BEACH VIEW HOUSE
Oatquarter, Kilronan, Inis Mor,
Aran Islands, Co Galway

### Aran Islands (Inismore)
TEL: **099 61141**   FAX: **099 61141**
EMAIL: **beachviewhouse@eircom.net**

Situated in middle of island near Dun Aengus. Scenic and tranquil surroundings. Ideal for Cliff walk's with views of Cliff's of Moher. Blue flag Beach, Restaurants and Pubs nearby.

| B&B | - | Ensuite | - | Dinner | - |
|-----|---|---------|---|--------|---|
| B&B | 6 | Standard | €30-€30 | Partial Board | - |
| Single Rate | | | €40-€41 | Child reduction | - |

**Open:** 5th May-6th September

---

**Kilronan 6km**

**Mrs Margaret Conneely**
CREIGMOUNT HOUSE
Creig-An-Cheirin, Kilronan,
Inis Mor, Aran Islands,
Co Galway

### Aran Islands (Inismore)
TEL: **099 61139**

Spectacular sea panorama from house set in unspoilt location. Historic monuments easily accessible. Qualified Cook/London City and Guilds Diploma.

| B&B | 2 | Ensuite | €30-€32 | Dinner | €26 |
|-----|---|---------|---------|--------|-----|
| B&B | 1 | Standard | €28-€30 | Partial Board | - |
| Single Rate | | | €42-€50 | Child reduction | - |

**Open:** 1st May-30th September

---

**In Kilronan**

**Marion Craven-Hernon**
CLAI BAN
Kilronan, Aran Islands,
Co Galway

### Aran Islands (Inismore)
TEL: **099 61111**   FAX: **099 61423**

Clai Ban is one of the nicest B&B's on Inismor. An easy 5 minute well-marked walk from Kilronan's centre. Panoramic views.

| B&B | 6 | Ensuite | €30-€35 | Dinner | - |
|-----|---|---------|---------|--------|---|
| B&B | - | Standard | | Partial Board | - |
| Single Rate | | | €50-€60 | Child reduction | 33.3% |

**Open:** All Year Except Christmas

**Bridie & Patrick McDonagh**
**AN CRUGAN**
Kilronan, Inis Mor, Aran Islands,
Co Galway

## Aran Islands (Inismore)

Tel: **099 61150** Fax: **099 61468**
Email: **ancrugan@eircom.net**
Web: **www.ancrugan.com**

Situated in Kilronan, the principal port and village of Inishmore. Convenient to Restaurants, Pubs, Beaches. Visa accepted. Hairdryers in bedrooms.

| B&B | 5 | Ensuite | €33 | Dinner | - |
|-----|---|---------|-----|--------|---|
| B&B | 1 | Standard | €30 | Partial Board | - |
| Single Rate | | | €50 | Child reduction | **50%** |

In Kilronan

**Open:** March-September

---

**Mrs Rita McDonagh**
**PORT ARAN HOUSE**
Upper Kilronan, Inismore,
Aran Islands, Co Galway

## Aran Islands (Inismore)

Tel: **099 61396** Fax: **099 61901**
Email: **portaran@eircom.net**

Friendly welcome awaits you at Portaran House overlooking Galway Bay, Connemara Coast and Clare Hills. Situated within walking distance of all amenities.

| B&B | 6 | Ensuite | €35 | Dinner | - |
|-----|---|---------|-----|--------|---|
| B&B | - | Standard | - | Partial Board | - |
| Single Rate | | | €50 | Child reduction | **50%** |

In Kilronan

**Open:** 1st April-30th September

---

**Mrs Teresa Faherty**
**AN DUN**
Inis Meain,
Aran Islands Inis Meain,
Co Galway

## Aran Islands Inis Meain

Tel: **099 73047** Fax: **099 73047**
Email: **andunininismeain@eircom.net**
Web: **inismeainaccommodation.com**

New house, wonderful scenic views all bedrooms. Purpose built, comfortable, hotel standard bedrooms, 2 dinning rooms.

| B&B | 4 | Ensuite | €28-€35 | Dinner | €15-€25 |
|-----|---|---------|---------|--------|---------|
| B&B | - | Standard | - | Partial Board | - |
| Single Rate | | | €40-€45 | Child reduction | **50%** |

Aran Islands

**Open:** All Year

---

**Cait Flaherty**
**ARD MHUIRIS**
Kilronan, Aran Islands,
Co Galway

## Aran Islands

Tel: **099 61208** Fax: **099 61333**
Email: **ardmhuiris@eircom.net**

5-7 minutes from Ferry - turn right, then left. View of Galway Bay, peaceful area. Walking distance from Restaurants, Pubs, Beaches.

| B&B | 6 | Ensuite | €30-€35 | Dinner | - |
|-----|---|---------|---------|--------|---|
| B&B | - | Standard | - | Partial Board | - |
| Single Rate | | | €50-€60 | Child reduction | **50%** |

Kilronan

**Open:** 1st March-1st November

---

**Joe & Maura Wolfe**
**MAN OF ARAN COTTAGES**
Kilmurvey, Inish Mor,
Aran Islands, Co Galway

## Aran Islands

Tel: **099 61301** Fax: **099 61324**
Email: **manofaran@eircom.net**
Web: **www.manofarancottage.com**

This historic thatched cottage on an acre of organically grown vegetables and herbs was built by Robert Flaherty as a set for his film "The Man of Aran".

| B&B | 1 | Ensuite | €37-€37 | Dinner | €30 |
|-----|---|---------|---------|--------|-----|
| B&B | 2 | Standard | €35-€35 | Partial Board | - |
| Single Rate | | | €45-€47 | Child reduction | - |

Kilronan 6.5km

**Open:** 1st March-31st October

In Athenry

**John & Barbara Coyne**
**CAHEROYAN HOUSE AND FARM**
**Athenry, Co Galway**

Tel: **091 844858**
Email: **caheroynhouseandfarm@eircom.net**
Web: **caheroyanhouseathenry.com**

Country manor house luxuriously restored 70 organic acres of peaceful lush walks, tennis court, river, Lime Kiln, all a 5 min walk from Athenry on Monivea Road.

| B&B | 4 | Ensuite | €35-€50 | Dinner | - |
|-----|---|---------|---------|--------|---|
| B&B | | Standard | | Partial Board | - |
| Single Rate | | | €40-€55 | Child reduction | **33.3%** |

**Open:** 1st January-23rd December

---

In Athenry

**Ms Marion E McDonagh**
**TEACH AN GHARRAIN**
**Ballygarraun Road, Athenry, Co Galway**

Tel: **091 844579**
Email: **mcdhaus@eircom.net**
Web: **www.mcdonaghsbandb.com**

Athenry a place to touch the past with the comforts of the present. Tranquil, quiet location. Galway City 20 mins, train service, Internet access. Take N6 to R348. **Stg: Ensuite £20-£21.25 Single Rate £27-£29.**

| B&B | 4 | Ensuite | €29-€31 | Dinner | - |
|-----|---|---------|---------|--------|---|
| B&B | | Standard | - | Partial Board | - |
| Single Rate | | | €40-€43.50 | Child reduction | **50%** |

**Open:** All Year

---

In Athenry

**Mr Paul Thompson**
**ARD RI**
**Swangate, Athenry, Co Galway**

Tel: **091 844050**

Galway City 12km. Train station Dublin-Galway line. Ideal for touring Connemara, Burren, Aran Islands, Heritage Town. Fishing, Golfing.

| B&B | 4 | Ensuite | €27.50-€31 | Dinner | - |
|-----|---|---------|------------|--------|---|
| B&B | - | Standard | - | Partial Board | - |
| Single Rate | | | €40-€43.50 | Child reduction | **50%** |

**Open:** 2nd January-20th December

---

Ballinasloe 3km

**Angela Lyons**
**NEPHIN**
**Portumna Road, Kellygrove, Ballinasloe, Co Galway**

Tel: **090 9642685**
Email: **angelalyonsbb@eircom.net**

Spacious house on landscaped gardens overlooking Golf Course. Complimentry Tea/Coffee. Hairdryers. Le Guide du Routard recommended. 1 mile off N6.

| B&B | 2 | Ensuite | €28.50-€31 | Dinner | - |
|-----|---|---------|------------|--------|---|
| B&B | 1 | Standard | €26.50-€28.50 | Partial Board | - |
| Single Rate | | | €38-€43.50 | Child reduction | **25%** |

**Open:** 15th April-14th November

---

Ballyconneely 1km

**Bernie O'Neill**
**MANNIN LODGE**
**Mannin Road, Ballyconneely, Co Galway**

Tel: **095 23586** Fax: **095 23861**
Email: **boneillmanninlodge@eircom.net**

Family run home. Convenient to Beaches, Golf Club, Pony Trekking. All with TV and Hairdryers. Clifden 10 minutes drive. Near Restuarants.

| B&B | 6 | Ensuite | €28-€31 | Dinner | €22-€22 |
|-----|---|---------|---------|--------|---------|
| B&B | - | Standard | - | Partial Board | €336 |
| Single Rate | | | €40-€43.50 | Child reduction | **25%** |

**Open:** 28th February-30th November

**Mrs Irene Carr**
VILLA DE PORRES
Barna Village, Galway,
Co Galway

### Barna Village
TEL: **091 592239**   FAX: **091 592239**

Off Coast Road. Close to sea food Restaurants. Beaches, Fishing, Barna Golf Club, Pony trekking. Private carpark. All rooms with TV, Hairdryers, Electric blankets. Tea/Coffee facilities.

| B&B | 4 | Ensuite | €32-€35 | Dinner | - |
| B&B | 1 | Standard | €28-€30 | Partial Board | - |
| Single Rate | | | €40-€45 | Child reduction | 25% |

Galway 8km

**Open:** 31st March-31st October

**Mrs Joan Codyre**
FREEPORT HOUSE
Barna Village, Co Galway

### Barna
TEL: **091 592199**   FAX: **091 592199**

Coast road R336. Seafront in Village. Overlooking Galway Bay. Breakfast menu, Home baking. Beside village Restaurants, Pubs, Barna Golf Club, Connemara, Aran Islands.

| B&B | 6 | Ensuite | €32-€35 | Dinner | - |
| B&B | - | Standard | | Partial Board | - |
| Single Rate | | | €40-€45 | Child reduction | 25% |

Galway City 8km

**Open:** 15th February-1st November

**Bernadette Ryan**
ABBEYVILLE
Freeport, Barna, Co Galway

### Barna
TEL: **091 592430**
EMAIL: **ryanbearna@eircom.net**
WEB: **www.abbeyvillebandb.com**

Attractive modern home. TV, Orthopaedic beds. Private Car parking. 200 meters Restaurants, Pubs. Located off the R336 in Barna village before traffic lights.

| B&B | 4 | Ensuite | €28-€40 | Dinner | - |
| B&B | - | Standard | - | Partial Board | - |
| Single Rate | | | €40-€45 | Child reduction | 25% |

Galway City 6km

**Open:** 1st January-21st December

**Colm & Una Conneely**
RADHARC NA NOILEAN
Annaghvane, Bealadangan,
Co Galway

### Beal A Daingin Connemara
TEL: **091 572137**   FAX: **091 572137**
EMAIL: **radharcnanoilean@eircom.net**

Friendly family home with sea & mountain views. Tea/Coffee, Scones on arrival. Aran Islands nearby, also Fishing, Walks, Golf. R336 from Galway to Casla, R374 to Annaghvane.

| B&B | 3 | Ensuite | €28-€30 | Dinner | - |
| B&B | - | Standard | - | Partial Board | - |
| Single Rate | | | €40-€43.50 | Child reduction | 33.3% |

Bealadangan 1km

**Open:** All Year Except Christmas

**Padraic & Angela O'Conghaile**
TEACH ANACH MHEAIN
Anach Mheain, Beal a Daingin,
Connemara, Co Galway

### Beal A Daingin Connemara
TEL: **091 572348**   FAX: **091 572348**
EMAIL: **padraicoc@eircom.net**

Modern family house. All bedrooms with Sea and Mountain view. Convenient to Aran Islands, Ferry, Golf, Fishing ,Walks, Beaches etc.

| B&B | 4 | Ensuite | €27.50-€31 | Dinner | - |
| B&B | - | Standard | | Partial Board | - |
| Single Rate | | | €40-€43.50 | Child reduction | 33.3% |

Lettermore 3km

**Open:** 1st May-30th September

### Mrs Barbara Madden
HILLSIDE HOUSE B&B
Kylesalia, Kilkieran,
Connemara, Co Galway

**Carna Connemara**

TEL: **095 33420**   FAX: **095 33624**
EMAIL: **hillsidehouse@oceanfree.net**
WEB: **www.connemara.net/hillside/**

Warm country home with panoramic sea/mountain views. Hill/coastal walks, beaches and Aran Island ferry nearby. Route R340 on Kilkieran/Carna road. AA ◆◆◆◆.

| B&B | 4 | Ensuite | €27.50-€31 | Dinner | - |
| B&B | - | Standard | | Partial Board | - |
| Single Rate | | | €40-€44 | Child reduction | - |

Kilkieran 3km

**Open:** 1st March-31st October

---

### Barbara Mulkerrin
TEACH NA TRA
Callowfeenish, Carna,
Co Galway

**Carna Connemara**

TEL: **095 32259**   FAX: **095 32259**
EMAIL: **info@teachnatra.com**
WEB: **www.teachnatra.com**

Farmhouse panoramic view of sea and mountain Cead Mile Fáilte. Tea coffee served on arrival.

| B&B | 4 | Ensuite | €30-€32.50 | Dinner | €20-€24 |
| B&B | - | Standard | - | Partial Board | |
| Single Rate | | | €40-€43.50 | Child reduction | 25% |

Carna 4km

**Open:** 1st March-31st October

---

### Mrs Tina Donoghue
DONOGHUE'S
Carraroe, Connemara,
Co Galway

**Carraroe**

TEL: **091 595174**   FAX: **091 595174**
EMAIL: **donoghuec@esatclear.ie**

Comfortable family home on spacious grounds. Beaches and Country Walks; daily trips to Aran Islands nearby. Credit Cards accepted.

| B&B | 2 | Ensuite | €27.50-€31 | Dinner | - |
| B&B | 1 | Standard | €25.50-€28.50 | Partial Board | - |
| Single Rate | | | €38-€43.50 | Child reduction | 50% |

Carraroe 1km

**Open:** 17th March-30th November

---

### Mrs Mary Lydon
CARRAROE HOUSE
Carraroe, Connemara,
Co Galway

**Carraroe Connemara**

TEL: **091 595188**
EMAIL: **carraroehouse@oceanfree.net**

Modern family home on outskirts of village. Ideal for touring Connemara, Aran Islands, near Beaches-Coral Beach. R336 from Galway to Casla, R343 to Carraroe.

| B&B | 4 | Ensuite | €27.50-€31 | Dinner | - |
| B&B | 1 | Standard | €25.50-€28.50 | Partial Board | - |
| Single Rate | | | €38-€43.50 | Child reduction | 50% |

Galway 40km

**Open:** 7th January-20th December

---

### Maura Campbell
AVONDALE
Cregboy, Claregalway,
Co Galway

**Claregalway**

TEL: **091 798349**

Comfortable home on N17 Galway/Sligo road. Fishing and Horse riding nearby. 5km from Galway Airport. Ideal for touring Connemara/Clare.

| B&B | 2 | Ensuite | €27.50-€31 | Dinner | - |
| B&B | 2 | Standard | €25.50-€28.50 | Partial Board | - |
| Single Rate | | | €38-€43.50 | Child reduction | 50% |

Galway 7km

**Open:** 1st May-31st October

Claregalway 1km

### Mary Gannon
**CASTLEGROVE HOUSE**
**Tuam Rd, Claregalway,**
**Co Galway**

**Claregalway**

TEL: **091 799169**
EMAIL: **m_gannon45@hotmail.com**
WEB: **www.castlegrove-house.com/**

Friendly family home on N17. Ideal touring base for Connemara and Clare. Lovely restaurants, lounge bars and other facilities 5 minutes walk. Galway City 9km.

| B&B | 4 | Ensuite | €30-€40 | Dinner | - |
| B&B | - | Standard | | Partial Board | - |
| Single Rate | | | €40-€45 | Child reduction | 25% |

**Open:** All Year

Galway City 10km

### Mrs Mary McNulty
**CREG LODGE**
**Claregalway, Co Galway**

**Claregalway**

TEL: **091 798862**
EMAIL: **creglodge@eircom.net**
WEB: **www.creglodge.ie**

Luxury family home on the N17 Galway/Sligo Road. 10km from Galway City and 5km from Airport. Restaurants/Pubs/Hotel within walking distance.

| B&B | 4 | Ensuite | €30-€35 | Dinner | - |
| B&B | - | Standard | - | Partial Board | - |
| Single Rate | | | €40-€45 | Child reduction | 25% |

**Open:** 10th January-20th December

Galway 12km

### Mr Niall Stewart
**GARMISCH**
**Loughgeorge, Claregalway,**
**Co Galway**

**Claregalway**

TEL: **091 798606**
EMAIL: **garmisch@eircom.net**

Luxury dormer bungalow on N17. Adjacent to Central Tavern Bar and Restaurant. Convenient for Fishing, Golfing and Touring. Galway Airport 6km.

| B&B | 4 | Ensuite | €28-€32 | Dinner | - |
| B&B | - | Standard | | Partial Board | - |
| Single Rate | | | €40-€44 | Child reduction | 50% |

**Open:** All Year

In Clarinbridge

### Mrs Dympna Callinan
**CLAREVILLE**
**Stradbally North, Clarinbridge,**
**Co Galway**

**Clarinbridge**

TEL: **091 796248**
EMAIL: **clareville@eircom.net**
WEB: **homepage.eircom.net/~clareville/**

Luxurious spacious dormer home situated in the heart of Oyster Country. 0.5km off N18, within walking distance of Village, Sea. Central to Burren, Connemara.

| B&B | 4 | Ensuite | €27.50-€34 | Dinner | - |
| B&B | - | Standard | - | Partial Board | - |
| Single Rate | | | €40-€47 | Child reduction | 25% |

**Open:** 1st March-30th November

### K Geraghty
**INISFREE B&B**
**Slievaun, Clarinbridge, Galway,**
**Co Galway**

**Clarinbridge**

TEL: **091 796655**

Conveniently located on the main N18. Within walking distance of Village and Restaurants. In the heart of Oyster Country and only 12 mins Galway.

| B&B | 3 | Ensuite | €29.50-€31 | Dinner | - |
| B&B | - | Standard | | Partial Board | - |
| Single Rate | | | €40-€43.50 | Child reduction | 25% |

In Clarinbridge

**Open:** All Year Except Christmas

**Clarinbridge 1km**

### Mrs Maura McNamara
**SPRING LAWN**
Stradbally, Clarinbridge,
Co Galway

**Clarinbridge**

Tel: **091 796045**   Fax: **091 796045**
Email: **springlawn2@hotmail.com**
Web: **www.surf.to/springlawn2**

Luxury family home on mature landscaped gardens. Located just off N18 near Village and Sea. Ideal base to visit Connemara, Aran Islands, Burren. Dillard Causin Guide recommended.

| B&B | 3 | Ensuite | €27.50-€31 | Dinner | - |
|---|---|---|---|---|---|
| B&B | - | Standard | | Partial Board | - |
| Single Rate | | | €40-€45 | Child reduction | 25% |

**Open:** 1st March-30th November

---

**Clarinbridge 1km**

### Mrs Teresa O'Dea
**KARAUN HOUSE**
Stradbally, Clarinbridge,
Co Galway

**Clarinbridge**

Tel: **091 796182**
Email: **tod_karaun@ireland.com**
Web: **www.go.to/karaun**

Irish Times Recommended. 1km off N18. Walk to Sea. Near Burren, Galway City, Connemara, Aran Islands. Tea/Coffee, Hairdryers, Electric blankets. Visa, Master Cards accepted.

| B&B | 2 | Ensuite | €27.50-€31 | Dinner | - |
|---|---|---|---|---|---|
| B&B | 1 | Standard | €25.50-€28.50 | Partial Board | - |
| Single Rate | | | €38-€45 | Child reduction | - |

**Open:** 15th January-15th December

---

**Cleggan 1km**

### William & Bernie Hughes
**COIS NA MARA**
Cleggan, Clifden, Co Galway

**Cleggan Connemara**

Tel: **095 44647**   Fax: **095 44016**
Email: **coisnamara@hotmail.com**
Web: **www.dirl.com/galway/cois-na-mara.htm**

Family home in scenic area. Daily boat trips to Inishbofin. Safe sandy Beaches and Pony trekking within walking distance. Access/Visa accepted.

| B&B | 4 | Ensuite | €27.50-€31 | Dinner | - |
|---|---|---|---|---|---|
| B&B | - | Standard | - | Partial Board | - |
| Single Rate | | | €40-€43.50 | Child reduction | 33.3% |

**Open:** 15th May-15th September

---

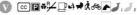

**Clifden 10km**

### Mrs Mary King
**CNOC BREAC**
Cleggan, Co Galway

**Cleggan Connemara**

Tel: **095 44688**
Email: **tking@gofree.indigo.ie**

Family home. Peaceful, scenic area. Beside sandy Beach. Fishing, Pony Riding. Bay Cruises arranged. Convenient for Inishbofin Ferry. Village 1km.

| B&B | 4 | Ensuite | €27.50-€31 | Dinner | - |
|---|---|---|---|---|---|
| B&B | - | Standard | | Partial Board | - |
| Single Rate | | | €40-€43.50 | Child reduction | 25% |

**Open:** 1st May-30th September

---

**Clifden 9km**

### Mrs Loretta O'Malley
**HARBOUR HOUSE**
Cleggan, Co Galway

**Cleggan Connemara**

Tel: **095 44702**
Email: **harbour.house@oceanfree.net**

Spacious family run home situated in pretty fishing Village of Cleggan from which to explore the wonderful land and seascapes.

| B&B | 4 | Ensuite | €27.50-€31 | Dinner | - |
|---|---|---|---|---|---|
| B&B | - | Standard | | Partial Board | - |
| Single Rate | | | €40-€43.50 | Child reduction | 25% |

**Open:** 1st February-31st October

Cleggan 1.5km

## Cleggan Connemara

**Ms Mary O'Malley**
WILD HEATHER
Cloon, Cleggan, Co Galway

TEL: **095 44617**
EMAIL: **cloon@oceanfree.net**
WEB: **www.wildheather.org**

Dine in scenic splendour in conservatory overlooking Bay and Islands. Relax by peat fires. Rest well and enjoy Connemara. Home baking. Information provided, Village 1.5km.

| B&B | 4 | Ensuite | €27.50-€31 | Dinner | - |
|-----|---|---------|------------|--------|---|
| B&B | | Standard | | Partial Board | - |
| Single Rate | | | €40-€43.50 | Child reduction | **25%** |

**Open:** 1st March-30th September

---

Clifden 1km

## Clifden Connemara

**Jane Andrews**
LIGHTHOUSE VIEW
Sky Road, Fakeeragh, Clifden,
Co Galway

TEL: **095 22113**

Friendly house on scenic sky road, opposite Clifden Castle. Ideal base for touring Connemara or just relaxing. Home baking. Warm welcome assured. 1km from Clifden. Child reduction for under 7.

| B&B | 4 | Ensuite | €28.50-€31 | Dinner | - |
|-----|---|---------|------------|--------|---|
| B&B | - | Standard | - | Partial Board | - |
| Single Rate | | | €40-€43.50 | Child reduction | **25%** |

**Open:** 7th January-18th December

---

Clifden 8km

## Clifden Connemara

**Mrs Noreen Conneely**
BEN BREEN HOUSE
Tooreen, Moyard, Co Galway

TEL: **095 41171**
EMAIL: **benbreenhouse@iolfree.ie**
WEB: **www.connemara.net**

Comfortable well heated home. Peat fires. Magnificent view sea/mountain. Peaceful and tranquil location. Convenient to Connemara National Park.

| B&B | 6 | Ensuite | €27.50-€31 | Dinner | €20-€20 |
|-----|---|---------|------------|--------|---------|
| B&B | - | Standard | - | Partial Board | €295 |
| Single Rate | | | €40-€43.50 | Child reduction | **25%** |

**Open:** 15th March-31st October

---

Clifden 5km

## Clifden Connemara

**Mrs Anne Conroy**
ROCKMOUNT HOUSE
Bayleek, Sky Road, Clifden,
Co Galway

TEL: **095 21763**
EMAIL: **rockmount@indigo.ie**
WEB: **www.rockmounthouse.com**

Breathtaking views of scenic Sky Road. Convenient to Sandy Beaches, Fishing, Cliff Walks and Golf. Peaceful location, ideal touring base. Breakfast menu. Warm welcome assured.

| B&B | 4 | Ensuite | €27.50-€31 | Dinner | €22 |
|-----|---|---------|------------|--------|-----|
| B&B | - | Standard | - | Partial Board | - |
| Single Rate | | | €45-€50 | Child reduction | **33.3%** |

**Open:** April-October

---

Clifden 4.5km

## Clifden Connemara

**Mr & Mrs Kevin & Sinead Conroy**
SEAFIELD HOUSE
Bayleek, Sky Road, Clifden,
Co Galway

TEL: **095 22102**
EMAIL: **seafieldhouse@msn.com**
WEB: **www.connemara.net/seafieldhouse**

Attractive, modern bungalow set on the scenic sky road. Spacious rooms ensuite with views of Atlantic seaboard. All local amenities close by.

| B&B | 4 | Ensuite | €27.50-€32.50 | Dinner | - |
|-----|---|---------|---------------|--------|---|
| B&B | - | Standard | - | Partial Board | - |
| Single Rate | | | €38-€45 | Child reduction | **33.3%** |

**Open:** 1st April-1st October

**John & Joan Coyne**
SEA VIEW
Westport Road, Clifden,
Co Galway

TEL: **095 22822**  FAX: **095 21394**
EMAIL: **seaviewhse@eircom.net**
WEB: **www.house4rent.ie/SeaView**

Modern bungalow in peaceful surroundings. Panoramic view of Streamstown Bay and Sky Road. Electric blankets, Orthopaedic beds. Ideal touring centre for Connemara. (N59).

| B&B | 5 | Ensuite | €28-€31 | Dinner | - |
|-----|---|---------|---------|--------|---|
| B&B | - | Standard | | Partial Board | - |
| Single Rate | | | €40-€45 | Child reduction | 50% |

Clifden 2km

**Open:** All Year

---

**Michael & Jane Delapp**
HEATHER LODGE
Westport Road, Clifden,
Co Galway

**Clifden Connemara**

TEL: **095 21331**  FAX: **095 22041**
EMAIL: **info@heatherlodge.ie**
WEB: **www.heatherlodge.ie**

Beautiful, peaceful country home. Spacious bedrooms overlook lake and mountain range. Superb breakfast menu with home baking. High standards maintained, highly recommended.

| B&B | 6 | Ensuite | €30-€35 | Dinner | - |
|-----|---|---------|---------|--------|---|
| B&B | - | Standard | | Partial Board | - |
| Single Rate | | | €40-€45 | Child reduction | 25% |

Clifden 1.5km

**Open:** 1st March-31st October

---

**Mrs Breege Feneran**
LOUGH FADDA HOUSE
Ballyconneely Road, Clifden,
Co Galway

**Clifden Connemara**

TEL: **095 21165**
EMAIL: **feneran@gofree.indigo.ie**
WEB: **pages.zdnet.com/loughfaddahouse/loughfaddahouse**

Spacious, well heated country home. Lovely quiet country walks in scenic area. Peat fires, Fishing & Pony Riding arranged. Credit Cards accepted.

| B&B | 6 | Ensuite | €28-€31 | Dinner | - |
|-----|---|---------|---------|--------|---|
| B&B | - | Standard | - | Partial Board | - |
| Single Rate | | | €40-€43.50 | Child reduction | 25% |

Clifden 3km

**Open:** 24th March-15th October

---

**Mrs Carmel Gaughan**
ARD AOIBHINN
Ardbear, Ballyconneely Road,
Clifden, Co Galway

**Clifden Connemara**

TEL: **095 21339**
EMAIL: **ardbear@eircom.net**
WEB: **www.ardaoibhinnclifden.com**

Modern bungalow in scenic surroundings on Clifden - Ballyconneely Road convenient to safe Beaches and Golf Links. Excellent touring base.

| B&B | 2 | Ensuite | €27.50-€31 | Dinner | - |
|-----|---|---------|------------|--------|---|
| B&B | 1 | Standard | €25.50-€28.50 | Partial Board | - |
| Single Rate | | | €38-€43.50 | Child reduction | 25% |

Clifden 1km

**Open:** 1st April-31st October

---

**Mrs Maureen Geoghegan**
ROSSFIELD HOUSE
Westport Road, Clifden,
Co Galway

**Clifden Connemara**

TEL: **095 21392**
EMAIL: **rossfieldhouse@eircom.net**

Family run home. Warm welcome. Breakfast menu. Home baking. Convenient to safe beaches and golf links. Excellent touring base. Orthopaedic beds. Peaceful location.

| B&B | 3 | Ensuite | €27.50-€31 | Dinner | - |
|-----|---|---------|------------|--------|---|
| B&B | - | Standard | | Partial Board | - |
| Single Rate | | | €40-€43.50 | Child reduction | 33.3% |

Clifden 1km

**Open:** 1st February-1st December

**Mrs Kathleen Hardman**
MALLMORE HOUSE
Ballyconneely Road, Clifden,
Co Galway

### Clifden Connemara

TEL: **095 21460**
EMAIL: **info@mallmore.com**
WEB: **www.mallmorecountryhouse.com**

Lovingly restored Georgian home. 35 acre woodland grounds, spacious rooms, superb views, open fires and award-winning breakfasts. AA ◆◆◆◆.

| B&B | 6 | Ensuite | €30-€35 | Dinner | - |
|------|---|---------|---------|--------|---|
| B&B | - | Standard | - | Partial Board | - |
| Single Rate | | | - | Child reduction | 25% |

Clifden 1.5km   ✖   🅿... **Open:** 7th March-1st October

---

**Mrs Bridie Hyland**
BAY VIEW
Westport Road, Clifden,
Co Galway

### Clifden Connemara

TEL: **095 21286**   FAX: **095 22938**
EMAIL: **info@connemara-clifden.com**
WEB: **www.connemara-clifden.com**

Frommer recommended. Overlooking Streamstown Bay. View from house described "most spectacular view in Ireland". Orthopaedic Beds, Electric Blankets, hairdryers.

| B&B | 4 | Ensuite | €28-€32 | Dinner | - |
|------|---|---------|---------|--------|---|
| B&B | - | Standard | - | Partial Board | - |
| Single Rate | | | €40-€43.50 | Child reduction | 50% |

Clifden 2km   Ⓥ ... **Open:** 1st February-10th December

---

**Oliver Joyce**
THE WILDERNESS
Emloughmore, Clifden,
Co Galway

### Clifden Connemara

TEL: **095 21641**
EMAIL: **thewilderness_b_b@hotmail.com**

Modern home located in peaceful scenic wilds of Connemara with mountain views, Turf fires. Warm friendly atmosphere. 8km from Clifden on N59 route.

| B&B | 4 | Ensuite | €30-€31 | Dinner | - |
|------|---|---------|---------|--------|---|
| B&B | - | Standard | - | Partial Board | - |
| Single Rate | | | €40-€43.50 | Child reduction | 25% |

Clifden 8km   Ⓥ ... **Open:** 17th March-31st October

---

**Mrs Margaret Kelly**
WINNOWING HILL
Ballyconneely Road, Clifden,
Co Galway

### Clifden Connemara

TEL: **095 21281**   FAX: **095 21287**
EMAIL: **winnowinghill@eircom.net**
WEB: **www.winnowinghill.com**

Situated on a tranquil hill overlooking the Twelve Bens, Clifden Town and Salt Lake. Views can also be enjoyed with a cup of tea from glass conservatory.

| B&B | 3 | Ensuite | €28-€32 | Dinner | - |
|------|---|---------|---------|--------|---|
| B&B | - | Standard | - | Partial Board | - |
| Single Rate | | | €40-€44 | Child reduction | 33.3% |

Clifden 1km   Ⓥ ... **Open:** 12th March-6th November

---

**Mrs Mary King**
KINGSTOWN HOUSE
Bridge Street, Clifden,
Co Galway

### Clifden Connemara

TEL: **095 21470**   FAX: **095 21530**

AA registered. Long established home in Town. Convenient to Beaches, Golf, Fishing, Riding. 2 mins walk Bus, 5 mins to Sea.

| B&B | 7 | Ensuite | €28-€32 | Dinner | - |
|------|---|---------|---------|--------|---|
| B&B | 1 | Standard | €27-€29 | Partial Board | - |
| Single Rate | | | €40-€44 | Child reduction | 25% |

n Clifden   Ⓥ ... **Open:** 1st January-31st December

**Clifden 8km**

### Odile LeDorven
**KER MOR**
Claddaghduff, Clifden,
Connemara, Co Galway

**Clifden Connemara**

TEL: **095 44954/44698**  FAX: **095 44773**
EMAIL: **kermor@eircom.net**
WEB: **www.kermor-irl.com**

Peaceful and friendly house on Streamstown Bay. Large bedrooms en-suite. Surprising healthy breakfast. Something special and different, Walking, Angling etc.

| B&B | 3 | Ensuite | €30-€32 | Dinner | - |
|-----|---|---------|---------|--------|---|
| B&B | - | Standard | | Partial Board | - |
| Single Rate | | | €42-€45 | Child reduction | - |

**Open:** 1st January-31st December

---

**Clifden 10km**

### Tina McDonagh
**DOONHILL LODGE**
Aillebrack, Ballyconneely,
Clifden, Co Galway

**Clifden Connemara**

TEL: **095 23726**  FAX: **095 23812**
EMAIL: **tandfmcdonaghdoonhilllodge@eircom.net**

Warm comfortable home, situated 0.5km from Connemara Golf Club. Walking distance to Beaches and Pony Trekking. Hairdryer, Tea/Coffee facilities and TV in rooms. Ballyconneely 2 km.

| B&B | 4 | Ensuite | €27.50-€31 | Dinner | - |
|-----|---|---------|------------|--------|---|
| B&B | - | Standard | | Partial Board | - |
| Single Rate | | | €40-€43.50 | Child reduction | 25% |

**Open:** 1st May-30th September

---

**Clifden**

### The McEvaddy Family
**BAYMOUNT HOUSE**
Seaview, Clifden, Co Galway

**Clifden Connemara**

TEL: **095 21459**  FAX: **095 21639**
EMAIL: **baymounthouse@eircom.net**
WEB: **www.baymount-connemara.com**

Spacious family home overlooking Clifden Bay. Magnificent Sea Views. Peaceful location. Hairdryers, Tea/coffee making facilities and TV in bedrooms.

| B&B | 10 | Ensuite | €25-€30 | Dinner | - |
|-----|----|---------|---------|--------|---|
| B&B | - | Standard | - | Partial Board | - |
| Single Rate | | | | Child reduction | 33.3% |

**Open:** 1st March-31st October

---

**Clifden 8km**

### Mrs Carmel Murray
**OCEAN VILLA**
Kingstown, Sky Road, Clifden,
Co Galway

**Clifden Connemara**

TEL: **095 21357**
EMAIL: **info@oceanvillaireland.com**
WEB: **www.oceanvillaireland.com**

Modern bungalow overlooking sea with panoramic hill and sea views. Tranquil location on famous Sky Road. All outdoor activities arranged. Recommended.

| B&B | 6 | Ensuite | €30-€32 | Dinner | - |
|-----|---|---------|---------|--------|---|
| B&B | - | Standard | - | Partial Board | - |
| Single Rate | | | - | Child reduction | - |

**Open:** 1st March-31st October

---

**Clifden 2km**

### Mrs Mary O'Donnell
**CREGG HOUSE**
Galway Road, Clifden,
Co Galway

**Clifden Connemara**

TEL: **095 21326**  FAX: **095 21326**
EMAIL: **cregghouse1@eircom.net**
WEB: **cregg-house.com**

On N59 landscaped garden. Spacious rooms, Breakfast menu. Owenglen River nearby. Ideal touring base. Recommended Elsie Dillard, Best B&B's Ireland.

| B&B | 5 | Ensuite | €27.50-€31 | Dinner | - |
|-----|---|---------|------------|--------|---|
| B&B | 1 | Standard | €25.50-€28.50 | Partial Board | - |
| Single Rate | | | €38-€43.50 | Child reduction | 25% |

**Open:** 22nd March-1st November

**Clifden**

### Clifden Connemara

Yvonne & Patricia Price
**HIGHFIELD LODGE**
Dooneen, Clifden, Co Galway

TEL: **095 22283**
EMAIL: **highfield@highfieldlodge.com**
WEB: **www.highfieldlodge.com**

Boasting stunning views of the 12 Benns to Clifden Bay. Only 4 minutes walk from town. The house offers spacious, comfortable accomodation with the feel of home!

| B&B | 4 | Ensuite | €28-€35 | Dinner | - |
| B&B | - | Standard | - | Partial Board | - |
| Single Rate | | | - | Child reduction | 25% |

Open: 8th March-30th September

**lifden 2km**

### Clifden Connemara

Margaret Pryce
**ATLANTIC VIEW**
Letternoosh, Westport Road,
Clifden, Co Galway

TEL: **095 21291**  FAX: **095 22051**
EMAIL: **info@atlantic-view.com**
WEB: **www.atlantic-view.com**

Overlooking the Atlantic Ocean on N59 near Clifden. Large spacious ensuite rooms with TV, Tea/Coffee, Hairdryer, Iron, Alarm Clock. Internet access available. Orthopaedic Beds.

| B&B | 4 | Ensuite | €28-€32 | Dinner | - |
| B&B | - | Standard | - | Partial Board | - |
| Single Rate | | | €40-€43.50 | Child reduction | 50% |

Open: All Year

**Clifden**

### Clifden

Mary Ryan
**DUN AENGUS HOUSE**
Sky Road, Clifden, Connemara,
Co Galway

TEL: **095 21069**  FAX: **095 21069**

Superbly located, 5 mins walk to town. Views described Best In Ireland. Own super angling boat. Delicious breakfasts.

| B&B | 6 | Ensuite | €27.50-€31 | Dinner | - |
| B&B | - | Standard | - | Partial Board | - |
| Single Rate | | | €40-€45 | Child reduction | 25% |

Open: All Year

**lonbur 1km**

### Clonbur Cong Connemara

Mrs Ann Lambe
**BALLYKINE HOUSE**
Clonbur, Co Galway

TEL: **094 9546150**  FAX: **094 9546150**
EMAIL: **ballykine@eircom.net**
WEB: **www.ballykinehouse-clonbur-cong.com**

200 yr old Guinness Lodge overlooking Lough Mask on Cong/Clonbur Rd, R345. Forest and Lakeside walks from house. Gateway to Connemara, Restaurants within walking distance.

| B&B | 4 | Ensuite | €28-€31 | Dinner | - |
| B&B | 1 | Standard | €28-€31 | Partial Board | - |
| Single Rate | | | €40-€43.50 | Child reduction | 25% |

Open: 1st April-1st November

**orr Na Móna 3km**

### Corr Na Móna

Mrs Sorcha Peirce
**GRASSHOPPER COTTAGE**
Dooras, Corr Na Móna,
Co Galway

TEL: **094 9548165**  FAX: **094 9548896**
EMAIL: **grasshoppercottage@eircom.net**
WEB: **www.troutfishingireland.com**

Lodge on shore of Lough Corrib off R345. Superb scenery. Angling centre (boat/ tackle hire). Ideal base for walking/touring Joyce Country and Connemara.

| B&B | 3 | Ensuite | €33-€36 | Dinner | - |
| B&B | 1 | Standard | €28-€31 | Partial Board | - |
| Single Rate | | | €42-€50 | Child reduction | 25% |

Open: 19th March-9th October

**In Craughwell**

**Mrs Peggy Gilligan**
AHAVEEN HOUSE
Cappanraheen, Craughwell,
Co Galway

### Craughwell

Tel: **091 846147**
Email: **ahaveen@eircom.net**

Comfortable home on spacious grounds just off N6 Galway-Dublin Road. Excellent restaurants, hunting, golf, ideal touring base, Burren Connemara.

| B&B | 4 | Ensuite | €31 | Dinner | - |
| B&B | 1 | Standard | €28.50 | Partial Board | - |
| Single Rate | | | €41-€43.50 | Child reduction | **50%** |

**Open:** 1st January-31st December

---

**Galway City 2km**

**Mrs Colette Cawley**
DUNGUAIRE
8 Lurgan Park, Murrough,
Dublin Road,
Galway City (East), Co Galway

### Galway City

Tel: **091 757043**
Email: **ccawley@eircom.net**
Bus No: **4E, 2E**

Warm friendly home. Convenient for touring Connemara, Burren and Aran Islands. Take Galway City east exit. House opposite Corrib Great Southern Hotel, GMIT, Merlin Park Hospital on N6.

| B&B | 3 | Ensuite | €28-€45 | Dinner | - |
| B&B | 1 | Standard | €26-€30 | Partial Board | - |
| Single Rate | | | €38-€50 | Child reduction | **50%** |

**Open:** 1st January-20th December

---

**Galway City 1km**

**Mrs Noreen Collins**
ST ANTHONY'S
Terryland Cross,
Headford Road, Galway,
Co Galway

### Galway City

Tel: **091 766477**
Email: **stanthonysgalway@eircom.net**
Bus No: **7**

Family run home. Warm welcome. Beside Shopping Centre. Cinema & Restaurants. Tea/Coffee facilities. Rooms ensuite. Private car park.

| B&B | 4 | Ensuite | €30-€35 | Dinner | - |
| B&B | - | Standard | - | Partial Board | - |
| Single Rate | | | €40-€45 | Child reduction | - |

**Open:** 1st January-20th December

---

**Galway 3km**

**Ms Rita Conway**
MOYTURA
4 Ballybane Road, Ballybane,
Galway, Co Galway

### Galway City

Tel: **091 757755**
Email: **moyturarc@eircom.net**
Web: **www.moyturagalway.com**

Beside Corrib Great Southern Hotel, GMIT, Merlin Park Hospital. Take Route 338 off N6 to "Galway City East". Lovely view of Galway Bay and Burren. Warm welcome.

| B&B | 3 | Ensuite | €30-€50 | Dinner | - |
| B&B | - | Standard | - | Partial Board | - |
| Single Rate | | | €40-€50 | Child reduction | **25%** |

**Open:** 1st January-20th December

---

**Galway City**

**Mrs Mary Corless**
COOLAVALLA
22 Newcastle Road, Galway,
Co Galway

### Galway City

Tel: **091 522415**
Email: **coolavalla@eircom.net**

Family house beside Hospital and University, opposite Presentation School. 6 mins walk City, 15 mins Salthill. Close to all amenities. Ideal touring base.

| B&B | 1 | Ensuite | €30-€33 | Dinner | - |
| B&B | 3 | Standard | €28-€31 | Partial Board | - |
| Single Rate | | | €45-€48 | Child reduction | - |

**Open:** 1st March-30th November

**Galway City 2km**

### Nora Corley
**LISNAGREE B&B**
**1 Cherry Park, New Castle,**
**Galway, Co Galway**

Tel: **091 520230**
Email: **lisnagree@hotmail.com**
Web: **www.lisnagreebandb.s5.com**
Bus No: **4**

Family run adjacent to the Westwood Hotel fourth left off N59. TV, Tea Coffee facilities in all bedrooms.

| | | | | | | |
|---|---|---|---|---|---|---|
| B&B | 4 | Ensuite | €30-€35 | Dinner | | - |
| B&B | - | Standard | | Partial Board | | - |
| Single Rate | | | €40-€44 | Child reduction | | 25% |

**Open:** 1st January-22nd December

**Galway 3km**

### Mary Egan
**AUBURN HOUSE**
**1 Merlin Gate, Dublin Road,**
**Galway, Co Galway**

Tel: **091 771018**
Email: **auburnhousegalway@eircom.net**
Web: **www.auburnhousegalway.com**

Beautifully appointed family run B&B. Close to Merlin Park hospital, Corrib Great Southern, TV, Tea/Coffee varied breakfast menu, home baking, visa accepted.

| | | | | | | |
|---|---|---|---|---|---|---|
| B&B | 2 | Ensuite | €35-€50 | Dinner | | - |
| B&B | 1 | Standard | €35-€45 | Partial Board | | - |
| Single Rate | | | €40-€50 | Child reduction | | 25% |

**Open:** All Year

**Galway 1km**

### Ms Frances Gallagher
**15 Beechmount Road**
**Highfield Park, Galway,**
**Co Galway**

Tel: **091 522078**
Bus No: **2**

Modern Semi-detached guesthouse overlooking open park. Conveniently located close to both Salthill and Galway. Excellent rates.

| | | | | | | |
|---|---|---|---|---|---|---|
| B&B | 3 | Ensuite | €28-€31 | Dinner | | - |
| B&B | 1 | Standard | €28.50 | Partial Board | | - |
| Single Rate | | | €41-€43.50 | Child reduction | | - |

**Open:** 1st June-31st September

**Galway 3km**

### Annette & Mike Grady
**KILBREE HOUSE**
**Circular Road, Dangan Upper,**
**Galway, Co Galway**

Tel: **091 527177**  Fax: **091 520404**
Email: **info@kilbree.com**
Web: **www.kilbree.com**
Bus No: **36**

Welcoming luxurious home N59 with excellent food. En route Connemara. Overlooks City and Lake near Hotels and Pubs. TV, Tea/Coffee and Hairdryer in all rooms.

| | | | | | | |
|---|---|---|---|---|---|---|
| B&B | 6 | Ensuite | €30-€50 | Dinner | | - |
| B&B | - | Standard | | Partial Board | | - |
| Single Rate | | | €40-€60 | Child reduction | | - |

**Open:** All Year

**Galway City**

### Helen Kathleen Hanlon
**CLOCHARD**
**4 Spires Gardens,**
**Shantalla Road, Galway,**
**Co Galway**

Tel: **091 521533**  Fax: **091 522536**
Email: **info@clochardgalway.com**
Web: **www.clochardgalway.com**

Warm friendly home. Quiet Historic Site within walking distance of City Centre and Beach. Close to University, Hospital and Shops. Hairdryers.

| | | | | | | |
|---|---|---|---|---|---|---|
| B&B | 4 | Ensuite | €32-€36 | Dinner | | - |
| B&B | - | Standard | | Partial Board | | - |
| Single Rate | | | €55-€60 | Child reduction | | - |

**Open:** 10th February-10th December

**Galway City**

**Mrs Maureen McCallion**
VILLA NOVA
40 Newcastle Road, Galway,
Co Galway

TEL: **091 524849**

Quiet bungalow off the main road. Beside Hospital & University & convenient to City Centre. Private car park.

| B&B | 4 | Ensuite | €27.50-€31 | Dinner | - |
|------|---|----------|-------------|--------|---|
| B&B | - | Standard | - | Partial Board | - |
| Single Rate | | | €40-€43.50 | Child reduction | - |

Galway City

**Open:** 1st January-30th November

---

**Galway City**

**Miss Bridget Phil McCarthy**
PETRA
201 Laurel Park, Newcastle,
Galway City, Co Galway

TEL: **091 521844**
EMAIL: **petrabandb@eircom.net**
BUS NO: **4, 5**

Convenient to City Bus. Train/Aran Ferry, University, Hospital. Adjacent to Oughterard/Clifden Road N59. Second left Sioban McKenna Rd, first right.

| B&B | 3 | Ensuite | €27.50-€34 | Dinner | - |
|------|---|----------|-------------|--------|---|
| B&B | 2 | Standard | €25.50-€30 | Partial Board | - |
| Single Rate | | | €38-€45 | Child reduction | - |

Galway 2km

**Open:** 1st February-30th November

---

**Galway City**

**Mrs Mary McLaughlin-Tobin**
ARAS MHUIRE
28 Maunsell's Road,
Taylor's Hill, Galway,
Co Galway

TEL: **091 526210**   FAX: **091 526210**
EMAIL: **mmtobin@eircom.net**
WEB: **www.arasmhuire.com**
BUS NO: **2**

Peaceful setting view of Galway's beautiful Cathedral. No.2W Bus passes door. Adjacent Ardilaun Hotel, Hospital, University, Golf, Horse Riding Arranged. Recommended, happy homely warm atmosphere.

| B&B | 2 | Ensuite | €27.50-€40 | Dinner | - |
|------|---|----------|-------------|--------|---|
| B&B | 1 | Standard | €25.50-€30 | Partial Board | - |
| Single Rate | | | €38-€45 | Child reduction | 25% |

In Galway

**Open:** All Year Except Christmas

---

**Galway City**

**Mrs Marcella Mitchell**
LIMA
Tuam Road, Galway City,
Co Galway

TEL: **091 757986**
BUS NO: **3**

Detached bungalow adjacent to City Centre, close to all amenities of a vibrant City. Private parking. TV, Tea/Coffee facilities all bedrooms. Beside AIB bank.

| B&B | 2 | Ensuite | €30-€32 | Dinner | - |
|------|---|----------|-------------|--------|---|
| B&B | 1 | Standard | - | Partial Board | - |
| Single Rate | | | €38-€41 | Child reduction | 25% |

In Galway

**Open:** 2nd January-20th December

---

**Galway City**

**Mary O'Brien**
ANACH-CUIN HOUSE
36 Wellpark Grove,
Galway City, Co Galway

TEL: **091 755120**
BUS NO: **2**

Town House, quiet and peaceful location as you enter City Centre, close to Restaurants and all amenities.

| B&B | 4 | Ensuite | €30-€32 | Dinner | - |
|------|---|----------|-------------|--------|---|
| B&B | - | Standard | - | Partial Board | - |
| Single Rate | | | €40-€43.50 | Child reduction | 25% |

Galway City 1.25km

**Open:** 1st March-31st October

**Michael O'Shaughnessy**
ABBEY LEE
3 Cuan Glas,
Bishop O'Donnell Road,
Galway, Co Galway

### Galway

Tel: **091 524768**
Email: **mroshaugh@oceanfree.net**
Web: **www.abbeylee.net**
Bus No: **2**

Family run, purpose built B&B. Tastefully appointed, warm friendly atmosphere. Ten minute walk to Galway Bay and Beach.

| B&B | 4 | Ensuite | €30-€40 | Dinner | - |
| B&B | - | Standard | | Partial Board | - |
| Single Rate | | | €40-€50 | Child reduction | 25% |

Galway 2km

**Open:** 1st January-31st December

---

**Ann Staed**
CARRAIG VILLA
Cloonacauneen, Castlegar,
Co Galway

### Galway City Castlegar Area

Tel: **091 799020**  Fax: **091 799370**
Email: **sstaed@iol.ie**
Web: **http://myhome.iolfree.ie/~staed/**

Luxurious friendly family home just off N17 in the tranquility of the countryside with pleasant country walk. Galway City 7 mins, airport 10 mins, racecourse 5 mins.

| B&B | 3 | Ensuite | €27.50-€32 | Dinner | - |
| B&B | 1 | Standard | €25.50-€29 | Partial Board | - |
| Single Rate | | | €38-€45 | Child reduction | 25% |

Galway 5km

**Open:** 1st January-30th November

---

**Mrs Phil Concannon**
WINACRE LODGE
Bushy Park, Galway,
Co Galway

### Galway City Dangan

Tel: **091 523459**
Email: **winacrelodge@eircom.net**

Modern friendly home, spectacular views of River Corrib on N59. Near Glenlo Abbey and Westwood Hotels. Private parking. TV, Tea/Coffee in bedrooms. Visa.

| B&B | 5 | Ensuite | €28-€40 | Dinner | - |
| B&B | - | Standard | - | Partial Board | - |
| Single Rate | | | €40-€50 | Child reduction | 50% |

Galway 3km

**Open:** 1st January-31st December

---

**Mrs Bernie McTigue**
ABBEY VIEW
Bushy Park, Galway,
Co Galway

### Galway City Dangan

Tel: **091 524488**  Fax: **091 524488**
Email: **abbeyview59@hotmail.com**

Frommer recommended. A warm welcome awaits you. View overlooks Glenlo Abbey Golf Course. Adjacent to Restaurants. Ideal for touring Connemara.

| B&B | 3 | Ensuite | €33-€40 | Dinner | - |
| B&B | 2 | Standard | €30-€33 | Partial Board | - |
| Single Rate | | | €38-€50 | Child reduction | 50% |

Galway 4km

**Open:** All Year

---

**Mrs Bridie Ward**
THE ARCHES
Woodstock, Bushy Park,
Galway, Co Galway

### Galway City Dangan

Tel: **091 527815**
Email: **thearches@oceanfree.net**

Dormer style home on N59 enroute to Connemara. 3km from Glenlo Abbey Hotel. Golf, Fishing, Horse riding nearby. Private parking. Ideal touring base.

| B&B | 4 | Ensuite | €30-€38 | Dinner | - |
| B&B | - | Standard | | Partial Board | - |
| Single Rate | | | €45-€55 | Child reduction | 25% |

Galway 6km

**Open:** 15th January-15th December

### Mary Beatty
SNAEFELL
6 Glenina Heights, Galway,
Co Galway

TEL: **091 751643**
BUS No: **2, 4,5**

Comfortable welcoming home with superb beds. Home made brown bread. Situated on N6 and main bus routes. Close to all amenities including Dog and Race Tracks.

| B&B | 3 | Ensuite | €30-€40 | Dinner | - |
|-----|---|---------|---------|--------|---|
| B&B | - | Standard | | Partial Board | - |
| Single Rate | | | €45-€45 | Child reduction | - |

Galway 1.5km

**Open:** 1st April-31st October

---

### Mrs Kathleen Burke
LISCARNA
22 Grattan Park, Coast Road,
Galway, Co Galway

TEL: **091 585086**

Modern detached home beside Beach on Coast Road, walking distance of City Centre, Leisureland. All rooms with shower/toilet, TV.

| B&B | 4 | Ensuite | €27.50-€31 | Dinner | - |
|-----|---|---------|------------|--------|---|
| B&B | - | Standard | - | Partial Board | - |
| Single Rate | | | - | Child reduction | 25% |

Galway City 1km

**Open:** 1st February-1st December

---

### Mrs Freda Cunningham
KYLE NA SHEE
37 Grattan Park, Galway City,
Co Galway

TEL: **091 583505**
EMAIL: **kylenashee@eircom.net**
WEB: **homepage.eircom.net/~kylenashee**

Detached home beside Beach on Coast road to Salthill. Quiet and close to all amenities. Walking distance of City Centre. Tea/Coffee & TV in all rooms.

| B&B | 3 | Ensuite | €30-€32.50 | Dinner | - |
|-----|---|---------|------------|--------|---|
| B&B | 1 | Standard | - | Partial Board | - |
| Single Rate | | | €41-€45 | Child reduction | 25% |

Galway City 1km

**Open:** 1st March-30th November

---

### Bernadette Donoghue
KILTEVNA
24 Grattan Park, Coast Road,
Galway, Co Galway

TEL: **091 588477**   FAX: **091 581173**
EMAIL: **kiltevnahouse@eircom.net**

Modern detached home beside Beach, off Coast road. Within walking distance City, Leisureland. All rooms with bathrooms, TV, Hairdryers. Le Guide de Routard recommended. Beside bus route.

| B&B | 4 | Ensuite | €30-€32 | Dinner | - |
|-----|---|---------|---------|--------|---|
| B&B | - | Standard | - | Partial Board | - |
| Single Rate | | | - | Child reduction | 25% |

In Galway City

**Open:** 1st February-30th November

---

### Mrs Pat Greaney
HIGH TIDE
9 Grattan Park, Coast Road,
Galway City, Co Galway

TEL: **091 584324/589470**  FAX: **091 584324 (man)**
EMAIL: **hightide@iol.ie**
WEB: **www.hightidegalway.ie**

Panoramic views of Galway Bay. Frommer/Inside Ireland/Sullivan Guides recommended. 10 min. walk to City Centre. Also local Bus. Breakfast menu. Tours arranged.

| B&B | 4 | Ensuite | €30-€32 | Dinner | - |
|-----|---|---------|---------|--------|---|
| B&B | - | Standard | - | Partial Board | - |
| Single Rate | | | - | Child reduction | 25% |

Galway City

**Open:** 1st February-1st December

### Ms Joan O'Dea
THE PERIWINKLE
14 Grattan Park, Grattan Road,
Galway, Co Galway

Tel: **091 584885**
Email: **periwinkle@eircom.net**
Web: **www.aperiwinkle.com**

Tastefully renovated modern family home beside beach. 10 mins walk to City Centre or Salthill. Close to all amenities. Ideal touring base. Breakfast menu.

| | | | Dinner | - |
|---|---|---|---|---|
| B&B | 4 | Ensuite | €32.50-€35 | |
| B&B | - | Standard | | Partial Board | - |
| Single Rate | | | €45-€47 | Child reduction | 25% |

Galway 1km

**Open:** 15th January-15th December

---

### Mrs Dolores Bane
THE BRANCHES
13 Woodhaven, Merlin Park,
Galway, Co Galway

Tel: **091 752712**   Fax: **091 735596**
Email: **branches13@eircom.net**
Web: **www.branchesgalway.com**
Bus No: **4**

New luxury accommodation 5 min City Centre beside Corrib Great Southern Hotel. Cable TV, Hairdryers all rooms. Car park. Enjoy Mikes Irish breakfast.

| | | | | Dinner | - |
|---|---|---|---|---|---|
| B&B | 3 | Ensuite | €30-€50 | Partial Board | - |
| B&B | 1 | Standard | €26-€30 | Child reduction | - |
| Single Rate | | | €38-€60 | | |

Galway City 2km

**Open:** All Year

---

### Mrs Olive Connolly
SEACREST
Coast Road, Roscam,
Merlin Park, Galway,
Co Galway

Tel: **091 757975**   Fax: **091 795587**
Email: **djcon@iol.ie**
Web: **http://www.iol.ie/~djcon/**

Overlooking Galway Bay, Indoor Pool. Hairdryers, Radios, Bedrooms ground floor level, New York Times, Boston Globe, Le Guide du Routard recommended.

| | | | | Dinner | - |
|---|---|---|---|---|---|
| B&B | 4 | Ensuite | €35-€40 | Partial Board | - |
| B&B | - | Standard | - | Child reduction | - |
| Single Rate | | | €45-€50 | | |

Galway City 5km

**Open:** 13th February-30th October

---

### Ms Peggy Kenny
CLOONIFF HOUSE
16 Woodhaven, Merlin Park,
Galway, Co Galway

Tel: **091 758815/582465**
Bus No: **4**

Luxurious family run house beside Corrib Southern Hotel. City Centre 5 mins drive, private parking. Close to Beach and all amenities. Ideal touring base.

| | | | | Dinner | - |
|---|---|---|---|---|---|
| B&B | 3 | Ensuite | €28-€55 | Partial Board | - |
| B&B | 1 | Standard | - | Child reduction | 25% |
| Single Rate | | | €40-€65 | | |

Galway City 2km

**Open:** 1st January-20th December

---

### Matt & Marie Kiernan
ALMARA HOUSE
2 Merlin Gate, Merlin Park,
Dublin Road, Galway,
Co Galway

Tel: **091 755345**   Fax: **091 771585**
Email: **matthewkiernan@eircom.net**
Web: **www.almarahouse.com**
Bus No: **4E**

Adj Shannon/Dublin junction. Tastefully appointed rooms. Hospitality tray, Radio alarms, Irons, Hairdryers, Mineal Water. Extensive Breakfast menu. Sparkling Diamond Award AA ◆◆◆◆ RAC ◆◆◆◆.

| | | | | Dinner | - |
|---|---|---|---|---|---|
| B&B | 4 | Ensuite | €30-€50 | Partial Board | - |
| B&B | - | Standard | - | Child reduction | - |
| Single Rate | | | €40-€60 | | |

Galway 2km

**Open:** 1st January-20th December

**Galway City 2km**

### Kathleen Laffey
**AVOCA HOUSE**
3 Merlin Gate, Geata Na Mara,
Merlin Park, Galway,
Co Galway

**Galway City Merlin Park**

TEL: **091 757866**   FAX: **091 764859**
EMAIL: **avocahouse1@eircom.net**
BUS NO: **4**

Family run B&B. 5 mins drive to city centre. Ideal touring base. Cable TV in all rooms. Private parking. Families welcome.

| B&B | 3 | Ensuite | €28-€50 | Dinner | - |
| B&B | 1 | Standard | €26-€45 | Partial Board | - |
| Single Rate | | | €45-€65 | Child reduction | 25% |

**Open:** 1st January-20th December

**Galway 3km**

### Juliette Manton
**WOODVIEW B&B**
10 Woodhaven, Merlin Park,
Galway, Co Galway

**Galway City Merlin Park**

TEL: **091 756843**
EMAIL: **juliette2@eircom.net**
BUS NO: **4**

One of Galway City's finest B&B's, family run. Luxurious home, quiet cul de sac. Adjacent to Corrib Great Southern Hotel.

| B&B | 4 | Ensuite | €30-€50 | Dinner | - |
| B&B | - | Standard | - | Partial Board | - |
| Single Rate | | | €40-€60 | Child reduction | 25% |

**Open:** All Year

**Galway City 3km**

### Liam & Yvonne O'Reilly
**CORRIB VIEW B&B**
12 Woodhaven, Merlin Park,
Galway, Co Galway

**Galway City Merlin Park**

TEL: **091 755667**
EMAIL: **corribview@eircom.net**
WEB: **www.corribview.net**
BUS NO: **4**

Luxurious residence, quiet cul-de-sac. Recommended as one of the Best B&B in the West. Bus route. City Centre 3km. Adjacent Corrib Great Southern Hotel, GMIT.

| B&B | 3 | Ensuite | €32.50-€50 | Dinner | - |
| B&B | - | Standard | - | Partial Board | - |
| Single Rate | | | €40-€65 | Child reduction | - |

**Open:** 1st January-20th December

**Galway City 3km**

### Maria and John Rabbitte
**GRANGE HOUSE**
15 Woodhaven, Merlin Park,
Galway, Co Galway

**Galway City Merlin Park**

TEL: **091 755470**   FAX: **091 755470**
EMAIL: **mrabbitte@eircom.net**
BUS NO: **4**

Luxurious home, personally run, quiet cul-de-sac. Convenient to City Bus Route. Adjacent Corrib Great Southern Hotel. Ideal touring base. Highly recommended.

| B&B | 4 | Ensuite | €30-€50 | Dinner | - |
| B&B | - | Standard | - | Partial Board | - |
| Single Rate | | | €40-€60 | Child reduction | 25% |

**Open:** 1st January-20th December

**Galway 2km**

### Noreen Cosgrove
**MAPLE HOUSE**
Dr Mannix Road, Salthill,
Co Galway

**Galway City Salthill**

TEL: **091 526136**
EMAIL: **maplehouse@eircom.net**

Purpose built luxury home. Peaceful location. Power showers. Adjacent Galway Bay, & Ardilaun hotels. Golf, Tennis, Leisureland. Parking. Hairdryers. On bus route.

| B&B | 4 | Ensuite | €28-€33 | Dinner | - |
| B&B | - | Standard | - | Partial Board | - |
| Single Rate | | | - | Child reduction | 25% |

**Open:** 1st January-20th December

**Ms Marie Cotter**
BAYBERRY HOUSE
9 Cuan Glas, Bishop
O'Donnell Road, Taylors Hill,
Galway, Co Galway

### Galway City Salthill

Tel: **091 525171/525212**
Email: **tcotter@iol.ie**
Web: **www.bayberryhouse.com**
Bus No: **2**

A charming purpose built B&B conveniently located at the top of Taylors Hill. A stay at Bayberry combines a Georgian style elegance with a warm welcome.

| B&B | 6 | Ensuite | €30-€40 | Dinner | - |
| B&B | - | Standard | | Partial Board | - |
| Single Rate | | | €40-€45 | Child reduction | 25% |

alway 2km

**Open:** 1st February-30th November

---

**Phil Flannery**
FLANNERY'S
54 Dalysfort Road, Salthill,
Galway, Co Galway

### Galway City Salthill

Tel: **091 522048**   Fax: **091 522048**
Email: **phil.flannery@iol.ie**
Web: **www.flannerysbedandbreakfast.com**
Bus No: **1**

Award winning house, charming garden, in quiet residential area. Great breakfasts, comfortable beds. Private parking. 5 mins to beach. German spoken.

| B&B | 3 | Ensuite | €30-€35 | Dinner | - |
| B&B | 1 | Standard | €26-€30 | Partial Board | - |
| Single Rate | | | €38-€41 | Child reduction | - |

alway 2km

**Open:** 1st March-15th November

---

**Mrs Nora Hanniffy**
ANNA REE HOUSE
49 Oaklands, Salthill, Galway,
Co Galway

### Galway City Salthill

Tel: **091 522583**
Email: **norahanniffy@eircom.net**

Modern home. Private parking. Rear of Church by Sacre Coeur Hotel. 5 mins walk Beach, Leisureland and Bus route. Electric blankets.

| B&B | 6 | Ensuite | €30-€32 | Dinner | - |
| B&B | - | Standard | - | Partial Board | - |
| Single Rate | | | €40-€43.50 | Child reduction | - |

**Open:** 1st April-31st October

---

**David & Rita Lenihan**
ATLANTIC SUNSET
Coast Road, Genetian Hill,
Salthill, Galway, Co Galway

### Galway City Salthill

Tel: **091 521425**
Bus No: **2**

Luxurious comfortable home in scenic peaceful surroundings overlooking Galway Bay and Bird sanctuary. Award winning gardens. Golf, Fishing, Beach, Leisureland closeby.

| B&B | 4 | Ensuite | €30-€40 | Dinner | - |
| B&B | - | Standard | - | Partial Board | - |
| Single Rate | | | - | Child reduction | 50% |

lthill 2km

**Open:** 12th February-12th December

---

**Mrs Teresa McDonagh**
ARD MHUIRE
Knocknacarra Road, Salthill,
Galway, Co Galway

### Galway City Salthill

Tel: **091 522344**   Fax: **091 529629**
Email: **teresa@ardmhuire.com**
Web: **www.ardmhuire.com**

Attractive, comfortable home within walking distance of the Seaside. Close to Leisureland, Golf, Tennis, Fishing, Horse riding etc.

| B&B | 6 | Ensuite | €30-€40 | Dinner | - |
| B&B | - | Standard | | Partial Board | - |
| Single Rate | | | €45-€50 | Child reduction | 25% |

lway 2km

**Open:** 1st January-20th December

**Marian Mitchell**
**CHESTNUT LODGE**
**35 Rockbarton Road, Salthill,**
**Co Galway**

TEL: **091 529988**

Luxurious home beside Galway Bay and Beach. Golf Club, Tennis Club and Leisureland. Ideal for touring Connemara, Aran Islands and the Burren.

| B&B | 3 | Ensuite | €27.30-€31 | Dinner | - |
|---|---|---|---|---|---|
| B&B | - | Standard | - | Partial Board | - |
| Single Rate | | | €40-€43.50 | Child reduction | - |

Galway 2km    **Open:** 1st May-31st September

---

**Mrs Nora O'Malley**
**ST KIERAN'S**
**33 Rockbarton Road, Salthill,**
**Galway, Co Galway**

TEL: **091 523333**
EMAIL: **michealomalley@hotmail.com**

Family run home beside all amenities. Within walking distance of Beach, Leisureland, Golf, GAA and Tennis Club. Home cooking. Tea or Coffee on arrival.

| B&B | 3 | Ensuite | €27.50-€31 | Dinner | - |
|---|---|---|---|---|---|
| B&B | 1 | Standard | €25.50-€28.50 | Partial Board | - |
| Single Rate | | | €38-€43.50 | Child reduction | - |

In Salthill    **Open:** 1st February-30th November

---

**Mrs Ann O'Toole**
**CLYDAGH**
**Knocknacarra Road, Salthill,**
**Galway, Co Galway**

TEL: **091 524205**
EMAIL: **clydagh@ireland.com**
WEB: **www.dirl.com/galway/clydagh.htm**
BUS NO: **2W**

Comfortable family home with private parking. Convenient to Beaches, Tennis, Golf. Bus route to City Centre. Ideal touring base for Connemara and Aran Island.

| B&B | 4 | Ensuite | €31-€35 | Dinner | - |
|---|---|---|---|---|---|
| B&B | - | Standard | - | Partial Board | - |
| Single Rate | | | €40-€45 | Child reduction | 33.3% |

Galway City 3km    **Open:** 1st March-31st October

---

**Catherine Quinlan**
**CAPPA VEAGH**
**76 Dalysfort Road, Salthill,**
**Co Galway**

TEL: **091 526518**
EMAIL: **cappaveaghbandb@eircom.net**
WEB: **www.cappaveaghbandb.com**
BUS NO: **1**

Comfortable clean family run B&B, walking distance to Salthill, 2km to Galway City, on direct bus route (No 1). A visit to Cappa Veagh leaves you refreshed.

| B&B | 4 | Ensuite | €33-€35 | Dinner | - |
|---|---|---|---|---|---|
| B&B | - | Standard | - | Partial Board | - |
| Single Rate | | | | Child reduction | 50% |

Galway 2km     **Open:** 1st March-31st October

---

**Trish Flynn**
**ADRIA**
**34 Beach Court, Lower Salthill,**
**Galway, Co Galway**

TEL: **091 589444**
EMAIL: **info@adriaguesthouse.com**
WEB: **www.adriaguesthouse.com**

Warm clean family business, friendly helpful land lady, tastefully decorated, spacious bedrooms. Quiet home with ample parking and good breakfast.

| B&B | 4 | Ensuite | €29-€50 | Dinner | - |
|---|---|---|---|---|---|
| B&B | - | Standard | - | Partial Board | - |
| Single Rate | | | €40-€60 | Child reduction | 25% |

In Galway City    **Open:** 31st January-31st December

**Ita Johnstone**
**ST JUDES**
**110 Lower Salthill, Galway,**
**Co Galway**

### Galway City Lower Salthill

Tᴇʟ: **091 521619**
Eᴍᴀɪʟ: **info@st-judes.com**
Wᴇʙ: **www.st-judes.com**
Bᴜs Nᴏ: **1**

Distinguished family residence, elegantly furnished. Private parking on City Bus route, short walk to Beach and all amenities. Breakfast menu.

| B&B | 6 | Ensuite | €35-€40 | Dinner | - |
|-----|---|---------|---------|--------|---|
| B&B | - | Standard | | Partial Board | - |
| Single Rate | | | €45-€55 | Child reduction | **25%** |

Galway 1.5km

**Open:** 15th January-15th December

---

**Mrs Christina Ruane**
**25 Grattan Court**
**Fr Griffin Road, Lower Salthill,**
**Galway, Co Galway**

### Galway City Lower Salthill

Tᴇʟ: **091 586513**

Modern detached house, quiet residential area. 10 mins walk Salthill, 5 mins Beach, Golf Club, 10 mins Hospital & University.

| B&B | 4 | Ensuite | €30-€32 | Dinner | - |
|-----|---|---------|---------|--------|---|
| B&B | - | Standard | - | Partial Board | - |
| Single Rate | | | - | Child reduction | **50%** |

Galway City

**Open:** 1st January-30th November

---

**Mrs Marie Dempsey**
**ACHILL LODGE**
**5 Cashelmara,**
**Knocknacarra Cross, Salthill,**
**Co Galway**

### Galway City Upper Salthill

Tᴇʟ: **091 584709**
Eᴍᴀɪʟ: **info@achill-lodge.com**
Wᴇʙ: **www.achill-lodge.com**
Bᴜs Nᴏ: **2**

Welcome to our highly recommended home over looking Galway Bay and bird sanctuary beside golf, horseriding, surfing, tennis and leisureland. Breakfast menu.

| B&B | 4 | Ensuite | €28-€40 | Dinner | - |
|-----|---|---------|---------|--------|---|
| B&B | - | Standard | - | Partial Board | - |
| Single Rate | | | €40-€50 | Child reduction | **25%** |

In Salthill

**Open:** 17th March-31st October

---

**Mrs Mary Duggan**
**KNOCKMOY HOUSE**
**7 Westbrook, Barna Road,**
**Galway, Co Galway**

### Galway City Upper Salthill

Tᴇʟ: **091 590674**
Bᴜs Nᴏ: **2**

Neo Georgian house overlooking Galway Bay. TV Lounge. Only 10 mins drive from Salthill, Golf, Tennis, Leisureland and Horse riding.

| B&B | 4 | Ensuite | €30-€32 | Dinner | - |
|-----|---|---------|---------|--------|---|
| B&B | - | Standard | | Partial Board | - |
| Single Rate | | | €40-€44 | Child reduction | **50%** |

Salthill 2km

**Open:** 15th March-31st October

---

**Mrs Christina Fahey**
**CASHELMARA LODGE**
**Knocknacarra Cross, Salthill,**
**Galway, Co Galway**

### Galway City Upper Salthill

Tᴇʟ: **091 520020**
Eᴍᴀɪʟ: **cashelmara@eircom.net**
Wᴇʙ: **www.galway.net/pages/cashelmara**
Bᴜs Nᴏ: **2**

New luxury accommodation. Beside Beach, Golf, Horseriding, Surfing, Tennis, Leisureland. Breakfast menu. Power Showers all rooms. Large balcony, views Galway Bay, weathered stone waterfall in garden.

| B&B | 4 | Ensuite | €28-€45 | Dinner | - |
|-----|---|---------|---------|--------|---|
| B&B | - | Standard | | Partial Board | - |
| Single Rate | | | €35-€50 | Child reduction | **25%** |

Galway 2km

**Open:** 1st February-30th November

### Galway City Upper Salthill

**Tom & Colette Keaveney**
THE CONNAUGHT
**Barna Road, Salthill, Galway,**
**Co Galway**

TEL: **091 525865** FAX: **091 525865**
EMAIL: **tcconnaught@eircom.net**
WEB: **www.theconnaught.net**
BUS NO: **2**

Luxurious family home, purpose built. All amenities close by. Touring base Connemara. Recommended "Best B&B's in Ireland/Guide de Routard. Home from home. Breakfast menu, Chef owner.

| B&B | 6 | Ensuite | €30-€35 | Dinner | - |
|-----|---|---------|---------|--------|---|
| B&B | - | Standard | - | Partial Board | - |
| Single Rate | | | €40-€45 | Child reduction | 33.3% |

Salthill 2km  **Open:** 12th March-15th November

---

### Galway City Upper Salthill

**Mrs Caroline Larkin**
KILBRACK HOUSE
**2 Woodfield, Barna Road,**
**Galway, Co Galway**

TEL: **091 590802** FAX: **091 590802**
EMAIL: **kilbracklarkin@eircom.net**
BUS NO: **2, 34**

Luxurious home overlooking Galway Bay. Golf, Fishing, Horseriding, Leisureland, Aquarium, Tennis and good Restaurants nearby. Ideal touring base for Aran Islands.

| B&B | 6 | Ensuite | €27.50-€40 | Dinner | - |
|-----|---|---------|------------|--------|---|
| B&B | - | Standard | - | Partial Board | - |
| Single Rate | | | €50 | Child reduction | 50% |

Salthill 2km  **Open:** 1st May-1st November

---

### Galway City Upper Salthill

**Padraig & Maureen O'Donnell**
SHAMROCK LODGE
**4 Carragh Drive, Knocknacarra Rd,**
**Upper Salthill, Galway,**
**Co Galway**

TEL: **091 521429** FAX: **091 521429**
EMAIL: **oods@eircom.net**
BUS NO: **2W**

Overlooking Bay, Beach, Golf, Tennis, Leisureland, TV, Hairdryers, Electric Blankets. Follow promenade, Golf Course, right at Spinnaker, 3rd left, 4th on right.

| B&B | 4 | Ensuite | €30-€35 | Dinner | - |
|-----|---|---------|---------|--------|---|
| B&B | - | Standard | - | Partial Board | - |
| Single Rate | | | €40-€45 | Child reduction | 25% |

Galway City 2km **Open:** 1st March-31st October

---

### Galway City Upper Salthill

**Kevin & Maire O'Hare**
ROSE VILLA
**10 Cashelmara,**
**Knocknacarra Cross, Salthill,**
**Co Galway**

TEL: **091 584200** FAX: **091 584200**
EMAIL: **kevin.ohare@ireland.com**
WEB: **www.rosevilla.utvinternet.ie**
BUS NO: **2**

New luxury accommodation overlooking Galway Bay and Bird sanctuary. Close to Golf, Fishing, Horse Riding, Surfing, Leisureland. Ideal touring base.

| B&B | 4 | Ensuite | €27.50-€40 | Dinner | - |
|-----|---|---------|------------|--------|---|
| B&B | - | Standard | - | Partial Board | - |
| Single Rate | | | €40-€50 | Child reduction | 25% |

Galway 3km **Open:** 1st February-1st December

---

### Galway City Upper Salthill

**Bernie Power**
FOUR WINDS LODGE
**Gentian Hill, Salthill, Galway,**
**Co Galway**

TEL: **091 526026**
EMAIL: **fourwindslodge@ireland.com**
WEB: **www.bedireland.com/fourwinds**
BUS NO: **2**

Traditional home. Overlooking Galway Bay. Enjoy breakfast in conservatory. Net access. Private parking & gardens. First right after Statoil after Golf Club. 4 star AA. Car hire can be arranged.

| B&B | 4 | Ensuite | €30-€50 | Dinner | - |
|-----|---|---------|---------|--------|---|
| B&B | - | Standard | - | Partial Board | - |
| Single Rate | | | €45-€65 | Child reduction | 50% |

Salthill 1.5km  **Open:** All Year Except Christmas

**Mrs Patty Wheeler**
WOODVILLE
Barna Rd, Salthill, Galway,
Co Galway

## Galway City Upper Salthill

Tel: **091 524260**  Fax: **091 524260**
Email: **woodville@esatclear.ie**
Web: **www.esatclear.ie/~woodville/intro.htm**
Bus No: **2**

Friendly home on Coast road overlooking Galway Bay. Ideal touring base, Restaurants, Beaches, 3 Golf Clubs, Tennis, Horseriding, Windsurfing, Canoeing. Bird santuary closeby.

| B&B | 4 | Ensuite | €27.50-€35 | Dinner | - |
| B&B | - | Standard | - | Partial Board | - |
| Single Rate | | | €40-€50 | Child reduction | 33.3% |

Galway City 2km

**Open:** 1st February-30th November

---

**Mrs Georgianna Darby**
MANDALAY BY THE SEA
10 Gentian/Blakes Hill, Galway,
Co Galway

## Galway City Upper Salthill - Gentian Hill

Tel: **091 524177**  Fax: **091 529952**
Email: **mandalay@esatclear.ie**

Luxurious balconied residence, panoramic view of Galway Bay. Recommended "Best B&B's in Ireland", Lonely Planet & Hidden Places of Ireland. Off 336 Coast road. 2 miles from Galway City.

| B&B | 4 | Ensuite | €29-€40 | Dinner | - |
| B&B | - | Standard | - | Partial Board | - |
| Single Rate | | | €58-€80 | Child reduction | 25% |

Salthill

**Open:** 1st January-31st December

---

**Mrs Mary McLoughlin**
SAILIN
Gentian Hill Coast Rd,
Upper Salthill, Galway,
Co Galway

## Galway City Upper Salthill - Gentian Hill Area

Tel: **091 521676**  Fax: **091 521676**
Email: **gentianhill@eircom.net**
Web: **homepage.eircom.net/~gentianhill**
Bus No: **2**

Located in bird sanctuary beside Galway Bay. Frommer recommended. Breakfast award. Secure parking. Hill walking information. 2nd left turn after Spinaker Hotel.

| B&B | 3 | Ensuite | €30-€33 | Dinner | - |
| B&B | - | Standard | - | Partial Board | - |
| Single Rate | | | €50-€50 | Child reduction | 50% |

Galway 3km

**Open:** 1st May-15th September

---

**Mrs Christina Connolly**
CLARE VILLA
38 Threadneedle Road, Salthill,
Co Galway

## Galway City Salthill Threadneedle Road

Tel: **091 522520**  Fax: **091 589684**
Email: **clarevilla@yahoo.com**

Spacious residence close to Beach, Tennis, Golf, Leisureland. On bus route. Complimentary Tea/Coffee 24 hours. Hairdryers. Lonely Planet recommended.

| B&B | 6 | Ensuite | €30-€35 | Dinner | - |
| B&B | - | Standard | - | Partial Board | - |
| Single Rate | | | €40-€50 | Child reduction | 25% |

Galway 2km

**Open:** 1st March-31st October

---

**Mrs Mary Geraghty**
MARLESS HOUSE
Threadneedle Road, Salthill,
Galway, Co Galway

## Galway City Salthill Threadneedle Road

Tel: **091 523931**  Fax: **091 529810**
Email: **marlesshouse@eircom.net**
Web: **www.marlesshouse.com**
Bus No: **1**

Luxurious Georgian style home just steps from Beach. Frommer recommended. TV, electric blankets, hairdryers, Tea/Coffee facilities in all rooms.

| B&B | 6 | Ensuite | €30-€35 | Dinner | - |
| B&B | - | Standard | - | Partial Board | - |
| Single Rate | | | €40-€50 | Child reduction | 25% |

Galway 2km

**Open:** 10th January-18th December

**Galway 2km**

**Mrs Mairead McGuire**
ATWESTPOINT
87 Threadneedle Road, Salthill,
Galway, Co Galway

### Galway City Salthill Threadneedle Road

Tel: **091 521026/582152** Fax: **091 582152**
Email: **westpointmac@netscape.net**
Web: **www.atwestpoint.com**
Bus No: **1, 2**

Purpose built family run B&B near Ardilaun and Galway Bay Hotels. Quality assured & multi recommendations. Sea view. Parking. Bus route, Beach, Leisureland, Tennis & Golf.

| B&B | 6 | Ensuite | €27.50-€40 | Dinner | €25-€25 |
|-----|---|---------|------------|--------|---------|
| B&B | - | Standard | | Partial Board | |
| Single Rate | | | €40-€45 | Child reduction | **25%** |

**Open:** 1st January-30th November

---

**In Galway**

**Mrs Teresa Burke**
LYNBURGH
Whitestrand Road,
Lower Salthill, Galway,
Co Galway

### Galway City Whitestrand

Tel: **091 581555** Fax: **091 581823**
Email: **tburke@iol.ie**
Web: **www.lynburgh.com**

Spacious residence overlooking Galway Bay. Beside Beach, walking distance to City, Leisureland, University & Aran Ferry. TV, Hairdryers and Tea/Coffee facilites.

| B&B | 6 | Ensuite | €30-€35 | Dinner | - |
|-----|---|---------|---------|--------|---|
| B&B | - | Standard | | Partial Board | - |
| Single Rate | | | €40-€45 | Child reduction | - |

**Open:** 15th January-15th December

---

**Galway 1km**

**Mrs Sara Davy**
ROSS HOUSE
14 Whitestrand Avenue,
Lower Salthill, Galway,
Co Galway

### Galway City Whitestrand

Tel: **091 587431** Fax: **091 581970**
Email: **rosshousebb@eircom.net**
Web: **www.rosshousebb.com**

Beside Galway Bay. All rooms en-suite, TV, Hairdryer, Hospitality tray. Ample safe offstreet parking. Ten minutes walking to City Centre. 5 minutes to Beach.

| B&B | 4 | Ensuite | €30-€32 | Dinner | - |
|-----|---|---------|---------|--------|---|
| B&B | - | Standard | - | Partial Board | - |
| Single Rate | | | | Child reduction | - |

**Open:** 1st January-24th December

---

**Galway 1km**

**Stella Faherty**
CONSILIO
4 Whitestrand Avenue,
Lower Salthill, Galway,
Co Galway

### Galway City Whitestrand

Tel: **091 586450** Fax: **091 586450**
Email: **consilio4@eircom.net**
Bus No: **1**

Friendly and comfortable home in quiet area between Galway and Salthill. Beside Beach and convenient to all City entertainment. No smoking house.

| B&B | 4 | Ensuite | €30-€32 | Dinner | - |
|-----|---|---------|---------|--------|---|
| B&B | - | Standard | | Partial Board | - |
| Single Rate | | | €40-€45 | Child reduction | - |

**Open:** All Year

---

**Galway City 1km**

**Kathleen Melvin**
LISKEA
16 Whitestrand Avenue,
Lower Salthill, Galway,
Co Galway

### Galway City Whitestrand

Tel: **091 584318** Fax: **091 584319**

Beside Galway Bay. Beach 100 yds. Short walk to City Centre. All rooms ensuite, Television, Hairdryer, Tea/Coffee.

| B&B | 4 | Ensuite | €30-€32 | Dinner | - |
|-----|---|---------|---------|--------|---|
| B&B | - | Standard | - | Partial Board | - |
| Single Rate | | | | Child reduction | - |

**Open:** All Year

**Galway 1km**

### Tim & Carmel O'Halloran
**RONCALLI HOUSE**
24 Whitestrand Avenue,
Galway, Co Galway

**Galway City Whitestrand**

Tel: **091 584159/589013**   Fax: **091 584159**
Email: **roncallihouse@eircom.net**

Warm comfortable home beside Galway Bay. Walking distance City Centre. Frommer, Lonely Planet, Ireland Guide, Birnbaum recommended. Breakfast Award.

| B&B | 6 | Ensuite | €30-€32 | Dinner | - |
| B&B | - | Standard | - | Partial Board | - |
| Single Rate | | | €40-€45 | Child reduction | 25% |

**Open:** All Year

---

**In Galway City**

### Ms Maureen Tarpey
**THE DORMERS**
Whitestrand Road, Galway,
Co Galway

**Galway City Whitestrand**

Tel: **091 585034**   Fax: **091 585034**

Bungalow, conveniently situated within walking distance to Leisureland/ University/ City/Beach. All rooms with shower/toilet/TV/hairdryers. Some rooms on ground floor.

| B&B | 6 | Ensuite | €30-€35 | Dinner | - |
| B&B | - | Standard | - | Partial Board | - |
| Single Rate | | | €40-€45 | Child reduction | 25% |

**Open:** 1st February-15th December

---

**In Galway**

### Mrs Bridie Thomson
**ROCK LODGE**
Whitestrand Road, Galway,
Co Galway

**Galway City Whitestrand**

Tel: **091 583789**   Fax: **091 583789**
Email: **rocklodgeguests@eircom.net**

Spacious residence beside Galway Bay. TV, Hairdryers, Tea/Coffee facilities. Private parking. 10 minutes walk City Centre. Beach 100 yds.

| B&B | 6 | Ensuite | €30-€32 | Dinner | - |
| B&B | - | Standard | - | Partial Board | - |
| Single Rate | | | €40-€50 | Child reduction | 25% |

**Open:** All Year

---

**Gort 2km**

### Paul & Marion Collins
**EALAMAR**
Coole Park, Gort, Co Galway

**Gort**

Tel: **091 631572**   Fax: **091 631572**
Email: **pmcoll@eircom.net**
Web: **www.galway.net/pages/ealamar/**

Country home, just off N18 on entrance to Coole National Park-Lakes, Gardens, Heritage. Ideal base for visiting Cliffs of Moher/Galway City/Connemara. Golf 3mls.

| B&B | 4 | Ensuite | €27.50-€31 | Dinner | - |
| B&B | - | Standard | - | Partial Board | - |
| Single Rate | | | €40-€43.50 | Child reduction | 33.3% |

**Open:** 1st May-31st October

---

**In Gort**

### Mrs Kathleen O'Connor
**THE ASHTREE**
Glenbrack, Galway Road, Gort,
Co Galway

**Gort**

Tel: **091 631380**
Email: **katoconnor@eircom.net**

Comfortable home on N18. Galway and Ennis 30 mins. The Burren, Coole Park, Thoorballylee and 18 hole Golf course nearby. Shannon Airport 1 hr.

| B&B | 3 | Ensuite | €31-€31 | Dinner | - |
| B&B | - | Standard | - | Partial Board | - |
| Single Rate | | | €40-€45 | Child reduction | 25% |

**Open:** 1st April-31st October

### Mrs Maureen Fawle
**HOLLYOAK**
Kinvara Road, Ballinderreen,
Kilcolgan, Co Galway

TEL: **091 637165**
EMAIL: **maureenfawle@oceanfree.net**

Warm, country home on N67 between Kinvara - Kilcolgan. Central Burren, Cliffs of Moher, Connemara. Banquets nightly in Dunguire Castle. Fodor Guide recommended.

| B&B | 2 | Ensuite | €28-€31 | Dinner | - |
| B&B | 1 | Standard | €25.50-€28.50 | Partial Board | - |
| Single Rate | | | €38-€43.50 | Child reduction | 25% |

Kinvara 4km

**Open:** 16th March-31st October

---

### Mary Flanagan
**MOUNTAIN VIEW**
Ballycleara, Kinvara, Co Galway

TEL: **091 637275**   FAX: **091 637275**
EMAIL: **mountainviewbandbkinvara@eircom.net**
WEB: **www.kinvara.com/mountainviewbb**

Comfortable modern country house on N67 near Dunguaire Castle with its nightly banquets. Tea/coffee facilities. General Burren, Cliffs of Moher, Commemara.

| B&B | 4 | Ensuite | €27.50-€31 | Dinner | - |
| B&B | - | Standard | - | Partial Board | - |
| Single Rate | | | €40-€43.50 | Child reduction | 33.3% |

Kinvara 1km

**Open:** 1st April-31st October

---

### Jim & Mary Killeen
**VILLA MARIA**
Ballyclery, Kinvara, Co Galway

TEL: **091 638117**
EMAIL: **villamariakinvara@eircom.net**
WEB: **www.kinvaraguesthouse.com**

Country home on the N67, near Dunguaire Castle with nightly banquets, central to Burren, Cliffs of Moher, Ailwee Cave, Connemara, Shannon Airport 1 hour drive.

| B&B | 4 | Ensuite | €27.50-€31 | Dinner | - |
| B&B | - | Standard | - | Partial Board | - |
| Single Rate | | | €40-€43.50 | Child reduction | 33.3% |

Kinvara 1km

**Open:** All Year

---

### Angela Larkin
**BARN LODGE B&B**
Kinvara Road, Toureen,
Ballindereen, Kilcolgan,
Co Galway

TEL: **091 637548**   FAX: **091 637548**
EMAIL: **angelalarkin@oceanfree.net**

Country home situated on N67. 50 yrds off main road on left. Between Ballindereen & kinvara. Scenic route to Burren Cliffs of Moher, Aran Islands, Banquets in Dunguaire Castle.

| B&B | 4 | Ensuite | €30-€31 | Dinner | - |
| B&B | - | Standard | - | Partial Board | - |
| Single Rate | | | - | Child reduction | 33.3% |

Kinvara 4km

**Open:** All Year Except Christmas

---

### Nancy Naughton
**KYLEMORE HOUSE**
Kylemore, Connemara,
Co Galway

TEL: **095 41143**   FAX: **095 41143**
EMAIL: **kylemorehouse@eircom.net**
WEB: **www.connemara.net/kylemorehouse**

Impressive Georgian house on the shores of Kylemore Lake. Ideal base walking. Spacious bedrooms. Home cooking. Horse riding, Beaches nearby. Recommended B&B Guide. On N59.

| B&B | 6 | Ensuite | €33-€38 | Dinner | - |
| B&B | - | Standard | - | Partial Board | - |
| Single Rate | | | €40-€55 | Child reduction | - |

Clifden 20km

**Open:** 1st March-31st October

**Leenane Connemara**

**Rita Hoult**
HILLCREST HOUSE
Clifden Road, Leenane,
Co Galway

Tel: 095 42244

Modern bungalow beside Killary harbour. Some of the finest scenery in Connemara. Assleagh Waterfall, choice of restaurants in village, Fishing, Walking nearby.

| B&B | 2 | Ensuite | €31 | Dinner | - |
| B&B | 1 | Standard | €28.50 | Partial Board | - |
| Single Rate | | | | Child reduction | - |

Leenane 2km

**Open:** 1st April-30th September

**Loughrea**

**Mrs Rose Plower**
LA RIASC
Clostoken, Loughrea,
Co Galway

Tel: 091 841069

Comfortable modern home, just off Dublin - Galway Road (N6). Galway side of Loughrea. Adjacent to award winning Restaurant "Meadow Court". Ideal touring base.

| B&B | 3 | Ensuite | €27.50-€31 | Dinner | - |
| B&B | 1 | Standard | €25.50-€28.50 | Partial Board | - |
| Single Rate | | | €38-€43.50 | Child reduction | 25% |

Loughrea 4km

**Open:** 10th January-20th December

**Moycullen**

**Áine Mulkerrins**
ARD IOSEF
Moycullen, Co Galway

Tel: 091 555149
Email: ardiosef@oceanfree.net

Friendly comfortable home on N59, 10km from Galway City. Fishing, Golf, Excellent Restaurants nearby. Breakfast menu. Ideal base for touring Connemara.

| B&B | 3 | Ensuite | €32-€38 | Dinner | - |
| B&B | 1 | Standard | €30-€36 | Partial Board | - |
| Single Rate | | | €40-€48 | Child reduction | 25% |

n Moycullen

**Open:** 1st April-31st October

**Oranmore**

**Mary Carney**
ARDFINNAN HOUSE
Maree Road, Oranmore,
Co Galway

Tel: 091 790749

Comfortable accommodation, orthopaedic beds, home baking, 5 mins from Galway City. Close to Restaurants, Beaches, Golf, Parks, Sailing. Heritage facilities

| B&B | 3 | Ensuite | €30-€35 | Dinner | - |
| B&B | - | Standard | - | Partial Board | - |
| Single Rate | | | €40-€45 | Child reduction | 25% |

n Oranmore

**Open:** All Year

**Oranmore**

**Mrs Patricia Collins**
CASTLE VIEW HOUSE
Galway Coast Road, Oranmore,
Co Galway

Tel: 091 794648
Email: patcollins101@hotmail.com
Web: www.geocities.com/pcollins100

Quiet country home, spacious bedrooms. Overlooking Galway Bay, Burren Mountains. Golf course and Horse riding nearby. Galway 7 mins drive.

| B&B | 4 | Ensuite | €28-€32 | Dinner | - |
| B&B | - | Standard | | Partial Board | - |
| Single Rate | | | €43-€43.50 | Child reduction | 25% |

n Oranmore

**Open:** 1st January-31st December

**Mrs Mary Curran**
BIRCHGROVE
Dublin Rd, Oranbeg,
Oranmore, Co Galway

### Oranmore

TEL: **091 790238**
EMAIL: **birchgrove@eircom.net**
WEB: **homepage.eircom.net/~birchgrove/**

Comfortable modern bungalow off N6. Friendly relaxed atmosphere. Quality Restaurants/Pubs nearby. Ideal touring base. Quiet location. Galway 8 minutes.

| B&B | 4 | Ensuite | €27.50-€31 | Dinner | €19 |
|---|---|---|---|---|---|
| B&B | - | Standard | - | Partial Board | |
| Single Rate | | | €40-€43.50 | Child reduction | 33.3% |

Oranmore 1km

**Open:** All Year

---

**Teresa Dundon**
MILLBROOK
Dublin Road, Oranmore,
Co Galway

### Oranmore

TEL: **091 794404**
EMAIL: **teresadundon@eircom.net**

Dormer bungalow on Dublin road, 5 mins walk from Oranmore Village. Sailing, Windsurfing, Golf nearby. Ideal touring base for Connemara, Burren.

| B&B | 3 | Ensuite | €30-€35 | Dinner | - |
|---|---|---|---|---|---|
| B&B | 1 | Standard | €28.50-€32 | Partial Board | - |
| Single Rate | | | €40-€45 | Child reduction | 25% |

In Oranmore

**Open:** 1st April-30th October

---

**Geraldine & Seamus Grady**
SHANLIN HOUSE
Maree Road, Oranmore,
Co Galway

### Oranmore

TEL: **091 790381**   FAX: **091 790381**
EMAIL: **ggrady@indigo.ie**
WEB: **www.shanlinhouse.com**

Friendly Georgian home. Walk to Village, Pubs, Restaurants, Irish Music. 5 mins to Golf Courses, Rinville Park. Galway City 10km. Centrally located to tour Connemara, Burren. Aran Islands.

| B&B | 4 | Ensuite | €30-€40 | Dinner | - |
|---|---|---|---|---|---|
| B&B | - | Standard | - | Partial Board | - |
| Single Rate | | | €40-€50 | Child reduction | 25% |

In Oranmore

**Open:** All Year

---

**Mrs Maureen Kelly**
COOLIBAH HOUSE
Dublin Road, Oranmore,
Co Galway

### Oranmore

TEL: **091 794996**

Comfortable modern home on N6, 100 mts east N18 & N6 roundabout. Ideal base for touring. Friendly and relaxing. 1km to Village.

| B&B | 3 | Ensuite | €30-€35 | Dinner | - |
|---|---|---|---|---|---|
| B&B | - | Standard | - | Partial Board | - |
| Single Rate | | | €40-€45 | Child reduction | 25% |

Oranmore 1km

**Open:** 2nd January-22nd December

---

**Marian McVicker**
THE BIRCHES
10 Carrowmoneash,
Oranmore, Co Galway

### Oranmore

TEL: **091 790394**
EMAIL: **thebirches@eircom.net**

Friendly family home. Quiet road off N6. Oranmore Lodge/Quality Hotels 200m. Pubs/Restaurants in Village. Galway 8km, Airport 3km. Ideal touring/golf base.

| B&B | 4 | Ensuite | €27.50-€35 | Dinner | - |
|---|---|---|---|---|---|
| B&B | - | Standard | - | Partial Board | - |
| Single Rate | | | €40-€43.50 | Child reduction | 25% |

Oranmore

**Open:** All Year Except Christmas

**Maureen Murphy**
**HILLVIEW**
**Moneymore, Oranmore,**
**Co Galway**

### Oranmore

Tel: **091 794341**
Email: **maureen@hillvieworanmore.com**
Web: **www.hillvieworanmore.com**

Dormer bungalow on N18. View of Clare hills. Ideal touring base for the Burren and Connemara. 18 hole Golf course nearby. Galway Airport 5km. Galway City 7km.

| B&B | 3 | Ensuite | €28-€32 | Dinner | €19 |
| B&B | 1 | Standard | €26-€29 | Partial Board | |
| Single Rate | | | €40-€45 | Child reduction | 25% |

Oranmore 1km

**Open:** 4th February-30th November

**Noeleen Murren**
**AVONDALE**
**Renville West, Oranmore,**
**Co Galway**

### Oranmore

Tel: **091 790527**
Email: **murrenwest@eircom.net**

Spacious warm house, large bedrooms, quiet location. Leisure park, golf, sailing 1km. Close to excellent restaurants. Galway City 10km, airport 8km.

| B&B | 3 | Ensuite | €30-€38 | Dinner | - |
| B&B | - | Standard | - | Partial Board | - |
| Single Rate | | | €40-€48 | Child reduction | 25% |

Oranmore 2km

**Open:** 1st April-1st December

**Mrs Mary Noone**
**ASHBROOK HOUSE**
**Dublin Road, Oranmore,**
**Co Galway**

### Oranmore

Tel: **091 794196** Fax: **091 794196**
Email: **mnoone@iol.ie**
Web: **www.ashbrookhouse.com**

Purpose built house 1 acre of landscaped gardens. Opposite Water Tower N6. Tea/Coffee, TV, Hairdryer all rooms. Golf, Sailing, Horse Riding nearby. Ideal touring Cliffs of Moher, Connemara.

| B&B | 4 | Ensuite | €30-€40 | Dinner | - |
| B&B | - | Standard | - | Partial Board | - |
| Single Rate | | | €40-€45 | Child reduction | - |

Oranmore 1km

**Open:** All Year

**Edwina Bunyan**
**THE WESTERN WAY**
**Camp Street, Oughterard,**
**Co Galway**

### Oughterard Connemara

Tel: **091 552475**
Email: **westernwaybb@hotmail.com**
Web: **www.oughterardtourism.com/westernway.htm**

Old style spacious town residence in picturesque Oughterard. Relaxed atmosphere. Walk to top class Restaurants and Pubs. Ideal base to tour Connemara.

| B&B | 3 | Ensuite | €28-€32 | Dinner | - |
| B&B | 1 | Standard | €26-€30 | Partial Board | - |
| Single Rate | | | €38-€45 | Child reduction | - |

In Oughterard

**Open:** 1st March-31st October

**Mrs Teresa Butler**
**CROSSRIVER**
**Glann Road, Oughterard,**
**Co Galway**

### Oughterard Connemara

Tel: **091 552676**
Email: **crossriver@eircom.net**
Web: **www.crossriverguesthouse.com**

Superbly situated adjacent to Owen Riff River. 300 yards from Lough Corrib, famous for brown trout. Own boats available. 3 minutes walk from Village. Many first class Restaurants.

| B&B | 4 | Ensuite | €30-€31 | Dinner | - |
| B&B | 2 | Standard | €28-€28.50 | Partial Board | - |
| Single Rate | | | €40-€45 | Child reduction | 50% |

In Oughterard

**Open:** 1st March-31st November

**Faherty Costelloe Family**
LAKELAND
Portacarron Bay, Oughterard,
Co Galway

Tel: **091 552121/552146**   Fax: **091 552146**
Email: **mayfly@eircom.net**
Web: **www.erin.ie/Lakeland**

Lakeshore lodge with private gardens to Lake. Complete Angling/Boating facility on site. 5 mins drive from Village. Golfing, Walking. Off the N59, 2nd right after Golf Club sign.

| B&B | 8 | Ensuite | €30-€35 | Dinner | - |
| B&B | 1 | Standard | €28-€30 | Partial Board | - |
| Single Rate | | | €40-€45 | Child reduction | - |

Oughterard 2km

**Open:** 1st March-30th November

---

**Ms Deirdre Forde**
CAMILLAUN
Eighterard, Oughterard,
Co Galway

Tel: **091 552678**   Fax: **091 552439**
Email: **camillaun@eircom.net**
Web: **www.camillaun.com**

Riverside setting. Lake boats moored in garden. A short walk to the Village by pedestrian way. Turn at the Lake Hotel, down street over bridge, next right.

| B&B | 4 | Ensuite | €35-€40 | Dinner | - |
| B&B | - | Standard | - | Partial Board | - |
| Single Rate | | | €47-€52 | Child reduction | 33.3% |

In Oughterard

**Open:** 1st March-31st October

---

**Mrs Brenda Joyce**
THE SUNSET
Killola, Rosscahill, Oughterard,
Co Galway

Tel: **091 550146**
Email: **thesunset@eircom.net**
Web: **www.bed-breakfast-connemara.com**

Modern country home in route N59. Ideal base for touring Connemara. Golfing, Fishing, Horse Riding available locally. Excellent home cooking.

| B&B | 3 | Ensuite | €32.50 | Dinner | - |
| B&B | - | Standard | - | Partial Board | - |
| Single Rate | | | €45 | Child reduction | 25% |

Oughterard 4km

**Open:** 1st March-30th November

---

**Ann Kelleher**
RIVER WALK HOUSE
Riverside, Oughterard,
Co Galway

Tel: **091 552788**   Fax: **091 557069**
Email: **riverwalk@eircom.net**
Web: **www.riverwalkhouse.com**

Comfortable friendly home in peaceful setting. Ideal base to tour Connemara and Aran Islands. 3 minutes walk to Oughterard Village. Fishing, Golf, Walking tours all nearby.

| B&B | 6 | Ensuite | €32-€35 | Dinner | - |
| B&B | - | Standard | - | Partial Board | - |
| Single Rate | | | €40-€45 | Child reduction | 25% |

In Oughterard

**Open:** All Year Except Christmas

---

**Mrs Dolores Leonard**
FOREST HILL
Glann Road, Oughterard,
Co Galway

Tel: **091 552549**
Email: **lakeshoreroad@eircom.net**
Web: **www.foresthillbb.com**

Quiet. Peaceful country home. Panoramic Connemara scenery. Ideal base for touring and walking. Central for exploring Irish National Park, Kylemore Abbey and Ashford Castle and Aran Islands.

| B&B | 6 | Ensuite | €27.50-€31 | Dinner | €19-€19 |
| B&B | - | Standard | - | Partial Board | - |
| Single Rate | | | €38-€43.50 | Child reduction | 33.3% |

Oughterard 4km

**Open:** 7th March-1st November

**Mrs Mary O'Halloran**
LAKESIDE
Ardnasilla, Oughterard,
Co Galway

### Oughterard Connemara

TEL: 091 552846   FAX: 091 552846
EMAIL: lakesideaccommodation@hotmail.com

Superbly situated on the shores of Lough Corrib. Fishing, Boating, 18 hole Golf, Pitch & Putt, Aughnanure Castle 1km. Dillard Causin, Michele Erdvig Guides. First class Restaurants 4km.

| B&B | 4 | Ensuite | €30-€32 | Dinner | - |
| B&B | - | Standard | | Partial Board | - |
| Single Rate | | | €40-€44 | Child reduction | 25% |

ughterard 4km   **Open:** 1st March-30th November

---

**Miss Brid Tierney**
GORTREVAGH HOUSE
Portacarron, Oughterard,
Co Galway

### Oughterard Connemara

TEL: 091 552129

Old style charm, beside Golf Course, 10 mins from Lough Corrib. Tennis and Horse Riding nearby. Traditional cooking, speciality vegetarian.

| B&B | 2 | Ensuite | €28-€31 | Dinner | €18 |
| B&B | 3 | Standard | €25.50-€28.50 | Partial Board | - |
| Single Rate | | | €38-€40 | Child reduction | - |

ughterard 1km   **Open:** All Year

---

**Mary & Tom Walsh**
THE WATERFRONT
Corrib View, Oughterard,
Connemara, Co Galway

### Oughterard Connemara

TEL: 091 552797   FAX: 091 552730
EMAIL: waterfront@galwayireland.net
WEB: www.galwayireland.net

Panoramic, Lakeside setting. Depart N59 at Golf course, towards Aughnanure Castle. Turn left, 0.5km. before the Castle towards Lake, drive along shore.

| B&B | 6 | Ensuite | €30-€34 | Dinner | - |
| B&B | - | Standard | - | Partial Board | - |
| Single Rate | | | €41-€46 | Child reduction | - |

ughterard 4km   **Open:** 3rd January-19th December

---

**Mrs Elizabeth Ryan**
AUVERGNE LODGE
Dominic Street, Portumna,
Co Galway

### Portumna

TEL: 090 9741138   FAX: 090 9741138
EMAIL: auvergnelodge@eircom.net

Warm friendly family home. Quiet area close to River Shannon, Lough Derg, Castle, Golf, Angling, Go Karting, Equestrian, Pubs, Restaurants, Hotel. TV, Tea/Coffee.

| B&B | 4 | Ensuite | €28-€31 | Dinner | - |
| B&B | - | Standard | | Partial Board | - |
| Single Rate | | | €40-€47 | Child reduction | 25% |

Portumna   **Open:** 1st January-21st December

---

**Mrs Noreen Conneely**
SEA BREEZE
Gurteen, Renvyle, Co Galway

### Renvyle Connemara

TEL: 095 43489   FAX: 095 43489
EMAIL: seabreezebandbrenvyle@eircom.net
WEB: www.connemara.net/seabreeze

Luxury accommodation in scenic location. Convenient to Kylemore Abbey, Connemara National Park. Scuba Divewest, Oceans Alive, Golf, Fishing, Horse Riding nearby. Guest Conservatory.

| B&B | 4 | Ensuite | €28-€31 | Dinner | - |
| B&B | - | Standard | | Partial Board | - |
| Single Rate | | | €40-€43.50 | Child reduction | 50% |

ifden 19km   **Open:** 1st January-20th December

**Conneely Family**
SUNNYMEADE
**Tully, Renvyle, Co Galway**

### Renvyle Connemara

TEL: **095 43491**  FAX: **095 43491**
EMAIL: **sunny@eircom.net**
WEB: **www.connemara.net/sunnymeade**

What a find! Renowned for its hospitality, overlooking sea and mountains. "Stress Free". Breakfast Menu. Convenient to Connemara Park, Kylemore Abbey, Restaurants.

| B&B | 4 | Ensuite | €27.50-€31 | Dinner | - |
| B&B | - | Standard | - | Partial Board | - |
| Single Rate | | | €40-€43.50 | Child reduction | - |

Clifden 19km

**Open:** 25th March-31st October

---

**Davin Family**
OLDE CASTLE HOUSE
**Curragh, Renvyle, Connemara, Co Galway**

### Renvyle Connemara

TEL: **095 43460**
EMAIL: **oldecastle@hotmail.com**
WEB: **geocities.com/olde-castle**

Traditional home situated in front of the sea beside 15th Century Renvyle Castle. Peaceful surroundings. House features in famous film Purple Taxi and Water Colour Challenge.

| B&B | 5 | Ensuite | €27.50-€31 | | €22-€25 |
| B&B | 1 | Standard | €25.50-€28.50 | Partial Board | €343 |
| Single Rate | | | €38-€43.50 | Child reduction | - |

Clifden 20km

**Open:** 12th March-7th November

---

**Catherine Burke**
IVY ROCK HOUSE
**Letterdyfe, Roundstone, Co Galway**

### Roundstone Connemara

TEL: **095 35872**  FAX: **095 35959**
EMAIL: **ivyrockhouse@eircom.net**

This newly refurbished Guesthouse overlooks the Sea and the Twelve Bens and is close to all amenities, Horseriding, Golf, Beaches.

| B&B | 5 | Ensuite | €30-€32 | Dinner | - |
| B&B | 1 | Standard | €29-€30 | Partial Board | - |
| Single Rate | | | €40-€45 | Child reduction | - |

Roundstone

**Open:** 16th March-31st October

---

**Christina Lowry**
ST. JOSEPH'S
**Roundstone, Connemara, Co Galway**

### Roundstone Connemara

TEL: **095 35865/35930**  FAX: **095 35865**
EMAIL: **christinalowry@eircom.net**
WEB: **www.connemara.net/conemara.org/stjosephsbb**

Spacious, 19th Century town house overlooking Roundstone Harbour. Home from home. Repeat business. Traditional welcome. Bike shed, Hill, Beach & Island walks.

| B&B | 6 | Ensuite | €29-€35 | Dinner | - |
| B&B | - | Standard | - | Partial Board | - |
| Single Rate | | | €40-€45 | Child reduction | 50% |

In Roundstone

**Open:** 1st January-15th December

---

**Linda Nee**
RUSH LAKE HOUSE
**Roundstone, Co Galway**

### Roundstone Connemara

TEL: **095 35915**  FAX: **095 35915**
EMAIL: **rushlakeguests@eircom.net**
WEB: **www.connemara.net/rushlakehouse**

Peaceful setting overlooking Sea and Mountains, walking distance from Village. Friendly and relaxed atmosphere in a family run home.

| B&B | 4 | Ensuite | €30-€35 | Dinner | - |
| B&B | - | Standard | - | Partial Board | - |
| Single Rate | | | €40-€45 | Child reduction | 25% |

In Roundstone

**Open:** 1st April-30th November

### Mrs Alice Concannon
**DUN LIOS**
**Park West, Spiddal, Co Galway**

Tel: **091 553165**
Email: **concass@indigo.ie**
Web: **www.dunlios.8m.com**

Friendly family home with views of Galway Bay. Gateway to Connemara, Aran Islands Restaurants, traditional music, beach, golf nearby "Rough Guide" recommended tea/coffee on arrival.

| B&B | 4 | Ensuite | €27.50-€31 | Dinner | - |
|-----|---|---------|-----------|--------|---|
| B&B | - | Standard | - | Partial Board | - |
| Single Rate | | | €40-€43.50 | Child reduction | 25% |

Spiddal 3km

**Open:** 1st May-31st October

### Mrs Maura Conneely (Ni Chonghaile)
**AN CALADH GEARR THATCH COTTAGE**
**Knock, Spiddal, Co Galway**

Tel: **091 593124**
Email: **cgthatchcot@eircom.net**

Think old, friendly, traditional, find it in our thatch cottage, overlooking Galway Bay, on route 336 west of Spiddal Village. Recommended- Rough guide to Ireland.

| B&B | 3 | Ensuite | €30-€32 | Dinner | - |
|-----|---|---------|---------|--------|---|
| B&B | - | Standard | - | Partial Board | - |
| Single Rate | | | €40-€44 | Child reduction | 25% |

Spiddal 5km

**Open:** 1st March-31st October

### Mrs Frances Cummins (Ui Chuimin)
**BRISEADH NA CARRAIGE**
**Pairc, Spiddal, Co Galway**

Tel: **091 553212**
Email: **frances@galwaybay.com**
Web: **www.galwaybay.com**

Guide du Routard recommended. Touring Connemara, Aran Islands, Galway Bay, Burren. Choice menu. Tea/Coffee arrival. Restaurants, Golf, Angling, Horse-riding, Beaches.

| B&B | 3 | Ensuite | €30-€32 | Dinner | - |
|-----|---|---------|---------|--------|---|
| B&B | - | Standard | - | Partial Board | - |
| Single Rate | | | - | Child reduction | 50% |

Spiddal 3km

**Open:** 1st February-15th December

### Sarah Curran
**SLIABH RUA HOUSE**
**Salahoona, Spiddal R336, Co Galway**

Tel: **091 553243**

Dormer, spacious, friendly, peaceful, home on seaside overlooking Galway Bay, Burren, Cliffs, close to all amenities, Aran Boat, Airport, 1.5 west of village.

| B&B | 4 | Ensuite | €28-€31 | Dinner | - |
|-----|---|---------|---------|--------|---|
| B&B | - | Standard | - | Partial Board | - |
| Single Rate | | | - | Child reduction | - |

Spiddal 1.5km

**Open:** 30th June-31st October

### Bartley & Vera Feeney
**ARDMOR COUNTRY HOUSE**
**Greenhill, Spiddal, Co Galway**

Tel: **091 553145/553596** Fax: **091 553596**
Email: **ardmorcountryhouse@yahoo.com**
Web: **www.ardmorcountryhouse.com**

Country home enjoying superb views. Spacious rooms, comfort assured. Relaxed and friendly atmosphere. Breakfast awards. Recommended Frommer, Sullivan, Rough Guide. AA ◆◆◆◆ Selected.

| B&B | 7 | Ensuite | €30-€33 | Dinner | - |
|-----|---|---------|---------|--------|---|
| B&B | - | Standard | - | Partial Board | - |
| Single Rate | | | €40-€45 | Child reduction | 33.3% |

In Spiddal

**Open:** 1st March-30th November

In Spiddal

**Eamonn & Siobhan Feeney**
**TUAR BEAG**
**Spiddal, Co Galway**

TEL: **091 553422**   FAX: **091 553010**
EMAIL: **tuarbeagbandb@eircom.net**
WEB: **www.tuarbeag.com**

Relax in comfort of unique home. Originally 1831 thatched cottage. Bay Views. Recommended AA ◆◆◆◆, Inside Ireland. Cooke/Rough Guides. R336 West village. Extensive breakfast menu.

| B&B | 6 | Ensuite | €27.50-€32 | Dinner | - |
| B&B | - | Standard | - | Partial Board | - |
| Single Rate | | | - | Child reduction | 50% |

**Open:** 1st February-15th November

---

In Spiddal

**Mrs Moya Feeney**
**CALA 'N UISCE**
**Greenhill, Spiddal, Co Galway**

TEL: **091 553324**   FAX: **091 553324**
EMAIL: **moyafeeney@iolfree.ie**
WEB: **www.geocities.com/spiddalgalway**

Dillard Causin recommended. Modern home on Seaward side of R336. Just west of Spiddal. Close to all amenities. Ideal for touring Connemara and Aran Islands.

| B&B | 5 | Ensuite | €30-€32 | Dinner | - |
| B&B | - | Standard | - | Partial Board | - |
| Single Rate | | | €42-€45 | Child reduction | - |

**Open:** 1st May-1st October

---

Spiddal 2km

**Mrs Sarah Flaherty**
**COIS CAOLAIRE**
**Ballintleva, Spiddal, Co Galway**

TEL: **091 553176**   FAX: **091 553624**
EMAIL: **coiscaolaire@vodafone.ie**

"Cead Mile Fáilte". Enjoy Irish hospitality in a family run home on the Coast R336 to Connemara. Scenic view of Galway Bay, Aran Island, Burren. Home Baking. Organic produce.

| B&B | 5 | Ensuite | €30-€32 | Dinner | - |
| B&B | - | Standard | - | Partial Board | - |
| Single Rate | | | €40-€50 | Child reduction | 50% |

**Open:** 1st March-30th October

---

**Mary Joyce**
**ARD NA GREINE**
**Cre Dubh, Spiddal, Co Galway**

TEL: **091 553039**   FAX: **091 553039**
EMAIL: **mjoyce81@hotmail.com**
WEB: **www.spiddal-commemara.com**

Friendly home, facing Atlantic. Restaurants, Pubs, Music, Bog walks, Golf, Beaches. Aran Islands ferry "Special places to stay in Ireland". Breakfast menu. Home cooking, TV.

| B&B | 3 | Ensuite | €30-€32 | Dinner | - |
| B&B | - | Standard | - | Partial Board | - |
| Single Rate | | | - | Child reduction | 25% |

**Open:** All Year

---

Spiddal 1.5km

**Mrs Maureen Keady (Ni Cheidigh)**
**COL-MAR HOUSE**
**Salahoona, Spiddal, Co Galway**

TEL: **091 553247**   FAX: **091 553247**

Peaceful country home. Set in private woods and colourful gardens. Warm hospitality, spacious, comfortable. Michelin, Routard, "Lonely Planets Cadogan" recommended. 1.5km west Spiddal off R336

| B&B | 5 | Ensuite | €27.50-€31 | Dinner | - |
| B&B | - | Standard | - | Partial Board | - |
| Single Rate | | | €43.50 | Child reduction | 50% |

**Open:** 1st May-30th September

**Mrs Patsy Mc Carthy**
SAILIN
**Coill Rua, Spiddal, Co Galway**

### Spiddal Connemara

TEL: **091 553308**
EMAIL: **sailincoillrua@hotmail.com**

Bungalow overlooking Galway Bay & Cliffs of Moher. Ideal for touring Connemara & Aran Islands. Canoeing, Angling & Horse Riding. Families welcome. Route 336.

| B&B | 3 | Ensuite | €27.50-€31 | Dinner | - |
| B&B | 1 | Standard | €25.50-€28.50 | Partial Board | - |
| Single Rate | | | €38-€43.50 | Child reduction | 33.3% |

Spiddal 2km

**Open:** 1st May-30th September

---

**Mrs Barbara O'Malley-Curran**
ARD AOIBHINN
**Spiddal, Connemara, Co Galway**

### Spiddal Connemara

TEL: **091 553179**   FAX: **091 553179**
EMAIL: **aoibhinn@gofree.indigo.ie**

0.5km west Village. Multi Guidebook recommended. Convenient Aran Ferry, Connemara/Burren Tours, Seafood Restaurants, Pubs, AA ◆◆◆, Craft Village, Aran sweaters, Bog/Seashore walks.

| B&B | 5 | Ensuite | €27.50-€31 | Dinner | - |
| B&B | - | Standard | - | Partial Board | - |
| Single Rate | | | €40-€45 | Child reduction | 50% |

n Spiddal

**Open:** 1st January-31st December

---

**Brian Clancy**
SUAN NA MARA
**Stripe, Furbo, Spiddal, Co Galway**

### Spiddal Furbo

TEL: **091 591512**   FAX: **091 591632**
EMAIL: **brian@suannamara.com**
WEB: **www.suannamara.com**

Luxury accommodation RAC ◆◆◆◆◆ Premier. National Winner Country Homes Award. Chef owned, Laundry, Internet, Aran Ferries. Beach, scenic walks. Route 336 west.

| B&B | 3 | Ensuite | €37.50-€40 | Dinner | - |
| B&B | 1 | Standard | €37.50-€37.50 | Partial Board | - |
| Single Rate | | | €52-€55 | Child reduction | - |

Spiddal 5.5km

**Open:** 1st February-20th December

---

**Mrs Josephine O'Connor**
KILMORE HOUSE
**Galway Road, Tuam, Co Galway**

### Tuam

TEL: **093 28118/26525**
EMAIL: **kilmorehouse@mail.com**
WEB: **www.ebookireland.com**

Spacious modern residence on farm. Warm hospitality. Frommer recommended. Peaceful rural setting. Knock, Connemara and Galway convenient. Restaurants, Pubs nearby.

| B&B | 7 | Ensuite | €27.50-€31 | Dinner | - |
| B&B | - | Standard | - | Partial Board | - |
| Single Rate | | | €40-€43.50 | Child reduction | 25% |

Tuam 1km

**Open:** 1st January-31st December

---

## SYMBOL

### LOOK OUT FOR THIS SYMBOL WHICH
### ALL MEMBERS OF TOWN & COUNTRY HOMES DISPLAY

Welcome to Mayo, "Ireland's best kept secret". Blue flag beaches, rivers, lakes and deep-sea fishing. Visitor attractions, great Golf courses, the most incredible Touring, Trekking and Walking countryside, but most of all the hospitality of the people of Mayo.

**Michael & Rowena Lavelle**
**REALT NA MARA**
Dooagh, Achill Island, Co Mayo

### Achill Island

Tel: **098 43005** Fax: **098 43006**
Email: **mglavell@gofree.indigo.ie**
Web: **www.realtnamara.com**

On main road in Dooagh Village overlooking the Bay. New modern B&B. Family run with many facilities such as Snooker Room, Sauna, Gym, Jacuzzi, Laundry room, Drying, Freezing facilities.

| B&B | 6 | Ensuite | €30-€35 | Dinner | - |
|-----|---|---------|---------|--------|---|
| B&B | - | Standard | - | Partial Board | - |
| Single Rate | | | €40-€60 | Child reduction | 25% |

Westport 55km

**Open:** 1st March-31st October

---

**Mrs Teresa McNamara**
**WEST COAST HOUSE**
School Road, Dooagh,
Achill Island, Co Mayo

### Achill Island

Tel: **098 43317** Fax: **098 43317**
Email: **westcoast@anu.ie**
Web: **www.achillcliff.com/westcoasthouse.htm**

AA ◆◆◆. Panoramic view, Tranquil setting. Orthopaedic beds. Hairdryer, Payphone, Breakfast menu, Drying room, Laundry service. Tours arranged. Fish Restaurant nearby.

| B&B | 5 | Ensuite | €28-€32 | Dinner | €19-€25 |
|-----|---|---------|---------|--------|---------|
| B&B | - | Standard | - | Partial Board | €350 |
| Single Rate | | | €40-€50 | Child reduction | 25% |

Keel 1km

**Open:** 1st March-11th November

---

**Mrs T Moran**
**WOODVIEW HOUSE**
Springvale, Achill Sound,
Co Mayo

### Achill Island

Tel: **098 45261**

Modern bungalow in quiet scenic surroundings with panoramic view of Sea and Mountains, 1km from House of Prayer.

| B&B | 3 | Ensuite | €27.50-€31 | Dinner | - |
|-----|---|---------|------------|--------|---|
| B&B | 3 | Standard | €25.50-€28.50 | Partial Board | - |
| Single Rate | | | €38-€43.50 | Child reduction | - |

Achill Sound 1km

**Open:** 1st January-30th November

---

**Mrs Ann Sweeney**
**FINNCORRY HOUSE**
Atlantic Drive, Bleanaskill Bay,
Achill Island, Co Mayo

### Achill Island

Tel: **098 45755** Fax: **098 45755**
Email: **achill_island@hotmail.com**
Web: **achill.mayo-ireland.ie/finncorry.htm**

Relax, enjoy traditional hospitality in luxuriously appointed modern home. Peaceful setting overlooking Bleanaskill Bay on spectacular Atlantic Drive. AA/RAC Approved-◆◆◆◆.

| B&B | 6 | Ensuite | €30-€31 | Dinner | - |
|-----|---|---------|---------|--------|---|
| B&B | - | Standard | - | Partial Board | - |
| Single Rate | | | €40-€43.50 | Child reduction | 25% |

Achill Sound 3km

**Open:** 1st March-31st October

**Geraldine Best**
GLENEAGLE HOUSE
Foxford Road, Ballina, Co Mayo

### Ballina

Tel: **096 70228**

Dormer bungalow, a home of genuine welcome. 5 mins walk from Town. Rooms ensuite with TV, Tea and Coffee facilities. Ideal for Fishing and Golfing.

| B&B | 3 | Ensuite | €27.50-€31 | Dinner | - |
| B&B | - | Standard | | Partial Board | - |
| Single Rate | | | €40-€43.50 | Child reduction | 50% |

n Ballina

**Open:** 1st March-30th November

**Mrs Josephine Corrigan**
GREEN HILL
Cathedral Close, Ballina, Co Mayo

### Ballina

Tel: **096 22767**
Email: **greenhillbandb@eircom.net**

Comfortable home in quiet location at rear of Cathedral, within walking distance of River Moy, Ridge Pool and Town Centre.

| B&B | 4 | Ensuite | €27.50-€31 | Dinner | - |
| B&B | 1 | Standard | €25.50-€28.50 | Partial Board | - |
| Single Rate | | | €38-€43.50 | Child reduction | 33.3% |

n Ballina

**Open:** 1st January-18th December

**Mrs Noelle Curry**
EVERGREEN
Foxford Road, Ballina, Co Mayo

### Ballina

Tel: **096 71343**
Email: **evergreen-curry@iol.ie**
Web: **ballina.mayo-ireland.ie/evergreen.htm**

Welcome to our comfortable bungalow in peaceful location walking distance of Town. Rooms ensuite with TV, Private car park.

| B&B | 3 | Ensuite | €27.50-€31 | Dinner | - |
| B&B | - | Standard | | Partial Board | - |
| Single Rate | | | €40-€43.50 | Child reduction | - |

Ballina 1km

**Open:** All Year Except Christmas

**Ms Dolores Jordan**
RED RIVER LODGE
Iceford, Quay Rd, Ballina, Co Mayo

### Ballina

Tel: **096 22841**
Email: **redriverlodge@eircom.net**
Web: **www.redriverlodgebnb.com**

Friendly country home on 1 acre gardens overlooking Moy Estuary on Scenic Quay Road. 3km from Quay Village. Recommended by International Guides.

| B&B | 4 | Ensuite | €27.50-€31 | Dinner | - |
| B&B | - | Standard | - | Partial Board | - |
| Single Rate | | | €40-€43.50 | Child reduction | - |

Ballina 6km

**Open:** 15th April-15th October

**Agnes & Brendan McElvanna**
CLADDAGH HOUSE
Sligo Rd, Ballina, Co Mayo

### Ballina

Tel: **096 71670**　Fax: **096 76756**
Email: **brenclad@eircom.net**
Web: **www.claddaghhouse.net**

Modern home, excellent views. Comfortable and spacious. Guest TV Lounge, complimentary Tea/Coffee. Hospitable and friendly atmosphere. Full Fire Safety Certificate.

| B&B | 6 | Ensuite | €27.50-€31 | Dinner | - |
| B&B | - | Standard | - | Partial Board | - |
| Single Rate | | | €40-€43.50 | Child reduction | 25% |

Ballina 4.8km

**Open:** 1st March-31st October

### Mary O'Dowd
**CNOC BREANDAIN**
Quay Road, Ballina, Co Mayo

TEL: **096 22145**
EMAIL: **nodowd@iol.ie**
WEB: **www.iol.ie/~cnocbreandain**

Country home overlooking Moy Estuary. Noted for good food and hospitality. Many recommendations. Breakfast menu. 2km past Quay Village towards Enniscrone.

| B&B | 4 | Ensuite | €28-€31 | Dinner | - |
| B&B | - | Standard | | Partial Board | - |
| Single Rate | | | €40-€43.50 | Child reduction | 25% |

Ballina 5km   **Open:** 1st May-31st August

### Breege Padden
**QUIGNALEGAN HOUSE**
Sligo Road N59, Ballina, Co Mayo

TEL: **096 71644**   FAX: **096 71644**
EMAIL: **quignaleganhouse@eircom.net**

Quality country home, Tea/Coffee, Breakfast choice, rooms ensuite, TV, group discounts, Guide du Routard recommended, Beach, Golf, Fishing, country walks, seaweed baths.

| B&B | 5 | Ensuite | €28-€31 | Dinner | - |
| B&B | - | Standard | - | Partial Board | - |
| Single Rate | | | €40-€43.50 | Child reduction | 33.3% |

Ballina 3km  **Open:** 1st March-31st October

### Mrs Mary Reilly
**BELVEDERE HOUSE**
Foxford Rd, Ballina, Co Mayo

TEL: **096 22004**
EMAIL: **belvederehse@eircom.net**

Modern Georgian style home on N26. Within walking distance from Town, Bus and Train. Ideal for Golf and Walking. Salmon Fishing on River Moy, Trout Fishing on Lough Conn.

| B&B | 4 | Ensuite | €27.50-€31 | Dinner | - |
| B&B | - | Standard | | Partial Board | - |
| Single Rate | | | €40-€43.50 | Child reduction | 25% |

In Ballina **Open:** 5th January-20th December

### Mrs Helen Smyth
**ASHLEAM HOUSE**
Mount Falcon, Foxford Rd, Ballina, Co Mayo

TEL: **096 22406**
EMAIL: **helensmyth@eircom.net**

Friendly country home half way between Ballina and Foxford old N26 off the N26 near Mount Falcon Castle. Beside the Moy. Ideal base for touring.

| B&B | 4 | Ensuite | €27.50-€31 | Dinner | - |
| B&B | - | Standard | | Partial Board | - |
| Single Rate | | | €40-€43.50 | Child reduction | 25% |

Ballina 4km   **Open:** 1st April-30th September

### Mr & Mrs Breda & David Walsh
**SUNCROFT**
3 Cathedral Close, Ballina, Co Mayo

TEL: **096 21573**   FAX: **096 21573**
EMAIL: **suncroftbb@eircom.net**

Town house in quiet location behind Cathedral. Town Centre and River Moy, Ridge Pool 300 mtrs. Le Guide De Routard recommended.

| B&B | 4 | Ensuite | €27.50-€31 | Dinner | - |
| B&B | 1 | Standard | €25.50-€28.50 | Partial Board | - |
| Single Rate | | | €38-€43.50 | Child reduction | 50% |

In Ballina  **Open:** 1st January-23rd December

**Ms Monica Clancy**
TEMPLECARRIG HOUSE
Neale, Ballinrobe, Co Mayo

### Ballinrobe

Tel: **094 9546818**
Email: **mclancy@oceanfree.net**
Web: **www.templecarrighouse.com**

Modern custom built house set in a rural landscape 200mts from Neale Village. Heritage display of old farm implements and a traditional cottage.

| B&B | 4 | Ensuite | €27.50-€31 | Dinner | - |
| B&B | - | Standard | - | Partial Board | - |
| Single Rate | | | €40-€43.50 | Child reduction | 50% |

Ballinrobe 5km      **Open:** 1st March-31st October

---

**Martin & Breege Kavanagh**
FRIARSQUARTER HOUSE
Convent Road, Ballinrobe, Co Mayo

### Ballinrobe

Tel: **094 9541154**
Email: **breege@friarshouse.com**
Web: **www.friarshouse.com**

Elegant house, period furnishings. Spacious gardens. Le Guide Du Routard recommended. 18 Champion Golf course. Touring Base. Connemara Knock N84.

| B&B | 3 | Ensuite | €31-€33 | Dinner | - |
| B&B | 1 | Standard | €30-€32 | Partial Board | - |
| Single Rate | | | €40-€45 | Child reduction | 25% |

n Ballinrobe      **Open:** All Year

---

**Anne Mahon**
RIVERSIDE HOUSE
Cornmarket, Ballinrobe, Co Mayo

### Ballinrobe

Tel: **094 9541674**   Fax: **094 9541674**
Email: **annmahon@iol.ie**

Modern home in Lake District. Championship Golf Course, Scenic Walks. Easy driving distance Ashford Castle, Westport, Knock Shrine, Galway, Connemara, Fishing.

| B&B | 3 | Ensuite | €30-€31 | Dinner | - |
| B&B | 1 | Standard | €27.50-€28.50 | Partial Board | - |
| Single Rate | | | €38-€43.50 | Child reduction | 50% |

Ballinrobe      **Open:** 15th January-15th December

---

**Eileen McHale**
THE YELLOW ROSE B&B
Belderrig, Ballina, Co Mayo

### Ballycastle

Tel: **096 43125**

The Yellow Rose B&B is situated 10km west of the CÈid Fields. Enjoy the breathtaking views from bedrooms overlooking the sea. Fresh seafood caught and served daily, wild salmon etc.

| B&B | 2 | Ensuite | €27.50-€31 | Dinner | €19-€19 |
| B&B | 1 | Standard | €25.50-€28.50 | Partial Board | €294 |
| Single Rate | | | €38-€43.50 | Child reduction | |

Ballycastle 12km      **Open:** All Year

---

**Mrs Carmel Murphy**
THE HAWTHORNS
Belderrig, Ballina, Co Mayo

### Ballycastle

Tel: **096 43148**   Fax: **096 43148**
Email: **camurphy@indigo.ie**

Enjoy warm friendly hospitality in the picturesque Village of Belderrig. Beside Sea/Fishing Port. Hill/Cliff Walking. Ceide Fields nearby.

| B&B | 2 | Ensuite | €27.50-€31 | Dinner | €19-€19 |
| B&B | 1 | Standard | €25.50-€28.50 | Partial Board | €294 |
| Single Rate | | | €38-€43.50 | Child reduction | 50% |

Ballycastle 10km      **Open:** 1st January-31st December

**Josephine Geraghty**
BRU CHIANN LIR
Tirrane, Clogher, Belmullet,
Ballina, Co Mayo

### Belmullet Peninsula

TEL: **097 85741**  FAX: **097 85741**
EMAIL: **bruclannlir@eircom.net**
WEB: **www.bruchlannlir.com**

Visit this unspoilt Peninsula location. Surrounded by Sea, Boat trips/Angling arranged. Quiet Blue Flag Beaches, Walks, Golf, Birdlife. We have it all.

| B&B | 5 | Ensuite | €30-€32.50 | Dinner | - |
| B&B | - | Standard | - | Partial Board | - |
| Single Rate | | | €40-€43.50 | Child reduction | 33.3% |

Belmullet 13km     **Open:** 1st May-30th September

---

**Ann Healy**
CHANNEL-DALE
Ballina Road, Belmullet,
Co Mayo

### Belmullet

TEL: **097 81377**
EMAIL: **ann.healy@oceanfree.net**

Scenic tranquill surroundings, panoramic view of Broadhaven Bay, 5 mins walk to town, central to golf, fishing, beaches, heritage centre, pubs, restaurants.

| B&B | 3 | Ensuite | €30-€32.50 | Dinner | - |
| B&B | - | Standard | - | Partial Board | - |
| Single Rate | | | - | Child reduction | 50% |

Belmullet 1km     **Open:** 1st April-30th September

---

**Ms Mairin Maguire-Murphy**
DROM CAOIN
Belmullet, Co Mayo

### Belmullet

TEL: **097 81195**  FAX: **097 81195**
EMAIL: **stay@dromcaoin.ie**
WEB: **www.belmullet-accommodation.com**

Panoramic view of Blacksod Bay and Achill Island: AIB Best Food Award, Vegetarian Option, King Beds, Internet Access: Carne Golf Links, Diving, Surfing, Blue Flag Beaches.

| B&B | 4 | Ensuite | €32-€35 | Dinner | - |
| B&B | - | Standard | - | Partial Board | - |
| Single Rate | | | €40-€43.50 | Child reduction | 33.3% |

Belmullet 1km     **Open:** 15th January-15th December

---

**Anne Reilly**
HIGHDRIFT
Haven View, Ballina Road,
Belmullet, Co Mayo

### Belmullet

TEL: **097 81260**  FAX: **097 81260**
EMAIL: **anne.reilly@ireland.com**

Quiet scenic surroundings overlooking the Atlantic and Broadhaven Bay. Turf fires. 5 mins walk to Town. Visit Mullet Peninsula and Ceide fields. Warm welcome.

| B&B | 3 | Ensuite | €30-€31 | Dinner | - |
| B&B | - | Standard | - | Partial Board | - |
| Single Rate | | | €40-€43.50 | Child reduction | 25% |

Belmullet 1km     **Open:** 1st April-10th October

---

**Veronica Reilly**
CHEZ NOUS
Church Road, Belmullet,
Co Mayo

### Belmullet

TEL: **097 82167**
EMAIL: **chez_nous_belmullet@esatclear.ie**

Old style house renovated to a high standard. Carne golf links, sea angling, blue flag beaches, ceide fields, walking.

| B&B | 3 | Ensuite | €30-€32.50 | Dinner | - |
| B&B | - | Standard | - | Partial Board | - |
| Single Rate | | | €40-€43.50 | Child reduction | 50% |

In Belmullet     **Open:** 1st January-20th December

**Mrs Bernie Collins**
DRUMSHINNAGH HOUSE
Rahins, Newport Road,
Castlebar, Co Mayo

### Castlebar

TEL: **094 9024211**   FAX: **094 9024211**
EMAIL: **berniecollins@oceanfree.net**

Tranquil location, near town. On Newport/Mulranny/Achill Island Road (R311). Superb touring base. Sauna available for guest use. Friendly welcome.

| B&B | 4 | Ensuite | €32-€35 | Dinner | - |
|-----|---|---------|---------|--------|---|
| B&B | - | Standard | - | Partial Board | - |
| Single Rate | | | €40-€45 | Child reduction | **50%** |

Castlebar 3km

**Open:** 15th March-31st October

---

**Bridget Cribbin**
DOOGARRY HOUSE B&B
Kilkenny Cross, Breaffy Road,
Castlebar, Co Mayo

### Castlebar

TEL: **094 9021793**
EMAIL: **doogarryhousebab@eircom.net**

Luxurious spacious home on N60. Walking distance of town. Ideal base for Golf, Fishing, Cycling, Walking. Visit Connemara, Knock, Ceide Fields, Ashford Castle.

| B&B | 3 | Ensuite | €27.50-€31 | Dinner | - |
|-----|---|---------|------------|--------|---|
| B&B | - | Standard | - | Partial Board | - |
| Single Rate | | | €40-€43.50 | Child reduction | **33.3%** |

Castlebar 2km

**Open:** All Year

---

**Mrs Maureen Daly**
WOODVIEW LODGE
Breaffy(Breaghwy), Castlebar,
Co Mayo

### Castlebar

TEL: **094 9023985**   FAX: **094 9023985**
EMAIL: **woodviewlodge@eircom.net**

Luxurious country home, quiet peaceful location. N60 on Claremorris road opposite Breaffy House Hotel. Rooms ensuite, Tea/Coffee, TV, Hairdryers.

| B&B | 4 | Ensuite | €31 | Dinner | - |
|-----|---|---------|-----|--------|---|
| B&B | - | Standard | - | Partial Board | - |
| Single Rate | | | - | Child reduction | **25%** |

Castlebar 4km

**Open:** All Year

---

**Mrs Kay McGrath**
WINDERMERE HOUSE
Westport Road N5, Islandeady,
Castlebar, Co Mayo

### Castlebar

TEL: **094 9023329**
EMAIL: **windermerehse@eircom.net**
WEB: **www.castlebar.mayo-ireland.ie/windermere.htm**

Luxurious spacious home. Bilberry Lake 1km. Home away from home. Brittany Ferries selected. Breakfast Menu. Trouser press, Hairdryers. Boat hire. Friendly and relaxed atmosphere.

| B&B | 5 | Ensuite | €27.50-€31 | Dinner | €20 |
|-----|---|---------|------------|--------|-----|
| B&B | - | Standard | - | Partial Board | - |
| Single Rate | | | €40-€43.50 | Child reduction | **33.3%** |

Castlebar 6km

**Open:** 1st January-31st December

---

**Mrs Eileen Pierce**
FOUR WINDS
Maryland, Breaffy Road,
Castlebar, Co Mayo

### Castlebar

TEL: **094 9021767**   FAX: **094 9021767**
EMAIL: **epierce_fourwinds@esatclear.ie**

Spacious house. Quiet location. N60 walking distance Town. TV, Hairdryers in bedrooms. Convenient to Breaffy House Hotel, Train Station. Visit Knock Shrine. Ballintubber Abbey.

| B&B | 5 | Ensuite | €28-€31 | Dinner | €14-€16 |
|-----|---|---------|---------|--------|---------|
| B&B | - | Standard | - | Partial Board | - |
| Single Rate | | | €40-€43.50 | Child reduction | **33.3%** |

n Castlebar

**Open:** 15th April-16th November

**In Castlebar**

**Mrs Teresa Quinn**
NEPHIN HOUSE
Westport Road, Castlebar,
Co Mayo

### Castlebar

Tel: **094 9023840**  Fax: **094 9023840**
Email: **quinnnephin@eircom.net**

Comfortable home. Beside Westport road roundabout. Walking distance from Town. T.F. Royal Hotel, Hospital. TV, Tea/Coffee, Hairdryers in rooms. Ideal touring base.

| B&B | 3 | Ensuite | €27.50-€31 | Dinner | - |
|-----|---|---------|------------|--------|---|
| B&B | - | Standard | - | Partial Board | - |
| Single Rate | | | - | Child reduction | 50% |

**Open:** 29th April-31st October

**Castlebar 4km**

**Mrs Breege Scahill**
MILLHILL HOUSE
Westport Road, Castlebar,
Co Mayo

### Castlebar

Tel: **094 9024279**
Email: **millhill@eircom.net**
Web: **homepage.eircom.net/~millhill**

Quality accommodation off main road. Easy to find. Take Westport road N5 from Castlebar. Sign on left. Convenient to Westport. Guest lounge, TV, Tea/Coffee facilities.

| B&B | 2 | Ensuite | €27.50-€31 | Dinner | - |
|-----|---|---------|------------|--------|---|
| B&B | 1 | Standard | €25.50-€28.50 | Partial Board | - |
| Single Rate | | | €38-€43.50 | Child reduction | 50% |

**Open:** 1st May-1st October

**Castlebar 2km**

**Mrs Bernadette Walsh**
ROCKSBERRY B&B
Westport Road, Castlebar,
Co Mayo

### Castlebar

Tel: **094 9027254**  Fax: **094 9027254**
Email: **rocksberrybb@eircom.net**
Web: **www.mayo-accommodation.com**

Award winning B&B 2002 (Lyons Tea Irish welcome of the Year). Home from home, spacious rooms. Ideal touring base for West Ireland. Boat/engine hire for local Lakes and angling advice.

| B&B | 4 | Ensuite | €30-€35 | Dinner | - |
|-----|---|---------|---------|--------|---|
| B&B | - | Standard | - | Partial Board | - |
| Single Rate | | | €40-€43.50 | Child reduction | 25% |

**Open:** 1st February-30th November

**Castlebar 1km**

**Mrs Nora Ward**
DEVARD
Westport Road, Castlebar,
Co Mayo

### Castlebar

Tel: **094 9023462**
Email: **devard@esatclear.ie**
Web: **www.noraward.com**

Bungalow on N5 Westport road, 2 doors from Spar Foodstore. Electric Blankets, Hairdryers, TV, Tea/Coffee in bedrooms. Award winning gardens.

| B&B | 5 | Ensuite | €27.50-€32 | Dinner | - |
|-----|---|---------|------------|--------|---|
| B&B | - | Standard | - | Partial Board | - |
| Single Rate | | | €40-€44 | Child reduction | 33.3% |

**Open:** 1st March-30th November

**Charlestown 1km**

**Philip & Carol O'Gorman**
ASHFORT
Galway/Knock Road,
Charlestown, Co Mayo

### Charlestown

Tel: **094 9254706**  Fax: **094 9255885**
Email: **ashfortbb@eircom.net**

Spacious, comfortable home. Quiet, central location routes N17/N5. Personal attention, Route planning, Genealogy guidance. Knock Airport 5 mins. Knock Shrine 20 min. Frommer Guide.

| B&B | 5 | Ensuite | €27.50-€32 | Dinner | - |
|-----|---|---------|------------|--------|---|
| B&B | - | Standard | - | Partial Board | - |
| Single Rate | | | €40-€45 | Child reduction | 25% |

**Open:** 1st May-31st October

**Pat & Carmel Conway**
CONWAYS B&B
Coilmore, Claremorris,
Co Mayo

### Claremorris

TEL: **094 9371117**
EMAIL: **coilmore@eircom.net**
WEB: **www.coilmore.com**

Set in mature secluded gardens on Ballyhaunis road N60. Close to Knock Shrine, Airport, Horse Riding, Golf, Swimming Pool. Home Baking. Choice of breakfast.

| | | | | | |
|---|---|---|---|---|---|
| B&B | 2 | Ensuite | €27.50-€31 | Dinner | - |
| B&B | 2 | Standard | €25.50-€28.50 | Partial Board | - |
| Single Rate | | | €38-€43.50 | Child reduction | 25% |

Claremorris 4km

**Open:** 1st January-31st December

---

**Mrs Ann Coakley**
HAZEL GROVE
Drumshiel, Cong, Co Mayo

### Cong Connemara

TEL: **094 9546060**  FAX: **094 9546060**
EMAIL: **hazelgrovecong@eircom.net**
WEB: **www.hazelgrove.net**

Warm friendly home, peaceful area between Lakes Corrib/Mask. Panoramic view of Connemara Mountains. Historic area. Forest walks. Ideal touring base for Connemara/Mayo.

| | | | | | |
|---|---|---|---|---|---|
| B&B | 5 | Ensuite | €27.50-€31 | Dinner | - |
| B&B | - | Standard | - | Partial Board | - |
| Single Rate | | | €40-€43.50 | Child reduction | 50% |

Cong 1km

**Open:** 1st February-30th November

---

**Christina Dunleavy**
ASHFIELD HOUSE
Caherduff, Neale, Ballinrobe,
Co Mayo

### Cong

TEL: **094 9546759**   FAX: **094 9546759**
EMAIL: **dunleavy8@eircom.net**

Tastefully decorated home. Near Ashford Castle, Cong Abbey, Quiet Man Heritage cottage, Golf, Equestrian Centre, Lough Corrib/Mask. Ideal base for touring Connemara. Guide du Routard recommended.

| | | | | | |
|---|---|---|---|---|---|
| B&B | 4 | Ensuite | €27.50-€31 | Dinner | - |
| B&B | - | Standard | - | Partial Board | - |
| Single Rate | | | €40-€43.50 | Child reduction | 25% |

Cong 2km

**Open:** 7th January-30th November

---

**Madge Gorman**
DRINGEEN BAY B&B
Cong, Co Mayo

### Cong Connemara

TEL: **094 9546103**
EMAIL: **dringeenbay@eircom.net**
WEB: **homepage.eircom.net/~dringeenbay**

Elegant home located off R345 Cong/Clonbur road. 300m from shore of Lough Mask. Scenic mountain views. Home baking. Forest walks, extensive gardens. Ideal base for touring Connemara.

| | | | | | |
|---|---|---|---|---|---|
| B&B | 3 | Ensuite | €27.50-€31 | Dinner | - |
| B&B | - | Standard | - | Partial Board | - |
| Single Rate | | | €40-€43.50 | Child reduction | 25% |

Cong 3km

**Open:** 1st May-30th September

---

**Mrs Ann Holian**
VILLA PIO
Gortacurra, Cross, Cong,
Co Mayo

### Cong

TEL: **094 9546403**  FAX: **094 9546403**
EMAIL: **villapiocong@hotmail.com**
WEB: **www.holiantravel.com**

Situated off R334 near Lough Corrib. Boat/Engine Hire. Ideal for walkers, cyclists and touring Connemara. Quiet Man film location and Ashford Castle. Taxi Service.

| | | | | | |
|---|---|---|---|---|---|
| B&B | 2 | Ensuite | €27.50-€31 | Dinner | - |
| B&B | 1 | Standard | €25.50-€28.50 | Partial Board | - |
| Single Rate | | | €38-€43.50 | Child reduction | 33.3% |

Cong 3km

**Open:** All Year

Cong 0.5km

**Mrs Kathy O'Connor**
DOLMEN HOUSE
Drumsheel, Cong, Co Mayo

### Cong
TEL: **094 9546466**  FAX: **094 9546993**

Luxurious house overlooking Connemara mountains. Excellent touring base, paradise for anglers, walkers etc. Routard recommended.

| B&B | 5 | Ensuite | €30-€31 | Dinner | - |
| B&B | - | Standard | | Partial Board | - |
| Single Rate | | | €40-€43.50 | Child reduction | 25% |

**Open:** 1st January-31st December

---

Cong 1km

**Mrs Bridie O'Toole**
HILL VIEW FARM
Drumshiel, Cong, Co Mayo

### Cong Connemara
TEL: **094 9546500**
EMAIL: **hillviewcong@hotmail.com**

Warm hospitality in a modern country home, quiet scenic area with magnificent views of mountains/old castle. Cycle storage, drying room, TV lounge, home baking.

| B&B | 4 | Ensuite | €27.50-€31 | Dinner | - |
| B&B | - | Standard | - | Partial Board | - |
| Single Rate | | | €40-€43.50 | Child reduction | 50% |

**Open:** 1st February-30th November

---

Cong 1.5km

**Kathleen Walsh**
INISHFREE HOUSE
Ashford, Cong, Co Mayo

### Cong
TEL: **094 9546082**
EMAIL: **inishfreecong@hotmail.com**

Country home between lakes Corrib/Mask on road 345 off N84 in the heart of Quiet Man Country. Near Ashford Castle and Cong Abbey.

| B&B | 4 | Ensuite | €27.50-€31 | Dinner | - |
| B&B | - | Standard | - | Partial Board | - |
| Single Rate | | | - | Child reduction | 50% |

**Open:** 1st January-20th December

---

In Crossmolina

**Mrs Nuala Gallagher-Matthews**
LAKE VIEW HOUSE
Ballina Road, Crossmolina, Co Mayo

### Crossmolina
TEL: **096 31296**
EMAIL: **lakeviewhouse@oceanfree.net**

Country home. Close to Lough Conn. Family Research/Archaeological Centres and Ceide Fields. Boat/Ghillie hire. Fishing arranged. Tea/Coffee facilities. Ideal touring base.

| B&B | 6 | Ensuite | €27.50-€31 | Dinner | - |
| B&B | - | Standard | - | Partial Board | - |
| Single Rate | | | €40-€43.50 | Child reduction | - |

**Open:** 1st May-31st October

---

Kiltimagh

**Michael & Carol Roache**
SHANNON'S B&B
Aiden Street, Kiltimagh, Co Mayo

### Kiltimagh
TEL: **094 9381350**
EMAIL: **shannonbedbreakfast@eircom.net**
WEB: **www.shannonbandb.com**

Family run B&B located in town centre. B&B comprises of 5 ensuite rooms. 4 of which are on the 2nd floor and 1 on ground floor with category 3 disabled access.

| B&B | 5 | Ensuite | €27.50-€35 | Dinner | - |
| B&B | - | Standard | - | Partial Board | - |
| Single Rate | | | €40-€46 | Child reduction | 50% |

**Open:** 1st January-31st December

Knock 1km

### Knock

**Maureen Carney & Family**
BURREN
Kiltimagh Road, Knock,
Co Mayo

TEL: **094 9388362**   FAX: **094 9388362**
EMAIL: **carneymaureenc@eircom.net**

On R323, west off N17. All ground floor rooms. Hairdryers, electric blankets, TV's. Lounge with tea/coffee making facilities. Private parking.

| | | | | | |
|---|---|---|---|---|---|
| B&B | 4 | Ensuite | €27.50-€31 | Dinner | - |
| B&B | - | Standard | - | Partial Board | - |
| Single Rate | | | €40-€43.50 | Child reduction | 33.3% |

**Open:** 1st June-31st August

---

n Knock

### Knock

**Mrs Kathleen Carty**
CARRAMORE HOUSE
Old Airport Road, Knock,
Co Mayo

TEL: **094 9388149**   FAX: **094 9388154**
EMAIL: **jcarty@cllr.mayococo.ie**

Family home 500 metres from Shrine. Electric blankets, TV, Hairdryers, Complimentry Tea/Coffee. Routes planned. Guidance on Genealogy Tracing. Convenient to bus stop. Own parking lot.

| | | | | | |
|---|---|---|---|---|---|
| B&B | 6 | Ensuite | €28-€32 | Dinner | - |
| B&B | - | Standard | - | Partial Board | - |
| Single Rate | | | €38-€43.50 | Child reduction | 33.3% |

**Open:** 17th March-31st October

---

n Knock

### Knock

**Ms Mary Coyne**
AISHLING HOUSE
Ballyhaunis Road, Knock,
Co Mayo

TEL: **094 9388558**

Spacious, warm & welcoming off N17. Tea/Coffee, Private parking. Ideal touring West, historical places, lakes, golf, horse riding. Beside Shrine. Near Airport.

| | | | | | |
|---|---|---|---|---|---|
| B&B | 5 | Ensuite | €27.50-€31 | Dinner | - |
| B&B | 1 | Standard | €25.50-€28.50 | Partial Board | - |
| Single Rate | | | €38-€43.50 | Child reduction | 33.3% |

**Open:** All Year

---

n Knock

### Knock

**Taffe Family**
ESKERVILLE
Claremorris Rd, Knock,
Co Mayo

TEL: **094 9388413**   FAX: **094 9388413**

Beige Dormer Bungalow situated on Claremorris/Galway Road. In Knock. N17. Private Parking. Mature Gardens. Credit cards. Children welcome.

| | | | | | |
|---|---|---|---|---|---|
| B&B | 4 | Ensuite | €27.50-€31 | Dinner | - |
| B&B | 1 | Standard | €25.50-€28.50 | Partial Board | - |
| Single Rate | | | €38-€43.50 | Child reduction | 33.3% |

**Open:** All Year

---

n Louisburgh

### Louisburgh

**Mrs Claire Kenny**
SPRINGFIELD HOUSE
Westport Rd, Louisburgh,
Co Mayo

TEL: **098 66289**

On main Louisburgh/Westport Road (R335). Safe sandy Beaches, Sea & River Fishing. Ideal area for Walking, Mountain Climbing & Cycling.

| | | | | | |
|---|---|---|---|---|---|
| B&B | 3 | Ensuite | €31-€31 | Dinner | - |
| B&B | 1 | Standard | €25.50-€28.50 | Partial Board | - |
| Single Rate | | | €38-€43.50 | Child reduction | 25% |

**Open:** 1st January-1st December

### Angela McGuinness
**LOUISBURGH LODGE**
Caher, Louisburgh, Co Mayo

**Louisburgh**
Tᴇʟ: **098 66202**
Eᴍᴀɪʟ: **ciaraann@eircom.net**

Spacious, modern family home, superb sea, mountain views, 2 minutes to town, 5 minutes to blue flag beach. Nearby ferries to Clare Island/Inisturk river fishing.

| B&B | 4 | Ensuite | €30-€35 | Dinner | - |
|-----|---|---------|---------|--------|---|
| B&B | - | Standard | | Partial Board | - |
| Single Rate | | | €40-€45 | Child reduction | 33.3% |

In Louisburgh

**Open:** 31st January-30th November

---

### Mrs Marian McNamara
**PONDEROSA**
Tooreen Road, Louisburgh,
Co Mayo

**Louisburgh**
Tᴇʟ: **098 66440**

Ideally located near all amenities. Tour Connemara, Achill Island, Ceide Fields, Knock Shrine etc. Near safe sandy beaches. River fishing, sea angling, surfing, mountain climbing. 3 mins town.

| B&B | 1 | Ensuite | €27.50-€31 | Dinner | - |
|-----|---|---------|------------|--------|---|
| B&B | 2 | Standard | €25.50-€28.50 | Partial Board | - |
| Single Rate | | | €38-€43.50 | Child reduction | 25% |

In Louisburgh

**Open:** 1st April-31st October

---

### Mrs Mary Sammin
**THE THREE ARCHES**
Askelane, Louisburgh, Co Mayo

**Louisburgh**
Tᴇʟ: **098 66484**
Eᴍᴀɪʟ: 3arches@gofree.indigo.ie
Wᴇʙ: http://gofree.indigo.ie/~3arches

Modern bungalow with panoramic view. Ideal touring centre for Clare Island. Croagh Patrick. Safe Sandy Beaches. Scenic Walks. Home Cooking.

| B&B | 2 | Ensuite | €28-€31 | Dinner | €25 |
|-----|---|---------|---------|--------|-----|
| B&B | 2 | Standard | €26-€29 | Partial Board | - |
| Single Rate | | | €40-€45 | Child reduction | 50% |

Louisburgh 3km

**Open:** 1st May-30th September

---

### Mrs Maureen McGovern
**ANCHOR HOUSE**
The Quay, Newport, Co Mayo

**Newport**
Tᴇʟ: **098 41178**  Fᴀx: **094 9024903**
Eᴍᴀɪʟ: **maureenanchorhouse@hotmail.com**

Quiet residential area on the Waterfront. Convenient to Town, Restaurants, Pubs. Ideal base for Touring, Golf, Fishing and Walking. TA Vouchers accepted. B&B from €28 to €45.

| B&B | 4 | Ensuite | €28-€35 | Dinner | - |
|-----|---|---------|---------|--------|---|
| B&B | 1 | Standard | €28-€30 | Partial Board | - |
| Single Rate | | | €38-€45 | Child reduction | - |

In Newport

**Open:** 1st March-1st October

---

### Catherine Walsh
**CLOONLARA LODGE**
Cloonlara, Swinford, Co Mayo

**Swinford**
Tᴇʟ: **094 9251452**  Fᴀx: **094 9253373**
Eᴍᴀɪʟ: **epwalsh@iol.ie**

Modern dormer bungalow in tranquil setting with large individually decorated rooms, breakfast menu.

| B&B | 4 | Ensuite | €30-€35 | Dinner | - |
|-----|---|---------|---------|--------|---|
| B&B | - | Standard | - | Partial Board | - |
| Single Rate | | | €40-€45 | Child reduction | 50% |

In Swinford

**Open:** 15th January-20th December

**Maria & Stephen Breen**
LINDEN HALL
**Altamount Street, Westport,
Co Mayo**

### Westport
Tel: **098 27005**
Email: **lindenhall@iol.ie**
Web: **www.lindenhallwestport.com**

Excellent location in Westport Town. Spacious period townhouse, TV & Tea/Coffee. Breakfast menu. Walk to hotels, bars & restaurants. Parking available.

| B&B | 4 | Ensuite | €27.50-€35 | Dinner | - |
| B&B | - | Standard | | Partial Board | - |
| Single Rate | | | €40-€45 | Child reduction | 50% |

Westport

**Open:** 10th January-11th December

---

**Mrs Amanda Brennan**
AURORA HOUSE
**Streamstown,
Louisburgh Road, Westport,
Co Mayo**

### Westport
Tel: **098 29077**
Email: **amandabrennan7@yahoo.co.uk**

Beautiful home with panoramic views of Croagh Patrick. Ideal base for Touring, Fishing, Golfing, Walking or Relaxing. 5km Croagh Patrick 6km sandy beach.

| B&B | 3 | Ensuite | €27.50-€31 | Dinner | - |
| B&B | - | Standard | - | Partial Board | - |
| Single Rate | | | €40-€43.50 | Child reduction | 50% |

estport 3km

**Open:** 1st April-31st October

---

**John & Mary Cafferkey**
HAZELBROOK
**Deerpark East,
Newport Road N59, Westport,
Co Mayo**

### Westport
Tel: **098 26865**
Email: **hazelbrookhouse@eircom.net**
Web: **www.hazelbrookhouse.com**

Welcoming home, superb for touring West Coast 4 mins walk to town. Le Guide du Routard recommended. Extensive Breakfast Menu. Private Parking. Aromatherapy/Massage/Reflexology available.

| B&B | 6 | Ensuite | €27.50-€31 | Dinner | - |
| B&B | - | Standard | - | Partial Board | - |
| Single Rate | | | €40-€45 | Child reduction | - |

Westport

**Open:** All Year

---

**Maire Dever**
WESTWOOD B&B
**Ballinrobe Road, Westport,
Co Mayo**

### Westport
Tel: **098 25520**
Email: **westwoodhouse@eircom.net**

Modern home. Adjacent to railway station. Ideally situated for touring Connemara Achill Island and Croagh Patrick. Private Car Park.

| B&B | 4 | Ensuite | €28-€31 | Dinner | - |
| B&B | - | Standard | - | Partial Board | - |
| Single Rate | | | - | Child reduction | 50% |

estport 1km

**Open:** 1st April-1st November

---

**Mary & John Doherty**
LUI-NA-GREINE
**Castlebar Road, Westport,
Co Mayo**

### Westport
Tel: **098 25536**

Bungalow on N5 scenic area within walking distance of Town. Spacious gardens. Car park. Recommended "Guide to Ireland", "En Irlande"

| B&B | 4 | Ensuite | €29-€31 | Dinner | - |
| B&B | 2 | Standard | €27.50-€28.50 | Partial Board | - |
| Single Rate | | | €38-€43.50 | Child reduction | 50% |

estport 1km

**Open:** 25th March-31st October

### Mrs Vera English
**HILLSIDE LODGE**
Castlebar Road, Westport,
Co Mayo

**Westport**

TEL: **098 25668**   FAX: **098 25668**
EMAIL: **veraandjohn@unison.ie**
WEB: **homepage.eircom.net/~hillsidelodge**

Warm welcoming family home just a short distance from Town. Ideal touring base for Achill,
Connemara and Knock. Take N5 from Westport past Shell Garage on left.

| | | | | | |
|---|---|---|---|---|---|
| B&B | 2 | Ensuite | €27.50-€31 | Dinner | - |
| B&B | 1 | Standard | €25.50-€28.50 | Partial Board | - |
| Single Rate | | | €38-€43.50 | Child reduction | 25% |

Westport 1km

**Open:** 1st February-30th November

---

### Maureen & Peter Flynn
**CEDAR LODGE**
Kings Hill, Newport Rd N59,
Westport, Co Mayo

**Westport**

TEL: **098 25417**
EMAIL: **info@cedarlodgewestport.com**
WEB: **www.cedarlodgewestport.com**

Welcoming peaceful bungalow, landscaped gardens (Award 2002). Irish hospitality. Great breakfast
menu, 6 min walk Town, near Golf. Frommer, Routard, Rough Guide, Best B&B's Recommended

| | | | | | |
|---|---|---|---|---|---|
| B&B | 4 | Ensuite | €30-€31 | Dinner | - |
| B&B | - | Standard | - | Partial Board | - |
| Single Rate | | | €40-€48 | Child reduction | - |

In Westport

**Open:** 1st January-24th December

---

### Mrs Angela Gavin
**CARRABAUN HOUSE**
Carrabaun, Leenane Road,
Westport, Co Mayo

**Westport**

TEL: **098 26196**   FAX: **098 28466**
EMAIL: **carrabaun@anu.ie**
WEB: **www.anu.ie/carrabaunhouse**

New spacious period house. Panoramic views. Hairdryer, TV, Trouser Press, Tea/Coffee, Electric
Blanket, Breakfast menu. Near Golfing, Museums,Pubs, Restaurants, N59. AA ◆◆◆◆

| | | | | | |
|---|---|---|---|---|---|
| B&B | 6 | Ensuite | €32-€32 | Dinner | - |
| B&B | - | Standard | - | Partial Board | - |
| Single Rate | | | | Child reduction | 25% |

Westport 1km

**Open:** 1st January-10th December

---

### John & Mary Gavin
**BEN GORM LODGE**
Murrisk Na Bol, Westport,
Co Mayo

**Westport**

TEL: **098 64791**
EMAIL: **gormlodge@eircom.net**
WEB: **www.bengormlodge.com**

Luxury home surrounded by sea and mountains. Rooms with panoramic views of Clew Bay/Croagh
Patrick. Warm welcome, homebaking, walk to pubs and restaurant.

| | | | | | |
|---|---|---|---|---|---|
| B&B | 4 | Ensuite | €30-€32 | Dinner | - |
| B&B | - | Standard | - | Partial Board | - |
| Single Rate | | | €40-€43.50 | Child reduction | 25% |

Westport 6km

**Open:** 15th March-15th November

---

### Mrs Maureen Geraghty
**ST BRENDANS**
Kilmeena, Westport, Co Mayo

**Westport**

TEL: **098 41209**

Dormer type house, 3 guest rooms. Close to all amenities, Fishing. Ideal touring base. 18 hole and
9 hole golf courses nearby. Minibus - Taxi on premises

| | | | | | |
|---|---|---|---|---|---|
| B&B | 3 | Ensuite | €27.50-€31 | Dinner | - |
| B&B | - | Standard | - | Partial Board | - |
| Single Rate | | | | Child reduction | 25% |

Westport 7km

**Open:** 15th April-30th September

**Mrs Teresa Geraghty**
ARD BAWN
**Leenane Road, Westport, Co Mayo**

Tel: **098 25150**

Comfortable family home. 1km Westport Town - 10 mins walk. Panoramic views of Croagh Patrick & Clew Bay. Ideal Base for touring Connemara, Achill Island. Horse Riding & Fishing nearby.

| B&B | 3 | Ensuite | €28-€31 | Dinner | - |
| B&B | 1 | Standard | €26.50-€30 | Partial Board | - |
| Single Rate | | | €39-€43.50 | Child reduction | 25% |

estport

**Open:** 17th March-31st October

---

**Mrs Bridget Gibbons**
BROADLANDS
**Quay Road, Westport, Co Mayo**

Tel: **098 27377**

Large bungalow, situated on the coast road to Louisburgh. Close to Town Centre, Westport Quay, Pubs & Restaurants.

| B&B | 5 | Ensuite | €29-€31 | Dinner | - |
| B&B | - | Standard | | Partial Board | - |
| Single Rate | | | €40-€45 | Child reduction | - |

Westport

**Open:** All Year

---

**Mrs Beatrice Gill**
SEA BREEZE
**Kilsallagh, Westport, Co Mayo**

Tel: **098 66548**
Email: **seabreeze@eircom.net**
Web: **http://homepage.eircom.net/~beatricegill/**

AA ◆◆◆. Comfortable, friendly home, breathtaking views. From Westport take R335 to avail of hospitality and delicious food. Close to Pubs, Turf Fires, Restaurants, Croagh Patrick, Beach.

| B&B | 3 | Ensuite | €27.50-€31 | Dinner | €25-€25 |
| B&B | - | Standard | | Partial Board | - |
| Single Rate | | | €40-€45 | Child reduction | 25% |

estport 12km

**Open:** 15th January-1st November

---

**Mary Hughes**
ROCKVILLE
**Moyhastin, Westport, Co Mayo**

Tel: **098 28949** Fax: **098 28949**
Email: **info@rockvilleguesthouse.com**
Web: **www.rockvilleguesthouse.com**

Majestic peaceful setting. Award winning gardens. View of Lake, Croagh Patrick and Clew Bay. Guest lounge, breakfast menu, electric blankets. Golf, Walking, Cycling.

| B&B | 4 | Ensuite | €30-€31 | Dinner | - |
| B&B | - | Standard | - | Partial Board | - |
| Single Rate | | | €40-€43.50 | Child reduction | 50% |

estport 2km

**Open:** 1st March-31st October

---

**Mary Jordan**
ROSMO HOUSE
**Rosbeg, Westport, Co Mayo**

Tel: **098 25925**
Email: **rosmohouse@unison.ie**

Purpose built house in Westport Harbour area. Quiet location on Coast Road to Louisburgh. Short distance Croagh Patrick, Pubs, Restaurants. Satellite, TV, Video, Power showers, Tea/Coffee. Car park.

| B&B | 5 | Ensuite | €27.50-€31 | Dinner | - |
| B&B | - | Standard | | Partial Board | - |
| Single Rate | | | €40-€43.50 | Child reduction | 50% |

Westport 1.5km

**Open:** 1st March-31st October

In Westport

**Robert & Sheila Kilkelly**
**ST ANTHONY'S**
**Distillery Rd, Westport,**
**Co Mayo**

**Westport**

TEL: **098 28887**  FAX: **098 25172**
EMAIL: **robert@st-anthonys.com**
WEB: **www.st-anthonys.com**

Enjoy a little luxury in an 1820 Built Town House. Private parking on one acre of grounds. Riverside. Tea/Coffee facilities. Two ensuites with Jacuzzi.

| B&B | 5 | Ensuite | €40 | Dinner | - |
| B&B | - | Standard | - | Partial Board | - |
| Single Rate | | | - | Child reduction | - |

**Open:** All Year

---

Westport 3km

**Ronan & Eithne Larkin**
**AODHNAIT**
**Rosbeg, Westport, Co Mayo**

**Westport**

TEL: **098 25784**
EMAIL: **aodhnait@eircom.net**
WEB: **www.aodhnait.ie**

Quiet country home on the shores of Clew Bay. Ideal base for Mayo/Connemara. Walking distance of Harbour. Home baking, Breakfast menu. First right turn after harbour.

| B&B | 4 | Ensuite | €30-€32 | Dinner | - |
| B&B | - | Standard | - | Partial Board | - |
| Single Rate | | | €40-€44 | Child reduction | 25% |

**Open:** 1st February-31st October

---

In Westport

**Mrs Margaret Madigan**
**ADARE HOUSE**
**Quay Road, Westport, Co Mayo**

**Westport**

TEL: **098 26102**  FAX: **098 26202**
EMAIL: **adarehouse@eircom.net**
WEB: **www.accommodation-westport-mayo.com**

Modern home T39/R335. 7 minutes walk Town, Pubs, Restaurants. Panoramic views. Orthopaedic beds. Guest Lounge. Tea/Coffee facilities. Breakfast menu.

| B&B | 6 | Ensuite | €27.50-€31 | Dinner | - |
| B&B | - | Standard | - | Partial Board | - |
| Single Rate | | | €40-€44 | Child reduction | 50% |

**Open:** 1st January-20th December

---

Westport 9km

**Mrs Bridie McDermott**
**CASHEL CAIRNS**
**Cashel, Ayle, Westport,**
**Co Mayo**

**Westport**

TEL: **098 35141**

Comfortable friendly accomodation in scenic surroundings. Touring base for Achill Island Bertra Strand Croagh Patrick. Ballintubber Abbey and Connemara.

| B&B | - | Ensuite | - | Dinner | - |
| B&B | 4 | Standard | €25.50-€28.50 | Partial Board | - |
| Single Rate | | | €38-€41.50 | Child reduction | 33.3% |

**Open:** All Year Except Christmas

---

Westport 1km

**Mrs Angela McDonagh**
**DOVEDALE**
**Rampart Wood,**
**Golf Course Rd, Westport,**
**Co Mayo**

**Westport**

TEL: **098 25154**  FAX: **098 25154**
EMAIL: **dovedale@ireland.com**
WEB: **www.dovedale-ireland.com**

Modern home set in woodland surroundings. Mature gardens. Private parking. 10 mins walk to Town Centre. Golf, Horse riding, Sailing. Route N59, Newport road 1km.

| B&B | 4 | Ensuite | €28-€32 | Dinner | - |
| B&B | - | Standard | - | Partial Board | - |
| Single Rate | | | €40-€44 | Child reduction | - |

**Open:** 1st April-31st October

**Mrs Mary Mitchell**
CILLCOMAN LODGE
Rosbeg, Westport, Co Mayo

### Westport

TEL: **098 26379**
EMAIL: **cillcomanlodge@eircom.net**
WEB: **www.cillcomanlodge.com**

Situated on Coast Road. Quiet location with parking facilities and garden. Guest TV lounge. Adjacent to Harbour, Pubs & Restaurants.

| B&B | 6 | Ensuite | €29-€31 | Dinner | - |
|---|---|---|---|---|---|
| B&B | - | Standard | | Partial Board | - |
| Single Rate | | | €40-€45 | Child reduction | **50%** |

estport 1.5km   **Open:** 1st April-20th October

---

**Mrs Ann O'Flaherty**
GLENDERAN
Rosbeg, Westport, Co Mayo

### Westport

TEL: **098 26585**
EMAIL: **glenderan@anu.ie**
WEB: **www.glenderan.com**

New house, quiet location beside Harbour. Walking distance Pubs/Restaurants. Satellite TV, Coffee/Tea, Hairdryers bedrooms. Car Park. T39/R335. Past Quays Pub, 200 mtrs turn left.

| B&B | 4 | Ensuite | €29-€31 | Dinner | - |
|---|---|---|---|---|---|
| B&B | 2 | Standard | €27-€29 | Partial Board | - |
| Single Rate | | | €40-€45 | Child reduction | **50%** |

estport 1.5km   **Open:** 1st March-31st October

---

**Marie O'Keefe**
LAKESIDE HOUSE
Leenane Rd, Westport,
Co Mayo

### Westport

TEL: **098 25670**
EMAIL: **lakesidehousewestport@eircom.net**
WEB: **www.littleireland.ie/lakesidehouse**

House beside trout fishing lake on road to Connemara N59. Spacious bedrooms. 2km from leisure centre and Westport House. 5km to Westport Golf Club.

| B&B | 3 | Ensuite | €27.50-€31 | Dinner | - |
|---|---|---|---|---|---|
| B&B | - | Standard | - | Partial Board | - |
| Single Rate | | | | Child reduction | - |

Vestport 2km   **Open:** 1st June-15th September

---

**Mrs Kay O'Malley**
RIVERBANK HOUSE
Rosbeg, Westport Harbour,
Co Mayo

### Westport

TEL: **098 25719**

Country peacefulness, on T39/R335. Walking distance Pubs/Restaurants, Home baking, Car Park, Tea/Coffee facilities. Recommended 300 best B&B Guide.

| B&B | 6 | Ensuite | €30-€31 | Dinner | - |
|---|---|---|---|---|---|
| B&B | 1 | Standard | €30-€31 | Partial Board | - |
| Single Rate | | | €40-€43.50 | Child reduction | **50%** |

Vestport 1.5km   **Open:** 12th March-31st October

---

**Mrs Marian O'Malley**
MOHER HOUSE
Liscarney, Westport, Co Mayo

### Westport

TEL: **098 21360**
EMAIL: **moherbandb@eircom.net**
WEB: **homepage.eircom.net/~moherhouse**

Country home on N59. Award winning garden 2003. Breakfast, Dinner, Veg Menu. Home cooking. Afternoon Tea on arrival. Peat fire in lounge. Off Western Way. Walkers Best B&B. Rough Guide.

| B&B | 3 | Ensuite | €28-€31 | Dinner | €20-€20 |
|---|---|---|---|---|---|
| B&B | 1 | Standard | €25.50-€28.50 | Partial Board | - |
| Single Rate | | | €38-€43.50 | Child reduction | **50%** |

Vestport 8km   **Open:** 17th March-31st October

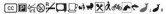

**In Westport**

### Mrs Noreen Reddington
**BROOKLODGE**
Deerpark East, Newport Rd,
Westport, Co Mayo

Westport

TEL: **098 26654**
EMAIL: **brooklodgebandb@eircom.net**
WEB: **homepage.eircom.net/~brooklodgebandb**

Modern home, quiet residential area. 5 minutes walk Town. Warm welcome, with Tea/Coffee on arrival. Recommended 400 Best B&B's Ireland.

| B&B | 5 | Ensuite | €27.50-€31 | Dinner | - |
|-----|---|---------|-----------|--------|---|
| B&B | - | Standard | | Partial Board | - |
| Single Rate | | | €40-€44 | Child reduction | **50%** |

**Open:** All Year Except Christmas

---

### Julie & Aiden Redmond
**HARMONY HEIGHTS**
Kings Hill, Newport Road,
Westport, Co Mayo

**Westport**

TEL: **098 25491**

**In Westport**

Original family home-traditional Irish hospitality. Elevated bungalow with veranda, flowers/shrubs. Route 59. Third turn left from Newport Road Bridge.

| B&B | 2 | Ensuite | €27.50-€31 | Dinner | - |
|-----|---|---------|-----------|--------|---|
| B&B | 1 | Standard | €25.50-€28.50 | Partial Board | - |
| Single Rate | | | €40-€43.50 | Child reduction | - |

**Open:** 1st March-31st October

---

### A Ruane
**ANNA LODGE**
6 Distillery Court, Westport,
Co Mayo

**Westport**

TEL: **098 28219**

**Westport**

Welcoming new Town house set in a cul-de-sac surrounded by the magnificent original Eighteenth Century Distillery walls.

| B&B | 3 | Ensuite | €30-€35 | Dinner | - |
|-----|---|---------|---------|--------|---|
| B&B | - | Standard | - | Partial Board | - |
| Single Rate | | | €40-€45 | Child reduction | - |

**Open:** 1st January-16th December

---

**Westport 1km**

### Mrs Marie Ruane
**WOODVIEW HOUSE**
Buckwaria, Castlebar Rd N5,
Westport, Co Mayo

**Westport**

TEL: **098 27879**
EMAIL: **truane@iol.ie**
WEB: **www.woodviewbb.com**

New home, quiet location on own ground. Peaceful wooded area. Private parking. Award winning Gardens and House. .5km off N5. Walking distance of Town. Breakfast Menu.

| B&B | 6 | Ensuite | €30-€33 | Dinner | - |
|-----|---|---------|---------|--------|---|
| B&B | - | Standard | | Partial Board | - |
| Single Rate | | | €45-€45 | Child reduction | **25%** |

**Open:** 1st February-30th November

---

**In Westport**

### Cora Sadik
**MOUNTAIN VIEW**
15 Deerpark View, Westport,
Co Mayo

**Westport**

TEL: **098 25575**
EMAIL: **sadiks@eircom.net**
WEB: **www.mountainviewmayo.com**

Modern family run home just five minutes walk to town centre. All rooms equipped with TV, Hairdryers, Tea/Coffee. Ideal for relaxing touring or golfing.

| B&B | 4 | Ensuite | €28-€31 | Dinner | - |
|-----|---|---------|---------|--------|---|
| B&B | - | Standard | - | Partial Board | - |
| Single Rate | | | €45-€50 | Child reduction | - |

**Open:** 1st January-20th December

**Mrs Valerie Sammon**
AILLMORE
Knockranny Village,
Castlebar Rd N5, Westport,
Co Mayo

### Westport

TEL: **098 27818**
EMAIL: **vsammon@eircom.net**
WEB: **http://westport.mayo-ireland.ie/Aillmore.htm**

Cosy, modern home in peaceful location. Just 10 mins walk to Town. Extensive Local/Irish history Library available. 500m off N5. Warm welcome assured.

| B&B | 4 | Ensuite | €32-€35 | Dinner | - |
| B&B | - | Standard | - | Partial Board | - |
| Single Rate | | | €45-€50 | Child reduction | 25% |

estport 1km

**Open:** 1st March-31st October

**Christine Scahill**
LURGAN HOUSE
Carnalurgan, Westport,
Co Mayo

### Westport

TEL: **098 27126** FAX: **098 27837**
EMAIL: **lurganhouse@eircom.net**
WEB: **www.bedbreakfastwestport.com**

Georgian house N59/R335. Spacious bedrooms. Central to suggested driving tours. Close to Pubs/Restaurants/Sandy Beaches/Golf/Fishing/Croagh Patrick.

| B&B | 3 | Ensuite | €27.50-€31 | Dinner | - |
| B&B | 1 | Standard | €25.50-€28.50 | Partial Board | - |
| Single Rate | | | €38-€43.50 | Child reduction | 50% |

estport 1km

**Open:** 1st January-30th November

**Sheridan Family**
ALTAMONT HOUSE
Ballinrobe Road, Westport,
Co Mayo

### Westport

TEL: **098 25226**

Pre-famine (1848). Tastefully modernised home, 5 minutes walk from Town Centre. Interesting Garden for guests use. Recommended "300 Best B&B's Ireland"

| B&B | 5 | Ensuite | €30-€31 | Dinner | - |
| B&B | 3 | Standard | €28-€30 | Partial Board | - |
| Single Rate | | | €38-€41 | Child reduction | 25% |

Westport

**Open:** 15th March-1st November

The county that gave Ireland its last High King and modern Ireland its first President.
Rich in wonderful landscape containing Rivers, Lakes, Mountains, Moorlands, Archaeological Features and Forest Park.
A fisherman's paradise, also numerous Golf Courses and other leisure activities.

---

**Mrs Catherine Harney**
**REESIDE**
**Barrymore, Athlone,**
**Co Roscommon**

### Athlone

TEL: **090 6492051**
EMAIL: **reeside@oceanfree.net**
WEB: **www.reeside.com**

Country Home on four acres. Road N61, beside Lough Ree & River Shannon. Close to Hodson Bay Hotel, Athlone Golf Club. Luxury cruiser available for trips on Lough Ree.

| B&B | 4 | Ensuite | €30-€31 | Dinner | - |
|-----|---|---------|---------|--------|---|
| B&B | - | Standard | - | Partial Board | - |
| Single Rate | | | €40-€43.50 | Child reduction | 50% |

Athlone 5km

**Open:** 1st January-20th December

---

**Gerald & Eleanor Kelly**
**LOUGHREE LODGE**
**Kiltoom, Athlone,**
**Co Roscommon**

### Athlone

TEL: **09064 89214**
EMAIL: **eleanorcousinskelly@hotmail.com**
WEB: **www.loughreelodge.com**

Spacious residence situated on beautiful landscaped gardens overlooking Lough Ree. On N61, 7km from Athlone. Relaxed friendly atmosphere. Close to Golf Club and Hodson Bay.

| B&B | 4 | Ensuite | €30-€31 | Dinner | - |
|-----|---|---------|---------|--------|---|
| B&B | - | Standard | - | Partial Board | - |
| Single Rate | | | €40-€43.50 | Child reduction | - |

Athlone 7km

**Open:** 31st March-31st October

---

**Mary Cooney**
**CESH CORRAN**
**Abbey Tce, Boyle,**
**Co Roscommon**

### Boyle

TEL: **071 9662265** FAX: **071 9662265**
EMAIL: **info@marycooney.com**
WEB: **www.marycooney.com**

Beautifully restored Edwardian town house on old Dublin/Sligo road, overlooking Boyle Abbey and River. Private parking. Near King House Forest Park, Lakes.

| B&B | 3 | Ensuite | €27.50-€35 | Dinner | - |
|-----|---|---------|-----------|--------|---|
| B&B | - | Standard | - | Partial Board | - |
| Single Rate | | | €45-€55 | Child reduction | 25% |

In Boyle

**Open:** All Year Except Christmas

---

**Brenda McCormack**
**ROSDARRIG**
**Dublin Road, Boyle,**
**Co Roscommon**

### Boyle

TEL: **071 9662040**
EMAIL: **rosdarrig@yahoo.co.uk**
WEB: **www.rosdarrig.com**

Modern home on edge of Town. Irish hospitality. Walk to Pubs/Restaurants. Views Curlieu mountains/surrounding farmland. Close to Boyle Abbey/Forest Park / Lakes/ King House.

| B&B | 5 | Ensuite | €28-€32 | Dinner | - |
|-----|---|---------|---------|--------|---|
| B&B | - | Standard | - | Partial Board | - |
| Single Rate | | | €40-€43.50 | Child reduction | 50% |

Boyle 1km

**Open:** 1st February-30th November

**Christina Mitchell**
ABBEY HOUSE
Boyle, Co Roscommon

### Boyle

TEL: **071 9664614/9662385**   FAX: **071 9662385**
EMAIL: **abbeyhouseboyle@eircom.net**

Victorian house nestled between Boyle River and Abbey. Within walking distance of Town Centre and Forest Park. Large mature gardens.

| B&B | 5 | Ensuite | €32-€32 | Dinner | - |
| B&B | 1 | Standard | €28.50-€30 | Partial Board | - |
| Single Rate | | | €40-€45 | Child reduction | 33.3% |

oyle 1km

**Open:** 1st March-1st November

**Mrs Rita Morgan**
ARMCASHEL B&B
Knock Rd, Castlerea,
Co Roscommon

### Castlerea

TEL: **094 9620117**
EMAIL: **morgan_rita@hotmail.com**

Modern spacious dormer bungalow on N60. Peaceful surroundings overlooking Clonalis Estate. Base for touring. Daily train to and from Dublin. Knock 25 mins. Galway 60 mins.

| B&B | 6 | Ensuite | €28-€31 | Dinner | - |
| B&B | - | Standard | | Partial Board | - |
| Single Rate | | | €40-€43.50 | Child reduction | 33.3% |

astlerea 1km

**Open:** 10th January-20th December

**Mrs Carmel Davis**
AVONDALE HOUSE
Rooskey, Carrick-on-Shannon,
Co Roscommon

### Rooskey

TEL: **071 9638095**
EMAIL: **avondalerooskey@eircom.net**

Luxury two storey house family run. Highly recommended. Peaceful surroundings. Situated near river Shannon, Famine Museum 12km. Fishing nearby. Midway Dublin/Donegal.

| B&B | 4 | Ensuite | €31 | Dinner | - |
| B&B | - | Standard | | Partial Board | - |
| Single Rate | | | €43.50 | Child reduction | 33.3% |

Rooskey Village

**Open:** 1st January-1st December

**Catherine Campbell**
WESTWAY
Galway Road, Roscommon,
Co Roscommon

### Roscommon

TEL: **090 6626927**
EMAIL: **westwayguests@eircom.net**
WEB: **www.westwayguests.com**

Easy to find on N63 within walking distance of Roscommon Town. Spacious bedrooms. Relax in our conservatory with complimentary tea and coffee.

| B&B | 4 | Ensuite | €27.50-€31 | Dinner | - |
| B&B | - | Standard | | Partial Board | - |
| Single Rate | | | | Child reduction | 50% |

oscommon

**Open:** 3rd January-20th December

**Noelle Hynes**
RIVERSIDE HOUSE
Riverside Avenue,
Circular Road, Roscommon,
Co Roscommon

### Roscommon

TEL: **090 6626897**

Modern dormer bungalow set in mature grounds in Roscommon Town within walking distance of Golf course, Castle and Museum.

| B&B | 2 | Ensuite | €27.50-€31 | Dinner | - |
| B&B | 2 | Standard | | Partial Board | - |
| Single Rate | | | €38-€43.50 | Child reduction | 50% |

Roscommon

**Open:** All Year

**Noreen O'Grady**
**THE VILLA**
**Galway Road, Roscommon,**
**Co Roscommon**

### Roscommon

Tel: **09066 25998**
Email: **noreen@thevillaguests.com**
Web: **www.thevillaguests.com**

Georgian home on N63, within walking distance town centre. TV. Tea/Coffee, Hairdryers in all bedrooms. Enjoy breakfast in conservatory overlooking gardens. Breakfast menu.

| B&B | 3 | Ensuite | €27.50-€31 | Dinner | - |
|-----|---|---------|-----------|--------|---|
| B&B | 2 | Standard | €26-€28.50 | Partial Board | - |
| Single Rate | | | - | Child reduction | 50% |

In Roscommon

**Open:** All Year

---

**Gerard & Teresa O'Hara**
**ROSS HOUSE B&B**
**No 2 Quarry View,**
**Roscommon, Co Roscommon**

### Roscommon

Tel: **090 6628891**
Email: **info@rosshouse.ie**
Web: **www.rosshouse.ie**

Welcome to our new family run B&B which offfers friendly comfortable accommodation with spacious en suite bedrooms, central heating, excellent showers and colour tv.

| B&B | 4 | Ensuite | €28-€35 | Dinner | - |
|-----|---|---------|---------|--------|---|
| B&B | - | Standard | - | Partial Board | - |
| Single Rate | | | €40-€60 | Child reduction | - |

Roscommon

**Open:** 1st January-31st December

---

## RESERVATIONS

- Confirm phone bookings in writing without delay with agreed deposit.

- To avoid misunderstandings later, check rate on booking and clarify any additional changes which may apply to your booking.

- Give details of any special requirements.

- State clearly day, date of arrival and departure date.

## SYMBOL

### LOOK OUT FOR THIS SYMBOL WHICH
### ALL MEMBERS OF TOWN & COUNTRY HOMES DISPLAY

*Midlands East*

Where Dreams Come True......

The East Coast & Midlands Region of Ireland stretches from the golden beaches of the East Coast to the mountains of Wicklow, the Cooley Peninsula and the Slieve Blooms, to the majestic Shannon in the Midlands, this the most varied of Ireland's holiday regions.

In this part of Ireland there is something for everyone - all types of activity holidays, including some of the finest parkland and links courses in the world; outstanding angling, both freshwater and sea; superb equestrian facilities, including the Irish Racing Classics; spectacular walking terrain, relaxing cruises and exciting adventure breaks.

WICKLOW MOUNTAINS NATIONAL PARK

The range of visitor attractions, ancient monuments including Newgrange, heritage sites such as Clonmacnoise and Glendalough, great houses and gardens, quality restaurants and interesting comfortable affordable accommodation make the East Coast and Midlands the ideal location for that well earned holiday break.

## Area Representatives

**KILDARE**
Mr Tony Donoghue WOODCOURTE HOUSE Trimolin Moone Athy Co Kildare
Tel: 05986 24167   Fax: 05986 24326

**LAOIS**
Mrs Lily Saunders ROSEDENE Limerick Road Portlaoise Co Laois
Tel: 0502 22345   Fax: 0502 22345

**LOUTH**
Mrs Marian Witherow KRAKOW 190 Ard Easmuinn Dundalk Co Louth
Tel: 042 9337535

**MEATH**
Mrs Anne Finnegan WOODTOWN HOUSE Woodtown West Athboy Co Meath
Tel: 046 9435022   Fax: 046 9435022
Mrs Ann Marie Russell SYCAMORES Dublin Road Navan Co Meath
Tel: 046 9023719   Fax: 046 9021261

**OFFALY**
Mt Liam Kirwin TREASCON LODGE Portarlington Co Offaly
Tel: 0502 43183   Fax: 0502 43183

**WESTMEATH**
Mr Jim Denby SHELMALIER HOUSE Cartrontory Athlone Co Westmeath
Tel: 090 6472245   Fax: 090 6473190

**WICKLOW**
Mrs Fiona Byrne GLEN NA SMOLE Ashtown Lane Marlton Road
Wicklow Co Wicklow  Tel: 0404 67945   Fax: 0404 68155
Mr Gerry Fulham ABHAINN MOR HOUSE Corballis Rathdrum Co Wicklow
Tel: 0404 46330

 ## Tourist Information Offices

**OPEN ALL YEAR**

REFER TO PAGE 5 FOR A LIST OF SERVICES AVAILABLE

Mullingar
Tel: 044 48650

Dundalk
Jocelyn Street
Tel: 042 9335484

Wicklow
Rialto House
Fitzwilliam Square
Tel: 0404 69117

Meath
Bru Na Boinne
Donore
041 9880305

Website: **www.eastcoastmidlands.ie**

On Dublin's doorstep. Renowned for Horse-racing, The Curragh, Naas, Punchestown and the National Stud. Rich in history, abounding in great houses, Japanese and Arcadian gardens and Forest Park. Excellent golf clubs and Peatland Interpretative Centre, Canals, Angling and Cruising - a visitors paradise.

---

### Agnes & Tony Donoghue

**Athy**

**WOODCOURTE HOUSE**
Timolin, Moone, Athy,
Co Kildare

TEL: **059 8624167**  FAX: **059 8624326**
EMAIL: **woodcourthouse@hotmail.com**
WEB: **www.woodcourthouse.com**

Country home with extensive gardens. In woodland setting. On N9. 35 miles Dublin, hourly bus service. Taxi available. Close to Golf courses, Race tracks, Fishing, Lovely Walks locally.

| B&B | 4 | Ensuite | €30-€32.50 | Dinner | €25-€25 |
|---|---|---|---|---|---|
| B&B | - | Standard | - | Partial Board | €350 |
| Single Rate | | | €40-€43.50 | Child reduction | **33.3%** |

Athy 5km

**Open:** All Year

---

### Mr Brian Lynch

**Clane**

**KERRY'S**
Dublin Road, Clane, Co Kildare

TEL: **045 892601**
EMAIL: **kerrysbb@hotmail.com**
BUS NO: **120, 123**

Peaceful home on Dublin's doorstep. Dublin 30 min, Airport/Ferries 40 mins, Pubs/Restaurants 1 min. Curragh/Naas/Punchestown race courses, Mondello nearby. Car park.

| B&B | 4 | Ensuite | €35-€35 | Dinner | - |
|---|---|---|---|---|---|
| B&B | - | Standard | - | Partial Board | - |
| Single Rate | | | €40-€50 | Child reduction | **25%** |

In Clane Village

**Open:** 2nd January-22nd December

---

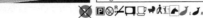

### Mrs Mary Lynch

**Clane**

**THE LAURELS**
Dublin Road, Clane, Co Kildare

TEL: **045 868274**

Dublin 30 mins drive.  Bus to and from City Centre.  Convenient to Airport/Ferries.

| B&B | 3 | Ensuite | €32-€32 | Dinner | - |
|---|---|---|---|---|---|
| B&B | - | Standard | - | Partial Board | - |
| Single Rate | | | €40-€43.50 | Child reduction | **50%** |

In Clane

**Open:** 1st May-30th September

---

### The Timoney Family

**Clane**

**SHRIFF LODGE**
Painstown on R407, Clane,
Co Kildare

TEL: **045 869282**  FAX: **045 869282**
EMAIL: **shrifflodge@eircom.net**
WEB: **homepage.eircom.net/~shrifflodge**

On R407, Dublin 20 miles, M4 9km. Convenient Airport/Ferries, Curragh, Naas, Punchestown Races. Donadea Forest Park, Golf KClub, Knockanally, Pinetrees.

| B&B | 3 | Ensuite | €31-€36 | Dinner | - |
|---|---|---|---|---|---|
| B&B | - | Standard | - | Partial Board | - |
| Single Rate | | | €38-€50 | Child reduction | - |

Clane 4.5km

**Open:** 10th April-20th October

**Ms Una Healy**
STRAFFAN B&B
**Dublin Rd, Straffan, Co Kildare**

### Clane/Straffan

TEL: **01 6272386**
EMAIL: **judj@gofree.indigo.ie**
BUS NO: **123, 120**

Spacious gardens, Power showers. Barberstown Castle and Kclub 2mins. Golf, Fishing, Mondello, Goffs nearby. Dublin 17 miles. Airport 45 mins. Exit M4 at Maynooth, Exit N7 at Kill.

| B&B | 3 | Ensuite | €32.50-€45 | Dinner | - |
| B&B | - | Standard | - | Partial Board | - |
| Single Rate | | | - | Child reduction | 25% |

Clane 4.8km

**Open:** 9th January-20th December

---

**The Foran Family**
HEATHERVILLE B&B
**Shaughlins Glen, Confey, Leixlip, Co Kildare**

### Leixlip

TEL: **01 6245156/6060923**
EMAIL: **forans@iol.ie**
BUS NO: **66**

Rural setting. 2 miles Leixlip, 12 miles Dublin, 30 mins Airport/Ferry. Secure parking. Exit M4/N4 into Leixlip Town. Right at traffic lights to T junction, left 1.2miles.

| B&B | 3 | Ensuite | €30-€35 | Dinner | - |
| B&B | - | Standard | - | Partial Board | - |
| Single Rate | | | €40-€45 | Child reduction | 50% |

Leixlip 3km

**Open:** 3rd January-16th December

---

**Mrs Maureen Downes**
AARONBEG
**Moyglare, Maynooth, Co Kildare**

### Maynooth

TEL: **01 6292074**
EMAIL: **aaronbeg@eircom.net**
WEB: **www.aaronbeg.com**
BUS NO: **66, 67**

New two storey purpose built bed & breakfast in rural area. Beside Moyglare Stud Farm. 30 mins from airport. Train and bus service from Maynooth to Dublin.

| B&B | 4 | Ensuite | €30-€35 | Dinner | - |
| B&B | - | Standard | - | Partial Board | - |
| Single Rate | | | €40-€43.50 | Child reduction | 50% |

Maynooth 2km

**Open:** 7th January-20th December

---

**Mrs Bridie Doherty**
TWO MILE HOUSE
**Naas, Co Kildare**

### Naas

TEL: **045 879824**
EMAIL: **twomilehousebb@yahoo.com**

Peaceful location - 200 yds off N9 Dublin/Waterford road. Dublin 30 mins drive. Convenient to Airport and Ferries.

| B&B | 3 | Ensuite | €30-€32 | Dinner | - |
| B&B | - | Standard | - | Partial Board | - |
| Single Rate | | | €40-€45 | Child reduction | 50% |

Naas 4km

**Open:** 1st February-30th November

---

**Kinane Family**
AVONDALE
**Dublin Road, Naas, Co Kildare**

### Naas

TEL: **045 876254**
EMAIL: **kinanev@indigo.ie**

Beside Naas town centre. 1/2 acre gardens. On bus route to Dublin. Use of iron, microwave, fridge. Hairdryers in all rooms. Fire safety certificate. Warm welcome.

| B&B | 4 | Ensuite | €35-€37.50 | Dinner | - |
| B&B | - | Standard | - | Partial Board | - |
| Single Rate | | | €50 | Child reduction | 25% |

In Naas

**Open:** 1st January-21st December

**Mrs Olive Hennessy**
DUN AONGHUS
Beggars End, Naas, Co Kildare

Naas

TEL: **045 875126**　FAX: **045 898069**
EMAIL: **dunaonghus@hotmail.com**

Tranquil location near town. Just off R410. 4 mins N7. Ideal for visiting Kildare, Dublin, Wicklow. Golf, Equestrian horseracing. 1 hour Airport and Ferryports.

| B&B | 4 | Ensuite | €32-€40 | Dinner | - |
| B&B | 2 | Standard | €30-€40 | Partial Board | - |
| Single Rate | | | €38-€50 | Child reduction | 25% |

Naas 2km

**Open:** 3rd January-22nd December

---

**Mrs Kathleen Garrett**
SEVEN SPRINGS
Hawkfield, Newbridge,
Co Kildare

Newbridge

TEL: **045 431677**

Bungalow, beside Newbridge and N7. Convenient to National Stud, Japanese Gardens, Curragh, Naas. Punchestown Race Course, Boat, Airport, Dog-racing & Mondello nearby.

| B&B | 3 | Ensuite | €32-€40 | Dinner | - |
| B&B | - | Standard | - | Partial Board | - |
| Single Rate | | | €40-€50 | Child reduction | 50% |

Newbridge 3km

**Open:** 30th January-30th November

---

**Mrs Breda Kelly**
BELLA VISTA
105 Moorefield Park,
Newbridge, Co Kildare

Newbridge

TEL: **045 431047**　FAX: **045 438259**
EMAIL: **belavista@eircom.net**
WEB: **www.bellavistaireland.com**

Long established residence in quiet residential area. Convenient to Curragh, Punchestown, Japanese Gardens. Rooms en-suite, TV, Video, Hairdryers, Tea- making facilities.

| B&B | 4 | Ensuite | €30-€40 | Dinner | - |
| B&B | - | Standard | - | Partial Board | - |
| Single Rate | | | €40-€48 | Child reduction | 25% |

In Newbridge

**Open:** All Year

---

## FREQUENTLY ASKED QUESTIONS

**Q. Are the prices based on per person sharing or a room rate?**
A. The price for bed & breakfast is per person sharing.

**Q. What does an "ensuite" room mean?**
A. An ensuite room means the room has a private bath/shower and toilet

**Q. What are the check-in times?**
A. The check-in times are normally between 2pm and 6pm, unless agreed with your host/hostess.

**Q. Where do I get directions to the B&B I have booked?**
A. Our website www.townandcountry.ie hosts directions to our homes. Alternatively, over 80% of our homes are accessible by email/fax and will be happy to forward directions on request.

Laois is a picturesque inland county. Rich in historical houses and garden's, heritage sites, Museums, Golfing, Angling, Bogs, canals and rivers. Discover the Slieve Bloom mountains, their waterfalls and nature trails. The visitors relax and enjoy peace and tranquillity.

---

### Borris-in-Ossory

**Moira Phelan**
CASTLETOWN HOUSE
**Donaghmore, Rathdowney,
Co Laois**

TEL: **0505 46415** FAX: **0505 46415**
EMAIL: **castletown@eircom.net**
WEB: **www.castletownguesthouse.com**

Welcome to our "Triple Tourism Award Winning" country home, situated 1km off R435 road at Donaghmore. Rathdowney Designer Outlet 4km. Tea on arrival.

| | | | | |
|---|---|---|---|---|
| B&B | 4 | Ensuite | €30-€35 | Dinner | - |
| B&B | - | Standard | - | Partial Board | - |
| Single Rate | | | €40-€43.50 | Child reduction | 33.3% |

Rathdowney 3km

**Open:** 1st January-20th December

---

### Mountmellick

**Abigail McEvoy**
GAROON HOUSE
**Birr Road, Mountmellick,
Co Laois**

TEL: **0502 24641**
EMAIL: **abigail@garoonhouse.com**
WEB: **www.garoonhouse.com**

Spacious, tastefully decorated home on large manicured grounds. Central location for touring any part of Ireland. Personally supervised breakfast menu.

| | | | | |
|---|---|---|---|---|
| B&B | 5 | Ensuite | €35-€35 | Dinner | - |
| B&B | - | Standard | - | Partial Board | - |
| Single Rate | | | €45-€45 | Child reduction | 25% |

Mountmellick 1km

**Open:** 1st April-30th September

---

### Portlaoise

**Kathleen Condon**
TALLTREES B&B
**Cork Road, Stradbally,
Portlaoise, Co Laois**

TEL: **0502 25412**
EMAIL: **epcon@dol.ie**

Friendly family run home, quiet surroundings, private parking, on euro route to midlands/west, an hour from Dublin, Tea/Coffe on arrival.

| | | | | |
|---|---|---|---|---|
| B&B | 4 | Ensuite | €27.50-€32.50 | Dinner | - |
| B&B | - | Standard | - | Partial Board | - |
| Single Rate | | | €40-€45 | Child reduction | 50% |

Stradbally 0.5km

**Open:** 1st January-31st December

---

### Portlaoise

**Maurice & Mary Murphy**
OAKVILLE
**Mountrath Road, Portlaoise,
Co Laois**

TEL: **0502 61970** FAX: **0502 61970**
EMAIL: **oakvillebandb@eircom.net**

Situated on R445 N7 west. Crossroads of Ireland. Shops, Restaurants, Pubs, Theatre nearby. Family run. Tour guide on premises. Italian spoken. Private carpark.

| | | | | |
|---|---|---|---|---|
| B&B | 3 | Ensuite | €32-€32 | Dinner | - |
| B&B | 1 | Standard | €30-€30 | Partial Board | - |
| Single Rate | | | €38-€44 | Child reduction | - |

Portlaoise 0.5km

**Open:** 20th January-18th December

In Portlaoise

**Mr Dermot O'Sullivan**
8 Kellyville Park
**Portlaoise, Co Laois**

Tel: **0502 22774**  Fax: **0502 80836**

Charming old house opposite the County Hall car park. 50 metres from Tourist Office. Private Car Park.

| B&B | 5 | Ensuite | €39-€39 | Dinner | - |
| B&B | - | Standard | | Partial Board | - |
| Single Rate | | | €55-€55 | Child reduction | 25% |

**Open:** 1st January-23rd December

Portlaoise 1km

**Mrs Lily Saunders**
ROSEDENE
**Limerick Road, Portlaoise, Co Laois**

Tel: **0502 22345**  Fax: **0502 22345**
Email: **rosedenebb@eircom.net**

Peaceful, relaxing home. Personal attention. Bedrooms have multichannel TV, Tea/Coffee, Hairdryers. Walk to Pubs, Restaurants. On N7 R445 West. Central location. Dublin 80km.

| B&B | 3 | Ensuite | €28-€32 | Dinner | - |
| B&B | - | Standard | - | Partial Board | - |
| Single Rate | | | €40-€43.50 | Child reduction | - |

**Open:** 1st February-20th December

**Carole England**
BALLAGHMORE HOUSE
**Ballaghmore, Borris-In-Ossory, Co Laois**

Tel: **0505 21366**  Fax: **0505 23669**
Email: **ballaghmorehse@eircom.net**
Web: **wwwballaghmorecountryhse.com**

Roscrea 5km

Spacious country house, situated on N7 Dublin-Limerick road, halfway between Borris-In-Ossory and Roscrea. Dublin 1.5 hrs, Limerick 1.25 hrs. Highly recommended.

| B&B | 6 | Ensuite | €35-€40 | Dinner | €25 |
| B&B | - | Standard | - | Partial Board | - |
| Single Rate | | | €48 | Child reduction | 50% |

**Open:** 2nd January-21st December

---

## TELEPHONE

- Operator assisted calls within Ireland     Dial 10
- International telephone operator     Dial 11818
- Directory Enquiries     Dial 11811

**FOR TROUBLE-FREE TELEPHONE CALLS FROM PUBLIC PAY PHONES IT IS ADVISABLE TO PURCHASE A TELEPHONE CALLCARD AVAILABLE IN POST OFFICES AND WHEREVER YOU SEE A CALLCARD SIGN.**
**TO DIAL IRELAND FROM ABROAD:** Country Access Code + 353 + Area Code (omit first zero) + Local Number

## SYMBOL

### LOOK OUT FOR THIS SYMBOL WHICH
### ALL MEMBERS OF TOWN & COUNTRY HOMES DISPLAY

Longford - this inland county is approximately 80 miles from Dublin. The county is rich in literary associations. The wonderful landscape is a blend of bogland, lakeland, pastureland and Wetland. Anglers can take advantage of the excellent facilities here.

**Miss Bridie Kenny**
ARDKEN
Ardagh, Co Longford

### Ardagh

TEL: **043 75029**  FAX: **043 75029**
EMAIL: **ardken@iol.ie**

Beautiful house in unique estate village. Winner of National Tidy Towns award. Identified as Heritage Village just off N4, N55.

| B&B | 4 | Ensuite | €27.50-€31 | Dinner | €30-€30 |
|-----|---|---------|------------|--------|---------|
| B&B | - | Standard | - | Partial Board | €300 |
| Single Rate | | | €40-€43.50 | Child reduction | 50% |

Longford Town 10km

**Open:** All Year

**Patricia Cumiskey**
LONGFORD COUNTRY HOUSE
Ennybegs Village, Co Longford

### Longford

TEL: **043 23320**  FAX: **043 23516**
EMAIL: **kc@iol.ie**
WEB: **www.longfordcountryhouse.com**

Enchanting tudor revival home in secluded gardens, parlour with open fire and library loft. Large bedrooms and showers, breakfast to suit guests. All home cooking. Delux suite.

| B&B | 5 | Ensuite | €39-€75 | Dinner | €25-€35 |
|-----|---|---------|---------|--------|---------|
| B&B | 1 | Standard | €35 | Partial Board | - |
| Single Rate | | | €50-€50 | Child reduction | 33.3% |

Longford 8km

**Open:** 1st March-31st October

**Mandy Etherton**
OLDE SCHOOLHOUSE
Garrowhill, Newtownforbes,
Co Longford

### Longford

TEL: **043 24854**
EMAIL: **mandy1@eircom.net**
WEB: **www.olde-schoolhouse.com**

"Rough Guide" recommended, unique old world charm, spacious, in the countryside. From Longford bypass (N4) take R198 towards Drumlish for 3 miles. Crossroads turn right.

| B&B | 3 | Ensuite | €28-€32 | Dinner | €18-€25 |
|-----|---|---------|---------|--------|---------|
| B&B | - | Standard | - | Partial Board | €350 |
| Single Rate | | | €40-€44 | Child reduction | 50% |

Longford

**Open:** 10th January-20th December

**Mrs Eileen Prunty**
EDEN HOUSE
Newtownforbes, Longford,
Co Longford

### Longford

TEL: **043 41160**

Peaceful home in picturesque village off Newtownforbes on N4. All facilities closeby. Refreshments on arrival. Orthopaedic beds, Electric blankets, TV.

| B&B | 4 | Ensuite | €31 | Dinner | - |
|-----|---|---------|-----|--------|---|
| B&B | 1 | Standard | €29 | Partial Board | - |
| Single Rate | | | €45 | Child reduction | 25% |

Longford 4km

**Open:** 15th January-15th December

The diversity of scenery, historical/archeological sites, sporting and shopping attractions within easy access from Dublin and Belfast ports/airports.

The tranquillity of the Boyne Valley and Newgrange, to the splendour and panoramic views of Carlingford Lough at the base of the Mourne Mountains makes Louth the ideal base for all tourists.

---

**Mrs Sheila Magennis**
CARRAIG MOR
Blakestown, Ardee, Co Louth

### Ardee

TEL: **041 6853513**   FAX: **041 6853513**
EMAIL: **info@carraigmor.com**
WEB: **www.carraigmor.com**

Spacious comfortable home N2 (Dublin/Derry) 2 km south Ardee. Restaurants, Golf, Fishing nearby. Central to Monasterboice, Mellifont, Newgrange. Dublin Airport 40mins. Belfast 1.5hrs

| B&B | 4 | Ensuite | €27.50-€31 | Dinner | - |
|-----|---|---------|------------|--------|---|
| B&B | - | Standard | - | Partial Board | - |
| Single Rate | | | €40-€43.50 | Child reduction | 50% |

Ardee 2km

Open: All Year

---

**Mrs Lyn Grills**
MOURNEVIEW
Belmont, Carlingford, Co Louth

### Carlingford

TEL: **042 9373551**   FAX: **042 9373551**
EMAIL: **info@mourneviewcarlingford.com**
WEB: **www.mourneviewcarlingford.com**

Enjoy home comforts in family run B&B. Tranquil. Views of Mourne and Cooley Mountains. Spacious rooms. Sign for Carlingford. Off Dublin/Belfast road (N1).

| B&B | 6 | Ensuite | €30-€32 | Dinner | - |
|-----|---|---------|---------|--------|---|
| B&B | - | Standard | - | Partial Board | - |
| Single Rate | | | €42.50-€43.50 | Child reduction | 50% |

Carlingford 2km

Open: 1st January-31st December

---

**Mrs Wendy Hanratty**
GROVE HOUSE
Grove Road, Carlingford, Co Louth

### Carlingford

TEL: **042 9373494**   FAX: **042 9383851**
EMAIL: **enquiries@grovehousecarlingford.com**
WEB: **www.grovehousecarlingford.com**

Purpose built B&B situated in the medieval town of Carlingford. TV and tea making facilities, electric blankets. Breakfast menu. Private parking. Large family rooms available.

| B&B | 4 | Ensuite | €32-€35 | Dinner | - |
|-----|---|---------|---------|--------|---|
| B&B | - | Standard | - | Partial Board | - |
| Single Rate | | | €45-€50 | Child reduction | 50% |

In Carlingford

Open: All Year

---

**Mrs Nuala Harold**
HARWOOD HEIGHTS
Mountain Park, Carlingford, Co Louth

### Carlingford

TEL: **042 9373379**
EMAIL: **harwoodheights@hotmail.com**
WEB: **www.harwood-heights.com**

Family run B&B. Scenic area overlooking medieval Carlingford. Ideal touring base. Bedrooms ensuite with tv and tea making facilities. Private car park.

| B&B | 3 | Ensuite | €32-€35 | Dinner | - |
|-----|---|---------|---------|--------|---|
| B&B | - | Standard | - | Partial Board | - |
| Single Rate | | | - | Child reduction | 50% |

In Carlingford

Open: All Year

### Marie McCarthy
**HIGHLANDS**
Irish Grange, Carlingford,
Co Louth

TEL: **042 9376104**
EMAIL: **thehighlands@eircom.net**
WEB: **www.thehighlandscarlingford.com**

Family run B&B offering luxury ensuite rooms, in a relaxed enviroment, overlooking Carlingford Lough. Spacious landscaped gardens. Private parking. On R173 South of Carlingford.

| B&B | 3 | Ensuite | €28-€33 | Dinner | - |
| B&B | - | Standard | - | Partial Board | - |
| Single Rate | | | €40-€44 | Child reduction | 50% |

Carlingford 3km          Open: 14th January-11th December

---

### Mrs Jackie Woods
**SHALOM**
Ghan Road, Carlingford,
Co Louth

TEL: **042 9373151**
EMAIL: **kevinwoods@eircom.net**
WEB: **www.jackiewoods.com**

Situated beside the Sea in the Medieval town of Carlingford. Overlooked by the Mourne Mountains on one side and the Cooley Mountains on the other.

| B&B | 5 | Ensuite | €28-€31 | Dinner | - |
| B&B | - | Standard | - | Partial Board | - |
| Single Rate | | | €40-€43.50 | Child reduction | 50% |

Carlingford          Open: All Year

---

### Mrs Mary Dolores McEvoy
**THE CROSS GARDEN**
Ganderstown, Clogherhead,
Drogheda, Route 166,
Co Louth

TEL: **041 9822675**

Overlooking Irish Sea, Modern dormer bungalow, on elevated site. Clogherhead one mile on Termonfeckin Road. All rooms private facilities. Warm welcome.

| B&B | 2 | Ensuite | €30-€31 | Dinner | - |
| B&B | 1 | Standard | €30-€30 | Partial Board | - |
| Single Rate | | | €40-€43.50 | Child reduction | 25% |

Drogheda 10km          Open: All Year

---

### Mrs Angela Kerrigan
**KILLOWEN HOUSE**
Woodgrange, Dublin Rd,
Drogheda, Co Louth

TEL: **041 9833547**   FAX: **041 9833547**
EMAIL: **killowen_house@hotmail.com**
WEB: **www.killowen-house.net**

Luxury home 50m off N1, near Hotels, 20 mins Airport, 40 mins City Centre. Good base touring Boyne Valley, near Newgrange, Monasterboice, Beach, Golf. Spacious rooms. All facilities.

| B&B | 3 | Ensuite | €35-€40 | Dinner | - |
| B&B | 1 | Standard | €32.50-€35 | Partial Board | - |
| Single Rate | | | €45-€60 | Child reduction | 25% |

Drogheda 3km          Open: 12th February-18th December

---

### Mrs Elizabeth Nallen
**ELEVENTH TEE HOUSE**
Golf Links Road, Bettystown,
Drogheda, Co Louth

TEL: **041 9827613**
EMAIL: **bettynallen@hotmail.com**

Situated in beautiful gardens adjoining Golf Course. Large Beach 0.5km. Bettystown 1.5km. Convenient Newgrange, Mosney. Airport 30 mins. 4km off N1, Road no R150.

| B&B | 3 | Ensuite | €32-€37 | Dinner | €40-€50 |
| B&B | 1 | Standard | - | Partial Board | - |
| Single Rate | | | €50-€60 | Child reduction | 25% |

Drogheda 5km          Open: 6th January-20th December

In Drogheda

**Peter & Mary Phillips**
ORLEY HOUSE
Bryanstown, Dublin Road,
Drogheda, Co Louth

**Drogheda**

TEL: **041 9836019**   FAX: **041 9836019**
EMAIL: **info@orleyhouse.com**
WEB: **www.orleyhouse.com**

Luxurious Town home off N1. Conservatory Dining Room. Airport 20 mins, near
Bus/Rail/Ferries/3 Golf Courses/Newgrange/Boynevalley/Hotels/Shops and Restaurants.

| B&B | 4 | Ensuite | €35-€40 | Dinner | €25-€30 |
|------|---|----------|---------|--------|---------|
| B&B | - | Standard | | Partial Board | - |
| Single Rate | | | €50-€60 | Child reduction | - |

**Open:** 1st January-31st December

---

Dundalk 4km

**Teresa Byrne**
HERITAGE
Haynestown, Dundalk,
Co Louth

**Dundalk**

TEL: **042 9335850**   FAX: **042 9382916**
EMAIL: **heritagedundalk@eircom.net**
WEB: **www.heritagedundalk.com**

Luxury home in peaceful setting, 700m from Roundabout to M1. Follow signposts for Haynestown
off N1 & N52. Convenient Fairways Hotel, Dundalk IT, Golf, Restaurants. 40 mins Dublin Airport.

| B&B | 3 | Ensuite | €30-€32 | Dinner | - |
|------|---|----------|---------|--------|---|
| B&B | 1 | Standard | €28-€28.50 | Partial Board | - |
| Single Rate | | | €43-€45 | Child reduction | 50% |

**Open:** 1st January-31st December

---

Dundalk 4km

**Mrs Evelyn Carolan**
LYNOLAN HOUSE
Haynestown, Dundalk,
Co Louth

**Dundalk**

TEL: **042 9336553**   FAX: **042 9336553**
EMAIL: **lynolan@indigo.ie**
WEB: **www.lynolan.com**

Luxury home in rural setting 700m from motorway roundabout, follow signs for Haynestown off
N1/N52. Convenient to Fairways Hotel, Darver Castle and restaurants.

| B&B | 6 | Ensuite | €29-€33 | Dinner | €20 |
|------|---|----------|---------|--------|-----|
| B&B | - | Standard | | Partial Board | - |
| Single Rate | | | €40-€44 | Child reduction | 50% |

**Open:** 1st January-31st December

---

**Mrs Patricia Murphy**
PINEWOODS
Dublin Road, Dundalk,
Co Louth

**Dundalk**

TEL: **042 9321295**
EMAIL: **olmurphy@eircom.net**

Traditional Irish welcome. Off M1 going north, turn right at traffic lights at Zerox factory. Take N132
for Castlebellingham. If travelling south from Newry-Belfast turn left at same traffic lights.

| B&B | 5 | Ensuite | €28-€35 | Dinner | - |
|------|---|----------|---------|--------|---|
| B&B | - | Standard | | Partial Board | - |
| Single Rate | | | €40-€50 | Child reduction | 25% |

Dundalk 3km

**Open:** All Year

---

Dundalk 5km

**Orla O'Grady**
GREENGATES B&B
Dublin Road, Blackrock,
Dundalk, Co Louth

**Dundalk**

TEL: **042 9322047**
EMAIL: **orla@greengatesblackrock.com**
WEB: **www.greengatesblackrock.com**

Luxurious modern home 1km Blackrock seaside, 1km Fairways Hotel and 45 mins to Dublin
Airport. Golf, Fishing, Horseriding nearby. Private off street parking.

| B&B | 4 | Ensuite | €30-€35 | Dinner | - |
|------|---|----------|---------|--------|---|
| B&B | - | Standard | - | Partial Board | - |
| Single Rate | | | €40-€50 | Child reduction | 50% |

**Open:** 1st January-31st December

**Brenda Rogers**
BLACKROCK HOUSE
Main Street, Blackrock Village,
Blackrock, Dundalk, Co Louth

Tel: **042 9321829**
Email: **blackrockhsedundalk@eircom.net**
Web: **www.blackrockhouse.net**

Home by shore. Lounge has panoramic view Dundalk Bay. First class Bars and Restaurants. Dundalk Golf Club, Fairways Htl, Bird Sanctuary nearby. 50 mins Dublin Airport/Belfast.

| B&B | 6 | Ensuite | €30-€35 | Dinner | - |
|------|---|---------|---------|--------|---|
| B&B | - | Standard | - | Partial Board | - |
| Single Rate | | | €40-€50 | Child reduction | - |

Dundalk 5km    **Open:** 5th January-16th December

---

**Briege Thornton**
FAIRLAWNS
Dublin Road, Dundalk,
Co Louth

Tel: **042 9323813**   Fax: **042 9323813**
Email: **info@fairlawnsdundalk.com**
Web: **www.fairlawnsdundalk.com**

Modern home just off Dublin/Belfast motorway, beside Fairways Hotel & Conference Centre. Close to seaside. 50 mins Dublin/Belfast Airports. Large private car park.

| B&B | 4 | Ensuite | €27.50-€32 | Dinner | - |
|------|---|---------|-----------|--------|---|
| B&B | - | Standard | - | Partial Board | - |
| Single Rate | | | €40-€43.50 | Child reduction | 50% |

Dundalk 2km    **Open:** 1st January-31st December

---

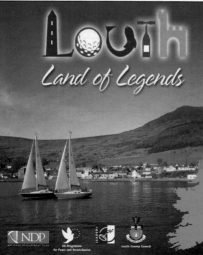

**Mrs Marian Witherow**
KRAKOW
190 Ard Easmuinn, Dundalk,
Co Louth

Tel: **042 9337535**
Email: **krakow@eircom.net**
Web: **www.krakowbandb.com**

Modern bungalow covenient to Railway Station and Derryhale Hotel. Walking distance to Town Centre. First turn right after Railway Stn. 2 directional signs- KRAKOW B&B.

| B&B | 5 | Ensuite | €30-€32.50 | Dinner | €19-€22 |
|------|---|---------|-----------|--------|---------|
| B&B | - | Standard | - | Partial Board | €294 |
| Single Rate | | | €42.50-€45 | Child reduction | |

In Dundalk    **Open:** All Year

---

Visit the stoneage passage tombs of Newgrange/Knowth, Christian sites of Kells and Hill of Tara. Navan - Capital town and Slane picturesque estate village. Trim Castle now open - Europe's largest Anglo Norman Castle. Craft shop and Visitors Centre. Activities: Golf, Equestrian, Fishing, Gardens, Fine Dining and Quaint Pubs.

### Ashbourne

**Mrs Kathleen Kelly**
BALTRASNA LODGE
**Baltrasna, Ashbourne, Co Meath**

Tel: **01 8350446**
Email: **baltrasnalodge@eircom.net**
Bus No: **103**

Luxury home on large grounds. Dublin City/Airport 20 mins. 3rd house R125 off N2. 1 single, 1 double, 2 family(2 double beds per room). Private guest entrance.

| | | | | | |
|---|---|---|---|---|---|
| B&B | 4 | Ensuite | €30-€33 | Dinner | - |
| B&B | - | Standard | - | Partial Board | - |
| Single Rate | | | - | Child reduction | 33.3% |

Ashbourne 1.5km

**Open:** 31st March-31st October

### Athboy

**Colin & Anne Finnegan**
WOODTOWN HOUSE
**Woodtown West, Athboy, Co Meath**

Tel: **046 9435022**  Fax: **046 9435022**
Email: **woodtown@iol.ie**
Web: **www.iol.ie/~woodtown**

Visit to remember oodles of atmosphere, inside and out. Convenient to Trim/Kells/Dublin /Airport. Travel 2 miles N51 Athboy/Delvin Road. Turn left follow signs.

| | | | | | |
|---|---|---|---|---|---|
| B&B | 2 | Ensuite | €32-€35 | Dinner | - |
| B&B | 2 | Standard | €28.50-€28.50 | Partial Board | - |
| Single Rate | | | €41-€43.50 | Child reduction | 25% |

Athboy 7km

**Open:** 1st April-30th September

### Bettystown

**Jean A.M. Strong**
WOODVIEW HOUSE
**Bettystown Cross, Bettystown, Co Meath**

Tel: **041 9827911**
Email: **bookings@woodview-house.com**
Web: **www.woodview-house.com**

Set in scenic woodland area. Near to beach, golf, tennis, equestrian centre. 25 mins Dublin Airport, 20 mins Newgrange & Boyne Valley region. Close to Baltray, Sea point, Laytown & Bettystown golf clubs.

| | | | | | |
|---|---|---|---|---|---|
| B&B | 4 | Ensuite | €35-€35 | Dinner | - |
| B&B | - | Standard | - | Partial Board | - |
| Single Rate | | | €40-€43.50 | Child reduction | 50% |

Drogheda 6km

**Open:** 6th January-18th December

### Julianstown

**Mrs Deirdre Cluskey**
KEENOGUE HOUSE
**Julianstown, Co Meath**

Tel: **041 9829118**  Fax: **041 9829980**
Email: **deirdrecluskey@hotmail.com**
Bus No: **100**

Modern bungalow on working farm just off the M1 motorway. Convenient to Newgrange and Boyne Valley. 15 mins Dublin Airport, 30 mins Dublin City.

| | | | | | |
|---|---|---|---|---|---|
| B&B | 4 | Ensuite | €32.50-€35 | Dinner | - |
| B&B | - | Standard | - | Partial Board | - |
| Single Rate | | | €45-€50 | Child reduction | - |

Drogheda 5km

**Open:** 2nd January-20th December

**Una Garvey**
SMITHSTOWN LODGE
Dublin Road, Drogheda,
Co Meath

TEL: **041 9829777/9829020**
EMAIL: **unagarvey@eircom.net**

Luxurious home 3 miles south of Drogheda on N1. 20 mins Dublin Airport, 5 mins to Beach and Golf, 20 mins Newgrange and Boyne Valley. Breakfast menu. Routard recommended.

| B&B | 6 | Ensuite | €30-€35 | Dinner | - |
|-----|---|---------|---------|--------|---|
| B&B | - | Standard | - | Partial Board | - |
| Single Rate | | | €40-€43.50 | Child reduction | - |

Drogheda 5km

**Open:** 1st January-31st December

---

**Mrs Maureen Kington**
BARDEN LODGE
Whitecross, Julianstown,
Co Meath

TEL: **041 9829369/9829910** FAX: **041 9829369**
EMAIL: **kington@eircom.net**
WEB: **www.dirl.com/meath/barden-lodge.htm**

A warm welcome awaits in this quiet country house off N1. Close to all amenities. 5 mins beach, 15 mins Dublin Airport, 25 mins Dublin City. Central for Newgrange, Boyne Valley & Hotels.

| B&B | 2 | Ensuite | €30-€35 | Dinner | - |
|-----|---|---------|---------|--------|---|
| B&B | 2 | Standard | €30-€35 | Partial Board | - |
| Single Rate | | | €40-€50 | Child reduction | - |

Drogheda 5km

**Open:** 1st January-31st December

---

**Tom & Marie Clarke**
BIRCHWOOD
Balrath, Kells, Co Meath

TEL: **046 9240688** FAX: **046 9240688**
EMAIL: **clarket@iol.ie**

Modern Country Farmhouse. Panoramic view, N52, Kells-Mullingar. Airport 1 hr. Good local restaurants. Convenient Newgrange, Loughcrew Cairns, Kells Cross, Golf Clubs.

| B&B | 4 | Ensuite | €32.50-€35 | Dinner | - |
|-----|---|---------|------------|--------|---|
| B&B | - | Standard | | Partial Board | - |
| Single Rate | | | €45-€45 | Child reduction | 25% |

Kells 1.5km

**Open:** 1st January-21st December

---

**Rosemary Murray**
WOODVIEW
Athboy Road, Kells, Co Meath

TEL: **046 9240200**
EMAIL: **rosemurray@eircom.net**

Quiet area, Kells Town. Tea/Coffee, TV in bedrooms. Walking distance Pubs, Restaurants. Golf, Fishing, Horseriding nearby. Convenient to Newgrange etc. 1hour Dublin Airport on R164.

| B&B | 2 | Ensuite | €32.50 | Dinner | - |
|-----|---|---------|--------|--------|---|
| B&B | 1 | Standard | €30 | Partial Board | - |
| Single Rate | | | €42.50-€43.50 | Child reduction | 50% |

In Kells

**Open:** 1st January-23rd December

---

**Peggy O'Reilly**
TEACH CUAILGNE
Carlanstown, Kells, Co Meath

TEL: **046 9246621** FAX: **046 9246046**
EMAIL: **pegreilly@eircom.net**
WEB: **www.teachcuailgne.com**

Luxury home. Bedrooms on ground floor. Carlanstown Village N52. 3km from Kells, Headfort Golf Club. Convenient to Airport, Newgrange, Lough Crew. Breakfast choice, Orthapaedic beds.

| B&B | 2 | Ensuite | €32.50-€35 | Dinner | - |
|-----|---|---------|------------|--------|---|
| B&B | 2 | Standard | €30-€30 | Partial Board | - |
| Single Rate | | | €40-€45 | Child reduction | 50% |

Kells 3km

**Open:** 1st January-20th December

**Pat & Pauline Boylan**
ATHLUMNEY MANOR
Athlumney, Duleek Road,
Navan, Co Meath

TEL: **046 9071388**
EMAIL: **stay@athlumneymanor.com**
WEB: **www.athlumneymanor.com**

Luxurious home overlooking Athlumney Castle. Rooms en-suite with TV, Coffee facilities, Phone, Hairdryer. 5 minutes walk to Town Centre. Secure parking. Half hourly bus to Dublin. On R153.

| B&B | 6 | Ensuite | €30-€33 | Dinner | - |
| B&B | - | Standard | | Partial Board | - |
| Single Rate | | | €40-€45 | Child reduction | 25% |

In Navan Town

Open: 1st January-31st December

---

**Teresa & Gerard Brennan**
VILLAGE B&B
Kilmessan Village, Navan,
Co Meath

TEL: **046 9025250**
EMAIL: **villagebnb@eircom.net**
WEB: **www.meathvillagebandb.com**

Scenic village off N3, beside Pubs/Hotel/Restaurant. Ideal base Hill of Tara (4km), Newgrange, Trim/Dunsany Castles, Boyne Drive. Dublin Airport/City 30 mins.

| B&B | 5 | Ensuite | €35-€38 | Dinner | - |
| B&B | - | Standard | - | Partial Board | - |
| Single Rate | | | €45-€50 | Child reduction | 50% |

Navan 10km

Open: All Year

---

**Nora Byrne**
ASH COTTAGE
Balerask Old, Navan, Co Meath

TEL: **046 9022115**
EMAIL: **ashcottage@hotmail.com**
WEB: **wwwashcottagenavan.com**

Family home, ensuite, tv, power showers, quiet road. Near town, good hotel, restaurant, pub, beside N3, and bus route Dublin, near fishing, golf, horse racing.

| B&B | 4 | Ensuite | €30-€35 | Dinner | - |
| B&B | - | Standard | - | Partial Board | - |
| Single Rate | | | €40-€43.50 | Child reduction | 25% |

Navan 2km

Open: 7th January-20th December

---

**Mrs Mary Callanan**
LIOS NA GREINE
Athlumney,
Duleek Road(R153), Navan,
Co Meath

TEL: **046 9028092**   FAX: **046 9028092**
EMAIL: **liosnagreine@eircom.net**

Luxury home 1km off N3 on Duleek/Ashbourne/Airport (R153). Rooms Ensuite with TV, Tea/Coffee facilities. 30 mins Dublin Airport. Nearby Newgrange, Trim Castle, Tara.

| B&B | 2 | Ensuite | €30-€33 | Dinner | - |
| B&B | 1 | Standard | €25.50-€32 | Partial Board | - |
| Single Rate | | | €40-€45 | Child reduction | 33.3% |

Navan 1km

Open: 1st January-23rd December

---

**Mrs Paula Casserly**
BOYNE DALE
Donaghmore, Slane Road,
Navan, Co Meath

TEL: **046 9028015**   FAX: **046 9028015**
EMAIL: **boynedale@iolfree.ie**

Exclusive B&B on Navan-Slane road. Groundfloor bedrooms. Extensive breakfast menu. Easy accessability to Dublin, with the advantages of being in the country.

| B&B | 3 | Ensuite | €27.50-€35 | Dinner | - |
| B&B | 2 | Standard | €25.50-€32 | Partial Board | - |
| Single Rate | | | €38-€45 | Child reduction | - |

Navan 2km

Open: 1st March-1st October

**Brian & Pauline Daly**
DALY'S B&B
Bloomfield House,
Duleek Road R153,
Mooretown, Navan, Co Meath

Tel: **046 9023219**

On Dublin's doorstep 30 mins. 2km off N3 on Kentown Duleek/Ashbourne/Airport (R153). Credit cards accepted. 15 mins Newgrange/Tara/Trim.

| B&B | 2 | Ensuite | €30-€33 | Dinner | - |
| B&B | 1 | Standard | €30-€30 | Partial Board | - |
| Single Rate | | | €40-€43.50 | Child reduction | 33.3% |

Navan 2km

Open: 20th January-20th December

---

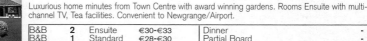

**Margaret Dunne**
DUNLAIR HOUSE
Old Road, Athlumney, Navan,
Co Meath

Tel: **046 9072551**
Email: **dunlair@hotmail.com**
Web: **homepage.eircom.net/~dunlair**

Luxury house, quiet location just off R153, 1 km Navan Town, Ensuite rooms with TV/Tea/Coffee facilities, convenient to Airport.

| B&B | 5 | Ensuite | €30-€33 | Dinner | - |
| B&B | - | Standard | | Partial Board | - |
| Single Rate | | | €40-€43.50 | Child reduction | 33.3% |

Navan 1km

Open: 6th January-20th December

---

**Mrs Nora Loughran**
MEADOW VIEW
Slane Road (N51), Navan,
Co Meath

Tel: **046 9023994/9073131**   Fax: **046 9073131**
Email: **meadowview@eircom.net**

Luxurious home minutes from Town Centre with award winning gardens. Rooms Ensuite with multi-channel TV, Tea facilities. Convenient to Newgrange/Airport.

| B&B | 2 | Ensuite | €30-€33 | Dinner | - |
| B&B | 1 | Standard | €28-€30 | Partial Board | - |
| Single Rate | | | €38-€45 | Child reduction | 33.3% |

n Navan

Open: 7th January-20th December

---

**Ann Marie Russell**
SYCAMORES
Dublin Road, Navan, Co Meath

Tel: **046 9023719**
Email: **annemarierussell@oceanfree.net**

Luxurious bungalow on N3 south of Navan. Private parking. Overlooking the river Boyne. Antique furnishings, Books, Paintings, Silver. Homecooking, good Restaurants. Beside hotel.

| B&B | 3 | Ensuite | €30-€33 | Dinner | - |
| B&B | - | Standard | - | Partial Board | - |
| Single Rate | | | €40-€43.50 | Child reduction | 25% |

n Navan

Open: 1st April-30th September

---

**Packie & Caroline McDonnell**
OCTAVE HOUSE
Somerville Road, Kentstown,
Navan, Co Meath

Tel: **041 9825592**  Fax: **041 9825592**
Email: **info@octavehouse.com**
Web: **www.octavehouse.com**

Luxurious, spacious home in tranquil village. Situated off N2 (R153). Newgrange 10km, Airport 25min. Pub closeby. Guest rooms on ground floor. Warm friendly welcome awaits you.

| B&B | 3 | Ensuite | €30-€34 | Dinner | - |
| B&B | - | Standard | | Partial Board | - |
| Single Rate | | | €40-€43.50 | Child reduction | 25% |

Navan/Slane 6km

Open: All Year

**Slane 2km**

### Mrs Lily Bagnall
**HILLVIEW HOUSE**
Gernonstown, Slane, Co Meath

TEL: **041 9824327**
EMAIL: **hillviewhouse@dol.ie**

Luxurious family home, situated on own grounds, beautiful landscaped gardens. Convenient to historic monuments and Towns. Tea and coffee facilities.

| | | | | | |
|---|---|---|---|---|---|
| B&B | 3 | Ensuite | €30-€35 | Dinner | - |
| B&B | - | Standard | | Partial Board | - |
| Single Rate | | | €40-€45 | Child reduction | - |

**Open:** 1st February-30th November

---

**Slane 4km**

### Roly Bond
**BONDIQUE HOUSE**
Cullen, Beauparc, Navan, Co Meath

TEL: **041 9824823**   FAX: **041 9824823**
EMAIL: **bondique@iol.ie**

Situated on N2, 4km south of Slane. Bru na Boinne/Newgrange 8km. Navan/Drogheda 10 mins. Dublin Airport/ City 30 mins.

| | | | | | |
|---|---|---|---|---|---|
| B&B | 2 | Ensuite | €30-€35 | Dinner | - |
| B&B | 2 | Standard | €28-€30 | Partial Board | - |
| Single Rate | | | €45-€50 | Child reduction | 25% |

**Open:** All Year

---

**Slane 6km**

### Mrs Ann Curtis
**WOODVIEW**
Flemington, Balrath, Co Meath

TEL: **041 9825694**
EMAIL: **info@meathtourism.ie**
WEB: **www.meathtourism.ie**

Luxury bungalow 6km south of Slane, 100 metres off N2 on R150. Convenient to Newgrange Visitor Centre. Dublin Airport 30 mins. Ferries 45 mins.

| | | | | | |
|---|---|---|---|---|---|
| B&B | 2 | Ensuite | €27.50-€31 | Dinner | - |
| B&B | 1 | Standard | €27.50-€31 | Partial Board | - |
| Single Rate | | | €40-€43.50 | Child reduction | 25% |

**Open:** 1st January-20th December

---

**In Slane Village**

### Mrs Mary Hevey
**BOYNE VIEW**
Slane, Co Meath

TEL: **041 9824121**
EMAIL: **info@meathtourism.ie**
WEB: **www.meathtourism.ie**

Georgian period house overlooking scenic Boyne Valley, close to all historical monuments. N2 Dublin Road Slane Village. Dublin Airport 45 minutes.

| | | | | | |
|---|---|---|---|---|---|
| B&B | 3 | Ensuite | €30-€35 | Dinner | - |
| B&B | - | Standard | - | Partial Board | - |
| Single Rate | | | €40-€45 | Child reduction | - |

**Open:** 10th January-22nd December

---

**Slane 2km**

### Olive Owens
**SAN GIOVANNI HOUSE**
Dublin Road, Slane, Co Meath

TEL: **041 9824147**
EMAIL: **newgrangebandb@ireland.com**

Large modern house on N2 in picturesque Boyne Valley, breathtaking view from house. 7km from Newgrange. 30 mins from Dublin Airport.

| | | | | | |
|---|---|---|---|---|---|
| B&B | 3 | Ensuite | €27.50-€31 | Dinner | - |
| B&B | - | Standard | €40-€43.50 | Partial Board | - |
| Single Rate | | | - | Child reduction | 33.3% |

**Open:** All Year Except Christmas

**Slane**

**Mrs Marie Warren**
CASTLE VIEW HOUSE
Slane, Co Meath

Tᴇʟ: **041 9824510**
Eᴍᴀɪʟ: **castleview@oceanfree.net**
Wᴇʙ: **www.meathtourism.ie**

Modern bungalow on N51 overlooking Slane Castle Demesne. Close to historical sites, friendly atmosphere. Ideal touring base. Dublin Airport 45 mins.

| B&B | 4 | Ensuite | €30-€35 | Dinner | - |
|---|---|---|---|---|---|
| B&B | - | Standard | | Partial Board | - |
| Single Rate | | | €40-€45 | Child reduction | - |

Slane Village

**Open:** 10th January-21st December

**Tara**

**Ms Joan Maguire**
SEAMROG
Hill of Tara, Tara, Co Meath

Tᴇʟ: **046 25296**

A warm friendly B&B located on the Hill of Tara with beautiful views, experience the awe of Tara and then relax with us in our home. 10km from Navan off the N3.

| B&B | 2 | Ensuite | €30-€31 | Dinner | - |
|---|---|---|---|---|---|
| B&B | 1 | Standard | €27-€28.50 | Partial Board | - |
| Single Rate | | | €38-€43.50 | Child reduction | 50% |

avan 10km

**Open:** 1st May-31st October

**Trim**

**Marie Keane**
TIGH CATHAIN
Longwood Road, Trim,
Co Meath

Tᴇʟ: **046 9431996** Fᴀx: **046 9431996**
Eᴍᴀɪʟ: **mariekeane@esatclear.ie**
Wᴇʙ: **www.tighcathaintrim.com**

Tudor style country house on 1 acre mature gardens on R160. Large luxury ensuite rooms with Tea/Coffee, TV, Private park, Trim Castle 1km, Airport 40 mins.

| B&B | 3 | Ensuite | €32-€34 | Dinner | - |
|---|---|---|---|---|---|
| B&B | - | Standard | | Partial Board | - |
| Single Rate | | | €44-€46 | Child reduction | 33.3% |

rim 1km

**Open:** 7th January-20th December

**Trim**

**Thomas O'Loughlin**
WHITE LODGE B&B
Lackanash,
Navan Road Junction, Trim,
Co Meath

Tᴇʟ: **046 9436549** Fᴀx: **046 9436549**
Eᴍᴀɪʟ: **whitelodgetrim@eircom.net**
Wᴇʙ: **www.whitelodgetrim.com**

Town house, large ground floor bedrooms with TV/Tea in rooms. Restaurants closeby. 700m Town Centre/Trim Castle. Airport 40 mins. Frommer/Dumont recommended.

| B&B | 5 | Ensuite | €30-€32 | Dinner | - |
|---|---|---|---|---|---|
| B&B | 1 | Standard | €28-€30 | Partial Board | - |
| Single Rate | | | €38-€45 | Child reduction | 25% |

n Trim

**Open:** 1st February-30th November

**Trim**

**Anne O'Regan**
CRANNMOR HOUSE
Dunderry Rd, Trim, Co Meath

Tᴇʟ: **046 9431635** Fᴀx: **046 9438087**
Eᴍᴀɪʟ: **cranmor@eircom.net**
Wᴇʙ: **www.crannmor.com**

Georgian country house with gardens on the outskirts of Trim "Heritage" town. Convenient to Golf, Fishing and Boyne Valley. 35 mins Airport.

| B&B | 4 | Ensuite | €32-€34 | Dinner | - |
|---|---|---|---|---|---|
| B&B | - | Standard | | Partial Board | - |
| Single Rate | | | €44-€46 | Child reduction | 25% |

rim 1.5km

**Open:** 20th January-20th December

A county of Ancient Kingdoms, Rolling Mountains, The mighty river Shannon and the most precious Irish Jewel "Clonmacnoise". Tour Castles, visit Peatlands, cruise the river Shannon and Grand canal. Play Golf and Fish and always feel welcome in the "Faithful County".

### Banagher

**Grainne Kirwan**
THE HARBOUR MASTERS HOUSE
Shannon Harbour, Banagher, Co Offaly

TEL: **0509 51532**
EMAIL: **gkirwan@iol.ie**
WEB: **www.goireland.com**

Historic Georgian House on canal side, no passing traffic. All rooms ensuite and views of boats old and new. Traditional pubs nearby. Follow signs in Banagher or at Clononey Castle. Finalist in Rural Tourism Awards.

| B&B | 5 | Ensuite | €30-€35 | Dinner | - |
| B&B | - | Standard | - | Partial Board | - |
| Single Rate | | | €42-€45 | Child reduction | 25% |

Banagher 3km

**Open:** 1st January-22nd December

### Cloghan

**Carmel Finneran**
THE GABLES B&B
Castle Street, Cloghan, Co Offaly

TEL: **0906-457355**
EMAIL: **cfinneran@eircom.net**

House in Village of Cloghan, 4 bedroom's ensuite. Bog tour 16km, Clonmacnoise 18km, Slieve Bloom mountains 18km. Boora Parklands 10km. Birr Castle 16km. N62 R357.

| B&B | 4 | Ensuite | €27.50-€31 | Dinner | - |
| B&B | - | Standard | - | Partial Board | - |
| Single Rate | | | €40-€43.50 | Child reduction | 25% |

Birr 16km

**Open:** 6th January-20th December

### Clonmacnoise

**Bernie Kenny**
MEADOW VIEW B&B
Clonmacnoise, Shannonbridge, Athlone, Co Offaly

TEL: **090 9674257**
EMAIL: **meadowviewaccom@eircom.net**

Purpose built family run B&B in a quiet setting. Located 1km from Clonmacnoise on the river Shannon. Spacious rooms. Friendly atmosphere. Lets Go Ireland and Lonely Planet recommended.

| B&B | 2 | Ensuite | €27.50-€31 | Dinner | - |
| B&B | 1 | Standard | €25.50-€28.50 | Partial Board | - |
| Single Rate | | | €38-€43.50 | Child reduction | 33.3% |

Shannonbridge 6km

**Open:** 1st January-31st December

### Edenderry

**Catherine & Dermot Byrne**
AUBURN LODGE
Colonel Perry Street, Edenderry, Co Offaly

TEL: **046 9731319**
EMAIL: **auburnlodge@eircom.net**

Townhouse Tea/Coffee, TV bedrooms. Gardens, Car park. Off N4 en route to the West. Airport, Ferryports 60 mins. Great Fishing, Golf. Central base for touring.

| B&B | 5 | Ensuite | €27.50-€31 | Dinner | €19 |
| B&B | - | Standard | - | Partial Board | - |
| Single Rate | | | - | Child reduction | 50% |

Town

**Open:** 1st January-31st December

**In Kinnitty**

### Christina Byrne
ARDMORE HOUSE
The Walk, Kinnitty, Co Offaly

**Kinnitty**

TEL: **0509 37009**
EMAIL: **ardmorehouse@eircom.net**
WEB: **www.kinnitty.net**

Victorian House, Slieve Bloom Mountains. 2 hours Airport, Ferryports. Brass beds, turf fire, home baking. Walking, Equestrian, Irish music, Birr Castle Gardens/Telescope. Clonmacnoise.

| B&B | 4 | Ensuite | €32-€38 | Dinner | - |
| B&B | 1 | Standard | €30-€35 | Partial Board | - |
| Single Rate | | | €40-€45 | Child reduction | 25% |

**Open:** All Year

---

**Portarlington 4km**

### Liam & Marguerite Kirwan
TREASCON LODGE
Portarlington, Co Offaly

**Portarlington**

TEL: **0502 43183**   FAX: **0502 43183**
EMAIL: **treasconlodge@eircom.net**

Country home on two acres. Tennis Court, Playground in quiet setting. Two rooms ensuite. Golf 5 mins. Wheelchair accessible room.

| B&B | 2 | Ensuite | €33-€33 | Dinner | - |
| B&B | 1 | Standard | €33-€33 | Partial Board | - |
| Single Rate | | | €45-€45 | Child reduction | 33.3% |

**Open:** 1st February-30th November

---

**Ballinasloe 10km**

### Mrs Patricia Corbett
RACHRA HOUSE (SHANNON VIEW)
Shannonbridge, via Athlone, Co Offaly

**Shannonbridge**

TEL: **090 9674249**
EMAIL: **rachrahouse@eircom.net**
WEB: **www.rachrahouse.shannonbridge.net**

Modern house in picturesque village overlooking rivers Shannon and Suck. Clonmacnoise 6km. Bog Railtours 3km. Fishing, Golf, Horse-Riding, Tennis.

| B&B | 3 | Ensuite | €27.50-€31 | Dinner | - |
| B&B | 1 | Standard | €25.50-€28.50 | Partial Board | - |
| Single Rate | | | €38-€43.50 | Child reduction | - |

**Open:** 1st May-31st October

---

**Tullamore 5km**

### Larry & Agnes Mealiffe
BALLINAMONA FARM
Tullamore, Co Offaly

**Tullamore**

TEL: **0506 51162**
EMAIL: **ballinamonafarm@hotmail.com**

House in peaceful rural countryside, 5km north of Tullamore off N52. Have a cup of tea on arrival and we will tell you about local attractions.

| B&B | 4 | Ensuite | €27.50-€31 | Dinner | - |
| B&B | - | Standard | | Partial Board | - |
| Single Rate | | | €40-€43.50 | Child reduction | 25% |

**Open:** 1st March-31st October

---

**Tullamore 4km**

### Mrs Anne O'Brien
GORMAGH
Durrow, Tullamore, Co Offaly

**Tullamore**

TEL: **0506 51468**
EMAIL: **gormagh@eircom.net**

Secluded Home, 5 mins drive North of Tullamore off N52 after sign for Silver River. Use of natural materials throughout the house is in harmony with wildflower gardens.

| B&B | 4 | Ensuite | €31-€31 | Dinner | - |
| B&B | 1 | Standard | - | Partial Board | - |
| Single Rate | | | €43.50-€43.50 | Child reduction | - |

**Open:** 1st February-15th December

A warm welcome awaits you in Westmeath, Ireland's undiscovered lakelands. Situated in the heart of Ireland with magnificent lakes, an anglers paradise, also Golfing, Horse-riding and Water-sports. Travel the Belvedere Fore, or Lough Ree Trails or explore the heritage sites/visitor attractions.

**Pat & Teresa Byrne**
BENOWN HOUSE
Glasson, Athlone,
Co Westmeath

**Athlone**
TEL: **090 6485406**   FAX: **090 6485776**
EMAIL: **stay@glasson.com**
WEB: **www.glasson.com**

Relaxing residence in picturesque village of Glasson adjacent to award winning Restaurants and Pubs. Excellent choice breakfast in spacious dining room. Ideal for touring.

| B&B | 5 | Ensuite | €30-€37 | Dinner | - |
| B&B | 1 | Standard | €28-€33 | Partial Board | - |
| Single Rate | | | €40-€52 | Child reduction | 25% |

Athlone 8km

**Open:** 1st February-30th November

---

**Eileen Cahill**
CORRACLOR LODGE
Roscommon Rd, Athlone,
Co Westmeath

**Athlone**
TEL: **090 6493307**
EMAIL: **eileenkellycahill@eircom.net**

Bungalow quiet Rd 3km Athlone, 5 mins off N6 Dublin-Galway and 2 mins off N61 Roscommon/Sligo Rd. 5 mins from Hodson Bay, private parking, golf course, fishing and horse riding nearby.

| B&B | 3 | Ensuite | €30-€32 | Dinner | - |
| B&B | - | Standard | - | Partial Board | - |
| Single Rate | | | €42.50-€43.50 | Child reduction | - |

Athlone 5km

**Open:** 1st February-20th December

---

**Sean & Carmel Corbett**
RIVERVIEW HOUSE
Summerhill, Galway Road (N6),
Athlone, Co Westmeath

**Athlone**
TEL: **090 6494532**   FAX: **090 6494596**
EMAIL: **riverviewhouse@hotmail.com**
WEB: **www.riverviewhousebandb.com**

Two storey red brick on N6 Galway Road. Five minutes drive from town centre. Private car park. Credit cards accepted. AA ◆◆◆◆.

| B&B | 4 | Ensuite | €32 | Dinner | - |
| B&B | - | Standard | - | Partial Board | - |
| Single Rate | | | €45 | Child reduction | 25% |

Athlone 2km

**Open:** 1st March-18th December

---

**Jim & Nancy Denby**
SHELMALIER HOUSE
Cartrontroy, Athlone,
Co Westmeath

**Athlone**
TEL: **090 6472245**   FAX: **090 6473190**
EMAIL: **shelmalier@eircom.net**
WEB: **www.shelmalierhouse.com**

Beautiful house and gardens in quiet location. Signposted off R446 and N55. All in room services. AA ◆◆◆◆. Award winning breakfast menu. Private Parking.

| B&B | 7 | Ensuite | €30-€32 | Dinner | - |
| B&B | - | Standard | - | Partial Board | - |
| Single Rate | | | €42-€45 | Child reduction | 33.3% |

Athlone 2km

**Open:** 1st February-20th December

### Mrs Maura Duggan
VILLA ST JOHN
Roscommon Road, Athlone,
Co Westmeath

TEL: **090 6492490**  FAX: **090 6492490**
EMAIL: **villastjohn@eircom.net**
WEB: **www.athlone.ie/villastjohn**

Ideally situated on N61 off N6. Convenient to Bars, Restaurants, Lough Ree, Clonmacnoise, 2 Golf courses. TV, Coffee, Hairdryers in bedrooms. Private secure parking at rear of house.

| B&B | 5 | Ensuite | €32 | Dinner | - |
| B&B | 3 | Standard | €30 | Partial Board | - |
| Single Rate | | | €42-€45 | Child reduction | **33.3%** |

Athlone 2km

**Open:** 6th January-20th December

---

### Brian & Mary Fagg
CORNAMAGH HOUSE & GARDENS
Cornamagh, Athlone,
Co Westmeath

TEL: **09064 74171**
EMAIL: **fagg@indigo.ie**

Enjoy the tranquility of our country home and garden. We are commended for our breakfast and comfortable beds. Near Athlone regional sports centre. N55.

| B&B | 5 | Ensuite | €28-€32 | Dinner | - |
| B&B | - | Standard | - | Partial Board | - |
| Single Rate | | | €40-€43.50 | Child reduction | **25%** |

Athlone 2km

**Open:** 15th March-31st October

---

### Mrs Catherine Fox
DE PORRES
Cornamaddy, Ballykeeran,
Athlone, Co Westmeath

TEL: **090  6475759**
EMAIL: **deporres@iol.ie**

Signposted off Cavan Rd N55. Quiet location, private carpark, beautiful gardens. Clonmacnoise, Restaurants, Lakes, Golf nearby. TV, Tea/Coffee rooms. Customer Service Award winner.

| B&B | 4 | Ensuite | €27.50-€31 | Dinner | - |
| B&B | - | Standard | - | Partial Board | - |
| Single Rate | | | €40-€43.50 | Child reduction | **25%** |

Athlone 2km

**Open:** 1st April-30th September

---

### Paul & Deirdre Foxe
INN BAY B&B
Annagh, The Pigeons, Athlone,
Co Westmeath

TEL: **090 6485284**  FAX: **090 6485284**
EMAIL: **foxed@eircom.net**

Superb location on Lough Ree shore. Farm, fishing, boat hire, tranquility. Best home cooking. Ideal stopover between east and west. Stunning views.

| B&B | 3 | Ensuite | €28-€31 | Dinner | €20-€20 |
| B&B | 1 | Standard | €25.50-€28.50 | Partial Board | - |
| Single Rate | | | €38-€43.50 | Child reduction | **50%** |

Athlone

**Open:** 1st January-23rd December

---

### Breda Grennan
FOUR SEASONS
Annagh, Ballykeeran, Athlone,
Co Westmeath

TEL: **090 6474470**
EMAIL: **grennanfourseasons@eircom.net**
WEB: **www.athlone.ie/fourseasonsb&b**

Sample the hospitality & welcome of Four Seasons in the heart of Ireland. Spacious family run B&B. First Class home within 10 minutes drive of Athlone. Tea/Coffee on arrival.

| B&B | 4 | Ensuite | €30-€32 | Dinner | - |
| B&B | - | Standard | - | Partial Board | - |
| Single Rate | | | €42-€45 | Child reduction | **50%** |

Athlone 7km

**Open:** 6th January-19th December

**Mrs Mary Linnane**
BURREN LODGE
Creggan, Dublin Road, Athlone,
Co Westmeath

TEL: **090 6475157**
EMAIL: **burrenlodge@iolfree.ie**
WEB: **www.iolfree.ie/~burrenlodge**

Close to roundabout at Texaco Filling Station/Centra. Adjacent Creggan Court Hotel on N6. 15 mins to Clonmacnoise. Regular daily bus service to Dublin from door. TV, Tea/Coffee.

| | | | | | |
|---|---|---|---|---|---|
| B&B | 3 | Ensuite | €32-€32 | Dinner | - |
| B&B | 1 | Standard | €30-€30 | Partial Board | - |
| Single Rate | | | €42-€45 | Child reduction | 33.3% |

Athlone 2km

**Open:** 1st January-31st December

---

**Ann Meade**
HARBOUR HOUSE
Ballykeeran, Athlone,
Co Westmeath

TEL: **090 6485063**　FAX: **090 6485933**
EMAIL: **ameade@indigo.ie**
WEB: **www.harbourhouse.ie**

Luxurious quiet home on Lough Ree, 1.5km off N55 in Ballykeeran, Fishing, Golf, Restaurants locally. Tea/Coffee/TV, hairdryer facilities.

| | | | | | |
|---|---|---|---|---|---|
| B&B | 6 | Ensuite | €28.50-€31 | Dinner | - |
| B&B | - | Standard | - | Partial Board | - |
| Single Rate | | | €40-€43.50 | Child reduction | 25% |

Athlone 5km

**Open:** 1st March-31st October

---

**Mrs Audrey O'Brien**
BOGGANFIN HOUSE
Roscommon Road, Athlone,
Co Westmeath

TEL: **090 6494255**　FAX: **090 6494255**
EMAIL: **bogganfinhouse@eircom.net**

Tudor style res, off N6, on N61, near roundabout opposite Renault Garage. Guide to Ireland recom, Customer Service Award. Adjacent to Town Lakes, Leisure Centre, Pubs.

| | | | | | |
|---|---|---|---|---|---|
| B&B | 5 | Ensuite | €28.50-€32 | Dinner | - |
| B&B | 1 | Standard | €27-€30 | Partial Board | - |
| Single Rate | | | €40-€45 | Child reduction | 25% |

Athlone 1.5km

**Open:** 20th January-20th December

---

**Carmel & Oliver O'Neill**
A GLASSON STONE LODGE
Glasson, Athlone,
Co Westmeath

TEL: **090 6485004**
EMAIL: **glassonstonelodge@eircom.net**
WEB: **www.glassonstonelodge.com**

Beautiful house and garden in quaint village in centre of Ireland, on N55. Good breakfast. TV, Tea/Coffee in room's. Near Clonmacnoise. Excellent Restaurants, Pubs 2 min walk. Golf, Fishing.

| | | | | | |
|---|---|---|---|---|---|
| B&B | 6 | Ensuite | €30-€35 | Dinner | - |
| B&B | - | Standard | - | Partial Board | - |
| Single Rate | | | €43.50-€45.50 | Child reduction | - |

Athlone 4km

**Open:** 1st March-30th November

---

**Des & Mary O'Neill**
AVONREE HOUSE
Coosan, Athlone,
Co Westmeath

TEL: **090 6475485**
EMAIL: **avonreehouse@eircom.net**

Close N6 (Exit Coosan No.3 Junction) and N55. Italian spoken. Two Golf Clubs-10mins. Non-smoking. Clonmacnoise 20 mins, Dublin 1hr 50 mins. Award winning garden.

| | | | | | |
|---|---|---|---|---|---|
| B&B | 5 | Ensuite | €30-€35 | Dinner | - |
| B&B | - | Standard | - | Partial Board | - |
| Single Rate | | | €40-€43.50 | Child reduction | - |

Athlone 1km

**Open:** 1st January-30th November

In Village

**Jimmy & Eileen Whelehan**
THE VILLAGE B&B
Killucan, Co Westmeath

TEL: **044 74760**   FAX: **044 74973**
EMAIL: **thevillageinn@oceanfree.net**

Follow B&B sign on route N4 North West of Kinnegad. Royal Canal Fishing 2 km. 50 minutes from Dublin Airport and Ferries.

| B&B | 3 | Ensuite | €32-€34 | Dinner | - |
|-----|---|---------|---------|--------|---|
| B&B | - | Standard | - | Partial Board | - |
| Single Rate | | | €45-€45 | Child reduction | - |

**Open:** All Year

---

In Moate

**Mrs May Glynn**
RAILWAY LODGE
Cartronkeel, Ballymore Rd,
Moate, Co Westmeath

TEL: **0902 81596**
EMAIL: **james.glynn@emea.tycohealthcare.com**

Bungalow situated in peaceful area with landscaped Gardens, private car parking, home cooking, rooms ensuite. Knowledge of German and French.

| B&B | 2 | Ensuite | €28-€31 | Dinner | - |
|-----|---|---------|---------|--------|---|
| B&B | 1 | Standard | €26-€28.50 | Partial Board | - |
| Single Rate | | | €38-€43.50 | Child reduction | 25% |

**Open:** 1st January-20th December

---

Moate 2km

**Mrs Ethna Kelly**
COOLEEN COUNTRY HOME
Ballymore Rd, Moate,
Co Westmeath

TEL: **09064 81044**

Picturesque bungalow set in private gardens. 2km off N6. Close to Golf, Pitch and Putt, Clonmacnoise, Heritage Centre. Home cooking, Turf fires.

| B&B | 3 | Ensuite | €27.50-€31 | Dinner | - |
|-----|---|---------|------------|--------|---|
| B&B | - | Standard | - | Partial Board | - |
| Single Rate | | | - | Child reduction | 50% |

**Open:** 15th January-15th December

---

**Mrs Mary Barry**
WOODSIDE
Dublin Road, Mullingar,
Co Westmeath

TEL: **044 41636**
EMAIL: **woodside8@eircom.net**

Attractive family home set in peaceful location 10 mins walking distance from town centre, all rooms ensuite. Residents lounge, near Mullingar Park Hotel.

| B&B | 5 | Ensuite | €32.50-€35 | Dinner | - |
|-----|---|---------|------------|--------|---|
| B&B | - | Standard | - | Partial Board | - |
| Single Rate | | | €40-€45 | Child reduction | 33.3% |

Mullingar 0.5km

**Open:** 1st January-20th December

---

Mullingar 1km

**Catherine Bennet**
TURNPIKE LODGE
Dublin Road, Petits Wood,
Mullingar, Co Westmeath

TEL: **044 44913**   FAX: **044 44913**
EMAIL: **turnpikelodge@iolfree.ie**
WEB: **www.iolfree.ie/~turnpikelodge**

Friendly family home. Two large family rooms, Residents lounge, relaxing atmosphere. 2 minutes drive off N4. Mullingar Park Hotel just 2 mins walk.

| B&B | 5 | Ensuite | €33-€35 | Dinner | - |
|-----|---|---------|---------|--------|---|
| B&B | - | Standard | - | Partial Board | - |
| Single Rate | | | €40-€50 | Child reduction | - |

**Open:** 1st January-31st December

**Mullingar 3km**

**Sean & Dympna Casey**
HILLTOP
**Delvin Road (N52 off N4),
Rathconnell, Mullingar,
Co Westmeath**

**Mullingar**

TEL: **044 48958**  FAX: **044 48958**
EMAIL: **hilltopcountryhouse@eircom.net**
WEB: **www.hilltopcountryhouse.com**

Unique modern Country home, Award winning garden/breakfast. One hour from Dublin. AA selected ◆◆◆◆, Recommended Frommer, Dillard/Cousin, Sullivan guides.

| B&B | 4 | Ensuite | €34-€34 | Dinner | - |
|------|---|----------|---------|--------|---|
| B&B | - | Standard | | Partial Board | - |
| Single Rate | | | €42-€45 | Child reduction | - |

**Open:** 1st March-30th October

---

**Mullingar 8km**

**Rita Fahey**
BALLINAFID LAKE HOUSE
**Ballinafid, Longford Road,
Mullingar, Co Westmeath**

**Mullingar**

TEL: **044 71162**
EMAIL: **rfahey@ireland.com**

Spacious bungalow on the N4 Longford Rd. 8km from Mullingar beside the Covert Pub opposite Ballinafid Lake. Guest sitting room. Laundry facilities, Gardens.

| B&B | 4 | Ensuite | €30-€31 | Dinner | - |
|------|---|----------|---------|--------|---|
| B&B | - | Standard | - | Partial Board | - |
| Single Rate | | | €40-€43.50 | Child reduction | 33.3% |

**Open:** 1st March-31st October

---

**Castletown Geogeghan 3km**

**Josephine Garvey**
GREENHILLS
**Castletown Geogeghan,
Mullingar, Co Westmeath**

**Mullingar**

TEL: **044 26353**  FAX: **044 26353**
EMAIL: **josgarvey@eircom.net**

Old restored spacious country house in the heart of the Lake District. Very warm welcome assured. Pets welcome. Tea/Coffee on arrival.

| B&B | 3 | Ensuite | €35-€35 | Dinner | €19-€19 |
|------|---|----------|---------|--------|---------|
| B&B | - | Standard | - | Partial Board | - |
| Single Rate | | | €43.50-€43.50 | Child reduction | 25% |

**Open:** All Year Except Christmas

---

**Larry & Barbara Ginnell**
MARLINSTOWN COURT
**Old Dublin Road, Mullingar,
Co Westmeath**

**Mullingar**

TEL: **044 40053**  FAX: **044 40057**
EMAIL: **marlinstownct@eircom.net**
WEB: **www.marlinstowncourt.com**

Situated in a beautiful setting on own grounds. 1 mile to town centre. All rooms en suite. Residents lounge. Secluded Parking. 2 mins off N4, 1 hour from Dublin. Beside Mullingar Park Hotel.

| B&B | 5 | Ensuite | €30-€35 | Dinner | - |
|------|---|----------|---------|--------|---|
| B&B | - | Standard | | Partial Board | - |
| Single Rate | | | €40-€50 | Child reduction | 33.3% |

**Mullingar 1.5km**

**Open:** 1st January-23rd December

---

**Ms Margaret Keogh**
RIVER VIEW
**Ballinalack, Cappagh,
Mullingar, Co Westmeath**

**Mullingar**

TEL: **044 71950**

Spacious modern house, landscaped gardens, ample parking on N4 Dublin Sligo Road. Rural setting overlooking river Inny 5km from lakes.

| B&B | 2 | Ensuite | €30-€35 | Dinner | - |
|------|---|----------|---------|--------|---|
| B&B | 1 | Standard | €25.50-€30 | Partial Board | - |
| Single Rate | | | €38-€45 | Child reduction | 25% |

**Mullingar 15km**

**Open:** 1st February-30th November

**Mrs May McCarthy**
MOORLAND
Marlinstown,
Curraghmore (Off N4),
Mullingar, Co Westmeath

TEL: **044 40905**
WEB: **www.moorlandhouse.com**

House off main Dublin Road. Six rooms with private facilities. Turf Fires, Electric Blankets. Warm welcome.

| B&B | 6 | Ensuite | €33 | Dinner | - |
|-----|---|---------|-----|--------|---|
| B&B | - | Standard | | Partial Board | - |
| Single Rate | | | €43.50 | Child reduction | 50% |

Mullingar 2.5km

**Open:** 1st January-22nd December

**Celine O'Brien**
MAPLES B&B
Petitswood Manor, Mullingar,
Co Westmeath

TEL: **044 33504**

Town house 5 bedroom 1000 metres from Mullingar town centre situated on old Dublin Road located in heart of lake district.

| B&B | 2 | Ensuite | €32-€34 | Dinner | - |
|-----|---|---------|---------|--------|---|
| B&B | 2 | Standard | - | Partial Board | - |
| Single Rate | | | €38-€41 | Child reduction | 50% |

Mullingar

**Open:** 1st January-15th December

Wicklow, the "Garden of Ireland", bounded on the east by sandy beaches and the west by lakes and mountains. Monastic site at Glendalough. Excellent facilities for Golf, Angling, Watersports and Walking. Convenient Dublin/Rosslare with easy access along N11 and N81.

---

In Arklow

**Deirdre Bishop-Power**
**VALENTIA**
Coolgreany Rd, Arklow,
Co Wicklow

**Arklow**

TEL: **0402 39200**   FAX: **0402 39200**
EMAIL: **valentiahouse@esatclear.ie**
WEB: **www.geocities.com/valentiahouse**

Comfortable family home. Lovely conservatory dining room. Ideal touring base for Garden of Ireland. Good beaches. 1hr to Dublin and Wexford. Easy walk to Town.

| B&B | 4 | Ensuite | €30-€45 | Dinner | - |
|-----|---|----------|---------|--------|---|
| B&B | | Standard | - | Partial Board | - |
| Single Rate | | | €45-€55 | Child reduction | 25% |

**Open:** All Year

---

Arklow

**Ms Frances Doyle**
**RIVER VIEW**
7 Riverview Heights, Vale Road,
Arklow, Co Wicklow

**Arklow**

TEL: **0402 32601**
EMAIL: **riverviewbandb@eircom.net**

Modern family home with scenic views and a warm welcome. Ideal base for touring Co. Wicklow. Private parking. 1 hour Dublin, close to all local amenities.

| B&B | 3 | Ensuite | €30-€35 | Dinner | - |
|-----|---|----------|---------|--------|---|
| B&B | - | Standard | - | Partial Board | - |
| Single Rate | | | €40-€45 | Child reduction | 50% |

**Open:** 1st February-1st December

---

Arklow 1km

**Ms Catherine Dunne**
**DOBAN**
Carrig Mor, Dublin Rd, Arklow,
Co Wicklow

**Arklow**

TEL: **0402 32580**
EMAIL: **doban@tinet.ie**
WEB: **www.arklow.ie/members/doban.asp**

Purpose built spacious home in quiet cul-de-sac. Award winning garden. Private parking. Convenient to all local amenities. Ideal tourist base.

| B&B | 2 | Ensuite | €30-€31 | Dinner | - |
|-----|---|----------|---------|--------|---|
| B&B | 1 | Standard | €30-€31 | Partial Board | - |
| Single Rate | | | €45-€45 | Child reduction | 50% |

**Open:** 2nd January-30th November

---

Arklow 1.5km

**Mrs Kathleen Hendley**
**SWANLAKE**
Sea Road, Arklow, Co Wicklow

**Arklow**

TEL: **0402 32377**
EMAIL: **swanlakearklow@eircom.net**
WEB: **homepage.eircom.net/~swanlakearklow**

Modern bungalow on coast road close to Arklow Bay Hotel and caravan park. Overlooking sea and beach. Close to Town Centre.

| B&B | 3 | Ensuite | €30-€35 | Dinner | - |
|-----|---|----------|---------|--------|---|
| B&B | - | Standard | - | Partial Board | - |
| Single Rate | | | €40-€43.50 | Child reduction | 25% |

**Open:** 1st April-30th October

**Mrs Rita Kelly**
FAIRY LAWN
**Wexford Road, Arklow,
Co Wicklow**

Tᴇʟ: **0402 32790**

1km from Arklow on the Wexford/Gorey Road. Tea/Coffee facilities in bedrooms. Recommended in the 300 Best B&B Guide. Credit Cards accepted.

| B&B | 3 | Ensuite | €30-€32.50 | Dinner | - |
|-----|---|---------|-----------|--------|---|
| B&B | 1 | Standard | €28-€30 | Partial Board | - |
| Single Rate | | | €40-€50 | Child reduction | 50% |

Arklow 1km

**Open:** 1st January-15th December

---

**Mrs Geraldine Nicholson**
PINEBROOK B&B
**5 Ticknock Close, Briggs Lane,
Arklow, Co Wicklow**

Tᴇʟ: **0402 31527**   Fᴀx: **0402 31527**
Eᴍᴀɪʟ: **pinebrook@eircom.net**
Wᴇʙ: **www.pinebrook.net**

Modern detached townhouse within walking distance of Town Centre. Very quiet area with secure parking. Close to all amenities including beach and swimming pool.

| B&B | 4 | Ensuite | €30-€32.50 | Dinner | - |
|-----|---|---------|-----------|--------|---|
| B&B | - | Standard | - | Partial Board | - |
| Single Rate | | | €45-€50 | Child reduction | 33.3% |

In Arklow

**Open:** All Year

---

**Maeve O'Connor**
THE GABLES
**Ballygriffin, Arklow, Co Wicklow**

Tᴇʟ: **0402 33402**
Eᴍᴀɪʟ: **maeve.oconnor@oceanfree.net**
Wᴇʙ: **www.gables-arklow.com**

Spacious country home. Landscaped gardens, Tea facilites. Electric blankets. Breakfast menu. Tennis court. Dublin/Rosslare one hour. Signposted roundabout Arklow.

| B&B | 4 | Ensuite | €30-€32.50 | Dinner | - |
|-----|---|---------|-----------|--------|---|
| B&B | - | Standard | - | Partial Board | - |
| Single Rate | | | €40-€45 | Child reduction | 50% |

Arklow 3km

**Open:** 1st March-1st November

---

**Mrs Nancy Joynt**
CARRIG LODGE
**Ballylusk, Ashford, Co Wicklow**

Tᴇʟ: **0404 40278**   Fᴀx: **0404 40278**
Eᴍᴀɪʟ: **carriglodge@oceanfree.net**
Wᴇʙ: **www.carriglodge.com**

Spacious country home. Ideal touring base. Close to Pubs, Restaurants and world famous Mount Usher Gardens. Dublin/Rosslare 1hr. Dun Laoghaire 30 mins.

| B&B | 3 | Ensuite | €32-€32 | Dinner | - |
|-----|---|---------|---------|--------|---|
| B&B | 1 | Standard | - | Partial Board | - |
| Single Rate | | | €45-€45 | Child reduction | - |

Ashford 2km

**Open:** 1st April-31st October

---

**Jean O'Shea Conlon**
MOUNT USHER VIEW
**Ashford, Co Wicklow**

Tᴇʟ: **0404 40543**

Dormer bungalow, mature gardens, bordering Mount Usher gardens, ten minutes to Druids Glen Golf Course, 5 mins drive to swimming pool with gym.

| B&B | 4 | Ensuite | €28.50-€31 | Dinner | - |
|-----|---|---------|-----------|--------|---|
| B&B | - | Standard | €25.50-€28.50 | Partial Board | - |
| Single Rate | | | €38-€43.50 | Child reduction | 25% |

In Ashford

**Open:** All Year

In Ashford

**Mrs Phil Pallas**
**PALLAS LODGE**
**Mont Alto, Ashford, Co Wicklow**

TEL: **0404 40184**   FAX: **0404 40184**
EMAIL: **philpallas@eircom.ie**

Beautiful quiet garden over looking village, parking. 1hr Rosslare Port, 30 mins Dun Laoghaire Port close to pubs restaurants, famous Mount Usher Gardens.

| B&B | 4 | Ensuite | €35-€35 | Dinner | - |
| B&B | - | Standard | - | Partial Board | - |
| Single Rate | | | - | Child reduction | - |

**Open:** All Year Except Christmas

---

Ashford 1km

**Mrs Áine Shannon**
**CARRIGLEN**
**Ballinahinch, Ashford,**
**Co Wicklow**

TEL: **0404 40627**
EMAIL: **carriglen@eircom.net**
WEB: **www.freewebs.com/carriglen**

500 metres Ashford Village/off Main road/on Devils Glen Glendalough road. 5 min walk Pubs/Restaurants. Mount Usher Gardens. Dublin 45 min, Dunlaoighre 35 min.

| B&B | 3 | Ensuite | €28.50-€31 | Dinner | - |
| B&B | - | Standard | - | Partial Board | - |
| Single Rate | | | €40-€43.50 | Child reduction | 25% |

**Open:** All Year

---

Wicklow 4km

**Aileen Synnott**
**ROSSANA**
**Ashford, Co Wicklow**

TEL: **0404 40163**
EMAIL: **rossana@eircom.net**

150 metres off N11, 50 mins Dublin, 30 mins Dun Laoghaire. Excellent Pubs, Restaurants. Close to Mount Usher gardens, Powerscourt, Glendalough, Tinakilly House Hotel.

| B&B | 3 | Ensuite | €30-€30 | Dinner | - |
| B&B | - | Standard | - | Partial Board | - |
| Single Rate | | | €43 | Child reduction | - |

**Open:** All Year

---

Avoca 2km

**Mrs Doreen Burns**
**GREENHILLS**
**Knockanree Lower, Avoca,**
**Co Wicklow**

TEL: **0402 35197**   FAX: **0402 35197**

Bungalow in scenic peaceful surroundings near Avoca - The location of "Ballykissangel". Ideal touring area. Convenient to Handweavers, Glendalough, Dublin, Rosslare.

| B&B | 3 | Ensuite | €32.50-€35 | Dinner | - |
| B&B | - | Standard | - | Partial Board | - |
| Single Rate | | | €40-€45 | Child reduction | - |

**Open:** 1st May-30th September

---

Avoca 2km

**Mervyn & Jackie Burns**
**ASHDENE**
**Knockanree Lower, Avoca,**
**Co Wicklow**

TEL: **0402 35327**   FAX: **0402 35327**
EMAIL: **burns@ashdeneavoca.com**
WEB: **www.ashdeneavoca.com**

Award winning home near Handweavers and Avoca (Ballykissangel). Restaurants locally. Tennis Court. Ideal touring base. Dublin/Rosslare 1.5 hrs. See website.

| B&B | 4 | Ensuite | €32.50-€35 | Dinner | - |
| B&B | 1 | Standard | €30-€30 | Partial Board | - |
| Single Rate | | | €40-€45 | Child reduction | 25% |

**Open:** 8th April-15th October

**Mrs Rose Gilroy**
**KOLIBA**
**Beech Road, Avoca,**
**Co Wicklow**

*Avoca*

TEL: **0402 32737**   FAX: **0402 32737**
EMAIL: **koliba@eircom.net**
WEB: **www.koliba.com**

Highly recommended country home. Panoramic views of Arklow Bay. Lonely Planet recommended. Dublin, Rosslare 1 hour. In Avoca, turn right facing "Fitzgeralds".

| B&B | 4 | Ensuite | €28-€31 | Dinner | - |
|-----|---|---------|---------|--------|---|
| B&B | - | Standard | | Partial Board | - |
| Single Rate | | | €40-€45 | Child reduction | 25% |

Avoca 5km

**Open:** 1st April-31st October

**Mrs Bernie Ivers**
**CHERRYBROOK COUNTRY HOME**
**Avoca, Co Wicklow**

*Avoca*

TEL: **0402 35179**   FAX: **0402 35765**
EMAIL: **cherrybandb@eircom.net**
WEB: **www.cherrybrookhouse.com**

Highly recommended home in Avoca. Home of Avoca Handweavers. Minutes walk from Fitzgeralds bar of Ballykissangel. Ideal location for Golf, Walking and Touring the Garden County. AA ◆◆◆.

| B&B | 5 | Ensuite | €30-€32.50 | Dinner | - |
|-----|---|---------|------------|--------|---|
| B&B | - | Standard | - | Partial Board | - |
| Single Rate | | | €45-€45 | Child reduction | - |

In Avoca

**Open:** 1st January-20th December

**Mrs Margaret McGraynor**
**GLENDALE HOUSE**
**Avoca, Co Wicklow**

*Avoca*

TEL: **0402 35780**   FAX: **0402 30938**
EMAIL: **glendhouse@eircom.net**
WEB: **homepage.eircom.net/~glendale**

Highly recommended select home. 5 mins walk to Ballykissangel's Fitzgeralds Pub. Delicious breakfasts in charming conservatory. Close to Avoca Handweavers, Avondale House, Glendalough.

| B&B | 4 | Ensuite | €30-€32 | Dinner | - |
|-----|---|---------|---------|--------|---|
| B&B | - | Standard | - | Partial Board | - |
| Single Rate | | | | Child reduction | - |

In Avoca

**Open:** 17th March-4th November

**Mrs Patricia Gyves**
**HAYLANDS HOUSE**
**Dublin Road, Blessington,**
**Co Wicklow**

*Blessington*

TEL: **045 865183**
EMAIL: **haylands@eircom.net**
BUS NO: **65**

AIB hospitality award winner. Spacious bungalow in quiet surroundings on N81 in scenic area. Dublin Airport and Ferries 55 mins. Ideal location for touring.

| B&B | 5 | Ensuite | €32.50-€32.50 | Dinner | - |
|-----|---|---------|---------------|--------|---|
| B&B | 1 | Standard | €30-€30 | Partial Board | - |
| Single Rate | | | €40-€43.50 | Child reduction | 25% |

In Blessington

**Open:** 1st February-30th November

**Mrs Kay Kelly**
**OLD RECTORY**
**Herbert Road, Bray,**
**Co Wicklow**

*Bray*

TEL: **01 2867515**   FAX: **01 2867515**

Gothic Victorian Rectory, picturesque setting near Bray, Bus, Ferry, Golf, Mountains, Sea. 20km Dublin (N11). Bus No. 145 to Rapid Rail.

| B&B | 3 | Ensuite | €32-€35 | Dinner | - |
|-----|---|---------|---------|--------|---|
| B&B | - | Standard | | Partial Board | - |
| Single Rate | | | €40-€50 | Child reduction | 25% |

Bray 1.5km

**Open:** 3rd January-21st December

**Bray/Greystones 3km**

**Alma Mayberry**
PINE COTTAGE
Windgates, Bray, Co Wicklow

### Bray

Tᴇʟ: **01 2872601**
Bᴜs Nᴏ: **84, 184**

Luxury home in own grounds off Bray/Greystones road R761. Ideal for touring Co Wicklow/Dublin City by rapid rail/car ferry. Featured in Ulster Tatler.

| B&B | 3 | Ensuite | €36-€40 | Dinner | - |
| B&B | - | Standard | | Partial Board | - |
| Single Rate | | | €50-€55 | Child reduction | - |

**Open:** 1st April-30th September

---

**In Bray**

**Mrs Kathleen Roseingrave**
IVERAGH
44 Meath Road, Bray,
Co Wicklow

### Bray

Tᴇʟ: **01 2863877**
Eᴍᴀɪʟ: **iveragh@hotmail.com**
Bᴜs Nᴏ: **84, 45**

Detached period residence beside sea. Close to Rapid Rail, Bus, Car Ferry, Sporting Amenities. Dun Laoghaire 6 mls, Dublin 12 mls. Airport 20 mls.

| B&B | 4 | Ensuite | €30-€32.50 | Dinner | - |
| B&B | - | Standard | | Partial Board | - |
| Single Rate | | | €40 | Child reduction | 25% |

**Open:** 17th March-31st October

---

**Enniskerry 1km**

**Mrs Kay Lynch**
CHERBURY
Monastery, Enniskerry,
Co Wicklow

### Enniskerry

Tᴇʟ: **01 2828679**
Eᴍᴀɪʟ: **cherbury@eircom.net**
Bᴜs Nᴏ: **44**

Large Bungalow, Landscaped gardens. Ideal base for touring Wicklow. Convenient Powerscourt, Glendalough, Golf, Car Ferry, Airport, Dublin 20km.

| B&B | 3 | Ensuite | €35-€40 | Dinner | - |
| B&B | - | Standard | - | Partial Board | - |
| Single Rate | | | - | Child reduction | - |

**Open:** 1st January-31st December

---

**Enniskerry 4km**

**Kay O'Connor**
OAKLAWN
Glaskenny, Enniskerry,
Co Wicklow

### Enniskerry

Tᴇʟ: **01 2860493**
Eᴍᴀɪʟ: **johnb@indigo.ie**
Wᴇʙ: **www.oaklawnhouse.com**
Bᴜs Nᴏ: **185**

Delightful house and gardens. Just off Glencree Road, idyllic country setting. Beside Powerscourt and Wicklow Way. Convenient Car Ferries, Airport, Dublin 25 km.

| B&B | 2 | Ensuite | €35-€40 | Dinner | - |
| B&B | 2 | Standard | €30-€35 | Partial Board | - |
| Single Rate | | | €40-€50 | Child reduction | 50% |

**Open:** 1st April-31st October

---

**In Annamoe**

**Mrs Carmel Hawkins**
CARMEL'S
Glendalough, Annamoe,
Co Wicklow

### Glendalough

Tᴇʟ: **0404 45297**   Fᴀx: **0404 45297**
Eᴍᴀɪʟ: **carmelsbandb@eircom.net**
Wᴇʙ: **homepage.eircom.net/~carmels**

When touring Wicklow stay at this hospitable well established home set in the heart of the Wicklow Mountains. To book contact Carmel directly at carmelsbandb@eircom.net

| B&B | 4 | Ensuite | €30-€33 | Dinner | - |
| B&B | - | Standard | | Partial Board | - |
| Single Rate | | | - | Child reduction | 25% |

**Open:** 1st March-31st October

**Mrs Valerie Merrigan**
GLENDALE
Glendalough, Co Wicklow

TEL: **0404 45410**　FAX: **0404 45410**
EMAIL: **merrigan@eircom.net**
WEB: **www.glendale-glendalough.com**

Country Home set in scenic Wicklow Mountains, situated 1.5km Glendalough. On Laragh to Annamoe Road, 0.5km from Shops, Restaurants and Pub.

| B&B | 4 | Ensuite | €32-€35 | Dinner | - |
|---|---|---|---|---|---|
| B&B | - | Standard | - | Partial Board | - |
| Single Rate | | | €50-€60 | Child reduction | 25% |

In Laragh

**Open:** 1st January-20th December

---

**Martha & Joe O'Neill**
GLENDALOUGH RIVER HOUSE
Derrybawn, Glendalough, Co Wicklow

TEL: **0404 45577**　FAX: **0404 45577**
EMAIL: **glendaloughriverhouse@hotmail.com**

200 year old stone restored courtyard. All bedrooms have beautiful river views. Located on walking trail to Glendalough. Excellent breakfast menu.

| B&B | 4 | Ensuite | €35-€45 | Dinner | - |
|---|---|---|---|---|---|
| B&B | - | Standard | - | Partial Board | - |
| Single Rate | | | €60 | Child reduction | - |

Laragh 1km

**Open:** 1st March-30th September

---

**Ms Mary Doyle**
LA CASA
Kilpedder Grove, Kilpedder, Greystones, Co Wicklow

TEL: **01 2819703**
EMAIL: **lacasabb@yahoo.com**
WEB: **www.lacasabb.com**
BUS NO: **184, 133**

Situated in Kilpedder village N11 route. 10 mins Greystones, Airport 1 hour, Ferries 30 mins. 184 bus Greystones/Bray, DART every 20 mins, Glendalough. 30 min drive, Powerscourt 15 min.

| B&B | 3 | Ensuite | €35-€37.50 | Dinner | - |
|---|---|---|---|---|---|
| B&B | - | Standard | - | Partial Board | - |
| Single Rate | | | - | Child reduction | - |

Greystones 5km

**Open:** 1st March-31st November

---

**Kathleen & Seamus Fallon**
BELVEDERE HOUSE AND GARDENS
Templecarrig, Greystones, Co Wicklow

TEL: **01 2875189**　FAX: **01 2875189**
EMAIL: **kfallon@iolfree.ie**
WEB: **www.belvederehouse.net**
BUS NO: **84, 184**

Country residence overlooking Greystones Harbour set in 5 acres of gardens, woodlands, river and walks. Ideal location for touring Dublin & Wicklow. Close to many golf courses.

| B&B | 3 | Ensuite | €35-€35 | Dinner | - |
|---|---|---|---|---|---|
| B&B | - | Standard | €35-€35 | Partial Board | - |
| Single Rate | | | €60-€60 | Child reduction | - |

Greystones 2km

**Open:** April-October

---

**Malcolm & Penny Hall**
GLANDORE
St Vincent Rd, Burnaby Estate, Greystones, Co Wicklow

TEL: **01 2874364**　FAX: **01 2874364**
BUS NO: **84**

House of great charm, set in mature gardens in beautiful old world estate. Five minutes from all amenities.

| B&B | 4 | Ensuite | €32 | Dinner | - |
|---|---|---|---|---|---|
| B&B | - | Standard | - | Partial Board | - |
| Single Rate | | | - | Child reduction | 33.3% |

In Greystones

**Open:** All Year

Greystones 6km

**Mary & Michael Hogan**
THORNVALE
Kilpedder, Greystones,
Co Wicklow

### Greystones

Tel: **01 2810410**
Email: **hoganwicklow@eircom.net**
Bus No: **184/133**

Modern family home on 1 acre gardens. Exit N11 (south bound) for Kilquade at Kilpedder, immediately right at 4x4 garage. Ideal for touring Wicklow & Dublin. DART at Greystones/Bray.

| B&B | 4 | Ensuite | €32.50-€35 | Dinner | - |
| B&B | - | Standard | | Partial Board | - |
| Single Rate | | | €45-€50 | Child reduction | - |

**Open:** 1st January-31st December

In Greystones

**Mrs Kathleen Nunan**
SILLAN LODGE
Church Lane, Greystones,
Co Wicklow

### Greystones

Tel: **01 2875535**
Email: **sillanlodge@hotmail.com**
Bus No: **84, 184**

Sillan Lodge is situated off a peaceful tree lined avenue, with extensive grounds, mountain and sea views. Close to City, Car Ferry and Rapid Rail service (DART). Scenic drives nearby.

| B&B | 2 | Ensuite | €34-€35 | Dinner | - |
| B&B | 1 | Standard | €30-€32 | Partial Board | - |
| Single Rate | | | €50-€60 | Child reduction | - |

**Open:** 1st March-31st October

In Rathdrum

**Pat & Daphne Cullen**
STIRABOUT LANE B&B
36 Main Street, Rathdrum,
Co Wicklow

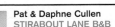

### Rathdrum

Tel: **0404 43142**   Fax: **0404 43142**
Email: **stiraboutlane@hotmail.com**
Web: **www.stiraboutlane.com**

Located in the heart of Rathdrum. Bedrooms ensuite, TV, Breakfast Menu, Guest Sitting Room. Mature garden to rear. Ideal location for touring Wicklow.

| B&B | 4 | Ensuite | €30-€35 | Dinner | - |
| B&B | - | Standard | | Partial Board | - |
| Single Rate | | | €40-€43.50 | Child reduction | 33.3% |

**Open:** 1st January-21st December

Rathdrum 2km

**Mr Gerry Fulham**
ABHAINN MOR HOUSE
Corballis, Rathdrum,
Co Wicklow

### Rathdrum

Tel: **0404 46330**
Email: **abhainnmor@eircom.net**
Web: **homepage.eircom.net/~wicklowbandb/**

Enjoy good food in a comfortable home with spacious gardens. Family rooms. Close to Glendalough and Avoca. 2km south of Rathdrum R752.

| B&B | 6 | Ensuite | €32-€34 | Dinner | €20-€20 |
| B&B | - | Standard | | Partial Board | €350 |
| Single Rate | | | €45-€48 | Child reduction | 33.3% |

**Open:** 2nd January-23rd December

Rathdrum 2km

**Mrs Ann Griffin**
LETTERMORE
Corballis, Rathdrum,
Co Wicklow

### Rathdrum

Tel: **0404 46506**   Fax: **0404 43183**
Email: **lettermore@eircom.net**
Web: **homepage.eircom.net/~lettermore**

Country home 2km south of Rathdrum, Avoca road(R752). Close Avondale, Meetings of Water, Avoca, Glendalough. From Airport M50 to Blessington, Hollywood, Wiclow Gap, Laragh, Rathdrum.

| B&B | 5 | Ensuite | €27.50-€31 | Dinner | €20-€20 |
| B&B | - | Standard | - | Partial Board | €294 |
| Single Rate | | | €40-€43.50 | Child reduction | 25% |

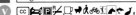

**Open:** 1st March-31st October

**Mrs Maeve Scott**
ST BRIDGET'S
Corballis, Rathdrum,
Co Wicklow

Tel: **0404 46477**
Email: **stbridgets@eircom.net**

Quiet countryside location. 2km south of Rathdrum town R753. Just 50 yds off Avoca road R752. All bedrooms on ground floor. Adjacent to Avondale, Avoca, Glendalough, Wicklow Mountains.

| B&B | 3 | Ensuite | €30-€32.50 | Dinner | - |
|-----|---|---------|------------|--------|---|
| B&B | - | Standard | | Partial Board | - |
| Single Rate | | | €40-€45 | Child reduction | 25% |

Rathdrum 2km

**Open:** 1st January-18th December

**Mrs Eileen Sheehan**
THE HAWTHORNS
Corballis, Rathdrum,
Co Wicklow

Tel: **0404 46683/46217** Fax: **0404 46217**
Email: **thehawthorns@eircom.net**
Web: **homepage.eircom.net/~thehawthorns**

Modern bungalow in award winning garden. 1/2 km from Rathdrum and railway station. Ideal centre for Golf, Fishing, Walking. 1hr to Airport and Ferries. Lonely Planet Recommended.

| B&B | 1 | Ensuite | €28-€32 | Dinner | - |
|-----|---|---------|---------|--------|---|
| B&B | 2 | Standard | €26-€30 | Partial Board | - |
| Single Rate | | | €40-€45 | Child reduction | 25% |

In Rathdrum

**Open:** 6th January-18th December

**Mrs Fiona Byrne**
GLEN NA SMOLE
Ashtown Lane, Marlton Road,
Wicklow, Co Wicklow

Tel: **0404 67945** Fax: **0404 67945**
Email: **byrneglen@eircom.net**
Web: **homepage.eircom.net/~byrneglen**

Comfortable family home. Award winning breakfasts. 2km Grand Hotel/Beehive Pub off Wicklow/Wexford Road. Golf, Fishing arranged. Low season discounts.

| B&B | 4 | Ensuite | €27.50-€31 | Dinner | €20 |
|-----|---|---------|------------|--------|-----|
| B&B | - | Standard | - | Partial Board | €295 |
| Single Rate | | | €40-€45 | Child reduction | 50% |

Wicklow 2km

**Open:** 1st April-1st November

**Mrs Rita Byrne**
ROSITA
Dunbur Park, Wicklow Town,
Co Wicklow

Tel: **0404 67059**

Luxurious spacious home overlooking Wicklow Bay. Take coast road, turn into Dunbur Park at pedestrian crossing. 5 minutes walk to Town.

| B&B | 4 | Ensuite | €32 | Dinner | - |
|-----|---|---------|-----|--------|---|
| B&B | - | Standard | - | Partial Board | - |
| Single Rate | | | €50 | Child reduction | - |

In Wicklow

**Open:** 1st March-31st October

**Elizabeth Dowling**
KILMANTIN HOUSE
Kilmantin Hill, Wicklow Town,
Co Wicklow

Tel: **0404 25081/67373**
Email: **kilmantinhouse@eircom.net**

Townhouse, centrally located to all amenities walking distance from town and coast line.

| B&B | 4 | Ensuite | €33-€33 | Dinner | - |
|-----|---|---------|---------|--------|---|
| B&B | - | Standard | - | Partial Board | - |
| Single Rate | | | €50-€55 | Child reduction | 33.3% |

In Wicklow

**Open:** 1st March-31st October

**Catherine Doyle**
DROM ARD
Ballynerrin Lr, Wicklow Town,
Co Wicklow

Wicklow

TEL: **0404 66056**
EMAIL: **dromardwicklow@excite.com**

Modern spilt-level home with splendid views of Mountains, Sea, Countryside. Within easy reach of Glendalough. Ideal base for touring South-East, Dublin-Rosslare.

| B&B | 3 | Ensuite | €30-€32.50 | Dinner | - |
|------|---|----------|------------|--------|---|
| B&B | 1 | Standard | €28-€30 | Partial Board | - |
| Single Rate | | | €43-€50 | Child reduction | 33.3% |

Wicklow 2km

**Open:** 1st February-30th November

---

**Mrs Lyla Doyle**
SILVER SANDS
Dunbur Road, Wicklow,
Co Wicklow

Wicklow

TEL: **0404 68243**
EMAIL: **lyladoyle@eircom.net**

Well heated home with panoramic views of Wicklow Bay. Extensive menu. Recommended by Frommer/Fran Sullivan/Elsie Dillards "300 Best B&B's".

| B&B | 4 | Ensuite | €33-€35 | Dinner | - |
|------|---|----------|---------|--------|---|
| B&B | 1 | Standard | €33-€33 | Partial Board | - |
| Single Rate | | | €45-€50 | Child reduction | 50% |

In Wicklow

**Open:** 1st March-1st December

---

**Mrs Sylvia Doyle**
SWALLOW'S REST
Ballynerrin, Wicklow Town,
Co Wicklow

Wicklow

TEL: **0404 68718**
EMAIL: **info@swallowsrest.ie**

Modern house with spectacular lake, sea and country view. Large spacious rooms, homely but with all modern facilities. Private grounds for guests use.

| B&B | 5 | Ensuite | €33-€33 | Dinner | - |
|------|---|----------|---------|--------|---|
| B&B | - | Standard | - | Partial Board | - |
| Single Rate | | | €45-€45 | Child reduction | 50% |

Wicklow 1km

**Open:** 1st March-31st October

---

**Mrs Helen Gorman**
THOMOND HOUSE
St Patricks Road Upr, Wicklow,
Co Wicklow

Wicklow

TEL: **0404 67940**   FAX: **0404 67940**
EMAIL: **thomondhouse@eircom.net**

House with balcony. Wonderful views Sea, Mountains. 1km past RC Church. Frommer, Lets Go, Lonely Planet, Rough Guide recommended. Golf arranged. Warm welcome.

| B&B | 2 | Ensuite | €32-€33 | Dinner | - |
|------|---|----------|---------|--------|---|
| B&B | 3 | Standard | €30-€31 | Partial Board | - |
| Single Rate | | | €38-€42 | Child reduction | - |

Wicklow 1km

**Open:** 1st April-30th September

---

**Mrs Patrica Klaue**
LISSADELL HOUSE
Ashtown Lane,
off Marlton Road, Wicklow,
Co Wicklow

Wicklow

TEL: **0404 67458**
EMAIL: **lissadellhse@eircom.net**
WEB: **www.geocities.com/lissadellhse**

Comfortable home, perfectly situated on outskirts of Wicklow Town 1.5km, turn right at Grand hotel (L29A Rd). Beach, Golf, Swimming Pool with Gym 5 mins drive.

| B&B | 2 | Ensuite | €34 | Dinner | - |
|------|---|----------|-----|--------|---|
| B&B | 2 | Standard | | Partial Board | - |
| Single Rate | | | €50-€55 | Child reduction | 25% |

Wicklow 1.5km

**Open:** 1st April-1st November

**Mrs Hilary McGowan**
ARCH HOUSE
**Ballynerrin, Wicklow Town,
Co Wicklow**

**Wicklow**

Tel: **0404 68176**
Email: **hilarymcgowan@eircom.net**

A dormer bungalow with a panoramic view of Wicklow Bay and Mountains. Golf, Fishing, Horseriding nearby. A friendly welcome awaits you.

| B&B | 3 | Ensuite | €30-€32 | Dinner | - |
|------|---|---------|---------|--------|---|
| B&B | - | Standard | - | Partial Board | - |
| Single Rate | | | €40-€45 | Child reduction | 50% |

icklow 1.5km

**Open:** 1st March-31st October

North West

iscover the North West and discover the best of Ireland! This is truly the greenest part of urope's Green Island...unspoilt, uncrowded and undiscovered.

the counties of Cavan, Donegal, Leitrim, Monaghan and Sligo there is a wealth of scenery, eritage and hospitality. With geography that ranges from wild Atlantic coast through gentle eandering rivers to sylvan lakeland, and a history that dates from Neolithic archaeology rough to modern Irish writing, every interest can be met.

## Glenveagh National Park

For the active there are classic links and parkland golf courses; superb equestrian centres; hill walking and mountain climbing; summer schools of every variety; wide open beaches, some with world class surfing; and at the end of every day Irish hospitality at its best in bars and restaurants.

## rea Representatives

**NEGAL**
 Mary Ita Boyle AVALON Glen Road Glenties Co Donegal
: 074 9551292
 s Breid Kelly ARDGLAS Lurgybrack Sligo Road Letterkenny Co Donegal
: 074 9122516   Fax: 074 9122516
 Majella Leonard OAKLANDS B&B 8 Oakland Park Gortlee Road
tterkenny Co Donegal
: 074 9125529

**IGO**
s Maeve Walsh CRUCKAWN HOUSE Ballymote/Boyle Rd Tubbercurry
 Sligo Tel: 071 9185188   Fax: 071 9185188

 ## Tourist Information Offices

OPEN ALL YEAR EXCEPT CARRICK-ON-SHANNON, CAVAN TOWN & MONAGHAN TOWN

REFER TO PAGE 5 FOR A LIST OF SERVICES AVAILABLE

Sligo Town
Aras Reddan
Temple Street
Tel: 071 9161201

Carrick-on-Shannon
The Old Barrel Store
Tel: 071 9620170

Cavan Town
1 Farnham Street
Tel: 049 4331942

Donegal Town
Quay Street
Tel: 074 9721148

Letterkenny
Neil T. Blaney Road
Tel: 074 9121160

Monaghan Town
Castle Meadow Court
Tel: 047 81122

Website: **www.irelandnorthwest.ie**

Cavan, a county rich in history and culture is also a haven for the lover of the quiet outdoors. The Angler, Golfer, Horse-rider and Hill-walker are all catered for. Swimming, Tennis, River Cruising and many other activities will make your visit an unforgettable one.

---

**Bawnboy 3km**

**Catherine O'Reilly**
LAKE AVENUE HOUSE
**Port, Bawnboy, Co Cavan**

### Ballyconnell

TEL: **049 9523298**   FAX: **049 9523298**
EMAIL: **lakeave@eircom.net**
WEB: **www.lakeavenuehouse.com**

Family run home offering luxury accomodation in a quiet scenic rural setting. Ideal Dublin-Donegal stop over. Off N87. Pubs, Restaurants, Golf, Fishing, Walks.

| B&B | 4 | Ensuite | €27.50-€31 | Dinner | - |
|-----|---|---------|-----------|--------|---|
| B&B | - | Standard | - | Partial Board | - |
| Single Rate | | | €40-€43.50 | Child reduction | **50%** |

**Open:** 14th January-19th December

---

**Belturbet 6km**

**James & Susan McCauley**
ROCKWOOD HOUSE
**Cloverhill, Belturbet, Co Cavan**

### Belturbet

TEL: **047 55351**   FAX: **047 55373**
EMAIL: **jbmac@eircom.net**

Lovely country house situated in secluded peaceful woodlands and surrounded by lawns and gardens on the N54, 2 miles from Butlersbridge, 6 miles Cavan.

| B&B | 4 | Ensuite | €30-€31 | Dinner | - |
|-----|---|---------|---------|--------|---|
| B&B | - | Standard | - | Partial Board | - |
| Single Rate | | | €40-€43.50 | Child reduction | **25%** |

**Open:** 10th January-23rd December

---

**Cavan 2km**

**Ben & Teresa Gaffney**
ROCKVILLA
**Moynehall, Cavan, Co Cavan**

### Cavan

TEL: **049 4361885**   FAX: **049 4361885**
EMAIL: **rockvilla@eircom.net**

Situated just off the N55 approaching from N3. Left at "Shell" gas station. Help with Genealogical research in Cavan. Ideal Dublin-Donegal stopover. Parking.

| B&B | 4 | Ensuite | €30-€31 | Dinner | - |
|-----|---|---------|---------|--------|---|
| B&B | - | Standard | - | Partial Board | - |
| Single Rate | | | €40-€43.50 | Child reduction | **25%** |

**Open:** 1st January-20th December

---

**Cavan 2.5km**

**Mrs Alacoque O'Brien**
BALLYCLOONE HOUSE
**Golf Links Road, Cavan,
Co Cavan**

### Cavan

TEL: **049 4362310**
EMAIL: **michaelobrien53@eircom.net**

Luxurious friendly accommodation, quiet road. Convenient to Town Centre, Golf Club, Equestrian Centre, Sports Complex. Hospital 500 metres.

| B&B | 2 | Ensuite | €31 | Dinner | - |
|-----|---|---------|-----|--------|---|
| B&B | 1 | Standard | €30.50 | Partial Board | - |
| Single Rate | | | €41-€43.50 | Child reduction | **25%** |

**Open:** 1st January-20th December

**Mrs Maura O'Reilly**
CLOONEEN HOUSE
Belturbet Rd. T52/R201,
Killeshandra, Co Cavan

### Killeshandra

TEL: **049 4334342**   FAX: **049 4334342**
EMAIL: **clooneen_house@esatclear.ie**

Turn right facing Ulster Bank. Dormer bungalow situated T52/R201. Ideal stopover between Dublin/Donegal. Belfast 2 1/2 hrs Help with Ancestral tracing. Killykeen Park, Walks, Fishing.

| B&B | 2 | Ensuite | €27.50-€31 | Dinner | - |
| B&B | 2 | Standard | €25.50-€28.50 | Partial Board | - |
| Single Rate | | | €38-€43.50 | Child reduction | 25% |

Killeshandra 2km

**Open:** 1st April-31st October

---

**Ethel & Donald Woodhouse**
GLENCLOY HOUSE
Drumgoon, Killeshandra,
Co Cavan

### Killeshandra

TEL: **049 4334315**
EMAIL: **glencloyhouse@eircom.net**
WEB: **www.glencloyhouse.com**

Modern spacious house convenient to lakes and forest park pool, room with balcony, friendly atmosphere, Tea Coffee. Tv all rooms.  One bedroom with whirlpol bath.

| B&B | 5 | Ensuite | €32-€38 | Dinner | - |
| B&B | - | Standard | - | Partial Board | - |
| Single Rate | | | €40-€43.50 | Child reduction | 25% |

Killeshandra 4km

**Open:** 1st February-10th December

---

**Mrs Emily McHugo**
THE WHITE HOUSE
Oldcastle Road, Virginia,
Co Cavan

### Virginia

TEL: **049 8547515**
EMAIL: **mchugo@esatclear.ie**
WEB: **www.mchugo.com**

Warm welcome, breakfast menu. Tea/Coffee bedrooms. Forest walks. Fish at Lough Ramor. Horseriding, Watersports. Visit Loughcrew, Newgrange, Fore Abbey.

| B&B | 4 | Ensuite | €30-€35 | Dinner | - |
| B&B | - | Standard | - | Partial Board | - |
| Single Rate | | | €40-€45 | Child reduction | 50% |

Virginia 1km

**Open:** 1st January-30th November

---

## FREQUENTLY ASKED QUESTIONS

**Q. Are the prices based on per person sharing or a room rate?**
A.  The price for bed & breakfast is per person sharing.

**Q. What does an "ensuite" room mean?**
A.  An ensuite room means the room has a private bath/shower and toilet

**Q. What are the check-in times?**
A.  The check-in times are normally between 2pm and 6pm, unless agreed with your host/hostess.

**Q. Where do I get directions to the B&B I have booked?**
A.  Our website www.townandcountry.ie hosts directions to our homes.
Alternatively, over 80% of our homes are accessible by email/fax and will be happy to forward directions on request.

Donegal is undoubtedly one of Ireland's most beautiful and rugged counties, with its spectacular scenery, rambling hills, magnificent mountains, lakes and its many blue-flag beaches, so too, has its heritage and culture. Noted for its hospitality and friendliness. Famous for it's tweed, hand knits and traditional music. Catering for all leisure and sporting activities.

---

Adara 1km

**Mrs Marian Bennett**
BAYVIEW COUNTRY HOUSE
**Portnoo Road, Ardara,**
**Co Donegal**

### Adara

TEL: **074 9541145**  FAX: **074 9541145**
EMAIL: **chbennett@eircom.net**

Spacious purpose built B&B overlooking bay, prize winning bread and scones. Award winning breakfasts. Tea coffee facilities, tv in rooms, credit cards.

| B&B | 4 | Ensuite | €27.50-€31 | Dinner | - |
| B&B | - | Standard | - | Partial Board | - |
| Single Rate | | | €40-€43.50 | Child reduction | 25% |

**Open:** 1st March-12th November

---

Ardara 2km

**Laurence & Fiona Breslin**
GORT NA MONA B&B
**Donegal Road, Cronkeerin,**
**Ardara, Co Donegal**

### Ardara

TEL: **074 9537777**  FAX: **074 9551622**
EMAIL: **laurencebreslin@unison.ie**
WEB: **www.gortnamonabandb.com**

New luxury purpose built B&B. Near beach, scenic walks. Mountain views. Home baking, home-made jam. Power showers. Tea/coffee on arrival. Warm welcome.

| B&B | 4 | Ensuite | €27.50-€31 | Dinner | - |
| B&B | - | Standard | - | Partial Board | - |
| Single Rate | | | €40-€43.50 | Child reduction | 25% |

**Open:** 15th March-1st November

---

Ardara 5km

**Mrs Eva Friel**
THALASSA COUNTRY HOME
**Narin - Portnoo, Co Donegal**

### Ardara Portnoo

TEL: **074 9545151**

Magnificent coastal region overlooking Ocean, Lake, Beaches, 18-hole Golf Course, Scenic Walks. Ancient Historic Monuments. Warm welcoming home. Recommended Guide de Routard.

| B&B | 4 | Ensuite | €27.50-€31.50 | Dinner | - |
| B&B | - | Standard | - | Partial Board | - |
| Single Rate | | | €40-€43.50 | Child reduction | 25% |

**Open:** 1st March-15th November

---

Ardara 1km

**Vincent & Susan McConnell**
ROSEWOOD COUNTRY HOUSE
**Killybegs Road, Ardara,**
**Co Donegal**

### Ardara

TEL: **074 9541168**  FAX: **074 9541168**
EMAIL: **jmccon@gofree.indigo.ie**

Recommended by Le Guide de Routard, Ireland's best 300 B&B's. Fresh baked muffins and home-made jam served for breakfast. Tea/Coffee served in Guest lounge on arrival. Credit cards.

| B&B | 6 | Ensuite | €27.50-€31 | Dinner | - |
| B&B | - | Standard | - | Partial Board | - |
| Single Rate | | | €40-€43.50 | Child reduction | 25% |

**Open:** 1st February-1st December

**Ardara**

**Mrs Norah Molloy**
**BRAE HOUSE**
**Front Street, Co Donegal**

Tel: **07495 41296**
Email: **braehouse@eircom.net**

Clean, friendly family home. Quiet, comfortable orthopaedic beds, TV, renowned for hospitality and excellent food. Easy to find, hard to leave, once been never forgotten.

| B&B | 4 | Ensuite | €27.50-€31 | Dinner | - |
|-----|---|---------|------------|--------|---|
| B&B | | Standard | - | Partial Board | - |
| Single Rate | | | - | Child reduction | - |

Ardara

**Open:** All Year

---

**Ballybofey Stranorlar**

**Peter & Miranda Byrne**
**DERGFIELD HOUSE**
**Ballybofey, Co Donegal**

Tel: **074 9132775**  Fax: **074 9132593**
Email: **derghouse@eircom.net**

Luxurious family run B&B set in private grounds. Ideal touring base. Excellent golfing, fishing and shopping locally. A warm welcome awaits you.

| B&B | 5 | Ensuite | €27.50-€32.50 | Dinner | - |
|-----|---|---------|---------------|--------|---|
| B&B | | Standard | - | Partial Board | - |
| Single Rate | | | €40-€43.50 | Child reduction | 50% |

Ballybofey 1km

**Open:** All Year Except Christmas

---

**Ballybofey Stranorlar**

**Judy McDermott**
**HILL TOP**
**Letterkenny Road, Stranorlar,**
**Co Donegal**

Tel: **074 9131185**
Email: **admiran@unison.ie**
Web: **www.hilltopBandB.net**

Comfortable home set among the rolling hills of Donegal. Good touring base. Golf and Fishing facilities available locally.

| B&B | 3 | Ensuite | €28-€31 | Dinner | - |
|-----|---|---------|---------|--------|---|
| B&B | | Standard | - | Partial Board | - |
| Single Rate | | | €40-€43.50 | Child reduction | 33.3% |

Ballybofey Stranorlar 1km

**Open:** 1st April-30th September

---

**Ballybofey Stranorlar**

**Mrs Gertrude Patton**
**FINN VIEW HOUSE**
**Lifford Road,**
**Ballybofey/Stranorlar,**
**Co Donegal**

Tel: **074 9131351**

Modern dormer bungalow. Ideal touring centre for Glenveagh National Park and Giants Causeway. Salmon Fishing, 18 hole Golf Course.

| B&B | 2 | Ensuite | €27.50-€31 | Dinner | - |
|-----|---|---------|------------|--------|---|
| B&B | 1 | Standard | €25.50-€28.50 | Partial Board | - |
| Single Rate | | | €38 | Child reduction | 25% |

Ballybofey Stranorlar 1km

**Open:** 1st May-30th September

---

**Ballyshannon**

**Mrs Mary Conlon**
**TEEVOGUE**
**Bundoran Road, Ballyshannon,**
**Co Donegal**

Tel: **071 9851386**  Fax: **071 9851386**
Email: **teevogue@iol.ie**
Web: **www.iol.ie/~teevoguebandb**

Bungalow overlooking Bay on N15. Spectacular view. Convenient to Donegal/Belleek China. Celtic Weave, rooms ensuite with T.V., Hairdryer. Homebaking, breakfast menu, Tea/Coffee facilities.

| B&B | 4 | Ensuite | €27.50-€31 | Dinner | €19-€19 |
|-----|---|---------|------------|--------|---------|
| B&B | | Standard | - | Partial Board | - |
| Single Rate | | | €40-€43.50 | Child reduction | 33.3% |

Ballyshannon 1km

**Open:** 1st April-31st October

**John & Clare Hughes**
RANDWICK
Bundoran Road, Ballyshannon,
Co Donegal

**Ballyshannon**

Tel: **071 9852545**   Fax: **071 9852545**
Email: **randwick9@eircom.net**

House on N15, magnificent views overlooking Erne Estuary. Le Guide du Routard. On parle francais. AIB Accommodation and Services Award 1998.

| B&B | 4 | Ensuite | €27.50-€31 | Dinner | €19-€19 |
|-----|---|---------|-------------|--------|---------|
| B&B | 1 | Standard | €25.50-€28.50 | Partial Board | |
| Single Rate | | | €38-€43.50 | Child reduction | 50% |

Ballyshannon 1km      **Open:** 1st March-31st December

---

**Siobain & George Luke**
ASPEN
Parkhill, Donegal Road,
Ballyshannon, Co Donegal

**Ballyshannon**

Tel: **071 9852065**   Fax: **071 9852065**
Email: **gluke@eircom.net**
Web: **homepage.eircom.net/~aspen**

Bungalow on N15 in scenic location. Non-smoking house, power showers, email facilities. Ballyshannon 1 mile, Belleek Pottery 4 miles, Donegal Castle 10 miles.

| B&B | 3 | Ensuite | €27.50-€31 | Dinner | €20-€20 |
|-----|---|---------|-------------|--------|---------|
| B&B | - | Standard | €25.50-€28.50 | Partial Board | €294 |
| Single Rate | | | €38-€43.50 | Child reduction | 50% |

Ballyshannon 2km      **Open:** 1st March-12th October

---

**Mrs Agnes McCaffrey**
CAVANGARDEN HOUSE
Donegal Road, Ballyshannon,
Co Donegal

**Ballyshannon**

Tel: **071 9851365**   Fax: **071 9851679**
Email: **cghouse@eircom.net**
Web: **www.littleireland.ie/cavangardenhouse**

Georgian house 1750, Donegal Road (route N15) on 380-acres, 0.5KM Driveway, Antique Furniture, Beach, Golf Course, Fishing, Belleek. Frommer recommended.

| B&B | 6 | Ensuite | €30-€35 | Dinner | - |
|-----|---|---------|----------|--------|---|
| B&B | - | Standard | - | Partial Board | - |
| Single Rate | | | €40-€43.50 | Child reduction | 50% |

Ballyshannon 3km      **Open:** 1st January-30th November

---

**Mrs B McCaffrey**
ROCKVILLE HOUSE
Belleek Road, Station Road,
Ballyshannon, Co Donegal

**Ballyshannon**

Tel: **071 9851106**
Email: **rockvillehouse@eircom.net**

Late 17th century home, overlooking River Erne. Convenient to Bundoran, Belleek Pottery, Rossnowlagh beaches. Important 12th century archaeological find on grounds.

| B&B | 4 | Ensuite | €30-€32 | Dinner | - |
|-----|---|---------|----------|--------|---|
| B&B | 2 | Standard | €28-€29 | Partial Board | - |
| Single Rate | | | €38-€43.50 | Child reduction | 25% |

In Ballyshannon      **Open:** All Year Except Christmas

---

**Karen McGee**
ELM BROOK
East Port, Ballyshannon,
Co Donegal

**Ballyshannon**

Tel: **071 9852615**
Email: **elmbrookbandb@eircom.net**

Spacious, modern home in peaceful location, yet convenient to all amenities. 3 mins walk Town Centre. Ideal touring base.

| B&B | 4 | Ensuite | €27.50-€31 | Dinner | - |
|-----|---|---------|-------------|--------|---|
| B&B | - | Standard | €25.50-€28.50 | Partial Board | - |
| Single Rate | | | €40-€43.50 | Child reduction | 33.3% |

In Ballyshannon      **Open:** 1st March-31st October

## Buncrana

**Mrs Marie Vaughan**
CALDRA
**Lisnakelly, Buncrana,
Inishowen, Co Donegal**

TEL: **074 9363703**
EMAIL: **caldrabandb@eircom.net**

Modern spacious family run home overlooking Lough Swilly and Town. Convenient to beaches, golf, fishing, parks, restaurants & pubs. Friendly warm atmosphere.

| B&B | 4 | Ensuite | €30-€31 | Dinner | - |
| B&B | - | Standard | - | Partial Board | - |
| Single Rate | | | €40-€43.50 | Child reduction | 50% |

Buncrana 1.5km          **Open:** All Year Except Christmas

## Bundoran

**Bernie Dillon**
GILLAROO LODGE
**West End, Bundoran,
Co Donegal**

TEL: **071 9842357**   FAX: **071 9842172**
EMAIL: **gillaroo@iol.ie**
WEB: **www.gillaroo.net**

Superbly located B&B on main road. Close to Beaches, Waterworld, Golf, Hillwalking. Angling Centre with angling guides, Tackle and Boat hire. Drying and Tackle room.

| B&B | 4 | Ensuite | €29-€32 | Dinner | - |
| B&B | 1 | Standard | €26-€30 | Partial Board | - |
| Single Rate | | | €39-€45 | Child reduction | 50% |

Bundoran          **Open:** 1st January-15th December

## Carrigans Near Derry

**Mrs J Martin**
MOUNT ROYD COUNTRY
HOME
**Carrigans, Co Donegal**

TEL: **074 9140163**   FAX: **074 9140400**
EMAIL: **jmartin@mountroyd.com**
WEB: **www.mountroyd.com**

Luxurious, triple RAC award winning ◆◆◆◆ house. AA top landlady finalist. En route to Giants Causeway, Innishowen, Derry City 8km on R236.

| B&B | 4 | Ensuite | €27.50-€31 | Dinner | - |
| B&B | - | Standard | - | Partial Board | - |
| Single Rate | | | €40-€43.50 | Child reduction | - |

Derry City 8km          **Open:** 1st February-31st December

## Carrigart

**Fidelma Cullen**
MEVAGH HOUSE
**Milford Road, Carrigart,
Letterkenny, Co Donegal**

TEL: **074 55693**   FAX: **074 55512**
EMAIL: **mevaghhouse@hotmail.com**

Family run B&B overlooking Mulroy Bay. 1/2km from Carraigart at entrance to Rosguill Peninsula and Atlantic Drive. Tea/coffee on arrival. Guest lounge. Scuba Diving available.

| B&B | 4 | Ensuite | €29-€31 | Dinner | - |
| B&B | - | Standard | - | Partial Board | - |
| Single Rate | | | €40-€43.50 | Child reduction | 33.3% |

Carrigart          **Open:** 1st March-31st October

## Carrigart

**Ann & Myles Gallagher**
SONAS
**Upper Carrick, Carrigart,
Letterkenny, Co Donegal**

TEL: **074 9155401**   FAX: **074 9155195**
EMAIL: **sonas1@indigo.ie**
WEB: **www.sonasbandb.com**

"Sonas" Modern Dormer Bungalow overlooking Bay combining modern facilities with old style hospitality. Ideal touring base. Home baking. Power showers.

| B&B | 5 | Ensuite | €27.50-€31 | Dinner | €21 |
| B&B | - | Standard | - | Partial Board | - |
| Single Rate | | | €40-€43.50 | Child reduction | 33.3% |

Carrigart 5km          **Open:** 1st January-20th December

**Fidelma McLaughlin**
FOUR ARCHES
Urris, Clonmany, Inishowen,
Co Donegal

### Clonmany Inishowen
Tel: **074 9376561**

Modern bungalow surrounded by Sea and Mountains. Ideal for touring Inishowen Peninsula. Near Mamore Gap. 20km from Malin Head. 20km from Buncrana Town.

| B&B | 5 | Ensuite | €27.50-€31 | Dinner | - |
| B&B | - | Standard | | Partial Board | - |
| Single Rate | | | €40-€43.50 | Child reduction | 50% |

Clonmany 5km

**Open:** 1st January-30th November

---

**Joan A Faulkner**
VILLAGE HOUSE
Culdaff, Co Donegal

### Culdaff
Tel: **074 9379972**
Email: **villagehouseculdaff@eircom.net**

Beautiful georgian house in seaside village. Spacious rooms. Gourmet breakfast.

| B&B | 4 | Ensuite | €30-€31 | Dinner | - |
| B&B | - | Standard | - | Partial Board | - |
| Single Rate | | | €40-€43.50 | Child reduction | 50% |

In Culdaff

**Open:** All Year

---

**Mrs Anne Lynch**
CEECLIFF HOUSE
Culdaff, Inishowen,
Co Donegal

### Culdaff
Tel: **074 9379159**

Family run home. Excellent views of Beach, River & Mountains. Close to all amenities.

| B&B | 3 | Ensuite | €27.50-€31 | Dinner | - |
| B&B | - | Standard | - | Partial Board | - |
| Single Rate | | | €40-€45 | Child reduction | - |

In Culdaff

**Open:** 1st January-23rd December

---

**Sile Callaghan**
THE GAP LODGE
Barnesmore Gap,
Donegal Town, Co Donegal

### Donegal Town
Tel: **074 9721956**
Email: **gaplodge@eircom.net**
Web: **www.littleireland.ie/gaplodge**

10 minutes drive from Donegal Town. Our spacious family run home is on the Letterkenny & Derry road, left side. Credit Cards accepted.

| B&B | 5 | Ensuite | €27.50-€31 | Dinner | - |
| B&B | - | Standard | €25.50-€28.50 | Partial Board | - |
| Single Rate | | | €38-€43.50 | Child reduction | 50% |

Donegal Town 8km

**Open:** 1st January-30th December

---

**Mrs Marie Campbell**
LYNDALE
Doonan, Donegal Town,
Co Donegal

### Donegal Town
Tel: **074 9721873**

Luxurious home  off (N56) next to Mill Park Hotel & Leisure Centre, Breakfast menu, Homebaking, TV, Electric Blankets,Hairdryers, Tea/Coffee. Donegal Town 5mins. "Petit Fute" recommended.

| B&B | 4 | Ensuite | €27.50-€40 | Dinner | - |
| B&B | - | Standard | | Partial Board | - |
| Single Rate | | | €40-€50 | Child reduction | 25% |

Donegal Town

**Open:** 1st February-30th November

**Breda Cannon**
**HEENEYS LODGE**
The Heeneys, Lough Eske,
Donegal Town, Co Donegal

### Donegal Town

TEL: **074 9723048**
EMAIL: **breda@henneyslodge.com**
WEB: **www.heeneyslodge.com**

Friendly spacious family home in scenic rural setting. Secure parking. Large family rooms available.
5 mins drive from Donegal Town and Harveys Point.

| B&B | 4 | Ensuite | €35 | Dinner | - |
|-----|---|---------|-----|--------|---|
| B&B | - | Standard | - | Partial Board | |
| Single Rate | | | €45 | Child reduction | 50% |

onegal Town 2km        **Open:** All Year Except Christmas

---

**Bernadette Dowds**
**ISLAND VIEW HOUSE**
Tullaghcullion, Donegal Town,
Co Donegal

### Donegal Town

TEL: **074 9722411**
EMAIL: **dowdsb@indigo.ie**
WEB: **www.eirbyte.com/islandview**

New two storey Georgian style house overlooking Donegal Bay. 10 minute walk to Town Centre.
Ideal base for touring North West Donegal.

| B&B | 4 | Ensuite | €27.50-€33 | Dinner | - |
|-----|---|---------|-----------|--------|---|
| B&B | - | Standard | - | Partial Board | - |
| Single Rate | | | €46 | Child reduction | 33.3% |

onegal Town 1km    **Open:** All Year Except Christmas

---

**Mrs Margaret Geary**
**KNOCKNAGOW**
Ballydevitt, Donegal,
Co Donegal

### Donegal Town

TEL: **074 9721052**

Modern bungalow situated in quiet countryside. Close to all amenities. Ideal touring base, excellent
Shops, Crafts, Restaurants nearby.

| B&B | 1 | Ensuite | €27.50-€31 | Dinner | - |
|-----|---|---------|-----------|--------|---|
| B&B | 2 | Standard | €25.50-€28.50 | Partial Board | |
| Single Rate | | | €38-€43.50 | Child reduction | 25% |

onegal 1km    **Open:** 1st April-30th September

---

**Mrs Mary J Harvey**
**CLYBAWN**
Station Road, Mountcharles,
Co Donegal

### Donegal Mountcharles

TEL: **074 9735076**

Modern bungalow in scenic location overlooking Donegal Bay.  Lake, River and Sea Fishing nearby.
Donegal Town 6km, Murvagh Golf Course 15km. Private  car park.

| B&B | 3 | Ensuite | €27.50-€31 | Dinner | - |
|-----|---|---------|-----------|--------|---|
| B&B | 1 | Standard | €25.50-€28.50 | Partial Board | |
| Single Rate | | | €38-€43.50 | Child reduction | 33.3% |

onegal 6km    **Open:** 1st April-30th September

---

**Philomena Jeffers**
**CULLENBEG HOUSE**
Tullaghcullion,
Ballyshannon Road,
Donegal Town, Co Donegal

### Donegal Town

TEL: **074 9723343**

Country house on elevated site overlooking Donegal Bay on R267 off N15. Ideal touring base.
Convenient to sandy beaches, Golfing and Fishing.

| B&B | 3 | Ensuite | €27.50-€33 | Dinner | - |
|-----|---|---------|-----------|--------|---|
| B&B | - | Standard | - | Partial Board | - |
| Single Rate | | | - | Child reduction | - |

onegal Town 1km    **Open:** 1st April-31st October

**Mrs Mary T Martin**
BAYSIDE
Mullinasole, Laghey,
Co Donegal

### Donegal Town

Tel: **074 9722768** Fax: **074 9722768**
Email: **bayside@campus.ie**

Coastal residence off N15 overlooking inlet of Donegal Bay. Golf Course and Beach 1km. Central touring location. Tea/coffee facilities.

| B&B | 5 | Ensuite | €27.50-€31 | Dinner | - |
|---|---|---|---|---|---|
| B&B | - | Standard | | Partial Board | - |
| Single Rate | | | €40-€43.50 | Child reduction | **50%** |

Donegal Town 6km

**Open:** 16th March-31st October

---

**Liam & Joan McCrea**
THE COVE LODGE
Drumgowan, Donegal Town,
Co Donegal

### Donegal Town

Tel: **074 9722302**
Email: **info@thecovelodge.com**
Web: **www.thecovelodge.com**

Charming country residence overlooking Donegal Bay, just off N15 on R267. Golf Course, Beaches. Craft village. Comfort and relaxation assured.

| B&B | 4 | Ensuite | €30-€40 | Dinner | - |
|---|---|---|---|---|---|
| B&B | - | Standard | - | Partial Board | - |
| Single Rate | | | €42-€52 | Child reduction | **25%** |

Donegal 2.5km

**Open:** 1st March-31st October

---

**Mrs Mary McGinty**
ARDEEVIN
Lough Eske, Barnesmore,
Donegal, Co Donegal

### Donegal Town Lough Eske

Tel: **074 9721790** Fax: **074 9721790**
Email: **seanmcginty@eircom.net**
Web: **members.tripod.com/~Ardeevin**

Charming country residence, magnificent view Lough Eske, Bluestack Mountains. Guide de Routard, Frommer recommended. AA ◆◆◆◆. RAC ◆◆◆◆. RAC Sparkling Diamond Award.

| B&B | 6 | Ensuite | €30-€32.50 | Dinner | - |
|---|---|---|---|---|---|
| B&B | - | Standard | €40-€45 | Partial Board | - |
| Single Rate | | | - | Child reduction | **25%** |

Donegal 8km

**Open:** 18th March-30th November

---

**Mrs Noreen McGinty**
THE ARCHES COUNTRY HOUSE
Lough Eske, Barnesmore,
Co Donegal

### Donegal Town Lough Eske

Tel: **074 9722029** Fax: **074 9722029**
Email: **archescountryhse@eircom.net**
Web: **www.archescountryhse.com**

AA ◆◆◆◆ luxurious residence - all rooms having panoramic views of Lough Eske/Bluestacks, Guide de Routard, Dumont, Michelin Green Guide, McQuillans Ire. Recommended.

| B&B | 6 | Ensuite | €30-€32.50 | Dinner | - |
|---|---|---|---|---|---|
| B&B | - | Standard | | Partial Board | - |
| Single Rate | | | €45-€50 | Child reduction | **25%** |

Donegal Town 8km

**Open:** All Year

---

**Ann McGlinchey**
EAS DUN LODGE
Greenans, Lough Eske,
Donegal, Co Donegal

### Donegal Town Lough Eske

Tel: **074 9722628**
Email: **info@easdunlodge.com**
Web: **www.easdunlodge.com**

Quiet location. Lovely view Bluestack Mountains. Close to lake and Harvey's Point Hotel and walking trails. Spacious bedrooms with TV, Tea/Coffee facilities.

| B&B | 3 | Ensuite | €27.50-€32.50 | Dinner | - |
|---|---|---|---|---|---|
| B&B | - | Standard | - | Partial Board | - |
| Single Rate | | | €40-€43.50 | Child reduction | **25%** |

Donegal

**Open:** 5th January-20th December

**Marie McGowan**
THE WATERS EDGE
Glebe, Donegal Town,
Co Donegal

### Donegal Town

Tel: **074 9721523**
Email: **thewatersedgebb2000@hotmail.com**
Web: **www.thewatersedge.ws**

Sligo road R267, opposite school, turn into cul-de-sac at Ballinderg House, 5th House down. Overlooking Bay/15th Century Abbey Ruins.

| B&B | 4 | Ensuite | €30-€35 | Dinner | - |
|-----|---|---------|---------|--------|---|
| B&B | - | Standard | - | Partial Board | - |
| Single Rate | | | - | Child reduction | - |

In Donegal

**Open:** 15th February-15th December

---

**Mrs Shona McNeice**
LAKELAND B&B
Birchill, Lough Eske,
Donegal Town, Co Donegal

### Donegal Town Lough Eske

Tel: **074 9722481**   Fax: **074 9722481**
Email: **mcneice@gofree.indigo.ie**
Web: **www.lakelandbedandbreakfast.com**

'Best Town & Country Home Award 2001'. Guide du Routard. Modern country home with superb panoramic view of Lough Eske and Blue Stack Mountains. Breakfast menu.

| B&B | 4 | Ensuite | €30-€32.50 | Dinner | - |
|-----|---|---------|------------|--------|---|
| B&B | - | Standard | - | Partial Board | - |
| Single Rate | | | €45 | Child reduction | 25% |

Donegal Town 5km

**Open:** 1st March-30th November

---

**Mrs Georgina Morrow**
HIGHFIELD
The Haugh, Lough Eske Road,
Donegal Town, Co Donegal

### Donegal Town

Tel: **074 9722393**
Email: **georginamorrow3@eircom.net**

Quiet elevated home with lovely view, close to Harvey's Point Country Hotel. Leave Donegal via N56, first turn right, signposted Lough Eske road for 2km.

| B&B | 3 | Ensuite | €30-€35 | Dinner | - |
|-----|---|---------|---------|--------|---|
| B&B | - | Standard | - | Partial Board | - |
| Single Rate | | | - | Child reduction | - |

Donegal 2km

**Open:** 1st February-30th November

---

**Mrs Bernie Mulhern**
MILLTOWN HOUSE
Ardlenagh, Sligo Road,
Donegal Town, Co Donegal

### Donegal Town

Tel: **074 9721985**   Fax: **074 9721985**
Email: **milltown@oceanfree.net**
Web: **www.milltownbandb.com**

Friendly, spacious home on R267 (off N15). Ideal touring base. Peaceful location, convenient Beaches, Golf, Fishing, Craft Village.

| B&B | 5 | Ensuite | €27.50-€31 | Dinner | - |
|-----|---|---------|------------|--------|---|
| B&B | - | Standard | - | Partial Board | - |
| Single Rate | | | €40-€43.50 | Child reduction | 33.3% |

Donegal 2km

**Open:** 1st March-30th November

---

**Breege & Martin Mulhern**
ROSEARL
The Glebe, Donegal Town,
Co Donegal

### Donegal Town

Tel: **074 9721462**
Email: **rosearl@eircom.net**

Modern spacious home in quiet residential area. 5 mins walk Town Centre. Golf, Beaches, Crafts nearby. Ideal touring base.

| B&B | 3 | Ensuite | €27.50-€35 | Dinner | - |
|-----|---|---------|------------|--------|---|
| B&B | 1 | Standard | €27.50-€35 | Partial Board | - |
| Single Rate | | | €40-€60 | Child reduction | 25% |

In Donegal

**Open:** All Year

### Mrs Eileen Mulhern
**ARDLENAGH VIEW**
Ardlenagh,
Sligo Road (R267 off N15),
Donegal PO, Co Donegal

**Donegal Town**

TEL: **074 9721646**
EMAIL: **ardlenaghview@eircom.net**
WEB: **www.ardlenaghview.com**

Spacious, elevated home, with view of Donegal Hills and Bay, 3 mins drive from Donegal Town on R267 off N15. Quiet location. Ideal touring base.

| B&B | 5 | Ensuite | €28-€32 | Dinner | - |
| B&B | - | Standard | | Partial Board | - |
| Single Rate | | | €40-€43.50 | Child reduction | 33.3% |

Donegal 2km

**Open:** All Year Except Christmas

---

### Ms Caroline Needham
**INCHBURGH B&B**
Coast Road, Doonan,
Donegal Town, Co Donegal

**Donegal Town**

TEL: **074 9721273**
EMAIL: **cneedham@eircom.net**

Bungalow on N56 situated 0.75km from Donegal Town. Peaceful location off main road. TV's, Tea/Coffee facilities in rooms.

| B&B | 3 | Ensuite | €30-€32.50 | Dinner | - |
| B&B | 1 | Standard | €27.50-€30 | Partial Board | - |
| Single Rate | | | €42.50-€43.50 | Child reduction | 50% |

In Donegal

**Open:** 1st February-30th November

---

### Martina & Patsy O'Sullivan
**DRUMCORROY HOUSE**
Druminin, Donegal Town,
Co Donegal

**Donegal Town**

TEL: **074 9722335**
EMAIL: **drumcorroyhouse@eircom.net**
WEB: **www.drumcorroyhouse.com**

Charming country farmhouse, 10 mins drive Donegal Town with superb panoramic view of Barnesmore Gap and Bluestack Mountains. 800m off N15. Traditional music if requested.

| B&B | 3 | Ensuite | €27.50-€31 | Dinner | - |
| B&B | 1 | Standard | €25.50-€28.50 | Partial Board | - |
| Single Rate | | | €38-€43.50 | Child reduction | 50% |

Donegal Town 5km

**Open:** 1st February-30th November

---

### Mr & Mrs Derek & Edith Little
**DUN ROAMIN**
Rosapenna, Downings,
Co Donegal

**Downings**

TEL: **074 9155716**
EMAIL: **info@littlebandb.com**
WEB: **www.littlebandb.com**

House on elevated site along Atlantic Drive beside Rosapenna Golf Links and panoramic views over Ards forrest, Muckish Mt, Sheephaven Bay, Downings beach.

| B&B | 3 | Ensuite | €30-€31 | Dinner | - |
| B&B | - | Standard | - | Partial Board | - |
| Single Rate | | | €40-€43.50 | Child reduction | 33.3% |

Downings 1.5km

**Open:** 1st March-31st October

---

### Mrs Roisin McHugh
**ROSMAN HOUSE**
Dunfanaghy, Co Donegal

**Dunfanaghy**

TEL: **074 9136273**   FAX: **074 9136273**
EMAIL: **rossman@eircom.net**
WEB: **www.rosmanhouse.ie**

Luxurious modern bungalow with spectacular views. 300 Best B&B's recommended. Breakfast menu, Electric blankets, Hairdryers, Radio Alarms.

| B&B | 5 | Ensuite | €30-€31 | Dinner | - |
| B&B | - | Standard | - | Partial Board | - |
| Single Rate | | | €40-€50 | Child reduction | 25% |

In Dunfanaghy

**Open:** 1st February-31st November

**In Dunfanaghy**

**Mrs Anne Marie Moore**
THE WHINS
Dunfanaghy, Letterkenny, Co Donegal

TEL: **074 9136481**   FAX: **074 9136481**
EMAIL: **annemarie@thewhins.com**
WEB: **www.thewhins.com**

Award winning home, with unique character. Recommended for comfort hospitality and "Fine Breakfasts" - New York Times. Opposite beach, Golf course.

| B&B | 4 | Ensuite | €27.50-€32 | Dinner | - |
| B&B | - | Standard | | Partial Board | - |
| Single Rate | | | €40-€50 | Child reduction | 25% |

**Open:** 11th February-6th November

---

**In Dunfanaghy**

**Bridget Moore**
CARRIGAN HOUSE
Kill, Dunfanaghy, Co Donegal

TEL: **074 9136276**   FAX: **074 9136276**
EMAIL: **carriganhouse@ireland.com**
WEB: **www.carriganhouse.com**

Superior accommodation in the beautiful scenic town of Dunfanaghy. Ideal touring base Glenveagh National Park, Dunlewey Lakeside. Tea/Coffee facilities. Breakfast menu.

| B&B | 4 | Ensuite | €27.50-€32 | Dinner | - |
| B&B | - | Standard | - | Partial Board | - |
| Single Rate | | | €40-€50 | Child reduction | 25% |

**Open:** 16th March-2nd October

---

**In Dungloe**

**Grace & John McCauley**
RADHARC AN OILEAIN
Quay Road, Dungloe, Co Donegal

TEL: **074 9521093/9522152**   FAX: **074 9522385**
EMAIL: **jmcauly@eircom.net**

Modern family run bunglow 5 minutes walk from town centre. Large well maintained gardens, peaceful surroundings panoramic view of west Donegal coast and Islands.

| B&B | 2 | Ensuite | €30-€32 | Dinner | - |
| B&B | 1 | Standard | €28-€30 | Partial Board | - |
| Single Rate | | | €38-€43.50 | Child reduction | 50% |

**Open:** 1st April-1st November

---

**Falcarragh 1km**

**Christina Cannon**
CUAN-NA-MARA
Ballyness, Falcarragh, Co Donegal

TEL: **074 35327**
EMAIL: **crisscannon@hotmail.com**

Dormer bungalow overlooking Ballyness Bay & Tory Island. Glenveagh National Park 16km. Golf, Fishing, miles of Beach locally. Electric blankets. Guide du Routard recommended.

| B&B | 2 | Ensuite | €27.50-€31 | Dinner | - |
| B&B | 2 | Standard | €25.50-€28.50 | Partial Board | - |
| Single Rate | | | €38-€43.50 | Child reduction | 50% |

**Open:** 1st June-30th September

---

**Glenties 1km**

**Mary Ita Boyle**
AVALON
Glen Road, Glenties, Co Donegal

TEL: **074 9551292**
EMAIL: **miboyle@eircom.net**
WEB: **http://homepage.eircom.net/~miboyle/**

Family run home, in a scenic location. Setting for Brian Friels play "Dancing at Lughnasa". Ideal place when touring the county. Coeliacs catered for.

| B&B | 3 | Ensuite | €28-€31 | Dinner | - |
| B&B | 1 | Standard | €27.50-€28.50 | Partial Board | - |
| Single Rate | | | €38-€42.50 | Child reduction | 33.3% |

**Open:** All Year Except Christmas

**Rosaleen Campbell & Conal Gallagher**
LISDANAR HOUSE
Mill Road, Glenties,
Co Donegal

### Glenties

Tel: **074 9551800**
Email: **lisdanar@eircom.net**
Web: **www.lisdanar.com**

Luxurious spacious home. Country setting yet only 2 mins walk to the village on N56. Half way between Glenveagh National Park and Slieve League. Many extras.

| | | | | | |
|---|---|---|---|---|---|
| B&B | 4 | Ensuite | €30-€34 | Dinner | - |
| B&B | - | Standard | | Partial Board | - |
| Single Rate | | | €45-€47 | Child reduction | - |

In Glenties

**Open:** 1st March-1st November

**Mrs Margaret McCafferty**
CLARADON COUNTRY HOUSE
Glen Road, Glenties,
Co Donegal

### Glenties

Tel: **074 9551113**   Fax: **074 9551113**
Email: **mccafferty@eircom.net**

Scenic mountain views/walks. Local Heritage/Museum/Beach/Golf 12km. Advice/Central for touring county. Fishing. 5 Tidy Towns wins. Genealogy help. On R253.

| | | | | | |
|---|---|---|---|---|---|
| B&B | 4 | Ensuite | €27.50-€31 | Dinner | - |
| B&B | - | Standard | - | Partial Board | - |
| Single Rate | | | €40-€43.50 | Child reduction | 33.3% |

Glenties 1km

**Open:** All Year

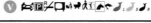

**Mrs Marguerite McLoone**
MARGUERITE'S
Lr Main Street, Glenties,
Co Donegal

### Glenties

Tel: **074 9551699**
Email: **mcloones@eircom.net**

Modern new house located in Town. Ideal base for touring. Beach/Golf 8 miles, local Museum, Scenic Walks, Fishing.

| | | | | | |
|---|---|---|---|---|---|
| B&B | 4 | Ensuite | €27.50-€31 | Dinner | - |
| B&B | - | Standard | - | Partial Board | - |
| Single Rate | | | €40-€43.50 | Child reduction | 33.3% |

In Glenties

**Open:** 1st January-31st December

**Mrs Mary Regan**
ARDLANN
Mill Rd, Glenties, Co Donegal

### Glenties

Tel: **074 9551271**
Email: **ardlann@eircom.net**

On N56. Spacious house with panoramic views from all rooms. Beside Museum, Hotel & Church. Touring base for "Highlands & Islands of Donegal". Golf/Beach 10km.

| | | | | | |
|---|---|---|---|---|---|
| B&B | 3 | Ensuite | €28-€31 | Dinner | - |
| B&B | 1 | Standard | €25.50-€28.50 | Partial Board | - |
| Single Rate | | | €38-€43.50 | Child reduction | 50% |

In Glenties

**Open:** 1st March-30th November

**Ms Mary Anderson**
CORNTON HOUSE
Old Fintra Road, Killybegs,
Co Donegal

### Killybegs

Tel: **074 9731588**
Email: **manderson@eircom.net**
Web: **homepage.eircom.net/~manderson**

Modern family home, quiet scenic location. Beautiful gardens, superb views. 1km Killybegs (10 mins walk). Ideal touring base, Angling, Pony trekking, Beach, Restaurants. 2003 NW Coastal Garden Winner.

| | | | | | |
|---|---|---|---|---|---|
| B&B | 4 | Ensuite | €30-€32.50 | Dinner | - |
| B&B | - | Standard | | Partial Board | - |
| Single Rate | | | €42.50-€45 | Child reduction | 33.3% |

Killybegs 1km

**Open:** 1st March-30th November

**Killybegs**

### Mrs Helena Cunningham
**OCEAN VIEW**
Largy, Killybegs, Co Donegal

TEL: **074 9731576**   FAX: **074 9731576**
EMAIL: **helenaoceanview@eircom.net**
WEB: **www.oceanviewhouse.info**

Luxurious home on elevated site 5km west of Killybegs. Spectacular views of Atlantic Ocean, Sligo Mountains. Beaches, Restaurants nearby. Slieve League 14km.

| B&B | 5 | Ensuite | €30-€45 | Dinner | - |
| B&B | - | Standard | | Partial Board | - |
| Single Rate | | | €45-€50 | Child reduction | 25% |

Killybegs 5km

**Open:** 1st May-30th September

---

**Killybegs**

### Mrs Ann Keeney
**HOLLYCREST LODGE**
Donegal Road, Killybegs,
Co Donegal

TEL: **074 9731470**
EMAIL: **hollycrest@hotmail.com**
WEB: **www.littleireland.ie/hollycrestlodge**

Recommended 300 Best B&B's. On main Donegal/Killybegs road, situated on right. Guests TV lounge. Bedrooms Tea/coffee facilities, Hairdryers and TV.

| B&B | 3 | Ensuite | €28-€31 | Dinner | - |
| B&B | 1 | Standard | €26-€29 | Partial Board | - |
| Single Rate | | | €38-€44 | Child reduction | 50% |

Killybegs 1km

**Open:** 1st February-31st October

---

**Killybegs**

### Phyllis Melly
**BANNAGH HOUSE**
Fintra Road, Killybegs,
Co Donegal

TEL: **074 9731108**
EMAIL: **bannaghhouse@eircom.net**
WEB: **www.bannaghhouse.com**

Modern bungalow on elevated site overlooking Killybegs Harbour and Fishing Fleet. Rooms ensuite. Private car park. Frommer recommended, 300 best B&B's.

| B&B | 4 | Ensuite | €30-€33 | Dinner | - |
| B&B | - | Standard | - | Partial Board | - |
| Single Rate | | | - | Child reduction | - |

In Killybegs

**Open:** 1st April-31st October

---

**Killybegs**

### Tully Family
**TULLYCULLION HOUSE**
Tullaghacullion, Killybegs,
Co Donegal

TEL: **074 9731842**   FAX: **074 9731842**
EMAIL: **tullys@gofree.indigo.ie**
WEB: **www.tullycullion.com**

New luxurious country home. Conservatory. Secluded, elevated 2 acre site. Panoramic view overlooking Killybegs Port/Hills/Farmland/Donkeys. Boat shaped signs (N56).

| B&B | 5 | Ensuite | €30-€40 | Dinner | - |
| B&B | - | Standard | | Partial Board | - |
| Single Rate | | | €40-€50 | Child reduction | 50% |

Killybegs 2km

**Open:** 1st March-1st November

---

**Killybegs**

### Catherine A Walsh
**OILEAN ROE HOUSE**
Fintra Rd, Killybegs,
Co Donegal

TEL: **074 9731192**
EMAIL: **walsh01@eircom.net**

Spacious 2 storey home, near Beach & Restaurants. Convenient to Slieve League, Glencolumbkille & Killybegs Harbour. TV in all rooms & Tea in lounge.

| B&B | 4 | Ensuite | €27.50-€31 | Dinner | - |
| B&B | - | Standard | - | Partial Board | - |
| Single Rate | | | €40-€43.50 | Child reduction | 50% |

Killybegs 1km

**Open:** 12th March-30th September

**Mrs Sophia Boyle**
BRIDGEBURN HOUSE
Trentagh, Letterkenny,
Co Donegal

Tel: **074 37167**
Email: **sophia@bridgeburnhouse.com**
Web: **www.bridgeburnhouse.com**

15 mins drive from Letterkenny N56 to village of Kilmacrennan, turn left at signpost for Churchill - 5km. Ideal for Glenveagh Park, Flaxmill, Glebe Gallery.

| B&B | 3 | Ensuite | €28-€31 | Dinner | €19-€19 |
|-----|---|---------|---------|--------|---------|
| B&B | 1 | Standard | €26-€28.50 | Partial Board | - |
| Single Rate | | | €40-€43.50 | Child reduction | 50% |

Letterkenny 9km

**Open:** 2nd January-20th December

---

**Mrs Elizabeth Cullen**
ARDLEE
Gortlee, Letterkenny,
Co Donegal

Tel: **074 9121943** Fax: **074 9121943**
Email: **lizcullen@eircom.net**

Modern house close to town Bus Station, Theatre, Hotels. TV, Tea tray in rooms. Turn left off Ramelton road opposite Aldi store, up Gortlee road, next left at top.

| B&B | 5 | Ensuite | €27.50-€31 | Dinner | - |
|-----|---|---------|------------|--------|---|
| B&B | 1 | Standard | €25.50-€28.50 | Partial Board | - |
| Single Rate | | | €38-€43.50 | Child reduction | 33.3% |

Letterkenny 1km

**Open:** 6th January-20th December

---

**Nuala Duddy**
PENNSYLVANIA HOUSE B&B
Curraghleas Mountain Top,
Letterkenny, Co Donegal

Tel: **074 9126808** Fax: **074 9128905**
Email: **info@accommodationdonegal.com**
Web: **www.accommodationdonegal.com**

Spacious rooms. Superb views. Central for touring Glenveigh National Park, Giants Causeway. Peaceful. Off N56. Laundry facilities. Electric blankets. Home baking. AA ◆◆◆◆.

| B&B | 4 | Ensuite | €45-€55 | Dinner | - |
|-----|---|---------|---------|--------|---|
| B&B | | Standard | - | Partial Board | - |
| Single Rate | | | - | Child reduction | - |

Letterkenny 2km

**Open:** All Year Except Christmas

---

**Danny & May Herrity**
TOWN VIEW
Leck Road, Letterkenny,
Co Donegal

Tel: **074 9121570/9125138**
Email: **townview@eircom.net**
Web: **www.townviewhouse.com**

Frommer & Guide du Routard listing. Food awards. 3 downstairs rooms. Teamaking, Hairdryers, Electric blankets. Cross bridge at Dunnes Stores, keep left for 1km.

| B&B | 6 | Ensuite | €31 | Dinner | - |
|-----|---|---------|-----|--------|---|
| B&B | - | Standard | | Partial Board | - |
| Single Rate | | | €43.50 | Child reduction | - |

Letterkenny 1km

**Open:** All Year

---

**Breid & Paddy Kelly**
ARDGLAS
Lurgybrack, Sligo Road,
Letterkenny, Co Donegal

Tel: **074 9122516** Fax: **074 9122516**
Email: **ardglas@yahoo.co.uk**
Web: **www.ardglas.com**

Spacious home panoramic views. 1km from Dryarch roundabout and Holiday Inn on N13 to Sligo. Ideal tour and golf base. TV, Hairdryer, Tea Facilities, Frommer.

| B&B | 6 | Ensuite | €27.50-€31 | Dinner | - |
|-----|---|---------|------------|--------|---|
| B&B | - | Standard | | Partial Board | - |
| Single Rate | | | €40-€43.50 | Child reduction | 33.3% |

Letterkenny 3km

**Open:** 1st April-14th October

**Majella Leonard**
OAKLANDS B&B
8 Oakland Park, Gortlee Road,
Letterkenny, Co Donegal

Tᴇʟ: **074 25529**
Eᴍᴀɪʟ: **oaklandhouse@hotmail.com**
Wᴇʙ: **www.bandbdonegal.net**

Family run B&B in quiet cul-de-sac opposite Aldi. 5 mins walk from Bars, Clubs, Restaurants. Ideal base for touring NW Region. Beside theatre and college.

| B&B | 4 | Ensuite | €30-€31 | Dinner | - |
| B&B | - | Standard | | Partial Board | - |
| Single Rate | | | €40-€43.50 | Child reduction | 50% |

Letterkenny 1km

**Open:** 7th January-7th December

---

**Mrs Mary McBride**
RINNEEN COUNTRY HOME
Woodland, Ramelton Road,
Letterkenny, Co Donegal

Tᴇʟ: **074 9124591**
Eᴍᴀɪʟ: **rinneencountryhome@eircom.net**

Modern home in peaceful countryside. Travel 5km on R245 & left 1km. Warm welcome & refreshments on arrival. Castlegrove Restaurant and Silver Tassie Hotel 2.5km. Ideal touring base.

| B&B | 4 | Ensuite | €27.50-€31 | Dinner | - |
| B&B | - | Standard | - | Partial Board | - |
| Single Rate | | | €40-€43.50 | Child reduction | 50% |

Letterkenny 6km

**Open:** 1st February-20th December

---

**Mrs Maureen McCleary**
GLENCAIRN HOUSE
Ramelton Road, Letterkenny,
Co Donegal

Tᴇʟ: **074 9124393/9125242**
Eᴍᴀɪʟ: **glencairnbb@hotmail.com**
Wᴇʙ: **www.glencairnhousebb.com**

Panoramic view from patio. On R245, near Mount Errigal Hotel/Silver Tassie and Golf. Central for touring. Guide du Routard recommended. All ground floor bedrooms, TV/Tea/Coffee/Hairdryer.

| B&B | 5 | Ensuite | €27.50-€31 | Dinner | - |
| B&B | 1 | Standard | €25.50-€28.50 | Partial Board | - |
| Single Rate | | | €38-€43.50 | Child reduction | 33.3% |

Letterkenny 2km

**Open:** 1st January-20th December

---

**Leonie McCloskey**
BLACKWOOD HOUSE
Ramelton Road, Letterkenny,
Co Donegal

Tᴇʟ: **074 26364**
Eᴍᴀɪʟ: **blackwoodbb@eircom.net**

Warm hospitality offered in this tastefully decorated home. Well situated on main Ramelton road R245. Home baking and breakfast menu available.

| B&B | 4 | Ensuite | €27.50-€31 | Dinner | - |
| B&B | - | Standard | | Partial Board | - |
| Single Rate | | | €40-€43.50 | Child reduction | 33.3% |

Letterkenny 2km

**Open:** 3rd January-23rd December

---

**Philomena McDaid**
LARKFIELD B&B
Drumnahoe, Letterkenny,
Co Donegal

Tᴇʟ: **074 21478**
Eᴍᴀɪʟ: **philomena21478@hotmail.com**
Wᴇʙ: **www.larkfield.net**

Quiet comfortable house. Secure private parking.AA ◆◆◆ - First left past Holiday Inn on N13 towards Letterkenny. Ideal for touring Giants Causeway, Glenveagh National Park.

| B&B | 2 | Ensuite | €27.50-€31 | Dinner | - |
| B&B | 1 | Standard | €25.50-€28.50 | Partial Board | - |
| Single Rate | | | €38-€41 | Child reduction | 50% |

Letterkenny 2km

**Open:** 3rd January-22nd December

**Letterkenny**

**Daniel & Genevieve McElwee**
FERN HOUSE
Lower Main Street,
Kilmacrennan, Letterkenny,
Co Donegal

TEL: **074 9139218**
EMAIL: **mailto@fern-house.com**
WEB: **www.fern-house.com**

Bright spacious two storey town house in village on N56 to Dunfanaghy. Glenveagh National Park 16K. Bars/Restaurants walking distance.

| B&B | 4 | Ensuite | €27.50-€31 | Dinner | - |
| B&B | - | Standard | | Partial Board | - |
| Single Rate | | | €40-€43.50 | Child reduction | 33.3% |

Letterkenny 9km

**Open:** 1st January-23rd December

**Letterkenny**

**Eugene & Ann O'Donnell**
WHITE PARK B&B
Ballyraine, Letterkenny,
Co Donegal

TEL: **074 9124067/9167597**   FAX: **074 9167597**
EMAIL: **whiteparkhouse@eircom.net**
WEB: **accommodationletterkenny.com**

On R245 to Ramelton. Large comfortable home. Spacious groundfloor rooms. Superb location for touring. 30 mins Glenveagh National Park & beach. 5 mins walk Mount Errigal Hotel, Pitch & Putt.

| B&B | 6 | Ensuite | €27.50-€31 | Dinner | - |
| B&B | - | Standard | - | Partial Board | - |
| Single Rate | | | €40-€43.50 | Child reduction | 25% |

Letterkenny

**Open:** 4th January-20th December

**Ramelton**

**Mervyn & Claire Hutton**
DONEGAL SHORE
Aughnagaddy, Ramelton,
Co Donegal

TEL: **074 9152006**
EMAIL: **huttomt@aol.com**
WEB: **www.donegalshore.com**

Warm welcome, great views from conservatory of our home off R245, 9km from Letterkenny. Fine A-La-Carte dinner menu, wine licence. French/Flemish spoken.

| B&B | 4 | Ensuite | €27.50-€31 | Dinner | €25 |
| B&B | - | Standard | - | Partial Board | - |
| Single Rate | | | €40-€43.50 | Child reduction | 50% |

Letterkenny 9km

**Open:** 1st March-20th December

**Raphoe**

**Mrs Shirley Chambers**
Strabane Road
Raphoe, Co Donegal

TEL: **074 9145410**

Modern house in peaceful location. 3 minutes walk from Raphoe, Beltony Stone Circle 4km. Tea making facilities. Ideal touring base Giants Causeway, Grianan Aileach.

| B&B | 4 | Ensuite | €27.50-€31 | Dinner | - |
| B&B | - | Standard | | Partial Board | - |
| Single Rate | | | €40-€43.50 | Child reduction | 33.3% |

In Raphoe

**Open:** 1st April-31st October

## RESERVATIONS

- Confirm phone bookings in writing without delay with agreed deposit.
- To avoid misunderstandings later, check rate on booking and clarify any additional changes which may apply to your booking.
- Give details of any special requirements.
- State clearly day, date of arrival and departure date.

# Approved
# Accommodation

**Look out for the quality shamrock approved sign whenever you're seeking accommodation and be sure of attaining the comfort you deserve when holidaying in Ireland.**

*This sign will be displayed at all premises which are approved to Irish Tourist Board standards by Tourism Accommodation Approvals Ltd., Coolcholly, Ballyshannon, Co. Donegal, Ireland. Tel: 071-9852760 Fax: 071-9852761 E-mail: taahomes@eircom.net*

www.taaireland.com

Co Leitrim with it's beautiful Lakelands, it's deep valleys and unspoiled terrain is famous for it's international coarse angling cruising and overseas tourists enjoy numerous festivals and attractions. Horse-riding, Golfing, Cycling, Hill-walking and other outdoor activities.

---

**Mrs Eileen Breen**
SUI MHUIRE
Cleendargen, Ballinamore,
Co Leitrim

### Ballinamore

TEL: **071 9644189**
EMAIL: **eileen_breen16@hotmail.com**

Situated 2.5 acres, scenic surroundings, Excellent fishing, golf, Entry/Exit drives. Situated route N202 Swanlinbar/Enniskillen Road. Highly recommended.

| B&B | 6 | Ensuite | €30-€32 | Dinner | €19-€19 |
|---|---|---|---|---|---|
| B&B | - | Standard | - | Partial Board | €294 |
| Single Rate | | | €40-€43.50 | Child reduction | 25% |

Ballinamore 2km

**Open:** 1st April-1st October

---

**Julie & Patrick Curran**
THE OLD RECTORY
Fenagh Glebe, Ballinamore,
Co Leitrim

### Ballinamore

TEL: **071 9644089**
EMAIL: **info@theoldrectoryireland.com**
WEB: **www.theoldrectoryireland.com**

The Old Rectory is an atmospheric 19th century Georgian Home on 50 acres of woodland overlooking Fenagh Lake and located beside Fenagh's historic Abbey's.

| B&B | 4 | Ensuite | €33-€35 | Dinner | - |
|---|---|---|---|---|---|
| B&B | - | Standard | - | Partial Board | - |
| Single Rate | | | €40-€43.50 | Child reduction | 25% |

Ballinamore 4.5km

**Open:** 1st February-1st December

---

**Damien Hamill**
HAMILLS B&B
High Street, Ballinamore,
Co Leitrim

### Ballinamore

TEL: **071 9644211**
EMAIL: **dhamill@gofree.indigo.ie**

Quietly situated in it's own grounds, in ideal town centre location, modern home with spacious comfortable rooms. A warm welcome awaits you.

| B&B | 4 | Ensuite | €28-€38 | Dinner | - |
|---|---|---|---|---|---|
| B&B | - | Standard | - | Partial Board | - |
| Single Rate | | | €40-€44 | Child reduction | 25% |

In Ballinamore

**Open:** 1st January-23rd December

---

**Mrs Valerie Cahill**
ATTYRORY LODGE
Dublin Road, Carrick-on-Shannon, Co Leitrim

### Carrick-on-Shannon

TEL: **071 9620955** FAX: **071 9620955**
EMAIL: **attyrorylodge@eircom.net**

Roots dating 100 years in Leitrim. Complimentary interior capturing warmth and history in style. Rough Guide recommended. Located on N4 Dublin/Sligo/Donegal route.

| B&B | 5 | Ensuite | €35 | Dinner | - |
|---|---|---|---|---|---|
| B&B | - | Standard | - | Partial Board | - |
| Single Rate | | | €45 | Child reduction | 25% |

Carrick-on-Shannon 1km

**Open:** 1st April-31st October

**Gerard & Jeanette Conefrey**
CANAL VIEW HOUSE
Keshcarrigan, Carrick-on-Shannon, Co Leitrim

### Carrick-on-Shannon

TEL: **071 9642056**   FAX: **071 9642261**
EMAIL: **canalviewcountryhome@eircom.net**

Delightful country home with breathtaking view of Cruisers passing. All rooms with pleasant outlook. Quiet walks and cycle routes. Fishing on doorstep. Music in Pubs.

| B&B | 6 | Ensuite | €32-€32 | Dinner | €20-€35 |
|-----|---|---------|---------|--------|---------|
| B&B | - | Standard | €32-€32 | Partial Board | €294 |
| Single Rate | | | €40-€40 | Child reduction | 33.3% |

In Keshcarrigan

**Open:** 1st January-31st December

---

**Martin Barnes & Ruth Cashill**
HARTLEY LODGE B&B
Hartley, Carrick-on-Shannon, Co Leitrim

### Carrick-on-Shannon

TEL: **071 9650883**
EMAIL: **hartleylodge@eircom.net**
WEB: **www.hartleylodge.com**

large classic style house, off road parking. All rooms ensuite, Tea/Coffee facilities & TV. Boating, Fishing, Walking, Golfing close by. Dinner on request.

| B&B | 5 | Ensuite | €35-€35 | Dinner | €18-€20 |
|-----|---|---------|---------|--------|---------|
| B&B | - | Standard | - | Partial Board | - |
| Single Rate | | | €45-€45 | Child reduction | - |

In Carrick-on-Shannon

**Open:** 3rd January-23rd December

---

**Aiden & Kathleen Meehan**
BLUEBELL HOUSE
Clooneen, Manorhamilton, Co Leitrim

### Manorhamilton

TEL: **071 9855384**
EMAIL: **bluebellbb@eircom.net**
WEB: **http://homepage.eircom.net/~bluebellbb/**

Friendly and spacious home, in tranquil setting with O'Donnell's Rock and Benbo mountain as spectacular views. Ideally situated in walking distance of town. Mobile no: 086 1542860.

| B&B | 3 | Ensuite | €30-€35 | Dinner | - |
|-----|---|---------|---------|--------|---------|
| B&B | - | Standard | - | Partial Board | - |
| Single Rate | | | €40-€50 | Child reduction | 25% |

Manorhamilton

**Open:** 1st February-31st November

---

## TELEPHONE

- Operator assisted calls within Ireland     Dial 10
- International telephone operator     Dial 11818
- Directory Enquiries     Dial 11811

**FOR TROUBLE-FREE TELEPHONE CALLS FROM PUBLIC PAY PHONES IT IS ADVISABLE TO PURCHASE A TELEPHONE CALLCARD AVAILABLE IN POST OFFICES AND WHEREVER YOU SEE A CALLCARD SIGN.**

**TO DIAL IRELAND FROM ABROAD:** Country Access Code + 353 + Area Code (omit first zero) + Local Number

## SYMBOL

### LOOK OUT FOR THIS SYMBOL WHICH
### ALL MEMBERS OF TOWN & COUNTRY HOMES DISPLAY

'County of the Little Hills'. The constant presence of the attractive lakes - Muckno, Gasslough, Erny and Darty has a special appeal to the sportsman. The intriguing roads winding around the hills serve to portray the dignified charm of pastoral landscape.

---

Carrickmacross 3km

**Margaret Flanagan**
SHANMULLAGH HOUSE
Killanny Rd (off Dundalk Rd),
Carrickmacross, Co Monaghan

### Carrickmacross

TEL: **042 9663038**  FAX: **042 9661915**
EMAIL: **flanagan@esatclear.ie**
WEB: **www.shanmullagh-house.com**

Artistically decorated home 2km Carrickmacross, exit N2 Dublin/Derry at Nuremore Hotel exit. Recommendations, Lonely Planet, Hidden Ireland, Elsie Dillard.

| B&B | 4 | Ensuite | €27.50-€31 | Dinner | - |
|-----|---|---------|------------|--------|---|
| B&B | - | Standard | - | Partial Board | - |
| Single Rate | | | €40-€43.50 | Child reduction | 33.3% |

**Open:** All Year

---

Carrickmacross 6.5km

**Ms Kate McCafferty**
ANDANTE B&B
Annamarron, Coolderry,
Carrickmacross, Co Monaghan

### Carrickmacross

TEL: **041 6855925**  FAX: **041 6855925**
EMAIL: **andant@eircom.net**
WEB: **www.andantebandb.com**

Spacious family run home along N2 bus route, close to golf courses, lakes, horse riding, 3 of our 4 rooms have walk in wardrobes. Dublin Airport 45 minutes.

| B&B | 3 | Ensuite | €30-€31 | Dinner | - |
|-----|---|---------|---------|--------|---|
| B&B | 1 | Standard | €30-€30 | Partial Board | - |
| Single Rate | | | €38-€43.50 | Child reduction | 25% |

**Open:** 7th January-22nd December

---

Castleblaney 1km

**Pat & Vera Conlon**
BLITTOGUE HOUSE B&B
Dublin Road, Castleblaney,
Co Monaghan

### Castleblaney

TEL: **042 9740476**
EMAIL: **blittogue.house@ireland.com**

New luxury family run home, near scenic Lough Muckno. Walking, Fishing, Golf, Horse Riding, Bowling, Boating, Skiing. On N2. Restaurants, pubs. Warm welcome.

| B&B | 3 | Ensuite | €30-€32.50 | Dinner | - |
|-----|---|---------|------------|--------|---|
| B&B | 2 | Standard | €27.50-€30 | Partial Board | - |
| Single Rate | | | €38-€43.50 | Child reduction | 25% |

**Open:** All Year

---

Castleblaney 1km

**Joan Loughman**
ROCKVILLE HOUSE
Dundalk Road, Castleblaney,
Co Monaghan

### Castleblaney

TEL: **042 9746161**  FAX: **042 9740226**
EMAIL: **rockvillehouse@hotmail.com**
WEB: **www.dirl.com/monaghan/rockville-house.htm**

Situated on the outskirts of the town of Castleblaney on the main Dublin to Derry N2 road. Lough Muckno Leisure Park is within walking distance.

| B&B | 3 | Ensuite | €30-€31 | Dinner | - |
|-----|---|---------|---------|--------|---|
| B&B | 1 | Standard | €28-€30 | Partial Board | - |
| Single Rate | | | €38-€43.50 | Child reduction | 25% |

**Open:** All Year

**Anna & Fergus Murray**
AN TEACH BAN
Main Street, Emyvale,
Co Monaghan

## Emyvale

TEL: **047 87198**   FAX: **047 87198**
EMAIL: **anteachban@eircom.net**
WEB: **www.anteachban.com**

Modern spacious family residence situated in the picturesque village of Emyvale on the N2, 11km north of Monaghan Town

| B&B | 4 | Ensuite | €27.50-€31 | Dinner | - |
|-----|---|---------|------------|--------|---|
| B&B | - | Standard | - | Partial Board | - |
| Single Rate | | | €40-€43.50 | Child reduction | 25% |

n Emyvale Village

**Open:** 1st February-30th November

**Maureen & Eugene Treanor**
GRANGEVIEW HOUSE
Mullinderg, Emyvale,
Co Monaghan

## Emyvale

TEL: **047 87358**   FAX: **047 87358**
EMAIL: **maureenttreanor@eircom.net**
WEB: **www.grangeviewhouse.com**

Situated on N2 Dublin/Derry Road. One hours drive to all main towns in Northern Ireland and Donegal. Hospitality tray on arrival.

| B&B | 3 | Ensuite | €27.50-€31 | Dinner | - |
|-----|---|---------|------------|--------|---|
| B&B | - | Standard | - | Partial Board | - |
| Single Rate | | | €40-€43.50 | Child reduction | 33.3% |

Monaghan 11km

**Open:** 3rd January-20th December

**Mrs Paula Trappe**
GROVE LODGE
Old Armagh Road, Latlurcan,
Co Monaghan

## Monaghan

TEL: **047 84677**
EMAIL: **grovelodge@eircom.net**

Modern spacious family residence centrally located to all amenities. Next door to Hillgrove Hotel. Turn off N2 at Monaghan cathedral. Highly recommended.

| B&B | 3 | Ensuite | €30-€35 | Dinner | - |
|-----|---|---------|---------|--------|---|
| B&B | - | Standard | - | Partial Board | - |
| Single Rate | | | €40-€43.50 | Child reduction | 25% |

n Monaghan

**Open:** 1st January-31st December

Sligo has surprising contrasting landscapes, spectacular scenery, dream for painters, writers, historians, and archaeologists.
Sligo has the second largest megalithic cemetery in Europe.
Sandy beaches - Golf - Fishing - Theatre - Equestrian - Water Sports - Traditional music, good restaurants and a warm welcome for visitors.

---

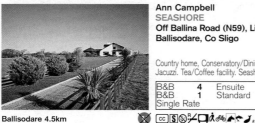

**Ann Campbell**
SEASHORE
Off Ballina Road (N59), Lisduff,
Ballisodare, Co Sligo

## Ballisodare

Tel: **071 9167827**   Fax: **071 9167827**
Email: **seashore@oceanfree.net**
Web: **www.seashoreguests.com**

Country home, Conservatory/Dining room overlooking Knocknarea, Ox Mountains, Ballisodare Bay. Tennis Court, Jacuzzi. Tea/Coffee facility. Seashore walks, birdwatching facility. AA ◆◆◆, Red Diamond Award 2002/03.

| | | | | | |
|---|---|---|---|---|---|
| B&B | 4 | Ensuite | €35-€37.50 | Dinner | - |
| B&B | 1 | Standard | - | Partial Board | - |
| Single Rate | | | €45-€50 | Child reduction | - |

**Ballisodare 4.5km**

**Open:** All Year

---

**Mrs Noreen & Peter Mullin**
MILLHOUSE
Keenaghan, Ballymote,
Co Sligo

## Ballymote

Tel: **071 9183449**
Email: **info@sligo-accommodation.com**
Web: **www.sligo-accommodation.com**

AIB "Best Overall" and Galtee breakfast award winning superb family home, peaceful location. Private tennis court. TV, Hairdryers. Megalithic tomb, Castle.

| | | | | | |
|---|---|---|---|---|---|
| B&B | 5 | Ensuite | €27.50-€31 | Dinner | - |
| B&B | - | Standard | - | Partial Board | - |
| Single Rate | | | €40-€43.50 | Child reduction | 25% |

**In Ballymote**

**Open:** 15th January-10th December

---

**Mrs Noeleen Henry**
HILLCREST
Ballindoon, Castlebaldwin,
Co Sligo

## Castlebaldwin

Tel: **071 9165559**   Fax: **071 9165559**
Email: **hillcrestfarm@eircom.net**
Web: **http:homepage.eircom.net/~hillcrestbandb/**

Quiet comfortable home overlookingg beautiful fishing lake of Lough Arrow and Carrowkeel Passage Tombs, off N4 at Castlebaldwin between Boyle and Sligo.

| | | | | | |
|---|---|---|---|---|---|
| B&B | 4 | Ensuite | €28-€33 | Dinner | €19 |
| B&B | - | Standard | - | Partial Board | - |
| Single Rate | | | €40-€43.50 | Child reduction | 50% |

**Castlebaldwin 4km**

**Open:** 14th March-31st October

---

**Mrs Geraldine Gibbons**
YEATS LODGE
Drumcliffe, Co Sligo

## Drumcliffe

Tel: **071 9173787**   Fax: **071 9173749**
Email: **gibbonsg@eircom.net**
Web: **www.yeatslodge.com**

500 mtrs to Bar & Restaurant, adjacent to Yeats Grave, Glencar Waterfall & Lake 5km, Fishing, Horse Riding, Watersports nearby.

| | | | | | |
|---|---|---|---|---|---|
| B&B | 4 | Ensuite | €32-€34 | Dinner | - |
| B&B | - | Standard | - | Partial Board | - |
| Single Rate | | | €42-€44 | Child reduction | 50% |

**Sligo 8km**

**Open:** 1st February-30th November

### Freda Monaghan
GLEBE HOUSE
Rathcormac, Drumcliffe,
Co Sligo

**Drumcliffe**

TEL: **071 9145074**
EMAIL: **fredamonaghan@sligoweb.zzn.com**

Situated in the heart of Yeats Country in the picturesque village of Rathcormac. 3 miles from Sligo N15 with Church, Shop, Pubs and Restaurant within walking.

| B&B | 2 | Ensuite | €30-€31 | Dinner | - |
| B&B | 1 | Standard | €30-€30 | Partial Board | - |
| Single Rate | | | €45-€45 | Child reduction | 25% |

Sligo 5km

**Open:** 1st February-30th November

### Mrs Masie Rooney
CASTLETOWN HOUSE
Drumcliffe, Co Sligo

**Drumcliffe**

TEL: **071 9163204**
EMAIL: **castletown_house@yahoo.ie**
WEB: **homepage.eircom.net/~castletownhouse/index.htm**

Situated beneath the bliss of Benbulben Mountains. Peaceful location. Hospitality, nearby W. B. Yeats grave. Glencar Waterfalls. Restaurants, Lisadell Hse.

| B&B | 3 | Ensuite | €30-€32 | Dinner | - |
| B&B | 1 | Standard | €27.50-€30 | Partial Board | - |
| Single Rate | | | €38-€43.50 | Child reduction | - |

Sligo 9km

**Open:** 1st April-31st October

### Mrs Maureen McGowan
MOUNT EDWARD LODGE
Off N15, Ballinfull, Grange,
Co Sligo

**Grange**

TEL: **071 9163263** FAX: **071 9163263**
EMAIL: **mountedwardlodge@eircom.net**
WEB: **www.littleireland.ie/mountedwardlodge**

Panoramic peaceful setting off N15. Views Sea, Mountains. Midway Sligo/Donegal. Breakfast conservatory, Breakfast menu. TV, Tea/Coffee, Electric blankets. Golf, Horseriding. Credit cards.

| B&B | 3 | Ensuite | €28-€31 | Dinner | --€25 |
| B&B | 2 | Standard | €26-€29 | Partial Board | - |
| Single Rate | | | €38-€43.50 | Child reduction | 25% |

Grange 2km

**Open:** 2nd January-22nd December

### Mrs Kathleen Neary
ROSSWICK
Grange, Co Sligo

**Grange**

TEL: **071 9163516**
EMAIL: **rosswick@eircom.net**

Family home, Personal attention. Panoramic view of Benbulben, Benwisken. Beaches, Horse riding, Hillwalking. Yeats Country closeby. TV, Hairdryer, Clock Radio all rooms. Breakfast menu.

| B&B | 2 | Ensuite | €27.50-€31 | Dinner | - |
| B&B | 1 | Standard | €25.50-€28.50 | Partial Board | - |
| Single Rate | | | €38-€43.50 | Child reduction | - |

n Grange

**Open:** 1st March-30th November

### Mrs Ita Connolly
IORRAS
Ballincar, Rosses Point Road,
Sligo, Co Sligo

**Rosses Point**

TEL: **071 9144911**
EMAIL: **connollyiorras@eircom.net**

Modern spacious home situated 2kms on Sligo to Rosses Point Road. TV, Tea/coffee in bedrooms. Golf, Sailing, Beach nearby. Breakfast menu.

| B&B | 4 | Ensuite | €32-€35 | Dinner | - |
| B&B | - | Standard | - | Partial Board | - |
| Single Rate | | | - | Child reduction | 50% |

Sligo 4km

**Open:** 1st February-30th November

**Mrs I Fullerton**
SEA PARK HOUSE
Rosses Point Road, Sligo,
Co Sligo

**Rosses Point**

TEL: **071 9145556** FAX: **071 9145556**
EMAIL: **seaparkhouse@eircom.net**

3.5km from Sligo on R291 Rosses Point rd. 3km Beach, Sailing, Golf. Extensive b'fast menu. TV, Tea/Coffee, Hairdryers in bedrooms. Many recommendations.

| B&B | 4 | Ensuite | €32-€35 | Dinner | - |
|---|---|---|---|---|---|
| B&B | - | Standard | - | Partial Board | - |
| Single Rate | | | - | Child reduction | 33.3% |

Sligo 3.5km

**Open:** 1st January-17th December

---

**Mrs Cait Gill**
KILVARNET HOUSE
Rosses Point, Co Sligo

**Rosses Point**

TEL: **071 9177202**
EMAIL: **kilvarnethouse@eircom.net**
WEB: **http://www.littleireland.ie/kilvarnethouse**

Modern comforts, traditional hospitality. In heart of Yeats Country, within walking distance of championship Golf Course, Yacht Club, Beaches, Restaurants.

| B&B | 4 | Ensuite | €35-€40 | Dinner | - |
|---|---|---|---|---|---|
| B&B | - | Standard | - | Partial Board | - |
| Single Rate | | | €45-€50 | Child reduction | - |

In Rosses Point

**Open:** 1st March-31st October

---

**Kelly Family**
SERENITY
Doonierin, Kintogher,
Rosses Point, Co Sligo

**Rosses Point**

TEL: **071 9143351**
EMAIL: **serenitysligo@eircom.net**

Award winner for hospitality. High quality food and accommodation. Superb Bay and Mountain views, cul-de-sac. Seaside location. You wont find a nicer place.

| B&B | 3 | Ensuite | €32-€40 | Dinner | - |
|---|---|---|---|---|---|
| B&B | - | Standard | - | Partial Board | - |
| Single Rate | | | - | Child reduction | - |

Rosses Point 5km

**Open:** 1st April-31st October

---

**Mrs Mary Scanlon**
PHILMAR HOUSE
Ballincar, Rosses Point Rd,
Sligo, Co Sligo

**Rosses Point**

TEL: **071 9145014**
EMAIL: **philmar-house-b-b@oceanfree.net**

Old style with modern comforts in quiet, scenic location. Large gardens for guests. Minutes from Golf course, Beaches, Sailing, Tennis.

| B&B | 2 | Ensuite | €32-€35 | Dinner | - |
|---|---|---|---|---|---|
| B&B | 2 | Standard | €30-€32 | Partial Board | - |
| Single Rate | | | - | Child reduction | 25% |

Sligo 4km

**Open:** All Year

---

**Mrs Renagh Burns**
OCHILLMORE HOUSE
Scarden-Beg, Strandhill Road,
Co Sligo

**Sligo**

TEL: **071 68032**

Dormer Bungalow on Strandhill/Airport Road. TV, Hairdryers, Electric Blankets, Tea making facilities. Close Beach, Airport, Golf, Megalithic Tombs, Mountains.

| B&B | 4 | Ensuite | €25-€26 | Dinner | - |
|---|---|---|---|---|---|
| B&B | - | Standard | - | Partial Board | - |
| Single Rate | | | €33-€35 | Child reduction | 50% |

Sligo 4km

**Open:** 1st January-31st December

**Mary Cadden**
LISSADELL
**Mailcoach Road (N15/N16),**
**Sligo, Co Sligo**

Tel: **071 9161937**

5 minute walk Town Centre. On N15/16. 200 yards off N4. TV, Hairdryers. Tea/Coffee facilities all rooms. Non-smoking.

| | | | | | |
|---|---|---|---|---|---|
| B&B | 3 | Ensuite | €32-€34 | Dinner | - |
| B&B | - | Standard | - | Partial Board | - |
| Single Rate | | | €42-€46 | Child reduction | - |

Sligo

**Open:** All Year Except Christmas

---

**Mary & Tommy Carroll**
ARD CUILINN LODGE
**Drumiskabole (R284), Sligo,**
**Co Sligo**

Tel: **071 9162925**
Email: **ardcuiln@esatclear.ie**
Web: **www.littleireland.ie/ardcuilinnlodge**

Luxury accommodation, tranquil scenic surroundings. Home cooking. Guide du Routard, Petit Fute recommended. Near Lough Gill, 1km off N4(Carrowroe roundabout) R284. Warm welcome.

| | | | | | |
|---|---|---|---|---|---|
| B&B | 2 | Ensuite | €29-€31 | Dinner | - |
| B&B | 1 | Standard | €27-€28.50 | Partial Board | - |
| Single Rate | | | | Child reduction | - |

Sligo 5km

**Open:** 10th March-25th October

---

**Mrs Mary Conway**
STONECROFT
**off Donegal Road (N15),**
**Kintogher, Sligo, Co Sligo**

Tel: **071 9145667**　Fax: **071 9145669**
Email: **stonecroft_sligo@yahoo.com**
Web: **www.stonecroftsligo.com**

Cosy home in Yeats country 300m off N15 Donegal Road. Near Drumcliffe Church. Superb views. Credit Cards, TV, Tea facilities.

| | | | | | |
|---|---|---|---|---|---|
| B&B | 5 | Ensuite | €38 | Dinner | - |
| B&B | - | Standard | - | Partial Board | - |
| Single Rate | | | €48 | Child reduction | 33.3% |

Sligo 4km

**Open:** 20th January-20th December

---

**Peter & Martha Davey**
CARBURY HOUSE
**Teesan, Sligo, Co Sligo**

Tel: **071 9143378**　Fax: **071 9147433**
Email: **carbury@indigo.ie**
Web: **www.carburyhouse.net**

Luxurious spacious home on N15. Warm welcome. All rooms ensuite, Orthopaedic beds, Clocks, TV, Power Showers. 3 kms from Sligo. Touring base Sligo/Donegal.

| | | | | | |
|---|---|---|---|---|---|
| B&B | 6 | Ensuite | €30-€35 | Dinner | - |
| B&B | - | Standard | - | Partial Board | - |
| Single Rate | | | €40-€45 | Child reduction | 50% |

Sligo 3km

**Open:** 7th January-23rd December

---

**Des & Nan Faul**
AISLING
**Cairns Hill, Sligo, Co Sligo**

Tel: **071 9160704**　Fax: **071 9160704**
Email: **aislingsligo@eircom.net**

Overlooking garden and sea. All rooms ground floor. Signposted 300m Sligo Park Hotel off N4. AA ◆◆◆, cosy. Listed in many Guides. Electric Blankets, TV's, Hairdryers.

| | | | | | |
|---|---|---|---|---|---|
| B&B | 3 | Ensuite | €32-€34 | Dinner | - |
| B&B | 1 | Standard | €29-€31 | Partial Board | - |
| Single Rate | | | €38-€46 | Child reduction | - |

Sligo 1km

**Open:** 1st January-20th December

**In Sligo**

### Florrie Gilmartin
**LOUGH GILL HOUSE**
Pearse Road, Sligo, Co Sligo

Tel: **071 9150045** Fax: **071 9153639**
Email: **loughgillbandb@eircom.net**
Web: **www.loughgillhouse.com**

The home where there is always a welcome, offers guests comfortable, homely atmosphere. Within walking distance of city. Close to all amenties.

| B&B | 4 | Ensuite | €33-€35 | Dinner | - |
| B&B | - | Standard | - | Partial Board | - |
| Single Rate | | | €43-€48 | Child reduction | - |

**Open:** All Year Except Christmas

---

**Sligo 1km**

### Geraldine Gorman
**GLENVALE**
Cornageeha,
Upper Pearse Road, Sligo,
Co Sligo

Tel: **071 9161706**
Email: **geraldinegorman@eircom.net**

Friendly family home on N4. 100 metres after Sligo Park Hotel. Private Parking. Close to Races, Sports Complex. Tea/Coffee, H/Dryer, TV, AA ◆◆◆ Award.

| B&B | 4 | Ensuite | €30-€32 | Dinner | - |
| B&B | - | Standard | - | Partial Board | - |
| Single Rate | | | €40-€45 | Child reduction | 25% |

**Open:** 5th January-22nd December

---

**Sligo 1.5km**

### Una Jenkins
**ABERCORN**
Rathbraughan Line, Sligo,
Co Sligo

Tel: **071 9146087**

Comfortable home in quiet location, 1.5km north of Sligo off N16. TV lounge, Tea/Coffee. Beaches, Golf, Horseriding, Fishing all within 5km.

| B&B | 2 | Ensuite | €28-€32 | Dinner | - |
| B&B | 1 | Standard | - | Partial Board | - |
| Single Rate | | | €38-€45 | Child reduction | - |

**Open:** 5th January-15th December

---

**Sligo 3km**

### Mrs Christina Jones
**CHESTNUT LAWN**
Cummeen, Strandhill Road,
Sligo, Co Sligo

Tel: **071 9162781** Fax: **071 9162781**

Modern spacious dormer bungalow situated 3km from Sligo Town on main Strandhill/Airport road. Close to Megalithic Tombs. Seaweed baths and beaches

| B&B | 2 | Ensuite | €30-€32 | Dinner | - |
| B&B | 1 | Standard | €28-€30 | Partial Board | - |
| Single Rate | | | €38-€43.50 | Child reduction | - |

**Open:** 1st March-31st October

---

**Sligo 2km**

### Mrs Veronica Kane
**GLENVIEW**
Cummeen, Strandhill Road,
Sligo, Co Sligo

Tel: **071 9170401/9162457** Fax: **071 9162457**

Modern bungalow Strandhill Road, Megalithic Tombs. Golf, Beaches, Airport, Colour TV, Hairdryers, Electric Blankets, Tea making facilities, Lets Go recommended.

| B&B | 4 | Ensuite | €27.50-€31 | Dinner | - |
| B&B | - | Standard | - | Partial Board | - |
| Single Rate | | | €40-€43.50 | Child reduction | 50% |

**Open:** 1st January-30th November

**Mrs Marie Kelly**
ST JUDE'S
Rathonoragh, Strandhill Road,
Sligo, Co Sligo

### Sligo

Tel: **071 9160858**   Fax: **071 9160858**
Email: **saintjudes@eircom.net**

Close Airport, Bus, Railway station. Surfing, Swimming, Seaweed baths nearby. Climb Knocknarea Mountain, Megalithic Tombs, Heritage & Genealogy society. Electric blankets, Tea facilities.

| B&B | 2 | Ensuite | €27.50-€31 | Dinner | - |
| B&B | 1 | Standard | €25.50-€28.50 | Partial Board | - |
| Single Rate | | | €38-€43.50 | Child reduction | - |

Sligo 3km

**Open:** 31st March-31st October

---

**Doreen MacEvilly**
TREE TOPS
Cleveragh Road,
(off Pearse Rd N4), Sligo Town,
Co Sligo

### Sligo Town

Tel: **071 9160160/9162301**   Fax: **071 9162301**
Email: **treetops@iol.ie**
Web: **www.sligobandb.com**

5 minutes walk Town Centre. T.V, Hairdryers, Direct Dial Telephones, Tea Facilities all rooms. Non smoking. Frommer, Guide du Routard recommended.

| B&B | 5 | Ensuite | €32-€34 | Dinner | - |
| B&B | - | Standard | - | Partial Board | - |
| Single Rate | | | €42-€46.50 | Child reduction | - |

Sligo

**Open:** 7th January-15th December

---

**Mary McGoldrick**
ST MARTIN DE PORRES
Drumshanbo Rd, Carraroe,
Sligo, Co Sligo

### Sligo

Tel: **071 9162793**
Email: **stmdeporres@eircom.net**

Peaceful rural setting, 1km off N4 at Carraroe roundabout on R284. Convenient to Lough Gill, Megalithic Tombs, Forest Walks. Secure parking. TV, Electric blankets.

| B&B | 4 | Ensuite | €28-€31 | Dinner | - |
| B&B | - | Standard | - | Partial Board | - |
| Single Rate | | | €40-€43.50 | Child reduction | 50% |

Sligo 4km

**Open:** 6th January-20th December

---

**Evelyn & Declan McPartland**
TEACH EAMAINN
off N16, Calry,
Old Manorhamilton Rd,
Co Sligo

### Sligo

Tel: **071 9143393**   Fax: **071 9143393**
Email: **info@teacheamonn.com**
Web: **www.teacheamonn.com**

Situated on two acres off R286. Tea room, over looking Knocknarae, Benbulben, Ox Mountains, Sligo Bay. T.V and powershower. Parties special rate.

| B&B | 6 | Ensuite | €27.50-€31 | Dinner | - |
| B&B | - | Standard | - | Partial Board | - |
| Single Rate | | | €40-€43.50 | Child reduction | - |

Sligo 2km

**Open:** 1st April-30th November

---

**Mel & Kathleen Noonan**
STRADBROOK
Cornageeha, Pearse Road,
Sligo, Co Sligo

### Sligo Town

Tel: **071 9169674/9150663**   Fax: **071 9169933**
Email: **stradbrook@eircom.net**
Web: **www.stradbrook.com**

Welcoming family home on N4. Sligo Park Hotel 100 metres. All facilities. Guide du Routard recommended. Beaches, Golf, Fishing nearby. Ideal base for touring Yeats Country/Donegal.

| B&B | 4 | Ensuite | €30-€32 | Dinner | - |
| B&B | - | Standard | - | Partial Board | - |
| Single Rate | | | €40-€45 | Child reduction | 50% |

Sligo 1.5km

**Open:** All Year

**Olivia Quigley**
**BENWISKIN LODGE**
**Shannon Eighter,**
**Off Donegal Road N15, Sligo,**
**Co Sligo**

### Sligo
Tel: **071 9141088**
Email: **pquigley@iol.ie**
Web: **www.benwiskin.com**

Welcoming character home, handcrafted country furniture throughout. 2km north Sligo in peaceful setting. Golf, Beaches, Horseriding, Angling, Seaweed Baths within 5km.

| | | | | |
|---|---|---|---|---|
| B&B | 4 | Ensuite | €30-€35 | Dinner | - |
| B&B | - | Standard | - | Partial Board | - |
| Single Rate | | | €40-€45 | Child reduction | - |

Sligo 2km

**Open:** 6th January-20th December

---

**Mrs Carmel Connolly**
**KNOCKNAREA HOUSE**
**Shore Road, Strandhill,**
**Co Sligo**

### Strandhill
Tel: **071 9168313/9168810**
Email: **connollyma@eircom.net**

Large family home beside Beach, Seaweed Baths, Golf, Surfing, Horse Riding, Airport. Ideal for peaceful scenic walks. TV and Tea/Coffee in all rooms.

| | | | | |
|---|---|---|---|---|
| B&B | 4 | Ensuite | €27.50-€31 | Dinner | - |
| B&B | - | Standard | - | Partial Board | - |
| Single Rate | | | €40-€43.50 | Child reduction | 25% |

Sligo 8km

**Open:** 1st March-31st October

---

**Ann Marie Kelly**
**MARDEL**
**Seafront, Strandhill, Co Sligo**

### Strandhill
Tel: **071 9168295**
Email: **mardel@oceanfree.net**

Welcoming family home on seafront overlooking Golf Course, beside Seaweed Baths, Airport, Surfing, Horse Riding, Megalithic Tombs, TV, Tea/Coffee in all rooms.

| | | | | |
|---|---|---|---|---|
| B&B | 4 | Ensuite | €27.50-€31 | Dinner | - |
| B&B | - | Standard | - | Partial Board | - |
| Single Rate | | | €40-€43.50 | Child reduction | - |

Sligo 8km

**Open:** 1st March-31st October

---

**Mrs Mary Brennan**
**EDEN VILLA**
**Ballina Road, Tubbercurry,**
**Co Sligo**

### Tubbercurry
Tel: **071 9185106**   Fax: **071 9185106**
Email: **edenvilla@ireland.com**
Web: **www.sligotourism.com/edenvilla**

A warm welcome awaits you at our luxurious family home. Tea/Coffee, Homebaking on arrival. Guest TV lounge with peat fire, breakfast menu. Ideal touring base. 250mtrs off N17.

| | | | | |
|---|---|---|---|---|
| B&B | 2 | Ensuite | €27.50-€31 | Dinner | €20 |
| B&B | 1 | Standard | €25.50-€28.50 | Partial Board | - |
| Single Rate | | | €38-€43.50 | Child reduction | 25% |

Tubbercurry 1km

**Open:** 1st February-1st December

---

**Mrs Monica Brennan**
**ROCKVILLE**
**Charlestown Road,**
**Tubbercurry, Co Sligo**

### Tubbercurry
Tel: **071 9185270**
Email: **rockville_monica@yahoo.com**
Web: **www.sligotourism.com/rockville**

Quiet, friendly Irish home on N17. Tea/Coffee, Home baking on arrival, Hairdryers, Electric blankets, Clock radios. Breakfast menu. Knock Airport 10 miles.

| | | | | |
|---|---|---|---|---|
| B&B | 3 | Ensuite | €28-€31 | Dinner | - |
| B&B | 1 | Standard | €26-€29 | Partial Board | - |
| Single Rate | | | €38-€43.50 | Child reduction | 33.3% |

In Tubbercurry

**Open:** 1st February-30th November

**Mrs Joan Brett**
ST ENDA'S
Charlestown Rd, Tubbercurry,
Co Sligo

### Tubbercurry

TEL: **071 9185100**
EMAIL: **st_endas@ireland.com**
WEB: **www.sligotourism.com/st_endas**

Friendly family home on N17. Scenic area. Home baking, Electric blankets. Gardens, Fishing and Golf nearby. Knock Airport 10 miles, Knock Shrine 22 miles.

| B&B | 4 | Ensuite | €28-€31 | Dinner | - |
| B&B | - | Standard | - | Partial Board | - |
| Single Rate | | | €40-€43.50 | Child reduction | **33.3%** |

Tubbercurry 1km    **Open:** 1st February-30th November

---

**Mrs Noreen Donoghue**
ROSSLI HOUSE
Doocastle, Tubbercurry,
Co Sligo

### Tubbercurry

TEL: **071 9185099**   FAX: **071 9185144**
EMAIL: **rossli@esatclear.ie**
WEB: **tubbercurrybandb.com**

Rural setting. Tea/Coffee. Hairdryers, Electric blankets. Laundry facilities. Conservatory. Frommer Guide, Le Guide du Routard, Interconnections listed. Travel 6km on Ballymote road.

| B&B | 4 | Ensuite | €27.50-€31 | Dinner | €20-€20 |
| B&B | - | Standard | - | Partial Board | - |
| Single Rate | | | €40-€43.50 | Child reduction | **25%** |

Tubbercurry 6km    **Open:** All Year

---

**Mrs Teresa Kelly**
PINEGROVE
Ballina Road, Tubbercurry,
Co Sligo

### Tubbercurry

TEL: **071 9185235**
EMAIL: **pinegrove@ireland.com**
WEB: **www.sligotourism.com**

Friendly atmosphere, home-baking, evening meals, electric blankets. Gardens, Fishing, Shooting & Golf. Knock Shrine. 300 metres off N17.

| B&B | 5 | Ensuite | €30-€35 | Dinner | - |
| B&B | - | Standard | - | Partial Board | - |
| Single Rate | | | €40-€43.50 | Child reduction | **33.3%** |

Tubbercurry    **Open:** 17th March-1st November

---

**Mrs Maeve Walsh**
CRUCKAWN HOUSE
Ballymote/Boyle Rd,
Tubbercurry, Co Sligo

### Tubbercurry

TEL: **071 9185188**   FAX: **071 9185188**
EMAIL: **cruckawn@esatclear.ie**
WEB: **www.sligotourism.com/cruckawn**

Award winning family home in peaceful suburb, overlooking Golf Course. AIB "Best Hospitality". Many recommendations, Guide de Routard. AA ◆◆◆. Sunlounge, Laundry. Off N17 on R294 road.

| B&B | 5 | Ensuite | €30-€35 | Dinner | - |
| B&B | - | Standard | - | Partial Board | - |
| Single Rate | | | €42-€45 | Child reduction | **25%** |

Tubbercurry    **Open:** 17th March-1st November

---

## TOWN & COUNTRY GIFT TOKENS

Why not share your experience of staying in a Town & Country home by buying our gift tokens. They are available in €10, €20 or €50 and can be used in any home featured in this guide.

Contact us on email: accounts@townandcountry.ie
Telephone: 071 9822222   Fax: 071 9822207

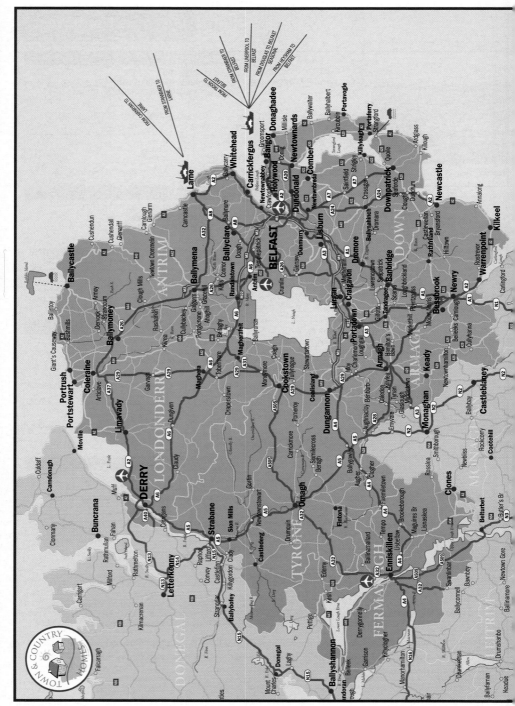

Northern Ireland

310

# Northern Ireland

Welcome to Northern Ireland! Gloriously green countryside, spectacular coast and mountains an ancient land with a rich historical and cultural tradition and some of the friendliest people anywhere.

Visit our capital city of Belfast, famous for its industrial heritage and birthplace of the Titanic, where you can experience a unique combination of award winning restaurants, traditional pubs, history and culture. Also well worth a visit is the city of Derry, one of the finest examples of a walled city in Europe and Armagh, the ecclesiastical capital of Ireland.

Northern Ireland is perfect for a host of outdoor pursuits. A day's walking amid spectacular scenery, an exhilarating horseback gallop along a quiet beach or a relaxing game of golf on one of our many famous courses. Alternatively you might consider a breathtaking bike ride on one of our new cycle routes, a peaceful afternoon boating or fishing or a leisurely stroll through the National Trust gardens of Mount Stewart.

The Majestic mountains of Mourne, the uncongested waterways of Lough Erne, the breathtaking Antrim coast with its world heritage site at the Giant's Causeway. The list is endless but whatever your preference seaside, town, city or countryside, there is a special place for you to stay.

Carrick-a-rede

## Area Representative

**ANTRIM**
Mrs Ann McHenry DIESKIRT FARM 104 Glen Road Glenariff
o Antrim BT44 0RG
Tel: 028 21771308  Fax: 028 21771185

**DOWN**
Mrs Liz McMorris SWAN LODGE 30 St Patricks Road Saul Downpatrick
o Down BT30 7JQ
Tel: 028 44615542  Fax: 087 07052501

**LONDONDERRY**
Mrs Averil Campbell KILLENNAN HOUSE 40 Killennan Road Drumahoe
o Londonderry BT47 3NG
Tel: 028 71301710  Fax: 028 71301710

## Tourist Information Offices
**OPEN ALL YEAR**

Armagh
Old Bank Building
40 English Street
BT61 7BA
Tel: 028 37521800

Belfast
Belfast Welcome
Centre
47 Donegall Place
BT1 5AD
Tel: 028 90246609

Derry
44 Foyle Street
BT48 6AT
Tel: 028 7126 7284

Dungannon
Killymaddy TIC
190 Ballygawley Road
BT70 1TF
Tel: 028 8776 7259

Enniskillen
Wellington Road
BT74 7EF
Tel: 028 6632 3110

Giant's Causeway
44 Causeway Road
BT57 8SU
Tel: 028 2073 1855

Larne
Narrow Gauge Road
BT40 1XB
Tel: 028 2826 0088

Newcastle Centre
10-14 Central
Promenade
BT33 0AA
Tel: 028 4372 2222

Website: **www.discovernorthernireland.com**

Causeway Coast and Glens an area of beauty, fusion of heritage and scenery. Breathtaking, rugged coastline merges into landscape of its deep silent glens and lush forest parks. Beaches, rivers, rolling lowlands, picturesque villages.
The capital city of Belfast, birthplace of Titanic, City Hall, traditional pubs, hotels, Ulster Folk and Transport Museum at Cultra.

---

**Valerie Brown**
GLENMORE HOUSE
White Park Road, Ballycastle,
Co Antrim BT54 6LR

### Ballycastle

TEL: **028 20763584**   FAX: **028 20762378**
EMAIL: **glenmorehouse@lineone.net**
WEB: **www.glenmore.biz**

New building with panoramic sea view on B15 Set on 90 acres for walks with fishing lake. Central for Causeway & Glens. TV & Tea making facilities in room. Private Parking. Euro accepted.

| | | | | | | |
|---|---|---|---|---|---|---|
| B&B | 6 | Ensuite | STG£20-£25 | - | Dinner | STG£15 - |
| B&B | - | Standard | - | - | Partial Board | - |
| Single Rate | | | STG£30-£36 | - | Child reduction | 33.3% |

Ballycastle 3km

**Open:** All Year

---

**Megan Donnelly**
PORTCAMPLEY
8 Harbour Rd, Ballintoy,
Ballycastle, Co Antrim
BT54 6NA

### Ballycastle

TEL: **028 207 68200**   FAX: **028 207 68200**
EMAIL: **m.donnelly@btconnect.com**
WEB: **www.portcampley.8k.com**

Spacious modern bungalow. Panoramic views of Rathlin Island and Scottish Coastline. Central to Causeway Coast and Glens. Home cooking and friendly atmosphere assured.

| | | | | | | |
|---|---|---|---|---|---|---|
| B&B | 5 | Ensuite | STG£18-£20 | €22-€25 | Dinner | STG£12.50 - |
| B&B | 1 | Standard | STG£16-£18 | - | Partial Board | - |
| Single Rate | | | STG£20-£25 | €25-€30 | Child reduction | 50% |

Ballycastle 6km

**Open:** All Year

---

**Mrs Jane Kane**
ISLANDARRAGH HOUSE
7 Islandarragh Road,
Cape Castle, Ballycastle,
Co Antrim BT54 6HX

### Ballycastle

TEL: **028 20762933**
EMAIL: **islandarraghhouse@talk21.com**

Refurbished 1920's farmhouse offering comfortable ensuite rooms and a hearty breakfast. Picturesque rural setting off A44. Close to Causeway coast.

| | | | | | | |
|---|---|---|---|---|---|---|
| B&B | 2 | Ensuite | STG£20-£20 | - | Dinner | - - |
| B&B | - | Standard | - | - | Partial Board | - |
| Single Rate | | | STG£22-£22 | - | Child reduction | 25% |

Ballycastle 5km

**Open:** 1st March-31st October

---

**Karen McArthur**
ROCK MANOR
87a Straid Road, Ballycastle,
Co Antrim BT54 6NW

### Ballycastle

TEL: **028 20768815**

Family run B&B close to the Causeway Coast. Large family rooms available. Landscaped gardens with private lake.

| | | | | | | |
|---|---|---|---|---|---|---|
| B&B | 2 | Ensuite | - | €27.50-€31 | Dinner | - - |
| B&B | - | Standard | - | - | Partial Board | - |
| Single Rate | | | - | €40-€43.50 | Child reduction | 50% |

Ballycastle 7km

**Open:** 1st April-1st November

## Ballymena

**Margaret & Andrew Neely**
NEELSGROVE FARM
51 Carnearney Rd, Ahoghill,
Ballymena, Co Antrim
BT42 2PL

TEL: **028 2587 1225**  FAX: **028 2587 8704**
EMAIL: **msneely@btinternet.com**
WEB: **www.neelsgrove.freeserve.co.uk**

Farmhouse set in 1 acre garden in a rural location. Excellent base for touring to North Coast, Glens of Antrim, Giants Causeway. Convenient to Galgorm Manor & Tullyglass Hotels.

| | | | | | Dinner | - | - |
|---|---|---|---|---|---|---|---|
| B&B | 2 | Ensuite | STG£21-£21 | €32-€32 | Dinner | - | - |
| B&B | 1 | Standard | STG£18-£18 | €28-€28 | Partial Board | - | - |
| Single Rate | | | STG£23-£26 | €36-€40 | Child reduction | - | - |

Ballymena 9km

Open: 1st January-30th November

---

## Belfast

**Mannix McAllister**
SOMERTON HOUSE
22 Lansdowne Rd, Belfast,
Co Antrim BT15 4DB

TEL: **028 90370717**  FAX: **028 90772462**
WEB: **www.somertonhouse.co.uk**
BUS NO: **64, 46, 48, 49**

Irish town house, family business. Beside Belfast Castle & Country Park Zoo, Ferries, Airport, 1.5miles city centre. Rooms TV, Tea/Coffee trays, morning news papers.

| | | | | | Dinner | - | - |
|---|---|---|---|---|---|---|---|
| B&B | 5 | Ensuite | STG£24.50 | €35 | Dinner | - | - |
| B&B | 4 | Standard | STG£20 | €30 | Partial Board | - | - |
| Single Rate | | | STG£25-£35 | €40-€50 | Child reduction | - | - |

Belfast 3.5km

Open: 5th January-22nd December

---

## Belfast

**Olive & Roger Nicholson**
RAVENHILL GUEST HOUSE
690 Ravenhill Road, Belfast,
Co Antrim BT6 0BZ

TEL: **028 90207444**  FAX: **028 90282590**
EMAIL: **roger@ravenhillguesthouse.com**
WEB: **www.ravenhillguesthouse.com**
BUS NO: **83, 84, 85, 86, 78, 79**

Warm welcoming Victorian home in South Belfast. Comfortable well equipped rooms. Delicious breakfast. Easy access to airports, ferries and motorways.

| | | | | | Dinner | - | - |
|---|---|---|---|---|---|---|---|
| B&B | 5 | Ensuite | STG£32.50 | - | Dinner | - | - |
| B&B | - | Standard | - | - | Partial Board | - | - |
| Single Rate | | | STG£42 | - | Child reduction | - | - |

Belfast 2km

Open: All Year Except Christmas

---

## Bushmills

**Mrs J Brown**
BROWNS COUNTRY HOUSE
174 Ballybogey Road,
Coleraine, Co Antrim BT52 2LP

TEL: **028 20732777**  FAX: **028 20731627**
EMAIL: **brownscountryhouse@hotmail.com**
WEB: **www.brownscountryhouse.co.uk**

Family run home near Giants Causeway. Reputation for superb breakfast & friendly atmosphere. Near to beaches & Golf links. Good touring base B62. Off B17 to Coleraine.

| | | | | | Dinner | - | - |
|---|---|---|---|---|---|---|---|
| B&B | 8 | Ensuite | STG£22-£23 | - | Dinner | - | - |
| B&B | - | Standard | - | - | Partial Board | - | - |
| Single Rate | | | STG£25-£27 | - | Child reduction | - | 33.3% |

Bushmills 4.5km

Open: 3rd January-19th December

---

## Bushmills

**Ann Carson**
CARNGLASS FARMHOUSE
170 Ballybogey Road,
Ballymoney, Co Antrim
BT53 6PQ

TEL: **028 20741762**  FAX: **028 20741762**
EMAIL: **stay@carnglass.com**
WEB: **www.carnglass.com**

A working farm which provides an excellent base for touring Bushmills and the Giants Causeway. Tea on arrival. Situated on the B62 near the B17.

| | | | | | Dinner | - | - |
|---|---|---|---|---|---|---|---|
| B&B | 2 | Ensuite | STG£20-£22 | - | Dinner | - | - |
| B&B | - | Standard | - | - | Partial Board | - | - |
| Single Rate | | | STG£25-£27 | - | Child reduction | - | 33.3% |

Bushmills 6.45km

Open: 1st February-30th November

---

Bushmills 6km

### Bushmills

**Mrs Aileen Kerr**
SPRINGFARM B&B
15 Isle Road, Dunseverick,
Bushmills, Co Antrim BT57 8TD

TEL: **028 207 31780**   FAX: **028 207 30355**
EMAIL: **springfarm@btinternet.com**

Traditional family run farmhouse. Spacious ground floor rooms. Off A2. Near Giants causeway, Bushmills Distillery, Dunluce Castle and Carrick-A-Rede Bridge.

| | | | | | | | |
|---|---|---|---|---|---|---|---|
| B&B | **3** | Ensuite | - | | €30-€32.50 | Dinner | - | - |
| B&B | - | Standard | - | | - | Partial Board | - | - |
| Single Rate | | | - | | €40-€45 | Child reduction | | **50%** |

**Open:** 1st January-23rd December

---

Bushmills 5km

### Bushmills

**Mrs Valerie McFall**
VALLEY VIEW COUNTRY HOUSE
6A Ballyclough Road,
Bushmills, Co Antrim BT57 8TU

TEL: **028 20741608/41319**   FAX: **028 20742739**
EMAIL: **valerie.mcfall@btinternet.com**
WEB: **www.valleyviewbushmills.com**

Attractive country house. Beautiful views. Friendly atmosphere, Tea on arrival. Close to Giants Causeway, Rope Bridge and Distillery. Off B17 to Coleraine.

| | | | | | | | |
|---|---|---|---|---|---|---|---|
| B&B | **7** | Ensuite | STG£20-£22 | €30-€33 | Dinner | - | - |
| B&B | - | Standard | - | | Partial Board | - | - |
| Single Rate | | | STG£25-£27 | €37.50-€40.50 | Child reduction | | **50%** |

**Open:** 2nd January-23rd December

---

Carrickfergus 2km

### Carrickfergus

**Mrs B Barron**
BEECHGROVE
412 Upper Road, Trooperslane,
Carrickfergus, Co Antrim
BT38 9PW

TEL: **028 93363304**   FAX: **028 93363304**
EMAIL: **enquiries @beechgrovefarm.co.uk**
WEB: **www.beechgrovefarm.co.uk**

Beechgrove is situated on the B90 about 2km north west of the historic town of Carrickfergus. All rooms are ensuite with tv & tea & coffee. Great views.

| | | | | | | |
|---|---|---|---|---|---|---|
| B&B | **6** | Ensuite | STG£21-£21 | - | Dinner | - | - |
| B&B | - | Standard | - | - | Partial Board | - | - |
| Single Rate | | | - | - | Child reduction | | **25%** |

**Open:** All Year

---

Crumlin 4km

### Crumlin

**Mr & Mrs C Kelly**
KEEF HALLA COUNTRY HOUSE
20 Tully Road, Nutts Corner,
Co Antrim BT29 4SW

TEL: **028 90825491**   FAX: **028 90825940**
EMAIL: **info@keefhalla.com**
WEB: **www.keefhalla.com**

Nearest 4 star guesthouse to Belfast International Airport. All rooms are ensuite with STV, Direct Dial Telephone, Tea/Coffee. A great base for touring Northern Ireland. Located on A26.

| | | | | | | |
|---|---|---|---|---|---|---|
| B&B | **7** | Ensuite | - | €40-€45 | Dinner | - | €25 |
| B&B | - | Standard | - | - | Partial Board | - | - |
| Single Rate | | | - | €60-€70 | Child reduction | | **50%** |

**Open:** 1st January-31st December

---

Crumlin 1.6km

### Crumlin

**Anne McKavanagh**
CALDHAME LODGE
102 Moira Rd, Nutts Corner,
Crumlin, Co Antrim BT29 4HG

TEL: **028 94423099**   FAX: **028 94423099**
EMAIL: **info@caldhamelodge.co.uk**
WEB: **www.caldhamelodge.co.uk**

Award winning hse, mins from Belfast Int. Airport. Luxurious home, digital TV, Tea/Coffee. Bridal suite/jacuzzi/4 poster bed. Restaurants & Pubs. 25 mins Belfast.

| | | | | | | |
|---|---|---|---|---|---|---|
| B&B | **8** | Ensuite | STG£25-£30 | - | Dinner | STG£18 | - |
| B&B | - | Standard | - | - | Partial Board | - | - |
| Single Rate | | | STG£40-£45 | - | Child reduction | | **50%** |

**Open:** 1st January-31st December

**Mrs Josephine McAuley**
GARRON VIEW
14 Cloughs Road, Cushendall,
Ballymena, Co Antrim
BT44 0SP

### Cushendall

Tel: **028 217 71018**
Email: **josiegarronview@yahoo.co.uk**
Bus No: **150**

Garron view is a working farm which offers a friendly welcome to all guests convenient to Giants Causeway and other tourist attractions. T.V. and Coffee making facilities in all rooms.

| B&B | 3 | Ensuite | STG£17-£17 | €28.50 | Dinner | STG£13 | - |
| B&B | - | Standard | STG£15-£15 | €25.50 | Partial Board | - | - |
| Single Rate | | | STG£18-£20 | €38-€40 | Child reduction | | 50% |

ushendall 1km

**Open:** All Year

---

**Nuala McAuley**
THE BURN B&B
63 Ballyeamon Road (B14),
Cushendall, Co Antrim
BT44 0SN

### Cushendall

Tel: **028 21771733**  Fax: **028 21771733**
Email: **theburn63@hotmail.com**
Web: **www.theburn-guesthouse.com**

Ideally situated to tour the "Glens" & beautiful Antrim coast, including the Giant's Causeway. Enjoy great hill walking. Return to a turf fire, tea and quietness.

| B&B | 3 | Ensuite | - | €27.50-€31.50 | Dinner | - | €18 |
| B&B | - | Standard | - | | Partial Board | - | €294 |
| Single Rate | | | - | €40-€43.50 | Child reduction | | 25% |

ushendall

**Open:** All Year

---

**Mrs Olive McAuley**
CULLENTRA HOUSE
16 Cloughs Road, Cushendall,
Co Antrim BT44 0SP

### Cushendall

Tel: **028 21771762**  Fax: **028 21771762**
Email: **cullentra@hotmail.com**
Bus No: **150**

Award winning B&B nestled amidst panoramic views of Antrim Coast and Glens. Close to Giants Causeway, Rope Bridge etc. Last B&B on Cloughs road.

| B&B | 3 | Ensuite | STG£18-£18 | €30-€31 | Dinner | STG£12 | €20 |
| B&B | - | Standard | - | - | Partial Board | - | - |
| Single Rate | | | STG£25-£25 | €40-€43.50 | Child reduction | | 33.3% |

ushendall 2km

**Open:** 1st January-31st December

---

**James & Ann McHenry**
DIESKIRT FARM
104 Glen Road, Glenariff,
Co Antrim BT44 0RG

### Glenariff

Tel: **028 21771308**  Fax: **028 21771185**
Email: **dieskirt@hotmail.com**
Web: **www.dieskirt.8k.com**
Bus No: **150, 218**

A working farm with private scenic walks, just off Antrim Coast Road (A2), and close to Giant's Causeway. 5 minute walk to Glenariffe Forest Park/Restaurant. Excellent breakfast.

| B&B | 3 | Ensuite | - | €27.50-€31 | Dinner | - | - |
| B&B | - | Standard | - | | Partial Board | - | - |
| Single Rate | | | - | €40-€43.50 | Child reduction | | 33.3% |

ushendall 8km

**Open:** 1st April-31st January

---

**Mrs Dulcibel Moore**
BROOK LODGE
79 Old Ballynahinch Rd,
Lisburn, Co Antrim BT27 6TH

### Lisburn

Tel: **028 92638454**  Fax: **028 92638454**

Brook Lodge is a farm guest house. Set in rural countryside over looking the Mourne mountains 4 rooms ensuite 2, standard.

| B&B | 4 | Ensuite | STG£22-£25 | - | Dinner | - | - |
| B&B | - | Standard | - | - | Partial Board | - | - |
| Single Rate | | | STG£22-£25 | - | Child reduction | | 25% |

sburn 3.5km

**Open:** 1st January-31st December

**In Randalstown**

**Sheila McLaughlin**
**LURGAN WEST LODGE**
**15A Old Staffordstown Road,**
**Randalstown, Co Antrim**
**BT41 3LD**

Tel: **028 94 479691**  Fax: **028 94 479691**
Email: **lurganwestlodge@btinternet.com**
Web: **lurganwestlodge.co.uk**

Modern town house on the outskirts of Randalstown. 10mins to Belfast International Airport. 20mins to Belfast/Larne Harbour.

| | | | | | | | |
|---|---|---|---|---|---|---|---|
| B&B | **2** | Ensuite | STG£25 | - | Dinner | - | - |
| B&B | **1** | Standard | STG£22.50-£22.50 | - | Partial Board | - | - |
| | | Single Rate | STG£23-£30 | - | Child reduction | | **50%** |

**Open:** All Year

**Giants Causeway**

**Telephoning from Republic of Ireland: 0044 28+ eight digit number**

Visitors can immerse in the ancient history of Ireland, amble through two cathedrals, stroll outside and visit the grave of one of Ireland's famous Kings Brian Buro. Try your hand at Road Bowls or if you prefer a faster pace the Ulster Rally in September.

**Mrs E Kee**
BALLINAHINCH HOUSE
47 Ballygroobany Rd, Richhill,
Co Armagh BT61 9NA

### Armagh
TEL: **028 388 70081**   FAX: **028 388 70081**
EMAIL: **info@ballinahinchhouse.com**
WEB: **www.ballinahinchhouse.com**

Victorian residence with picturesque setting in countryside. Ideal base for touring Northern Ireland. Visit website for more details. Discounts for block bookings and extended stay.

| | | | | | | |
|---|---|---|---|---|---|---|
| B&B | 2 | Ensuite | STG£25–£26.25 | - | Dinner | - |
| B&B | - | Standard | - | - | Partial Board | - |
| Single Rate | | | STG£30–£31.50 | - | Child reduction | 25% |

**Open:** 4th January–20th December

---

**Alice McBride**
HILLVIEW LODGE
33 Newtownhamilton Rd,
Armagh, Co Armagh BT60 2PL

### Armagh
TEL: **028 3752 2000**   FAX: **028 3752 8276**
EMAIL: **alice@hillviewlodge.com**
WEB: **www.hillviewlodge.com**

Luxury accommodation with Golf Driving Range and Disabled facilities. Follow A29 south stay with Tall Stone Wall take left onto B31 Hillview Lodge is on right.

| | | | | | | |
|---|---|---|---|---|---|---|
| B&B | 6 | Ensuite | STG£25 | - | Dinner | - |
| B&B | - | Standard | - | - | Partial Board | - |
| Single Rate | | | STG£30 | - | Child reduction | 50% |

Armagh 1km

**Open:** All Year

---

**Kathleen McGeown**
NI EOGHAIN LODGE
32 Ennislare Road, Armagh,
Co Armagh BT60 2AX

### Armagh
TEL: **028 37 525633**   FAX: **028 37 511246**
EMAIL: **nieoghainlodge@amserve.com**

Country house, award winning garden. Breakfast menu. Italian spoken. A29 south for 4km, Ennislare Rd left opposite cottages. House and garden well signed.

| | | | | | | |
|---|---|---|---|---|---|---|
| B&B | 3 | Ensuite | - | €28–€31 | Dinner | €15 |
| B&B | - | Standard | - | - | Partial Board | - |
| Single Rate | | | - | - | Child reduction | 50% |

Armagh 4km

**Open:** 1st April–30th September

---

**Mrs Maureen Oliver**
FAIRYLANDS COUNTRY HOUSE
25 Navan Fort Road, Armagh,
Co Armagh BT60 4PN

### Armagh
TEL: **028 37510315**
EMAIL: **reservations@fairylands.net**
WEB: **www.fairylands.net**

Purpose built family run B&B in countryside, approx 1 mile from Armagh just off A28 Enniskillen Road. 10 mins walk from Navan Fort.

| | | | | | | |
|---|---|---|---|---|---|---|
| B&B | 5 | Ensuite | STG£20–£20 | - | Dinner | - |
| B&B | - | Standard | - | - | Partial Board | - |
| Single Rate | | | STG£25–£25 | - | Child reduction | 50% |

Armagh 1km

**Open:** 1st January–22nd December

**Elizabeth & Larry Nugent**
**DUNDRUM HOUSE**
116 Dundrum Road, Tassagh,
Keady, Co Armagh BT60 2NG

### Keady

TEL: **028 37531257**   FAX: **028 37539821**
EMAIL: liz@dundrumhouse.com
WEB: www.dundrumhouse.com

Early 18th century country manor, recently renovated to its former glory, with many classic georgian features. 6 miles from Armagh City. Tea/Coffee on arrival.

| | | | | | | |
|---|---|---|---|---|---|---|
| B&B | 3 | Ensuite | STG£22.50 | €33-€35 | Dinner | - | - |
| B&B | - | Standard | - | - | Partial Board | - |
| Single Rate | | | STG£28 | €40-€45 | Child reduction | 50% |

Keady 3km        Open: All Year

---

## SYMBOL

**LOOK OUT FOR THIS SYMBOL WHICH
ALL MEMBERS OF TOWN & COUNTRY HOMES DISPLAY**

---

## APPROVED ACCOMMODATION SIGNS

Northern Ireland
Tourist Board

### Approved Accommodation Signs

These signs will be displayed at most premises which are approved by Failte Ireland, the National Tourism Development Authority and Northern Ireland Tourist Board Standards.

### Panneaux d'homologation des établissements

Ces panneaux sont affichés dans la plupart des établissements homologués selon les normes de l'Office du tourisme irlandais.

### Plakette fúr Geprúfte Unterkunft

Diese Plaketten werden an den meisten Häusern angezeigt, die von auf die Einhaltung der Normen der irischen Fremdenverkehrsbehörde überprüft und zugelassen wurden.

### Borden voor goedgekeurde accommodatie

Deze borden vindt u bij de meeste huizen die zijn goedgekeurd door voor de normen van de Ierse Toeristenbond.

### Simbolo di sistemazione approvata

Questi simboli saranno esposti nella maggior parte delle case approvate (associazione dei Bed & Breakfast approvati per qualità), rispondenti agli standard dell'Ente del Turismo Irlandese.

### Símbolo de alojamiento aprobado

Estos símbolos se muestran en los establecimientos que han sido aprobados por bajos los estandars de la Oficina de Turismo Irlandesa.

### Skyltar för Godkänd logi

Dessa skyltar finns vid de flesta gästhus som har godkänts (Föreningen för kvalitetsgodkända gästhus AB), enligt irländska turisföreningens normer.

The land that gave the world St Patrick, shamrocks and a hundred Irish tunes. The enchantment of the Down Region persists after 9,000 years of Celtic, Christian, Viking, Norman and modern civilisations. Come on Down and you'll see the Ireland you dreamed of.

---

**Norman & Esther Kerr**
MOURNEVIEW
32 Drumnascamph Road,
Laurencetown Gilford,
Co Down BT63 6DU

### Banbridge

TEL: 028 40626270   FAX: 028 40626270
EMAIL: info.mourneview@btconnect.com
WEB: www.mourneview.co.uk

Situated on A50 between Banbridge and Gilford. Ideal base to see Co Down Coast/Mourne Mountains/Linen homelands. 30 mins to Airports/Belfast. Excellent Restaurants nearby.

| | | | | | | |
|---|---|---|---|---|---|---|
| B&B | 4 | Ensuite | STG£20-£20 | - | Dinner | - - |
| B&B | - | Standard | - | - | Partial Board | - - |
| Single Rate | | | STG£25-£25 | - | Child reduction | 25% |

nbridge 5km    Ⓥ    **Open:** 2nd January-20th December

---

**Mrs Mary McGlue**
HEATH HALL
160 Moyadd Rd, Kilkeel,
Co Down BT34 4HJ

### Down

TEL: 028 41762612
EMAIL: emcglue@hotmail.com
WEB: www.kingdomofdown.com

House between Irish sea and mountains close to golf course all rooms have tv's, hairdryers and teas made friendly relaxed atmosphere.

| | | | | | | |
|---|---|---|---|---|---|---|
| B&B | 3 | Ensuite | STG£20-£22.50 | - | Dinner | - - |
| B&B | 2 | Standard | STG£19-£20 | - | Partial Board | - - |
| Single Rate | | | STG£20-£22.50 | - | Child reduction | - - |

keel 1 mile    **Open:** 3rd January-20th December

---

**Janis Bailey**
PHEASANTS HILL
37 Killyleagh Road,
Downpatrick, Co Down
BT30 9BL

### Downpatrick

TEL: 028 44 617246/838707   FAX: 028 44 617246
EMAIL: info@pheasantshill.com
WEB: www.pheasantshill.com

Winner AA Best Breakfast Award Ireland. AA Premier collection. 5 diamond grading. Luxury farmhouse/Rare breeds farm near Strangford Lough/Mourne Mtns.

| | | | | | | |
|---|---|---|---|---|---|---|
| B&B | 3 | Ensuite | STG£25-£32.50 | - | Dinner | - - |
| B&B | - | Standard | - | - | Partial Board | - - |
| Single Rate | | | STG£42-£45 | - | Child reduction | 50% |

ownpatrick 4km    **Open:** 4th January-11th December

---

**Mrs Patricia Forsythe**
ROSEBANK COUNTRY HOUSE
108 Ballydugan Road,
Downpatrick, Co Down
BT30 8HF

### Downpatrick

TEL: 028 44617021
EMAIL: jbforsy@yahoo.co.uk
WEB: www.rosebankcountryhouse.com
BUS NO: 15

Luxurious accomodation, warm welcome. Good food. Spacious ensuite bedrooms. TV, Tea/Coffee, guest lounge. On main A25, scenic route to Mournes Historic Downpatrick. Best Ulster Welcome Award Winner.

| | | | | | | |
|---|---|---|---|---|---|---|
| B&B | 3 | Ensuite | STG£22.50-£22.50 | - | Dinner | - - |
| B&B | - | Standard | - | - | Partial Board | - - |
| Single Rate | | | STG£30-£30 | - | Child reduction | 33.3% |

ownpatrick 4.8km    Ⓥ    **Open:** 1st January-31st December

## Downpatrick

**John & Liz McMorris**
SWAN LODGE
30 St Patricks Road, Saul,
Downpatrick, Co Down
BT30 7JQ

TEL: **028 44615542**   FAX: **087 07052501**
EMAIL: **breaks@swanldg.force9.co.uk**
WEB: **www.swanldg.force9.co.uk**

Superbly situated overlooking Strangford Lough, St Patricks Heritage area. Ideal touring base. Luxury family home in scenic surroundings. Excellent cuisine.

| | | | | | | |
|---|---|---|---|---|---|---|
| B&B | 3 | Ensuite | STG£23.50-£23.50 | - | Dinner | STG£15 - |
| B&B | - | Standard | | - | Partial Board | - |
| Single Rate | | STG£30 | | - | Child reduction | 25% |

Downpatrick 4km

**Open:** 1st January-31st December

## Dromore

**Mrs Rhoda Mark**
THE MAGGI MINN
11 Bishops Well Rd, Dromore,
Co Down BT25 1ST

TEL: **028 92693520**   FAX: **028 92693520**
EMAIL: **maggiminn@lycos.co.uk**
BUS NO: **38**

Country house situated in farmland, off the main A1 Belfast/Dublin Road, signposted from A1 at Dromore panoramic views of Mourne mountains, home cooking.

| | | | | | | |
|---|---|---|---|---|---|---|
| B&B | 1 | Ensuite | STG£25-£30 | €37.50-€45 | Dinner | - - |
| B&B | 2 | Standard | STG£20-£25 | €30-€37.50 | Partial Board | - - |
| Single Rate | | STG£30-£40 | | €45-€60 | Child reduction | 25% |

Dromore 3km

**Open:** 1st January-31st December

## Gilford

**Mrs Margaret Gamble**
MOUNT PLEASANT
38 Banbridge Road, Gilford,
Co Down BT63 6DJ

TEL: **028 38831522**   FAX: **028 38830701**
EMAIL: **contact@mountpleasantgilford.com**
WEB: **www.mountpleasantgilford.com**
BUS NO: **62**

Georgian house built 1760. Parapet Battlements. Spacious grounds, 10 mins from Dublin Road, to Belfast A1 Road. Warm family welcome special diets catered for.

| | | | | | | |
|---|---|---|---|---|---|---|
| B&B | - | Ensuite | - | - | Dinner | - - |
| B&B | 3 | Standard | STG£23-£23 | - | Partial Board | - - |
| Single Rate | | STG£20-£25 | | - | Child reduction | 25% |

Banbridge 7.2km

**Open:** All Year

## Kilkeel

**Trainor Family**
HILL VIEW HOUSE
18 Bog Rd, Attical, Kilkeel,
Co Down BT34 4HT

TEL: **028 417 64269**   FAX: **028 417 64269**
EMAIL: **trainor18@btopenworld.com**
WEB: **www.hillviewhouse.co.uk**

Luxury farmhouse in Mourne Mountains offering hospitality since 1903. TV, Tea/Coffee. Sign for Hillview and Attical Village on A2 & B27. Located at top of hill through village.

| | | | | | | |
|---|---|---|---|---|---|---|
| B&B | 2 | Ensuite | STG£22.50-£25 | - | Dinner | - - |
| B&B | 1 | Standard | STG£20-£24 | - | Partial Board | - - |
| Single Rate | | STG£23-£28 | | - | Child reduction | 25% |

Kilkeel 4km

**Open:** 10th January-20th December

## Newcastle

**Mrs Jan Joyce and Mrs Pam Horrox**
OAKLEIGH HOUSE
30 Middle Tollymore Rd,
Newcastle, Co Down BT33 0JJ

TEL: **028 43723353/43726816**   FAX: **028 43723353**
EMAIL: **jan@oakleigh-ireland.com**
WEB: **www.oakleigh-ireland.com**

A family run bungalow at the foot of the Mourne Mountains, close to Tollymore Forest Park and the Royal Co. Down golf course. Warm welcome assured.

| | | | | | | |
|---|---|---|---|---|---|---|
| B&B | 3 | Ensuite | STG£20-£20 | - | Dinner | - - |
| B&B | - | Standard | - | - | Partial Board | - - |
| Single Rate | | STG£25-£25 | | - | Child reduction | - |

Newcastle 1.25km

**Open:** 5th January-19th December

**Mrs Geraldine Bailie**
**BALLYNESTER HOUSE**
1a Cardy Rd(off Mountstewart
Rd), Newtownards, Co Down
**BT22 2LS**

Tel: **028 42788386** Fax: **028 42788986**
Email: **geraldine.bailie@virgin.net**
Web: **www.ballynesterhouse.com**

AA ◆◆◆◆◆, Award winner "Landlady of the Year Runnerup". Enjoy hospitality at its best! In tranquil surroundings, lough views. Beside Mount Stewart National Trust Est.

| B&B | 3 | Ensuite | STG£25 | - | Dinner | - | - |
|-----|---|---------|--------|---|--------|---|---|
| B&B | - | Standard | - | - | Partial Board | - | - |
| Single Rate | | | STG£30 | - | Child reduction | | - |

ewtownards 5.5km    Ⓥ [cc icons...]    **Open:** 3rd January-22nd December

---

**Leslie Bryan**
**TRASNAGH HOUSE**
23 Ballybryan Road,
Greyabbey, Co Down
**BT22 2RB**

Tel: **028 42788111**
Email: **trasnaghhouse@hotmail.com**

Off A20 great views of Strangford Lough. Comfortable spacious rooms excellent facilities and breakfasts Greyabbey 3km Mountstewart 5km Portaferry 15km.

| B&B | 2 | Ensuite | STG£23-£23 | - | Dinner | - | - |
|-----|---|---------|------------|---|--------|---|---|
| B&B | - | Standard | - | - | Partial Board | - | - |
| Single Rate | | | STG£30-£30 | - | Child reduction | | 50% |

reyabbey 2.5km    Ⓥ [icons...]    **Open:** 1st January-31st December

Fermanagh is best defined by sheer diversity and quality of all the county has to offer. Cruising, hill walking, lakes and rivers teeming with fish, splendid subterranean waterways and secretive caves, forest parks and nature reserves, megalithic tombs, stately homes, restaurants, welcoming pubs.

---

**Rosemary Armstrong**
ARCH HOUSE TULLYHONA
**59 Marble Arch Road,**
**Florencecourt, Enniskillen,**
**Co Fermanagh BT92 1DE**

### Enniskillen

TEL: **028 66348452**
EMAIL: **tullyguest60@hotmail.com**
WEB: **www.archhouse.com**

◆◆◆◆ 15 Awards. Restaurant home cooking. Laundry, Internet. Marble Arch Caves/F/C Castle/Belleek Pottery. Follow signs for caves from Enniskillen. A4 3 miles left A32. 4 miles then 2 miles right on right. ROI 048.

| | | | | | | | |
|---|---|---|---|---|---|---|---|
| B&B | 6 | Ensuite | STG£20-£23 | €30-€35 | Dinner | STG£7 | €10 |
| B&B | - | Standard | | - | Partial Board | | - |
| Single Rate | | | STG£20-£30 | €30-€45 | Child reduction | | 50% |

Enniskillen 8km  Open: All Year

---

**Catherine Corrigan**
CORRIGAN SHORE GUEST HOUSE
**Clonatrig, Bellanaleck,**
**Enniskillen, Co Fermanagh**
**BT92 2AR**

### Enniskillen

TEL: **028 6634 8572**

Shore of Lough Erne. Rooms ensuite, TV, Tea/Coffee facilities. Caves, National Trust, Museum, Restaurant. From town A4, A509 3.5 miles, left Shore Guest House, 2 miles.

| | | | | | | | |
|---|---|---|---|---|---|---|---|
| B&B | 5 | Ensuite | STG£20-£20 | - | Dinner | - | - |
| B&B | - | Standard | - | - | Partial Board | - | - |
| Single Rate | | | STG£25-£25 | - | Child reduction | | 50% |

Enniskillen 8km   Open: 10th January-15th December

---

**Joan Foster**
WILLOWBANK HOUSE
**60 Bellevue Road, Enniskillen,**
**Co Fermanagh BT44 4JH**

### Enniskillen

TEL: **028 66 328582** FAX: **028 66 328582**
EMAIL: **joan@willowbankhouse.com**
WEB: **www.willowbankhouse.com**

Exclusive B/B on shores of Lough Erne. Panoramic views. Ground floor bedrooms. Extensive breakfast menu. Willowbank sign on A4 1 mile from Enniskillen. AA ◆◆◆◆.

| | | | | | | | |
|---|---|---|---|---|---|---|---|
| B&B | 5 | Ensuite | - | €35-€45 | Dinner | STG£13.50 | €20 |
| B&B | - | Standard | - | - | Partial Board | | - |
| Single Rate | | | - | €45-€45 | Child reduction | | 50% |

Enniskillen 5.5km  Open: All Year Except Christmas

---

**Mrs Dorothy Hassard**
BAYVIEW GUEST HOUSE
**Tully, Churchill, Enniskillen,**
**Co Fermanagh BT93 6HP**

### Enniskillen

TEL: **028 68641250**
EMAIL: **dorothy.hassard@lineone.net**

Modern farm house on working dairy farm overlooking lower Lough Erne 10 miles from Enniskillen 12 miles from Belleek on A46 Road with shore walks.

| | | | | | | | |
|---|---|---|---|---|---|---|---|
| B&B | 2 | Ensuite | STG£20-£25 | €30-€40 | Dinner | - | - |
| B&B | 2 | Standard | STG£18-£22.50 | €28-€35 | Partial Board | - | - |
| Single Rate | | | STG£25-£25 | €40-€50 | Child reduction | | - |

Enniskillen 16km  Open: 1st February-30th November

**Wendy McChesney**
MOUNTVIEW
61 Irvinestown Road,
Enniskillen, Co Fermanagh
BT74 6DN

TEL: **028 66323147**  FAX: **028 66329611**
EMAIL: **wendy@mountviewguests.com**
WEB: **mountviewguests.com**

Victorian house in large garden 1km from town. All ensuite with TV, Kettle, Hairdryers. Snooker Room. Convenient to lake, Fishing, Golf, Nattrust Caves, Restaurants.

| | | | | | | Dinner | - | - |
|---|---|---|---|---|---|---|---|---|
| B&B | 3 | Ensuite | STG£23-£24 | | - | Dinner | - | - |
| B&B | - | Standard | - | | - | Partial Board | - | - |
| Single Rate | | | STG£34-£35 | | - | Child reduction | - | - |

Enniskillen 1km

**Open:** 3rd January-18th December

**Sharon Weir**
DROMARD HOUSE
Tamlaght, Enniskillen,
Co Fermanagh BT74 4HS

TEL: **028 66387250**
EMAIL: **dromardhouse@yahoo.co.uk**
WEB: **www.dromardhouse.com**

Come and enjoy our warm, friendly hospitality, beautiful situation, pretty ensuite rooms and woodland path to the lake shore of our lovely farm. AA ◆◆◆◆.

| | | | | | Dinner | - | - |
|---|---|---|---|---|---|---|---|
| B&B | 4 | Ensuite | STG£20 | €30-€31 | Dinner | - | - |
| B&B | - | Standard | - | - | Partial Board | - | - |
| Single Rate | | | STG£25 | €40-€43.50 | Child reduction | | 50% |

Enniskillen 3km

**Open:** All Year

Head north-west to a region that is extraordinary in a multitude of ways. It offers the lively Maiden City, the rolling Atlantic beaches and such a spectrum of things to do and see that you will want to stay longer.

---

**Mrs Ann Millar**
GLENLEARY FARMHOUSE
12 Glenleary Rd, Coleraine,
Co Londonderry BT51 3QY

### Coleraine

TEL: **028 70342919**  FAX: **028 70352130**
EMAIL: **glenleary.farm@virgin.net**
WEB: **glenlearyfarm.co.uk**
BUS NO: **116**

A warm welcome 5 minutes south of Coleraine just off A29. For a scenic peaceful view near all area tourist attractions with 2 restaurants nearby.

| | | | | | | | |
|---|---|---|---|---|---|---|---|
| B&B | 2 | Ensuite | STG£20-£25 | - | Dinner | STG£12 | - |
| B&B | 2 | Standard | STG£18-£23 | - | Partial Board | STG£38 | - |
| Single Rate | | | STG£21-£26 | - | Child reduction | | 50% |

Coleraine 1.4km

**Open:** All Year Except Christmas

---

**Margaret Moore**
KILLEAGUE LODGE
157 Drumcroone Road,
Coleraine, Co Londonderry
BT51 3SG

### Coleraine

TEL: **028 70868229**  FAX: **028 70868229**
EMAIL: **killeaguelodge@bushinternet.com**
WEB: **www.beds4thenight.co.uk**

Relax and be spoiled on our dairy farm, 5 miles south of Coleraine on A29. Convenient to Giants Causeway. Laundry facilities, hospitality award winner.

| | | | | | | | |
|---|---|---|---|---|---|---|---|
| B&B | 3 | Ensuite | STG£22.50-£25 | - | Dinner | - | - |
| B&B | - | Standard | - | - | Partial Board | - | - |
| Single Rate | | | STG£27-£27 | - | Child reduction | | 33.3% |

Coleraine 8km

**Open:** 1st January-20th December

---

**Mrs Elizabeth Rose Morrison**
BELLEVUE COUNTRY HOUSE
43 Greenhill Road, Aghadowey,
Coleraine, Co Londonderry
BT51 4EU

### Coleraine

TEL: **028 70 868797**  FAX: **028 70 868780**
EMAIL: **info@bellevuecountryhouse.co.uk**
WEB: **www.bellevuecountryhouse.co.uk**

Listed country house, beautiful views of the blue hills of county Antrim. Convenient to Giant's Causeway, Sperrins and Donegal. On B66 off A29, 7 miles south of Coleraine. AA ◆◆◆◆.

| | | | | | | | |
|---|---|---|---|---|---|---|---|
| B&B | 3 | Ensuite | STG£22.50-£25 | - | Dinner | - | - |
| B&B | - | Standard | - | - | Partial Board | - | - |
| Single Rate | | | STG£25-£25 | - | Child reduction | | 50% |

Coleraine 11km

**Open:** 1st February-30th November

---

**Mrs Averil Campbell**
KILLENNAN HOUSE
40 Killennan Road, Drumahoe,
Co Londonderry BT47 3NG

### Derry

TEL: **028 71301710**  FAX: **028 71301710**
EMAIL: **averil@killennan.co.uk**
WEB: **www.killennan.co.uk**

Warm welcome, 19th century country house, beautiful gardens. 10 mins from Derry, Airport. Ideal touring base. Off A6 to Belfast, take B118 Eglinton.

| | | | | | | | |
|---|---|---|---|---|---|---|---|
| B&B | 3 | Ensuite | STG£20 | €32 | Dinner | - | - |
| B&B | - | Standard | - | | Partial Board | - | - |
| Single Rate | | | STG£25 | €39 | Child reduction | | 50% |

Derry 8km

**Open:** All Year Except Christmas

**Mrs Florence Sloan**
DRUMCOVITT HOUSE
704 Feeny Road, Feeny, Derry,
Co Londonderry BT47 4SU

### Feeny
TEL: **028 77781224**　FAX: **028 77781224**
EMAIL: **drumcovitt.feeny@btinternet.com**
WEB: **www.drumcovitt.com**

Georgian farm house 103 hectares. Log fires, oil heating, gracious rooms. Walks, Birds, Selfcater, Visit Sperrin, Causeway, Donegal, Derry 14km. A6/B74 1km east Feeny.

| | | | | | | | | |
|---|---|---|---|---|---|---|---|---|
| B&B | - | Ensuite | - | | - | Dinner | - | - |
| B&B | 3 | Standard | STG£23-£27 | | - | Partial Board | - | - |
| Single Rate | | | STG£23-£27 | | - | Child reduction | | 25%-50% |

Dungiven 5km

Open: 1st January-23rd December

**Mrs Maureen McKean**
BRAEHEAD HOUSE
22 Brae Head Rd, Londonderry,
Co Londonderry BT48 9XE

### Londonderry
TEL: **028 712 63195**　FAX: **028 712 63195**

Georgian farmhouse on mixed farm overlooking River Foyle and Golf Course, panoramic views. TV, tea/coffee in rooms. Kennels available. 5 mins drive from Derry City on A40.

| | | | | | | | |
|---|---|---|---|---|---|---|---|
| B&B | 2 | Ensuite | STG£22 | €40 | Dinner | - | - |
| B&B | 1 | Standard | - | - | Partial Board | - | - |
| Single Rate | | | STG£20 | €38 | Child reduction | | 50% |

Derry 3km

Open: 6th January-15th December

The changing landscape embodies all that is great about Tyrone. From its mountains and moorlands in the northwest to the softer scenery of the south you'll find walking trails, forest parks, the American Folk Park and open-air visitor attractions.

---

**Mrs Annette McGarrity**
**GLENVAR**
111 Tullyvar Road, Aughnacloy, Co Tyrone BT69 6BL

### Aughnacloy

TEL: **028 855 57062**   FAX: **028 855 57062**
EMAIL: **glenvar.guesthouse@btopenworld.com**

Two star luxurious purpose design guesthouse, immaculate ensuite rooms, tranquill setting in wonderful countryside. Experience the "real home from home" A5 route.

| | | | | | | |
|---|---|---|---|---|---|---|
| B&B | 5 | Ensuite | - | --€35 | Dinner | - | €20 |
| B&B | - | Standard | - | - | Partial Board | - | - |
| Single Rate | | - | | --€45 | Child reduction | | 33.3% |

Aughnacloy 3km

**Open:** All Year

---

**Mrs Joan Davison**
**FORTVIEW**
36 Tullyboy Rd, Cookstown, Co Tyrone BT45 7YE

### Cookstown

TEL: **028 867 62640**   FAX: **028 867 64230**
EMAIL: **john_davison@btopenworld.com**
WEB: **www.smoothhound.co.uk/hotels/fortview**

Comfortable welcoming home on working farm 5km north of Cookstown. Signposted on A29 Cookstown - Moneymore carriageway. Spotless rooms, one on ground floor.

| | | | | | | |
|---|---|---|---|---|---|---|
| B&B | 2 | Ensuite | STG£20-£20 | €30-€30 | Dinner | - | - |
| B&B | 1 | Standard | - | - | Partial Board | - | - |
| Single Rate | | STG£16-£25 | | €26-€38 | Child reduction | | 33.3% |

Cookstown 5km

**Open:** All Year

---

**Mrs Mary Montgomery**
**CLANABOGAN HOUSE**
85 Clanabogan road, Omagh, Co Tyrone BT78 1SL

### Omagh

TEL: **028 82241171**   FAX: **028 82241171**
EMAIL: **info@clanaboganhouse.freeserve.co.uk**
WEB: **www.clanaboganhouse.freeserve.co.uk**

A restored period residence set in 5 acres of woodland and gardens. Bar, Golf, Driving range and Pony stables on site. Spacious rooms. Friendly relaxed atmosphere.

| | | | | | | |
|---|---|---|---|---|---|---|
| B&B | 8 | Ensuite | STG£25 | - | Dinner | - | - |
| B&B | - | Standard | - | - | Partial Board | - | - |
| Single Rate | | STG£25 | | - | Child reduction | | 50% |

Omagh 1.5km

**Open:** All Year

---

**Louie Reid**
**GREENMOUNT LODGE**
58 Greenmount Road, Gortaclare, Omagh, Co Tyrone BT79 0YE

### Omagh

TEL: **028 82841325**   FAX: **028 82840019**
EMAIL: **greenmountlodge@lineone.net**
WEB: **www.greenmountlodge.com**

Luxury ◆◆◆◆ guesthouse set in mature woodlands. Guest laundry facilities. Off A5 south of Omagh, turn right after Carrickkeel Pub. 1 mile on left.

| | | | | | | |
|---|---|---|---|---|---|---|
| B&B | 8 | Ensuite | STG£20-£25 | €30-€32 | Dinner | - | €20 |
| B&B | - | Standard | - | - | Partial Board | - | - |
| Single Rate | | - | | €40 | Child reduction | | 50% |

Omagh 12km

**Open:** 1st January-31st December

Telephoning from Republic of Ireland: 0044 28+ eight digit number

# Northern Ireland...
# You'll be amazed!

Northern Ireland our doors are always open and you'll find a welcome renowned roughout the world. Take some time, come in, relax and find out what brings eople back again and again. Our B&Bs provide a down to earth, warm, family mosphere, every bit as comforting as the Ulster Fry in the morning. Your hosts will fer a superb source of advice on what to see and do in the local area.

e natural, unspoilt landscape is e envy of many. From the cturesque beauty and fresh aters of the Fermanagh lakes; ough the rugged splendour of e Sperrin and Mourne Mountains, ong the golden beaches of the own and Antrim coasts, right up to e phenomenon that is the Giant's auseway. Thousands of years of story and a host of myths and gends are just waiting to be plored - follow the trail of St

Patrick through Co Down or hear how the Giant's Causeway was formed by the mythical Finn MacCool.

You will find truly world class golf and fishing on hand across Northern Ireland. Royal Portrush and Royal County Down were recently voted among the world's top 20 courses. While the loughs and rivers provide some of the most varied and bountiful game, coarse and marine fish species.

Take a break in two European cities with a rising reputation. The rebirth of Belfast and Derry continues apace with fantastic venues attracting world class events, fabulous restaurants offering fresh local produce and superb shops to suit all tastes.

Come to Northern Ireland and embrace the homely feel. You'll be guaranteed to leave with the smile you were greeted with.

reland

**Building
Sustainable
Prosperity**

To find out more about visiting Northern Ireland visit:
**www.discovernorthernireland.com**
or call us on:
**+44 (0) 28 9024 6609**
or **+353 1 679 1977**

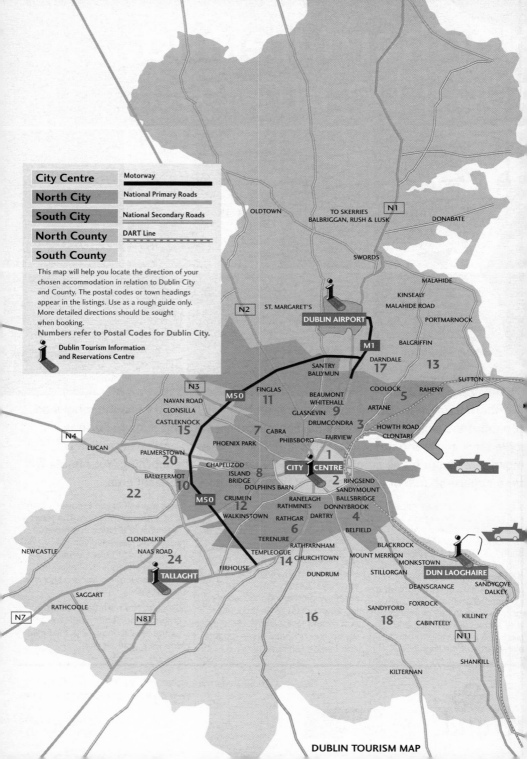

DUBLIN TOURISM MAP

# Dublin

Dublin, Ireland's capital, steeped in history and buzzing with youthful energy. From its gracious Georgian Squares and terraces, mountain walks and sandy beaches to the intimacy of its pub and cafe life, Dublin is a thriving centre for culture. It is home to a great literary tradition where the cosmopolitan and charming converge in an atmosphere of delightful diversity.

Fine museums and art galleries chronicle its long and colourful past while the pubs and cafes buzz with traditional entertainment. Dublin's attractions are many from castles, museums and art galleries to the lively spirit of Temple Bar within a half hour of the city centre there are mountain walks, stately homes and gardens, sandy beaches and quaint fishing villages.

During your stay with us you will sample some of the charm of Dublin and particularly the warmth and wit of its people that has never ceased to win the heart of the visitor.

## Area Representatives

**DUBLIN**

Mrs Rita Kenny SEAVIEW 166 Bettyglen Raheny Dublin 5
Tel: 01 8315335

Mrs Noreen McBride 3 Rossmore Grove Off Wellington Lane Templogue Dublin 6W
Tel: 01 4902939  Fax: 01 4929416

Mrs Margaret McLoughlin-O'Connell LOYOLA 18 Charleville Road Phibsboro Dublin 7
Tel: 01 8389973

## Tourist Information Offices

REFER TO PAGE 5 FOR A LIST OF SERVICES AVAILABLE

Dublin

Dublin Tourism Centre
Suffolk Street
Dublin 2
Information: 1850 230 330
Reservations: 1800 668 668
http://www.visitdublin.com

14 Upper O'Connell St.,
Dublin 1

Arrivals Hall
Dublin Airport

Dun Laoghaire Harbour
Ferry Terminal Building
Dun Laoghaire
Co Dublin

Baggot Street Bridge
Dublin 2

The Square Towncentre
Tallaght, Dublin 24

**Mrs Mary O'Reilly**
RATHLEEK
13 Brookwood Rd, Artane,
Dublin 5

### Artane

Tel: **01 8310555**
Bus No: **42, 42B, 42C, 27**

10 mins Beaumont Hospital, City Centre, Irish Ferries, Car Ferry, Connolly Station, Central Bus Station. Dart. Sea Front. Tea, TV, Radio, Hairdryer all rooms.

| | | | | Dinner | - |
|---|---|---|---|---|---|
| B&B | - | Ensuite | - | | |
| B&B | 3 | Standard | €30-€30 | Partial Board | - |
| Single Rate | | | €41-€41 | Child reduction | - |

Dublin 4km

**Open:** 1st March-31st October

---

**Kevin & Anne Rogers**
BLAITHIN B&B
18 St Brendans Avenue,
Artane, Dublin 5

### Artane

Tel: **01 8483817**  Fax: **01 8674029**
Email: **blakevin@eircom.net**
Bus No: **27, 42**

Luxurious family home. Excellent rooms with Tea/Coffee, TV. Close to Seafront, Golf. City 10 min. Buses at door. Airport 15 min, Ferry 10min. Safe Parking.

| | | | | Dinner | - |
|---|---|---|---|---|---|
| B&B | 3 | Ensuite | €35-€40 | | |
| B&B | 1 | Standard | €30-€35 | Partial Board | - |
| Single Rate | | | €55-€65 | Child reduction | - |

Dublin 5km

**Open:** 7th January-30th October

---

**Eve Mitchell**
ASHBROOK HOUSE
River Road, Ashtown,
Castleknock, Dublin 15,
Co Dublin

### Castleknock

Tel: **01 838 5660**  Fax: **01 838 5660**
Email: **evemitchell@hotmail.com**
Bus No: **39, 37, 38, 70**

A beautiful old Georgian House situated on 10 acres close to Phoenix pk. & M50. 15 mins from city centre & Airport. Secure car parking.

| | | | | Dinner | - |
|---|---|---|---|---|---|
| B&B | 4 | Ensuite | €45-€45 | | |
| B&B | - | Standard | - | Partial Board | - |
| Single Rate | | | €60-€60 | Child reduction | - |

In Dublin

**Open:** 2nd January-20th December

---

**Caroline & Paul Connolly**
KINCORA LODGE
54 Kincora Court, Clontarf,
Dublin 3

### Clontarf

Tel: **01 8330220**  Fax: **01 8330007**
Email: **info@kincoralodge.com**
Web: **www.kincoralodge.com**
Bus No: **130**

Modern home quiet area. Parking. 15 mins Airport, City Centre, Ferrypoint. Theatre, Golf Courses, Beach, Park within walking distance. TV, Tea/Coffee facilities, Beautician on premises.

| | | | | Dinner | - |
|---|---|---|---|---|---|
| B&B | 3 | Ensuite | €32.50-€45 | | |
| B&B | - | Standard | - | Partial Board | - |
| Single Rate | | | €60-€75 | Child reduction | 25% |

Dublin 4km

**Open:** 6th January-21st December

---

**Mrs Eileen Cummiskey Kelly**
GARRYBAWN
18 Copeland Avenue, Clontarf,
Dublin 3

### Clontarf

Tel: **01 8333760**
Bus No: **20, 20B, 42, 31**

Near Point Theatre, Airport, Ferryport, City Centre. 2km Croke Park, 1km Buses to Centre no.'s 20, 20B, 42, 31.

| | | | | Dinner | - |
|---|---|---|---|---|---|
| B&B | 2 | Ensuite | €30-€35 | | |
| B&B | 1 | Standard | €27.50-€30 | Partial Board | - |
| Single Rate | | | €38-€50 | Child reduction | 25% |

Dublin 3km

**Open:** All Year

**Mrs Susan Delahunty**
GLENBROOK
34 Howth Road, Clontarf,
Dublin 3

Clontarf

TEL: **01 8331117/8532265**
EMAIL: **delahunty@dol.ie**
BUS NO: **29A,31,31A,31B,32,32A,32B**

Victorian town house, close to City, Ferryport, Airport, Bus and Rail Terminals. Beach and Golf courses nearby.

| | | | | | |
|---|---|---|---|---|---|
| B&B | 2 | Ensuite | €38-€45 | Dinner | - |
| B&B | - | Standard | | Partial Board | - |
| Single Rate | | | €40-€50 | Child reduction | 25% |

Dublin City 3km

**Open:** 31st March-31st October

---

**Miss M Dereymont**
18 Seacourt
St Gabriel's Road, Clontarf,
Dublin 3

Clontarf

TEL: **01 8333313**
BUS NO: **130**

Georgian residence, convenient to City, Airport, Ferry, Restaurants, Point Theatre. Non smoking. Adults only. Closes 1 am (opposite St. Gabriel's Church). Shops nearby.

| | | | | | |
|---|---|---|---|---|---|
| B&B | 1 | Ensuite | €47.50-€47.50 | Dinner | - |
| B&B | 2 | Standard | €42.50-€42.50 | Partial Board | - |
| Single Rate | | | €75-€80 | Child reduction | - |

Dublin 5km

**Open:** 1st April-31st October

---

**John & Delia Devlin**
ANNAGH HOUSE
301 Clontarf Road, Clontarf,
Dublin 3

Clontarf

TEL: **01 8338841**   FAX: **01 8338841**
EMAIL: **annaghhouse@eircom.net**
BUS NO: **130**

Charming Victorian house, convenient to City, Airport, Ferryport, Restaurants, Pubs, Theatres, Golf, Beach. Superb location to explore culture of Dublin. Bus route.

| | | | | | |
|---|---|---|---|---|---|
| B&B | 3 | Ensuite | €37-€39 | Dinner | - |
| B&B | - | Standard | - | Partial Board | - |
| Single Rate | | | - | Child reduction | - |

Dublin 5km

**Open:** All Year Except Christmas

---

**Jackie Egan**
VALENTIA HOUSE
37 Kincora Court, Clontarf,
Dublin 3

Clontarf

TEL: **01 8338060**   FAX: **01 8339990**
EMAIL: **jackieegan@esatclear.ie**
WEB: **www.valentiahouse.com**
BUS NO: **130**

Family run home, convenient City/Airport/Ferry/Point Theatre/Beach/Golf Clubs/Restaurants. 130 Bus Abbey St. to Clontarf road Bus Depot. Left here, right at crossroads, first right & first right.

| | | | | | |
|---|---|---|---|---|---|
| B&B | 3 | Ensuite | €35-€45 | Dinner | - |
| B&B | - | Standard | | Partial Board | - |
| Single Rate | | | €70-€80 | Child reduction | 25% |

Dublin City 4km

**Open:** 1st January-21st December

---

**Mrs Moira Kavanagh**
SPRINGVALE
69 Kincora Drive,
Off Kincora Grove, Clontarf,
Dublin 3

Clontarf

TEL: **01 8333413**   FAX: **01 8333413**
EMAIL: **moira_kav@hotmail.com**
WEB: **www.springvaledublin.com**
BUS NO: **29A,31,32,130, DART**

Modern house, quiet residential area. 15 mins Airport, Car Ferry, City, Point Theatre. Frommer Recommended. Tea/coffee facilities. 4 rooms with shower only.

| | | | | | |
|---|---|---|---|---|---|
| B&B | - | Ensuite | €30-€32 | Dinner | - |
| B&B | 4 | Standard | | Partial Board | - |
| Single Rate | | | €38-€43 | Child reduction | - |

Dublin 4km

**Open:** 1st January-22nd December

### Catherine Kennedy
**SLIEVENAMON MANOR**
302 Clontarf Road, Clontarf,
Dublin 3, Co Dublin

Clontarf

TEL: **01 8331025**  FAX: **01 8535020**
EMAIL: **johnandcassiekennedy@eircom.net**
BUS No: **130**

Victorian residence overlooking Dublin Bay. Located in a high amenity area within walking distance. Frequent public transport a few paces from the front door. 130 Bus Lr. Abbey St.

| B&B | 3 | Ensuite | €35-€45 | Dinner | - |
|---|---|---|---|---|---|
| B&B | - | Standard | - | Partial Board | - |
| Single Rate | | | €55-€65 | Child reduction | 50% |

Dublin City 5km

**Open:** 6th January-18th December

---

### Mrs Eileen P Kelly
**TORC HOUSE**
17 Seacourt,
St Gabriels Road (off Seafield Rd), Clontarf, Dublin 3

Clontarf

TEL: **01 8332547**
EMAIL: **pkellytorc@eircom.net**
BUS No: **130**

Detached Georgian house, residential area. Convenient City, Airport, Ferry Port, Beach, Golf, Rose Gardens, Point Theatre. Frommer/Sullivan Guide recommended.

| B&B | 2 | Ensuite | €36-€36 | Dinner | - |
|---|---|---|---|---|---|
| B&B | 1 | Standard | €33-€33 | Partial Board | - |
| Single Rate | | | €50-€55 | Child reduction | - |

Dublin City 5km

**Open:** 1st March-31st October

---

### Mrs Mary Wright
**LAWRENCE HOUSE**
26 St Lawrence Rd, Clontarf,
Dublin 3

Clontarf

TEL: **01 8332525**  FAX: **01 8332525**
EMAIL: **info@lawrence-house.com**
WEB: **www.lawrence-house.com**
BUS No: **130, 31, 32, 29A, 31A, 32B**

Gracious Victorian house. 10 minutes to City, DART, Car Ferry, Airport and Point Theatre. Private car parking. Buses 130, 31, 31A, 32, 32B, 29A to St Lawrence Rd.

| B&B | 4 | Ensuite | €35-€40 | Dinner | - |
|---|---|---|---|---|---|
| B&B | - | Standard | - | Partial Board | - |
| Single Rate | | | €60-€60 | Child reduction | - |

Dublin 2.5km

**Open:** 1st January-23rd December

---

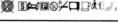

### Irene Coyle Ryan
**BLANFORD HOUSE**
37 Lambay Road,
off Griffith Ave, Drumcondra,
Dublin 9

Drumcondra

TEL: **01 8378036**
BUS No: **11, 11A, 13A**

Town house near Airport, Ferry Port, Botanic Gardens. Forbairt, Point Theatre. Dublin City University. Bonsecours Hospital. Mater Hospital.

| B&B | 1 | Ensuite | €30-€31 | Dinner | - |
|---|---|---|---|---|---|
| B&B | 3 | Standard | €27.50 | Partial Board | - |
| Single Rate | | | €38-€43.50 | Child reduction | - |

Dublin City 3km

**Open:** 2nd January-20th December

---

### Mrs Cait Cunningham Murray
30 Walnut Ave
**Courtlands Estate,**
off Griffith Ave, Drumcondra,
Dublin 9

Drumcondra

TEL: **01 8379327**
BUS No: **3,16,16A,41,41A,13A**

Modern home, off Griffith Ave overlooking park. Off N1 convenient to Airport, City Centre and B&I Ferry. Very quiet location. Smoke free home.

| B&B | 2 | Ensuite | €31-€31 | Dinner | - |
|---|---|---|---|---|---|
| B&B | 1 | Standard | €28-€28 | Partial Board | - |
| Single Rate | | | - | Child reduction | - |

Dublin City 4km

**Open:** 1st April-30th September

## Mrs Roma Gibbons
JOYVILLE
24 St Alphonsus Road,
Drumcondra, Dublin 9

**Drumcondra**

TEL: **01 8303221**
BUS NO: **3,11,11A,16,16A ,41,41B**

Victorian town house off main Airport road. Convenient to Car Ferry, Botanic Gardens, City Centre.

| B&B | - | Ensuite | - | Dinner | - |
|-----|---|---------|---|--------|---|
| B&B | 4 | Standard | €29-€29 | Partial Board | - |
| Single Rate | | | €35-€35 | Child reduction | - |

Dublin City 1km

**Open:** 7th January-20th December

---

## Mrs Ann Griffin
MUCKROSS HOUSE
Claude Road, off Whitworth Rd,
Drumcondra, Dublin 9

**Drumcondra**

TEL: **01 8304888**
EMAIL: **muckrosshouse01@eircom.net**
WEB: **www.muckrosshousedublin.com**
BUS NO: **13,40,40A,40B**

Situated off main Airport road (N1). Convenient to City Centre, Airport, Car Ferry & Point Depot. Private enclosed car parking.

| B&B | 5 | Ensuite | €32.50-€35 | Dinner | - |
|-----|---|---------|-----------|--------|---|
| B&B | - | Standard | - | Partial Board | - |
| Single Rate | | | €45 | Child reduction | 25% |

Dublin 1km

**Open:** 2nd January-20th December

---

## Mrs Gemma Rafferty
GREEN-VIEW
36 Walnut Avenue, Courtlands,
Off Griffith Ave, Drumcondra,
Dublin 9

**Drumcondra**

TEL: **01 8376217**
BUS NO: **3,13A,16,16A,41A, 41B**

Peaceful location opposite Park off M1. 10 mins City Centre, Airport, Car Ferry, Golf Courses.

| B&B | 2 | Ensuite | €31-€31 | Dinner | - |
|-----|---|---------|---------|--------|---|
| B&B | 1 | Standard | €28-€28.50 | Partial Board | - |
| Single Rate | | | - | Child reduction | - |

Dublin City 4km

**Open:** 20th March-15th November

---

## Mrs Teresa Ryan
PARKNASILLA
15 Iona Drive, Drumcondra,
Dublin 9

**Drumcondra**

TEL: **01 8305724**
BUS NO: **11,16,16A,41,13,19,19A,3.**

Edwardian detached residence, off main Airport Road N1, 10 minutes to City Centre, Airport, Car Ferry, Bus & Rail Terminals.

| B&B | 2 | Ensuite | €32.50-€32.50 | Dinner | - |
|-----|---|---------|---------------|--------|---|
| B&B | 2 | Standard | €30-€30 | Partial Board | - |
| Single Rate | | | €38-€43 | Child reduction | 25% |

Dublin 1.5km

**Open:** 7th January-20th December

---

## Mrs Margaret McLoughlin-O'Connell
LOYOLA
18 Charleville Road, Phibsboro,
Dublin 7

**Phibsboro**

TEL: **01 8389973**
EMAIL: **loyola18@eircom.net**
WEB: **www.loyola18.com**
BUS NO: **10, 38, 120, 121, 122**

Victorian house convenient to Rail, Bus, Airport, Car Ferry Terminals. Zoo, Public Parks, Mater Hospital, Link Roads.

| B&B | 2 | Ensuite | €35-€35 | Dinner | - |
|-----|---|---------|---------|--------|---|
| B&B | 2 | Standard | €32.50-€32.50 | Partial Board | - |
| Single Rate | | | €37.50-€45 | Child reduction | 25% |

Dublin City 1km

**Open:** 15th January-15th December

**Mrs Maureen Flynn**
FOUR SEASONS
15 Grange Park Green,
Raheny, Dublin 5

Raheny

Tel: **01 8486612**   Fax: **01 8672216**
Email: **eflynn@iol.ie**
Web: **www.abbeydrive.com**
Bus No: **29A, 31, 32, Aerdart**

Convenient to City Centre, Car Ferry, Airport, DART and Bus. Private parking. Restaurants in Village. TV lounge with Tea/Coffee, Hairdryers in rooms.

| B&B | 4 | Ensuite | €32-€33 | Dinner | - |
|-----|---|---------|---------|--------|---|
| B&B | - | Standard | - | Partial Board | - |
| Single Rate | | | - | Child reduction | - |

Dublin City 7km

**Open:** 15th January-15th December

**Mrs Eileen Keane**
BREIFNE
23 Bettyglen, Raheny, Dublin 5

Raheny

Tel: **01 8313976**
Bus No: **31, 31A, 32**

Large detached house overlooking sea. Private parking. 10km Dublin Airport, 6km B&I Car Ferry, 4km City Centre, Guest Lounge.

| B&B | 3 | Ensuite | €30-€34 | Dinner | - |
|-----|---|---------|---------|--------|---|
| B&B | 1 | Standard | €30-€32 | Partial Board | - |
| Single Rate | | | €40-€44 | Child reduction | 33.3% |

In Raheny

**Open:** 1st January-20th December

**Mrs Rita Kenny**
SEAVIEW
166 Bettyglen, Raheny,
Dublin 5, Co Dublin

Raheny

Tel: **01 8315335**
Email: **rita.kenny@ireland.com**
Bus No: **31, 31A, 32, 32B**

Large semi detached house overlooking Sea. Private parking. Convenient to Airport, Car Ferry, DART, Buses, Golf Courses. Orthopaedic beds, Room rate.

| B&B | 2 | Ensuite | €32 | Dinner | - |
|-----|---|---------|-----|--------|---|
| B&B | 1 | Standard | €32 | Partial Board | - |
| Single Rate | | | - | Child reduction | - |

Dublin City 5km

**Open:** 7th January-20th December

**Mrs Rosaleen Hobbs**
HAZELWOOD
2 Thormanby Woods,
Thormanby Road, Howth,
Dublin 13

**Howth**

TEL: **01 8391391**   FAX: **01 8391391**
EMAIL: **hobbs@eircom.net**
WEB: **www.hazelwood.net**
BUS NO: **31B, DART**

Modern dormer bungalow in own grounds. Ample car parking. Convenient Golf, Beach, Restaurants, Scenic Cliff Walks & Fishing Village. City centre 25mins.

| B&B | 6 | Ensuite | €34 | Dinner | - |
| B&B | - | Standard | - | Partial Board | - |
| Single Rate | | | - | Child reduction | 50% |

Howth 1.5km

**Open:** 10th January-20th December

---

**Ms Patricia Butterly**
BROOKFIELD LODGE B&B
Blakes Cross, Lusk, Co Dublin

**Lusk**

TEL: **01 8430043**   FAX: **01 8430177**
EMAIL: **trishb@indigo.ie**
BUS NO: **100**

Country home, 8 minutes Dublin Airport. AA ◆◆◆. From airport take M1 to Belfast. Take R132 direction Skerries, follow for 3km. Ignore sign for Lusk at Esso garage, continue for 400mts. On left.

| B&B | 3 | Ensuite | €28-€50 | Dinner | - |
| B&B | - | Standard | - | Partial Board | - |
| Single Rate | | | - | Child reduction | - |

Swords 4km

**Open:** 3rd January-30th November

---

**Deirdre Fairbrother**
GREENLANDS BED &
BREAKFAST
Corduff, Lusk, Co Dublin

**Lusk**

TEL: **01 8430130**

Custom built B&B, ground floor accom, from airport take M1 to Belfast. Take R132 Skerries direction for 3km. Ignore sign for Lusk at Esso garage. Continue on 1km B&B on right, own transport needed.

| B&B | 5 | Ensuite | €28.50-€45 | Dinner | - |
| B&B | - | Standard | - | Partial Board | - |
| Single Rate | | | €40-€58 | Child reduction | - |

Lusk 2km

**Open:** 2nd January-30th November

---

**Leo & Kay Fynes**
HILLVIEW HOUSE
Ballaghtown, Lusk, Co Dublin

**Lusk**

TEL: **01 8438218**   FAX: **01 8438218**
EMAIL: **lfynes@indigo.ie**
WEB: **www.hillviewhouselusk.com**
BUS NO: **33**

Hillview House is ideally situated in a tranquil country setting yet only 15 minutes to Dublin Airport and 30 minutes to Dublin City.

| B&B | 4 | Ensuite | €38-€42 | Dinner | - |
| B&B | - | Standard | - | Partial Board | - |
| Single Rate | | | €50-€55 | Child reduction | 50% |

Lusk 3km

**Open:** 3rd January-20th December

---

**Freda Rigney**
IVY BUNGALOW
Ballough, Lusk, Co Dublin

**Lusk**

TEL: **01 8437031**
EMAIL: **ivybungalowlusk@yahoo.com**

Quaint country home off Belfast Dublin road. 10 mins North of Dublin Airport. City Centre 30 mins. Peaceful surroundings. Ground floor accommodation. Pub 300 yards.

| B&B | 3 | Ensuite | €36.50-€47 | Dinner | - |
| B&B | 1 | Standard | €34-€35 | Partial Board | - |
| Single Rate | | | €40-€57.50 | Child reduction | - |

Swords 9km

**Open:** 3rd January-21st December

**Malahide**

**Mrs Monica Fitzsimons**
PEBBLE MILL
Kinsealy, Malahide, Co Dublin

TEL: **01 8461792**
EMAIL: **pat.fitzsimons@esatlink.com**
BUS NO: **42, 43**

Country home on 4 Acres. Golf, Horseriding, Yachting, Castle closeby. Airport 7mins, B&I 20 mins.
Room rates. TV, Hairdryers, Tea/Coffee all rooms.

| B&B | 3 | Ensuite | €35 | Dinner | - |
| B&B | - | Standard | - | Partial Board | - |
| Single Rate | | | - | Child reduction | 50% |

Malahide 3km

**Open:** 1st April-30th September

---

**Malahide**

**Emma Gaule S.R.N.**
CARA
104 Biscayne, off Coast Rd,
Malahide, Co Dublin

TEL: **01 8452041**   FAX: **01 8452041**
EMAIL: **egaule@eircom.net**
WEB: **www.gaule.ie**
BUS NO: **42, 32A, 102, 230** AIRPORT

Comfortable home. Pass Grand Hotel, 2nd turn right after Island View Hotel, keep right 3rd left.
Beach, restaurants, tv, tea/coffee, triple room with bathroom. City Airport bus route 20 mins.

| B&B | 1 | Ensuite | €30-€34 | Dinner | - |
| B&B | 2 | Standard | €30-€33 | Partial Board | - |
| Single Rate | | | €45-€55 | Child reduction | 25% |

Malahide 1km

**Open:** 1st February-15th November

---

**Malahide**

**Maura & Jim Halpin**
HEATHER VIEW
Malahide Road, Kinsealy,
Co Dublin

TEL: **01 8453483**   FAX: **01 8453818**
EMAIL: **hview@eircom.net**
BUS NO: **42,43,**AIRPORT 230

Luxury country home on R107, Airport 6km. Castle 1km, M50 3km. Parking. All rooms TV,
Clockradio, Hairdryer, Tea/Coffee. Breakfast menu.

| B&B | 5 | Ensuite | €35-€36 | Dinner | - |
| B&B | - | Standard | - | Partial Board | - |
| Single Rate | | | - | Child reduction | 25% |

Malahide 3km

**Open:** 5th January-18th December

---

**Malahide**

**Olive Hopkins**
EVERGREEN
Kinsealy Lane, Malahide,
Co Dublin

TEL: **01 8460185**
EMAIL: **evergreendub@eircom.net**
WEB: **www.evergreendublin.com**
BUS NO: **42**

Luxury home on 1 acre. Private parking. Malahide/Restaurants 1 mile. TV, Hairdryers all rooms.
Turn right before main entrance to Malahide Castle/Park. Airport 10 mins. Ferry/City 20 mins.

| B&B | 4 | Ensuite | €32-€34 | Dinner | - |
| B&B | 1 | Standard | €30-€32 | Partial Board | - |
| Single Rate | | | €43-€47 | Child reduction | 33.3% |

Malahide 2km

**Open:** 13th January-17th December

---

**Malahide**

**Jean Moodley**
SONAS
39 The Old Golf Links,
Malahide, Co Dublin

TEL: **01 8451953**   FAX: **01 8457032**
EMAIL: **jmoodley@indigo.ie**
BUS NO: **42, 32A, 102, 230, DART**

Luxury home in quiet cul de sac. Homely atmosphere, second right after Grand Hotel. Bus and
train to Dublin and bus to Airport. 15 mins to Airport.

| B&B | 3 | Ensuite | €35-€38 | Dinner | - |
| B&B | 1 | Standard | €32.50-€36 | Partial Board | - |
| Single Rate | | | - | Child reduction | 50% |

In Malahide

**Open:** 15th January-30th November

**In Malahide Village**

**Mrs Mary Sweeney**
SOMERTON
**The Mall, Malahide Village,**
**Co Dublin**

TEL: **01 8454090**
EMAIL: **somerton@iol.ie**
BUS NO: **32A, 42, 102, 230, DART**

In heart of Malahide village. All social amenities within short walking distance. City Centre within easy reach by bus or train. True Irish welcome assured. Home from home comforts.

| B&B | 4 | Ensuite | €40-€40 | Dinner | - |
| B&B | - | Standard | - | Partial Board | - |
| Single Rate | | | - | Child reduction | 25% |

**Open:** 2nd January-14th December

---

**Malahide 3km**

**Mrs Anne Askew**
HOWTH VIEW
**9 Beach Park,**
**on Blackberry Lane,**
**Portmarnock, Co Dublin**

TEL: **01 8460665**   FAX: **01 8169895**
EMAIL: **howthview@oceanfree.net**
WEB: **www.howthview.com**
BUS NO: **32, 32A, 32B, 102, 230, DART.**

Second right after Portmarnock Hotel. Fourth house on the right. Modern detached house. Convenient to several Golf courses, Airport, Ferryport and Beach.

| B&B | 4 | Ensuite | €30-€35 | Dinner | - |
| B&B | - | Standard | - | Partial Board | - |
| Single Rate | | | €40-€50 | Child reduction | 25% |

**Open:** All Year

---

**Malahide 3km**

**Mrs Margaret Creane**
ROBINIA
**452 Strand Rd, Portmarnock,**
**Co Dublin**

TEL: **01 8462987**
EMAIL: **robiniabb@eircom.net**
WEB: **homepage.eircom.net/~robinia**
BUS NO: **32, 32A, 102, 230**

Modern home overlooking Beach. Convenient to Golf, City, Malahide Castle. On Airport and City Bus route.

| B&B | 2 | Ensuite | €35-€37 | Dinner | - |
| B&B | 1 | Standard | €34-€35 | Partial Board | - |
| Single Rate | | | - | Child reduction | - |

**Open:** 1st January-20th December

---

**Malahide 1.5km**

**Marie D'Emidio**
SOUTHDALE
**143 Heather Walk,**
**Portmarnock, Co Dublin**

TEL: **01 8463760**   FAX: **01 8463760**
EMAIL: **southdale@eircom.net**
WEB: **www.portmarnock.info/southdale**
BUS NO: **32, 32A, 32B, 102, 230**

A pleasant friendly family home. Beach and Golf within walking distance. Airport 15 mins, City 30 min. Bus and Rail service.

| B&B | 4 | Ensuite | €32.50-€35 | Dinner | - |
| B&B | - | Standard | - | Partial Board | - |
| Single Rate | | | €45-€50 | Child reduction | - |

**Open:** 1st January-23rd December

---

**Malahide 2km**

**Mrs Mary Lee**
TARA
**14 Portmarnock Crescent,**
**Portmarnock, Co Dublin**

TEL: **01 8462996**
BUS NO: **32,32A,DART,102,230**

First turn right after Sands Hotel then sharp left. Near Beach, City Bus Route, convenient to Golf Club, Airport, Ferryport.

| B&B | 1 | Ensuite | €32-€34 | Dinner | - |
| B&B | 2 | Standard | €30-€32 | Partial Board | - |
| Single Rate | | | €40-€50 | Child reduction | - |

**Open:** 1st March-30th November

**Portmarnock 1km**

### Aileen Lynch
**OAKLEIGH**
30 Dewberry Park,
Portmarnock, Co Dublin

TEL: **01 8461628**
EMAIL: **aileenlynch@eircom.net**
BUS NO: **32, 32A, 102, DART(AIRPORT 230)**

Past Sands Hotel, 1st right, Wendell Ave, Then 2nd right. Beach, Restaurants, Golf. Airport 15 mins, City 30 mins. Malahide Castle 2 miles.

| B&B | 3 | Ensuite | €32.50-€35 | Dinner | - |
|-----|---|---------|------------|--------|---|
| B&B | - | Standard | | Partial Board | - |
| Single Rate | | | €50-€60 | Child reduction | - |

**Open:** 1st March-31st October

---

**Malahide 3km**

### Mrs Kathleen O'Brien
**CLARA**
22 Beach Park, Portmarnock,
Co Dublin

TEL: **01 8461936**
BUS NO: **32,32A,102,230**

Comfortable family home. Second turn right after the Portmarnock Hotel and Golf links "Blackberry Lane". Next right into Beachpark and right again.

| B&B | 2 | Ensuite | €30-€32 | Dinner | - |
|-----|---|---------|---------|--------|---|
| B&B | 1 | Standard | €28-€30 | Partial Board | - |
| Single Rate | | | - | Child reduction | - |

**Open:** 1st January-30th November

---

**Malahide 2km**

### Mrs Margaret Treanor
**SEAGLADE HOUSE**
off Coast Road,
At Round Tower, Portmarnock,
Co Dublin

TEL: **01 8462458**  FAX: **01 8460179**
BUS NO: **32/32A/32B/DART/102 AIRBUS**

Spacious home in secluded grounds of 3 acres, directly overlooking Irish Sea. Dublin Airport 15 mins, City Centre 30 mins.

| B&B | 6 | Ensuite | €34-€36 | Dinner | - |
|-----|---|---------|---------|--------|---|
| B&B | - | Standard | - | Partial Board | - |
| Single Rate | | | €60-€60 | Child reduction | - |

**Open:** 5th January-21st December

---

**Skerries**

### Ms Teresa Boylan
**RONNIE'S**
9 Thomas Hand Street,
Skerries, Co Dublin

TEL: **01 8491411**
BUS NO: **33**

Comfortable family home situated in the town of Skerries. From Dublin airport go left. N1 take right turn for Lusk. Take left for Skerries left under railway arch. I'm on the left. Convient to rail & bus.

| B&B | - | Ensuite | - | Dinner | - |
|-----|---|---------|---|--------|---|
| B&B | 3 | Standard | €27.50-€30 | Partial Board | - |
| Single Rate | | | €38.50-€41 | Child reduction | - |

**Open:** 1st March-30th September

---

**Skerries 1km**

### Mrs Violet Clinton
**THE REEFS**
Balbriggan Coast Road,
Skerries, Co Dublin

TEL: **01 8491574**  FAX: **01 8491574**
EMAIL: **info@thereefsskerries.com**
WEB: **www.thereefsskerries.com**
BUS NO: **33 OR 33A**

Spacious comfortable home overlooking the Sea. Golf nearby. "Ireland Guide" recommended. Convenient to Dublin City and Newgrange. Airport 20 kms.

| B&B | 4 | Ensuite | €32-€35 | Dinner | - |
|-----|---|---------|---------|--------|---|
| B&B | - | Standard | | Partial Board | - |
| Single Rate | | | €50-€50 | Child reduction | 25% |

**Open:** 1st April-30th September

**In Skerries**

### Mary Halpin
GREENVALE
Holmpatrick, Skerries,
Co Dublin

TEL: **01 8490413**
EMAIL: **halpinm@indigo.ie**
WEB: **www.greenvaleskerries.ie**
BUS NO: **33**

Large Victorian House overlooking Sea and Islands in quiet location close to Town Centre. Dublin 30 kms, Airport 20 kms.

| B&B | 3 | Ensuite | €35-€40 | Dinner | - |
|-----|---|---------|---------|--------|---|
| B&B | - | Standard | - | Partial Board | - |
| Single Rate | | | €50 | Child reduction | 25% |

Open: 15th January-15th December

---

**Howth 2km**

### Mrs Geraldine Conlan
THE MEADOWS
257 Sutton Park, Sutton,
Dublin 13

TEL: **01 8390257**
EMAIL: **conlanbb@eircom.net**
BUS NO: **31,32,DART**

Highly rated Bed & Breakfast. 15 mins from Dublin City by Dart Train. 15 mins from Airport.

| B&B | - | Ensuite | - | Dinner | - |
|-----|---|---------|---|--------|---|
| B&B | 3 | Standard | €32.50-€32.50 | Partial Board | - |
| Single Rate | | | €40-€41 | Child reduction | - |

Open: 7th January-30th November

---

**Dublin City 10km**

### Eileen Hobbs
HILLVIEW
39 Sutton Park, Dublin Road,
Sutton, Dublin 13

TEL: **01 8324584**
EMAIL: **eileenhobbs@eircom.net**
BUS NO: **31, 32**

Friendly comfortable home, peaceful surroundings. 5 minutes walk to Dart/Bus. Convenient to Point Theatre, City centre, Ferry. 10 minutes to Howth. 15 minutes to Airport.

| B&B | 3 | Ensuite | €36-€38 | Dinner | - |
|-----|---|---------|---------|--------|---|
| B&B | 1 | Standard | €35-€36 | Partial Board | - |
| Single Rate | | | €45-€48 | Child reduction | 25% |

Open: 15th January-15th December

---

**Dublin 10km**

### Mrs Mary McDonnell
DUN AOIBHINN
30 Sutton Park, Sutton,
Dublin 13

TEL: **01 8325456**   FAX: **01 8325213**
EMAIL: **mary_mcdonnell@ireland.com**
WEB: **www.dunaoibhinn.com**
BUS NO: **31, 32, DART, AERDART**

Luxurious detached home in quiet residential area facing amenity park. Adjacent coast road. City Centre 10km, Airport 12km. Howth 3km. Dart/Bus 5 mins walk.

| B&B | 3 | Ensuite | €30-€35 | Dinner | - |
|-----|---|---------|---------|--------|---|
| B&B | - | Standard | - | Partial Board | - |
| Single Rate | | | €45-€50 | Child reduction | - |

Open: 7th January-15th December

---

**Howth Village 3km**

### Mrs Eileen Staunton
AZURE
20 Offington Drive, Sutton,
Dublin 13

TEL: **01 8324442**   FAX: **01 8324442**
EMAIL: **spotta@iol.ie**
BUS NO: **31, 31A, 31B**

Friendly family home in quiet area on Howth Peninsula. One mile before Howth. Restaurants, walking nearby. Close to Bus, DART. 20 mins to City, Airport & Ferry.

| B&B | 3 | Ensuite | €34-€34 | Dinner | - |
|-----|---|---------|---------|--------|---|
| B&B | 1 | Standard | €34-€34 | Partial Board | - |
| Single Rate | | | €43-€43.50 | Child reduction | 25% |

Open: 10th January-10th December

**Mrs Eileen Sutton**
SUTTONS B&B
154 Sutton Park, Sutton,
Dublin 13, Co Dublin

TEL: **01 8325167**   FAX: **01 8395516**
EMAIL: **suttonsbandb@iol.ie**
WEB: **www.suttonsbandb.com**
BUS NO: **DART, 31/32, AERDART**

Excellent spacious accommodation close to Seafront & Dart Station. 15 mins Airport, Point Theatre, City Centre, Ferry, Golfing, Fishing, Restaurants, Amenities nearby

| B&B | 2 | Ensuite | €33-€35 | Dinner | - |
| B&B | 1 | Standard | | Partial Board | - |
| Single Rate | | | €40-€45 | Child reduction | - |

Dublin 10km

**Open:** 6th January-16th December

**Helen Webster**
CORNERVILLE
83 Offington Avenue, Sutton,
Dublin 13

TEL: **01 8393585**
EMAIL: **cornerville_sutton@yahoo.co.uk**
BUS NO: **31A, 31B**

Bright modern home with warm Irish welcome. Big bedrooms, big bathrooms. Close to all amenities, Airport 15 mins, city 10km, walk to Dart. Home from home.

| B&B | 3 | Ensuite | €37.50-€37.50 | Dinner | - |
| B&B | - | Standard | - | Partial Board | - |
| Single Rate | | | | Child reduction | - |

Dublin 10km

**Open:** 1st February-30th November

**Mrs Sarah Byrne**
ASHMORE
Chapel Lane, Rolestown,
Swords, Co Dublin

TEL: **01 8404391**
EMAIL: **ashmorehouse@hotmail.com**

Quiet country home 15 min Dublin Airport. From Airport take R132 North (in direction of Swords) left at next roundabout R108 (in direction of Naul/St. Margaret's) and follow signs for Ashmore B+B.

| B&B | 3 | Ensuite | €32.50-€35 | Dinner | - |
| B&B | - | Standard | - | Partial Board | - |
| Single Rate | | | - | Child reduction | 25% |

Swords 7km

**Open:** 1st February-29th November

**Gabrielle Mary Leonard**
STELLAMARIS
22 Watery Lane, Swords,
Co Dublin

TEL: **01 8403976**   FAX: **01 8403976**
BUS NO: **41, 41B, 33, 33B**

Town house, 5 minutes walk from Swords main street. 5 minutes drive from Airport. 30 mins from Dublin City Centre. Frequent buses. Good taxi service.

| B&B | 3 | Ensuite | €35-€35 | Dinner | - |
| B&B | - | Standard | - | Partial Board | - |
| Single Rate | | | - | Child reduction | - |

In Swords

**Open:** 1st January-20th December

**Mrs Rosemarie Barrett O'Neill**
BLACKBRIDGE AIRPORT LODGE
Lissenhall, Swords, Co Dublin

TEL: **01 8407276**
EMAIL: **blackbridge.lodge@indigo.ie**
BUS NO: **41,41B,41C,33**

Situated just off Belfast/Dublin Road. 3.5km Airport, 12km City. Room rates, reliable transport arranged, private car park.

| B&B | 4 | Ensuite | €27.50-€40 | Dinner | - |
| B&B | - | Standard | - | Partial Board | - |
| Single Rate | | | €40-€65 | Child reduction | 50% |

Swords 1km

**Open:** 10th January-21st December

**Catherine Cavanagh**
RIVERSDALE
Balheary Road, Swords,
Co Dublin

TEL: **01 8404802**   FAX: **01 8404802**
EMAIL: **michaelc@indigo.ie**
WEB: **www.balheary.com**
BUS NO: **41, 41A, 33, 33B, 001** TO AIRPORT

Airport 6 mins City 20 mins Ground Floor Accommodation wifi and ~Free Email Internet Access. Quiet location. Walking distance Swords, Private Car Park. Transport arranged. **Stg: Ensuite £20-£28 Single Rate £33-£40.**

| B&B | 4 | Ensuite | €30-€40 | Dinner | - |
| B&B | - | Standard | - | Partial Board | - |
| Single Rate | | | €50-€60 | Child reduction | **50%** |

In Swords 0.5km        **Open:** 1st January-22nd December

**Kathleen Kenegan**
CEDAR HOUSE
Jugback Lane, Swords,
Co Dublin

TEL: **01 8402757**   FAX: **01 8402041**
BUS NO: **41, 33, 41B**

Situated 5 mins walk from Swords main st. Modern town house, 5 mins drive from Airport. 30 mins from City Centre. Carpark. Home from home.

| B&B | 4 | Ensuite | €35-€40 | Dinner | - |
| B&B | - | Standard | - | Partial Board | - |
| Single Rate | | | €45-€55 | Child reduction | **33.3%** |

In Swords    **Open:** 1st January-20th December

**Betty Keane**
HALF ACRE
Hynestown, Naul, Co Dublin

TEL: **01 8413306**

Country home, 12 mins Dublin Airport. Coast 5 mins, Dublin City Centre 30 mins. Tea/Coffee all rooms. Private Car Park. From Dublin Airport, take M1 north. Take 3rd exit for Naul on left.

| B&B | 3 | Ensuite | €32-€36 | Dinner | - |
| B&B | - | Standard | - | Partial Board | - |
| Single Rate | | | €45-€50 | Child reduction | - |

Balbriggan 8km    **Open:** 1st April-30th September

**Margaret Farrell**
HOLLYWOOD B&B
Hollywood, Ballyboghil,
Co Dublin

TEL: **01 8433359**   FAX: **01 8433359**
EMAIL: **hwood@indigo.ie**
WEB: **www.hollywoodbb.com**

Airport 15 mins.Take M1 for Belfast. First exit off for Skerries. Go 2km. You meet Esso garage on left. Turn next left onto road R129. I am between Ballyboghil and Naul.

| B&B | 6 | Ensuite | €30-€32 | Dinner | - |
| B&B | - | Standard | - | Partial Board | - |
| Single Rate | | | €42-€45 | Child reduction | - |

Ballyboghil 3km    **Open:** 6th January-30th November

## TELEPHONE

- Operator assisted calls within Ireland       Dial 10
- International telephone operator              Dial 11818
- Directory Enquiries                          Dial 11811

**FOR TROUBLE-FREE TELEPHONE CALLS FROM PUBLIC PAY PHONES IT IS ADVISABLE TO PURCHASE A TELEPHONE CALLCARD AVAILABLE IN POST OFFICES AND WHEREVER YOU SEE A CALLCARD SIGN.**
**TO DIAL IRELAND FROM ABROAD:** Country Access Code + 353 + Area Code (omit first zero) + Local Number

### Carmel Chambers
25 Anglesea Road
Ballsbridge, Dublin 4

Tel: **01 6687346**   Fax: **01 6687346**
Email: **avlenireland@yahoo.com**
Bus No: **7A, 7, 8, 45, 84,63**

Edwardian home. Located in popular Ballsbridge, close to Bus, Rail (Dart), Embassies, Art Galleries, Trinity College, Point Theatre & RDS.

| B&B | 1 | Ensuite | €40-€40 | Dinner | - |
| B&B | 3 | Standard | €35-€35 | Partial Board | - |
| Single Rate | | | €38-€55 | Child reduction | - |

City Centre 2km

**Open:** 1st January-31st December

---

### Mrs Therese Clifford Sanderson
CAMELOT
37 Pembroke Park,
Ballsbridge, Dublin 4

Tel: **01 6680331**   Fax: **01 6671916**
Bus No: **10, 46A**

Victorian home, friendly atmosphere. Close to City Centre, RDS, American Embassy, Museums, Art Galleries, Universities. Fine Restaurants within walking distance.

| B&B | 3 | Ensuite | €45-€45 | Dinner | - |
| B&B | - | Standard | - | Partial Board | - |
| Single Rate | | | €60-€60 | Child reduction | - |

Dublin 2km

**Open:** 1st January-15th December

---

### Ms Catherine Foy
ADARE
20 Pembroke park, Ballsbridge,
Dublin 4

Tel: **01 6683075**
Email: **catherinefoy@eircom.net**
Web: **www.adarehouse.com**
Bus No: **10,46,46A,46B,46C**

Victorian house just minutes walk from City Centre. Warm, friendly athmosphere. Close to RDS, Universities, Embassies, RTE, Landsdowne Stadium. Serviced by Aircoach.

| B&B | 3 | Ensuite | €38-€46 | Dinner | - |
| B&B | - | Standard | - | Partial Board | - |
| Single Rate | | | €55-€60 | Child reduction | 25% |

n Ballsbridge

**Open:** 1st January-31st December

---

### Leslie Griffin
AARON COURT
144 Merrion Road, Ballsbridge,
Dublin 4

Tel: **01 2602631**
Email: **aaroncourt@yahoo.com**
Web: **www.aaroncourt.ie**
Bus No: **5, 7, 8, 45, DART**

Elegant family residence in the heart of Ballsbridge. All rooms en-suite, direct dial phones, TV. RDS, Point, Restaurant, Embassies.

| B&B | 6 | Ensuite | €40-€65 | Dinner | - |
| B&B | - | Standard | - | Partial Board | - |
| Single Rate | | | €60-€120 | Child reduction | 25% |

n Ballsbridge

**Open:** All Year

---

### Teresa Muldoon
OAK LODGE
4 Pembroke Park,
Off Clyde Rd, Ballsbridge,
Dublin 4

Tel: **01 6606096**   Fax: **01 6606096**
Email: **oaklodgebandb@hotmail.com**
Web: **www.oaklodge.ie**
Bus No: **10, 46, Air Coach**

Victorian home close to RDS, Universities, Embassies, Dart. Breakfast menu. Direct Air Coach from Airport. Nearest stop Sachs Hotel. Child rate negotiable.

| B&B | 3 | Ensuite | €35-€40 | Dinner | - |
| B&B | 1 | Standard | - | Partial Board | - |
| Single Rate | | | €38-€70 | Child reduction | - |

City Centre 1.5km

**Open:** 17th January-30th November

Dublin 3km

**Joan Donnellan**
HAZELHURST
**166 Stillorgan Rd, Donnybrook,**
**Dublin 4**

TEL: **01 2838509**   FAX: **01 2600346**
EMAIL: **hazelhurst@iolfree.ie**
BUS NO: **10, 46A**

Luxurious spacious residence situated on N11. Adjacent Embassies, UCD, Montrose Hotel, RTE, RDS, main route to Ferry. Private car park. AA ◆◆◆◆.

| | | | | | |
|---|---|---|---|---|---|
| B&B | 5 | Ensuite | €40-€50 | Dinner | - |
| B&B | - | Standard | | Partial Board | - |
| Single Rate | | | €65-€75 | Child reduction | - |

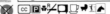

**Open:** 1st March-30th November

---

Donnybrook 1.5km

**Helen Martin**
MONTROSE LODGE
**164 Stillorgan Road,**
**Donnybrook, Dublin 4**

TEL: **01 2691590**   FAX: **01 2691590**
EMAIL: **montroselodge1@eircom.net**
WEB: **www.montroselodge.com**
BUS NO: **3,10, 46, 46A/B/C, 746,** AIR COACH

Spacious home situated on N11. Adjacent to UCD, RTE, Jury's Montrose Hotel, RDS and on main route to ferry. Ideally located for business & leisure. Secure parking.

| | | | | | |
|---|---|---|---|---|---|
| B&B | 4 | Ensuite | €40-€45 | Dinner | - |
| B&B | - | Standard | - | Partial Board | - |
| Single Rate | | | €60-€65 | Child reduction | 25% |

**Open:** 10th March-30th November

---

Dublin 2.2km

**Mrs Mai Bird**
ST DUNSTANS
**25A Oakley Rd, Ranelagh,**
**Dublin 6**

TEL: **01 4972286**
BUS NO: **11,11A,11B,13B,44,48**

Edwardian townhouse. Frommer recommended. Convenient City Centre, RDS, Ferry, Jurys, Universities. Launderette, Restaurants, Banks and Post Office in immediate vicinity.

| | | | | | |
|---|---|---|---|---|---|
| B&B | - | Ensuite | - | Dinner | - |
| B&B | 3 | Standard | €30-€30 | Partial Board | - |
| Single Rate | | | €35-€40 | Child reduction | - |

**Open:** All Year Except Christmas

---

Rathfarnham 1.5km

**Claire Gilroy**
**62 Marion Crescent**
**Rathfarnham, Dublin 14**

TEL: **01 4950572/4943872**   FAX: **01 4950572**
EMAIL: **cgilroy42@hotmail.com**
BUS NO: **15B**

We live in a detached house we have two standard bedrooms and one en suite room. We live in a quiet cul de sac with a large front garden.

| | | | | | |
|---|---|---|---|---|---|
| B&B | 1 | Ensuite | €32-€35 | Dinner | - |
| B&B | 2 | Standard | €28-€30 | Partial Board | - |
| Single Rate | | | €40-€45 | Child reduction | 25% |

**Open:** 1st January-31st December

---

Dublin 3km

**Mrs Aida Boyle**
ST JUDES
**6 Fortfield Tce,**
**Upper Rathmines, Dublin 6**

TEL: **01 4972517**
EMAIL: **stjudesdublin@hotmail.com**
BUS NO: **14A, 13**

Beautiful Victorian home, well maintained, quiet locality. Spacious bedrooms. 7 min Shops, Restaurants, Banks, Pubs, Churches, Parks, Walks, Point Theatre 6km RDS 3km.

| | | | | | |
|---|---|---|---|---|---|
| B&B | 2 | Ensuite | €35-€38 | Dinner | - |
| B&B | 3 | Standard | €30-€34 | Partial Board | - |
| Single Rate | | | €35-€50 | Child reduction | - |

**Open:** 5th January-20th December

**Nola Martini**
PINEHILL
Sandyford Village, Dublin 18

TEL: **01 2952061**   FAX: **01 2958291**
EMAIL: **martini@indigo.ie**
WEB: **www.martini.pair.com**
BUS No: **44, 114, DART**

Charming Cottage style home with modern amenities. Close to Leopardstown Race Course (Stillorgan), Dun Laoghaire Ferry Port.

| B&B | 3 | Ensuite | €40-€45 | Dinner | - |
| B&B | 1 | Standard | €35-€40 | Partial Board | - |
| Single Rate | | | €40-€50 | Child reduction | - |

Dublin City 8km

**Open:** 4th January-20th December

---

**Mrs Dolores Abbott Murphy**
14 Sandymount Castle Park
off Gilford Road, Sandymount,
Dublin 4

TEL: **01 2698413**
BUS No: **3**

Quiet safe location beside Village, Sea, Bus, Rail (DART), Embassies, Museums, Art Galleries, Point Theatre, RDS, UCD, Trinity, St Vincents Hospital.

| B&B | 1 | Ensuite | €37-€37 | Dinner | - |
| B&B | 2 | Standard | €33-€33 | Partial Board | - |
| Single Rate | | | €45-€45 | Child reduction | - |

Dublin 2km

**Open:** 1st May-30th September

---

**Mrs Kathleen Lee**
ARDAGH HOUSE
6 St Annes Road Sth,
South Circular Road, Dublin 8

TEL: **01 4536615**
EMAIL: **kaylee@oceanfree.net**
BUS No: **19, 121, 122**

Home overlooking Grand Canal. Convenient to all places of interest. Bus 19, 121, 122. Road opposite John Player and Sons. 2.5km to City Centre. Easy access to N1, N4, N7, N11, M50.

| B&B | 3 | Ensuite | €32.50-€35 | Dinner | - |
| B&B | 1 | Standard | €30-€32.50 | Partial Board | - |
| Single Rate | | | €40-€45 | Child reduction | - |

Dublin City 2.5km

**Open:** 10th March-31st October

---

**Mrs Noreen Devine**
CLARENDON B&B
293 Orwell Park Grove,
Templeogue, Dublin 6W

TEL: **01 4500007**   FAX: **01 4565725**
BUS No: **150, 54A, 15A**

From M50 motorway take N81 for Templeogue exit at Spawell roundabout onto Wellington Lane, straight through next roundabout, see B&B sign on right at rear of house.

| B&B | 4 | Ensuite | €33-€35 | Dinner | - |
| B&B | - | Standard | - | Partial Board | - |
| Single Rate | | | €40-€45 | Child reduction | 25% |

Dublin 6km

**Open:** 15th January-15th December

---

**Ms Maura Leahy**
ABBEY COURT
7 Glendown Court,
Off Templeville Rd,
Templeogue, Dublin 6W

TEL: **01 4562338**

Comfortable, friendly, smoke-free home in quiet cul-de-sac. Near M50, N4, N7 and Car Ferry. Leisure facilities locally.

| B&B | 2 | Ensuite | €33-€35 | Dinner | - |
| B&B | 1 | Standard | €30-€32 | Partial Board | - |
| Single Rate | | | €40-€45 | Child reduction | 25% |

Dublin 6km

**Open:** All Year

**Mrs Noreen McBride**
3 Rossmore Grove
**Off Wellington Lane,**
**Templeogue, Dublin 6W**

TEL: **01 4902939**   FAX: **01 4929416**
EMAIL: **denismb@iol.ie**
BUS NO: **150, 54A**

Frommer, AA recommended. 20 mins City & Airport. Bus every 10 mins to City. Near Restaurant & M50. Located off N81 at Spawell roundabout first right Rossmore Rd.

| B&B | 2 | Ensuite | €30-€33 | Dinner | - |
| B&B | 2 | Standard | €30-€33 | Partial Board | - |
| Single Rate | | | €40-€45 | Child reduction | - |

**Dublin 6km**

**Open:** 20th February-10th December

**Mrs Mary McGreal**
SEEFIN
**28 Rossmore Grove,**
**Templeogue, Dublin 6W**

TEL: **01 4907286**   FAX: **01 4907286**
EMAIL: **mcgreal_28@yahoo.co.uk**
BUS NO: **150, 54A**

Modern home in cul-de-sac off Wellington Lane. 1/2km from Spawell roundabout on N81. On Ferry and Bus Routes. 5mins M50 motorway. Restaurants, Pubs, Sporting facilities locally.

| B&B | 2 | Ensuite | €30-€35 | Dinner | - |
| B&B | 1 | Standard | €30-€32 | Partial Board | - |
| Single Rate | | | €40-€45 | Child reduction | - |

**Dublin City 6km**

**Open:** 1st March-31st October

**Mrs Ellie Kiernan**
LOUGHKIERN
**65 Rockfield Ave, Terenure,**
**Dublin 12, Co Dublin**

TEL: **01 4551509**
BUS NO: **15A, 150**

Comfortable modern family home. 25 mins to City. Convenient to Restaurants, Sports Centre, Bus, Park, Links Road and Ferry Terminal.

| B&B | 1 | Ensuite | €34-€36 | Dinner | - |
| B&B | 2 | Standard | €32-€34 | Partial Board | - |
| Single Rate | | | €38-€44 | Child reduction | 25% |

**Dublin City 5km**

**Open:** All Year Except Christmas

**Mrs Mary Corbett Monaghan**
ASHBERRY
46 Windsor Park,
Off Stradbrook Road,
Blackrock, Co Dublin

Tᴇʟ: **01 2843711**
Eᴍᴀɪʟ: **monaghanwindsor@eircom.net**
Bᴜs Nᴏ: **46A, 7**

Bright comfortable family home close to Monkstown Village, excellent restaurants, 46A bus stop and Salthill and Monkstown Dart station. Ideal location.

| B&B | 2 | Ensuite | €35-€40 | Dinner | - |
| B&B | 1 | Standard | €32.50-€32.50 | Partial Board | - |
| Single Rate | | | €40-€50 | Child reduction | - |

Dun Laoghaire 2km

**Open:** 1st April-31st October

---

**Monica & Michael Leydon**
AARONA
150 Clonkeen Rd,
Deansgrange, Blackrock,
Co Dublin

Tᴇʟ: **01 2893972**
Eᴍᴀɪʟ: **aarona.bandb.ireland@gmx.net**
Bᴜs Nᴏ: **45**

Exquisitely situated beside all amenities. Bus to City Centre. Dun Laoghaire, Ferry Port 5 mins. Highest standards maintained in friendly family atmosphere.

| B&B | 3 | Ensuite | €35-€35 | Dinner | - |
| B&B | - | Standard | - | Partial Board | - |
| Single Rate | | | €50-€50 | Child reduction | - |

Dun Laoghaire 2km

**Open:** 1st January-22nd December

---

**Steve & Maria Gavin**
LYNDEN
2 Mulgrave Tce, Dun Laoghaire,
Co Dublin

Tᴇʟ: **01 2806404**   Fᴀx: **01 2302258**
Eᴍᴀɪʟ: **lynden@iol.ie**
Bᴜs Nᴏ: **7,7A,8,45A,46A, 59,111,DART**

Georgian house. Quiet location. Adjacent Buses, Train, Shops. Car Ferry 5 mins walk. Early breakfasts. parking, TV & tea making facilities.

| B&B | 2 | Ensuite | €32-€35 | Dinner | - |
| B&B | 2 | Standard | €27-€30 | Partial Board | - |
| Single Rate | | | €38-€55 | Child reduction | 50% |

In Dun Laoghaire

**Open:** All Year

---

**John Goldrick**
LISSADELL
212 Glenageary Road Upper,
Glenageary, Co Dublin

Tᴇʟ: **01 2350609**   Fᴀx: **01 2350454**
Eᴍᴀɪʟ: **lissadellguesthouse@eircom.net**
Wᴇʙ: **lissadellaccommodation.com**
Bᴜs Nᴏ: **7, 7A, 45A, 59, 111**

Luxurious spacious residence, variety of fresh breakfasts, full office works facilities, free internet. Guest library, relax in beautiful gardens, Dart 5 mins walk.

| B&B | 5 | Ensuite | €30-€45 | Dinner | - |
| B&B | - | Standard | - | Partial Board | - |
| Single Rate | | | €45-€60 | Child reduction | 25% |

Dun Laoghaire 1km

**Open:** All Year

---

**Mrs Ann Harkin**
7 Claremont Villas
(Off Adelaide Road),
Glenageary, Dun Laoghaire,
Co Dublin

Tᴇʟ: **01 2805346**   Fᴀx: **01 2805346**
Eᴍᴀɪʟ: **harkinann@hotmail.com**
Wᴇʙ: **www.claremonthouse.net**
Bᴜs Nᴏ: **7, 59, DART**

Victorian home built 1876. 2 mins walk to train (DART) near ferry, bus, own restaurant "Daniels". Quiet cul-de-sac. Ample parking on St. Early breakfast.

| B&B | 4 | Ensuite | €34-€38 | Dinner | - |
| B&B | 1 | Standard | €30-€32 | Partial Board | - |
| Single Rate | | | €40-€55 | Child reduction | 50% |

Dun Laoghaire 1km

**Open:** All Year Except Christmas

In Dun Laoghaire

**Mary O'Farrell**
**WINDSOR LODGE**
3 Islington Ave, Sandycove,
**Dun Laoghaire, Co Dublin**

TEL: **01 2846952**  FAX: **01 2846952**
EMAIL: **winlodge@eircom.net**
BUS NO: **7, DART**

Victorian Home beside Dublin Bay. Close to all amenities. 5 minutes Stena Ferry. Beside Bus/Dart. 20 minutes City Centre.

| B&B | 4 | Ensuite | €32-€40 | Dinner | - |
|------|---|---------|---------|--------|---|
| B&B | - | Standard | - | Partial Board | - |
| Single Rate | | | - | Child reduction | 50% |

**Open:** 1st January-20th December

Dalky 2km

**Mrs Bridie O'Leary**
**ROSEMONT**
51 Bellevue Road, Glenageary,
**Dun Laoghaire, Co Dublin**

TEL: **01 2851021**  FAX: **01 2851021**
EMAIL: **rosemont51@eircom.net**
BUS NO: **59, 7, 7A**

Comfortable home, Private Parking. Located, from Dun Laoghaire, Ferryport is on left, take 2nd right turn, its Link Road, continue to Adelaide Rd, take left at T junction & right onto Bellevue Road.

| B&B | 3 | Ensuite | €31-€35 | Dinner | - |
|------|---|---------|---------|--------|---|
| B&B | 1 | Standard | €29-€32 | Partial Board | - |
| Single Rate | | | €39-€47 | Child reduction | 25% |

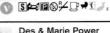

**Open:** 1st April-31st October

In Dun Laoghaire

**Des & Marie Power**
**ARIEMOND**
47 Mulgrave Street,
**Dun Laoghaire, Co Dublin**

TEL: **01 2801664**  FAX: **01 2801664**
EMAIL: **ariemond@hotmail.com**
BUS NO: **7, 46A, DART**

Georgian house Town Centre. Ferry five minutes walk. Beside Buses and Train. Dublin City centre 15 minutes. Golf and Rock climbing nearby.

| B&B | 3 | Ensuite | €35 | Dinner | - |
|------|---|---------|-----|--------|---|
| B&B | 2 | Standard | €30 | Partial Board | - |
| Single Rate | | | €50-€58 | Child reduction | - |

**Open:** 5th January-20th December

Dun Laoghaire 5km

**Mr Bearnard Reynolds**
**ABIGAILS**
4 Wyattville Park,
Loughlinstown, Dun Laoghaire,
Co Dublin

TEL: **01 2824157**  FAX: **01 2814792**
EMAIL: **mrsimeldareynolds@eircom.net**
BUS NO: **45, 84, 111**

Quiet bright modern home in Cul De Sac. 5km from Dun Laoghaire Car Ferry. Beach nearby. Golf, pubs, restaurants, easy reach City Centre. Dart. Late night buses. Off street parking.

| B&B | 2 | Ensuite | €30-€40 | Dinner | - |
|------|---|---------|---------|--------|---|
| B&B | 1 | Standard | €25.50-€35 | Partial Board | - |
| Single Rate | | | €38-€45 | Child reduction | 25% |

**Open:** 1st February-30th November

Killiney 1km

**Marguerite Kennedy**
**GLENAIRE LODGE**
3 Coundon Court,
Killiney Avenue, Killiney,
Co Dublin

TEL: **01 2856322**  FAX: **01 2856322**
EMAIL: **glenairelodge@eircom.net**
WEB: **www.glenairelodge.com**
BUS NO: **7**

Access to city on Dart, near Dun Laoghaire car ferry, gateway to Wicklow for golfing and walking. Rooms with hairdryer, ironing board and trouser press.

| B&B | 4 | Ensuite | €35-€45 | Dinner | - |
|------|---|---------|---------|--------|---|
| B&B | - | Standard | - | Partial Board | - |
| Single Rate | | | €50-€60 | Child reduction | - |

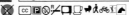

**Open:** All Year

Dun Laoghaire 2km

**Ms Betty MacAnaney**
70 Avondale Rd
**Killiney, Co Dublin**

TEL: **01 2859952**   FAX: **01 2859952**
EMAIL: **mcananey@hotmail.com**
WEB: **www.macananey.com**
BUS NO: **59**

Quiet area, 4 minute drive to Car Ferry. 12-minute walk to Glenageary Dart Station. Dalkey close by. Easy reach City Centre & Co. Wicklow. Private Parking.

| | | | | | Dinner | - |
|---|---|---|---|---|---|---|
| B&B | 3 | Ensuite | €31-€33 | | Partial Board | - |
| B&B | 1 | Standard | €30-€32 | | Child reduction | 25% |
| Single Rate | | | €40-€45 | | | |

**Open:** 1st February-30th November

---

Dun Laoghaire 2km

**Paul & Lucia Marié**
THE WILLOWS
51 Watson Road, Killiney,
Co Dublin

TEL: **01 2855430**
EMAIL: **lucia@gofree.indigo.ie**
WEB: **www.willowskilliney.com**
BUS NO: **7, 45A, 111**

Elegant friendly home in quiet location. Dart and Bus to city. Near Dun-Laoghaire ferry, M50, and N11. Golf, beach and mountains close by.

| | | | | | Dinner | - |
|---|---|---|---|---|---|---|
| B&B | 3 | Ensuite | €35-€40 | | Partial Board | - |
| B&B | - | Standard | - | | Child reduction | - |
| Single Rate | | | €50-€60 | | | |

**Open:** 1st January-20th December

---

In Rathcoole

**Mrs Ann Eagers**
BANNER HOUSE
Main St, Rathcoole, Co Dublin

TEL: **01 4589337**   FAX: **01 4589337**
BUS NO: **69**

Modern family home, 100 yds off N7. Convenient to Pub/Restaurant, beside bus stop. Conservatory for guests use. Golf & Horseriding nearby. Airport, City Centre, 30 mins.

| | | | | | Dinner | - |
|---|---|---|---|---|---|---|
| B&B | 3 | Ensuite | €35-€35 | | Partial Board | - |
| B&B | - | Standard | - | | Child reduction | - |
| Single Rate | | | €50-€50 | | | |

**Open:** 1st February-30th November

---

Rathcoole 2km

**Elizabeth Freeland**
HILLBROOK
Redgap, Rathcoole, Co Dublin

TEL: **01 4580060**
EMAIL: **lizfreeland@hotmail.com**
BUS NO: **69**

Welcoming home in scenic countryside, adjacent to Golf, Horse Riding, Pitch & Putt. Off N7 convenient to all main routes.

| | | | | | Dinner | - |
|---|---|---|---|---|---|---|
| B&B | 3 | Ensuite | €30-€35 | | Partial Board | - |
| B&B | - | Standard | - | | Child reduction | 25% |
| Single Rate | | | €40-€45 | | | |

**Open:** 1st February-30th November

---

Rathcoole 1.5km

**Elizabeth Keogh**
BEARNA RUA LODGE
Redgap, Rathcoole, Co Dublin

TEL: **01 4589920**   FAX: **01 4589920**
EMAIL: **bearnarualodge@hotmail.com**
WEB: **www.bearnarualodge.com**
BUS NO: **69**

Panoramic view, peaceful rural setting yet only 30 mins from Airport/Dublin City. Adjacent to Forest walks, Horseriding, Golf. Off N7. 1.5km from Village.

| | | | | | Dinner | - |
|---|---|---|---|---|---|---|
| B&B | 4 | Ensuite | €32.50-€35 | | Partial Board | - |
| B&B | - | Standard | - | | Child reduction | - |
| Single Rate | | | €43-€45 | | | |

**Open:** 1st February-30th November

**Mrs Mary Spillane**
GREENACRES
**Kilteel Road, Rathcoole,
Co Dublin**

**Rathcoole**

Tel: **01 4580732**  Fax: **01 4580732**
Bus No: **69**

Bungalow 2 miles from Rathcoole on Kilteel Rd, opposite Beech Park Golf Club. Riding Stables locally.

| B&B | 4 | Ensuite | €33-€35 | Dinner | - |
| B&B | 1 | Standard | €30-€33 | Partial Board | - |
| Single Rate | | | €42-€45 | Child reduction | - |

Rathcoole 3km

Ⓥ

**Open:** 1st March-1st November

---

**Aidan Finn**
CORGLASS
**15 Shanganagh Grove,
Shankill, Dublin 18,**

**Shankill**

Tel: **01 2820370**
Bus No: **45, 84, Airport Shuttle Bus**

Semi detached house on main bus and dart routes. All amenities very close. Proximity to beach and countryside while ameniable to Dublin.

| B&B | 2 | Ensuite | €35-€45 | Dinner | - |
| B&B | - | Standard | - | Partial Board | - |
| Single Rate | | | €45-€50 | Child reduction | 25% |

Shankill 0.5km

Ⓥ

**Open:** 1st January-31st December

---

## TELEPHONE

- Operator assisted calls within Ireland     Dial 10
- International telephone operator     Dial 11818
- Directory Enquiries     Dial 11811

**FOR TROUBLE-FREE TELEPHONE CALLS FROM PUBLIC PAY PHONES IT IS ADVISABLE TO PURCHASE A TELEPHONE CALLCARD AVAILABLE IN POST OFFICES AND WHEREVER YOU SEE A CALLCARD SIGN.**

**TO DIAL IRELAND FROM ABROAD:** Country Access Code + 353 + Area Code (omit first zero) + Local Number

---

## BOOKINGS

We recommend your first and last night is pre-booked. Your hosts will make a booking for you at your next selected home for the cost of the phone call. When travelling in high season (July, August), it is essential to pre-book your accommodation – preferably the evening before, or the following morning to avoid disappointment.

---

**WHEN TRAVELLING OFF-SEASON IT IS ADVISABLE TO CALL
AHEAD AND GIVE A TIME OF ARRIVAL TO ENSURE YOUR HOSTS
ARE AT HOME TO GREET YOU.**

## IRELAND

Failte Ireland
Baggot Street Bridge
Dublin 2
Tel: 1850 23 03 30
Fax: 01 602 4100

## NORTHERN IRELAND

### BELFAST

Failte Ireland
Northern Ireland Tourist Board
53 Castle Street
Belfast BT1 1GH
Tel: 028 9032 7888
Fax: 028 9024 0201

### DERRY

Failte Ireland
Northern Ireland Tourist Board
44 Foyle Street
Derry
BT48 6AT
Tel: 028 71369501
Fax: 028 71369501
* if dialing Northern Ireland from
Republic of Ireland dial 048
instead of 028

## EUROPE

### AUSTRIA

Tourism Ireland
Libellenweg 1
A-1140 Vienna
Tel: 01- 501596000
Fax: 01 -911 3765

### BELGIUM

Tourism Ireland
Avenue Louise 327 Louizalaan
1050 Brussels
Tel: +32 2 275 0171
Fax: +32 2 642 9851

### BRITAIN

Tourism Ireland
Nations House
103 Whigmore Street
London W1U 1QS
Tel: 0800 039 7000
Fax: 0207 493 9065

### CANADA

2 Bloor St West
Suite 3403
Toronto M4W 3E2
Tel: 1 800 223 6470
Fax: 01 416 925 6033

## FINLAND

Tourism Ireland
Tel: 0800 41 969
Fax: 09 9646 022

## FRANCE

Tourism Ireland
33 Rue de Miromesnil
75008 Paris
Tel: +33 1 70 20 00 20
Fax: +33 1 47 42 01 64

## GERMANY

Tourism Ireland
Gutleustrasse 32, D-60329
Frankfurt am Main
Tel: +49 69 668 00950
Fax: +49 69 923 18588

## ITALY

Tourism Ireland
Via Santa Maria Segreta 6
20123 Milano
Tel: +39 02 4829 6060
Fax: +39 02 869 0396

## THE NETHERLANDS

Tourism Ireland
Spuistraat 104
1012 VA Amsterdam
Tel: +31 20 504 0689
Fax: +31 20 620 8089

## NORDIC REGION

Tourism Ireland
Nyhavn 16
3rd Floor
DK1051
Copenhagen K
Denmark
Tel: 80 60 15 18
Fax: 33 32 44 01

## NORWAY

Tourism Ireland
Tel: +80 03 50 18
Fax: +47 22 20 26 41

## SPAIN

Tourism Ireland
Paseo de la Castellana 46
3a Planta, 28046
Madrid
Tel: +34 91 745 6420
Fax: +34 91 577 6934

## SWEDEN

Tourism Ireland
Tel: 0200 15 91 01
Fax: 08 233 727

## SWITZERLAND

Tourism Ireland
Mettlenstrasse 22
Ch-8142 Uitikon
Switzerland
Tel: +41 44 210 4153
Fax: +41 44 492 1475

## USA

Tourism Ireland
345 Park Avenue
New York
NY 10154
Tel: 800 223 6470
Fax: 212 371 9052

## SOUTH AFRICA

Tourism Ireland
c/o Development Promotions
Everite House, Level 7
20 De Korte Street
Braamfontein 2001
Gauteng
Tel: +27 11 339 48 65
Fax: +27 11 339 24 74

## NEW ZEALAND

Tourism Ireland
Level 6
18 Shortland Street
Private Bag 92136
Auckland
Tel: +64 9 977 2255
Fax: +64 9 977 2256

## AUSTRALIA

Tourism Ireland
Level 5
36 Carrington Street
Sydney NSW 2000
Tel: +61 2 9299 6177
Fax: +61 2 9299 6323

## JAPAN

Tourism Ireland
Woody 21
23 Aizumi-cho
Shinjuku-ku
Tokyo 160-0005
Tel: +81 3 5363 6515

Der Führer ist in acht geographische Regionen gegliedert, die wiederum in die einzelnen Grafschaften aufgeteilt sind (Karte der Regionen und Grafschaften s. S. 2). Die Regionen sind: **Südost, Cork/Kerry, Shannonside, Westirland, östliche Midlands, Nordwest, Nordirland, Dublin.**

## Übernachtung und Frühstück

Der Preis für Übernachtung und Frühstück gilt pro Person in einem Doppel-bzw. Zweibettzimmer. Siehe erläuternde Hinweise zu den Angaben für jeden Eintrag in unserem Führer.

## Buchungsverfahren

Es ist empfehlenswert, die erste und letzte Übernachtung immer im voraus zu buchen.

## Verfügbarkeit von Zimmern in Dublin

In der Hochsaison - Mai bis Oktober - ist es schwierig, in Dublin Zimmer zu finden, wenn man Unterkunft nicht im voraus gebucht hat.
Wir empfehlen dringend, die Unterkunft weit im voraus zu buchen, wenn Sie die Hauptstadt während dieser Monate besuchen wollen.
Verlassen Sie sich nie darauf, dass Sie in Dublin kurzfristig Zimmer finden können. Reservieren Sie immer im voraus.

## Weitere Reservierungen

Wenn Sie in Irland sind und bei der Suche nach weiterer Unterkunft Probleme auftreten, dann kontaktieren Sie eine beliebige Touristeninformationsstelle oder holen Sie sich Rat oder Hilfe bei Ihrem Gastgeber/Ihrer Gastgeberin in Town and Country Homes. Sie/Er wird Ihnen gerne bei der Buchung weiterer Übernachtungen helfen (zum Preis eines Telefongesprächs).

## Buchungen mit Kreditkarte

Kreditkarten werden in Pensionen akzeptiert, die das [cc] Symbol anzeigen.
Telefonische Reservierungen können durch Angabe einer gültigen Kreditkartennummer garantiert werden.

## Reisebürogutscheine

Bitte legen Sie Ihre Unterkunftsgutscheine bei Ihrer Ankunft vor. Die Gutscheine gelten nur in Häusern, die mit dem Symbol (V) gekennzeichnet sind. Die Standardgutscheine beziehen sich auf Übernachtung und Frühstück in einem Zimmer mit eigenem Bad. Der Zuschlag für ein Zimmer mit Bad/Waschgelegenheit beträgt maximal **€2.00** pro Person bzw. sollte **€5.00** für ein Zimmer, das von drei oder mehr Personen geteilt wird, nicht überschreiten.
"En-suite" Gutscheine beziehen sich auf ein Zimmer mit eigenem Bad. Eine zusätzliche Gebühr fällt nicht an. Hoch-/Nachsaisonzuschlag: für die Monate Juli und August sollten alle Reisebürogutscheine einen Zimmerzuschlag enthalten. Weitere Informationen sind beim Hauptbüro erhältlich.

## Zuschlag für Dublin

In den Monaten Juni, Juli, August und September wird für die Stadt und die Grafschaft Dublin (Dublin City und County) ein Zimmerzuschlag in Höhe von **€7.50** auf Reisebürogutscheine erhoben. Die Gebühr ist direkt an den Vermieter zu zahlen und ist nicht in dem Zimmergutschein enthalten.

## Stornierungsverfahren

Bitte erkundigen Sie sich bei der Buchung nach den Bedingungen für den Fall, daß Sie eine bestätigte Reservierung absagen müssen. Die Person, die die Buchung vornimmt, haftet für die vereinbarte Stornierungsgebühr.

Bitte benachrichtigen Sie die Pension so bald wie möglich telefonisch, wenn Sie Ihren Aufenthalt absagen müssen. Sollte die Absage oder Änderung einer Buchung so kurzfristig erfolgen, daß eine Neuvermietung nicht möglich ist, werden folgende Gebühren in Rechnung gestellt:

- Absage 7 - 14 Tage vor Ankunft: 50% der Ü/F-Kosten für die erste Übernachtung
- Absage 24 Std. - 6 Tage vor Ankunft: 75% der Ü/F-Kosten für die erste Übernachtung
- Keine Ankunft: 100% der Ü/F-Kosten für die erste Übernachtung

## Späte Ankunft

Bitte beachten Sie, daß eine spätere **Ankunft nach 18.00 Uhr ausdrücklich mit der Pension vereinbart werden muß.**

## Anzahlungen in bar / mit Kreditkarte

Bei Vorausbuchungen wird man Sie möglicherweise um Angabe einer Scheck- oder Kreditkartennummer als Sicherheit für die Ankunft bitten. Bitte erkundigen Sie sich nach den Bedingungen.

## Ankunft/Abreise:

Bitte teilen Sie mit, wenn Sie sehr früh ankommen.
- Zimmer verfügbar zwischen 14.00 und 18.00 Uhr
- Die Abreise sollte nicht später als 11.00 Uhr erfolgen
- Ankunft nach Möglichkeit vor 18.00 Uhr.

## Kinderermäßigung

Ermäßigung wird gewährt, wenn Kinder das Zimmer der Eltern teilen oder wenn drei oder mehr Kinder ein Zimmer teilen. Ein oder zwei Kinder in einem separaten Zimmer zahlen den vollen Preis. Bitte fragen Sie bei der Reservierung, ob das Haus für Kinder geeignet ist.
In einigen Häusern stehen Kinderbetten ⬅ zur Verfügung, für die u. U. eine kleine Gebühr erhoben wird.

## Abendmahlzeiten

Können im voraus gebucht werden, nach Möglichkeit vor 12 Uhr mittags.
Imbisse ⊠ werden auf Anfrage serviert.

## Haustiere

Mit Ausnahme von Blindenhunden sind Haustiere aus Hygienegründen nicht im Haus erlaubt.

## Behinderte Personen / Rollstuhlfahrer

Es werden nur solche Häuser als behindertengerecht aufgeführt, die von den zustandigen irischen Behörden ("Comhairle", "National Rehabilitation Board") als solche genehmigt wurden.

e guide est divisé en huit régions géographiques
bdivisées en comtés (voir la carte des régions et
mtés page 2). Les régions sont les suivantes: **Sud-Est,
rk/Kerry, Shannonside, Irlande Ouest, Centre-Est,
rd-Ouest, Irlande du Nord, Dublin.**

## hambre et petit déjeuner

Le tarif "chambre et petit déjeuner" est établi sur la
base de deux personnes par chambre. Voir les notes
au verso comportant des précisions sur chacune des
inscriptions de notre guide.

## éservations

Nous vous recommandons de toujours réserver
l'avance votre hébergement de la première et de la
dernière nuitée.

## sponibilité des chambres à Dublin

Il est parfois difficile de trouver des chambres à Dublin
et dans le comté de Dublin sans réservation préalable.
Lors d'un séjour dans la capitale nous vous
recommandons vivement de réserver votre
hébergement longtemps à l'avance.
Ne comptez en aucun cas trouver des chambres à
Dublin à la dernière minute. Réservez toujours à
l'avance.

## éservations pour les nuitées suivantes

En pleine saison touristique, en cas de difficulté à
trouver des chambres lors d'un séjour en Irlande,
contactez l'office de tourisme le plus proche ou
demandez des conseils ou de l'aide à votre hôte ou
hôtesse Town and Country. Moyennant le prix de la
communication téléphonique, il ou elle vous aidera à
réserver l'hébergement de la nuitée ou des nuités
suivante(s) avant de quitter le B&B.

## éservations par carte de crédit

Les cartes de crédit sont acceptées par les
établissements affichant le symbole $\boxed{\text{CC}}$ .
Les réservations téléphoniques sont confirmées sur
simple communication de votre numéro de carte de
crédit en cours de validité. Vérifiez les termes et
conditions lors de la réservation.

## ons d'agents de voyage

Ceux-ci sont à présenter dès l'arrivée. Les bons ne
sont acceptés que par les établissements affichant le
symbole $\text{ⓥ}$ . Les bons standard assurent
l'hébergement et le petit déjeuner en chambre sans
salle de bain. Supplément pour salle de bain privée:
maximum **€2.00** par personne. Le supplément par
chambre de 3 personnes ou plus ne doit en aucun
cas dépasser **€5.00** par chambre.
Les bons "en suite" concernent les chambres avec
salle de bain, sans aucun supplément.
Supplément basse/haute saison: Un supplément est
à inclure sur tous les bons pour les mois de juillet et
août. Pour tout renseignement complémentaire,
contacter le Bureau central."

## upplément - Dublin:

Un supplément de **€7.50** par chambre est prélevé à
Dublin et dans le comté de Dublin au cours des mois
de Juin. Juillet, Août et Septembre sur les bons

d'agents de voyage. Ce supplément est à régler
directement au prestataire de l'hébergement et n'est
pas compris dans le montant du bon.

## Annulations

Après confirmation d'une réservation, renseignez
vous auprès de l'établissement sur ses conditions
d'annulation. La personne effectuant la réservation
devra régler les frais d'annulation convenus.

Nous vous demandons d'informer immédiatement en
cas d'annulation. Une pénalité financière s'applique
s'il est nécessaire d'annuler ou de modifier une
réservation sans préavis suffisant:

- Préavis de 7-14 jours – 50% de la première nuitée.
- Préavis de 24 heures à 6 jours: 75% de la première nuitée.
- Absence: 100% de la première nuitée.

## Arrivées tardives

Nous vous demandons de noter que les arrivées
tardives - soit après 18.00 heures, ne sont possibles
qu'avec l'accord spécifique de l'établissement. Nous
vous serions reconnaissants de bien vouloir informer
votre hôte//hôtesse de votre heure d'arrivée.

## Réservations à l'avance

En cas de réservation à l'avance, un chèque ou un
numéro de carte de crédit pourront être demandés
pour garantir la disponibilité de votre hébergement à
votre arrivée. Vérifiez les termes et conditions.

## Arrivées/départs

Prévenir de toute arrivée en avance.
- Les chambres sont mises à disposition entre 14.00
  heures et 18.00 heures.
- Les chambres sont à libérer avant 11.00 heures.
- Les réservations sont à honorer avant 18.00 heures.

## Réductions pour les enfants

Celle-ci est consentie lorsque les enfants partagent
la chambre des parents ou lorsqu'une chambre est
occupée par trois enfants ou plus. Le tarif normal
s'applique lorsqu'un ou deux enfants occupent des
chambres séparées. Veuillez vérifier lors de la
réservation que l'établissement convient aux enfants.
Certains établissements peuvent mettre des lits $\text{🛏}$
d'enfant à votre disposition. Un léger supplément
pourra être demandé.

## Repas du soir

A réserver à l'avance, de préférence avant midi le
même jour. Collations servies $\boxed{\text{✗}}$ sur demande dans
certains établissements.

## Animaux domestiques

A l'exception des chiens d'aveugle et pour des
raisons d'hygiène, les animaux domestiques ne sont
pas admis à l'intérieur des établissements.

## Personnes handicapées/Utilisateurs de fauteuils roulants.

Seuls les établissements approuvés par Comhairle
ou, par le passé, par le National Rehabilitation Board,
seront indiqués.

La guía está dividida en ocho regiones geográficas que se encuentran subdivididas en condados (véase la página 2 para el mapa de regiones y condados). Las regiones son: **Sureste, Cork/Kerry, Shannonside, Oeste de Irlanda, Región central este, Noroeste, Irlanda del Norte, Dublín.**

## Casas de huéspedes

El precio de las casas de huéspedes se establece por persona en régimen compartido. Véase nota aclaratoria a la vuelta para más información acerca de cada caso individual en nuestra guía.

## Procedimiento de reservas

Se recomienda **reservar** siempre con anticipación **el alojamiento de la primera y última noche.**

### Disponibilidad de alojamiento en Dublín

A menos que se haya reservado con antelación, es difícil encontrar alojamiento en la ciudad y el condado de Dublín. Si se visita la capital, recomendamos firmemente hacer la reserva del alojamiento **con mucha anticipación.**

No confíe en encontrar habitaciones disponibles a corto plazo en Dublín; haga siempre su reserva por anticipado.

### Reservas posteriores

En caso de que tenga problemas para encontrar alojamiento en temporada alta una vez se encuentre en Irlanda, póngase en contacto con una oficina de turismo o consulte a la dueña de la casa de Town and Country Homes. Por el coste de una llamada telefónica, él/ ella le ayudará. Le recomendamos asegurarse el alojamiento de las noches siguientes antes de dejar la casa de huéspedes.

## Reservas con tarjetas de crédito

Las casas con el símbolo cc aceptan tarjetas de crédito.
Se podrán garantizar las reservas realizadas mediante llamadas telefónicas indicando un número de tarjeta de crédito en vigor. Consulte las condiciones al hacer su reserva.

## Vales de agencias de viaje

Le rogamos presente los vales a su llegada. Los vales sólo serán validos en aquellas casas que muestren el símbolo Ⓥ .
**Los vales estándar** cubren la habitación en casa de huéspedes sin baño privado. Para **ampliar a la categoría de habitaciones con baño privado** (en suite) el recargo será de **2,00€** máximo **por persona.** El recargo máximo para 3 ó más personas compartiendo **no excederá de 5,00€ por habitación. Los vales en suite** cubren la estancia en una habitación con instalaciones privadas completas. No se ha de pagar ningún recargo adicional.
Suplementos de temporada alta/ baja: En los meses de julio y agosto se debe incluir un suplemento en todos los vales. Para más información, consulte en la oficina central.

## Suplemento para Dublín

Se aplica un suplemento por habitación para la ciudad y el condado de Dublín de **7,50€** los meses de **junio, julio, agosto y septiembre** en los viajes

con vales de agencia de viajes. Esto se paga directamente a la persona que proporciona el alojamiento y no está incluido en el vale.

## Política de cancelaciones

Cuando se haya confirmado una reserva, le rogamos consulte con el establecimiento la política de cancelaciones al realizar la reserva. La persona que realice la reserva es responsable del recargo por cancelación acordado. Rogamos llame inmediatamente si desea hacer una cancelación. De hacerse necesaria una cancelación o cambio en la reserva sin haberlo notificado con suficiente antelación, se aplicará un recargo en concepto de penalización.
- 7-14 días de antelación – 50% de la primera noche
- 24 horas – 6 días de antelación – 75% de la primera noche
- No asistencia – 100% de la primera noche

## Llegadas después de las 6pm

Le rogamos que las llegadas tardías **(después de las 6 de la tarde) se realicen por acuerdo especial con la casa.** Rogamos que a ser posible se indique la hora de llegada al dueño.

## Reservas por adelantado

Para realizar reservas por adelantado, se le podrá pedir un cheque o número de tarjeta de crédito para garantizar la llegada. Consulte las condiciones.

## Horas de entrada/ salida

Le rogamos comunique llegadas tempranas.
- Las habitaciones están disponibles de 2:00 a 6:00 de la tarde.
- La hora de salida no deberá realizarse más tarde de las 11:00 de la mañana.
- Las habitaciones deberán ocuparse antes de las 6:00 de la tarde.

## Descuento para niños

Se aplica cuando los niños comparten la habitación de los padres o cuando tres o más niños comparten una habitación. Se aplica la tarifa completa cuando uno o dos niños ocupan habitaciones separadas. Le rogamos compruebe que la casa es adecuada para niños cuando realice la reserva. En algunas casas se encuentran disponibles cunas 🛏 - puede haber un recargo nominal.

## Cenas

Reserve con antelación preferentemente antes de las 12 del mediodía de ese mismo día. Comidas ligeras disponibles ✖ a petición suya.

## Animales domésticos

Con la excepción de perros-guía, por cuestiones de higiene, no se permite la entrada de animales domésticos en las casas.

## Discapacitados/ sillas de ruedas

Solamente se incluyen aquellas casas cuyas instalaciones han sido aprobadas por la Comhairle (agencia de ámbito nacional para garantizar la provisión de información y consejo adecuados al consumidor) o por la Nacional Rehabilitation Board (Instituto nacional de rehabilitación) anteriormente.

# Uso di questa guida

guida è divisa in otto regioni geografiche che sono a
volta suddivise in contee (vedi pagina 2 per mappa
le regioni e contee). Le regioni sono: **Sud Est,
rk/Kerry, Shannonside, Ovest, Centro Est, Nord
est, Irlanda del Nord, Dublino.**

## d & Breakfast

Il prezzo per Bed & Breakfast è per persona in
condivisione. Vedere note esplicative a tergo per
dettagli completi su ogni voce nella nostra guida.

## odalità di prenotazione

Si consiglia sempre di prenotare in anticipo la prima
e l'ultima notte del vostro soggiorno.

## mere disponibili a Dublino

Può essere difficile trovare camere nella città e nella
contea di Dublino se non si prenota in anticipo. Se si
visita la capitale, consigliamo caldamente di
prenotare il vostro alloggio con notevole anticipo.
Non contate mai di trovare camere a Dublino a breve
preavviso. Prenotate sempre in anticipo.

## enotazioni successive

Durante l'alta stagione, se dovessero sorgere dei
problemi nel trovare un alloggio una volta in Irlanda, si
prega di contattare qualsiasi ufficio turistico o cercare
consiglio e assistenza tramite il personale del luogo
dove si alloggia (Town and Country Homes). Costoro
saranno in grado di aiutarvi a trovare una
sistemazione per eventuali notti successive per il
costo di una telefonata. Raccomandiamo di
assicurarvi la sistemazione per le notti successive
prima di lasciare il B&B.

## enotazioni con carta di credito

Si accettano carte di credito nelle case con il
simbolo [CC].
Le prenotazioni telefoniche possono essere garantite
comunicando un numero di carta di credito valida. Si
prega di controllare i termini e le condizioni al
momento della prenotazione.

## oucher delle agenzie di viaggio

Presentare il voucher al momento dell'arrivo. I
voucher sono validi solo nelle case indicate con il
simbolo Ⓥ.
Normalmente i voucher includono pernottamento e
prima colazione in camera senza servizi privati. Per le
camere con servizi privati (en-suite) il supplemento
massimo è di **€2.00** per persona. Il supplemento
massimo per tre o più persone in condivisione non
dovrebbe superare **€5.00** per camera.
I voucher "en-suite" includono una camera con
servizi privati completi. Non è previsto nessun altro
supplemento.
Supplemento Bassa/Alta Stagione: Per i mesi di
luglio e agosto un supplemento va incluso su tutti i
voucher. Per ulteriori informazioni si prega di fare
riferimento all'Ufficio Centrale.

## Supplemento Dublino

Un supplemento camera di **€7.50** per la città e la
contea di Dublino viene applicato per i mesi di
giugno, luglio, agosto e settembre sui vouchers delle
Agenzie viaggi. Tale supplemento va pagato
direttamente a chi fornisce la sistemazione e non è
incluso nel voucher.

## Prassi di annullamento

Una volta che la prenotazione è stata confermata,
controllare la prassi di annullamento dei proprietari
della casa al momento della prenotazione. La persona
che effettua la prenotazione risponde della penale di
annullamento convenuta. Telefonare immediatamente
nel caso di un annullamento. Nell'eventualità che sia
necessario annullare o modificare una prenotazione
senza preavviso sufficiente verrà applicata una
penale.
• 7-14 giorni di preavviso – 50% della prima notte
• 24 ore – 6 giorni di preavviso – 75% della prima notte
• Mancato arrivo – 100% della prima notte

## Arrivi a tarda ora

NB: Arrivi a tarda ora e cioè dopo le **ore 18.00 solo
previo accordo speciale con i proprietari della
casa.** Si prega di comunicare l'orario dell'arrivo ai
proprietari della casa.

## Prenotazioni in anticipo

Per prenotazioni in anticipo potrà essere richiesto un
assegno o numero di Carta di Credito per garantire
l'arrivo. Si prega di controllare i Termini e Condizioni.

## Arrivo/Partenza:

Avvisare se si prevede di arrivare in anticipo.
• Le camere sono disponibili fra le 14.00 e le 18.00.
• Partenza: non oltre le 11.00.
• Le camere vanno occupate entro le 18.00.

## Riduzione per bambini

Si applica se i bambini condividono la camera dei
genitori o se tre o più bambini condividono la stessa
camera. La tariffa intera si applica se uno o due
bambini occupano una camera separata. Controllare
al momento della prenotazione che la casa sia adatta
ad ospitare bambini. In alcune case sono disponibili
lettini:➡ potrebbe esserci un addebito simbolico.

## Pasti serali

Prenotare in anticipo preferibilmente non più tardi di
mezzogiorno del giorno stesso. Spuntini disponibili
☒ su richiesta.

## Animali domestici

Ad eccezione dei cani guida per ciechi, per motivi
igienici, gli animali non sono ammessi nei locali.

## Disabili/invalidi

Saranno elencati solo locali in case approvate da
Comhairle o in passato dal National Rehabilitation
Board (ente nazionale riabilitazione).

De gids is onderverdeeld in acht geografische streken die weer in graafschappen zijn onderverdeeld (zie pagina 2 voor een kaart van de streken en graafschappen). De streken zijn: **Zuidoosten, Cork/Kerry, Shannonside, West Ierland, Centraal Ierland, het Noordwesten, Noord Ierland, Dublin.**

### Logies en ontbijt

De prijs voor logies en ontbijt is per persoon op één kamer. Zie de toelichting aan de ommezijde voor meer informatie over ieder huis in onze gids.

### Reserveren

U wordt geadviseerd de logies voor de eerste en laatste nacht altijd van tevoren te reserveren.

### Beschikbaarheld kamers in Dublin

In de stad en het graafschap Dublin is het vaak moeilijk logies te vinden, tenzij u van tevoren hebt gereserveerd. Als u de hoofdstad bezoekt, raden wij u sterk aan **vroeg te reserveren**. U kunt er niet op rekenen in Dublin op korte termijn logies te vinden. Reserveer altijd van te voren.

### Voorwaarts reserveren

Indien u in het hoogseizoen problemen ondervindt bij het zoeken naar logies terwijl u in Ierland bent, kunt u contact opnemen met een vreemdelingenbureau of de host/hostess van Town and Country Homes. Zij/hij helpt u bij het reserveren van logies voor de volgende nacht(en) voor de prijs van een telefoongesprek. Wij raden u aan logies te vinden voor de volgende nacht(en) alvorens het huis te verlaten.

### Reserveringen met creditcard

Creditcards worden geaccepteerd in huizen met het symbool [cc].
Telefoonreserveringen kunnen worden gegarandeerd door een geldig creditcard nummer op te geven.

### Bonnen van reisbureaus

Overhandig uw bon bij aankomst. Bonnen zijn alleen geldig in huizen met het symbool ⓥ.
Standaard bonnen zijn geldig voor Bed & Breakfast in een kamer zonder privé-faciliteiten. Voor opwaardering tot een kamer met badkamer betaalt u een maximale toeslag van €2.00 per persoon.
De maximale toeslag voor 3 of meer personen op één kamer is nooit meer dan €5.00 per kamer.
Bonnen voor kamers met badkamer zijn voor kamers met volledige privé-faciliteiten.
Geen extra kosten worden in rekening gebracht.
Laag-/hoogseizoentoeslag: Voor de maanden juli en augustus dient op alle bonnen een toeslag te worden meegerekend. Voor nadere informatie gelieve contact op te nemen met het hoofdkantoor.

### Toeslag in Dublin.

In de maanden juni, juli, augustus en september wordt in de stad en het graafschap Dublin een kamertoeslag van **€7.50** berekend. Deze toeslag dient rechtstreeks aan de verlener van de accommodatie te worden betaald en is niet bij de bon inbegrepen.

### Annuleringsbeleid

U dient het annuleringsbeleid van het huis ten tijde van reservering te controleren. De persoon die de reservering maakt is verantwoordelijk voor de overeengekomen annuleringsboete.
In geval van annulering dient u onmiddellijk te telefoneren. Mocht het nodig zijn een reservering the annuleren of te wijzigen zonder voldoende voorafgaande kennisgeving, is een financiële boete van toepassing.
- 7 - 14 dagen kennisgeving – 50% van de eerste nacht
- 24 uur – 6 dagen kennisgeving – 75% van de eerste nacht
- gast verschijnt niet – 100% van de eerste nacht.

### Late aankomst

Een late aankomst **(na 18.00 uur) dient speciaal met het huis afgesproken te worden.**

### Reserveringen

Voor reserveringen kunt u om een creditcard worden gevraagd om aankomst te garanderen. Gelieve algemene voorwaarden te controleren.

### Aankomst / Vertrek

Een vroege aankomst graag vooraf meedelen
- Kamers worden tussen 14.00 en 18.00 uur beschikbaar gesteld
- Vertrek - niet later dan 11.00 uur
- Gereserveerde kamers dienen om 18.00 uur te zijn ingenomen.

### Kinderkorting

Een kinderkorting is van toepassing indien kinderen de kamer met hun ouders delen of indien 3 of meer kinderen de kamer delen. Het volle tarief is van toepassing wanneer 1 of 2 kinderen aparte kamers innemen. Controleer bij de reservering dat het huis geschikt is voor kinderen. Wiegen zijn in sommige huizen beschikbaar 🛏-soms tegen een nominaal tarief.

### Avondmaaltijden

Deze dienen vooraf te worden gereserveerd, liefst voor 12.00 uur op de betreffende dag.
Lichte maaltijden ✗ zijn op verzoek beschikbaar.

### Huisdieren

In het belang van hygiëne worden huisdieren niet binnenshuis toegelaten, met uitzondering van blindengeleidehonden.

### Gehandicapten/rolstoelgebruikers

Uitsluitend huizen die door Comhairle (of in het verleden door de National Rehabilitation Board) zijn goedgekeurd verschijnen op de lijst.

nna guidebok har indelats i åtta geografiska
jioner, dessa regioner har sedan indelats i
dskap (se sid. 2 för kartor för regionerna och
dskapen). Regionerna är: **Cork/Kerry,
annonside, västra Irland, östra inlandet,
rdväst, Nordirland, Dublin, Sydöst.**

## d & Breakfast
Priset som uppges för Bed & Breakfast gäller per
person som delar ett rum. Se förklaringen till
guiden på nästa sida.

## kning
Vi rekommenderar att logi för första och sista
natten alltid bokas i förväg.

## gi i Dublin City
Det kan vara svårt att få tag i rum i Dublin City och
länet Dublin om ni inte har bokat rum i förväg. Om
ni planerar att besöka huvudstaden
rekommenderar vi att ni bokar all logi i god tid.
Räkna aldrig med att hitta rum i Dublin med kort
varsel. Boka alltid i förväg.

## darebokning:
Var vänlig ta kontakt med vilket
turistinformationskontor som helst om ni skulle ha
problem med logi under högsäsongen, eller också
kan ni be värden/värdinnan i Town & Country
Homes om hjälp. Han/hon hjälper gärna till med
förhandsbokningar av logi för gäster, för
kostnaden av ett telefonsamtal. För att undvika
besvikelse rekommenderar vi att denna service
utnyttjas innan ni lämnar hemmet.

## kning med kreditkort
Kreditkort accepteras på ställen som har
symbolen ⌐CC⌐.
Telefonbokning kan garanteras genom att ett
giltigt kreditkortsnummer uppges. Kontrollera
reglerna när ni bokar.

## esebyråkuponger
Var vänlig att visa kupongerna vid ankomsten.
Kuponger gäller endast på de gästhus som
uppvisar ❶ symbolen.
Standardkuponger täcker Bed and Breakfast med
rum utan privat badrum. Önskas privat badrum
tillkommer en extra kostnad på **€2.00** per person.
Den högsta avgiften är **€5.00** per rum för 3 eller
flera personer som delar ett rum. Det finns
kuponger som täcker kostnaden för rum med
privat badrum. Inga andra kostnader tillkommer.

## ctra tillägg för Dublin:
Ett extra tillägg på **€7.50** per rum gäller i juni, juli,
augusti och september för Dublin City och länet
Dublin, med resebyråkupongerna. Detta tillägg
betalas direkt till den som hyr ut rummen och är
inte medräknat i kupongerna.

## Avbeställningsregler
Var vänlig kontrollera avbeställningsreglerna med
hemmet när du bokar och bekräftar bokningen.
Personen som gör bokningen är ansvarig för
avbeställningsavgiften.
Var vänlig meddela värden/värdinnan omedelbart
om en avbeställning måste göras. Om det skulle
bli nödvändigt att avbeställa eller ändra en
bokning utan tillräcklig förvarsel tillkommer en
avgift enligt nedan:

- 7-14 dagars varsel - 50% av första nattens
  kostnad
- 24 timmars varsel - 75% av första nattens
  kostnad
- Utebliven ankomst - 100% av första nattens
  kostnad.

## Sen ankomst
Var vänlig observera att sen ankomst, efter kl.
18.00, måste bestämmas enligt specialavtal med
hemmet. Var vänlig meddela ankomsttiden till
värden/värdinnan.

## Förhandsbokning
En check eller ett kreditkortsnummer kan krävas
för att garantera ankomst. Läs bokningsreglerna.

## In-/Utcheckning:
Var vänlig meddela om tidig ankomst.
- Rummen kan intagas mellan kl. 14.00 och 18.00.
- Utcheckning måste göras innan kl. 11.00.
- Bokade rum måste intagas före kl. 18.00.

## Rabatt För Barn
Gäller där barn delar rum med föräldrar, eller om
3 eller fler barn delar ett rum.
Fullt pris när 1 eller 2 barn bor i separat rum.
Kontrollera att huset är lämpligt för barn när ni
bokar.
Barnsängar finns ➡️på vissa ställen och kan lånas
för en liten avgift.

## Kvällsmåltider
Beställs i förväg, helst före kl. 12.00 dagen ifråga.
Lätta måltider ⊠ serveras efter önskemål.

## Sällskapsdjur
Förutom guidehundar för blinda tillåts inga djur
inne i husen av hygieniska skäl.

## Rörelsehindrad person/rullstolsbunden person
Endast hem som har godkänts av Comhairle
(Rådgivningsnämnden) eller som tidigare
godkänts av det irländska rehabilieringsförbundet,
upptages i listan över hem.

| Area/Town | County | Page |
|---|---|---|
| **A** | | |
| Abbeyfeale | Limerick | 169 |
| Achill Island | Mayo | 218 |
| Adara | Donegal | 282 |
| Adare | Limerick | 169 |
| Annaghdown | Galway | 182 |
| Annascaul (Dingle Peninsula) | Kerry | 87 |
| Aran Islands | Galway | 183 |
| Aran Islands (Inismore) | Galway | 182 |
| Aran Islands Inis Meain | Galway | 183 |
| Ardagh | Longford | 247 |
| Ardara Portnoo | Donegal | 282 |
| Ardee | Louth | 248 |
| Ardfert | Kerry | 87 |
| Ardmore | Waterford | 32 |
| Arklow | Wicklow | 268 |
| Armagh | Armagh | 317 |
| Artane | DublinNorthCity | 330 |
| Arthurstown | Wexford | 44 |
| Ashbourne | Meath | 252 |
| Ashford | Wicklow | 269 |
| Askeaton | Limerick | 172 |
| Askeaton Pallaskenry | Limerick | 172 |
| Athboy | Meath | 252 |
| Athenry | Galway | 184 |
| Athlone | Roscommon | 236 |
| Athlone | Westmeath | 262 |
| Athy | Kildare | 242 |
| Aughnacloy | Tyrone | 326 |
| Avoca | Wicklow | 270 |
| **B** | | |
| Bagenalstown | Carlow | 10 |
| Ballina | Mayo | 219 |
| Ballinamore | Leitrim | 298 |
| Ballinasloe | Galway | 184 |
| Ballincollig | Cork | 54 |
| Ballinhassig Kinsale | Cork | 54 |
| Ballinrobe | Mayo | 221 |
| Ballinskelligs | Kerry | 87 |
| Ballisodare | Sligo | 302 |
| Ballsbridge | DublinSouthCity | 343 |
| Ballybofey Stranorlar | Donegal | 283 |
| Ballybunion | Kerry | 88 |
| Ballycastle | Antrim | 312 |
| Ballycastle | Mayo | 221 |
| Ballyconneely Connemara | Galway | 184 |
| Ballyconnell | Cavan | 280 |
| Ballycotton | Cork | 54 |
| Ballyduff | Kerry | 89 |
| Ballyhooly | Cork | 54 |
| Ballylongford | Kerry | 89 |
| Ballymacarbry Nire Valley | Waterford | 32 |
| Ballymena | Antrim | 313 |
| Ballymote | Sligo | 302 |
| Ballyneety | Limerick | 172 |
| Ballyshannon | Donegal | 283 |
| Ballyvaughan | Clare | 142 |
| Ballyvourney | Cork | 55 |
| Baltimore | Cork | 55 |
| Banagher | Offaly | 259 |
| Banbridge | Down | 319 |
| Bandon | Cork | 55 |
| Bantry | Cork | 56 |
| Barna | Galway | 185 |
| Barna Village | Galway | 185 |
| Beal A Daingin Connemara | Galway | 185 |
| Belfast | Antrim | 313 |
| Belmullet | Mayo | 222 |
| Belmullet Peninsula | Mayo | 222 |
| Belturbet | Cavan | 280 |
| Bennettsbridge | Kilkenny | 12 |
| Bettystown | Meath | 252 |
| Birdhill | Tipperary | 20 |
| Blackrock | DublinSouthCounty | 347 |
| Blarney | Cork | 58 |
| Blessington | Wicklow | 271 |
| Borris-in-Ossory | Laois | 245 |
| Borrisokane | Tipperary | 20 |
| Boyle | Roscommon | 236 |
| Bray | Wicklow | 271 |
| Bruff | Limerick | 172 |
| Bunclody | Wexford | 44 |
| Buncrana | Donegal | 285 |
| Bundoran | Donegal | 285 |
| Bunratty | Clare | 143 |
| Bushmills | Antrim | 313 |
| **C** | | |
| Caherdaniel Ring of Kerry | Kerry | 89 |
| Cahir | Tipperary | 20 |
| Cahirciveen | Kerry | 90 |
| Callan | Kilkenny | 12 |
| Cappoquin | Waterford | 32 |
| Carlingford | Louth | 248 |
| Carlow | Carlow | 10 |
| Carlow Town | Carlow | 11 |
| Carna Connemara | Galway | 186 |
| Carraroe | Galway | 186 |
| Carraroe Connemara | Galway | 186 |
| Carrickfergus | Antrim | 314 |
| Carrickmacross | Monaghan | 300 |
| Carrick-on-Shannon | Leitrim | 298 |
| Carrick-on-Suir | Tipperary | 22 |
| Carrigaline Cork Ferryport Airport | Cork | 63 |
| Carrigans Near Derry | Donegal | 285 |
| Carrigart | Donegal | 285 |
| Carrigtwohill | Cork | 63 |
| Cashel | Tipperary | 22 |
| Castlebaldwin | Sligo | 302 |
| Castlebar | Mayo | 223 |
| Castleblaney | Monaghan | 300 |
| Castledermot | Carlow | 11 |
| Castlegregory | Kerry | 92 |
| Castlegregory Dingle Peninsula | Kerry | 91 |
| Castleisland | Kerry | 93 |
| Castleknock | DublinNorthCity | 330 |
| Castlemaine | Kerry | 94 |
| Castlerea | Roscommon | 237 |
| Castletownbere | Cork | 63 |
| Castletownberehaven Ardgroom | Cork | 64 |
| Cavan | Cavan | 280 |
| Charlestown | Mayo | 224 |
| Clane | Kildare | 242 |
| Clane/Straffan | Kildare | 243 |
| Claregalway | Galway | 186 |
| Claremorris | Mayo | 225 |
| Clarinbridge | Galway | 187 |
| Cleggan Connemara | Galway | 188 |
| Clifden Connemara | Galway | 189 |
| Cloghan | Offaly | 259 |
| Clogherhead | Louth | 249 |
| Clonakilty | Cork | 64 |
| Clonbur Cong Connemara | Galway | 193 |
| Clonmacnoise | Offaly | 259 |
| Clonmany Inishowen | Donegal | 286 |
| Clonmel | Tipperary | 26 |
| Clontarf | DublinNorthCity | 330 |
| Cobh | Cork | 66 |
| Coleraine | Londonderry | 324 |
| Cong | Mayo | 225 |
| Cong Connemara | Mayo | 225 |
| Conna | Cork | 67 |
| Cookstown | Tyrone | 326 |
| Cork City | Cork | 68 |
| Cork City Airport Kinsale Road | Cork | 68 |
| Cork City Bishopstown | Cork | 68 |
| Cork City Dennehy's Cross-Wilton | Cork | 69 |
| Cork City Douglas | Cork | 69 |
| Cork City Lower Glanmire Road | Cork | 69 |
| Cork City Wilton University | Cork | 70 |
| Corofin | Clare | 147 |
| Corr Na Móna | Galway | 193 |
| Craughwell | Galway | 194 |
| Crookhaven Mizen Head | Cork | 70 |
| Crossmolina | Mayo | 226 |
| Crumlin | Antrim | 314 |
| Culdaff | Donegal | 286 |
| Cushendall | Antrim | 315 |
| **D** | | |
| Derry | Londonderry | 324 |
| Dingle | Kerry | 94 |
| Donegal Mountcharles | Donegal | 287 |
| Donegal Town | Donegal | 286 |
| Donegal Town Lough Eske | Donegal | 288 |
| Donnybrook | DublinSouthCity | 344 |
| Doolin | Clare | 148 |
| Doolin/Cliffs of Moher | Clare | 149 |
| Down | Down | 319 |
| Downings | Donegal | 290 |
| Downpatrick | Down | 319 |
| Drimoleague Skibbereen | Cork | 71 |
| Drogheda | Louth | 249 |
| Dromore | Down | 320 |
| Drumcliffe | Sligo | 302 |
| Drumcondra | DublinNorthCity | 332 |
| Dun Laoghaire | DublinSouthCounty | 347 |
| Dundalk | Louth | 250 |
| Dunfanaghy | Donegal | 290 |
| Dungarvan | Kilkenny | 12 |
| Dungarvan | Waterford | 33 |
| Dungloe | Donegal | 291 |
| Dunmore East | Waterford | 34 |
| **E** | | |
| Edenderry | Offaly | 259 |
| Emyvale | Monaghan | 301 |
| Ennis | Clare | 151 |
| Enniscorthy | Wexford | 44 |
| Enniskerry | Wicklow | 272 |
| Enniskillen | Fermanagh | 322 |
| Ennistymon | Clare | 155 |
| **F** | | |
| Falcarragh | Donegal | 291 |
| Feeny | Londonderry | 325 |
| Fermoy | Cork | 71 |
| Freshford | Kilkenny | 13 |
| **G** | | |
| Galway | Galway | 195 |
| Galway City | Galway | 194 |
| Galway City Castlegar Area | Galway | 197 |
| Galway City Dangan | Galway | 197 |
| Galway City Glenina Heights | Galway | 198 |
| Galway City Grattan Park | Galway | 198 |
| Galway City Lower Salthill | Galway | 199 |
| Galway City Merlin Park | Galway | 199 |
| Galway City Salthill | Galway | 200 |
| Galway City Salthill Threadneedle Road | Galway | 205 |
| Galway City Upper Salthill | Galway | 203 |
| Galway City Upper Salthill - Gentian Hill | Galway | 205 |
| Galway City Upper Salthill - Gentian Hill Area | Galway | 205 |

| Area/Town | County | Page |
|---|---|---|
| alway City Whitestrand | Galway | 206 |
| ilford | Down | 320 |
| en of Aherlow | Tipperary | 27 |
| enariff | Antrim | 315 |
| enbeigh | Kerry | 101 |
| enbeigh Ring of Kerry | Kerry | 102 |
| endalough | Wicklow | 272 |
| engarriff | Cork | 71 |
| enties | Donegal | 291 |
| in | Limerick | 173 |
| oleen | Cork | 72 |
| orey | Wexford | 45 |
| ort | Galway | 207 |
| raiguenamanagh | Kilkenny | 13 |
| range | Sligo | 303 |
| reystones | Wicklow | 273 |
| owth | DublinNorthCounty | 335 |
| ch Dingle Peninsula | Kerry | 102 |
| nishannon near Kinsale | Cork | 72 |
| lianstown | Meath | 252 |
| eady | Armagh | 318 |
| ells | Meath | 253 |
| enmare | Kerry | 102 |
| enmare Lauragh | Kerry | 108 |
| ilgarvan | Kerry | 109 |
| ilkee | Clare | 156 |
| ilkeel | Down | 320 |
| ilkenny | Kilkenny | 13 |
| ilkenny City | Kilkenny | 14 |
| illaloe | Clare | 156 |
| illarney | Kerry | 110 |
| illarney Aghadoe | Kerry | 114 |
| illarney Ballycasheen | Kerry | 124 |
| illarney Beaufort | Kerry | 115 |
| illarney Cork Road | Kerry | 111 |
| illarney Countess Road | Kerry | 115 |
| illarney Fossa | Kerry | 113 |
| illarney Gap of Dunloe | Kerry | 110 |
| illarney Muckross Road | Kerry | 111 |
| illarney Ross Road | Kerry | 117 |
| illarney Town | Kerry | 110 |
| illarney Tralee Road | Kerry | 110 |
| illeshandra | Cavan | 281 |
| illimer | Clare | 157 |
| illiney | DublinSouthCounty | 348 |
| illorglin | Kerry | 127 |
| illorglin Ring of Kerry | Kerry | 127 |
| illybegs | Donegal | 292 |
| ilmallock | Limerick | 173 |
| ilmore Quay | Wexford | 45 |
| ilrane | Wexford | 46 |
| ilrush | Clare | 157 |
| iltimagh | Mayo | 226 |
| innegad | Westmeath | 265 |
| innitty | Offaly | 260 |
| insale | Cork | 72 |
| invara | Galway | 208 |
| nock | Mayo | 227 |
| ylemore Connemara | Galway | 208 |
| ahinch | Clare | 158 |
| eenane Connemara | Galway | 209 |
| eixlip | Kildare | 243 |
| etterkenny | Donegal | 294 |
| imerick | Limerick | 175 |

| Area/Town | County | Page |
|---|---|---|
| Limerick City | Limerick | 174 |
| Limerick City Castletroy | Limerick | 174 |
| Limerick City Ennis Road | Limerick | 174 |
| Lisburn | Antrim | 315 |
| Liscannor | Clare | 160 |
| Lisdoonvarna | Clare | 160 |
| Lismore | Waterford | 35 |
| Listowel | Kerry | 129 |
| Londonderry | Londonderry | 325 |
| Longford | Longford | 247 |
| Loughrea | Galway | 209 |
| Louisburgh | Mayo | 227 |
| Lusk | DublinNorthCounty | 335 |
| **M** | | |
| Macroom | Cork | 78 |
| Malahide | DublinNorthCounty | 336 |
| Mallow | Cork | 79 |
| Manorhamilton | Leitrim | 299 |
| Maynooth | Kildare | 243 |
| Midleton | Cork | 81 |
| Milltown | Kerry | 130 |
| Miltown Malbay | Clare | 163 |
| Mitchelstown | Cork | 82 |
| Moate | Westmeath | 265 |
| Monaghan | Monaghan | 301 |
| Mountmellick | Laois | 245 |
| Mountshannon | Clare | 163 |
| Moycullen | Galway | 209 |
| Mullingar | Westmeath | 265 |
| Murroe | Limerick | 176 |
| **N** | | |
| Naas | Kildare | 243 |
| Navan | Meath | 254 |
| Navan/Slane | Meath | 255 |
| Nenagh | Tipperary | 27 |
| Nenagh Lough Derg | Tipperary | 29 |
| New Ross | Wexford | 46 |
| Newbridge | Kildare | 244 |
| Newcastle | Down | 320 |
| Newcastle West | Limerick | 176 |
| Newmarket-on-Fergus | Clare | 164 |
| Newport | Mayo | 228 |
| Newtownards | Down | 321 |
| **O** | | |
| O'Brien's Bridge | Clare | 165 |
| Omagh | Tyrone | 326 |
| Oranmore | Galway | 209 |
| Oughterard Connemara | Galway | 211 |
| **P** | | |
| Patrickswell | Limerick | 177 |
| Phibsboro | DublinNorthCity | 333 |
| Portarlington | Offaly | 260 |
| Portlaoise | Laois | 245 |
| Portmagee | Kerry | 130 |
| Portmarnock | DublinNorthCounty | 337 |
| Portumna | Galway | 213 |
| **Q** | | |
| Quin | Clare | 165 |
| **R** | | |
| Raheny | DublinNorthCity | 334 |
| Ramelton | Donegal | 296 |
| Randalstown | Antrim | 316 |
| Ranelagh | DublinSouthCity | 344 |
| Raphoe | Donegal | 296 |
| Rathcoole | DublinSouthCounty | 349 |
| Rathdrum | Wicklow | 274 |
| Rathfarnham | DublinSouthCity | 344 |
| Renvyle Connemara | Galway | 213 |
| Rooskey | Roscommon | 237 |

| Area/Town | County | Page |
|---|---|---|
| Roscommon | Roscommon | 237 |
| Roscrea | Laois | 246 |
| Roscrea | Tipperary | 29 |
| Rosses Point | Sligo | 303 |
| Rosslare Harbour | Wexford | 47 |
| Roundstone Connemara | Galway | 214 |
| **S** | | |
| Sandyford Village | DublinSouthCity | 345 |
| Sandymount | DublinSouthCity | 345 |
| Schull | Cork | 82 |
| Shankill | DublinSouthCounty | 350 |
| Shannon | Clare | 165 |
| Shannonbridge | Offaly | 260 |
| Skerries | DublinNorthCounty | 338 |
| Skibbereen | Cork | 82 |
| Skibbereen Town | Cork | 82 |
| Slane | Meath | 256 |
| Sligo | Sligo | 304 |
| Sligo Town | Sligo | 305 |
| Sneem Ring of Kerry | Kerry | 131 |
| South Circular Road | DublinSouthCity | 345 |
| Spiddal Connemara | Galway | 215 |
| Spiddal Furbo | Galway | 217 |
| Strandhill | Sligo | 308 |
| Sutton | DublinNorthCounty | 339 |
| Swinford | Mayo | 228 |
| Swords | DublinNorthCounty | 340 |
| Swords/Airport | DublinNorthCounty | 340 |
| Swords/Balbriggan | DublinNorthCounty | 341 |
| Swords/Ballyboghil | DublinNorthCounty | 341 |
| **T** | | |
| Tara | Meath | 257 |
| Templeogue | DublinSouthCity | 345 |
| Terenure | DublinSouthCity | 346 |
| Terryglass | Tipperary | 29 |
| Thomastown | Kilkenny | 19 |
| Thurles | Tipperary | 29 |
| Timoleague | Cork | 83 |
| Tipperary | Tipperary | 30 |
| Tralee | Kerry | 132 |
| Tralee Ballyard | Kerry | 135 |
| Tralee Fenit Road | Kerry | 133 |
| Tralee Killarney Road | Kerry | 134 |
| Tramore | Waterford | 35 |
| Trim | Meath | 257 |
| Tuam | Galway | 217 |
| Tubbercurry | Sligo | 308 |
| Tullamore | Offaly | 260 |
| Tulla-Quin | Clare | 168 |
| Tullow | Carlow | 11 |
| **U** | | |
| Union Hall Glandore | Cork | 84 |
| **V** | | |
| Valentia Island | Kerry | 136 |
| Virginia | Cavan | 281 |
| **W** | | |
| Waterford | Waterford | 38 |
| Waterville | Kerry | 137 |
| Waterville Ring Of Kerry | Kerry | 137 |
| Westport | Mayo | 229 |
| Wexford | Wexford | 50 |
| Wicklow | Wicklow | 275 |
| **Y** | | |
| Youghal | Cork | 84 |

# Ireland

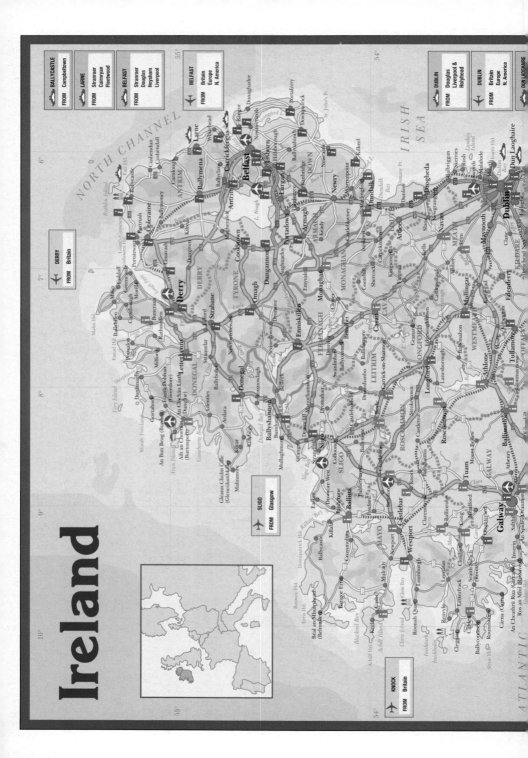